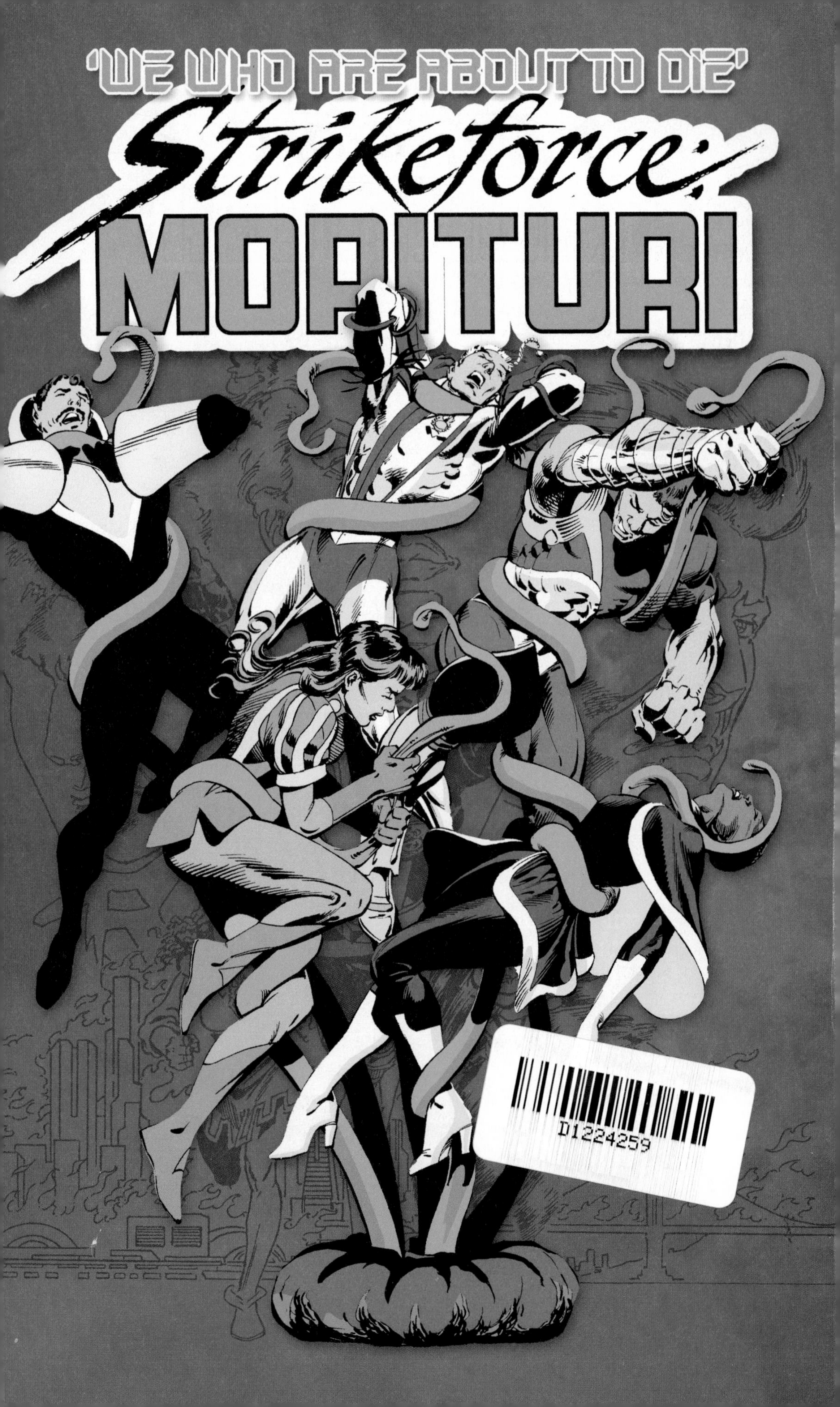
'WE WHO ARE ABOUT TO DIE'
Strikeforce:
MORITURI

'WE WHO ARE ABOUT TO DIE'
Strikeforce: MORITURI

WRITER
Peter B. Gillis

PENCILERS
Brent Anderson & Whilce Portacio

INKER
Scott Williams

COLORIST
Christie Scheele

LETTERERS
Jim Novak, Janice Chiang & Phil Felix

EDITOR
Carl Potts

COVER ARTISTS
Brent Anderson & Tom Smith

COLLECTION EDITOR: Mark D. Beazley
ASSISTANT EDITORS: Alex Starbuck & Nelson Ribeiro
EDITOR, SPECIAL PROJECTS: Jennifer Grünwald
SENIOR EDITOR, SPECIAL PROJECTS: Jeff Youngquist
RESEARCH: Roger Ott
LAYOUT: Jeph York
PRODUCTION: ColorTek & Joe Frontirre
COLOR RECONSTRUCTION: Digikore
BOOK DESIGNER: Arlene So
SENIOR VICE PRESIDENT OF SALES: David Gabriel
SVP OF BRAND PLANNING & COMMUNICATIONS: Michael Pasciullo

EDITOR IN CHIEF: Axel Alonso
CHIEF CREATIVE OFFICER: Joe Quesada
PUBLISHER: Dan Buckley
EXECUTIVE PRODUCER: Alan Fine

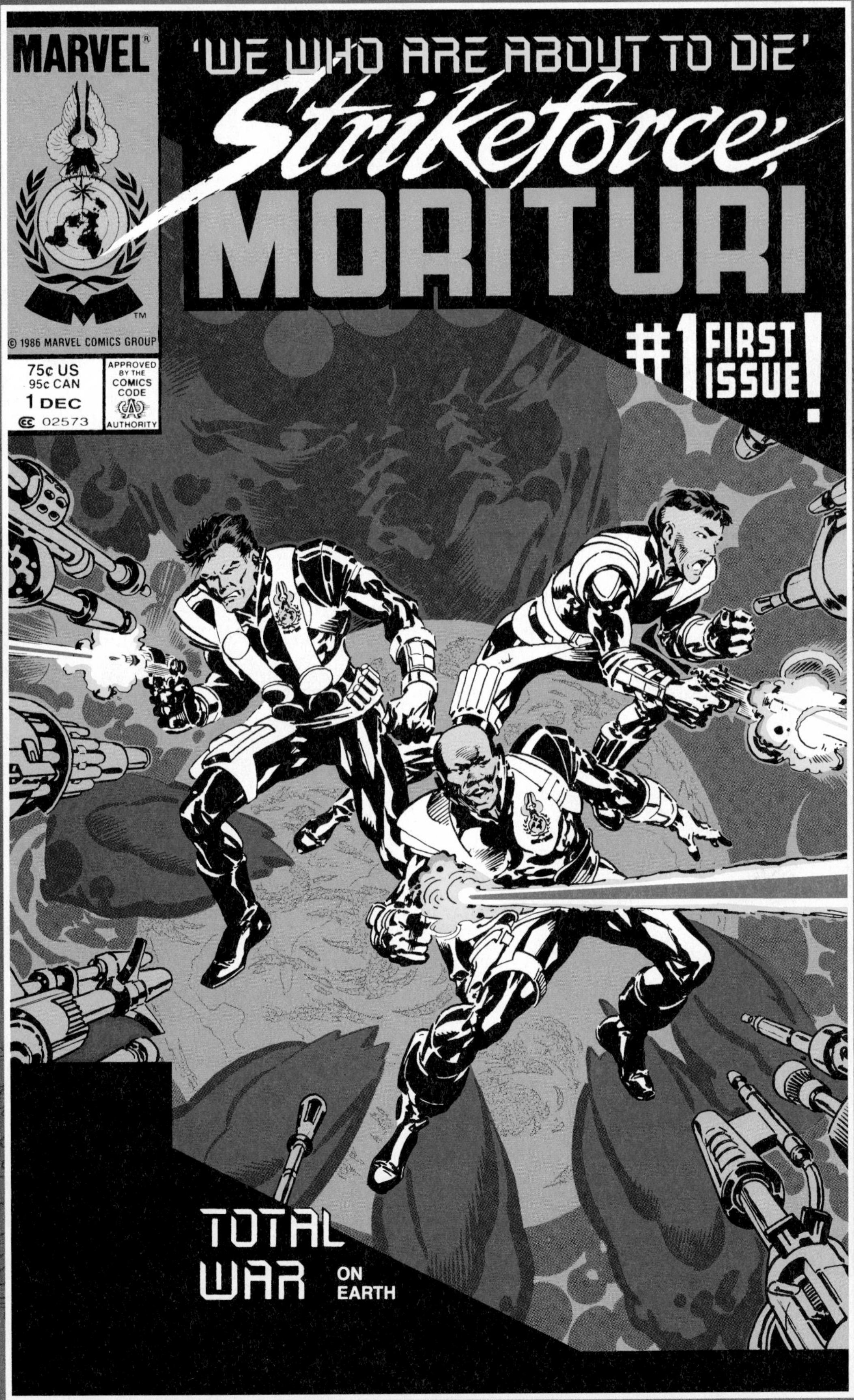

MARVEL
'WE WHO ARE ABOUT TO DIE'
Strikeforce:
MORITURI
© 1986 MARVEL COMICS GROUP
75¢ US
95¢ CAN
1 DEC
02573
APPROVED BY THE COMICS CODE AUTHORITY
#1 FIRST ISSUE!
TOTAL
WAR ON
EARTH

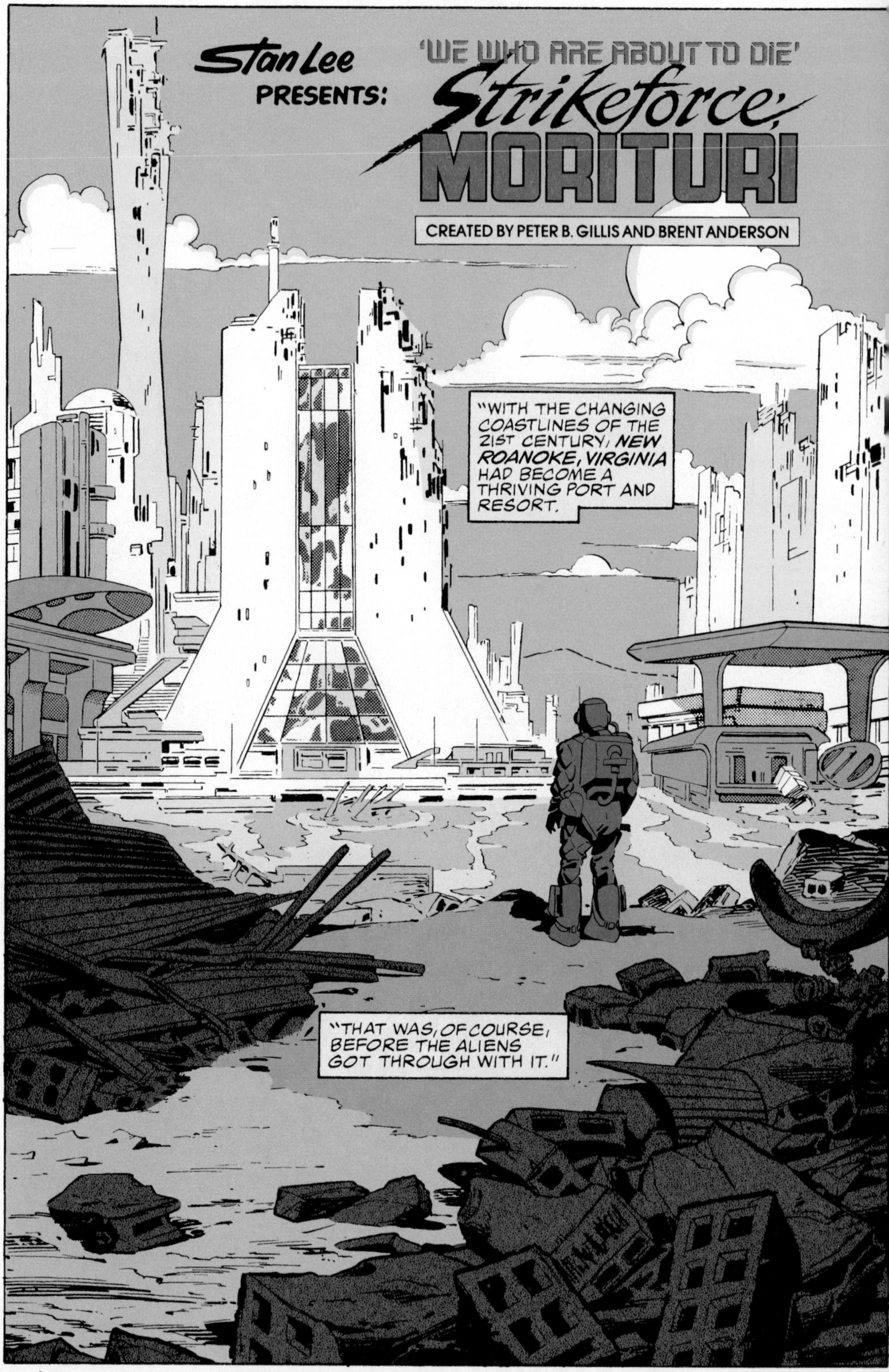
Stan Lee PRESENTS:
'WE WHO ARE ABOUT TO DIE'
Strikeforce: MORITURI
CREATED BY PETER B. GILLIS AND BRENT ANDERSON
"WITH THE CHANGING COASTLINES OF THE 21ST CENTURY, NEW ROANOKE, VIRGINIA HAD BECOME A THRIVING PORT AND RESORT.
"THAT WAS, OF COURSE, BEFORE THE ALIENS GOT THROUGH WITH IT."

peter b. **GILLIS** WRITER
brent **ANDERSON** PENCILER
scott **WILLIAMS** INKER
jim **NOVAK** LETTERER
max **SCHEELE** COLORER
carl **POTTS** EDITOR
jim **SHOOTER** EDITOR IN CHIEF

ART ON PAGES 5, 6, & 10 by WILCE PORTACIO

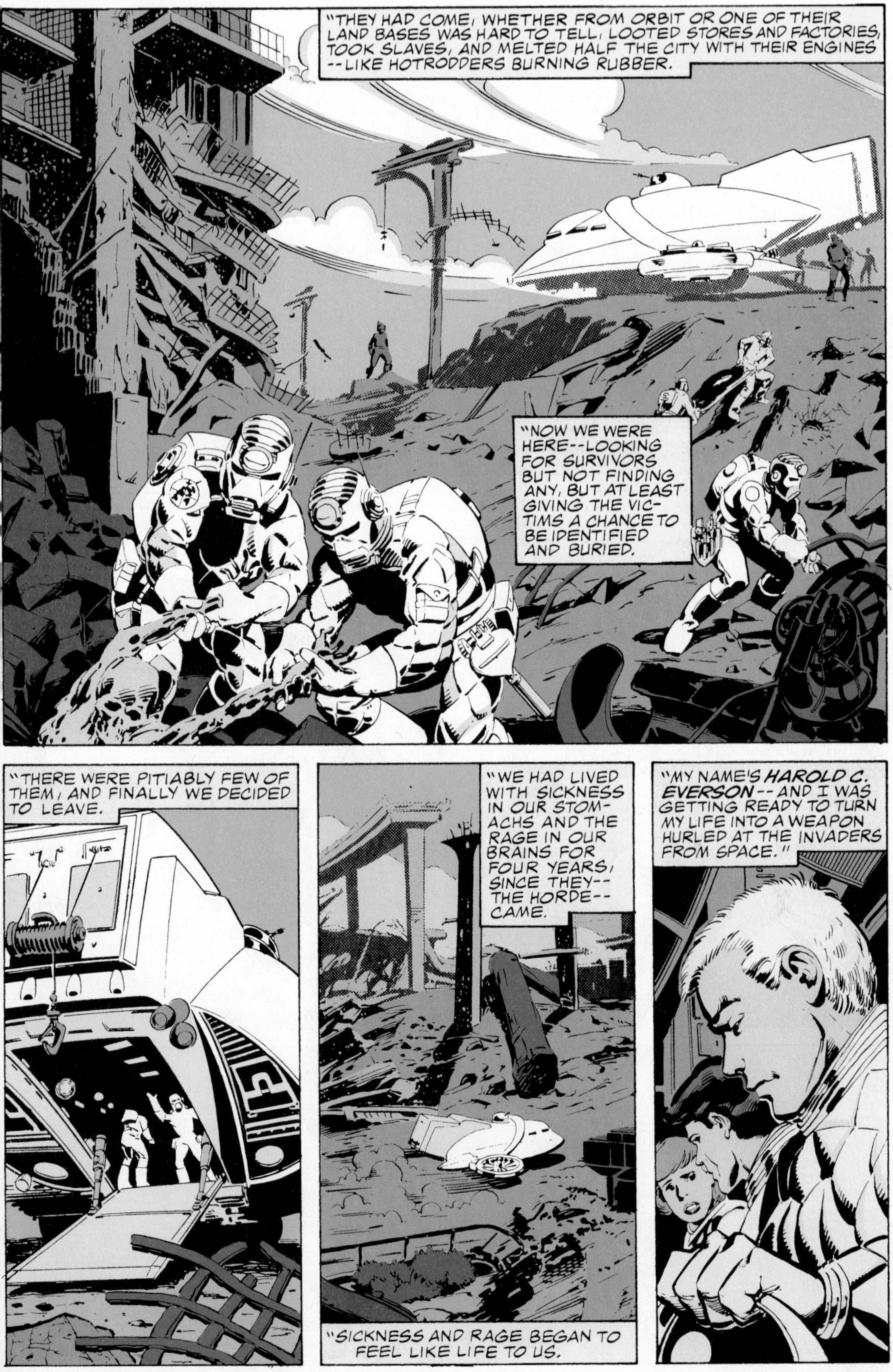
"THEY HAD COME, WHETHER FROM ORBIT OR ONE OF THEIR LAND BASES WAS HARD TO TELL, LOOTED STORES AND FACTORIES, TOOK SLAVES, AND MELTED HALF THE CITY WITH THEIR ENGINES --LIKE HOTRODDERS BURNING RUBBER.
"NOW WE WERE HERE--LOOKING FOR SURVIVORS BUT NOT FINDING ANY, BUT AT LEAST GIVING THE VICTIMS A CHANCE TO BE IDENTIFIED AND BURIED.
"THERE WERE PITIABLY FEW OF THEM, AND FINALLY WE DECIDED TO LEAVE.
"WE HAD LIVED WITH SICKNESS IN OUR STOMACHS AND THE RAGE IN OUR BRAINS FOR FOUR YEARS, SINCE THEY--THE HORDE--CAME.
"SICKNESS AND RAGE BEGAN TO FEEL LIKE LIFE TO US.
"MY NAME'S **HAROLD C. EVERSON** --AND I WAS GETTING READY TO TURN MY LIFE INTO A WEAPON HURLED AT THE INVADERS FROM SPACE."

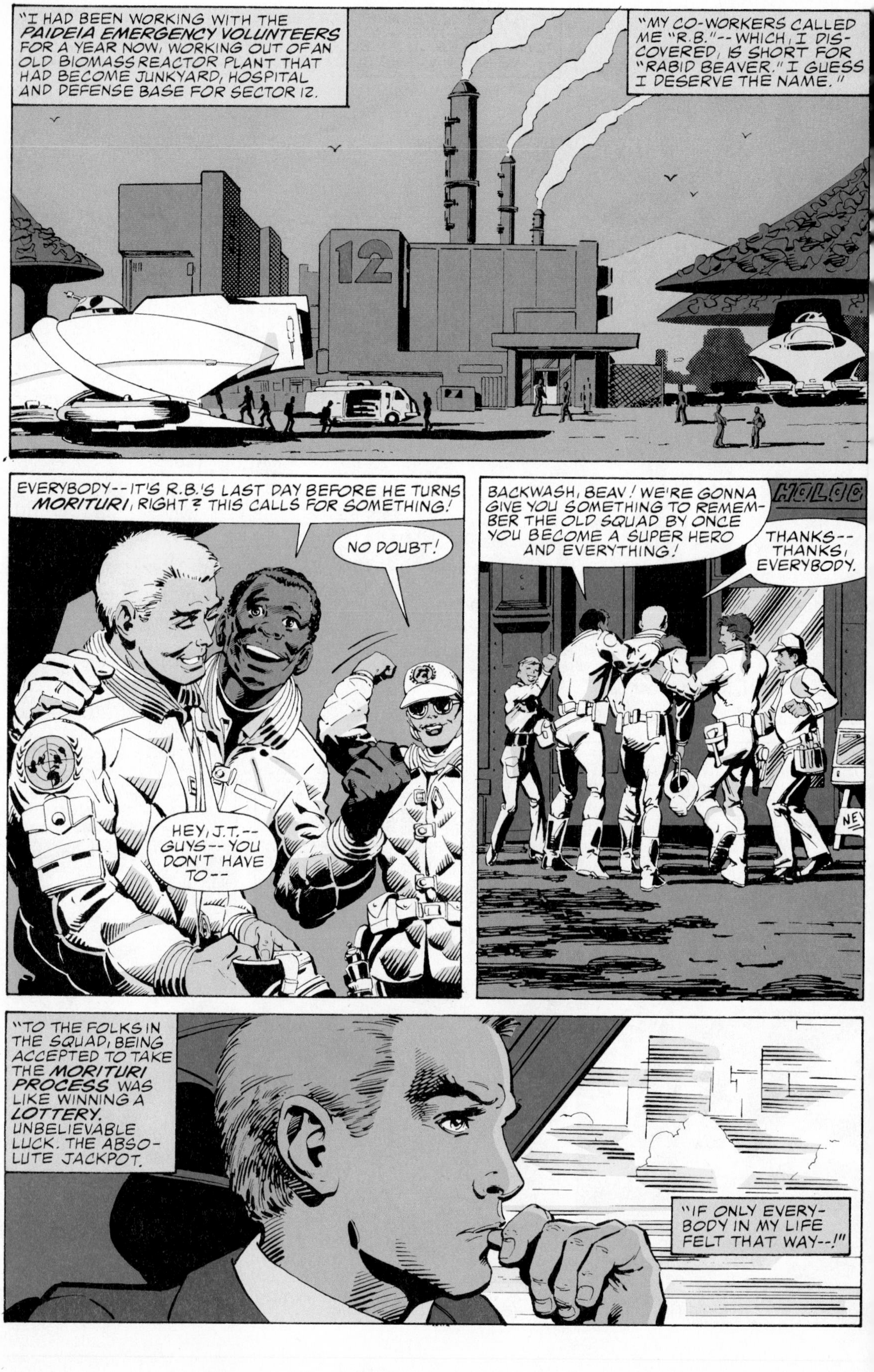
"I HAD BEEN WORKING WITH THE PAIDEIA EMERGENCY VOLUNTEERS FOR A YEAR NOW, WORKING OUT OF AN OLD BIOMASS REACTOR PLANT THAT HAD BECOME JUNKYARD, HOSPITAL AND DEFENSE BASE FOR SECTOR 12.
"MY CO-WORKERS CALLED ME "R.B."-- WHICH, I DISCOVERED, IS SHORT FOR "RABID BEAVER." I GUESS I DESERVE THE NAME."
12
EVERYBODY--IT'S R.B.'S LAST DAY BEFORE HE TURNS MORITURI, RIGHT? THIS CALLS FOR SOMETHING!
NO DOUBT!
HEY, J.T.-- GUYS-- YOU DON'T HAVE TO--
BACKWASH, BEAV! WE'RE GONNA GIVE YOU SOMETHING TO REMEMBER THE OLD SQUAD BY ONCE YOU BECOME A SUPER HERO AND EVERYTHING!
THANKS-- THANKS, EVERYBODY.
HOLOC
"TO THE FOLKS IN THE SQUAD, BEING ACCEPTED TO TAKE THE MORITURI PROCESS WAS LIKE WINNING A LOTTERY. UNBELIEVABLE LUCK. THE ABSOLUTE JACKPOT.
"IF ONLY EVERYBODY IN MY LIFE FELT THAT WAY--!"

ALEXANDRIA VIRGINIA 07:03

HAROLD! COME HERE!

GOOD TO SEE YOU, HAL.

HI, MOM! HI, DAD!

I'M SO GLAD YOU'RE HERE, HAROLD! WE'VE MISSED YOU!

WE'LL EAT DINNER AT 6. HOPE YOU CAN HOLD OUT TILL THEN.

SURE, DAD--!

I'M GLAD YOU'RE WILLING TO HEAR US OUT, HAL.

OF COURSE, DAD--BUT MY MIND'S MADE UP. WE'VE GOT TO FIGHT FOR OUR HOME.

I'M NOT DENYING THAT, SON. THERE'S JUST NO REASON YOU SHOULD GIVE UP SO MUCH FOR THIS--THIS TERRIBLE THING.

HAROLD--YOUR WRITING IS COMING ALONG SO WELL, THE REVIEWS ON THE LOCAL NET SAY YOU HAVE GREAT PROMISE--!

HAROLD--THERE ARE OTHER WAYS OF FIGHTING THE ALIENS...

AND THIS WAY IS MINE! A REAL WAY, NOT JUST HAULING BODIES!

SO YOU'RE THROWING EVERY-THING AWAY FOR A CHANCE TO GRAB SOME GLORY! I DON'T UNDERSTAND THAT, HAL!

IF YOU THINK THAT'S WHY I'M DOING IT-- THEN YOU DON'T UNDERSTAND ME, DAD, NOT AT ALL.

JUSTIN--HE'S GOING OFF TO BECOME A DEAD MAN-- OUR SON'S--

"AND IT WAS THOSE WORDS THAT STUNG MY EYES.

"IN MY ROOM, I PICKED THE BOOK UP-- READ IT AGAIN--

"-- WAITED FOR THE SINGING IN MY BLOOD TO RISE AGAIN--!"

The Last Stand of THE BLACK WATCH

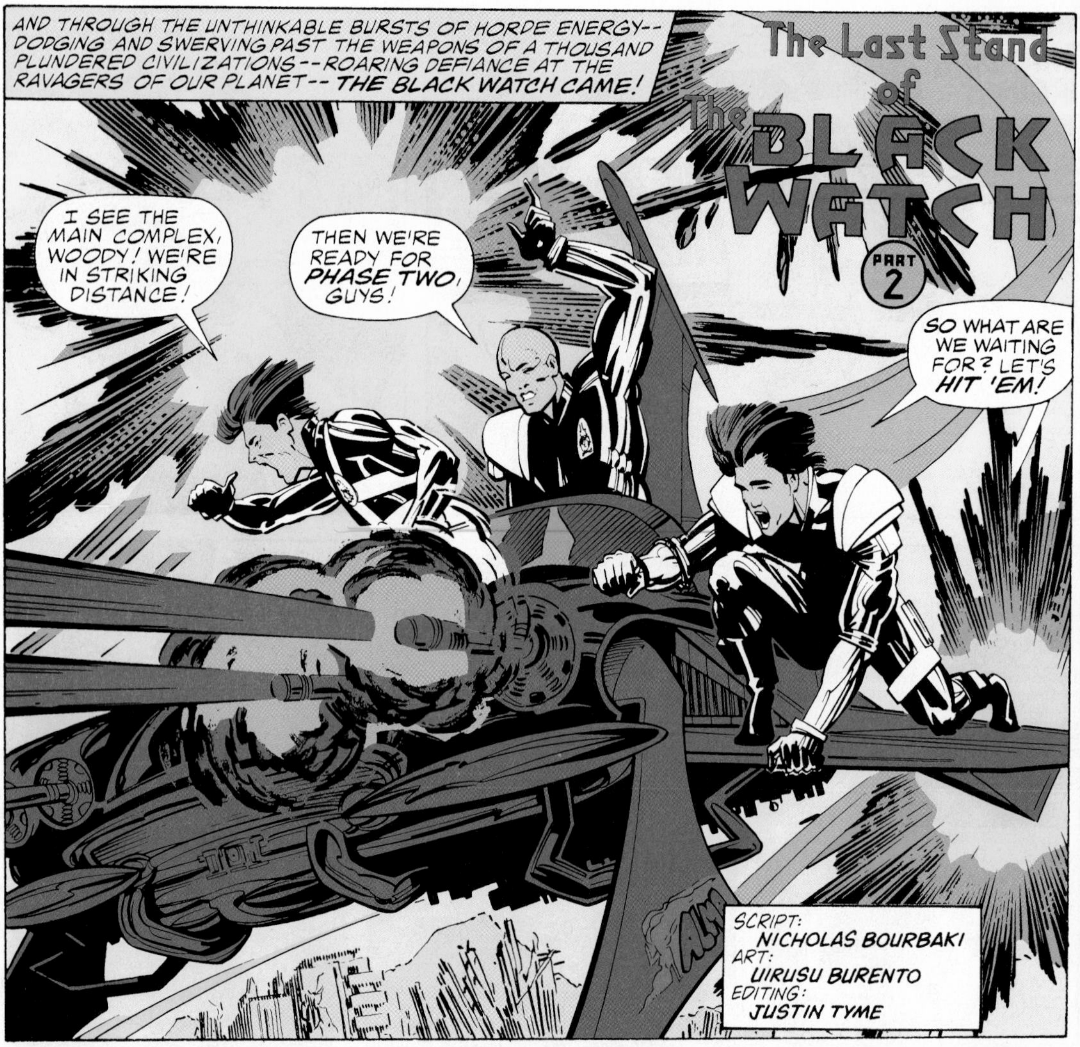
AND THROUGH THE UNTHINKABLE BURSTS OF HORDE ENERGY--DODGING AND SWERVING PAST THE WEAPONS OF A THOUSAND PLUNDERED CIVILIZATIONS--ROARING DEFIANCE AT THE RAVAGERS OF OUR PLANET--THE BLACK WATCH CAME!
The Last Stand of The BLACK WATCH
PART 2
I SEE THE MAIN COMPLEX, WOODY! WE'RE IN STRIKING DISTANCE!
THEN WE'RE READY FOR PHASE TWO, GUYS!
SO WHAT ARE WE WAITING FOR? LET'S HIT 'EM!
SCRIPT: NICHOLAS BOURBAKI
ART: UIRUSU BURENTO
EDITING: JUSTIN TYME

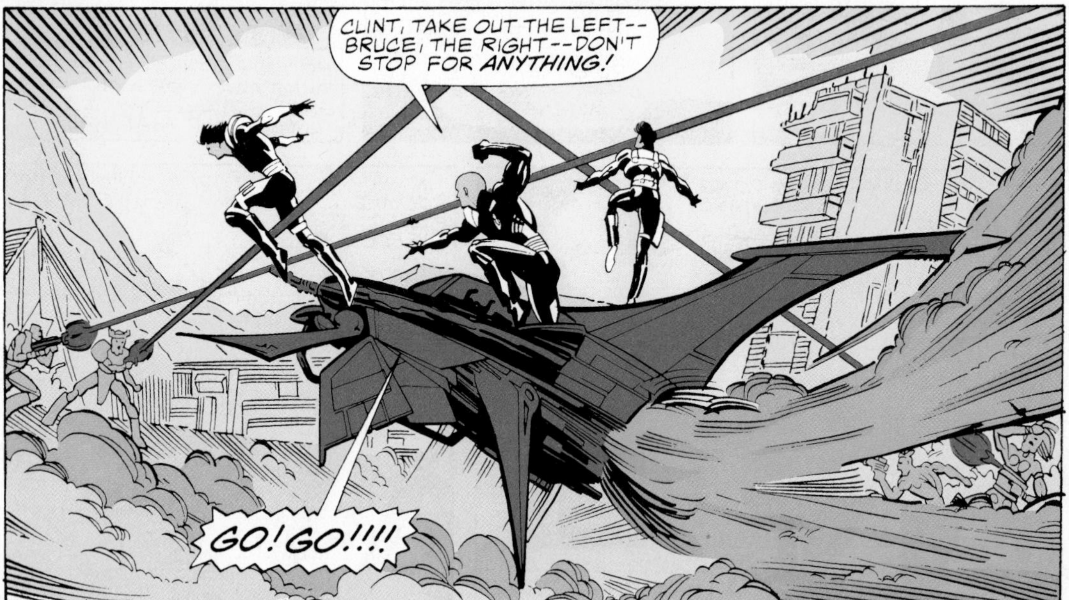
CLINT, TAKE OUT THE LEFT--BRUCE, THE RIGHT--DON'T STOP FOR ANYTHING!
GO! GO!!!!

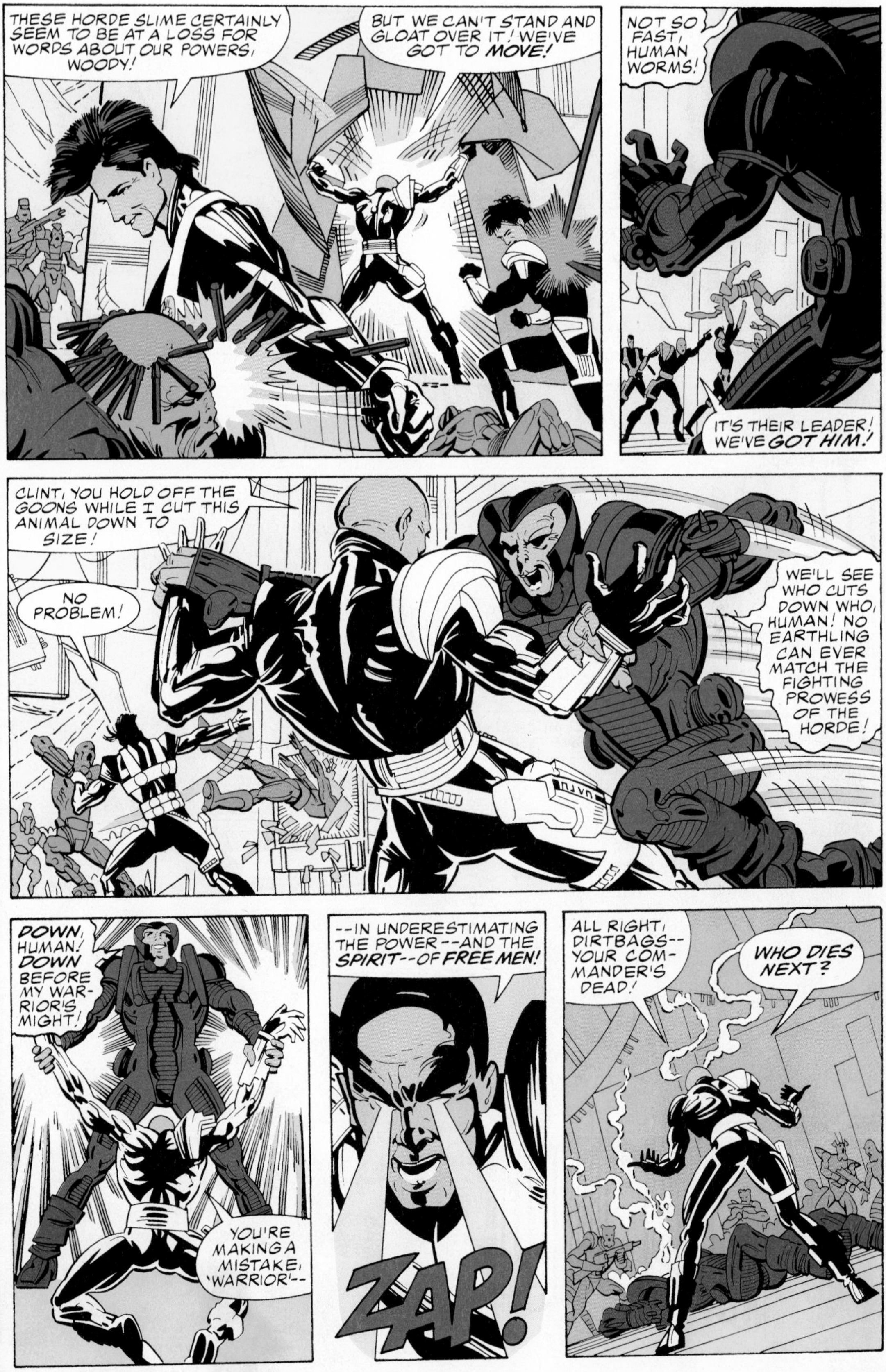
THESE HORDE SLIME CERTAINLY SEEM TO BE AT A LOSS FOR WORDS ABOUT OUR POWERS, WOODY!
BUT WE CAN'T STAND AND GLOAT OVER IT! WE'VE GOT TO MOVE!
NOT SO FAST, HUMAN WORMS!
IT'S THEIR LEADER! WE'VE GOT HIM!
CLINT, YOU HOLD OFF THE GOONS WHILE I CUT THIS ANIMAL DOWN TO SIZE!
NO PROBLEM!
WE'LL SEE WHO CUTS DOWN WHO, HUMAN! NO EARTHLING CAN EVER MATCH THE FIGHTING PROWESS OF THE HORDE!
DOWN, HUMAN! DOWN BEFORE MY WARRIOR'S MIGHT!
YOU'RE MAKING A MISTAKE, 'WARRIOR'--
--IN UNDERESTIMATING THE POWER--AND THE SPIRIT--OF FREE MEN!
ZAP!
ALL RIGHT, DIRTBAGS-- YOUR COMMANDER'S DEAD!
WHO DIES NEXT?

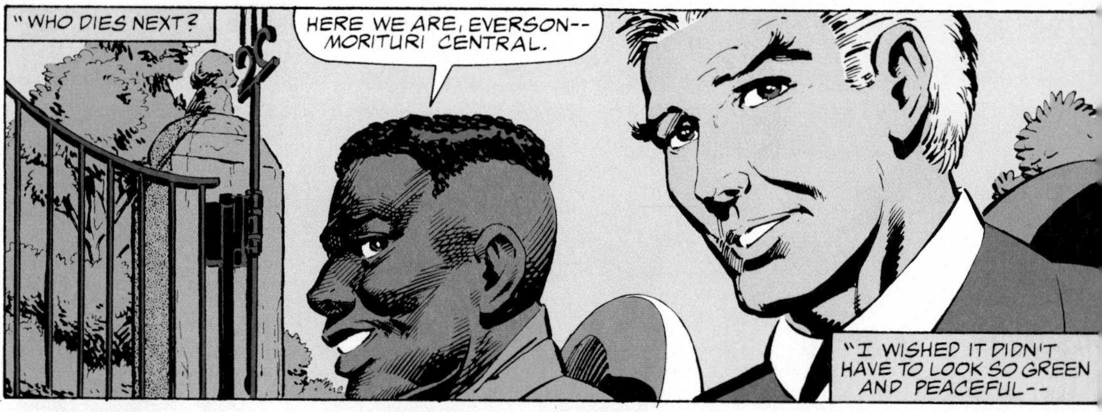
"WHO DIES NEXT?
HERE WE ARE, EVERSON--
MORITURI CENTRAL.
"I WISHED IT DIDN'T HAVE TO LOOK SO GREEN AND PEACEFUL--

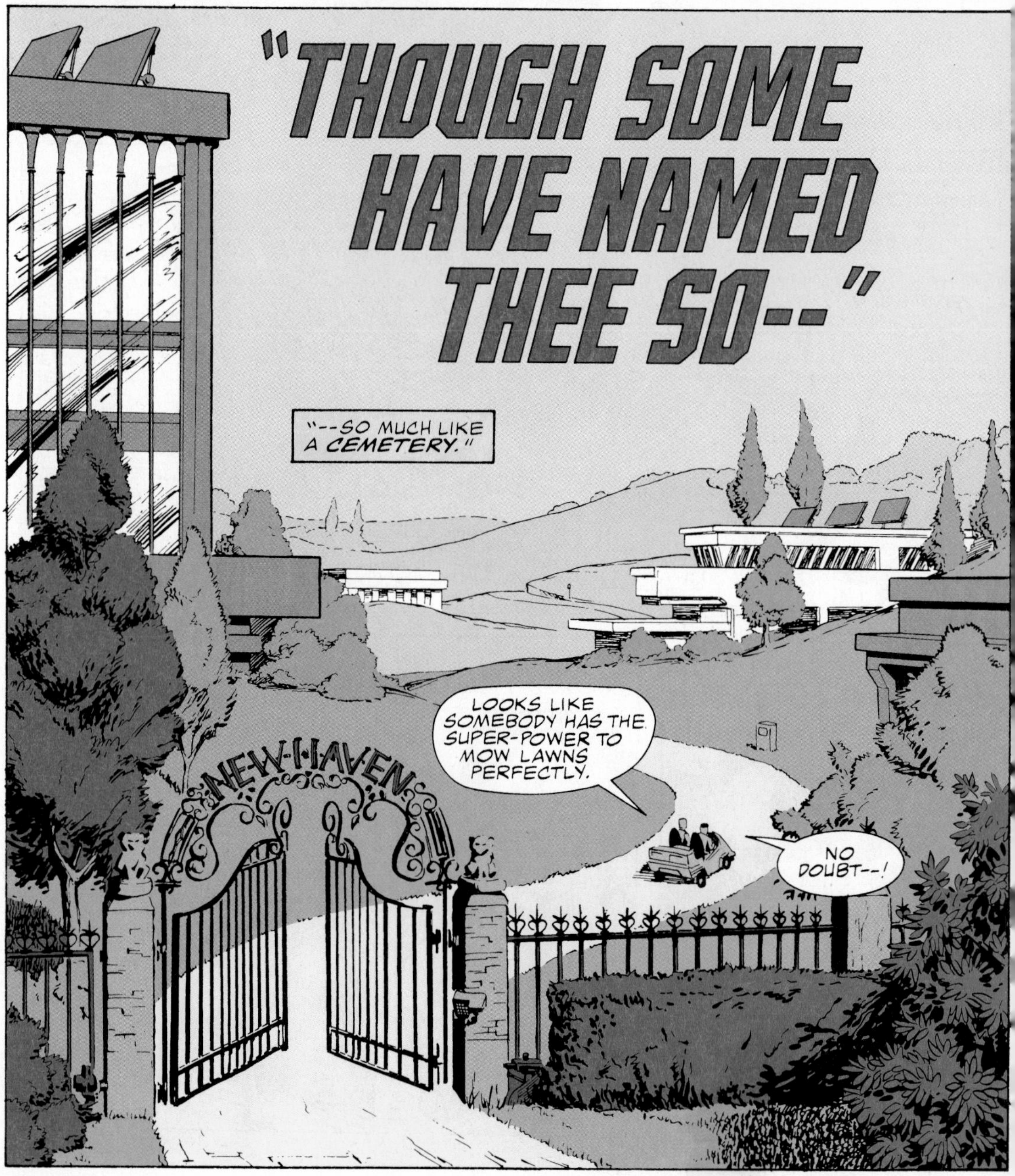
"THOUGH SOME HAVE NAMED THEE SO--"
"--SO MUCH LIKE A CEMETERY."
NEW HAVEN
LOOKS LIKE SOMEBODY HAS THE SUPER-POWER TO MOW LAWNS PERFECTLY.
NO DOUBT--!

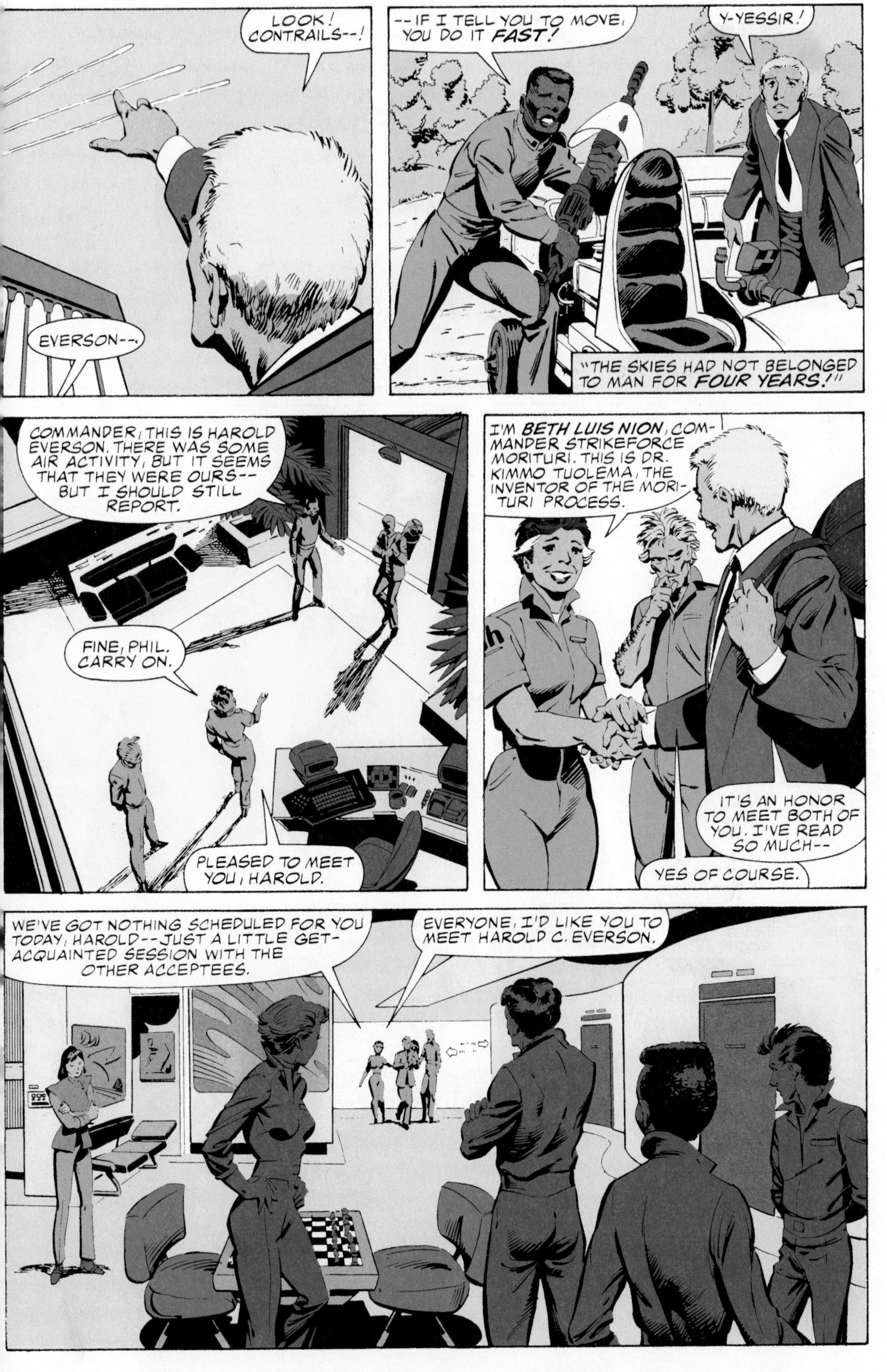
LOOK! CONTRAILS--!
EVERSON--.
--IF I TELL YOU TO MOVE, YOU DO IT FAST!
Y-YESSIR!
"THE SKIES HAD NOT BELONGED TO MAN FOR FOUR YEARS!"
COMMANDER, THIS IS HAROLD EVERSON. THERE WAS SOME AIR ACTIVITY, BUT IT SEEMS THAT THEY WERE OURS-- BUT I SHOULD STILL REPORT.
FINE, PHIL. CARRY ON.
PLEASED TO MEET YOU, HAROLD.
I'M BETH LUIS NION, COMMANDER STRIKEFORCE MORITURI. THIS IS DR. KIMMO TUOLEMA, THE INVENTOR OF THE MORITURI PROCESS.
IT'S AN HONOR TO MEET BOTH OF YOU. I'VE READ SO MUCH--
YES OF COURSE.
WE'VE GOT NOTHING SCHEDULED FOR YOU TODAY, HAROLD--JUST A LITTLE GET-ACQUAINTED SESSION WITH THE OTHER ACCEPTEES.
EVERYONE, I'D LIKE YOU TO MEET HAROLD C. EVERSON.

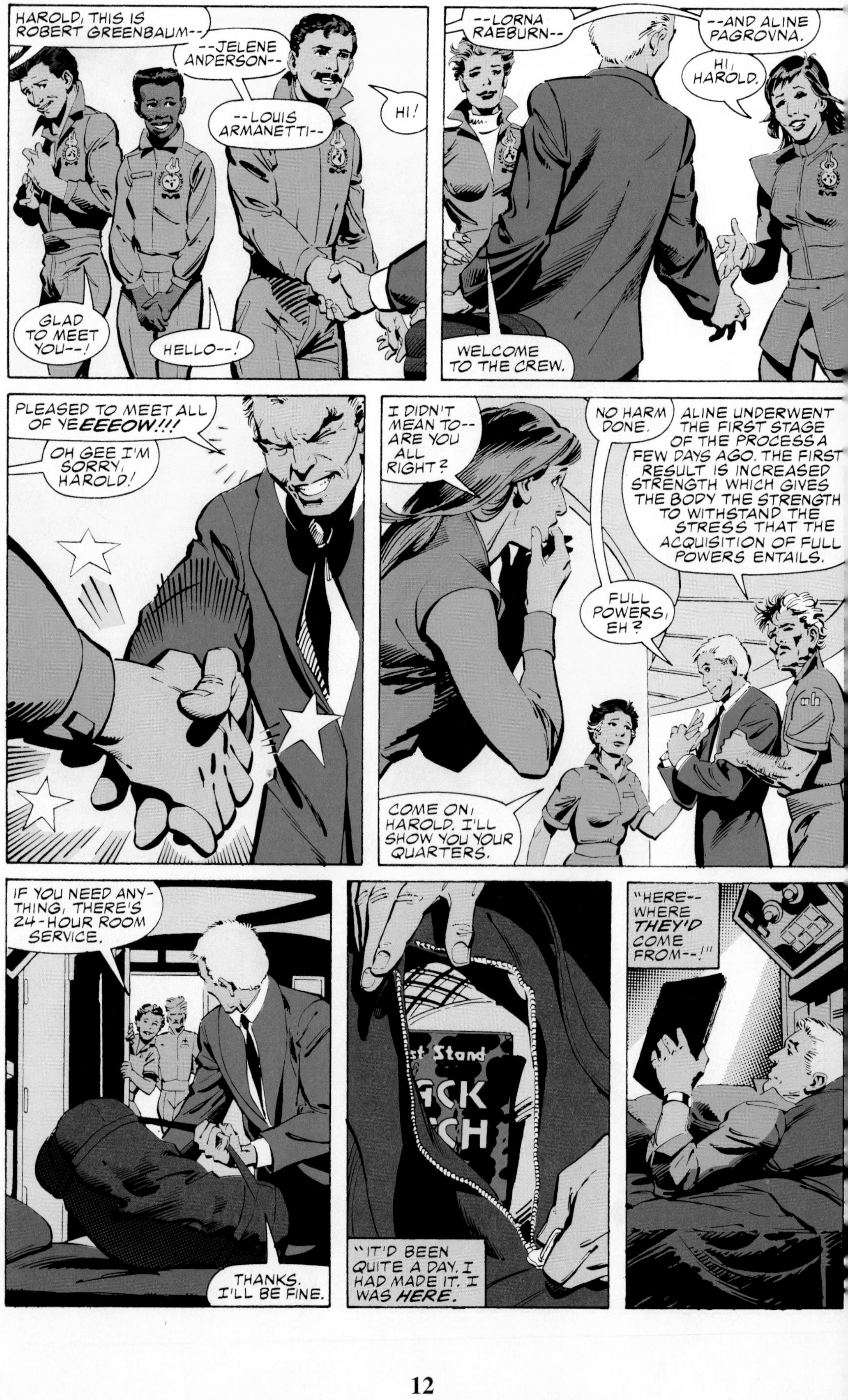
HAROLD, THIS IS ROBERT GREENBAUM--
--JELENE ANDERSON--
--LOUIS ARMANETTI--
HI!
GLAD TO MEET YOU--!
HELLO--!
--LORNA RAEBURN--
--AND ALINE PAGROVNA.
HI, HAROLD.
WELCOME TO THE CREW.
PLEASED TO MEET ALL OF YE**EEEOW!!!**
OH GEE I'M SORRY, HAROLD!
I DIDN'T MEAN TO-- ARE YOU ALL RIGHT?
NO HARM DONE.
ALINE UNDERWENT THE FIRST STAGE OF THE PROCESS A FEW DAYS AGO. THE FIRST RESULT IS INCREASED STRENGTH WHICH GIVES THE BODY THE STRENGTH TO WITHSTAND THE STRESS THAT THE ACQUISITION OF FULL POWERS ENTAILS.
FULL POWERS, EH?
COME ON, HAROLD. I'LL SHOW YOU YOUR QUARTERS.
IF YOU NEED ANYTHING, THERE'S 24-HOUR ROOM SERVICE.
THANKS. I'LL BE FINE.
"IT'D BEEN QUITE A DAY. I HAD MADE IT. I WAS **HERE**.
"HERE-- WHERE **THEY'D** COME FROM--!"

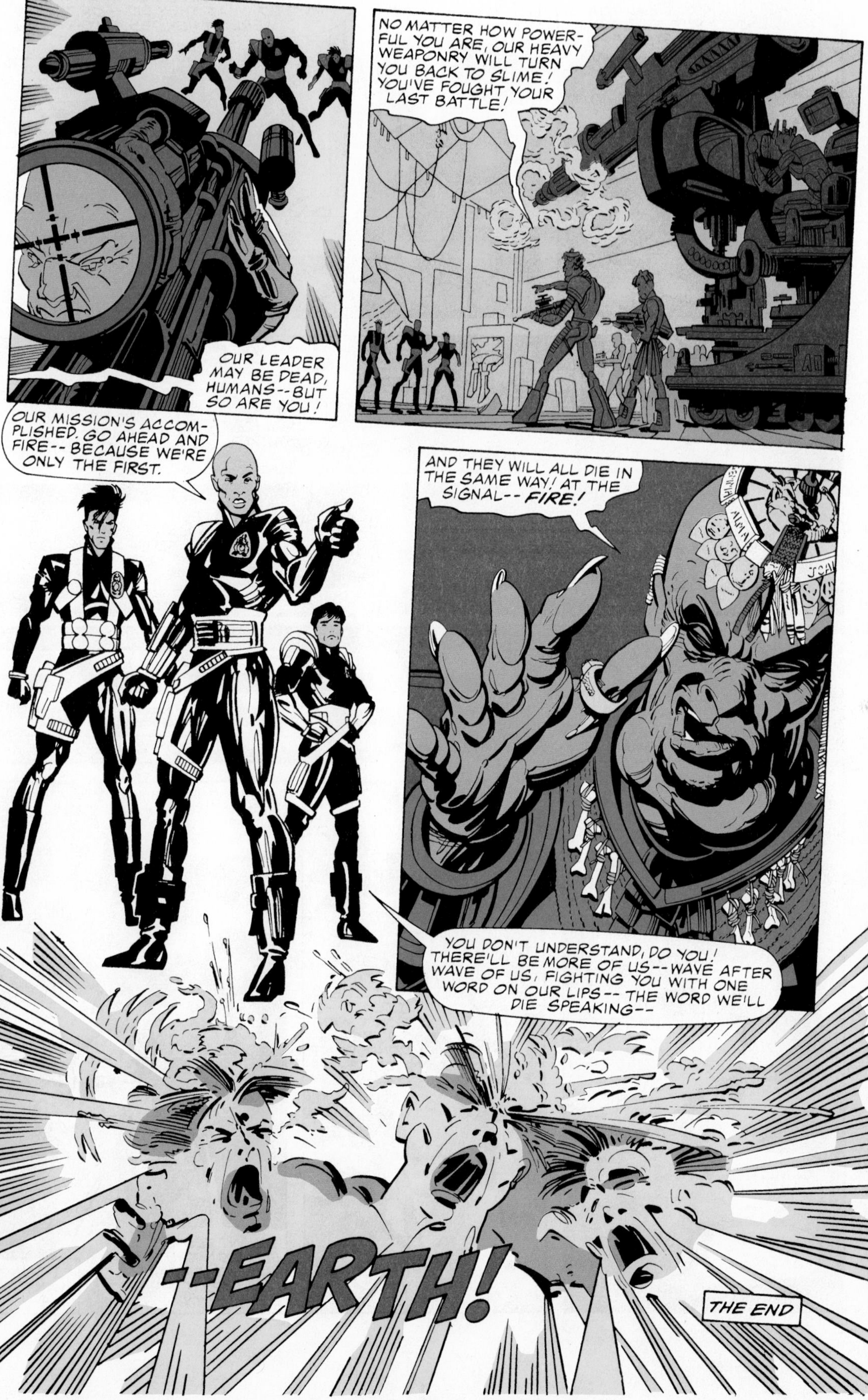
OUR LEADER MAY BE DEAD, HUMANS--BUT SO ARE YOU!
NO MATTER HOW POWERFUL YOU ARE, OUR HEAVY WEAPONRY WILL TURN YOU BACK TO SLIME! YOU'VE FOUGHT YOUR LAST BATTLE!
OUR MISSION'S ACCOMPLISHED. GO AHEAD AND FIRE-- BECAUSE WE'RE ONLY THE FIRST.
AND THEY WILL ALL DIE IN THE SAME WAY! AT THE SIGNAL--*FIRE!*
YOU DON'T UNDERSTAND, DO YOU! THERE'LL BE MORE OF US--WAVE AFTER WAVE OF US, FIGHTING YOU WITH ONE WORD ON OUR LIPS--THE WORD WE'LL DIE SPEAKING--
--EARTH!
THE END

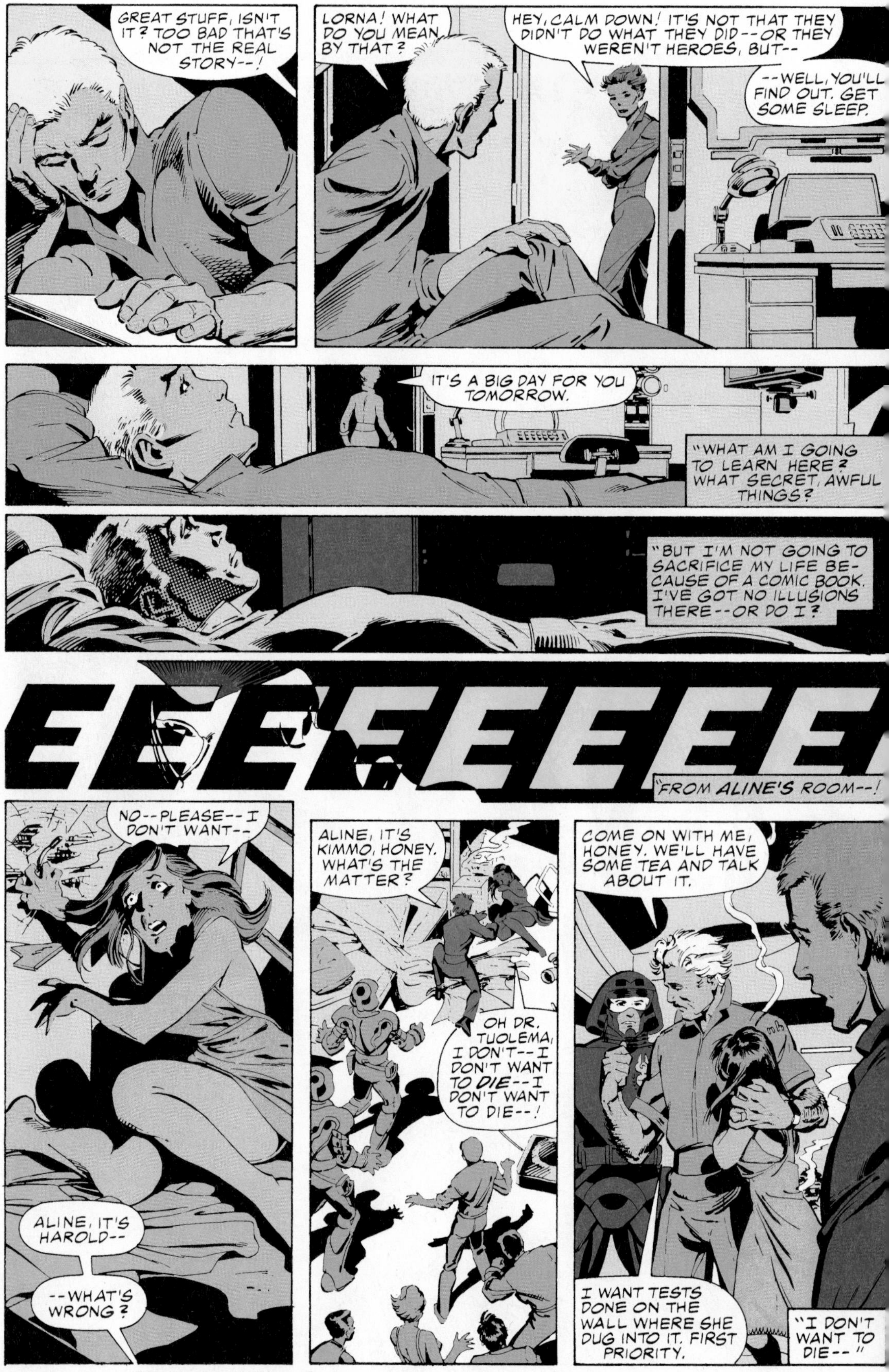
GREAT STUFF, ISN'T IT? TOO BAD THAT'S NOT THE REAL STORY--!
LORNA! WHAT DO YOU MEAN BY THAT?
HEY, CALM DOWN! IT'S NOT THAT THEY DIDN'T DO WHAT THEY DID--OR THEY WEREN'T HEROES, BUT--
--WELL, YOU'LL FIND OUT. GET SOME SLEEP.
IT'S A BIG DAY FOR YOU TOMORROW.
"WHAT AM I GOING TO LEARN HERE? WHAT SECRET, AWFUL THINGS?
"BUT I'M NOT GOING TO SACRIFICE MY LIFE BECAUSE OF A COMIC BOOK. I'VE GOT NO ILLUSIONS THERE--OR DO I?
EEEEEEE
"FROM ALINE'S ROOM--!
NO--PLEASE--I DON'T WANT--
ALINE, IT'S HAROLD--
--WHAT'S WRONG?
ALINE, IT'S KIMMO, HONEY. WHAT'S THE MATTER?
OH DR. TUOLEMA, I DON'T--I DON'T WANT TO DIE--I DON'T WANT TO DIE--!
COME ON WITH ME, HONEY. WE'LL HAVE SOME TEA AND TALK ABOUT IT.
I WANT TESTS DONE ON THE WALL WHERE SHE DUG INTO IT. FIRST PRIORITY.
"I DON'T WANT TO DIE--"

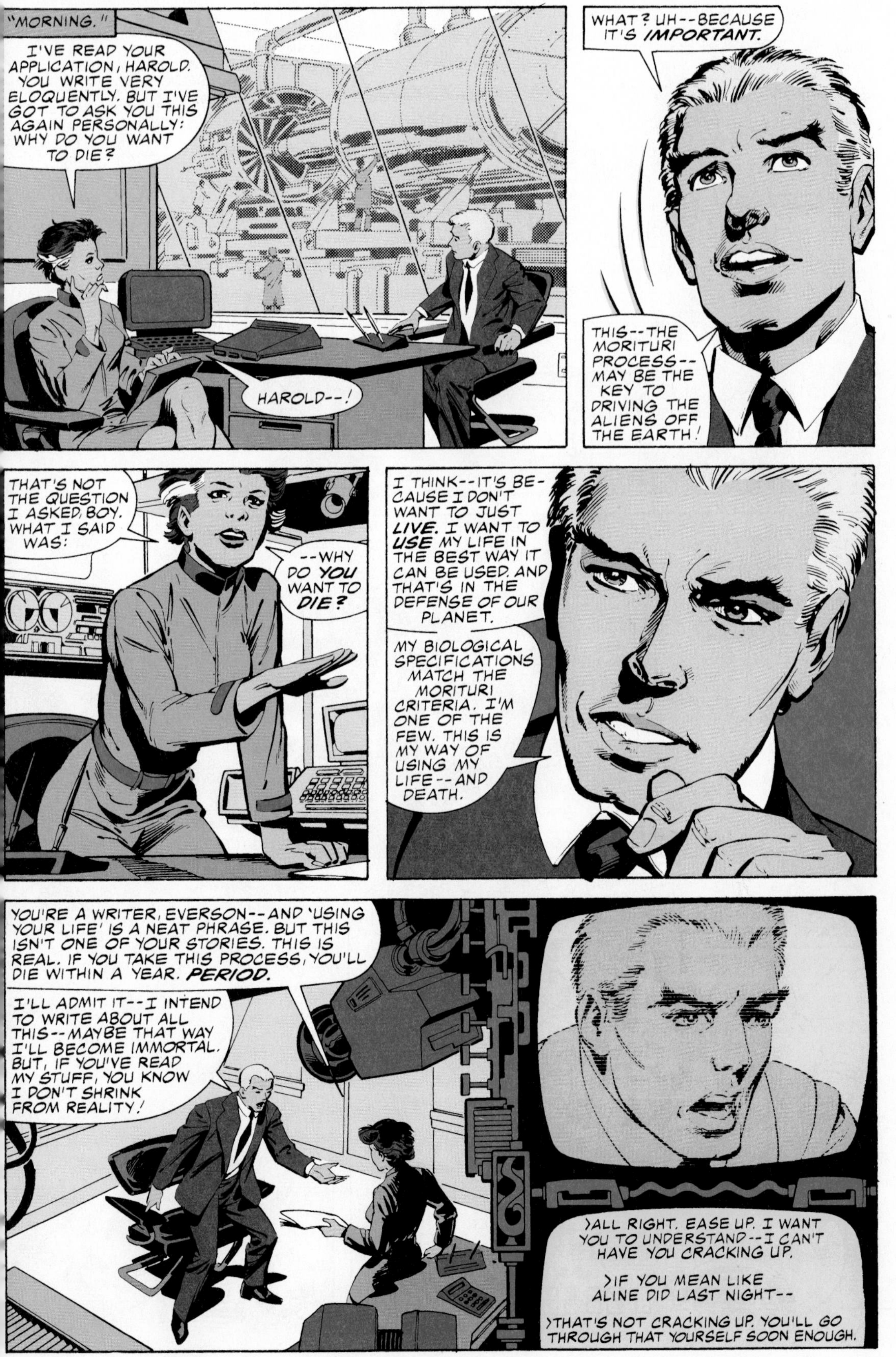

"MORNING."
I'VE READ YOUR APPLICATION, HAROLD. YOU WRITE VERY ELOQUENTLY. BUT I'VE GOT TO ASK YOU THIS AGAIN PERSONALLY: WHY DO YOU WANT TO DIE?
HAROLD--!
WHAT? UH--BECAUSE IT'S IMPORTANT.
THIS--THE MORITURI PROCESS--MAY BE THE KEY TO DRIVING THE ALIENS OFF THE EARTH!
THAT'S NOT THE QUESTION I ASKED, BOY. WHAT I SAID WAS:
--WHY DO YOU WANT TO DIE?
I THINK--IT'S BECAUSE I DON'T WANT TO JUST LIVE. I WANT TO USE MY LIFE IN THE BEST WAY IT CAN BE USED. AND THAT'S IN THE DEFENSE OF OUR PLANET.
MY BIOLOGICAL SPECIFICATIONS MATCH THE MORITURI CRITERIA. I'M ONE OF THE FEW. THIS IS MY WAY OF USING MY LIFE--AND DEATH.
YOU'RE A WRITER, EVERSON--AND 'USING YOUR LIFE' IS A NEAT PHRASE. BUT THIS ISN'T ONE OF YOUR STORIES. THIS IS REAL. IF YOU TAKE THIS PROCESS, YOU'LL DIE WITHIN A YEAR. PERIOD.
I'LL ADMIT IT--I INTEND TO WRITE ABOUT ALL THIS--MAYBE THAT WAY I'LL BECOME IMMORTAL. BUT, IF YOU'VE READ MY STUFF, YOU KNOW I DON'T SHRINK FROM REALITY!
>ALL RIGHT. EASE UP. I WANT YOU TO UNDERSTAND--I CAN'T HAVE YOU CRACKING UP.
>IF YOU MEAN LIKE ALINE DID LAST NIGHT--
>THAT'S NOT CRACKING UP. YOU'LL GO THROUGH THAT YOURSELF SOON ENOUGH.

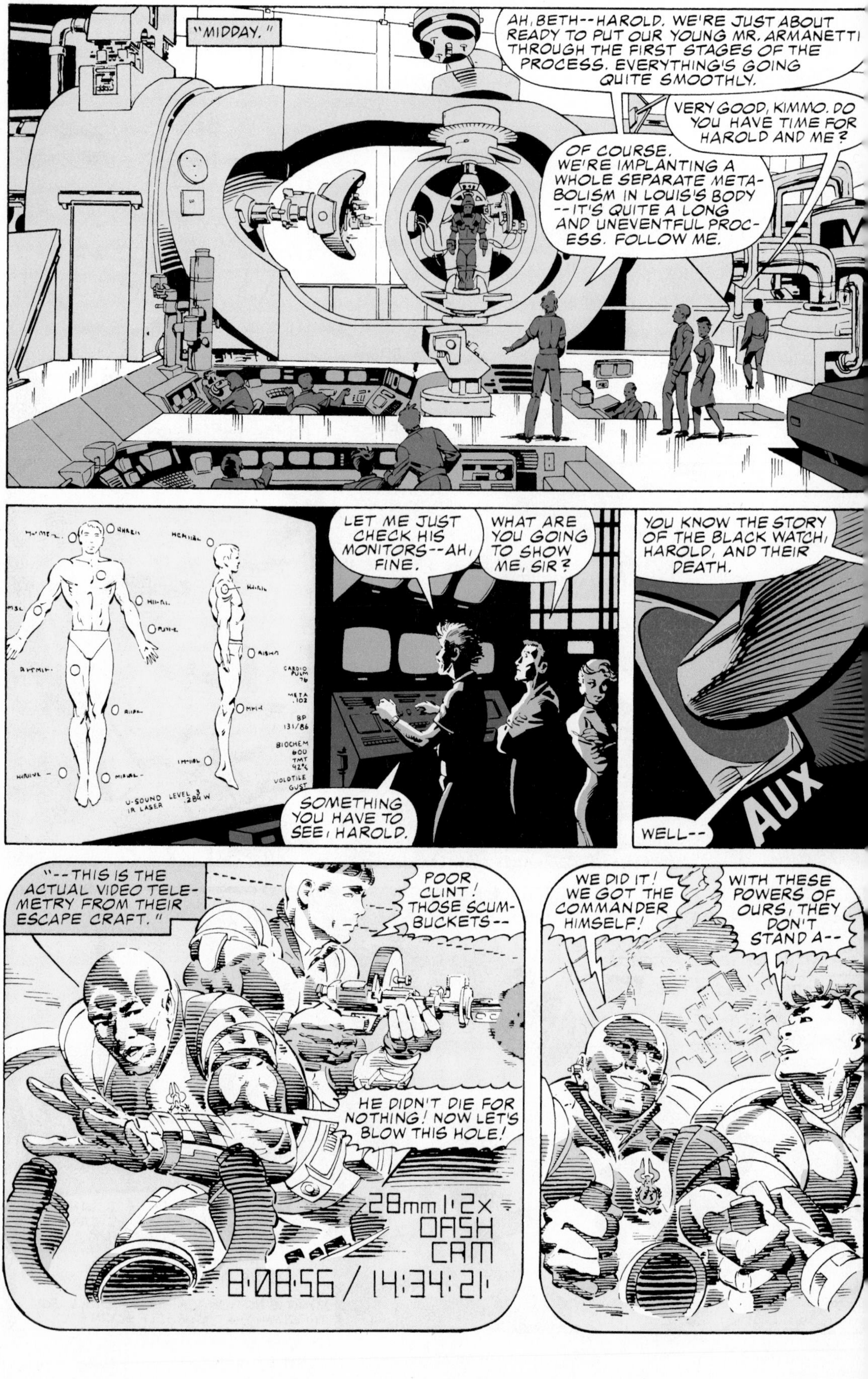
"MIDDAY."
AH, BETH--HAROLD. WE'RE JUST ABOUT READY TO PUT OUR YOUNG MR. ARMANETTI THROUGH THE FIRST STAGES OF THE PROCESS. EVERYTHING'S GOING QUITE SMOOTHLY.
VERY GOOD, KIMMO. DO YOU HAVE TIME FOR HAROLD AND ME?
OF COURSE. WE'RE IMPLANTING A WHOLE SEPARATE METABOLISM IN LOUIS'S BODY --IT'S QUITE A LONG AND UNEVENTFUL PROCESS. FOLLOW ME.
LET ME JUST CHECK HIS MONITORS--AH, FINE.
WHAT ARE YOU GOING TO SHOW ME, SIR?
SOMETHING YOU HAVE TO SEE, HAROLD.
YOU KNOW THE STORY OF THE BLACK WATCH, HAROLD, AND THEIR DEATH.
WELL--
AUX
"--THIS IS THE ACTUAL VIDEO TELEMETRY FROM THEIR ESCAPE CRAFT."
POOR CLINT! THOSE SCUMBUCKETS--
HE DIDN'T DIE FOR NOTHING! NOW LET'S BLOW THIS HOLE!
28mm 1:2x
DASH CAM
8:08:56 / 14:34:21
WE DID IT! WE GOT THE COMMANDER HIMSELF!
WITH THESE POWERS OF OURS, THEY DON'T STAND A--

WOODY! WHAT'S WRONG?

DON'T-- KNOW! DON'T--

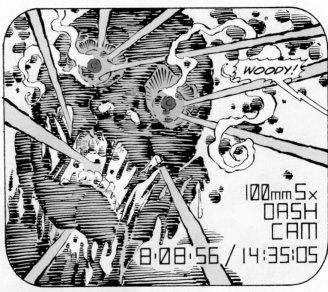

WOODY!

100mm 5x
DASH
CAM
8:08:56 / 14:35:05

CAN YOU HEAR ME? BASE! PLEASE! HEL--

14:35:12
END TRANSMISSION
0

THE MORITURI METABOLISM IS FUNDAMENTALLY INCOMPATIBLE WITH THE HUMAN-- AND WOODY'S BODY REJECTED IT CATASTROPHICALLY. AS ANY BODY MUST.

JUST AS IT'S IMPOSSIBLE TO PREDICT JUST WHAT POWERS A PERSON WILL DEVELOP, IT'S IMPOSSIBLE TO SAY JUST WHEN THIS REJECTION WILL OCCUR. ONE CAN'T EXPECT A GREATER SPAN THAN A YEAR.

THE HORDE NUKED THE ESCAPE SHIP IN RETALIATION-- OTHERWISE THE DATA WOULD BE MORE-- COMPLETE.

THAT'S THE PRICE WE'RE ASKING YOU TO PAY, EVERSON. THINK CAREFULLY ABOUT IT.

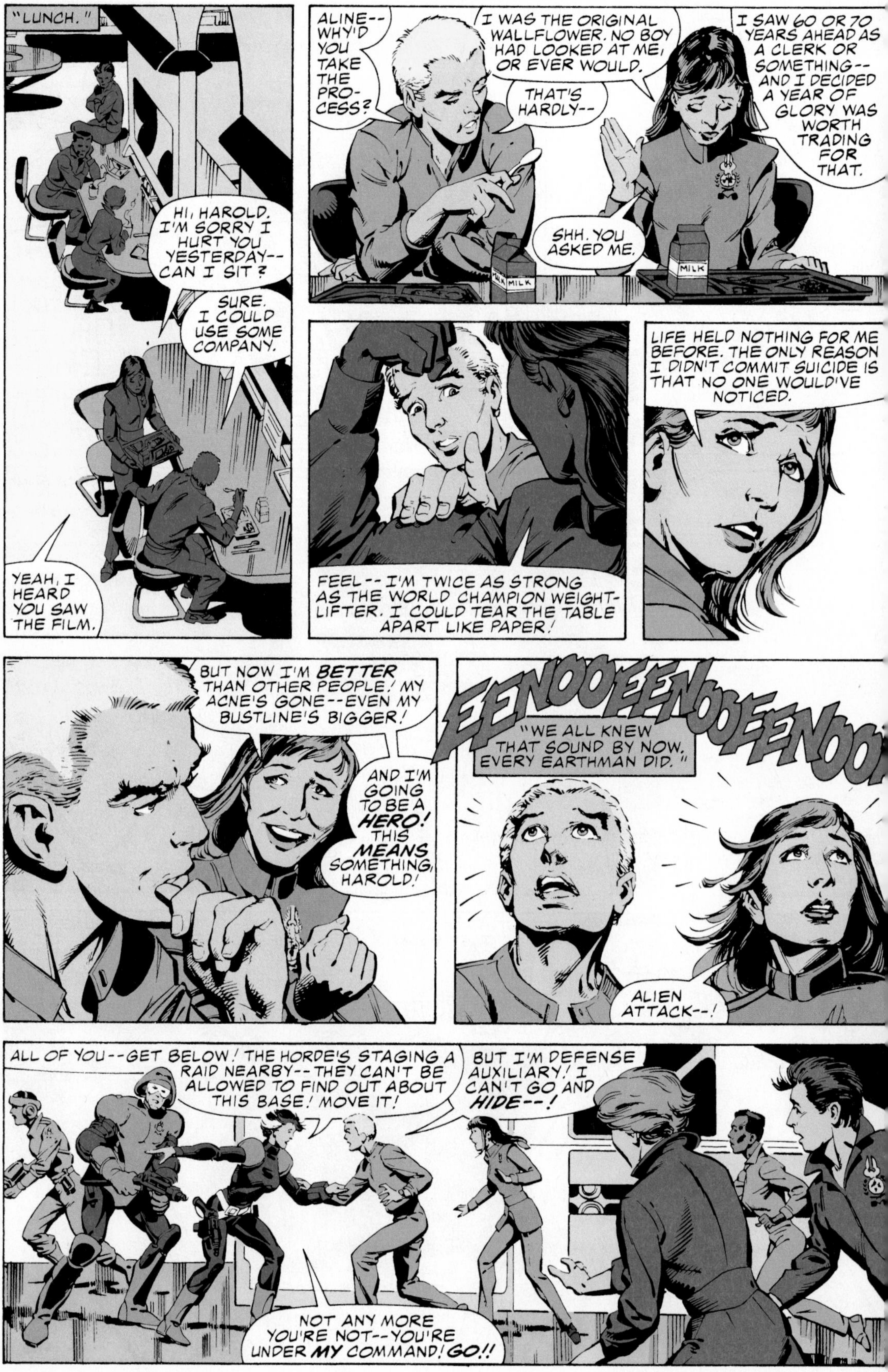
"LUNCH."
HI, HAROLD. I'M SORRY I HURT YOU YESTERDAY--CAN I SIT?
SURE. I COULD USE SOME COMPANY.
YEAH, I HEARD YOU SAW THE FILM.
ALINE--WHY'D YOU TAKE THE PROCESS?
I WAS THE ORIGINAL WALLFLOWER. NO BOY HAD LOOKED AT ME, OR EVER WOULD.
THAT'S HARDLY--
I SAW 60 OR 70 YEARS AHEAD AS A CLERK OR SOMETHING--AND I DECIDED A YEAR OF GLORY WAS WORTH TRADING FOR THAT.
SHH. YOU ASKED ME.
MILK
MILK
MILK
FEEL--I'M TWICE AS STRONG AS THE WORLD CHAMPION WEIGHT-LIFTER. I COULD TEAR THE TABLE APART LIKE PAPER!
LIFE HELD NOTHING FOR ME BEFORE. THE ONLY REASON I DIDN'T COMMIT SUICIDE IS THAT NO ONE WOULD'VE NOTICED.
BUT NOW I'M BETTER THAN OTHER PEOPLE! MY ACNE'S GONE--EVEN MY BUSTLINE'S BIGGER!
AND I'M GOING TO BE A HERO! THIS MEANS SOMETHING, HAROLD!
EENOOEENOOEENOOEENOO
"WE ALL KNEW THAT SOUND BY NOW. EVERY EARTHMAN DID."
ALIEN ATTACK--!
ALL OF YOU--GET BELOW! THE HORDE'S STAGING A RAID NEARBY--THEY CAN'T BE ALLOWED TO FIND OUT ABOUT THIS BASE! MOVE IT!
BUT I'M DEFENSE AUXILIARY! I CAN'T GO AND HIDE--!
NOT ANY MORE YOU'RE NOT--YOU'RE UNDER MY COMMAND! GO!!

"THEY PUT US IN A BUNKER A HUNDRED FEET DOWN. LIKE GOLD BULLION. AND I WOULDN'T HAVE IT."

WE SHOULDN'T BE COWERING IN A HOLE WHILE OTHERS FIGHT FOR US! I DIDN'T COME HERE TO BE A COWARD!

HMM-- YES--!

NONE OF US IS READY YET, HAROLD--NOT EVEN ALINE! WHAT GOOD WOULD IT DO IF WE GOT OURSELVES KILLED NOW?

THERE! THE WIZ DOES IT AGAIN! TUNED THIS RADIO RIGHT INTO THE MILITARY CHANNELS!

I SEE 'EM, COMMANDER --TYPICAL HORDE PLUNDER PARTY. TWO SEMI-PORTA-BLES AND A SCREEN GENERATOR. MAKING MY RUN NOW.

ROGER. TWO AND THREE ARE FOLLOWING YOU IN LOW.

YOU HEAR THAT? THAT'S THE COMMANDER'S VOICE! WE CAN'T SIT HERE WHILE SHE FIGHTS! I'M GOING!

AND SO AM I. MY FAMILY WAS IN SAN DIEGO.

NO ARGUMENT HERE--BUT THIS DOOR IS BUILT AGAINST EVEN MY STRENGTH.

BUT THEY CAN'T KEEP US--I'VE GOT TO PULL--!

WHAT THE--?

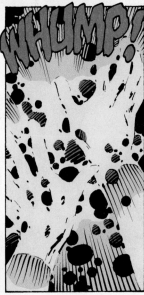

WHUMP!

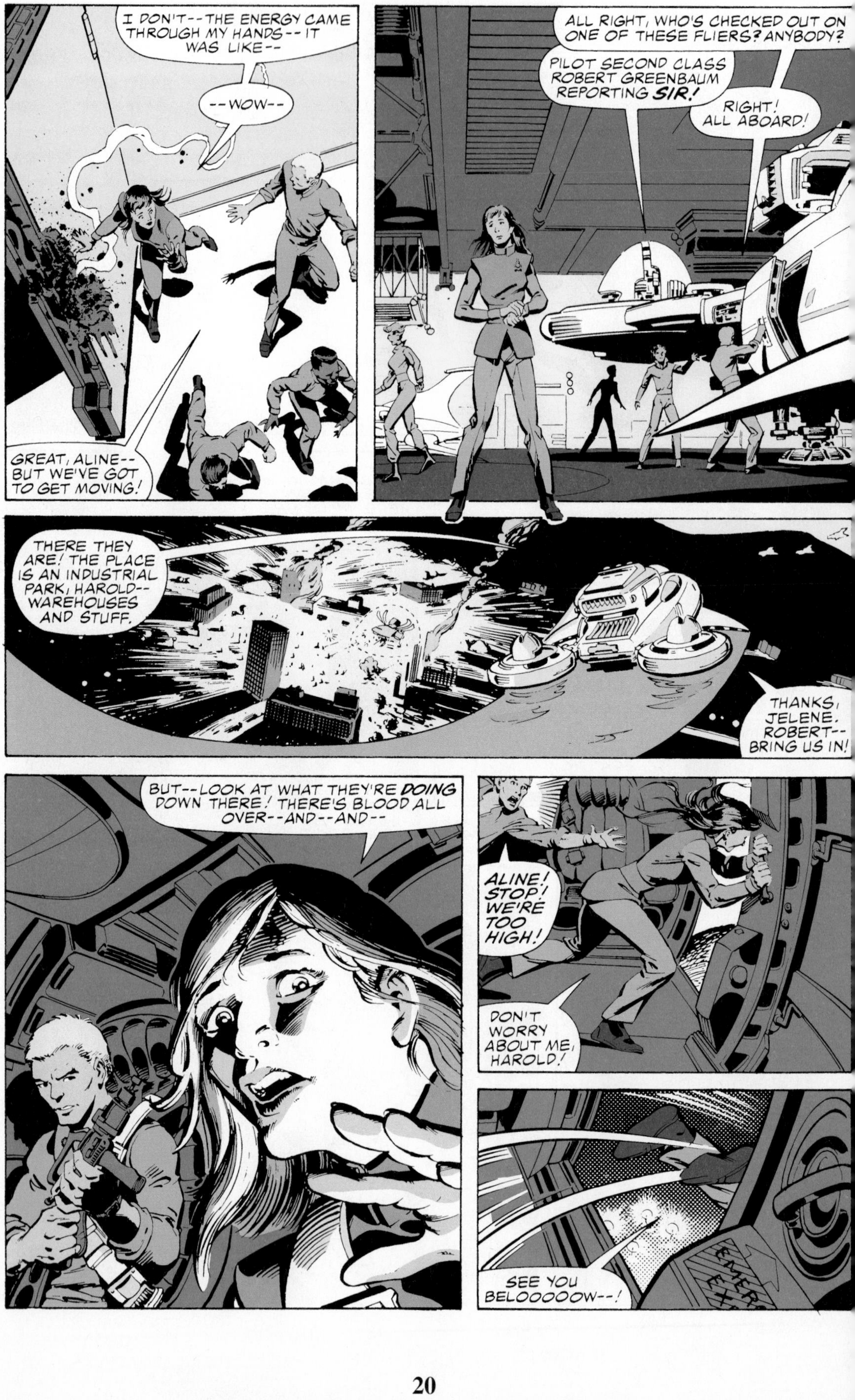
I DON'T--THE ENERGY CAME THROUGH MY HANDS--IT WAS LIKE--
--WOW--
GREAT, ALINE--BUT WE'VE GOT TO GET MOVING!
ALL RIGHT, WHO'S CHECKED OUT ON ONE OF THESE FLIERS? ANYBODY?
PILOT SECOND CLASS ROBERT GREENBAUM REPORTING SIR!
RIGHT! ALL ABOARD!
THERE THEY ARE! THE PLACE IS AN INDUSTRIAL PARK, HAROLD--WAREHOUSES AND STUFF.
THANKS, JELENE. ROBERT--BRING US IN!
BUT--LOOK AT WHAT THEY'RE DOING DOWN THERE! THERE'S BLOOD ALL OVER--AND--AND--
ALINE! STOP! WE'RE TOO HIGH!
DON'T WORRY ABOUT ME, HAROLD!
SEE YOU BELOOOOOW--!

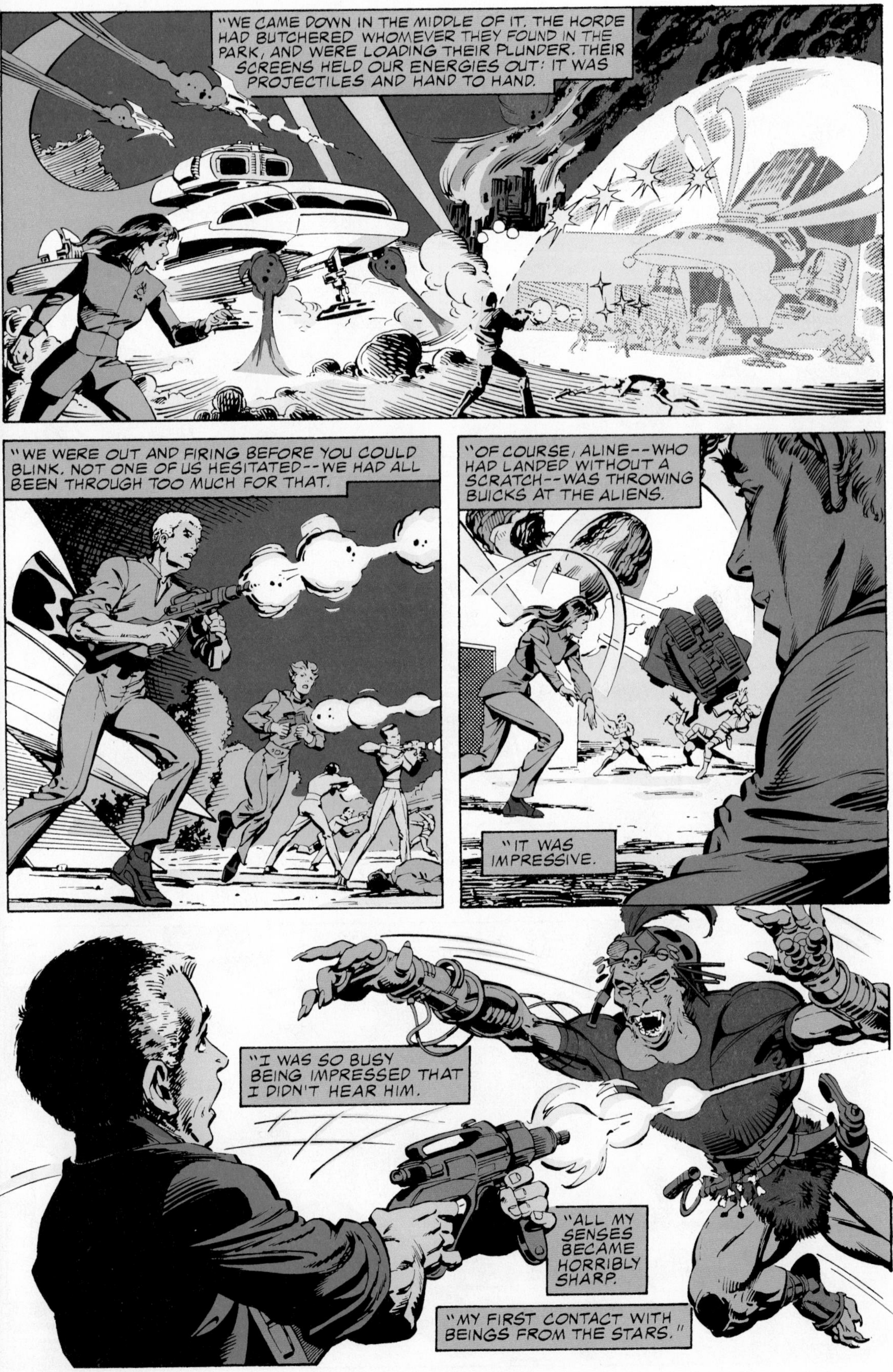
"WE CAME DOWN IN THE MIDDLE OF IT. THE HORDE HAD BUTCHERED WHOMEVER THEY FOUND IN THE PARK, AND WERE LOADING THEIR PLUNDER. THEIR SCREENS HELD OUR ENERGIES OUT: IT WAS PROJECTILES AND HAND TO HAND.
"WE WERE OUT AND FIRING BEFORE YOU COULD BLINK. NOT ONE OF US HESITATED--WE HAD ALL BEEN THROUGH TOO MUCH FOR THAT.
"OF COURSE, ALINE--WHO HAD LANDED WITHOUT A SCRATCH--WAS THROWING BUICKS AT THE ALIENS.
"IT WAS IMPRESSIVE.
"I WAS SO BUSY BEING IMPRESSED THAT I DIDN'T HEAR HIM.
"ALL MY SENSES BECAME HORRIBLY SHARP.
"MY FIRST CONTACT WITH BEINGS FROM THE STARS."

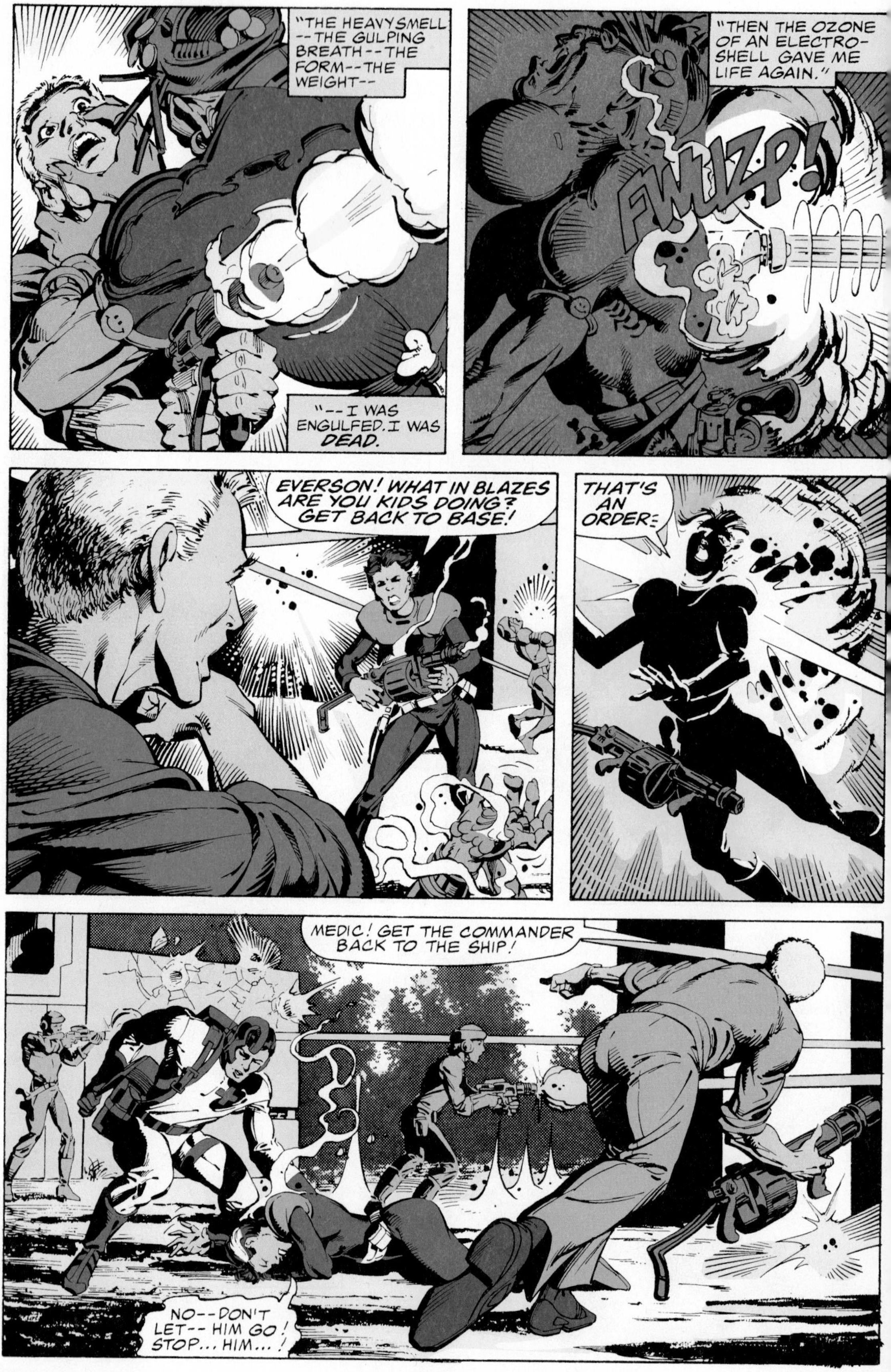
"THE HEAVYSMELL --THE GULPING BREATH--THE FORM--THE WEIGHT--
"--I WAS ENGULFED. I WAS DEAD.
"THEN THE OZONE OF AN ELECTRO-SHELL GAVE ME LIFE AGAIN."
FWUZP!
EVERSON! WHAT IN BLAZES ARE YOU KIDS DOING? GET BACK TO BASE!
THAT'S AN ORDER=
MEDIC! GET THE COMMANDER BACK TO THE SHIP!
NO--DON'T LET--HIM GO! STOP... HIM...!

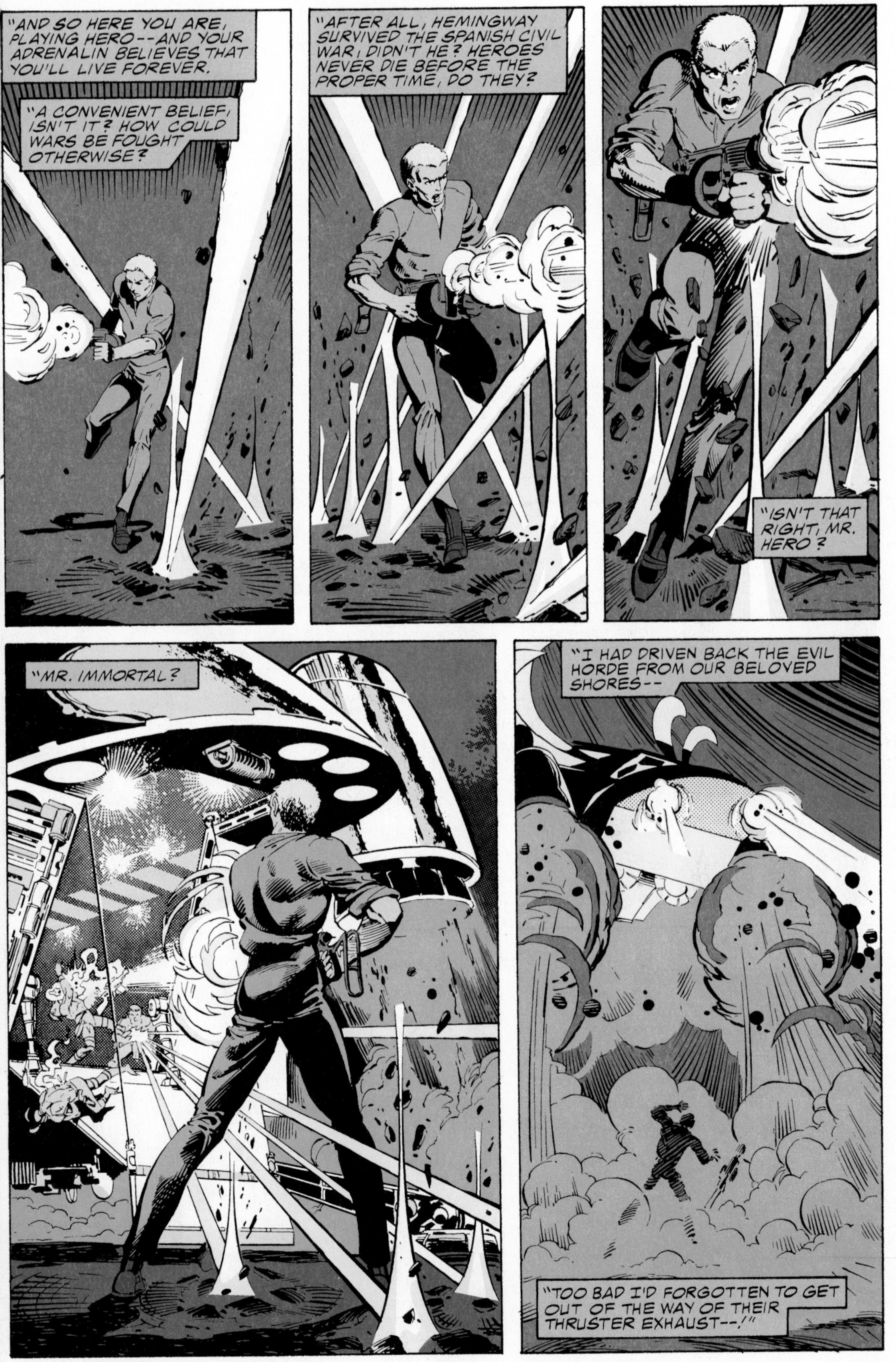
"AND SO HERE YOU ARE, PLAYING HERO--AND YOUR ADRENALIN BELIEVES THAT YOU'LL LIVE FOREVER.
"A CONVENIENT BELIEF, ISN'T IT? HOW COULD WARS BE FOUGHT OTHERWISE?
"AFTER ALL, HEMINGWAY SURVIVED THE SPANISH CIVIL WAR, DIDN'T HE? HEROES NEVER DIE BEFORE THE PROPER TIME, DO THEY?
"ISN'T THAT RIGHT, MR. HERO?
"MR. IMMORTAL?
"I HAD DRIVEN BACK THE EVIL HORDE FROM OUR BELOVED SHORES--
"TOO BAD I'D FORGOTTEN TO GET OUT OF THE WAY OF THEIR THRUSTER EXHAUST--!"

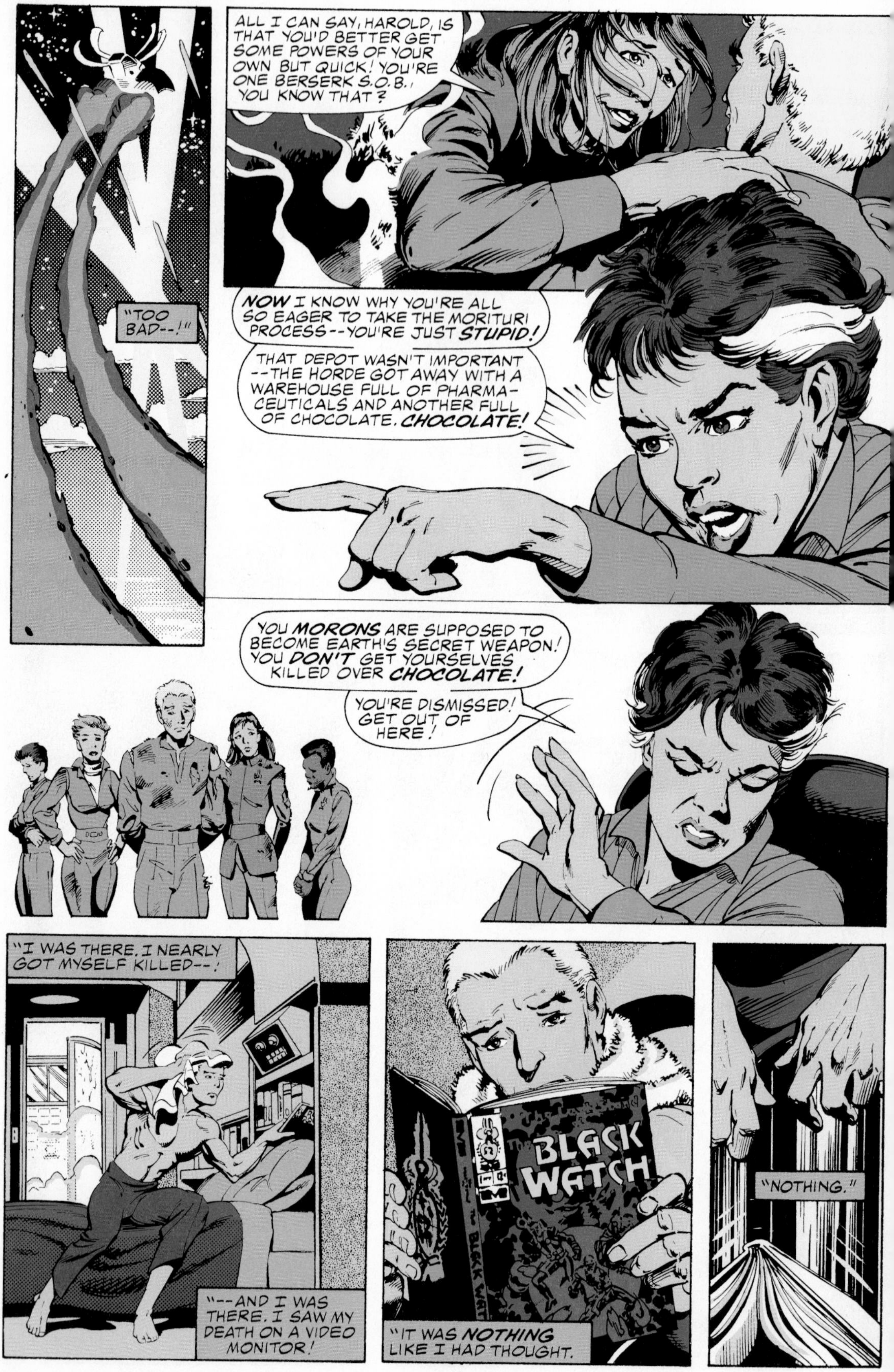
"TOO BAD--!"
ALL I CAN SAY, HAROLD, IS THAT YOU'D BETTER GET SOME POWERS OF YOUR OWN BUT QUICK! YOU'RE ONE BERSERK S.O.B., YOU KNOW THAT?
NOW I KNOW WHY YOU'RE ALL SO EAGER TO TAKE THE MORITURI PROCESS--YOU'RE JUST STUPID!
THAT DEPOT WASN'T IMPORTANT--THE HORDE GOT AWAY WITH A WAREHOUSE FULL OF PHARMACEUTICALS AND ANOTHER FULL OF CHOCOLATE. CHOCOLATE!
YOU MORONS ARE SUPPOSED TO BECOME EARTH'S SECRET WEAPON! YOU DON'T GET YOURSELVES KILLED OVER CHOCOLATE!
YOU'RE DISMISSED! GET OUT OF HERE!
"I WAS THERE. I NEARLY GOT MYSELF KILLED--!
"--AND I WAS THERE. I SAW MY DEATH ON A VIDEO MONITOR!
BLACK WATCH
"IT WAS NOTHING LIKE I HAD THOUGHT.
"NOTHING."

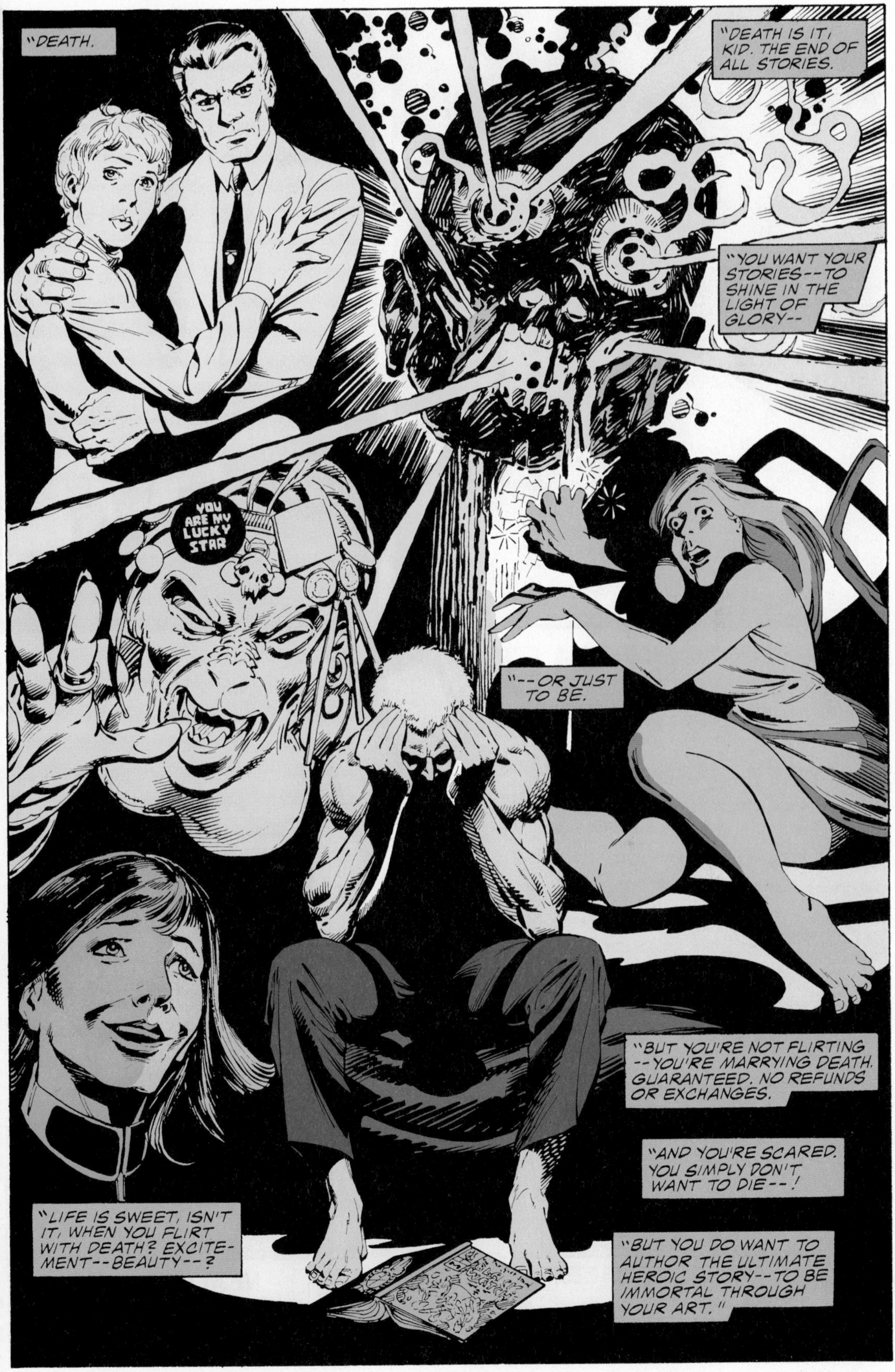
"DEATH.
YOU ARE MY LUCKY STAR
"DEATH IS IT, KID. THE END OF ALL STORIES.
"YOU WANT YOUR STORIES--TO SHINE IN THE LIGHT OF GLORY--
"--OR JUST TO BE.
"LIFE IS SWEET, ISN'T IT, WHEN YOU FLIRT WITH DEATH? EXCITE-MENT--BEAUTY--?
"BUT YOU'RE NOT FLIRTING --YOU'RE MARRYING DEATH. GUARANTEED. NO REFUNDS OR EXCHANGES.
"AND YOU'RE SCARED. YOU SIMPLY DON'T WANT TO DIE--!
"BUT YOU DO WANT TO AUTHOR THE ULTIMATE HEROIC STORY--TO BE IMMORTAL THROUGH YOUR ART."

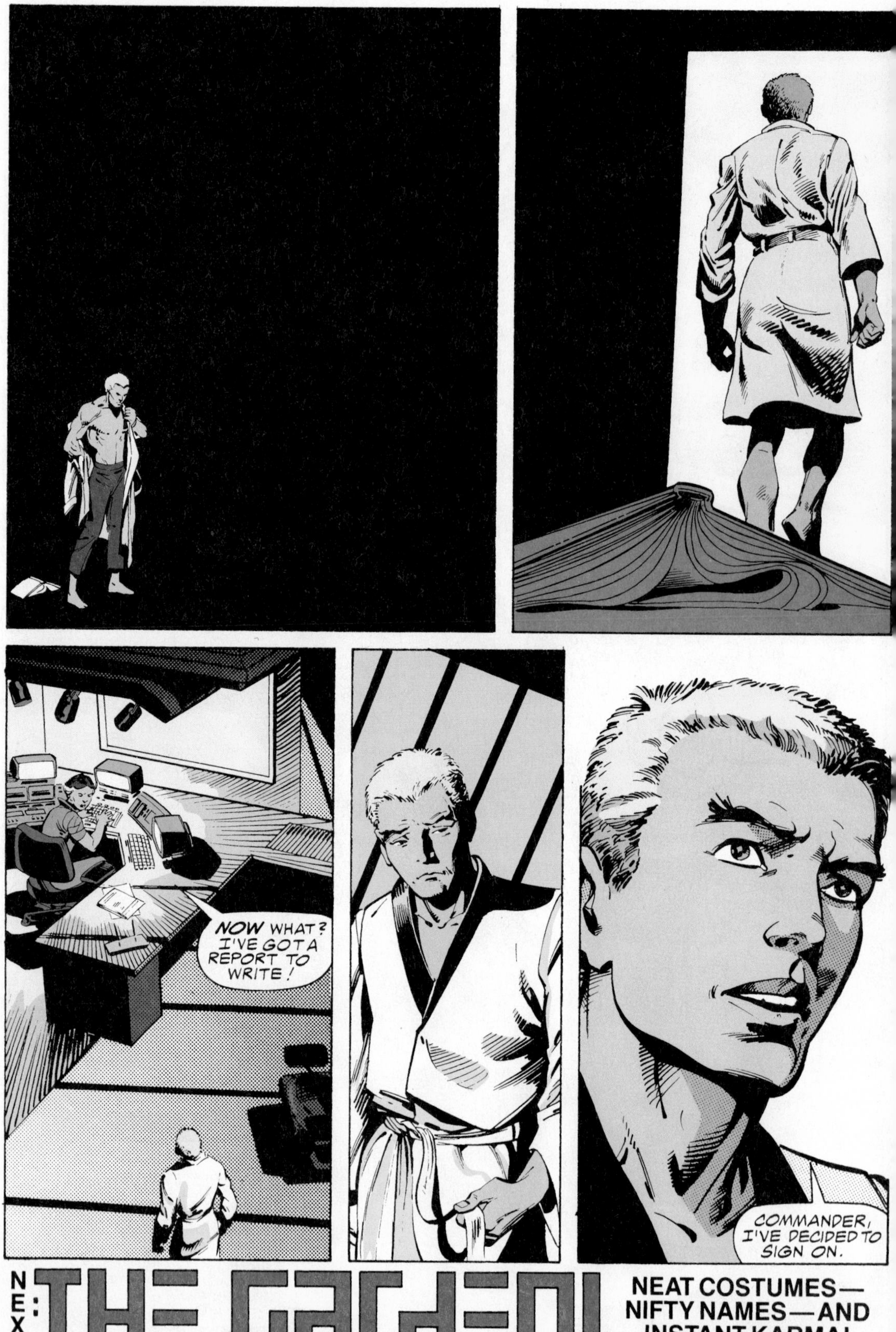
NOW WHAT? I'VE GOT A REPORT TO WRITE!
COMMANDER, I'VE DECIDED TO SIGN ON.

NEXT: THE GARDEN!

NEAT COSTUMES— NIFTY NAMES—AND INSTANT KARMA! DON'T MISS IT!

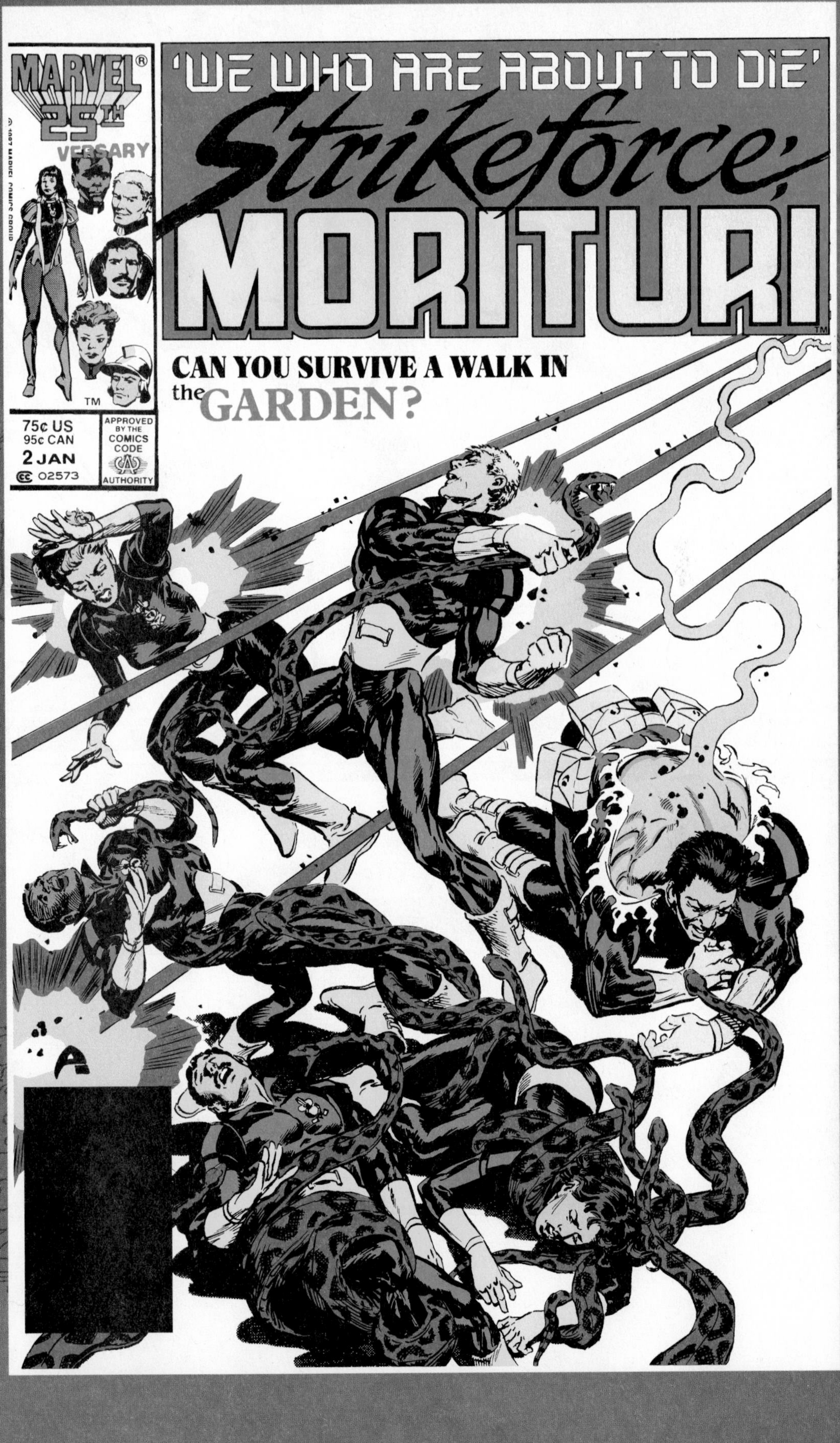
MARVEL®
25TH
VERSARY
TM
'WE WHO ARE ABOUT TO DIE'
Strikeforce:
MORITURI
TM
CAN YOU SURVIVE A WALK IN the GARDEN?
75¢ US
95¢ CAN
2 JAN
02573
APPROVED BY THE COMICS CODE AUTHORITY

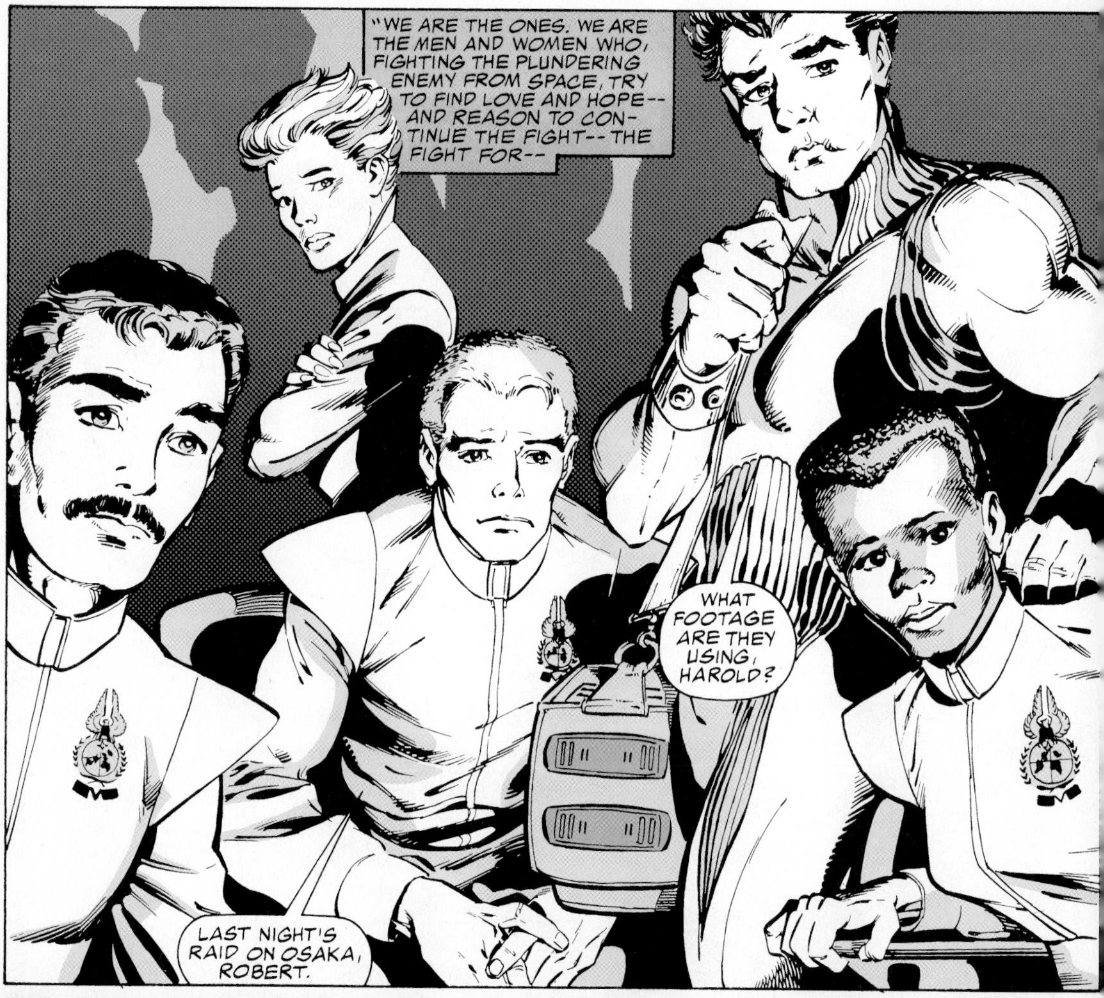
"WE ARE THE ONES. WE ARE THE MEN AND WOMEN WHO, FIGHTING THE PLUNDERING ENEMY FROM SPACE, TRY TO FIND LOVE AND HOPE-- AND REASON TO CONTINUE THE FIGHT-- THE FIGHT FOR--
WHAT FOOTAGE ARE THEY USING, HAROLD?
LAST NIGHT'S RAID ON OSAKA, ROBERT.

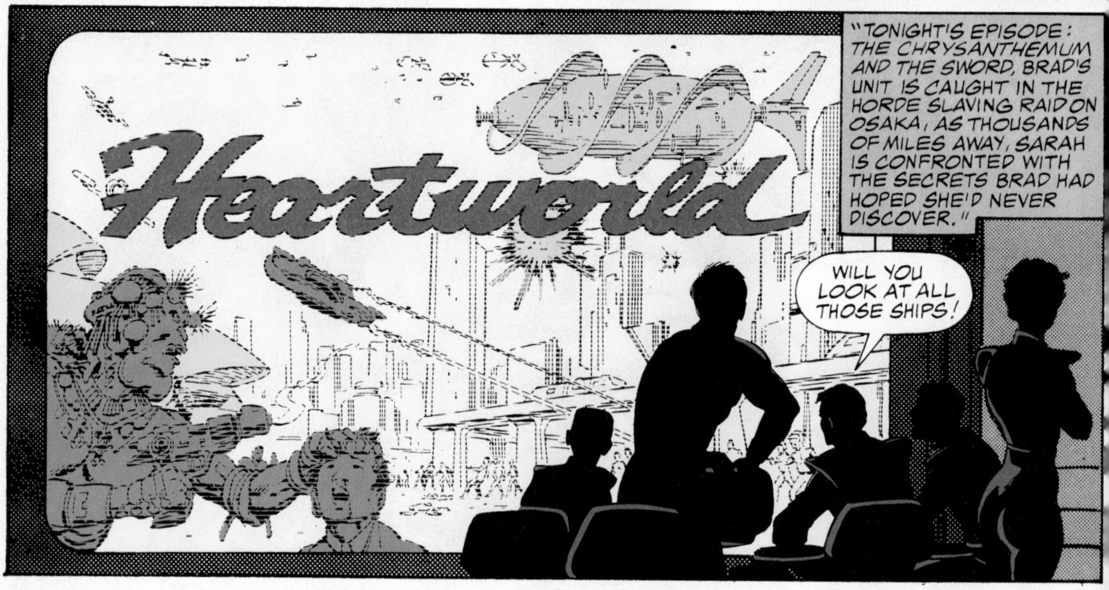
Heartworld
"TONIGHT'S EPISODE: THE CHRYSANTHEMUM AND THE SWORD. BRAD'S UNIT IS CAUGHT IN THE HORDE SLAVING RAID ON OSAKA, AS THOUSANDS OF MILES AWAY, SARAH IS CONFRONTED WITH THE SECRETS BRAD HAD HOPED SHE'D NEVER DISCOVER."
WILL YOU LOOK AT ALL THOSE SHIPS!

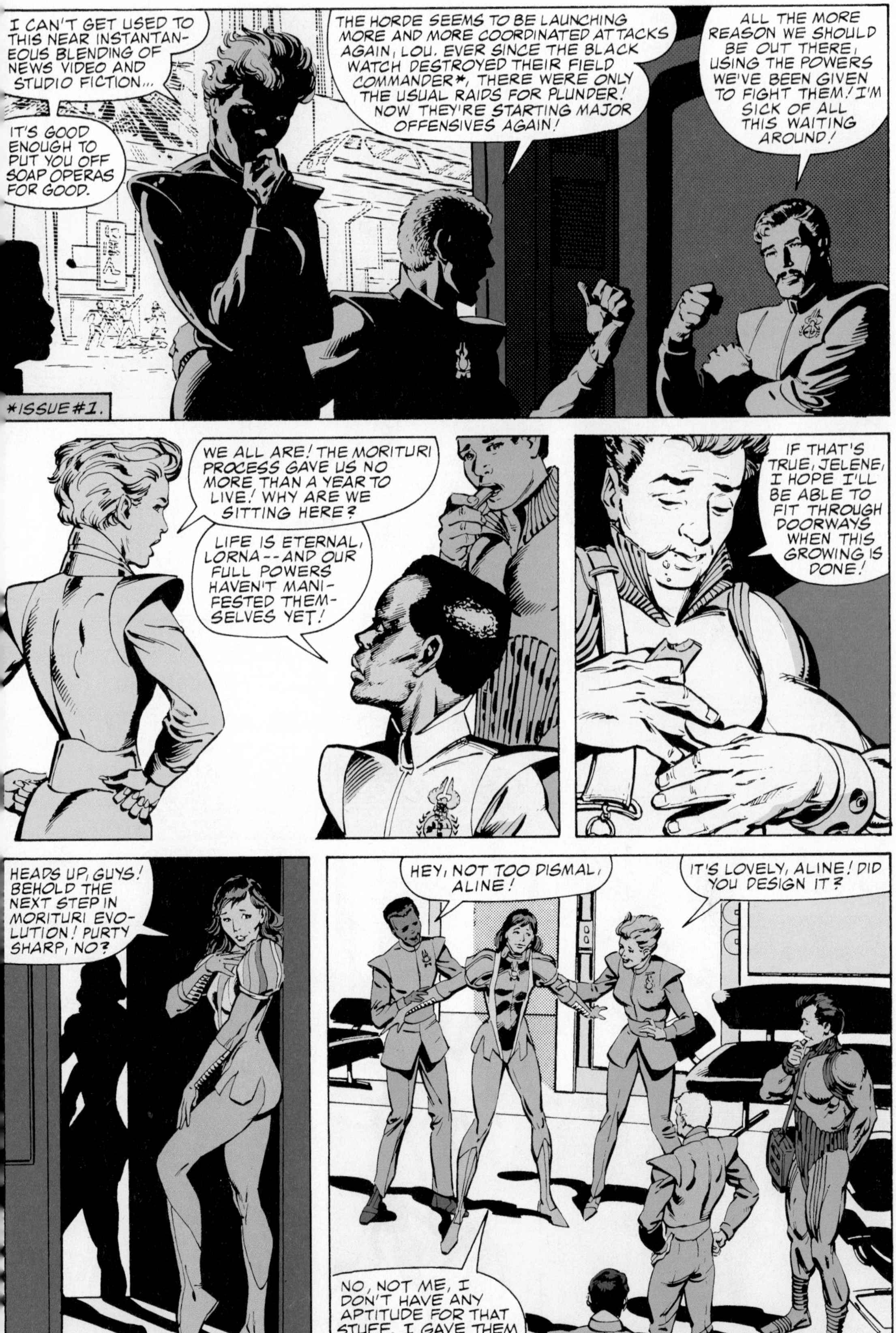
I CAN'T GET USED TO THIS NEAR INSTANTANEOUS BLENDING OF NEWS VIDEO AND STUDIO FICTION...
IT'S GOOD ENOUGH TO PUT YOU OFF SOAP OPERAS FOR GOOD.
THE HORDE SEEMS TO BE LAUNCHING MORE AND MORE COORDINATED ATTACKS AGAIN, LOU. EVER SINCE THE BLACK WATCH DESTROYED THEIR FIELD COMMANDER*, THERE WERE ONLY THE USUAL RAIDS FOR PLUNDER! NOW THEY'RE STARTING MAJOR OFFENSIVES AGAIN!
ALL THE MORE REASON WE SHOULD BE OUT THERE, USING THE POWERS WE'VE BEEN GIVEN TO FIGHT THEM! I'M SICK OF ALL THIS WAITING AROUND!
*ISSUE #1.
WE ALL ARE! THE MORITURI PROCESS GAVE US NO MORE THAN A YEAR TO LIVE! WHY ARE WE SITTING HERE?
LIFE IS ETERNAL, LORNA--AND OUR FULL POWERS HAVEN'T MANIFESTED THEMSELVES YET!
IF THAT'S TRUE, JELENE, I HOPE I'LL BE ABLE TO FIT THROUGH DOORWAYS WHEN THIS GROWING IS DONE!
HEADS UP, GUYS! BEHOLD THE NEXT STEP IN MORITURI EVOLUTION! PURTY SHARP, NO?
HEY, NOT TOO DISMAL, ALINE!
IT'S LOVELY, ALINE! DID YOU DESIGN IT?
NO, NOT ME, I DON'T HAVE ANY APTITUDE FOR THAT STUFF. I GAVE THEM THE IDEA AND THEY JUST DESIGNED IT.

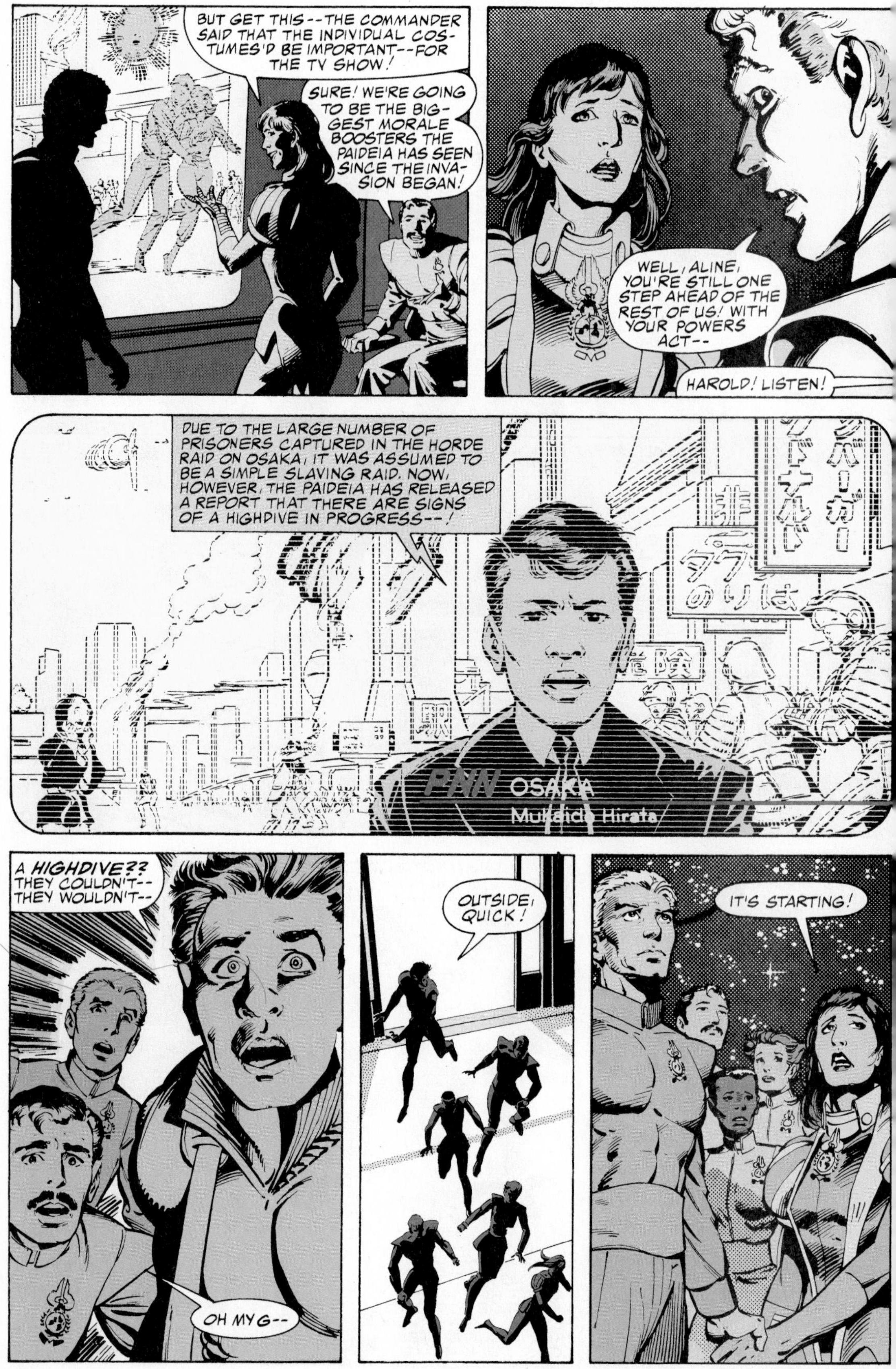
BUT GET THIS--THE COMMANDER SAID THAT THE INDIVIDUAL COSTUMES'D BE IMPORTANT--FOR THE TV SHOW!
SURE! WE'RE GOING TO BE THE BIGGEST MORALE BOOSTERS THE PAIDEIA HAS SEEN SINCE THE INVASION BEGAN!
WELL, ALINE, YOU'RE STILL ONE STEP AHEAD OF THE REST OF US! WITH YOUR POWERS ACT--
HAROLD! LISTEN!
DUE TO THE LARGE NUMBER OF PRISONERS CAPTURED IN THE HORDE RAID ON OSAKA, IT WAS ASSUMED TO BE A SIMPLE SLAVING RAID. NOW, HOWEVER, THE PAIDEIA HAS RELEASED A REPORT THAT THERE ARE SIGNS OF A HIGHDIVE IN PROGRESS--!
PNN OSAKA
Mukaido Hirata
A HIGHDIVE?? THEY COULDN'T--THEY WOULDN'T--
OH MY G--
OUTSIDE, QUICK!
IT'S STARTING!

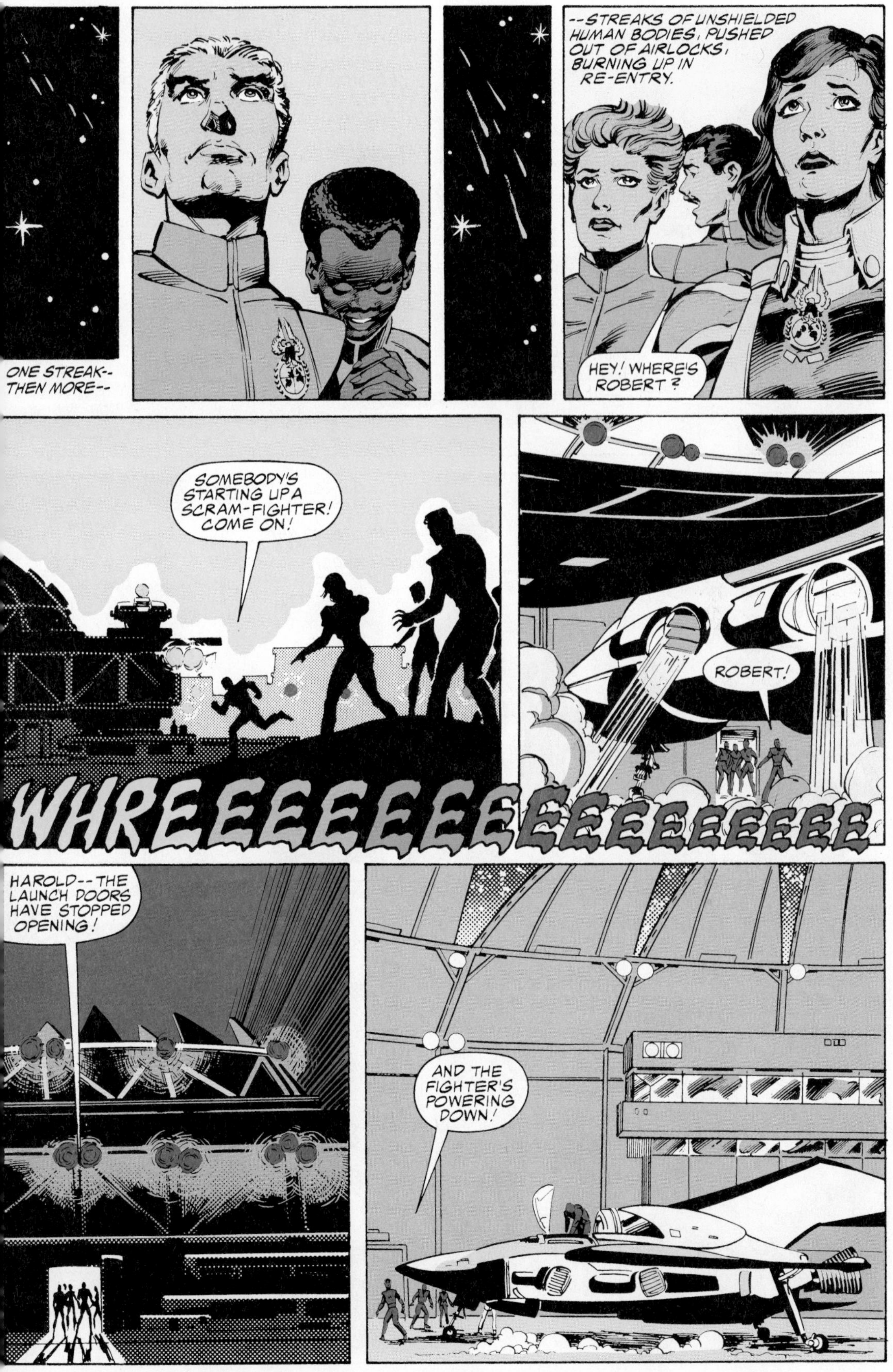
ONE STREAK--
THEN MORE--
--STREAKS OF UNSHIELDED HUMAN BODIES, PUSHED OUT OF AIRLOCKS, BURNING UP IN RE-ENTRY.
HEY! WHERE'S ROBERT?
SOMEBODY'S STARTING UP A SCRAM-FIGHTER! COME ON!
ROBERT!
WHREEEEEEEEEEEEEEEEEE
HAROLD--THE LAUNCH DOORS HAVE STOPPED OPENING!
AND THE FIGHTER'S POWERING DOWN!

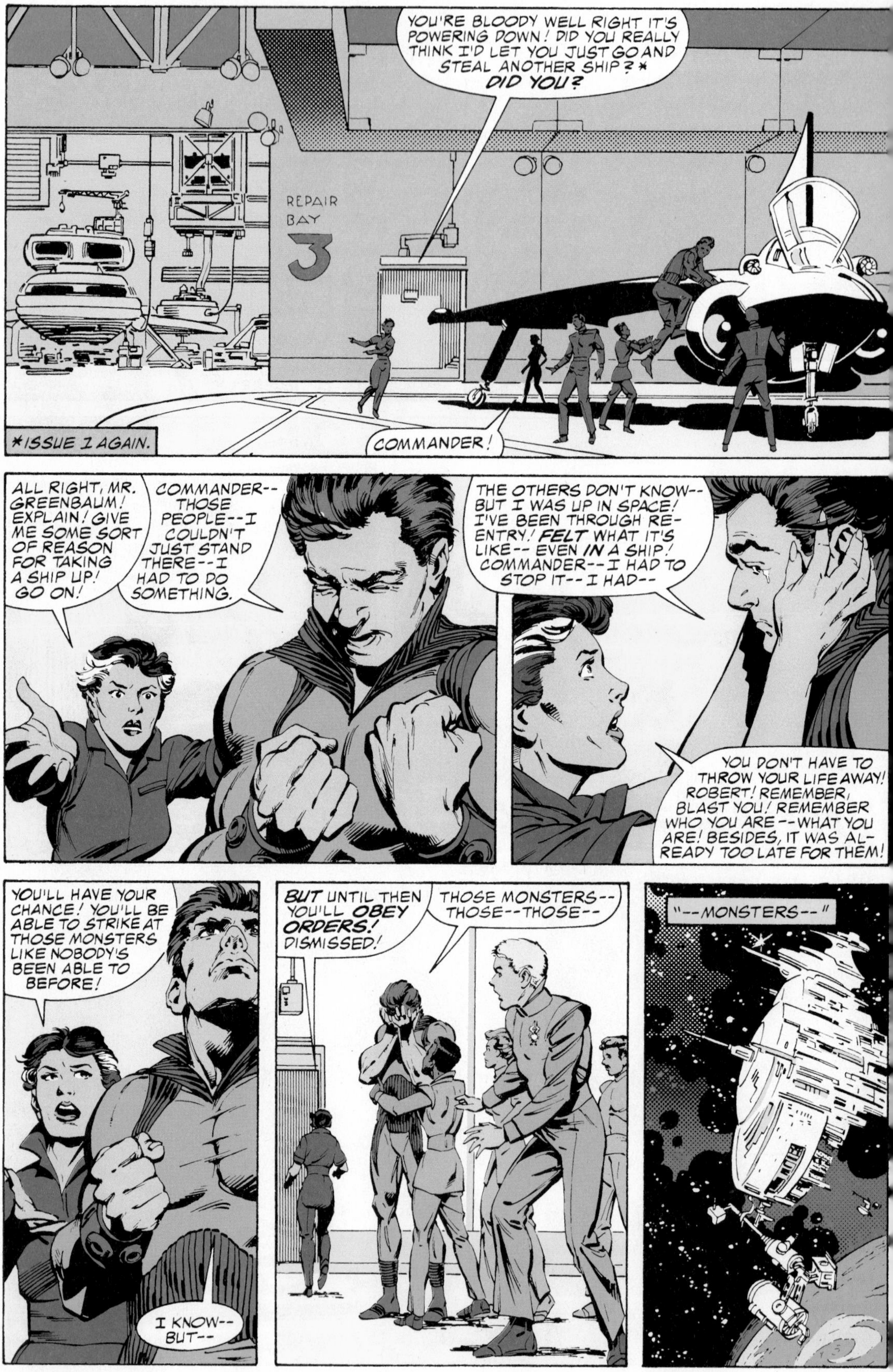
YOU'RE BLOODY WELL RIGHT IT'S POWERING DOWN! DID YOU REALLY THINK I'D LET YOU JUST GO AND STEAL ANOTHER SHIP?* DID YOU?
REPAIR BAY 3
*ISSUE 1 AGAIN.
COMMANDER!
ALL RIGHT, MR. GREENBAUM! EXPLAIN! GIVE ME SOME SORT OF REASON FOR TAKING A SHIP UP! GO ON!
COMMANDER-- THOSE PEOPLE--I COULDN'T JUST STAND THERE--I HAD TO DO SOMETHING.
THE OTHERS DON'T KNOW-- BUT I WAS UP IN SPACE! I'VE BEEN THROUGH RE-ENTRY! FELT WHAT IT'S LIKE-- EVEN IN A SHIP! COMMANDER--I HAD TO STOP IT--I HAD--
YOU DON'T HAVE TO THROW YOUR LIFE AWAY! ROBERT! REMEMBER, BLAST YOU! REMEMBER WHO YOU ARE--WHAT YOU ARE! BESIDES, IT WAS ALREADY TOO LATE FOR THEM!
YOU'LL HAVE YOUR CHANCE! YOU'LL BE ABLE TO STRIKE AT THOSE MONSTERS LIKE NOBODY'S BEEN ABLE TO BEFORE!
I KNOW-- BUT--
BUT UNTIL THEN YOU'LL OBEY ORDERS! DISMISSED!
THOSE MONSTERS-- THOSE--THOSE--
"--MONSTERS--"

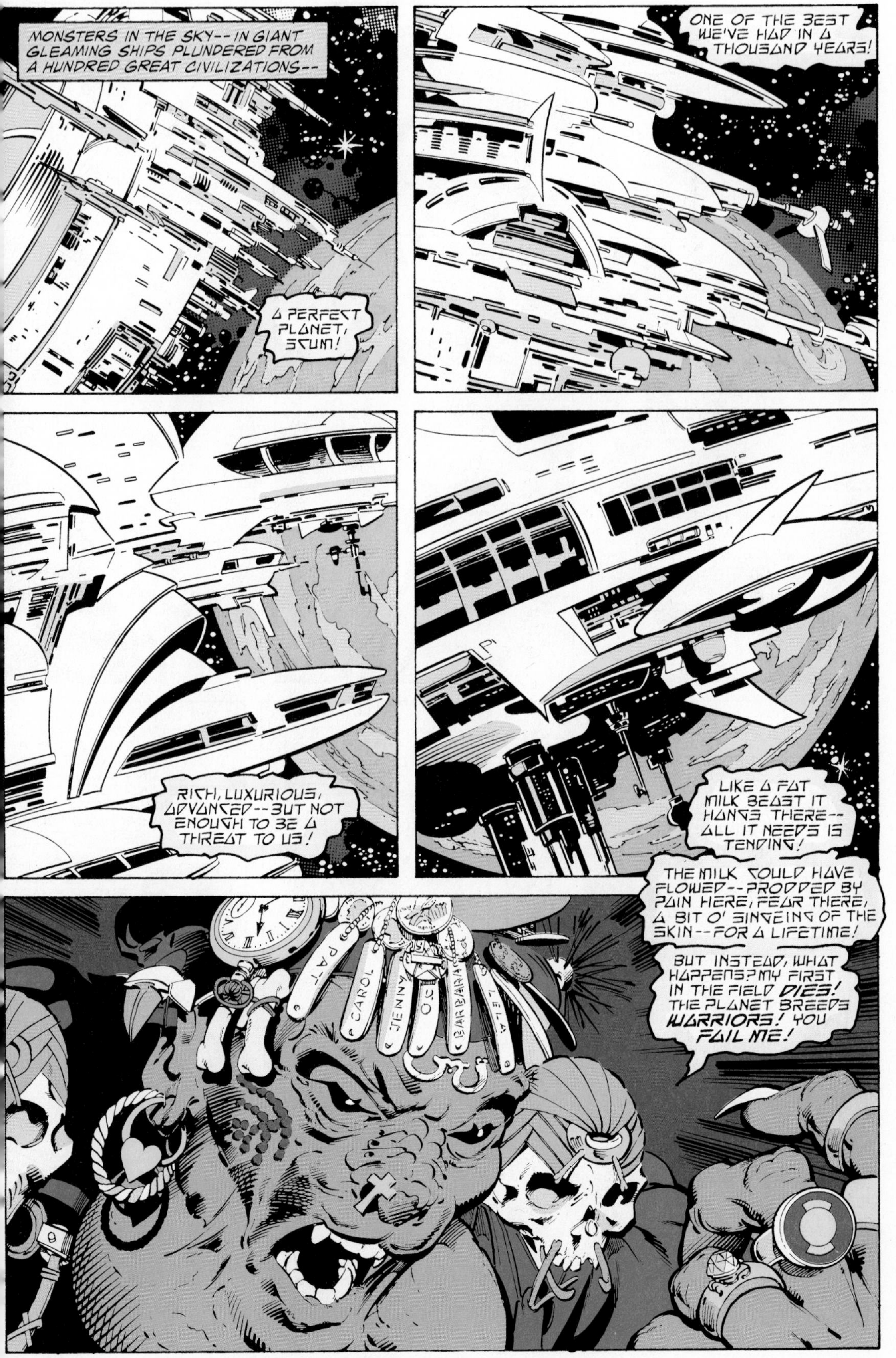
MONSTERS IN THE SKY--IN GIANT GLEAMING SHIPS PLUNDERED FROM A HUNDRED GREAT CIVILIZATIONS--
A PERFECT PLANET, SCUM!
ONE OF THE BEST WE'VE HAD IN A THOUSAND YEARS!
RICH, LUXURIOUS, ADVANCED--BUT NOT ENOUGH TO BE A THREAT TO US!
LIKE A FAT MILK BEAST IT HANGS THERE--ALL IT NEEDS IS TENDING!
THE MILK COULD HAVE FLOWED--PRODDED BY PAIN HERE, FEAR THERE, A BIT O' SINGEING OF THE SKIN--FOR A LIFETIME!
BUT INSTEAD, WHAT HAPPENS? MY FIRST IN THE FIELD DIES! THE PLANET BREEDS WARRIORS! YOU FAIL ME!
PAT
CAROL
JENNY
JO
BARBARA
LELA

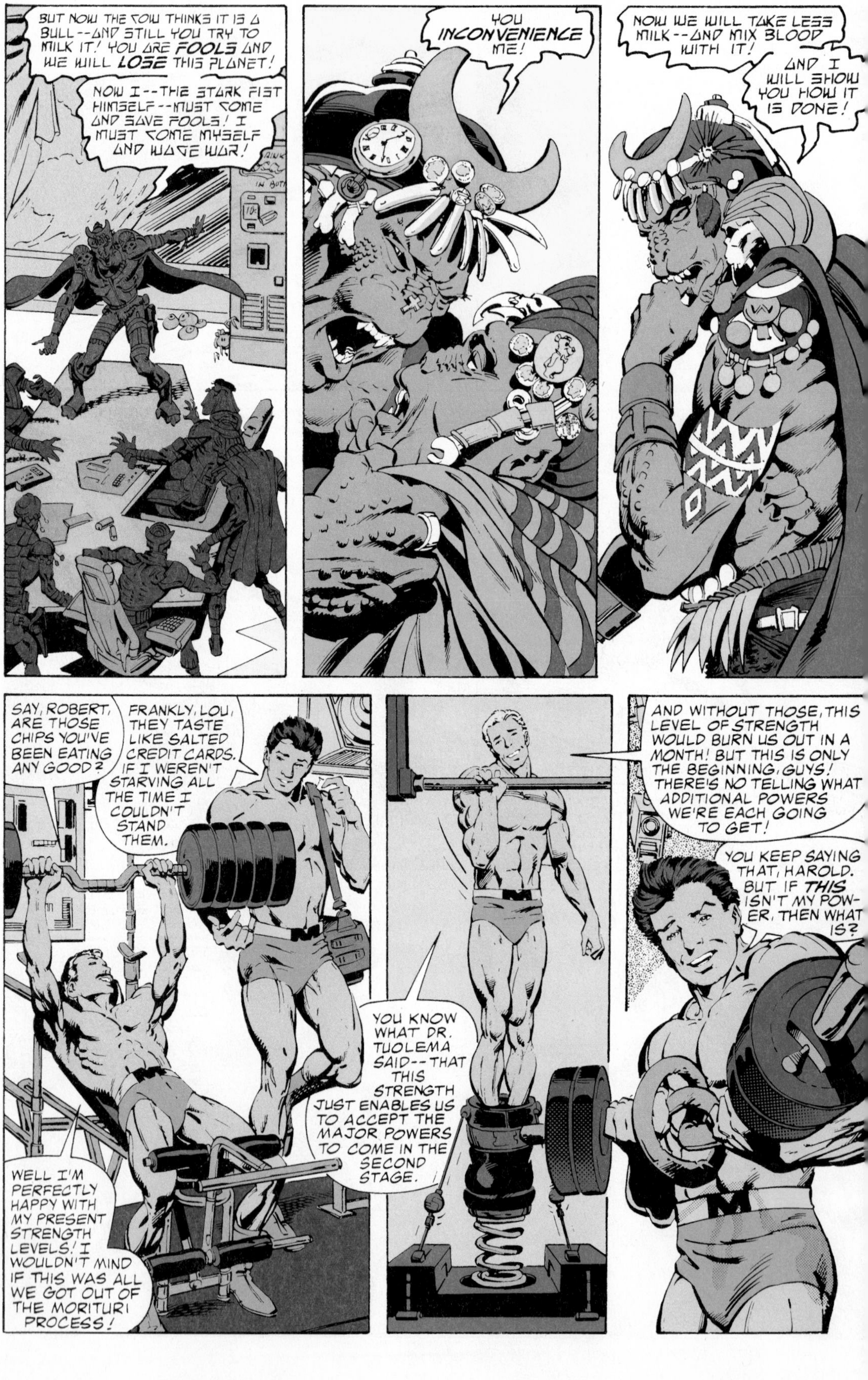
BUT NOW THE COW THINKS IT IS A BULL--AND STILL YOU TRY TO MILK IT! YOU ARE FOOLS AND WE WILL LOSE THIS PLANET!
NOW I--THE STARK FIST HIMSELF--MUST COME AND SAVE FOOLS! I MUST COME MYSELF AND WAGE WAR!
YOU INCONVENIENCE ME!
NOW WE WILL TAKE LESS MILK--AND MIX BLOOD WITH IT!
AND I WILL SHOW YOU HOW IT IS DONE!
SAY, ROBERT, ARE THOSE CHIPS YOU'VE BEEN EATING ANY GOOD?
FRANKLY, LOU, THEY TASTE LIKE SALTED CREDIT CARDS. IF I WEREN'T STARVING ALL THE TIME I COULDN'T STAND THEM.
WELL I'M PERFECTLY HAPPY WITH MY PRESENT STRENGTH LEVELS! I WOULDN'T MIND IF THIS WAS ALL WE GOT OUT OF THE MORITURI PROCESS!
YOU KNOW WHAT DR. TUOLEMA SAID--THAT THIS STRENGTH JUST ENABLES US TO ACCEPT THE MAJOR POWERS TO COME IN THE SECOND STAGE.
AND WITHOUT THOSE, THIS LEVEL OF STRENGTH WOULD BURN US OUT IN A MONTH! BUT THIS IS ONLY THE BEGINNING, GUYS! THERE'S NO TELLING WHAT ADDITIONAL POWERS WE'RE EACH GOING TO GET!
YOU KEEP SAYING THAT, HAROLD. BUT IF THIS ISN'T MY POWER, THEN WHAT IS?

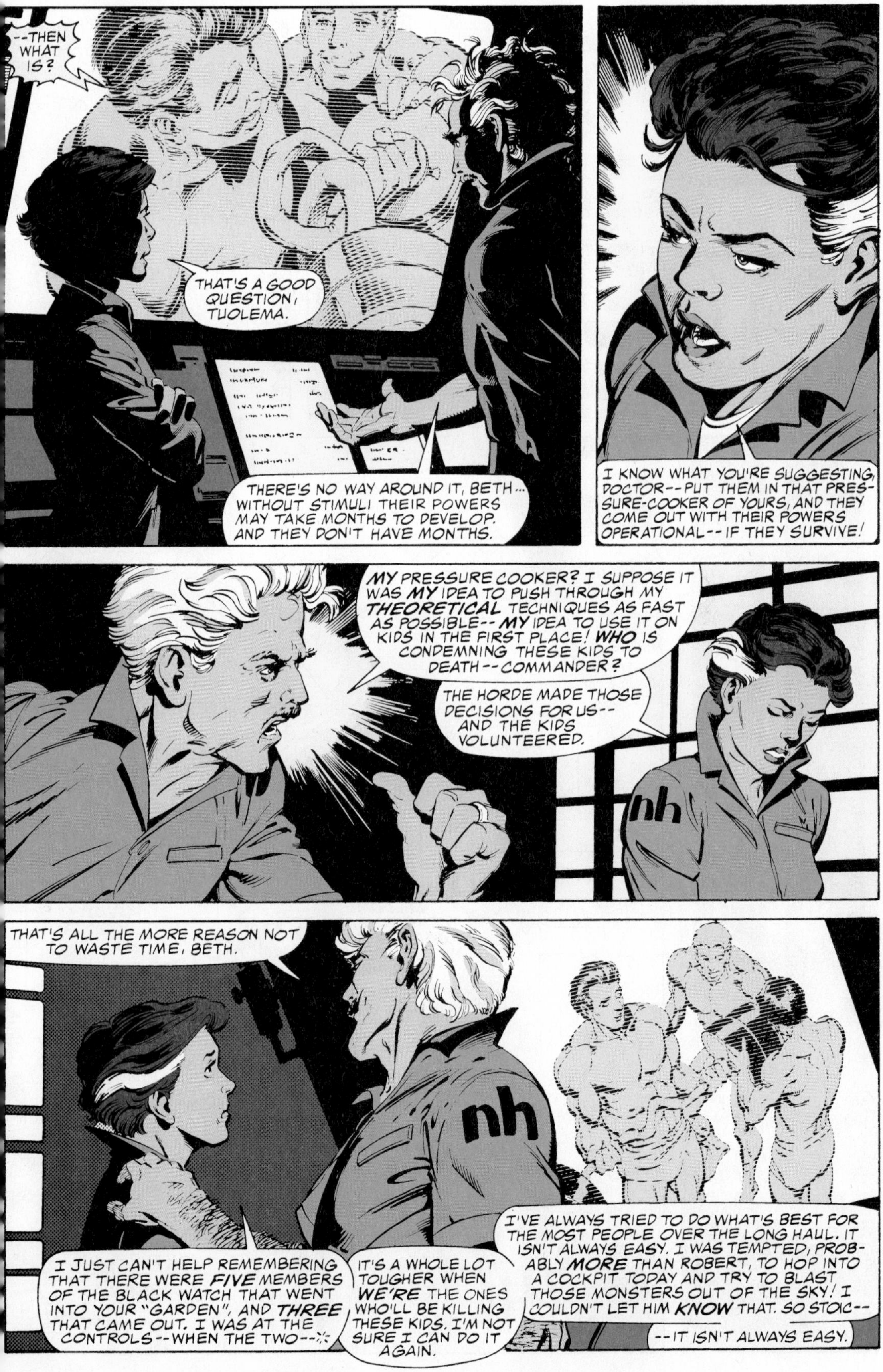
--THEN WHAT IS?
THAT'S A GOOD QUESTION, TUOLEMA.
THERE'S NO WAY AROUND IT, BETH... WITHOUT STIMULI THEIR POWERS MAY TAKE MONTHS TO DEVELOP. AND THEY DON'T HAVE MONTHS.
I KNOW WHAT YOU'RE SUGGESTING, DOCTOR-- PUT THEM IN THAT PRESSURE-COOKER OF YOURS, AND THEY COME OUT WITH THEIR POWERS OPERATIONAL-- IF THEY SURVIVE!
MY PRESSURE COOKER? I SUPPOSE IT WAS MY IDEA TO PUSH THROUGH MY THEORETICAL TECHNIQUES AS FAST AS POSSIBLE-- MY IDEA TO USE IT ON KIDS IN THE FIRST PLACE! WHO IS CONDEMNING THESE KIDS TO DEATH -- COMMANDER?
THE HORDE MADE THOSE DECISIONS FOR US-- AND THE KIDS VOLUNTEERED.
nh
THAT'S ALL THE MORE REASON NOT TO WASTE TIME, BETH.
nh
I JUST CAN'T HELP REMEMBERING THAT THERE WERE FIVE MEMBERS OF THE BLACK WATCH THAT WENT INTO YOUR "GARDEN", AND THREE THAT CAME OUT. I WAS AT THE CONTROLS--WHEN THE TWO--
IT'S A WHOLE LOT TOUGHER WHEN WE'RE THE ONES WHO'LL BE KILLING THESE KIDS. I'M NOT SURE I CAN DO IT AGAIN.
I'VE ALWAYS TRIED TO DO WHAT'S BEST FOR THE MOST PEOPLE OVER THE LONG HAUL. IT ISN'T ALWAYS EASY. I WAS TEMPTED, PROBABLY MORE THAN ROBERT, TO HOP INTO A COCKPIT TODAY AND TRY TO BLAST THOSE MONSTERS OUT OF THE SKY! I COULDN'T LET HIM KNOW THAT. SO STOIC--
--IT ISN'T ALWAYS EASY.

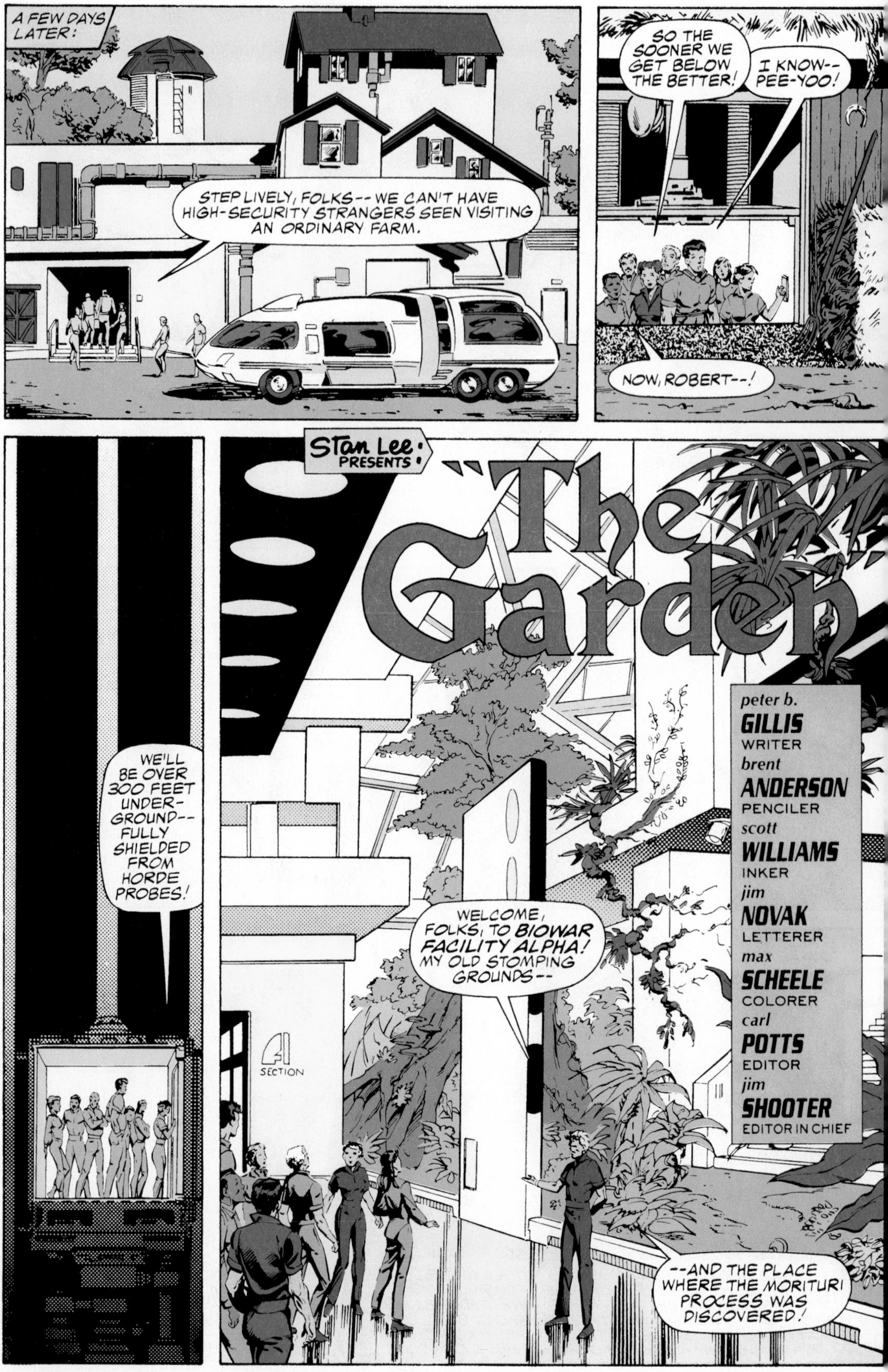
A FEW DAYS LATER:
STEP LIVELY, FOLKS-- WE CAN'T HAVE HIGH-SECURITY STRANGERS SEEN VISITING AN ORDINARY FARM.
SO THE SOONER WE GET BELOW THE BETTER!
I KNOW-- PEE-YOO!
NOW, ROBERT--!
WE'LL BE OVER 300 FEET UNDER-GROUND-- FULLY SHIELDED FROM HORDE PROBES!
STAN LEE PRESENTS:
"The Garden"
peter b. GILLIS WRITER
brent ANDERSON PENCILER
scott WILLIAMS INKER
jim NOVAK LETTERER
max SCHEELE COLORER
carl POTTS EDITOR
jim SHOOTER EDITOR IN CHIEF
WELCOME, FOLKS, TO BIOWAR FACILITY ALPHA! MY OLD STOMPING GROUNDS--
A1 SECTION
--AND THE PLACE WHERE THE MORITURI PROCESS WAS DISCOVERED!

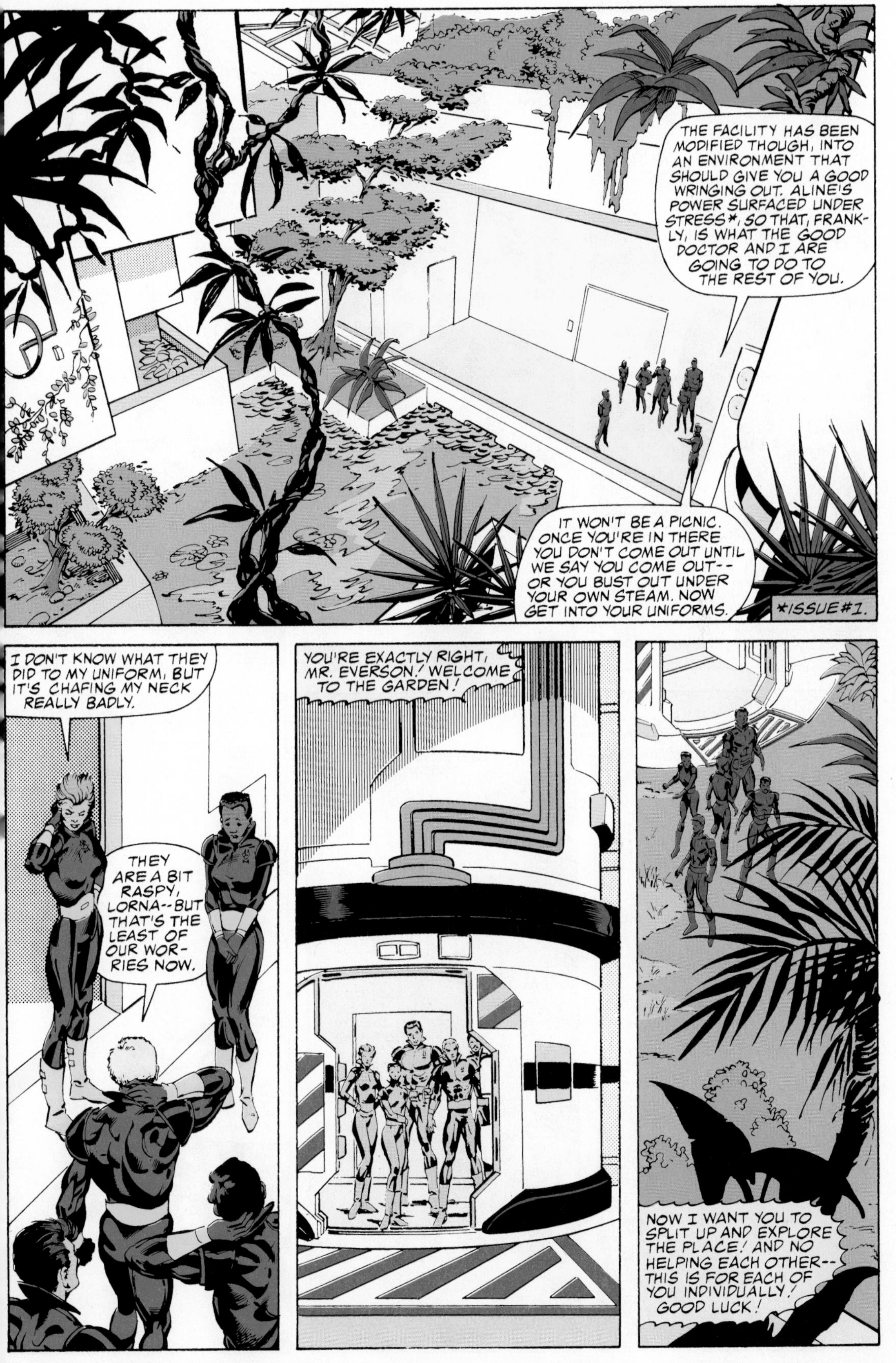
THE FACILITY HAS BEEN MODIFIED THOUGH, INTO AN ENVIRONMENT THAT SHOULD GIVE YOU A GOOD WRINGING OUT. ALINE'S POWER SURFACED UNDER STRESS*, SO THAT, FRANKLY, IS WHAT THE GOOD DOCTOR AND I ARE GOING TO DO TO THE REST OF YOU.
IT WON'T BE A PICNIC. ONCE YOU'RE IN THERE YOU DON'T COME OUT UNTIL WE SAY YOU COME OUT-- OR YOU BUST OUT UNDER YOUR OWN STEAM. NOW GET INTO YOUR UNIFORMS.
*ISSUE #1.
I DON'T KNOW WHAT THEY DID TO MY UNIFORM, BUT IT'S CHAFING MY NECK REALLY BADLY.
THEY ARE A BIT RASPY, LORNA--BUT THAT'S THE LEAST OF OUR WORRIES NOW.
YOU'RE EXACTLY RIGHT, MR. EVERSON! WELCOME TO THE GARDEN!
NOW I WANT YOU TO SPLIT UP AND EXPLORE THE PLACE! AND NO HELPING EACH OTHER-- THIS IS FOR EACH OF YOU INDIVIDUALLY! GOOD LUCK!

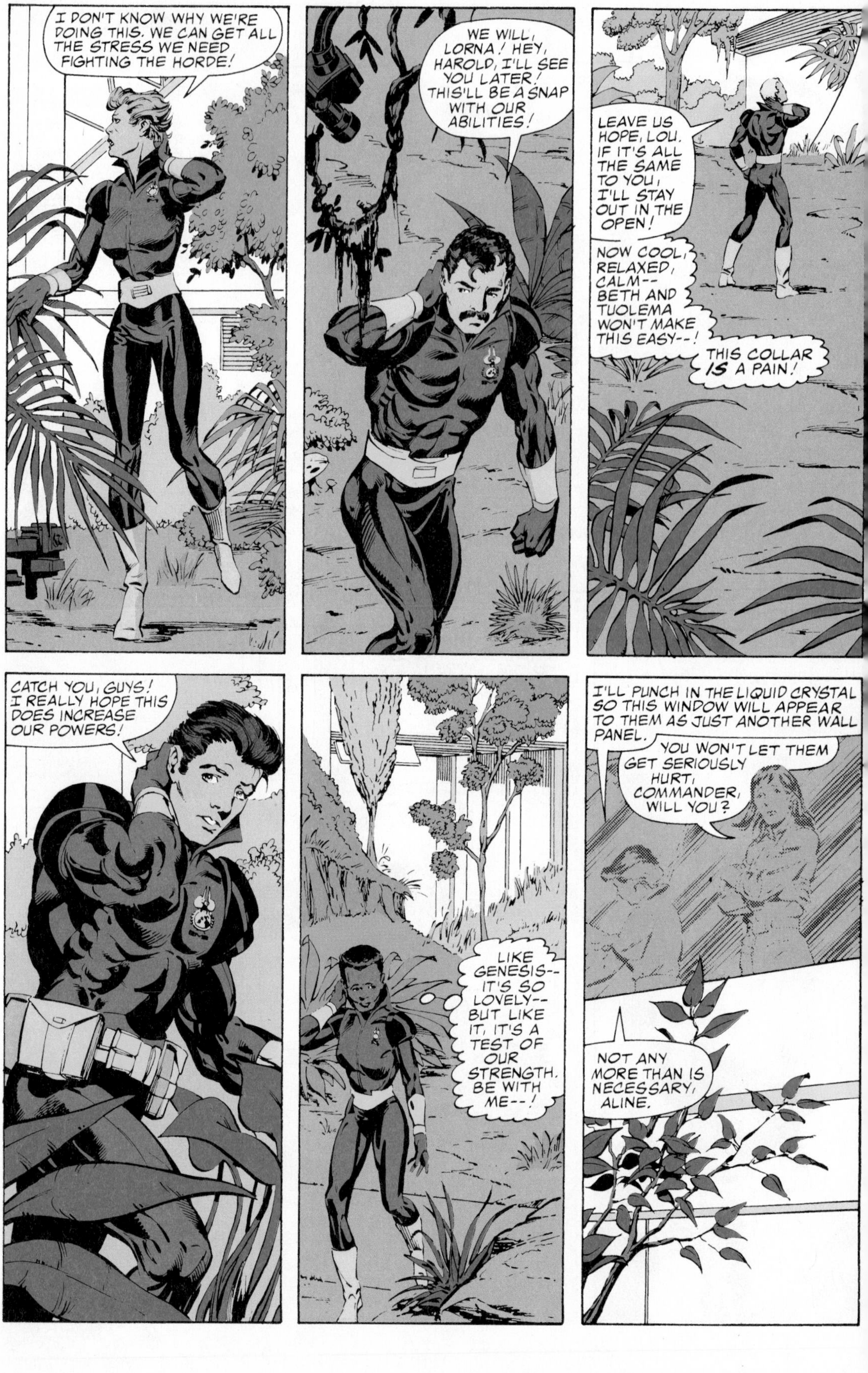
I DON'T KNOW WHY WE'RE DOING THIS. WE CAN GET ALL THE STRESS WE NEED FIGHTING THE HORDE!
WE WILL, LORNA! HEY, HAROLD, I'LL SEE YOU LATER! THIS'LL BE A SNAP WITH OUR ABILITIES!
LEAVE US HOPE, LOU. IF IT'S ALL THE SAME TO YOU, I'LL STAY OUT IN THE OPEN!
NOW COOL, RELAXED, CALM-- BETH AND TUOLEMA WON'T MAKE THIS EASY--!
THIS COLLAR *IS* A PAIN!
CATCH YOU, GUYS! I REALLY HOPE THIS DOES INCREASE OUR POWERS!
LIKE GENESIS-- IT'S SO LOVELY-- BUT LIKE IT, IT'S A TEST OF OUR STRENGTH. BE WITH ME--!
I'LL PUNCH IN THE LIQUID CRYSTAL SO THIS WINDOW WILL APPEAR TO THEM AS JUST ANOTHER WALL PANEL.
YOU WON'T LET THEM GET SERIOUSLY HURT, COMMANDER, WILL YOU?
NOT ANY MORE THAN IS NECESSARY, ALINE.

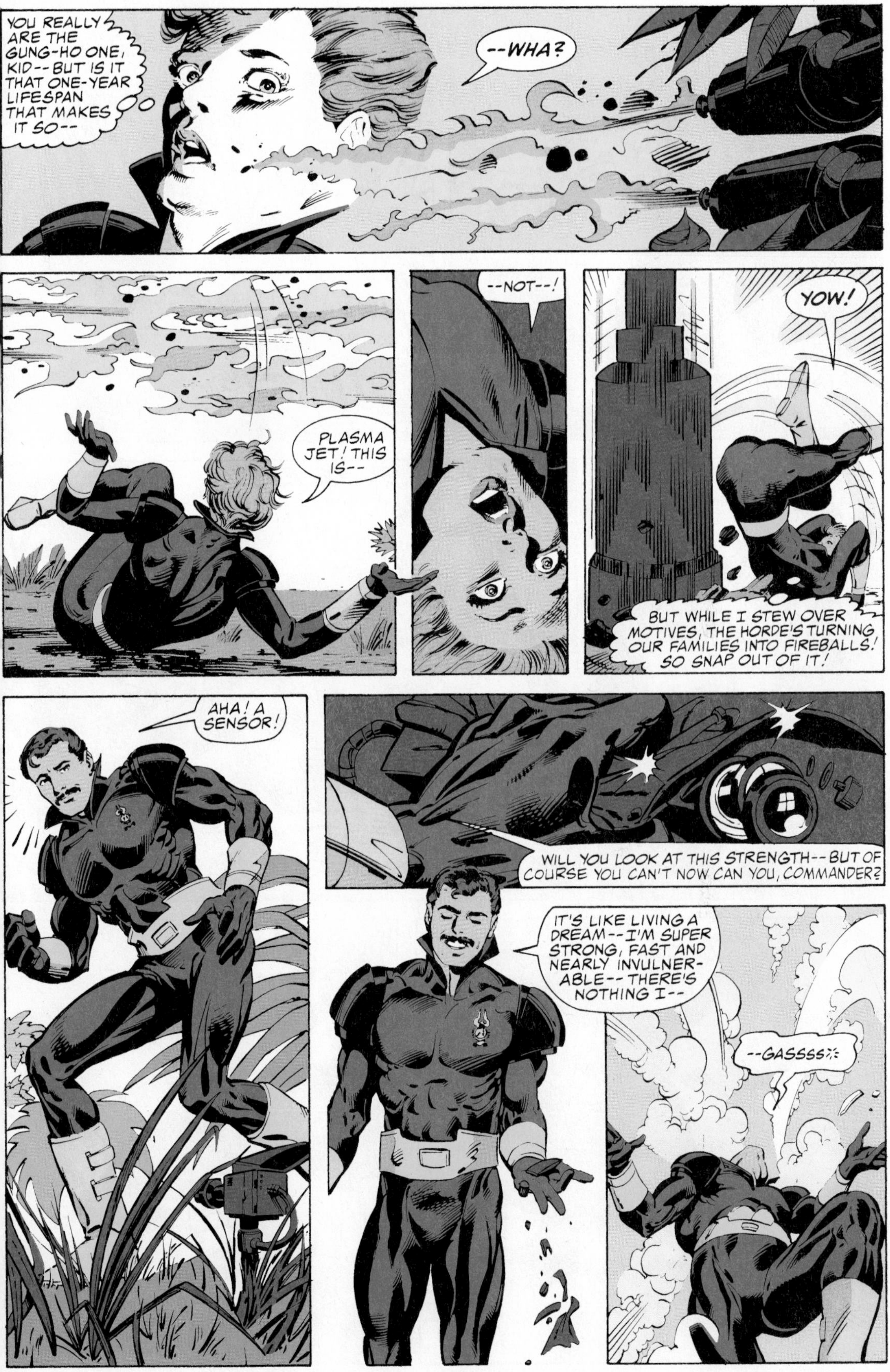
YOU REALLY ARE THE GUNG-HO ONE, KID-- BUT IS IT THAT ONE-YEAR LIFESPAN THAT MAKES IT SO--
--WHA?
PLASMA JET! THIS IS--
--NOT--!
YOW!
BUT WHILE I STEW OVER MOTIVES, THE HORDE'S TURNING OUR FAMILIES INTO FIREBALLS! SO SNAP OUT OF IT!
AHA! A SENSOR!
WILL YOU LOOK AT THIS STRENGTH-- BUT OF COURSE YOU CAN'T NOW CAN YOU, COMMANDER?
IT'S LIKE LIVING A DREAM-- I'M SUPER STRONG, FAST AND NEARLY INVULNER-ABLE-- THERE'S NOTHING I--
--GASSSS

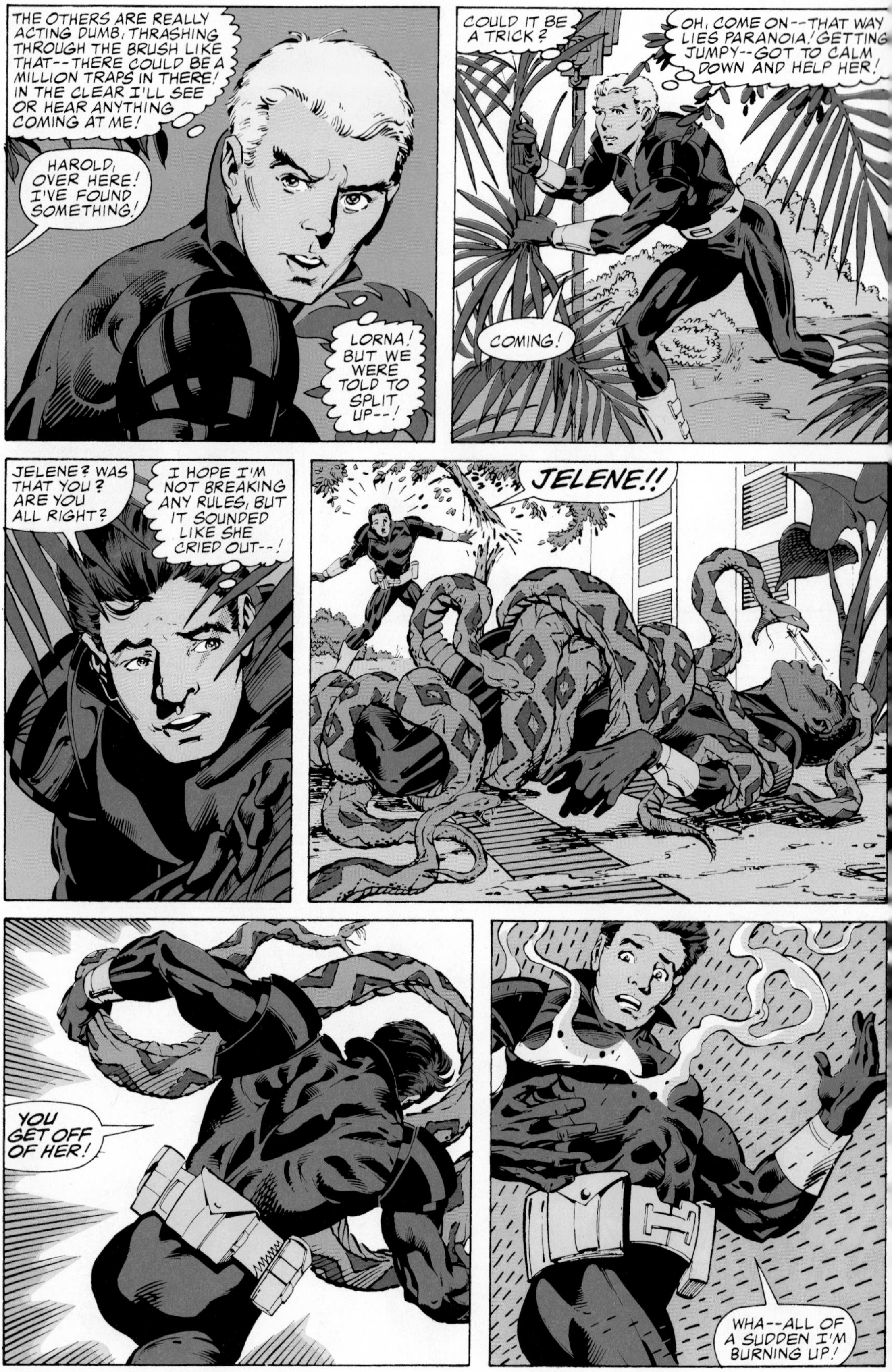
THE OTHERS ARE REALLY ACTING DUMB, THRASHING THROUGH THE BRUSH LIKE THAT--THERE COULD BE A MILLION TRAPS IN THERE! IN THE CLEAR I'LL SEE OR HEAR ANYTHING COMING AT ME!
HAROLD, OVER HERE! I'VE FOUND SOMETHING!
LORNA! BUT WE WERE TOLD TO SPLIT UP--!
COULD IT BE A TRICK?
OH, COME ON--THAT WAY LIES PARANOIA! GETTING JUMPY--GOT TO CALM DOWN AND HELP HER!
COMING!
JELENE? WAS THAT YOU? ARE YOU ALL RIGHT?
I HOPE I'M NOT BREAKING ANY RULES, BUT IT SOUNDED LIKE SHE CRIED OUT--!
JELENE!!
YOU GET OFF OF HER!
WHA--ALL OF A SUDDEN I'M BURNING UP!

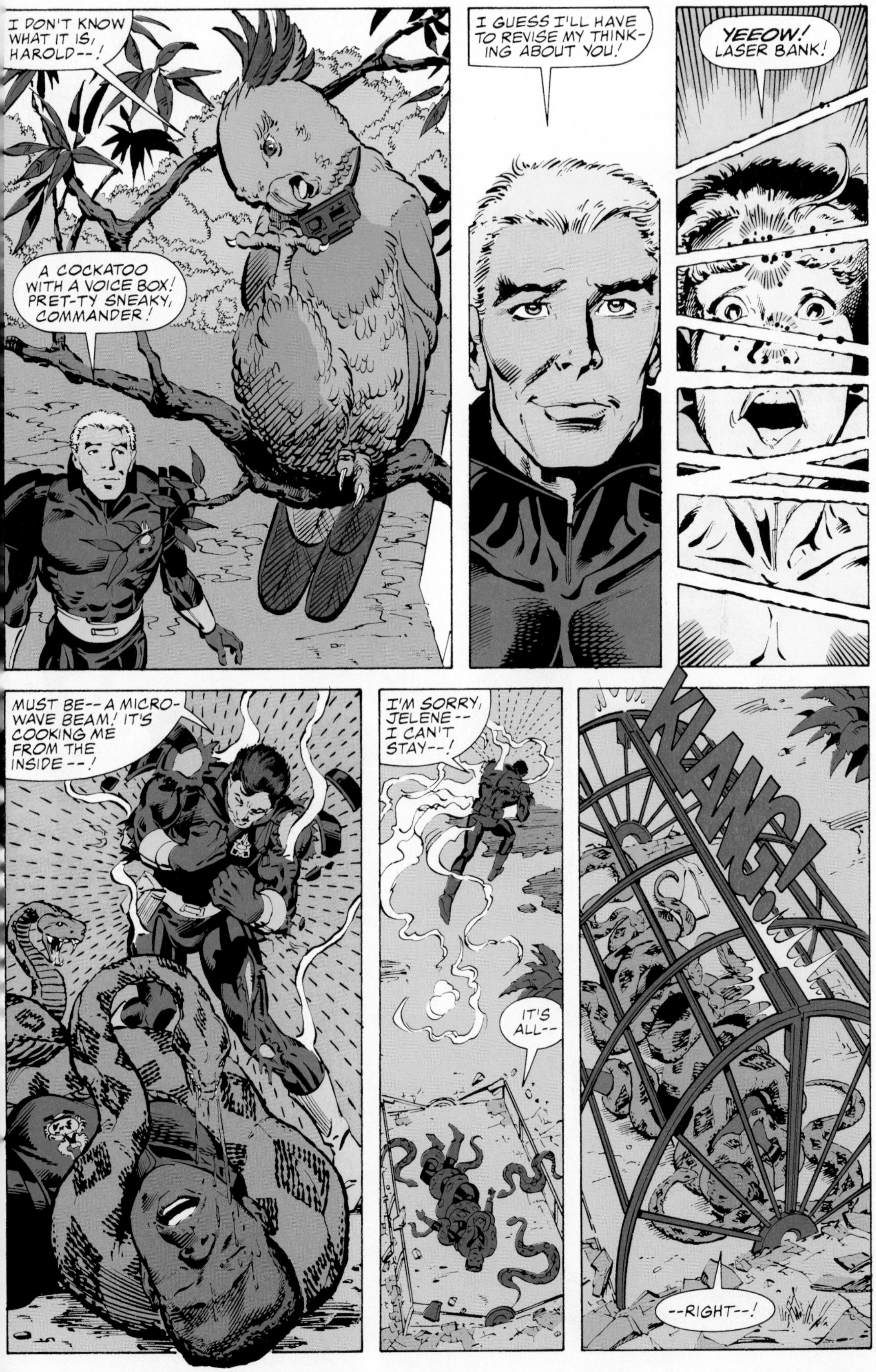

I DON'T KNOW WHAT IT IS, HAROLD--!
A COCKATOO WITH A VOICE BOX! PRET-TY SNEAKY, COMMANDER!
I GUESS I'LL HAVE TO REVISE MY THINKING ABOUT YOU!
YEEOW! LASER BANK!
MUST BE--A MICRO-WAVE BEAM! IT'S COOKING ME FROM THE INSIDE--!
I'M SORRY, JELENE--I CAN'T STAY--!
IT'S ALL--
KLANG!
--RIGHT--!

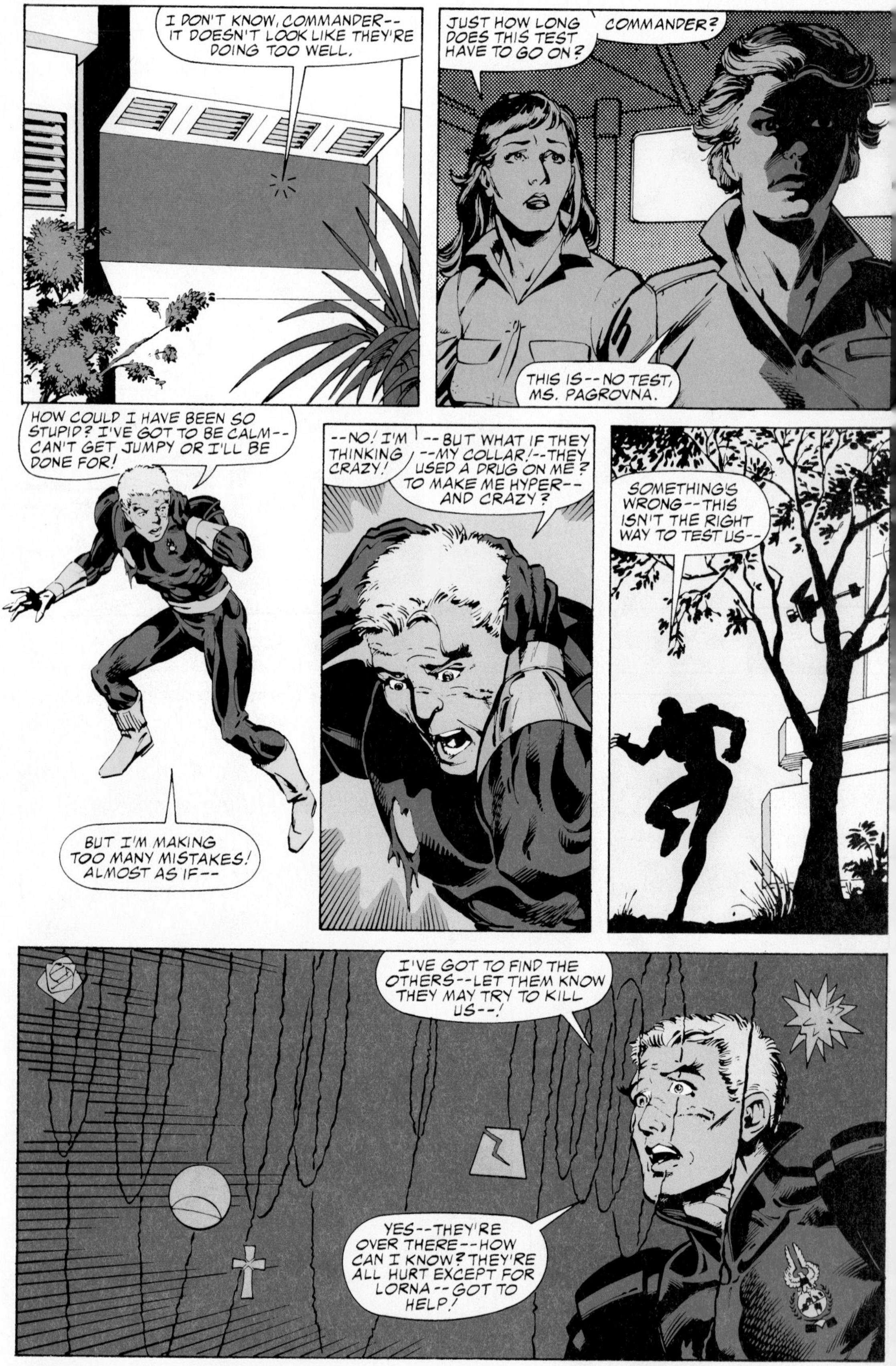
I DON'T KNOW, COMMANDER-- IT DOESN'T LOOK LIKE THEY'RE DOING TOO WELL.
JUST HOW LONG DOES THIS TEST HAVE TO GO ON?
COMMANDER?
THIS IS--NO TEST, MS. PAGROVNA.
HOW COULD I HAVE BEEN SO STUPID? I'VE GOT TO BE CALM--CAN'T GET JUMPY OR I'LL BE DONE FOR!
BUT I'M MAKING TOO MANY MISTAKES! ALMOST AS IF--
--NO! I'M THINKING CRAZY!
--BUT WHAT IF THEY --MY COLLAR!--THEY USED A DRUG ON ME? TO MAKE ME HYPER--AND CRAZY?
SOMETHING'S WRONG--THIS ISN'T THE RIGHT WAY TO TEST US--
I'VE GOT TO FIND THE OTHERS--LET THEM KNOW THEY MAY TRY TO KILL US--!
YES--THEY'RE OVER THERE--HOW CAN I KNOW? THEY'RE ALL HURT EXCEPT FOR LORNA--GOT TO HELP!

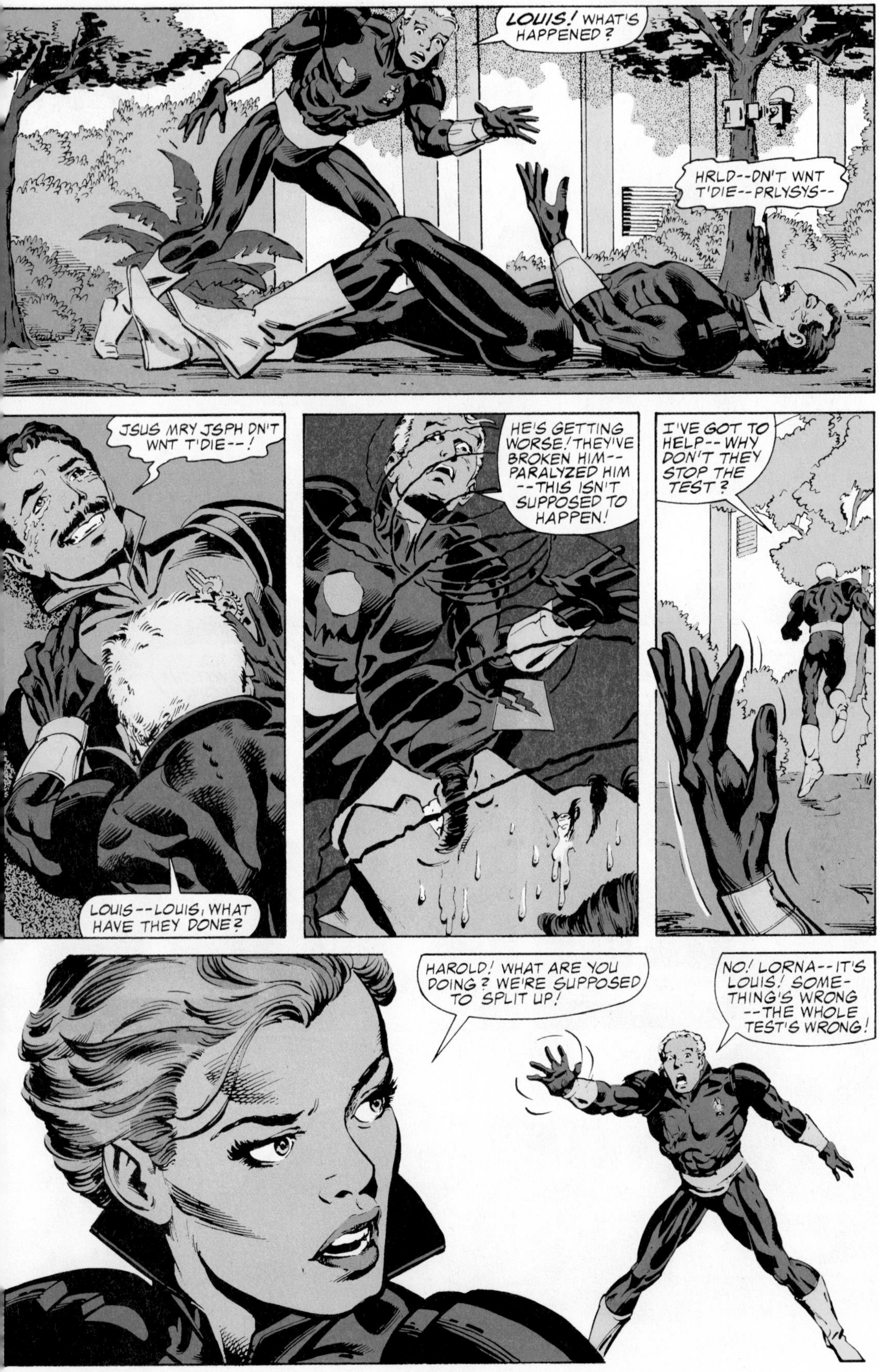
LOUIS! WHAT'S HAPPENED?
HRLD--DN'T WNT T'DIE--PRLYSYS--
JSUS MRY JSPH DN'T WNT T'DIE--!
LOUIS--LOUIS, WHAT HAVE THEY DONE?
HE'S GETTING WORSE! THEY'VE BROKEN HIM--PARALYZED HIM--THIS ISN'T SUPPOSED TO HAPPEN!
I'VE GOT TO HELP--WHY DON'T THEY STOP THE TEST?
HAROLD! WHAT ARE YOU DOING? WE'RE SUPPOSED TO SPLIT UP!
NO! LORNA--IT'S LOUIS! SOMETHING'S WRONG--THE WHOLE TEST'S WRONG!

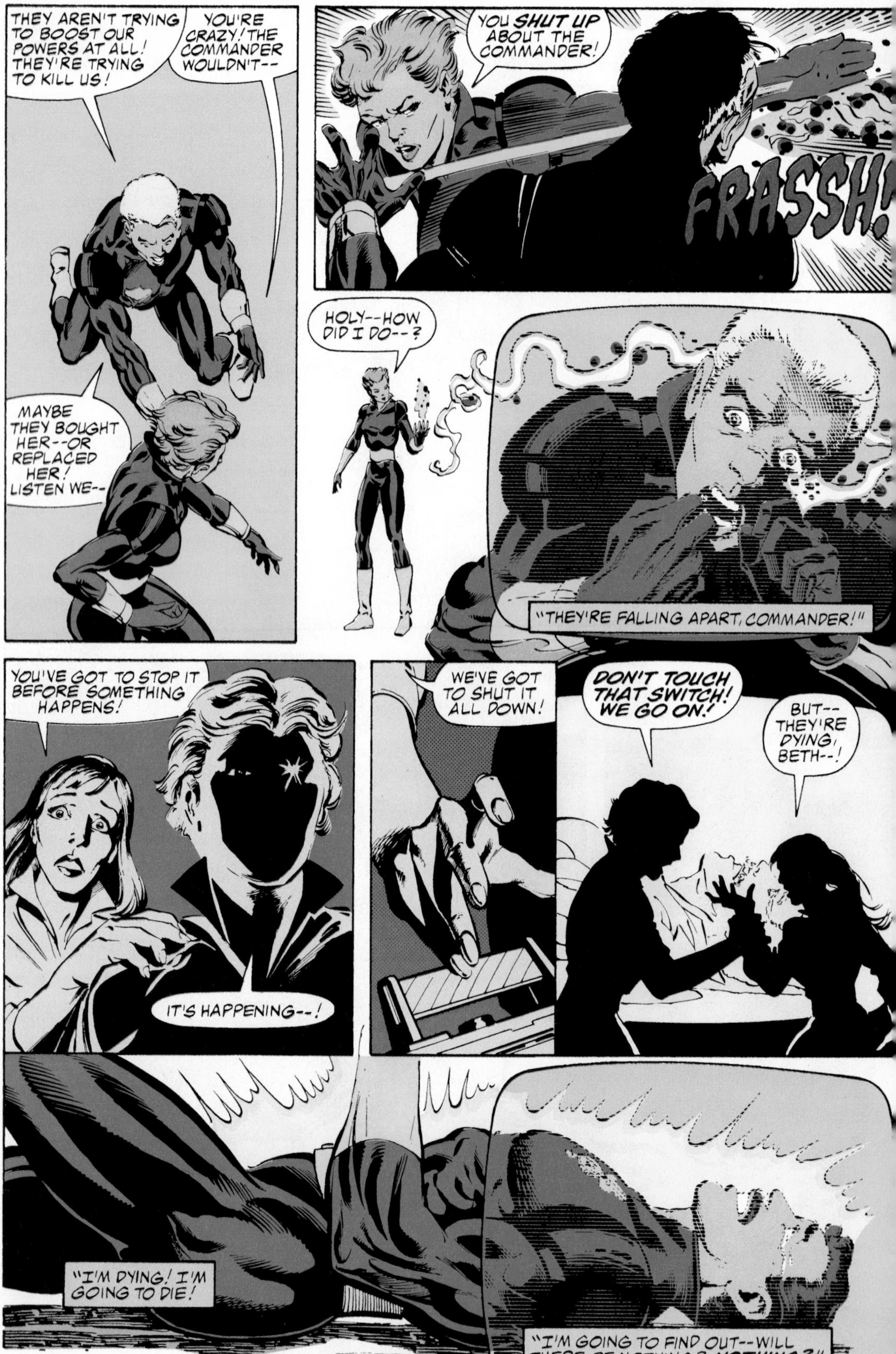

THEY AREN'T TRYING TO BOOST OUR POWERS AT ALL! THEY'RE TRYING TO KILL US!
YOU'RE CRAZY! THE COMMANDER WOULDN'T--
MAYBE THEY BOUGHT HER--OR REPLACED HER! LISTEN WE--
YOU SHUT UP ABOUT THE COMMANDER!
FRASSH!
HOLY--HOW DID I DO--?
"THEY'RE FALLING APART, COMMANDER!"
YOU'VE GOT TO STOP IT BEFORE SOMETHING HAPPENS!
IT'S HAPPENING--!
WE'VE GOT TO SHUT IT ALL DOWN!
DON'T TOUCH THAT SWITCH! WE GO ON!
BUT--THEY'RE DYING, BETH--!
"I'M DYING! I'M GOING TO DIE!
"I'M GOING TO FIND OUT--WILL THERE BE NOTHING? NOTHING?"

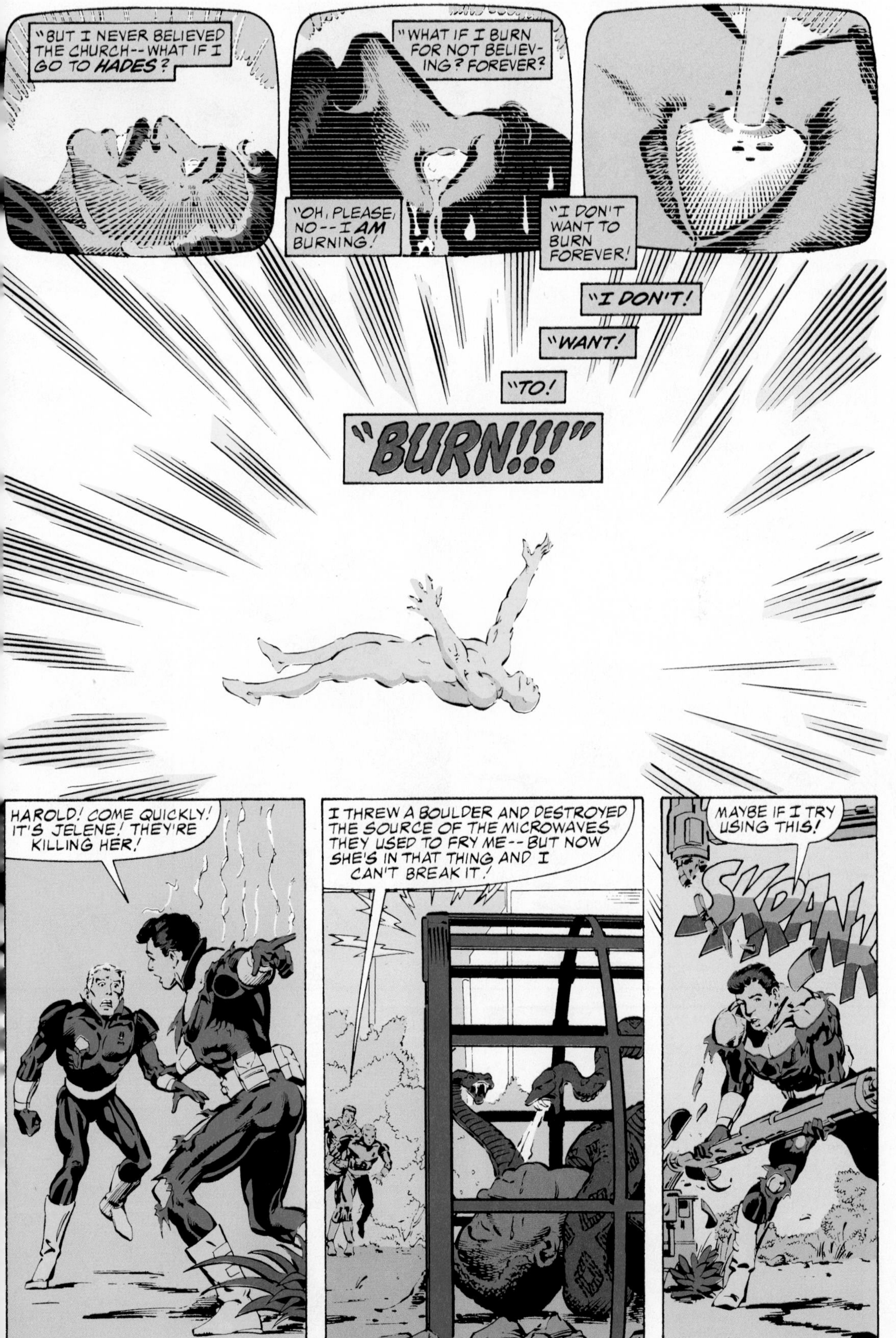
"BUT I NEVER BELIEVED THE CHURCH--WHAT IF I GO TO HADES?
"WHAT IF I BURN FOR NOT BELIEVING? FOREVER?
"OH, PLEASE, NO--I AM BURNING!
"I DON'T WANT TO BURN FOREVER!
"I DON'T!
"WANT!
"TO!
"BURN!!!"
HAROLD! COME QUICKLY! IT'S JELENE! THEY'RE KILLING HER!
I THREW A BOULDER AND DESTROYED THE SOURCE OF THE MICROWAVES THEY USED TO FRY ME--BUT NOW SHE'S IN THAT THING AND I CAN'T BREAK IT!
MAYBE IF I TRY USING THIS!

'NGH! ELECTRIC FIELD--!

CAN'T-- TAKE IT! MICRO-WAVES SAPPED-- TOO MUCH OF MY-- STRENGTH!

'S ALL RIGHT, ROBERT--'S NOT THE SNAKES' FAULT--MAYBE GOD --JUS' WAN'S ME HOME W'HIM--!

JELENE!!

MOVE OUT OF THE WAY, ROBERT!

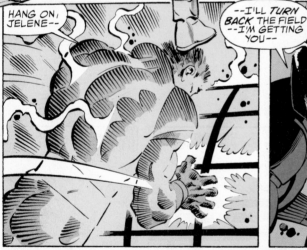

HANG ON, JELENE--

--I'LL TURN BACK THE FIELD --I'M GETTING YOU--

--OUT--!

STOP THE TEST, COMMANDER! YOU'RE PUSHING THEM UNTIL THEIR POWERS SHOW-- BUT JELENE'S NOT SHOWING ANYTHING! PLEASE!

WE-- KEEP GOING.

BUT WHAT IF HER POWERS DON'T WORK THAT WAY? WHAT IF THEY COME UP--AND AREN'T ADE-QUATE? THEN, EVEN IF YOU SUCCEED, YOU'VE KILLED HER!

WHAT?

STOP THE TEST! STOP--THE--TEST!

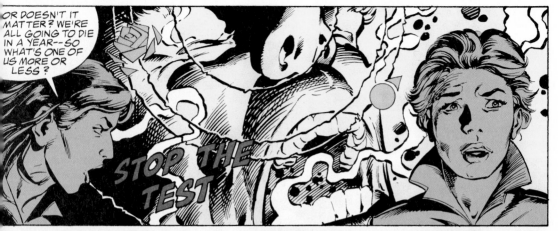

OR DOESN'T IT MATTER? WE'RE ALL GOING TO DIE IN A YEAR--SO WHAT'S ONE OF US MORE OR LESS?

STOP THE TEST

IT'S OK, ISN'T IT? TO TEST TO DESTRUCTION? TO FIND OUT JUST HOW MUCH STRESS IT TAKES TO BRING FORTH THE MORITURI POWERS? COMMANDER--THAT'S *JELENE* OUT THERE! YOU CAN'T KILL HER FOR *RESULTS!*

WE--GO ON.

MURDERER!!

I *KNOW* WHERE YOU ARE--

--I CAN *SENSE* YOU--

--MURDERER!!

HAROLD!

47

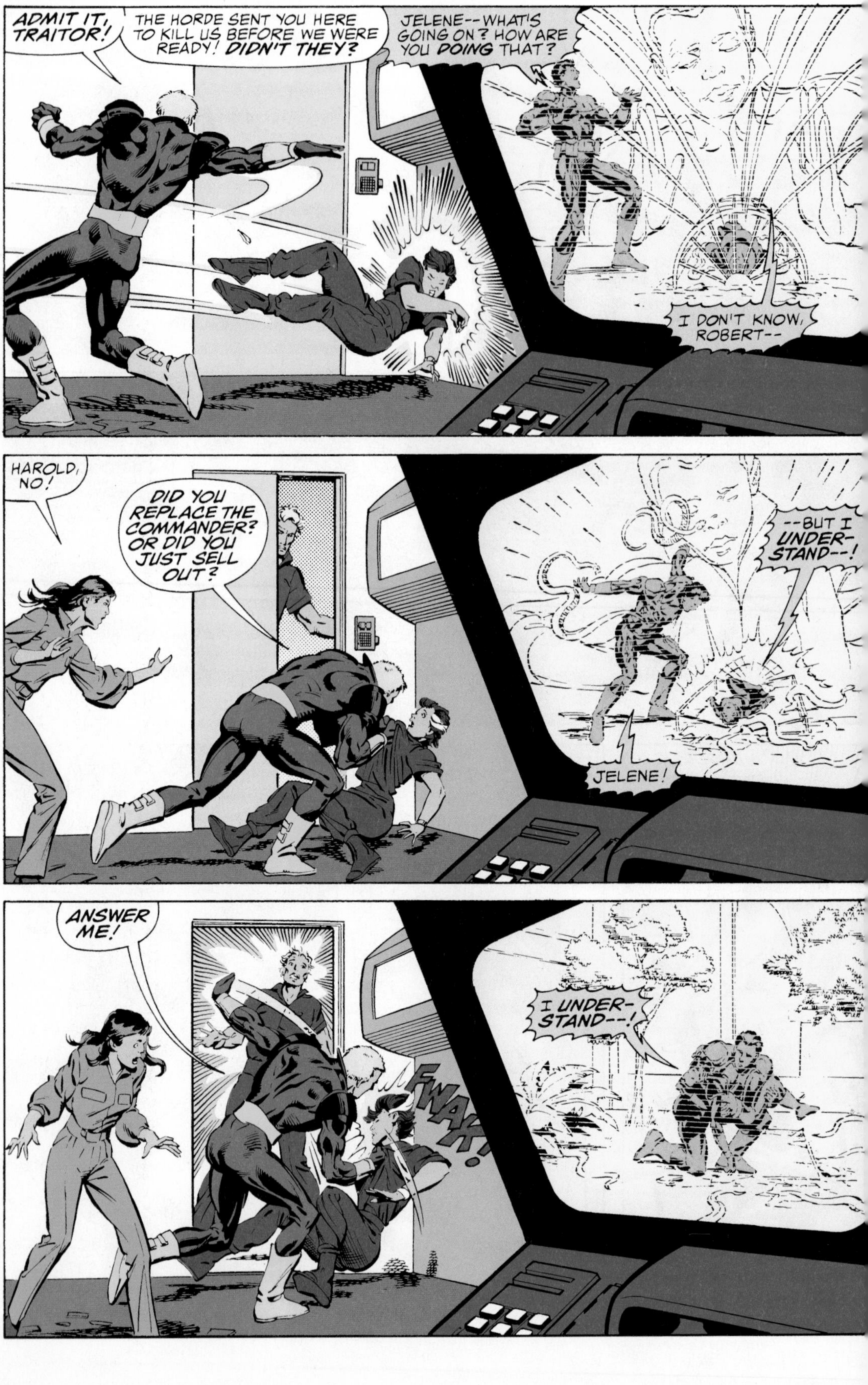
ADMIT IT, TRAITOR!
THE HORDE SENT YOU HERE TO KILL US BEFORE WE WERE READY! DIDN'T THEY?
JELENE--WHAT'S GOING ON? HOW ARE YOU DOING THAT?
I DON'T KNOW, ROBERT--
HAROLD, NO!
DID YOU REPLACE THE COMMANDER? OR DID YOU JUST SELL OUT?
--BUT I UNDERSTAND--!
JELENE!
ANSWER ME!
FWAK!
I UNDERSTAND--!

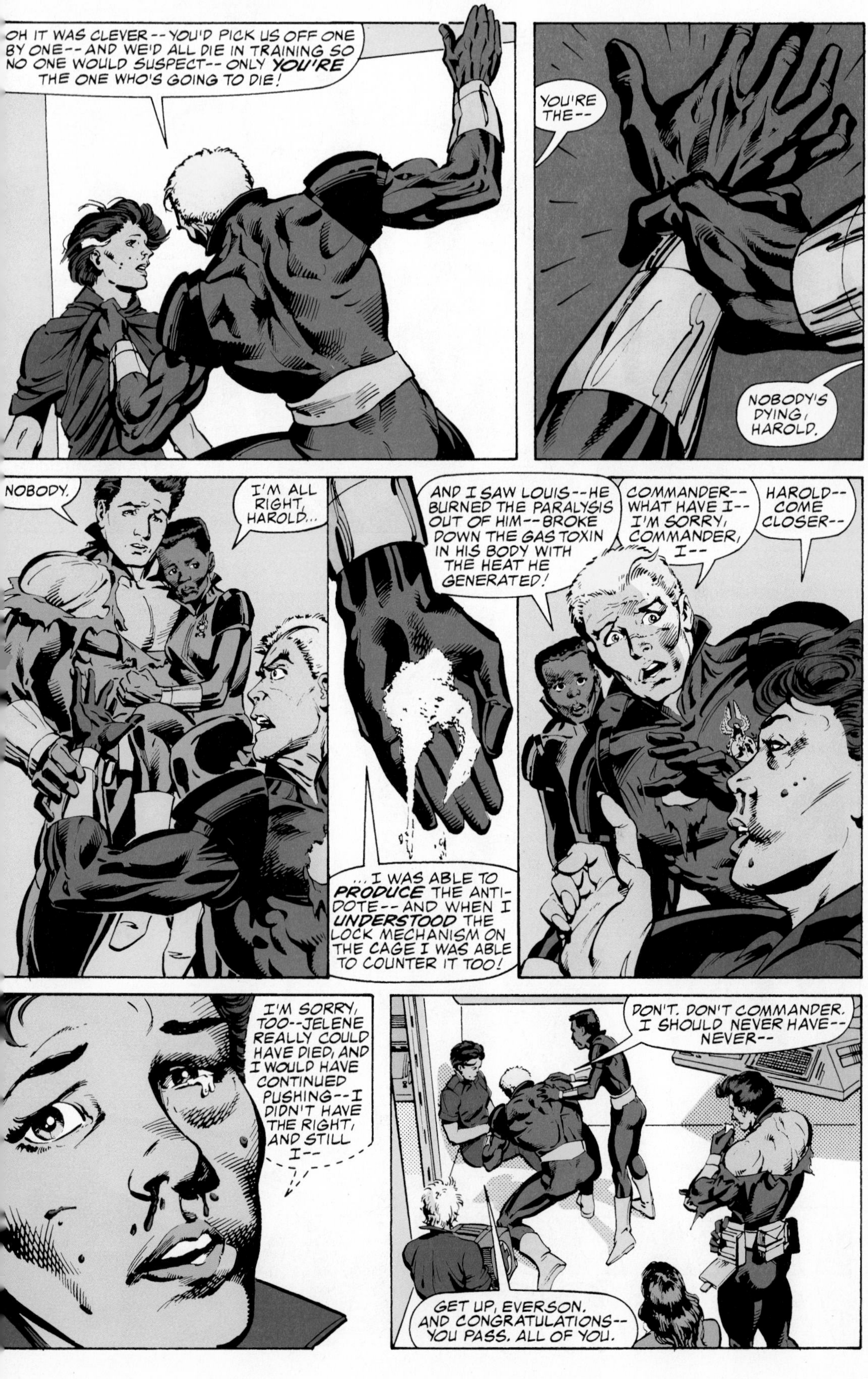
OH IT WAS CLEVER -- YOU'D PICK US OFF ONE BY ONE -- AND WE'D ALL DIE IN TRAINING SO NO ONE WOULD SUSPECT -- ONLY YOU'RE THE ONE WHO'S GOING TO DIE!
YOU'RE THE --
NOBODY'S DYING, HAROLD.
NOBODY.
I'M ALL RIGHT, HAROLD...
AND I SAW LOUIS -- HE BURNED THE PARALYSIS OUT OF HIM -- BROKE DOWN THE GAS TOXIN IN HIS BODY WITH THE HEAT HE GENERATED!
... I WAS ABLE TO PRODUCE THE ANTI-DOTE -- AND WHEN I UNDERSTOOD THE LOCK MECHANISM ON THE CAGE I WAS ABLE TO COUNTER IT TOO!
COMMANDER -- WHAT HAVE I -- I'M SORRY, COMMANDER, I --
HAROLD -- COME CLOSER --
I'M SORRY, TOO -- JELENE REALLY COULD HAVE DIED, AND I WOULD HAVE CONTINUED PUSHING -- I DIDN'T HAVE THE RIGHT, AND STILL I --
DON'T. DON'T COMMANDER. I SHOULD NEVER HAVE -- NEVER --
GET UP, EVERSON, AND CONGRATULATIONS -- YOU PASS. ALL OF YOU.

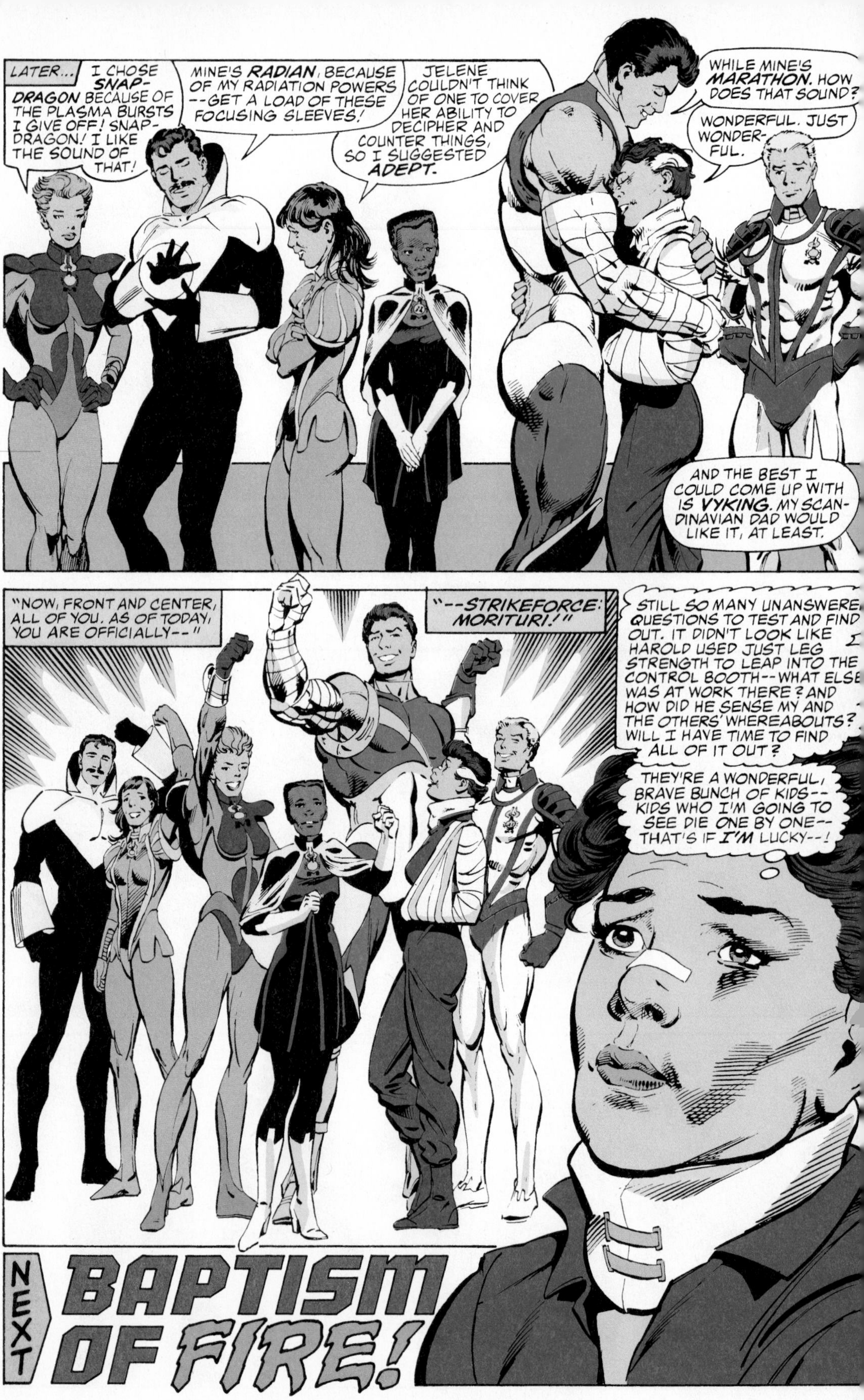

LATER...
I CHOSE SNAP-DRAGON BECAUSE OF THE PLASMA BURSTS I GIVE OFF! SNAP-DRAGON! I LIKE THE SOUND OF THAT!
MINE'S RADIAN, BECAUSE OF MY RADIATION POWERS --GET A LOAD OF THESE FOCUSING SLEEVES!
JELENE COULDN'T THINK OF ONE TO COVER HER ABILITY TO DECIPHER AND COUNTER THINGS, SO I SUGGESTED ADEPT.
WHILE MINE'S MARATHON. HOW DOES THAT SOUND?
WONDERFUL. JUST WONDER-FUL.
AND THE BEST I COULD COME UP WITH IS VYKING. MY SCAN-DINAVIAN DAD WOULD LIKE IT, AT LEAST.
"NOW, FRONT AND CENTER, ALL OF YOU. AS OF TODAY, YOU ARE OFFICIALLY--"
"--STRIKEFORCE: MORITURI!"
STILL SO MANY UNANSWERE QUESTIONS TO TEST AND FIND OUT. IT DIDN'T LOOK LIKE HAROLD USED JUST LEG STRENGTH TO LEAP INTO THE CONTROL BOOTH--WHAT ELSE WAS AT WORK THERE? AND HOW DID HE SENSE MY AND THE OTHERS' WHEREABOUTS? WILL I HAVE TIME TO FIND ALL OF IT OUT?
THEY'RE A WONDERFUL, BRAVE BUNCH OF KIDS-- KIDS WHO I'M GOING TO SEE DIE ONE BY ONE-- THAT'S IF I'M LUCKY--!
NEXT
BAPTISM OF FIRE!

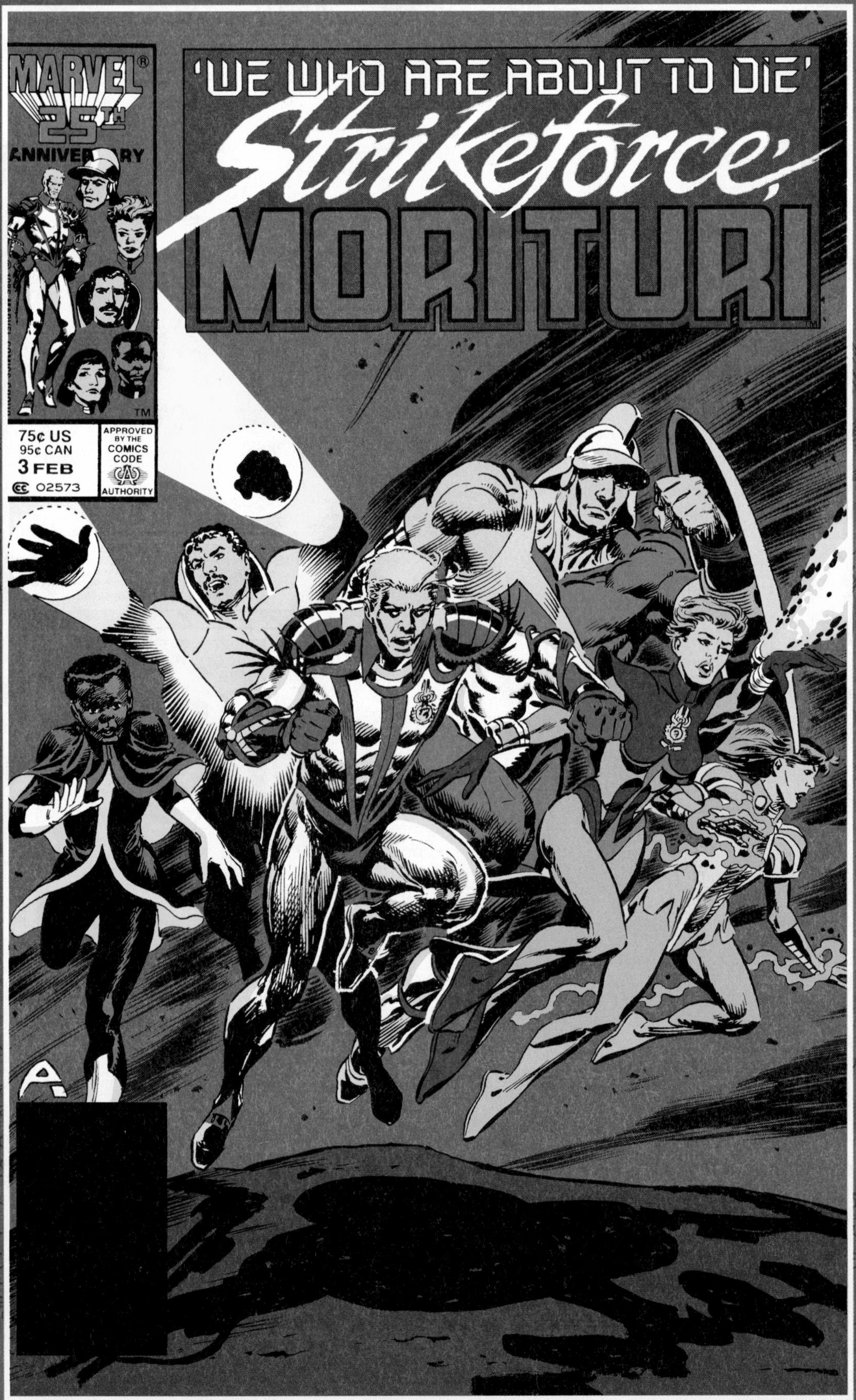
MARVEL®
25TH ANNIVERSARY
'WE WHO ARE ABOUT TO DIE'
Strikeforce:
MORITURI
75¢ US
95¢ CAN
3 FEB
02573
APPROVED BY THE COMICS CODE AUTHORITY

peter b. **GILLIS** WRITER · brent **ANDERSON** PENCILER · scott **WILLIAMS** INKER · janice **CHIANG** LETTERER · max **SCHEELE** COLORER · carl **POTTS** EDITOR · jim **SHOOTER** EDITOR IN CHIEF

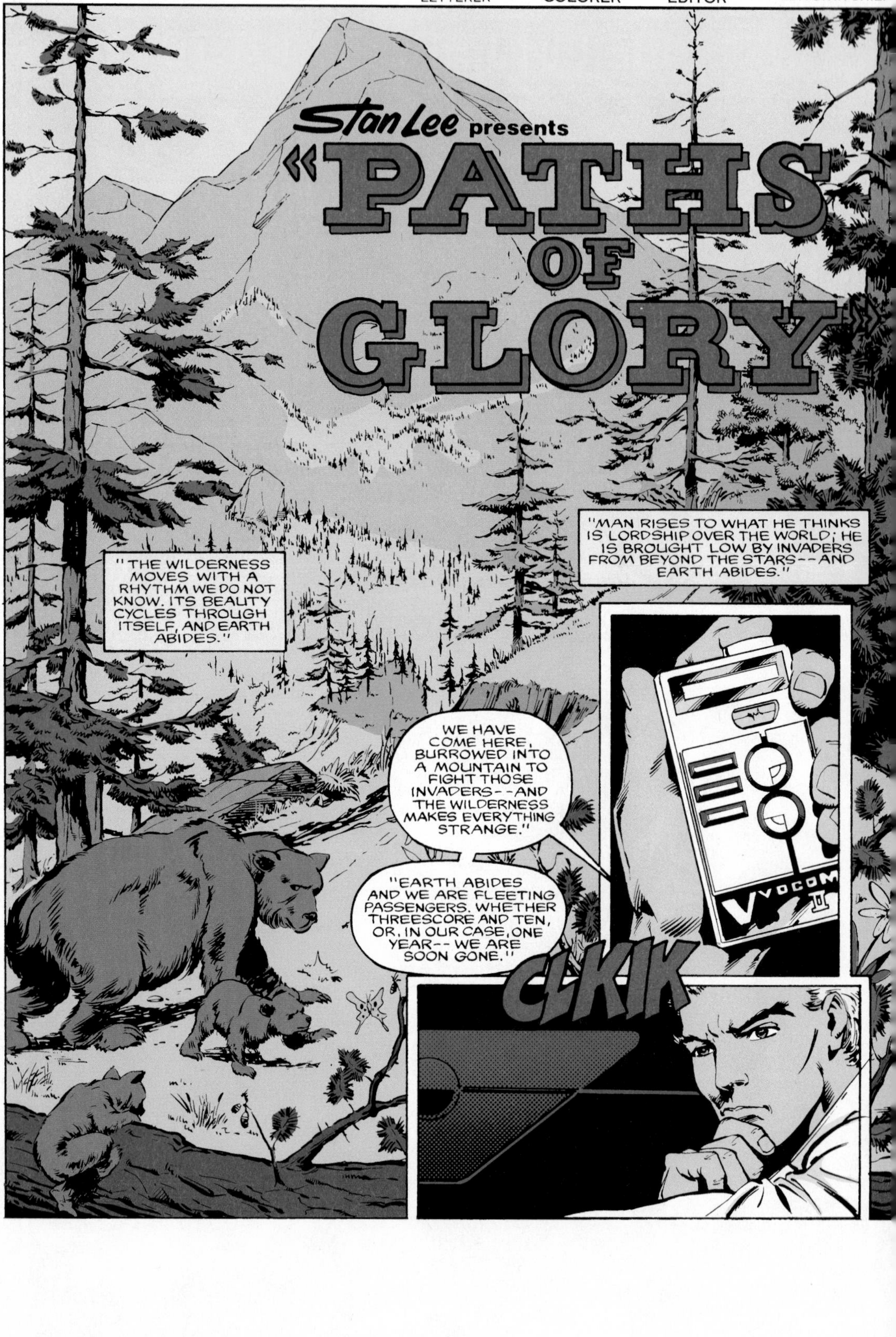

Stan Lee presents
"PATHS OF GLORY"
"THE WILDERNESS MOVES WITH A RHYTHM WE DO NOT KNOW. ITS BEAUTY CYCLES THROUGH ITSELF, AND EARTH ABIDES."
"MAN RISES TO WHAT HE THINKS IS LORDSHIP OVER THE WORLD; HE IS BROUGHT LOW BY INVADERS FROM BEYOND THE STARS--AND EARTH ABIDES."
WE HAVE COME HERE, BURROWED INTO A MOUNTAIN TO FIGHT THOSE INVADERS--AND THE WILDERNESS MAKES EVERYTHING STRANGE."
"EARTH ABIDES AND WE ARE FLEETING PASSENGERS. WHETHER THREESCORE AND TEN, OR, IN OUR CASE, ONE YEAR-- WE ARE SOON GONE."
VOCOM II
CLKIK

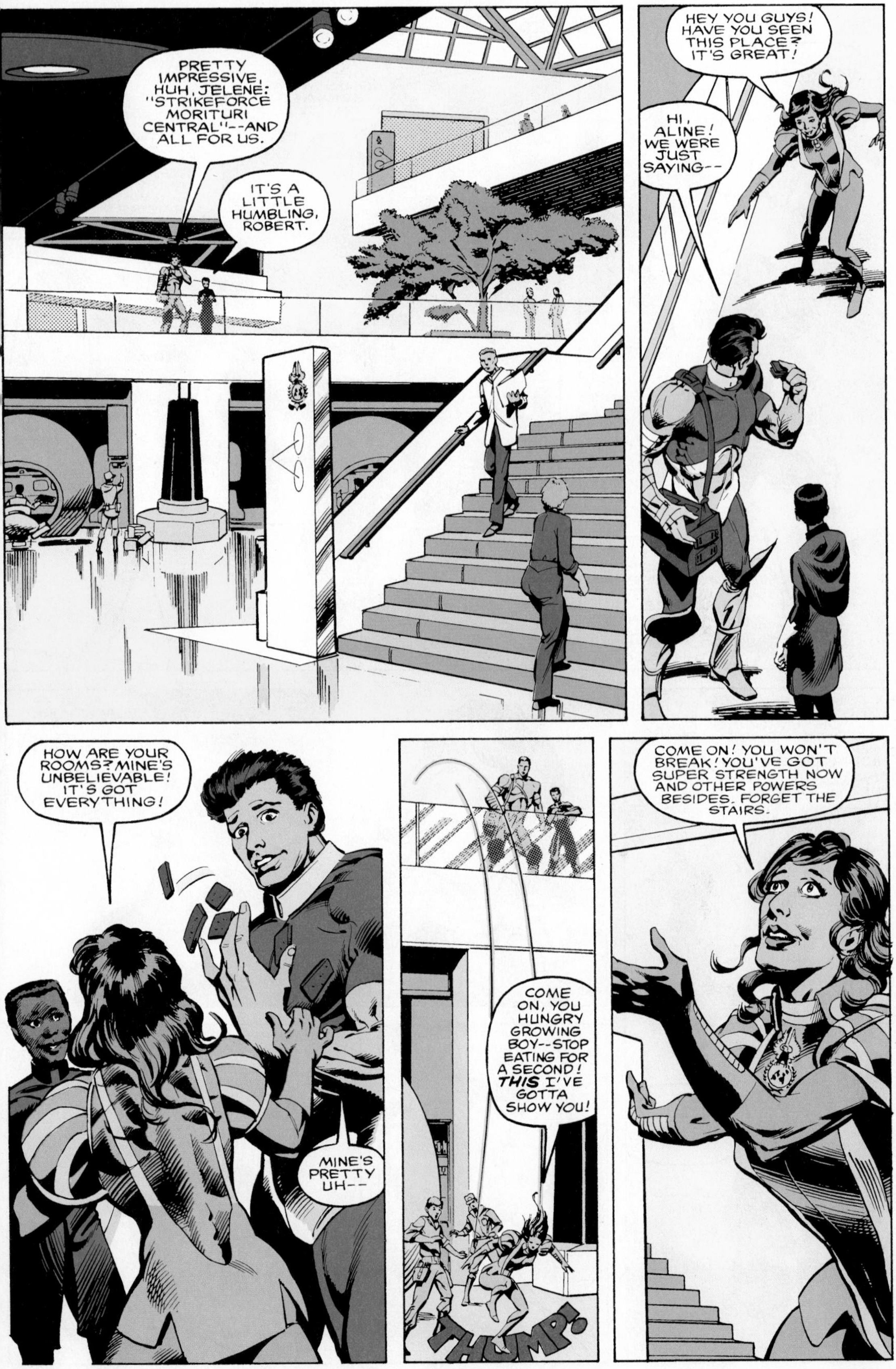
PRETTY IMPRESSIVE, HUH, JELENE: "STRIKEFORCE MORITURI CENTRAL"--AND ALL FOR US.
IT'S A LITTLE HUMBLING, ROBERT.
HEY YOU GUYS! HAVE YOU SEEN THIS PLACE? IT'S GREAT!
HI, ALINE! WE WERE JUST SAYING--
HOW ARE YOUR ROOMS? MINE'S UNBELIEVABLE! IT'S GOT EVERYTHING!
MINE'S PRETTY UH--
COME ON, YOU HUNGRY GROWING BOY--STOP EATING FOR A SECOND! THIS I'VE GOTTA SHOW YOU!
THUMP!
COME ON! YOU WON'T BREAK! YOU'VE GOT SUPER STRENGTH NOW AND OTHER POWERS BESIDES. FORGET THE STAIRS.

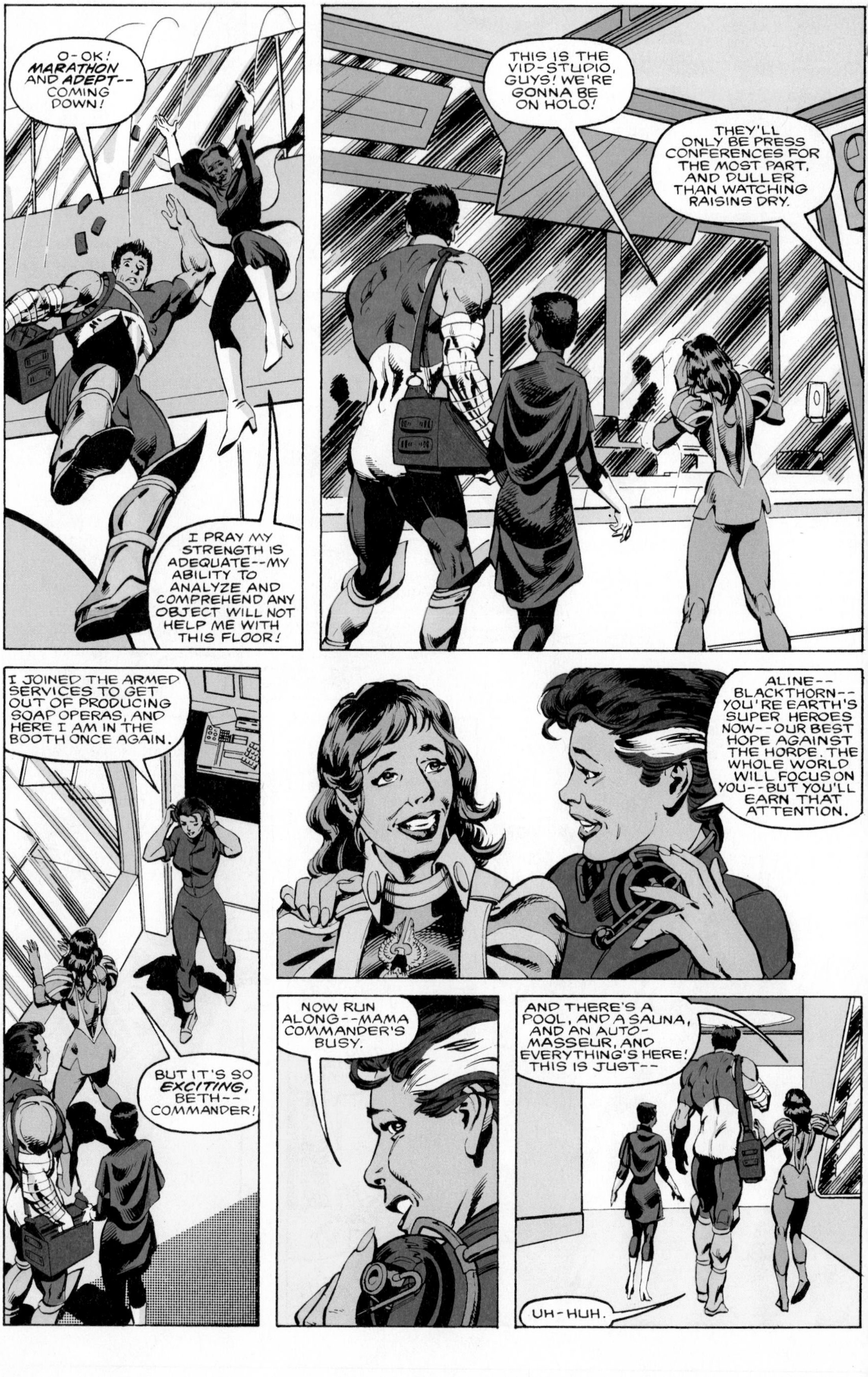
O-OK! MARATHON AND ADEPT--COMING DOWN!
I PRAY MY STRENGTH IS ADEQUATE--MY ABILITY TO ANALYZE AND COMPREHEND ANY OBJECT WILL NOT HELP ME WITH THIS FLOOR!
THIS IS THE VID-STUDIO, GUYS! WE'RE GONNA BE ON HOLO!
THEY'LL ONLY BE PRESS CONFERENCES FOR THE MOST PART, AND DULLER THAN WATCHING RAISINS DRY.
I JOINED THE ARMED SERVICES TO GET OUT OF PRODUCING SOAP OPERAS, AND HERE I AM IN THE BOOTH ONCE AGAIN.
BUT IT'S SO EXCITING, BETH--COMMANDER!
ALINE--BLACKTHORN--YOU'RE EARTH'S SUPER HEROES NOW--OUR BEST HOPE AGAINST THE HORDE. THE WHOLE WORLD WILL FOCUS ON YOU--BUT YOU'LL EARN THAT ATTENTION.
NOW RUN ALONG--MAMA COMMANDER'S BUSY.
AND THERE'S A POOL, AND A SAUNA, AND AN AUTO-MASSEUR, AND EVERYTHING'S HERE! THIS IS JUST--
UH-HUH.

AND-- SSSH.

ALL RIGHT, RADIAN: FOCUS AND AMPLIFY. TRY TO NARROW THE FREQUENCY SPREAD.

OKAY, YOU CAN STOP. DEPOWER AND COME OUT.

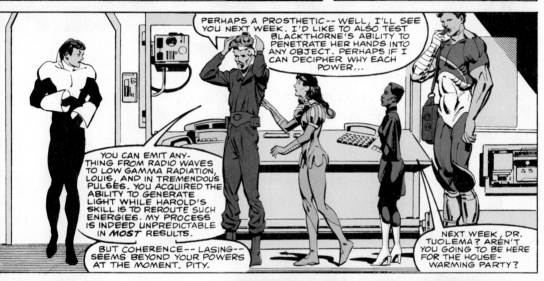

PERHAPS A PROSTHETIC-- WELL, I'LL SEE YOU NEXT WEEK. I'D LIKE TO ALSO TEST BLACKTHORNE'S ABILITY TO PENETRATE HER HANDS INTO ANY OBJECT. PERHAPS IF I CAN DECIPHER WHY EACH POWER...

YOU CAN EMIT ANY- THING FROM RADIO WAVES TO LOW GAMMA RADIATION, LOUIS, AND IN TREMENDOUS PULSES. YOU ACQUIRED THE ABILITY TO GENERATE LIGHT WHILE HAROLD'S SKILL IS TO REROUTE SUCH ENERGIES. MY PROCESS IS INDEED UNPREDICTABLE IN *MOST* RESULTS.

BUT COHERENCE-- LASING-- SEEMS BEYOND YOUR POWERS AT THE MOMENT. PITY.

NEXT WEEK, DR. TUOLEMA? AREN'T YOU GOING TO BE HERE FOR THE HOUSE- WARMING PARTY?

SORRY, BLACKTHORN. I'VE GOT TO GET BACK TO NEW HAVEN AND BEGIN DEVELOPING YOUR--

DR. TUOL

--REPLACEMENTS--!

DR. TUOLEMA

REPLACEMENTS-- OF COURSE--WITH OUR POWERS KILLING US INSIDE OF A YEAR, OF COURSE THEY'LL NEED-- REPLACEMENTS--!

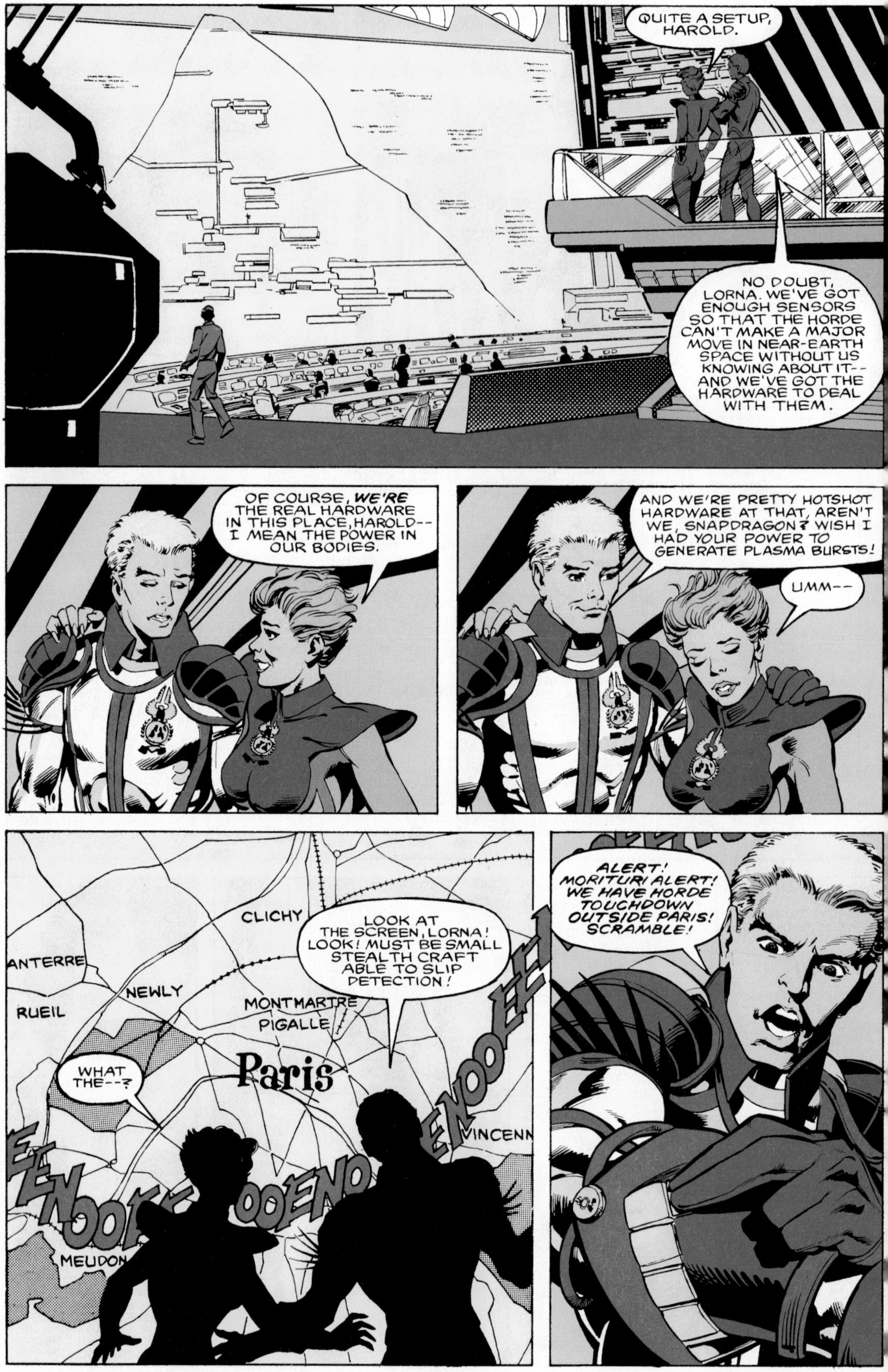
QUITE A SETUP, HAROLD.
NO DOUBT, LORNA. WE'VE GOT ENOUGH SENSORS SO THAT THE HORDE CAN'T MAKE A MAJOR MOVE IN NEAR-EARTH SPACE WITHOUT US KNOWING ABOUT IT--AND WE'VE GOT THE HARDWARE TO DEAL WITH THEM.
OF COURSE, WE'RE THE REAL HARDWARE IN THIS PLACE, HAROLD--I MEAN THE POWER IN OUR BODIES.
AND WE'RE PRETTY HOTSHOT HARDWARE AT THAT, AREN'T WE, SNAPDRAGON? WISH I HAD YOUR POWER TO GENERATE PLASMA BURSTS!
UMM--
CLICHY
ANTERRE
NEWLY
RUEIL
MONTMARTRE
PIGALLE
Paris
VINCENN
MEUDON
LOOK AT THE SCREEN, LORNA! LOOK! MUST BE SMALL STEALTH CRAFT ABLE TO SLIP DETECTION!
WHAT THE--?
ALERT! MORITURI ALERT! WE HAVE HORDE TOUCHDOWN OUTSIDE PARIS! SCRAMBLE!

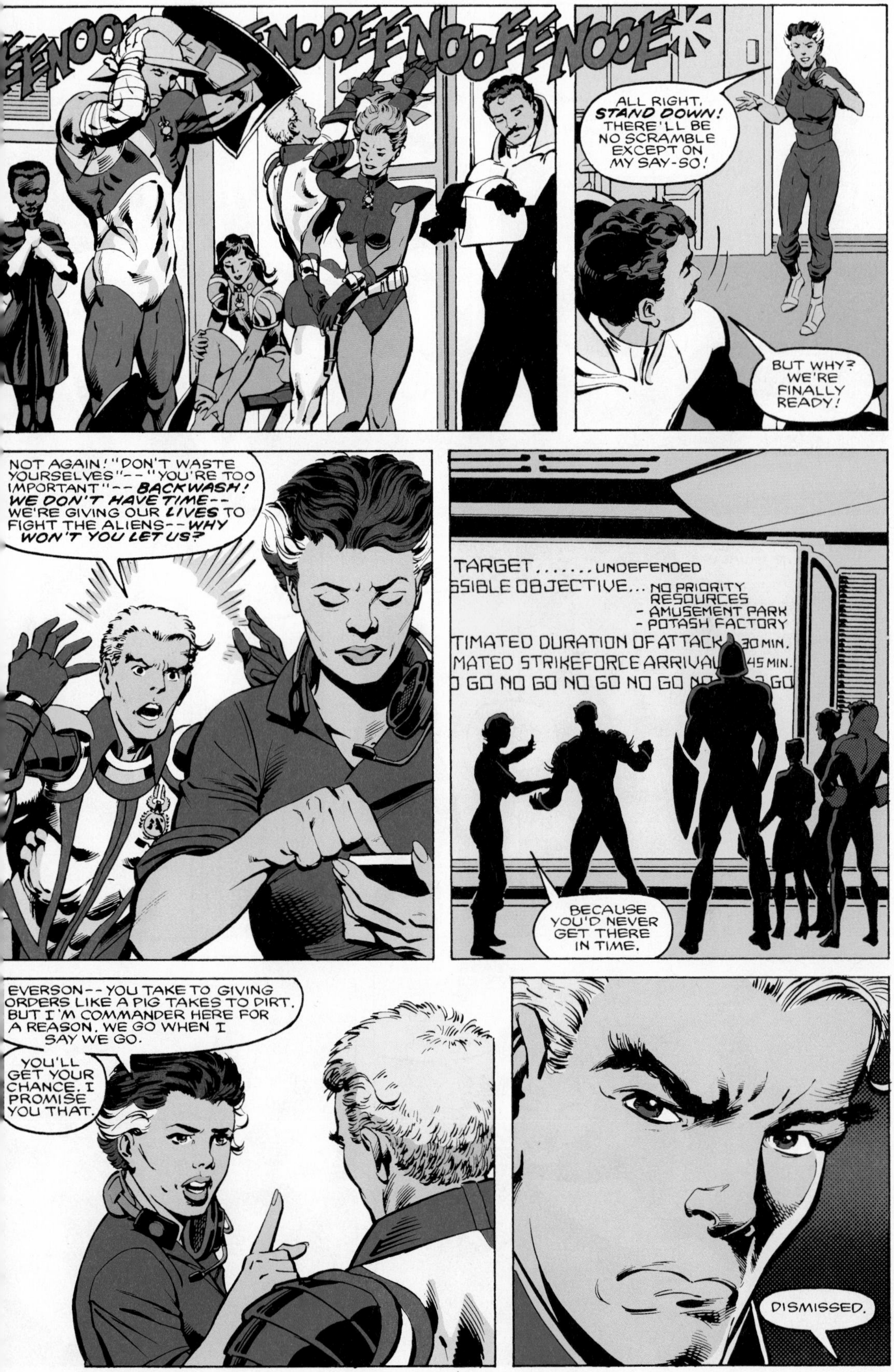
ENOOE ENOOE ENOOE ENOOE ENOOE
ALL RIGHT, STAND DOWN! THERE'LL BE NO SCRAMBLE EXCEPT ON MY SAY-SO!
BUT WHY? WE'RE FINALLY READY!
NOT AGAIN! "DON'T WASTE YOURSELVES"--"YOU'RE TOO IMPORTANT"--BACKWASH! WE DON'T HAVE TIME--WE'RE GIVING OUR LIVES TO FIGHT THE ALIENS--WHY WON'T YOU LET US?
TARGET.......UNDEFENDED
SSIBLE OBJECTIVE... NO PRIORITY RESOURCES
- AMUSEMENT PARK
- POTASH FACTORY
TIMATED DURATION OF ATTACK 30 MIN.
MATED STRIKEFORCE ARRIVAL 45 MIN.
BECAUSE YOU'D NEVER GET THERE IN TIME.
EVERSON--YOU TAKE TO GIVING ORDERS LIKE A PIG TAKES TO DIRT. BUT I'M COMMANDER HERE FOR A REASON. WE GO WHEN I SAY WE GO.
YOU'LL GET YOUR CHANCE. I PROMISE YOU THAT.
DISMISSED.

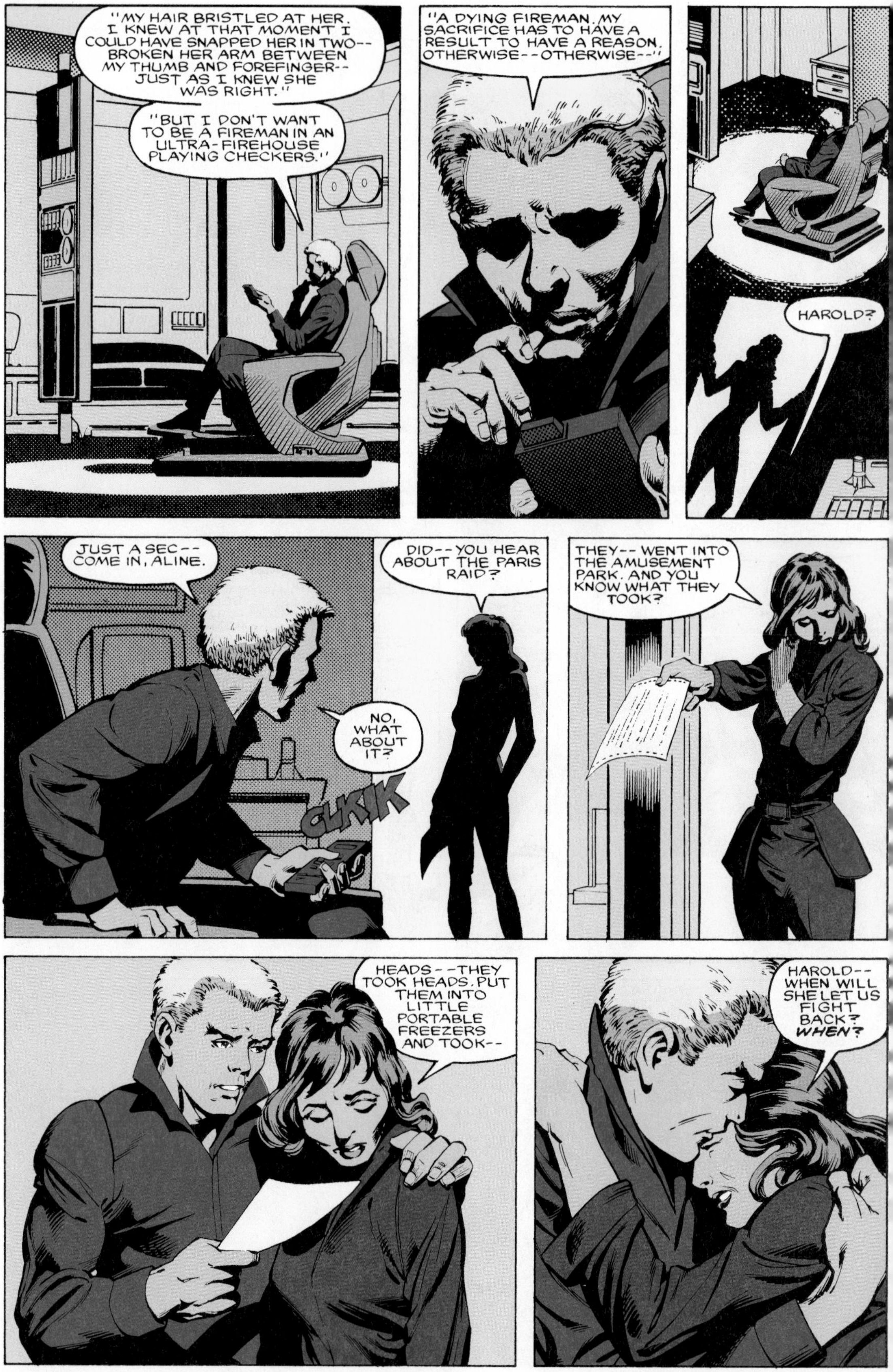
"MY HAIR BRISTLED AT HER. I KNEW AT THAT MOMENT I COULD HAVE SNAPPED HER IN TWO-- BROKEN HER ARM BETWEEN MY THUMB AND FOREFINGER-- JUST AS I KNEW SHE WAS RIGHT."
"BUT I DON'T WANT TO BE A FIREMAN IN AN ULTRA-FIREHOUSE PLAYING CHECKERS."
"A DYING FIREMAN. MY SACRIFICE HAS TO HAVE A RESULT TO HAVE A REASON. OTHERWISE--OTHERWISE--"
HAROLD?
JUST A SEC-- COME IN, ALINE.
NO, WHAT ABOUT IT?
CLKIK
DID--YOU HEAR ABOUT THE PARIS RAID?
THEY-- WENT INTO THE AMUSEMENT PARK. AND YOU KNOW WHAT THEY TOOK?
HEADS--THEY TOOK HEADS. PUT THEM INTO LITTLE PORTABLE FREEZERS AND TOOK--
HAROLD-- WHEN WILL SHE LET US FIGHT BACK? *WHEN?*

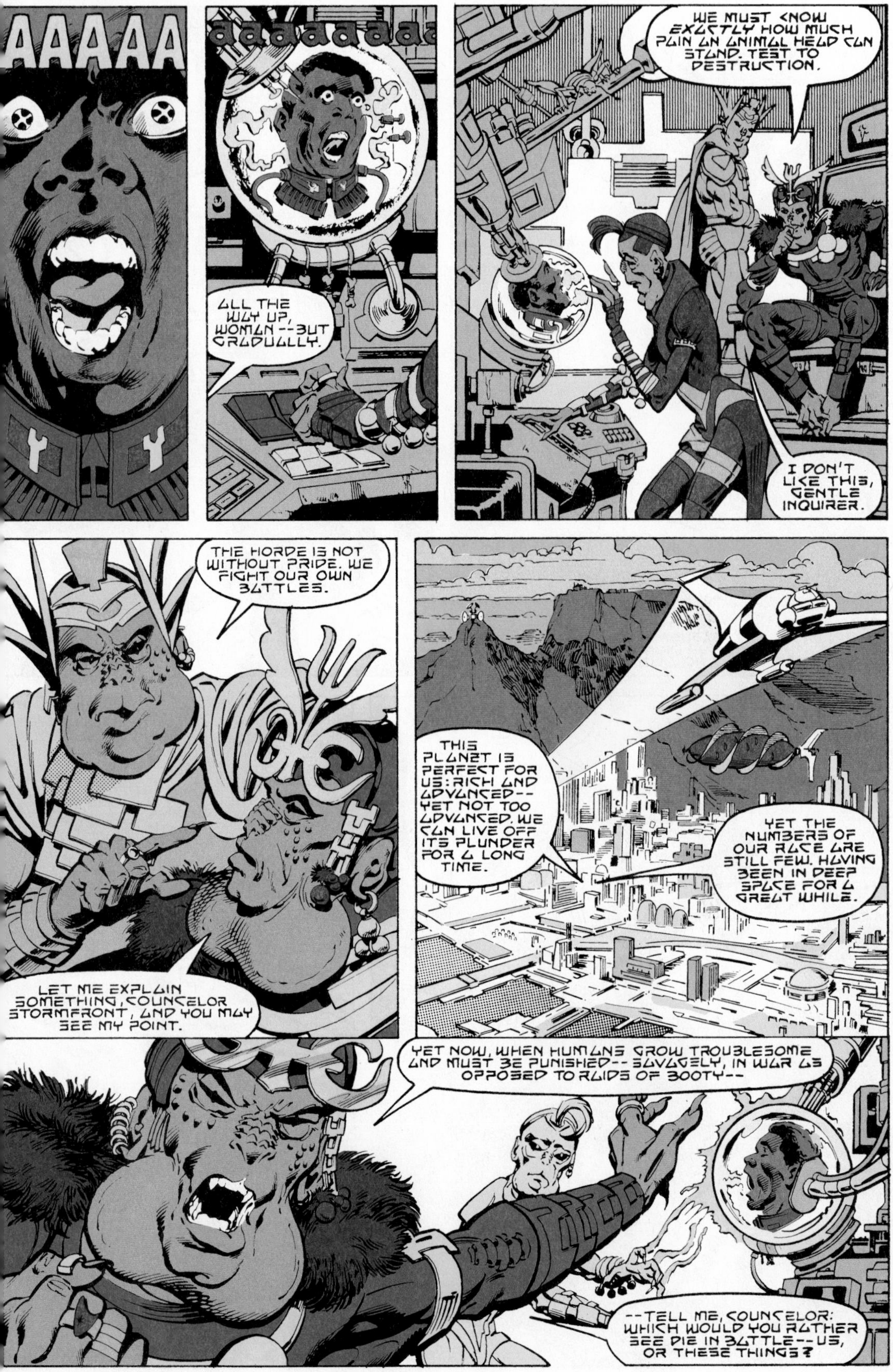
AAAAA
AAAAAAAAA
ALL THE WAY UP, WOMAN --BUT GRADUALLY.
WE MUST KNOW EXACTLY HOW MUCH PAIN AN ANIMAL HEAD CAN STAND. TEST TO DESTRUCTION.
I DON'T LIKE THIS, GENTLE INQUIRER.
THE HORDE IS NOT WITHOUT PRIDE. WE FIGHT OUR OWN BATTLES.
LET ME EXPLAIN SOMETHING, COUNCELOR STORMFRONT, AND YOU MAY SEE MY POINT.
THIS PLANET IS PERFECT FOR US: RICH AND ADVANCED-- YET NOT TOO ADVANCED. WE CAN LIVE OFF ITS PLUNDER FOR A LONG TIME.
YET THE NUMBERS OF OUR RACE ARE STILL FEW, HAVING BEEN IN DEEP SPACE FOR A GREAT WHILE.
YET NOW, WHEN HUMANS GROW TROUBLESOME AND MUST BE PUNISHED-- SAVAGELY, IN WAR AS OPPOSED TO RAIDS OF BOOTY--
--TELL ME, COUNCELOR: WHICH WOULD YOU RATHER SEE DIE IN BATTLE-- US, OR THESE THINGS?

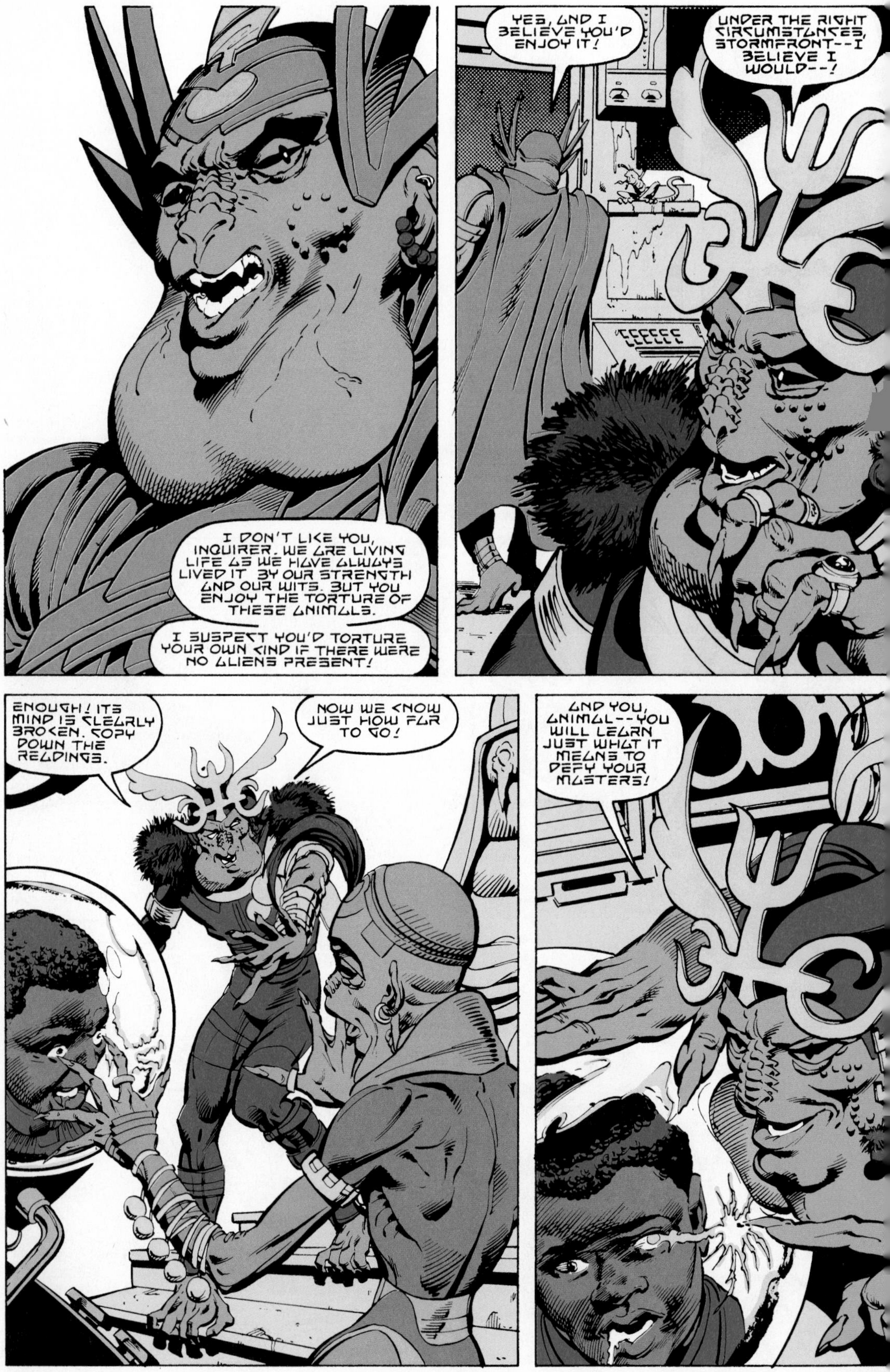
I DON'T LIKE YOU, INQUIRER. WE ARE LIVING LIFE AS WE HAVE ALWAYS LIVED IT BY OUR STRENGTH AND OUR WITS. BUT YOU ENJOY THE TORTURE OF THESE ANIMALS.
I SUSPECT YOU'D TORTURE YOUR OWN KIND IF THERE WERE NO ALIENS PRESENT!
YES, AND I BELIEVE YOU'D ENJOY IT!
UNDER THE RIGHT CIRCUMSTANCES, STORMFRONT--I BELIEVE I WOULD--!
ENOUGH! ITS MIND IS CLEARLY BROKEN. COPY DOWN THE READINGS.
NOW WE KNOW JUST HOW FAR TO GO!
AND YOU, ANIMAL--YOU WILL LEARN JUST WHAT IT MEANS TO DEFY YOUR MASTERS!

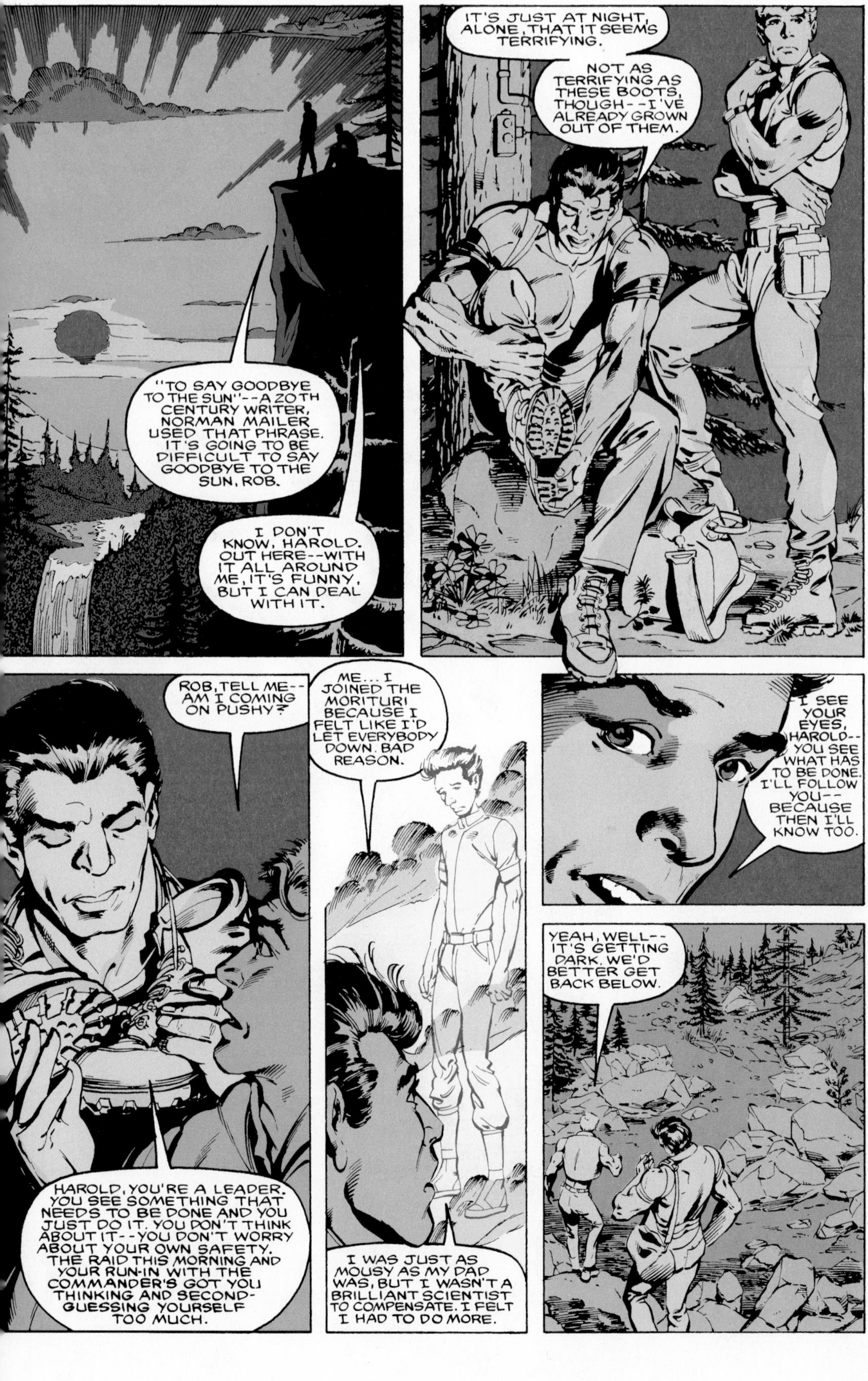
"TO SAY GOODBYE TO THE SUN"--A 20TH CENTURY WRITER, NORMAN MAILER USED THAT PHRASE. IT'S GOING TO BE DIFFICULT TO SAY GOODBYE TO THE SUN, ROB.
I DON'T KNOW, HAROLD. OUT HERE--WITH IT ALL AROUND ME, IT'S FUNNY, BUT I CAN DEAL WITH IT.
IT'S JUST AT NIGHT, ALONE, THAT IT SEEMS TERRIFYING.
NOT AS TERRIFYING AS THESE BOOTS, THOUGH--I'VE ALREADY GROWN OUT OF THEM.
ROB, TELL ME--AM I COMING ON PUSHY?
HAROLD, YOU'RE A LEADER. YOU SEE SOMETHING THAT NEEDS TO BE DONE AND YOU JUST DO IT. YOU DON'T THINK ABOUT IT--YOU DON'T WORRY ABOUT YOUR OWN SAFETY. THE RAID THIS MORNING AND YOUR RUN-IN WITH THE COMMANDER'S GOT YOU THINKING AND SECOND-GUESSING YOURSELF TOO MUCH.
ME... I JOINED THE MORITURI BECAUSE I FELT LIKE I'D LET EVERYBODY DOWN. BAD REASON.
I WAS JUST AS MOUSY AS MY DAD WAS, BUT I WASN'T A BRILLIANT SCIENTIST TO COMPENSATE. I FELT I HAD TO DO MORE.
I SEE YOUR EYES, HAROLD--YOU SEE WHAT HAS TO BE DONE. I'LL FOLLOW YOU--BECAUSE THEN I'LL KNOW TOO.
YEAH, WELL--IT'S GETTING DARK. WE'D BETTER GET BACK BELOW.

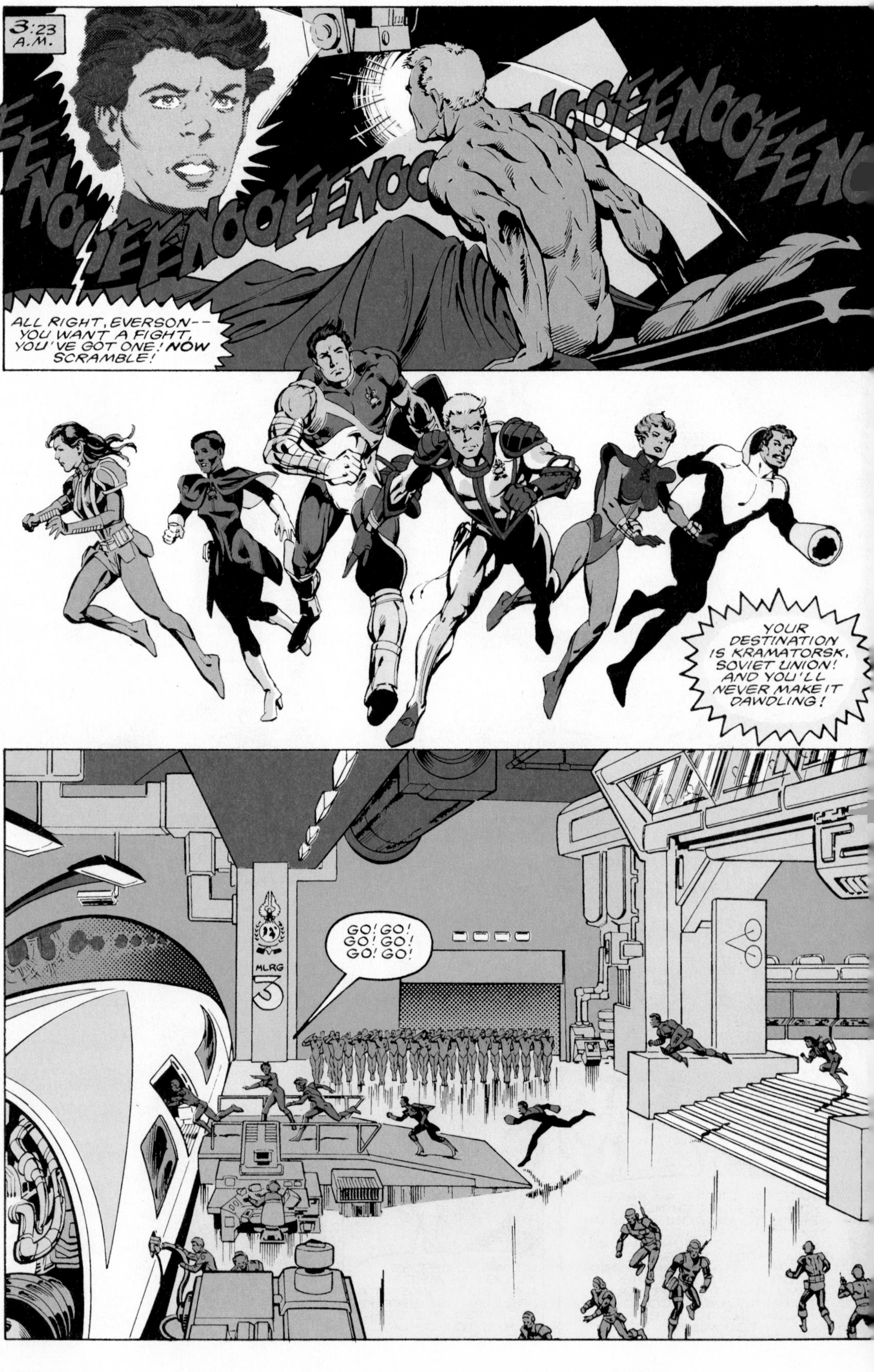
3:23 A.M.
EEENOOEENOOEENOOEENOOEENOOEENOOEENC
ALL RIGHT, EVERSON-- YOU WANT A FIGHT, YOU'VE GOT ONE! NOW SCRAMBLE!
YOUR DESTINATION IS KRAMATORSK, SOVIET UNION! AND YOU'LL NEVER MAKE IT DAWDLING!
MLRG
GO! GO! GO! GO! GO! GO!

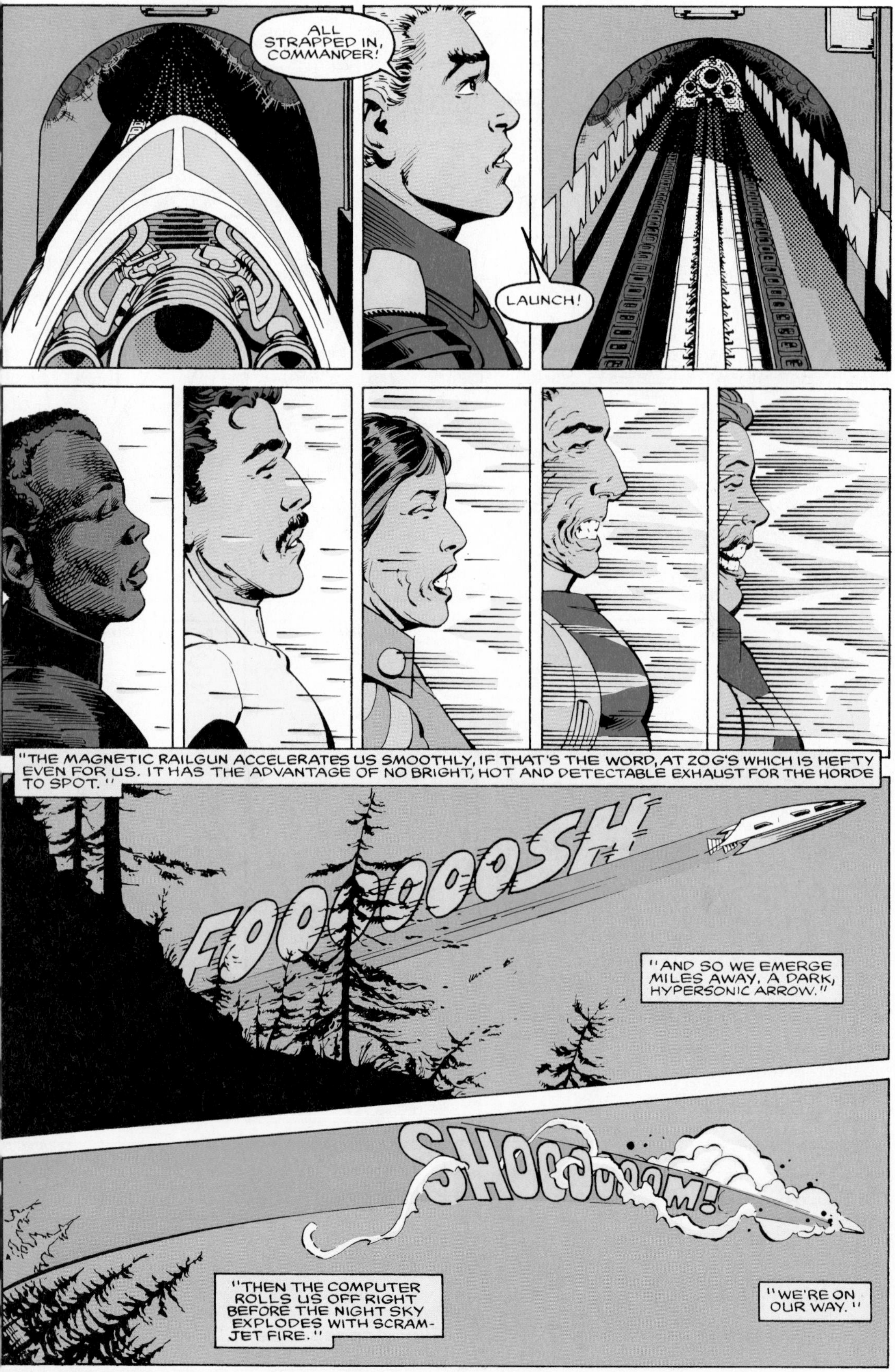
ALL STRAPPED IN, COMMANDER!
LAUNCH!
MMMMMMMNNNNNN
"THE MAGNETIC RAILGUN ACCELERATES US SMOOTHLY, IF THAT'S THE WORD, AT ZOG'S WHICH IS HEFTY EVEN FOR US. IT HAS THE ADVANTAGE OF NO BRIGHT, HOT AND DETECTABLE EXHAUST FOR THE HORDE TO SPOT."
FOOOOOOOSH!
"AND SO WE EMERGE MILES AWAY, A DARK, HYPERSONIC ARROW."
SHOOOOOOOM!
"THEN THE COMPUTER ROLLS US OFF RIGHT BEFORE THE NIGHT SKY EXPLODES WITH SCRAM-JET FIRE."
"WE'RE ON OUR WAY."

IT FEELS-- I FEEL ALIVE, READY, EVERYTHING EVEN IN THIS CRAMPED LITTLE--

--HOW ARE THE OTHERS STANDING THE HEAT--?

NO. NO! IT'S ME! I'M GLOWING! I'M SURGING!

IT'S TOO SOON! NOT NOW! NOT YET!

THE PROCESS CAN'T KILL ME NOW--! NOT LIKE THE BLACK WATCH--!*

*SEE ISSUE #1.

KRAMATORSK COMING UP REAL QUICK. THERE ARE HORDE LEPER-CRAFT EVERYWHERE. THAT MEANS THEY'RE FROM AN EARTH BASE AND NOT ORBIT.. BUT WHY SO MANY?

THE BANKS SAY KRAMATORSK IS WHERE WE'RE TRYING TO REBUILD SOME OF THE NUCLEAR ARSENAL WE DISMANTLED IN THE DECADES BEFORE THE ALIENS CAME.

I THINK THEY MEAN TO TEACH US A LESSON--!

I COULD DIE ANY SECOND--!

HOW CAN I TAKE RESPONSIBILITY-- LEAD, WHEN I COULD BE GONE?

HANG ON, CAMPERS! DISENGAGING POD-PAC--

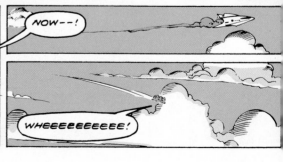

NOW--!

WHEEEEEEEEEEE!

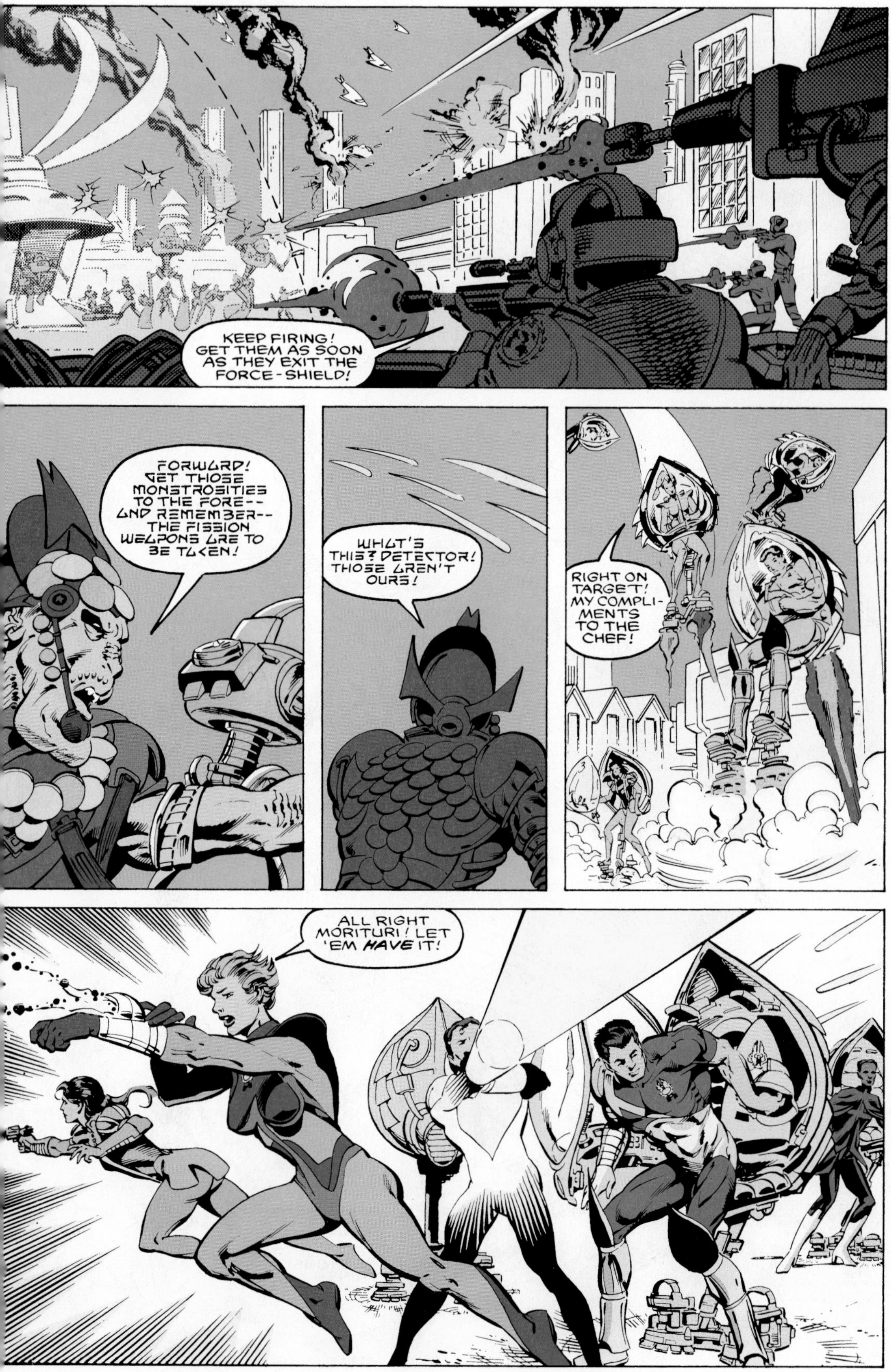

KEEP FIRING! GET THEM AS SOON AS THEY EXIT THE FORCE-SHIELD!
FORWARD! GET THOSE MONSTROSITIES TO THE FORE-- AND REMEMBER-- THE FISSION WEAPONS ARE TO BE TAKEN!
WHAT'S THIS? DETECTOR! THOSE AREN'T OURS!
RIGHT ON TARGET! MY COMPLIMENTS TO THE CHEF!
ALL RIGHT MORITURI! LET 'EM *HAVE* IT!

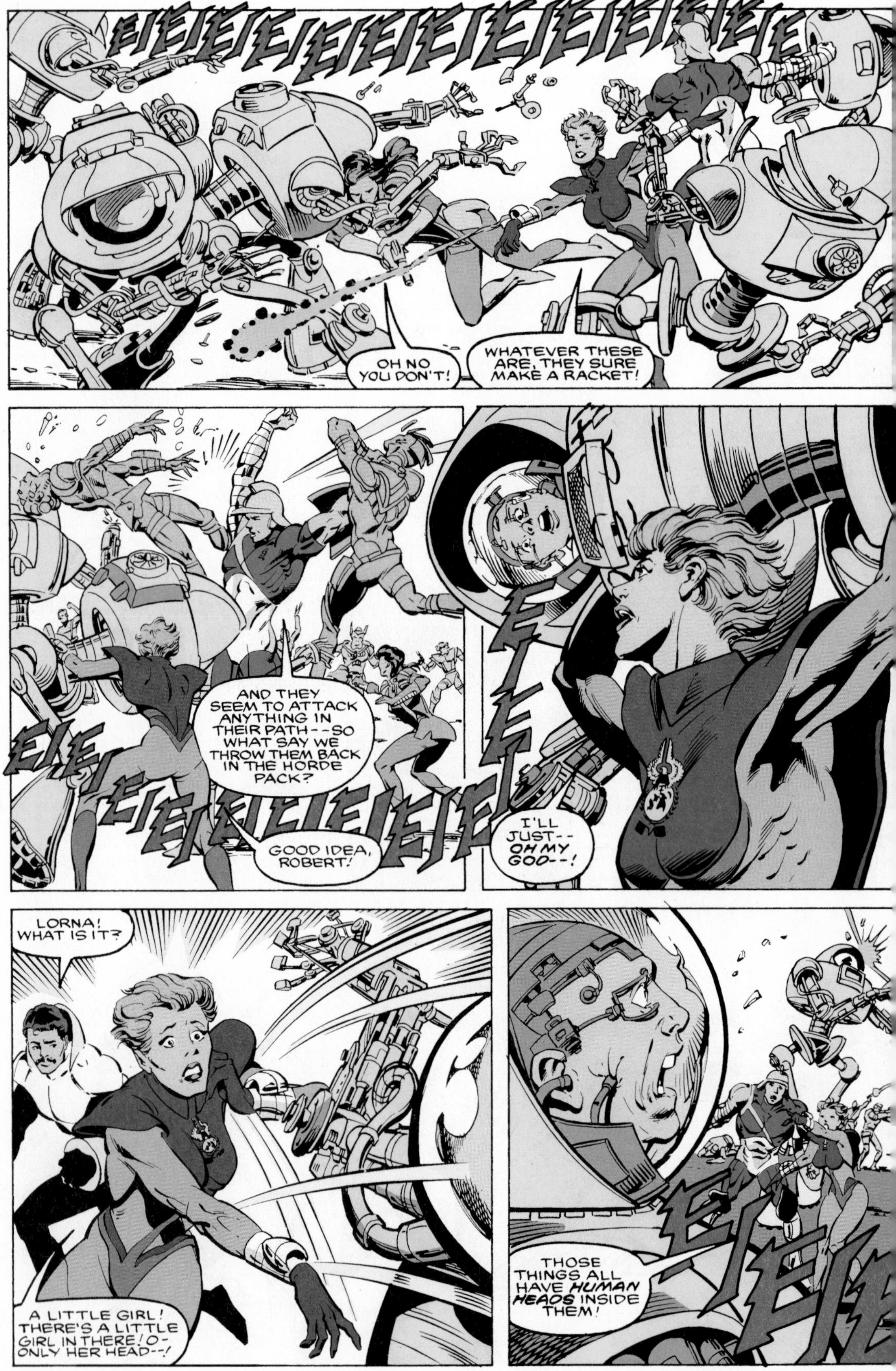
EIEIEIEIEIEIEIEIEIEIEIEIEIEIEIE
OH NO YOU DON'T!
WHATEVER THESE ARE, THEY SURE MAKE A RACKET!
AND THEY SEEM TO ATTACK ANYTHING IN THEIR PATH--SO WHAT SAY WE THROW THEM BACK IN THE HORDE PACK?
GOOD IDEA, ROBERT!
I'LL JUST--OH MY GOD--!
LORNA! WHAT IS IT?
A LITTLE GIRL! THERE'S A LITTLE GIRL IN THERE! O-ONLY HER HEAD--!
THOSE THINGS ALL HAVE HUMAN HEADS INSIDE THEM!

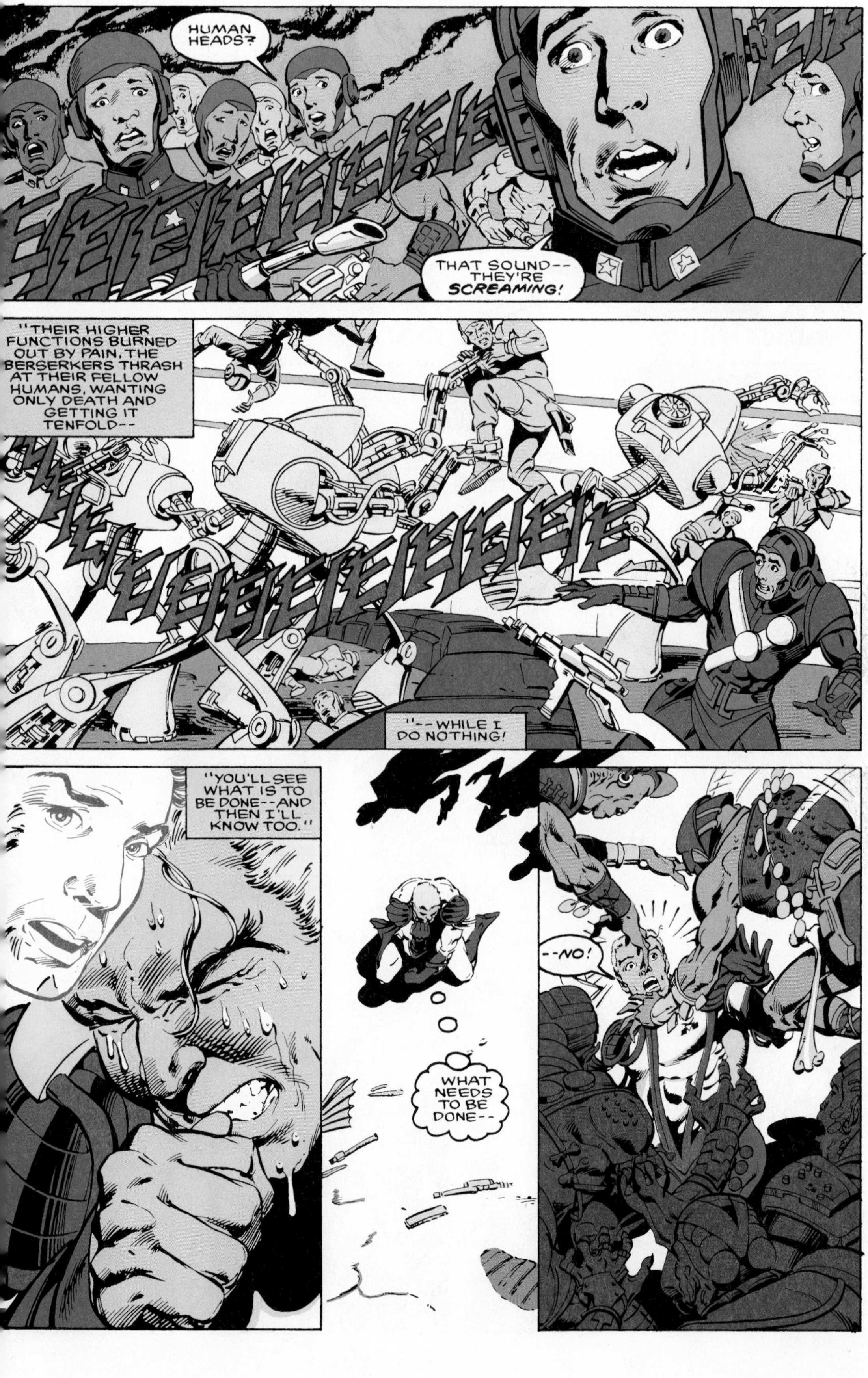
HUMAN HEADS?
THAT SOUND-- THEY'RE SCREAMING!
"THEIR HIGHER FUNCTIONS BURNED OUT BY PAIN, THE BERSERKERS THRASH AT THEIR FELLOW HUMANS, WANTING ONLY DEATH AND GETTING IT TENFOLD--
"--WHILE I DO NOTHING!
"YOU'LL SEE WHAT IS TO BE DONE--AND THEN I'LL KNOW TOO."
WHAT NEEDS TO BE DONE--
--NO!

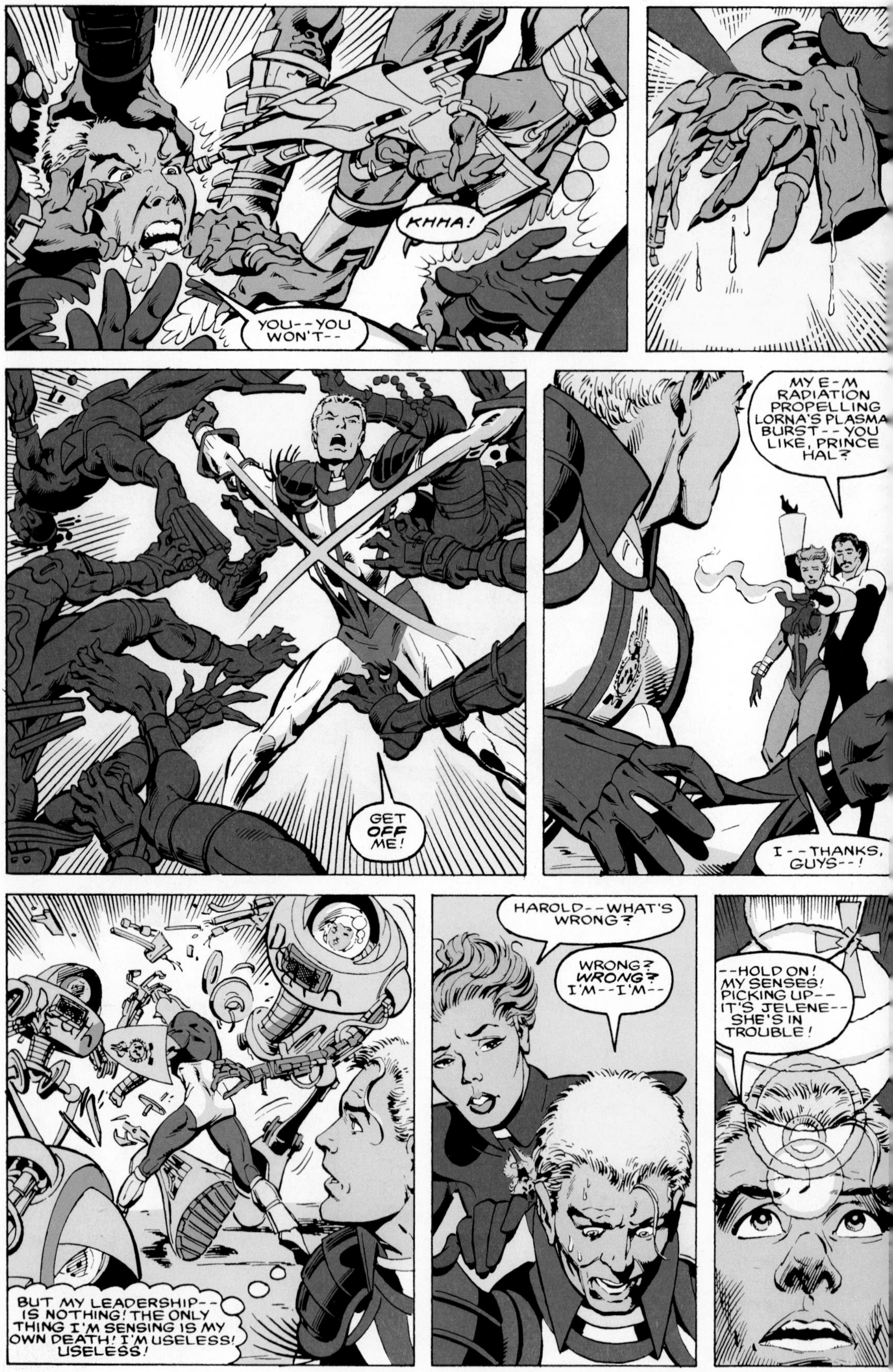
KHHA!
YOU--YOU WON'T--
GET OFF ME!
MY E-M RADIATION PROPELLING LORNA'S PLASMA BURST--YOU LIKE, PRINCE HAL?
I--THANKS, GUYS--!
BUT MY LEADERSHIP--IS NOTHING! THE ONLY THING I'M SENSING IS MY OWN DEATH! I'M USELESS! USELESS!
HAROLD--WHAT'S WRONG?
WRONG? WRONG? I'M--I'M--
--HOLD ON! MY SENSES! PICKING UP--IT'S JELENE--SHE'S IN TROUBLE!

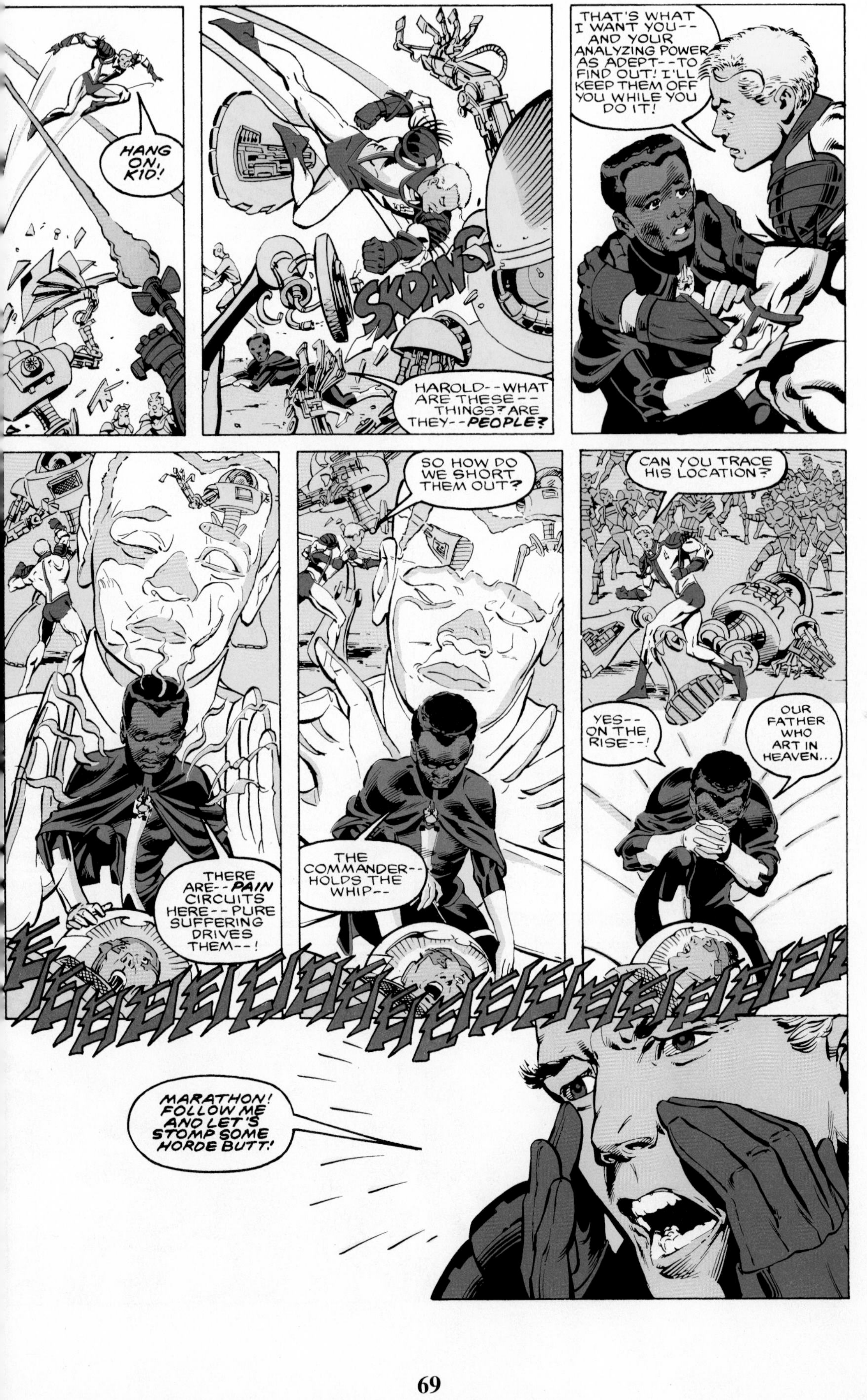
HANG ON, KID!
SKDANG!
HAROLD--WHAT ARE THESE--THINGS? ARE THEY--PEOPLE?
THAT'S WHAT I WANT YOU--AND YOUR ANALYZING POWER AS ADEPT--TO FIND OUT! I'LL KEEP THEM OFF YOU WHILE YOU DO IT!
THERE ARE--PAIN CIRCUITS HERE--PURE SUFFERING DRIVES THEM--!
SO HOW DO WE SHORT THEM OUT?
THE COMMANDER--HOLDS THE WHIP--
CAN YOU TRACE HIS LOCATION?
YES--ON THE RISE--!
OUR FATHER WHO ART IN HEAVEN...
EEEEEEEEEEEEEEEEEEEEEEEEEEEE
MARATHON! FOLLOW ME AND LET'S STOMP SOME HORDE BUTT!

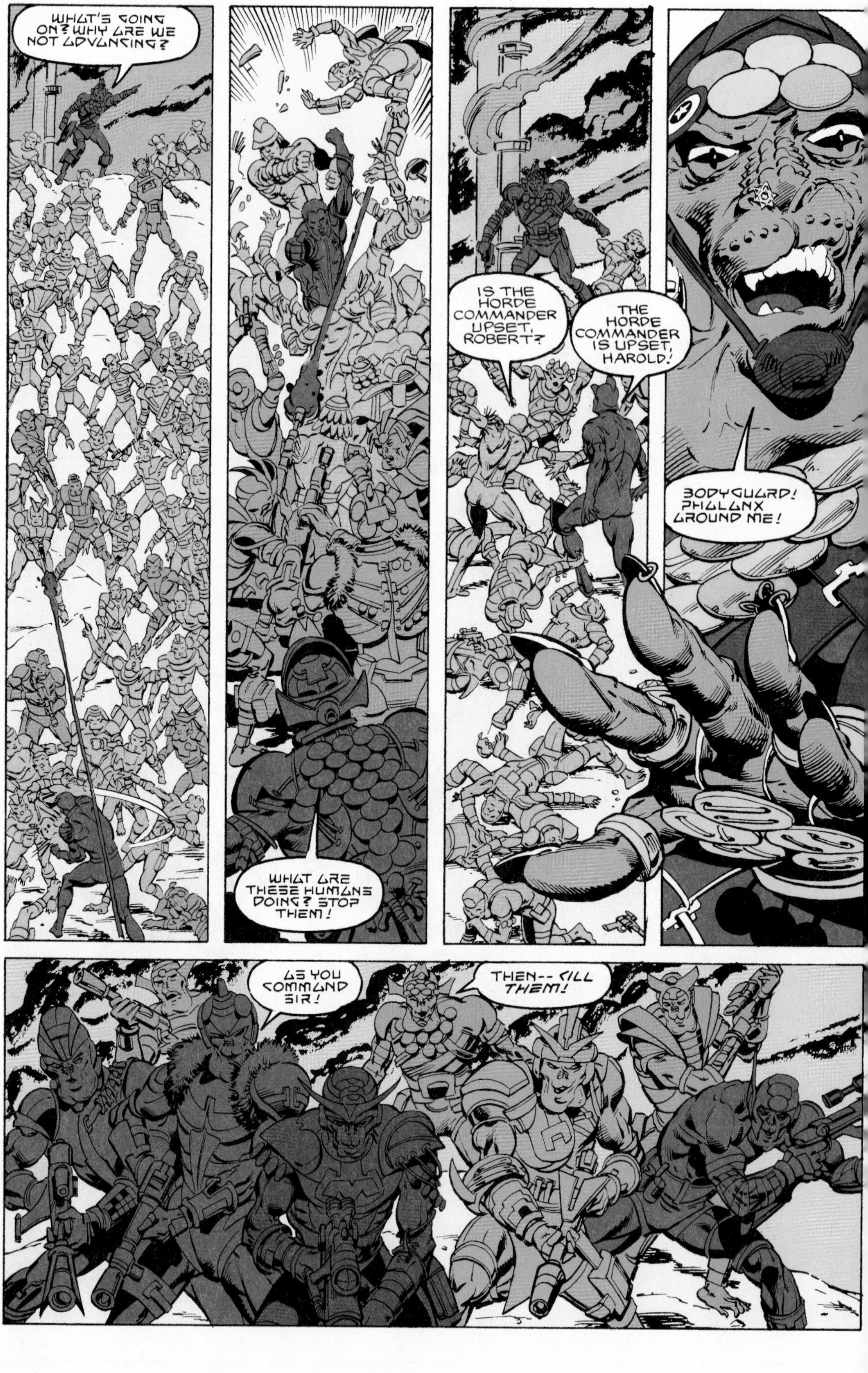
WHAT'S GOING ON? WHY ARE WE NOT ADVANCING?
WHAT ARE THESE HUMANS DOING? STOP THEM!
IS THE HORDE COMMANDER UPSET, ROBERT?
THE HORDE COMMANDER IS UPSET, HAROLD!
BODYGUARD! PHALANX AROUND ME!
AS YOU COMMAND SIR!
THEN-- KILL THEM!

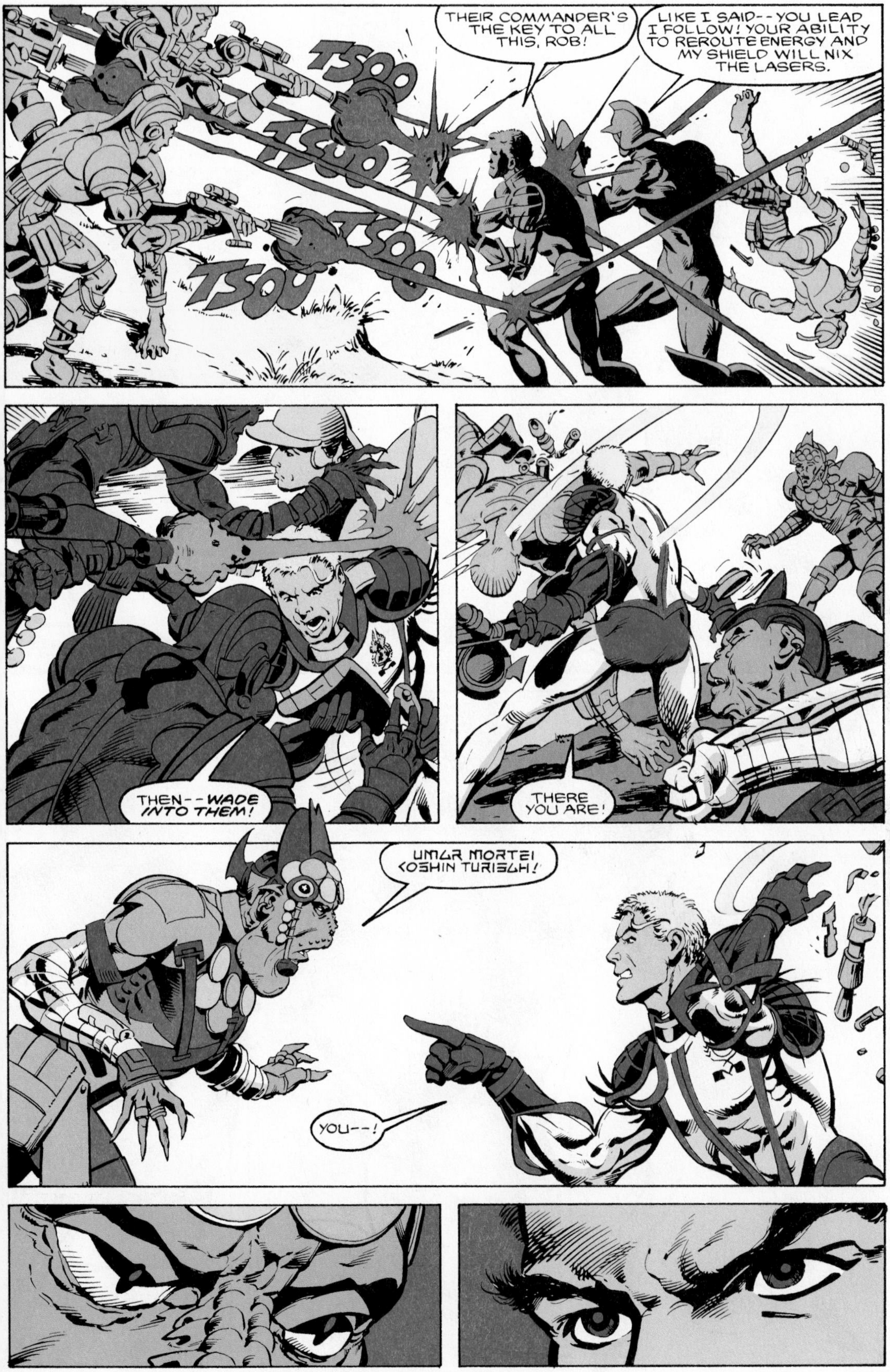
THEIR COMMANDER'S THE KEY TO ALL THIS, ROB!
LIKE I SAID--YOU LEAD I FOLLOW! YOUR ABILITY TO REROUTE ENERGY AND MY SHIELD WILL NIX THE LASERS.
TSOO
TSOO
TSOO
TSOO
THEN--WADE INTO THEM!
THERE YOU ARE!
UMGR MORTEI KOSHIN TURISGH!
YOU--!

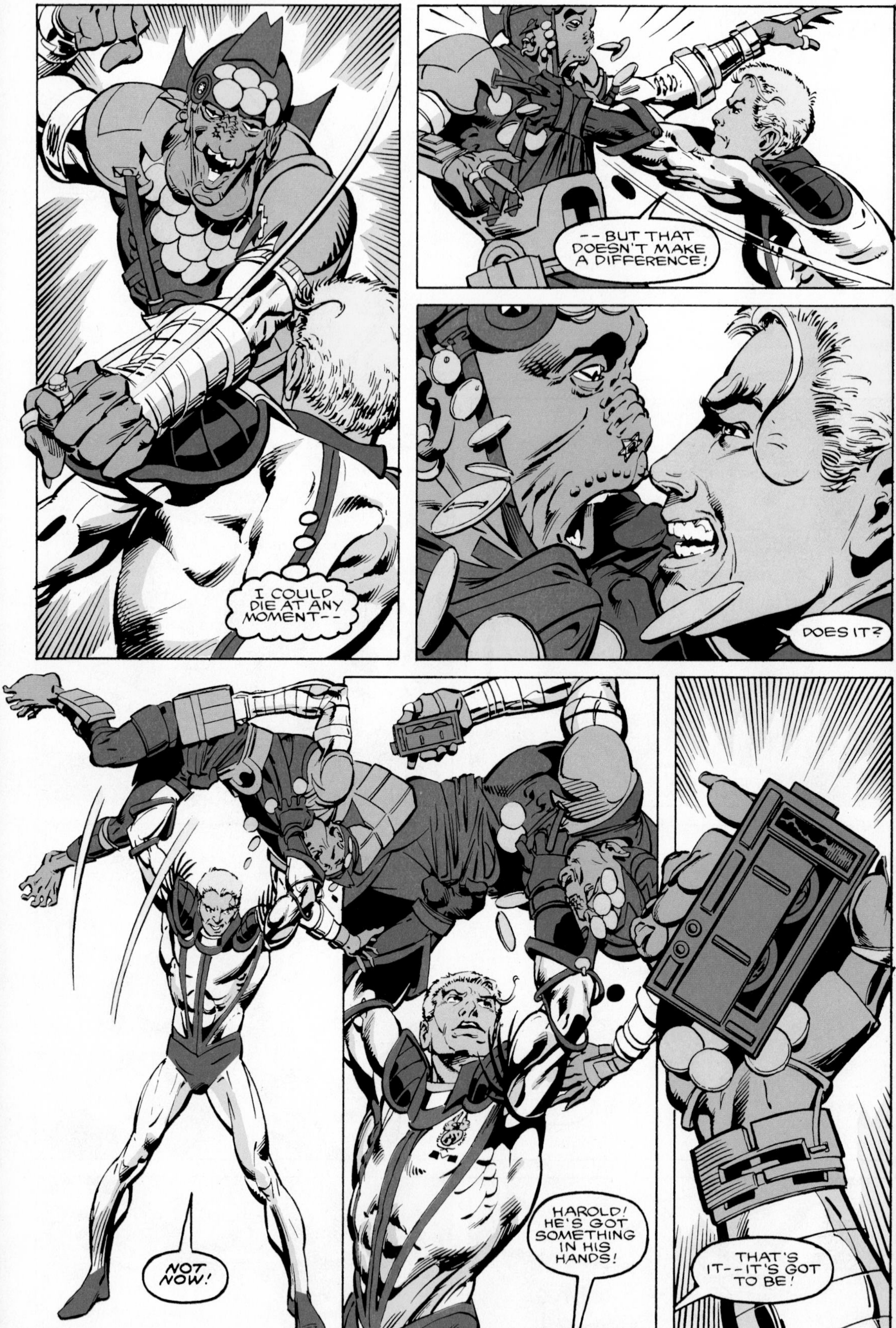
I COULD DIE AT ANY MOMENT--
--BUT THAT DOESN'T MAKE A DIFFERENCE!
DOES IT?
NOT NOW!
HAROLD! HE'S GOT SOMETHING IN HIS HANDS!
THAT'S IT--IT'S GOT TO BE!

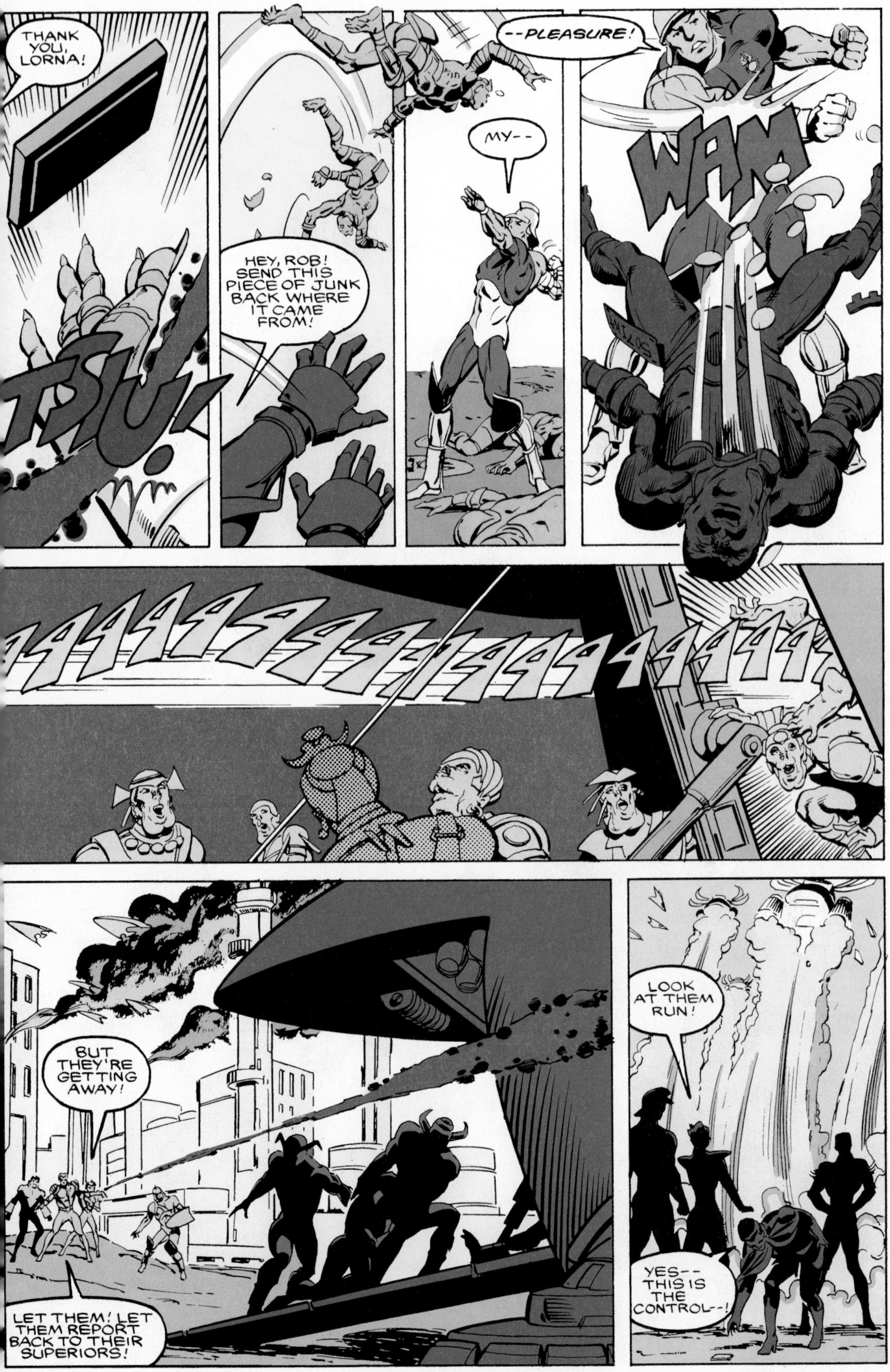
THANK YOU, LORNA!
TSU!
HEY, ROB! SEND THIS PIECE OF JUNK BACK WHERE IT CAME FROM!
MY--
--PLEASURE!
WAM
BUT THEY'RE GETTING AWAY!
LET THEM! LET THEM REPORT BACK TO THEIR SUPERIORS!
LOOK AT THEM RUN!
YES-- THIS IS THE CONTROL--!

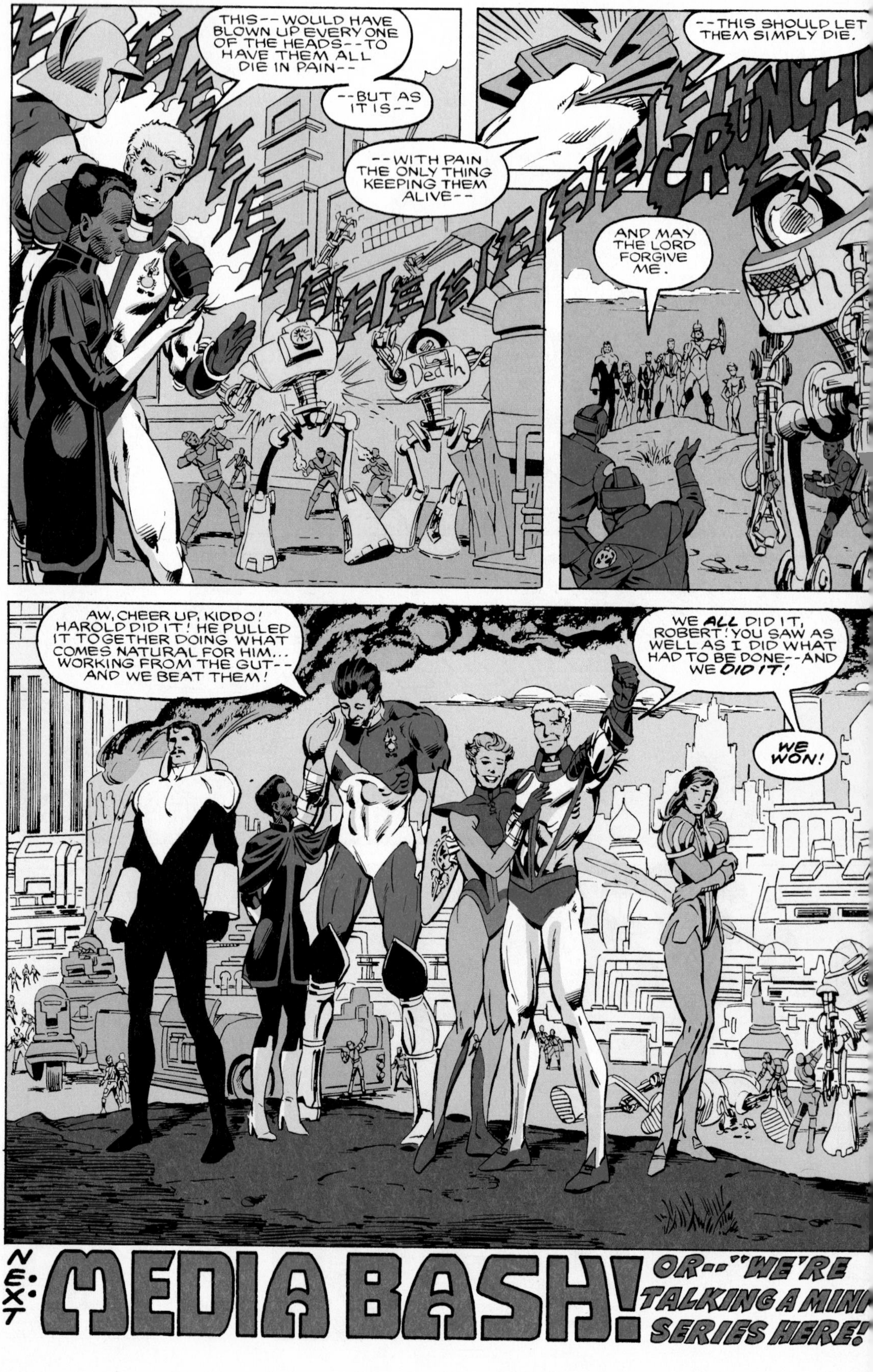

THIS-- WOULD HAVE BLOWN UP EVERY ONE OF THE HEADS--TO HAVE THEM ALL DIE IN PAIN--
--BUT AS IT IS--
--WITH PAIN THE ONLY THING KEEPING THEM ALIVE--
--THIS SHOULD LET THEM SIMPLY DIE.
CRUNCH!
AND MAY THE LORD FORGIVE ME.
AW, CHEER UP, KIDDO! HAROLD DID IT! HE PULLED IT TOGETHER DOING WHAT COMES NATURAL FOR HIM... WORKING FROM THE GUT--AND WE BEAT THEM!
WE ALL DID IT, ROBERT! YOU SAW AS WELL AS I DID WHAT HAD TO BE DONE--AND WE DID IT!
WE WON!
NEXT: MEDIA BASH! OR--"WE'RE TALKING A MINI SERIES HERE!

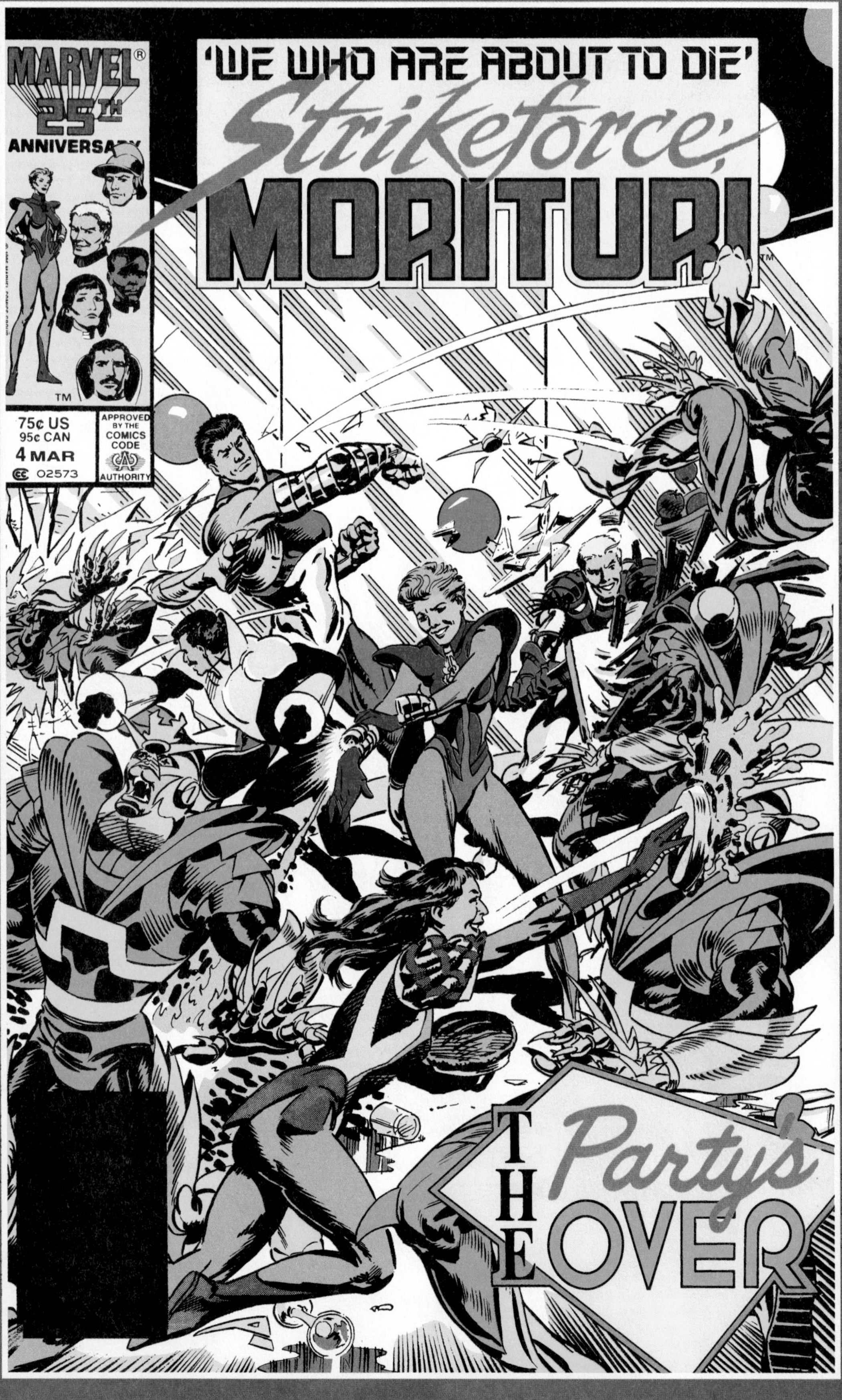
MARVEL®
25TH
ANNIVERSARY
TM
75¢ US
95¢ CAN
4 MAR
02573
APPROVED BY THE COMICS CODE AUTHORITY
'WE WHO ARE ABOUT TO DIE'
Strikeforce:
MORITURI™
THE Party's OVER

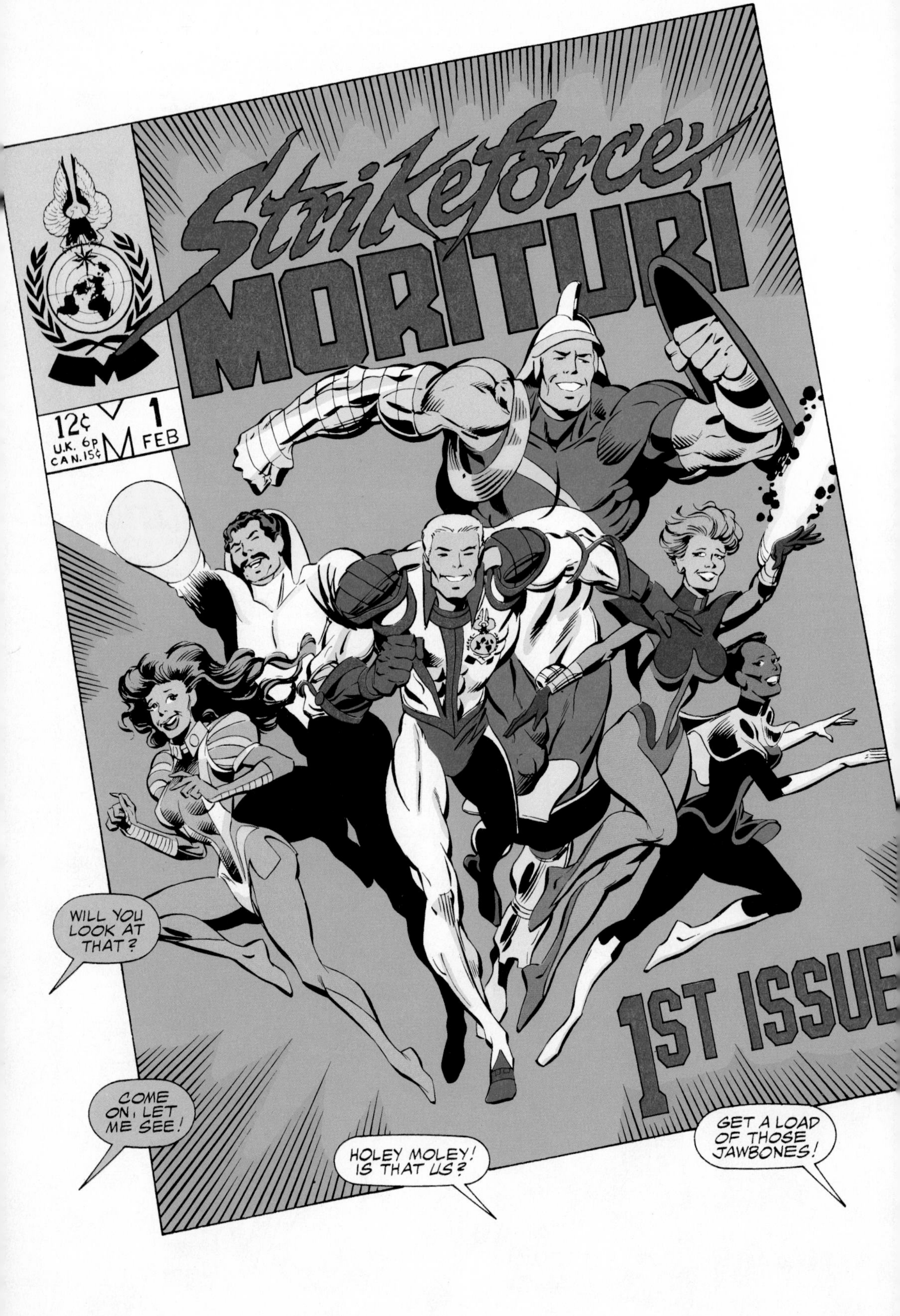
Strikeforce: MORITURI
12¢ U.K. 6p CAN. 15¢
1 FEB
1ST ISSUE
WILL YOU LOOK AT THAT?
COME ON, LET ME SEE!
HOLEY MOLEY! IS THAT US?
GET A LOAD OF THOSE JAWBONES!

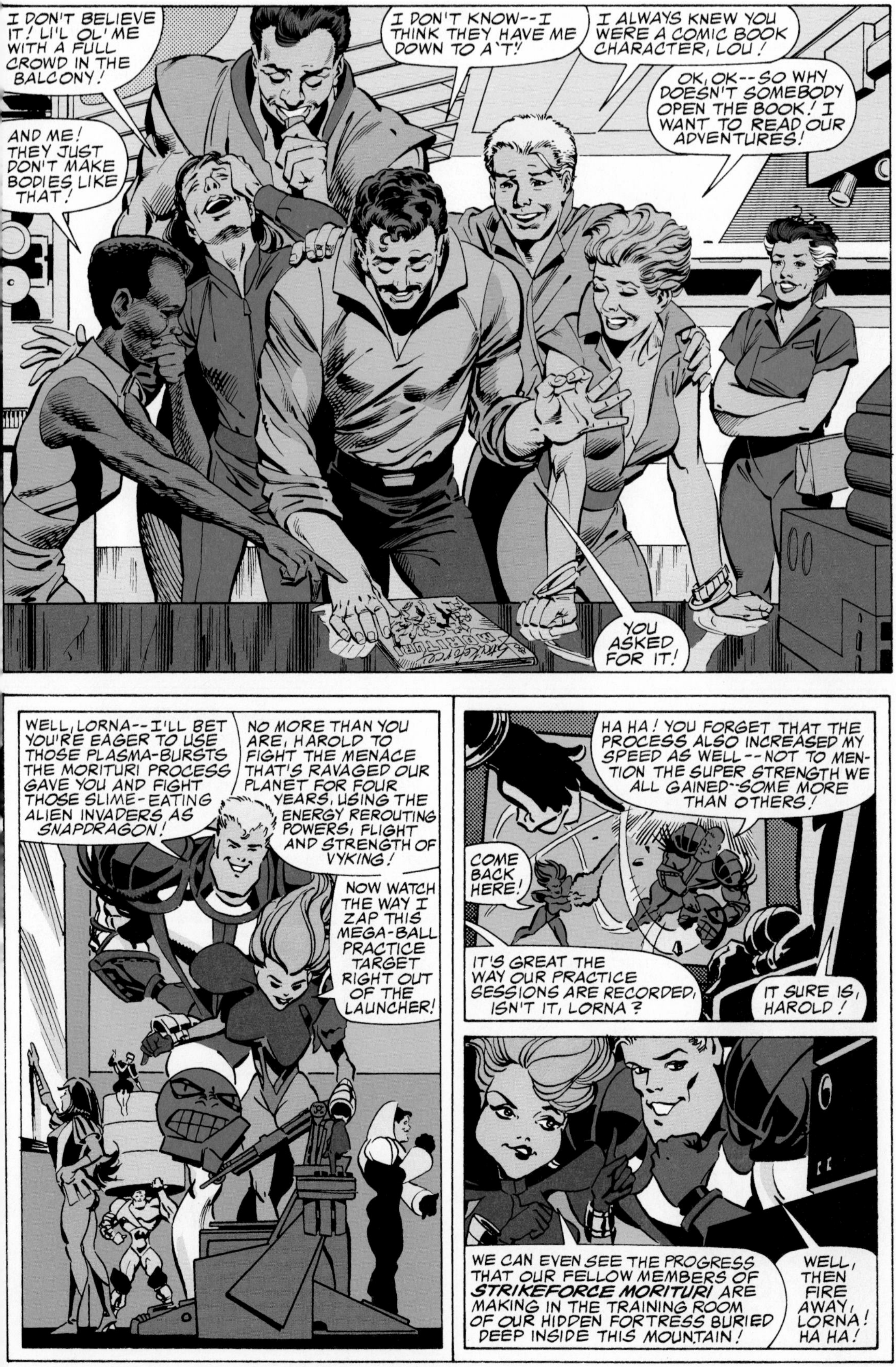
I DON'T BELIEVE IT! LI'L OL' ME WITH A FULL CROWD IN THE BALCONY!
AND ME! THEY JUST DON'T MAKE BODIES LIKE THAT!
I DON'T KNOW--I THINK THEY HAVE ME DOWN TO A 'T'!
I ALWAYS KNEW YOU WERE A COMIC BOOK CHARACTER, LOU!
OK, OK--SO WHY DOESN'T SOMEBODY OPEN THE BOOK! I WANT TO READ OUR ADVENTURES!
YOU ASKED FOR IT!
WELL, LORNA--I'LL BET YOU'RE EAGER TO USE THOSE PLASMA-BURSTS THE MORITURI PROCESS GAVE YOU AND FIGHT THOSE SLIME-EATING ALIEN INVADERS AS SNAPDRAGON!
NO MORE THAN YOU ARE, HAROLD TO FIGHT THE MENACE THAT'S RAVAGED OUR PLANET FOR FOUR YEARS, USING THE ENERGY REROUTING POWERS, FLIGHT AND STRENGTH OF VYKING!
NOW WATCH THE WAY I ZAP THIS MEGA-BALL PRACTICE TARGET RIGHT OUT OF THE LAUNCHER!
HA HA! YOU FORGET THAT THE PROCESS ALSO INCREASED MY SPEED AS WELL--NOT TO MENTION THE SUPER STRENGTH WE ALL GAINED--SOME MORE THAN OTHERS!
COME BACK HERE!
IT'S GREAT THE WAY OUR PRACTICE SESSIONS ARE RECORDED, ISN'T IT, LORNA?
IT SURE IS, HAROLD!
WE CAN EVEN SEE THE PROGRESS THAT OUR FELLOW MEMBERS OF STRIKEFORCE MORITURI ARE MAKING IN THE TRAINING ROOM OF OUR HIDDEN FORTRESS BURIED DEEP INSIDE THIS MOUNTAIN!
WELL, THEN FIRE AWAY, LORNA! HA HA!

WHO WRITES THIS STUFF?

IT'S LIKE A NIGHTMARE! THE READERS WILL THINK WE'RE ABSOLUTE MORONS!

COME ON, STOP COMPLAINING! LET'S SEE WHAT THEY DO WITH THE REST OF US!

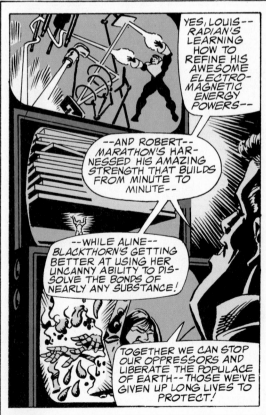

YES, LOUIS-- RADIAN'S LEARNING HOW TO REFINE HIS AWESOME ELECTRO-MAGNETIC ENERGY POWERS--

--AND ROBERT-- MARATHON'S HARNESSED HIS AMAZING STRENGTH THAT BUILDS FROM MINUTE TO MINUTE--

--WHILE ALINE-- BLACKTHORN'S GETTING BETTER AT USING HER UNCANNY ABILITY TO DISSOLVE THE BONDS OF NEARLY ANY SUBSTANCE!

TOGETHER WE CAN STOP OUR OPPRESSORS AND LIBERATE THE POPULACE OF EARTH--THOSE WE'VE GIVEN UP LONG LIVES TO PROTECT!

SNAPDRAGON! WHAT'S HAPPENED TO THE VIDEO MONITOR? SOMETHING'S INTERRUPTED THE SIGNAL!

IT CAN'T BE, VYKING-- BUT IT IS! IT'S THE COMMANDER OF THE EVIL ALIEN HORDE HIMSELF!

ACCURSED MORITURI! YOU MAY HAVE GAINED SUPER POWERS BY A PROCESS THAT WILL KILL YOU INSIDE OF A YEAR BY SPONTANEOUSLY BURNING UP FROM THE INSIDE-- BUT YOU WON'T LIVE EVEN THAT LONG TO CAUSE US ANY MORE TROUBLE! REMEMBER WHAT HAPPENED TO YOUR PREDECESSORS THE BLACK WATCH?

WE'RE ABOUT TO LAUNCH ANOTHER OF OUR RAIDS WHERE WE STEAL YOUR EARTHLY RESOURCES TO FEED OUR GREED --AND IF YOU TRY TO STOP US, YOU WILL BE DESTROYED!!!

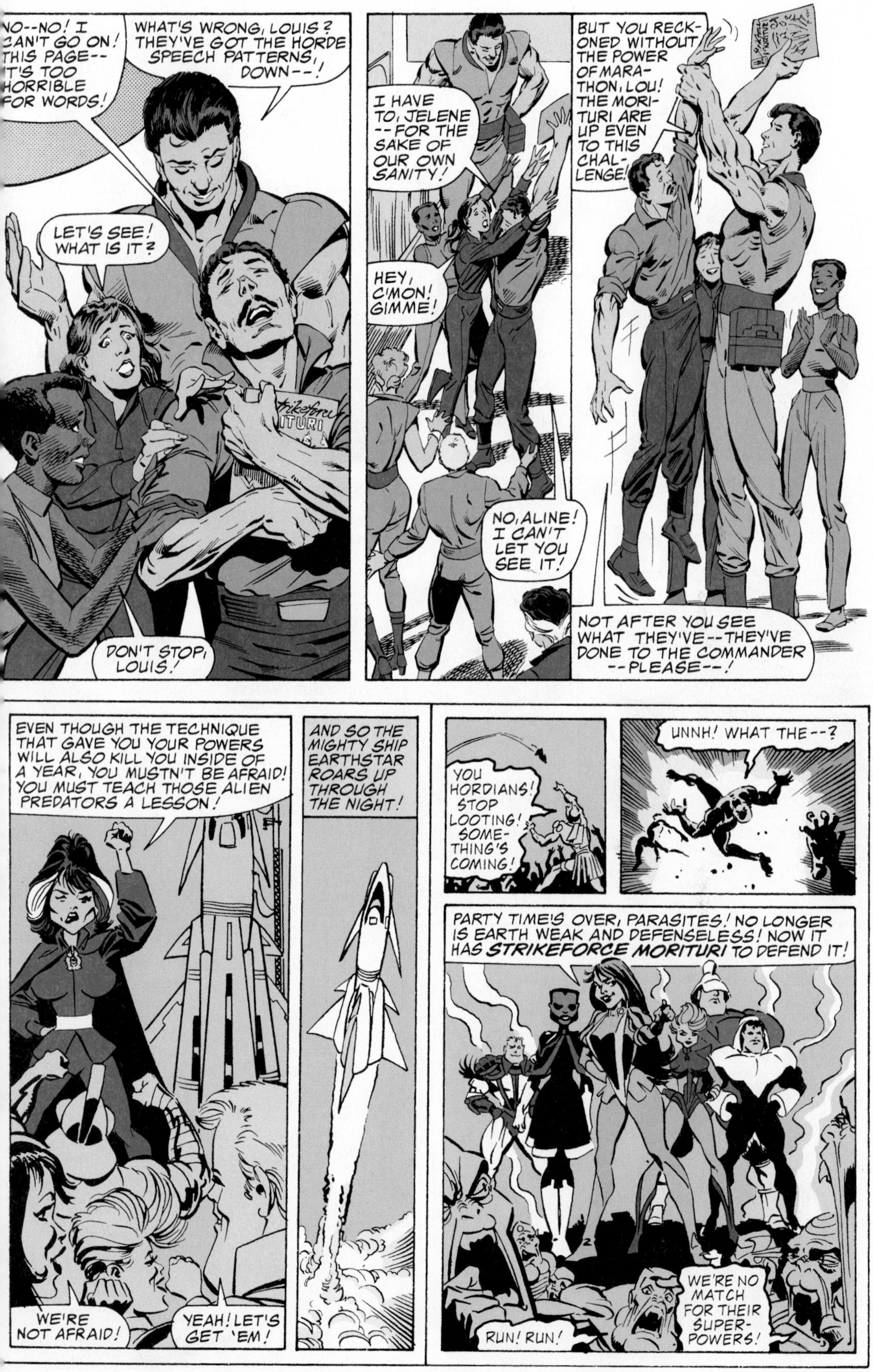
NO--NO! I CAN'T GO ON! THIS PAGE-- IT'S TOO HORRIBLE FOR WORDS!
WHAT'S WRONG, LOUIS? THEY'VE GOT THE HORDE SPEECH PATTERNS, DOWN--!
LET'S SEE! WHAT IS IT?
DON'T STOP, LOUIS!
I HAVE TO, JELENE --FOR THE SAKE OF OUR OWN SANITY!
HEY, C'MON! GIMME!
NO, ALINE! I CAN'T LET YOU SEE IT!
BUT YOU RECKONED WITHOUT THE POWER OF MARATHON, LOU! THE MORITURI ARE UP EVEN TO THIS CHALLENGE!
NOT AFTER YOU SEE WHAT THEY'VE--THEY'VE DONE TO THE COMMANDER --PLEASE--!
EVEN THOUGH THE TECHNIQUE THAT GAVE YOU YOUR POWERS WILL ALSO KILL YOU INSIDE OF A YEAR, YOU MUSTN'T BE AFRAID! YOU MUST TEACH THOSE ALIEN PREDATORS A LESSON!
WE'RE NOT AFRAID!
YEAH! LET'S GET 'EM!
AND SO THE MIGHTY SHIP EARTHSTAR ROARS UP THROUGH THE NIGHT!
YOU HORDIANS! STOP LOOTING! SOMETHING'S COMING!
UNNH! WHAT THE--?
PARTY TIME'S OVER, PARASITES! NO LONGER IS EARTH WEAK AND DEFENSELESS! NOW IT HAS STRIKEFORCE MORITURI TO DEFEND IT!
RUN! RUN!
WE'RE NO MATCH FOR THEIR SUPER-POWERS!

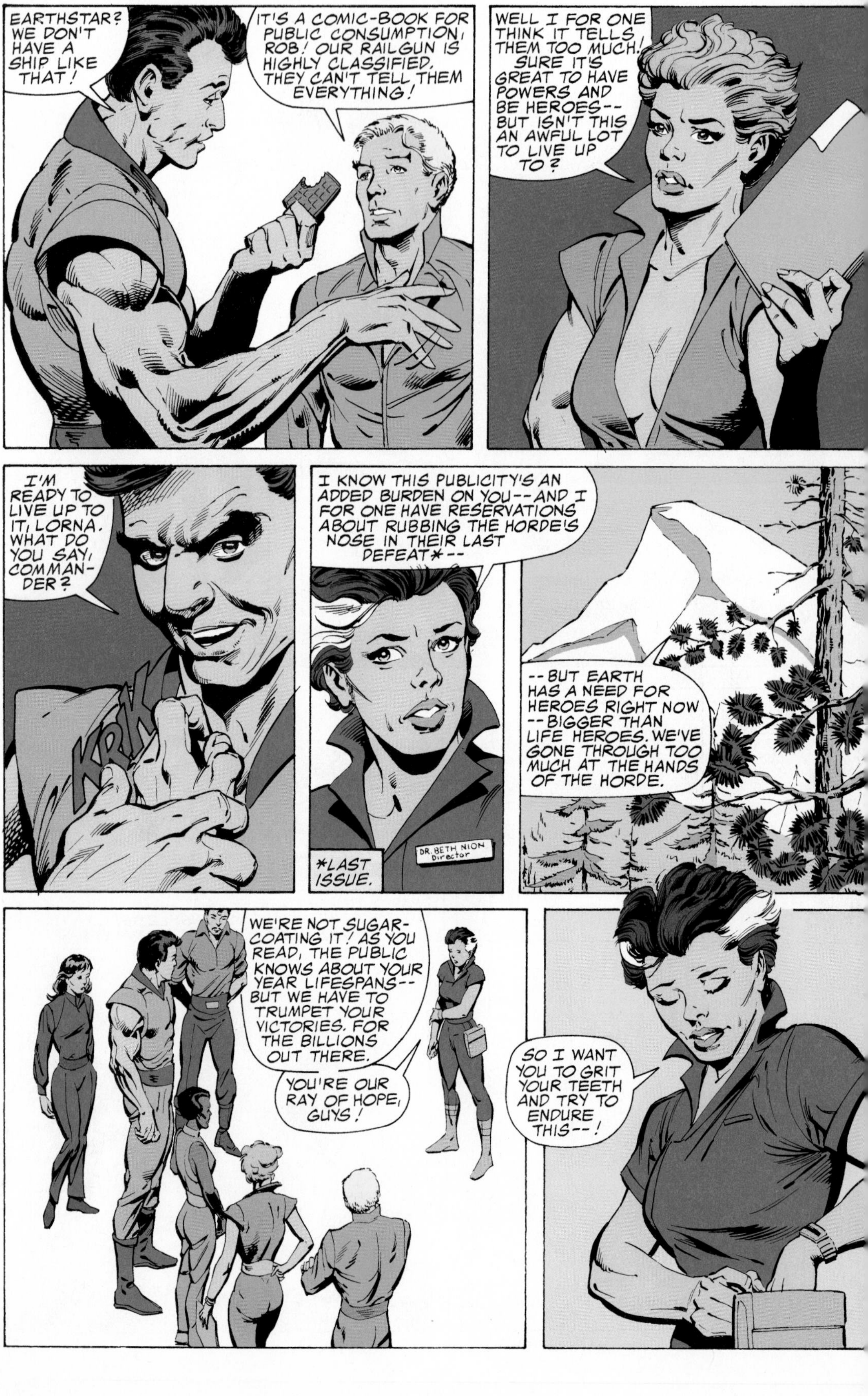
EARTHSTAR? WE DON'T HAVE A SHIP LIKE THAT!
IT'S A COMIC-BOOK FOR PUBLIC CONSUMPTION, ROB! OUR RAILGUN IS HIGHLY CLASSIFIED. THEY CAN'T TELL THEM EVERYTHING!
WELL I FOR ONE THINK IT TELLS THEM TOO MUCH! SURE IT'S GREAT TO HAVE POWERS AND BE HEROES-- BUT ISN'T THIS AN AWFUL LOT TO LIVE UP TO?
I'M READY TO LIVE UP TO IT, LORNA. WHAT DO YOU SAY, COMMANDER?
KRK
I KNOW THIS PUBLICITY'S AN ADDED BURDEN ON YOU--AND I FOR ONE HAVE RESERVATIONS ABOUT RUBBING THE HORDE'S NOSE IN THEIR LAST DEFEAT*--
DR. BETH NION Director
*LAST ISSUE.
--BUT EARTH HAS A NEED FOR HEROES RIGHT NOW --BIGGER THAN LIFE HEROES. WE'VE GONE THROUGH TOO MUCH AT THE HANDS OF THE HORDE.
WE'RE NOT SUGAR-COATING IT! AS YOU READ, THE PUBLIC KNOWS ABOUT YOUR YEAR LIFESPANS-- BUT WE HAVE TO TRUMPET YOUR VICTORIES. FOR THE BILLIONS OUT THERE.
YOU'RE OUR RAY OF HOPE, GUYS!
SO I WANT YOU TO GRIT YOUR TEETH AND TRY TO ENDURE THIS--!

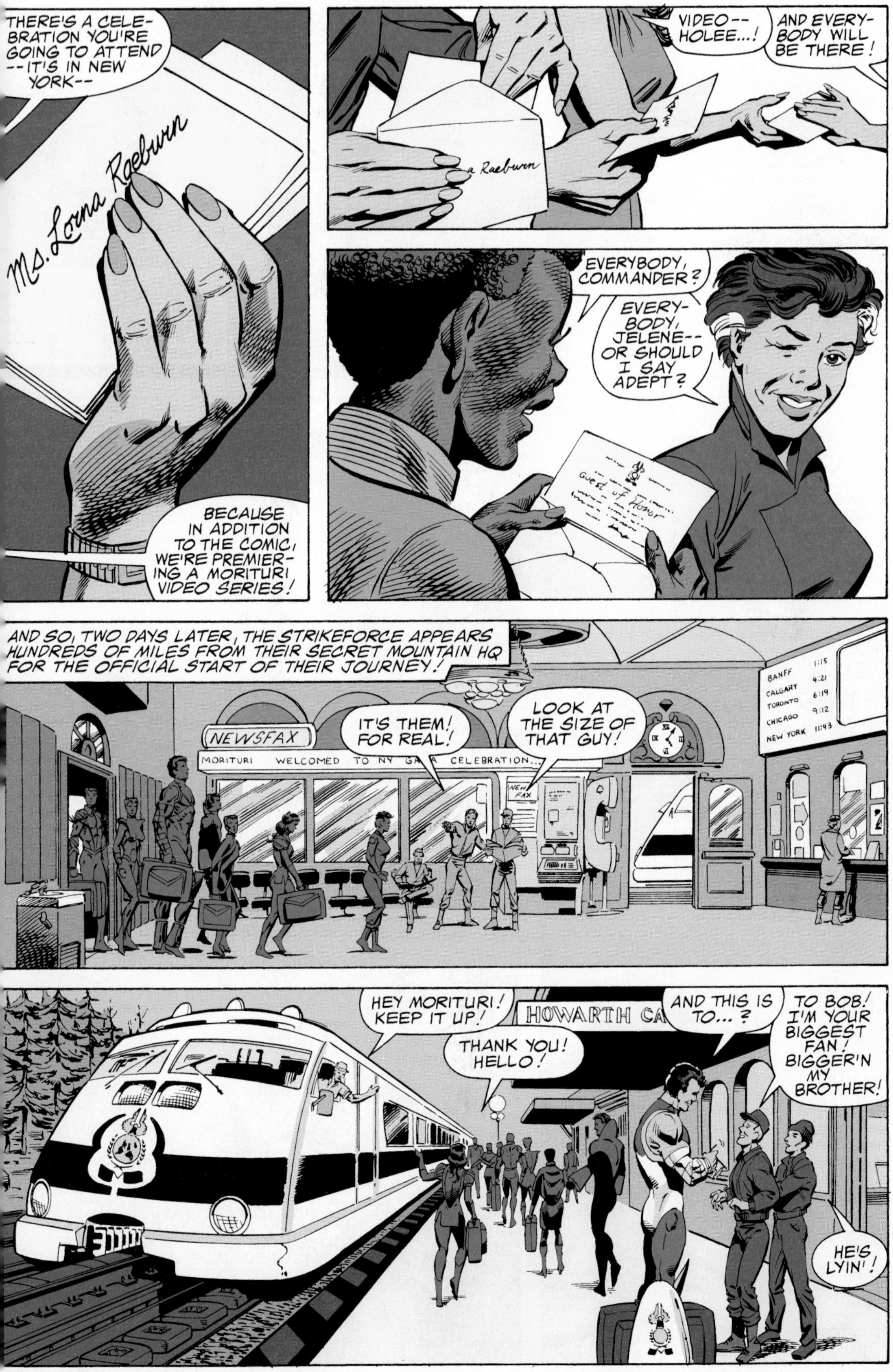
THERE'S A CELEBRATION YOU'RE GOING TO ATTEND --IT'S IN NEW YORK--
Ms. Lorna Raeburn
BECAUSE IN ADDITION TO THE COMIC, WE'RE PREMIERING A MORITURI VIDEO SERIES!
VIDEO-- HOLEE...!
AND EVERYBODY WILL BE THERE!
a Raeburn
EVERYBODY, COMMANDER?
EVERYBODY, JELENE-- OR SHOULD I SAY ADEPT?
Guest of Honor
AND SO, TWO DAYS LATER, THE STRIKEFORCE APPEARS HUNDREDS OF MILES FROM THEIR SECRET MOUNTAIN HQ FOR THE OFFICIAL START OF THEIR JOURNEY!
NEWSFAX
MORITURI WELCOMED TO NY GA A CELEBRATION...
IT'S THEM! FOR REAL!
LOOK AT THE SIZE OF THAT GUY!
BANFF 1:15
CALGARY 4:21
TORONTO 6:19
CHICAGO 9:12
NEW YORK 11:43
HEY MORITURI! KEEP IT UP!
THANK YOU! HELLO!
HOWARTH CA
AND THIS IS TO...?
TO BOB! I'M YOUR BIGGEST FAN! BIGGER'N MY BROTHER!
HE'S LYIN'!

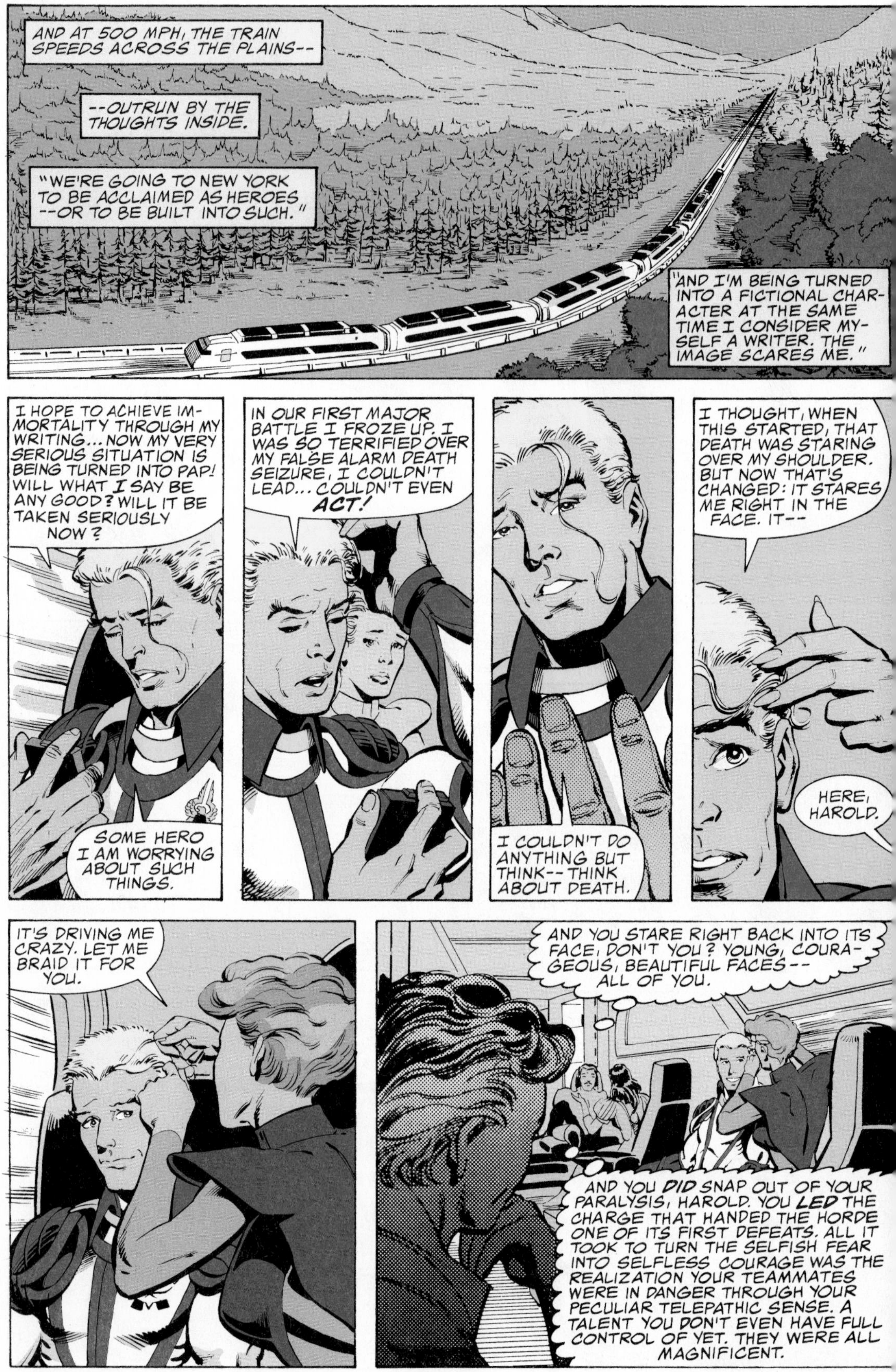
AND AT 500 MPH, THE TRAIN SPEEDS ACROSS THE PLAINS--
--OUTRUN BY THE THOUGHTS INSIDE.
"WE'RE GOING TO NEW YORK TO BE ACCLAIMED AS HEROES --OR TO BE BUILT INTO SUCH."
"AND I'M BEING TURNED INTO A FICTIONAL CHARACTER AT THE SAME TIME I CONSIDER MYSELF A WRITER. THE IMAGE SCARES ME."
I HOPE TO ACHIEVE IMMORTALITY THROUGH MY WRITING... NOW MY VERY SERIOUS SITUATION IS BEING TURNED INTO PAP! WILL WHAT I SAY BE ANY GOOD? WILL IT BE TAKEN SERIOUSLY NOW?
SOME HERO I AM WORRYING ABOUT SUCH THINGS.
IN OUR FIRST MAJOR BATTLE I FROZE UP. I WAS SO TERRIFIED OVER MY FALSE ALARM DEATH SEIZURE, I COULDN'T LEAD... COULDN'T EVEN ACT!
I COULDN'T DO ANYTHING BUT THINK-- THINK ABOUT DEATH.
I THOUGHT, WHEN THIS STARTED, THAT DEATH WAS STARING OVER MY SHOULDER. BUT NOW THAT'S CHANGED: IT STARES ME RIGHT IN THE FACE. IT--
HERE, HAROLD.
IT'S DRIVING ME CRAZY. LET ME BRAID IT FOR YOU.
AND YOU STARE RIGHT BACK INTO ITS FACE, DON'T YOU? YOUNG, COURAGEOUS, BEAUTIFUL FACES-- ALL OF YOU.
AND YOU DID SNAP OUT OF YOUR PARALYSIS, HAROLD. YOU LED THE CHARGE THAT HANDED THE HORDE ONE OF ITS FIRST DEFEATS. ALL IT TOOK TO TURN THE SELFISH FEAR INTO SELFLESS COURAGE WAS THE REALIZATION YOUR TEAMMATES WERE IN DANGER THROUGH YOUR PECULIAR TELEPATHIC SENSE. A TALENT YOU DON'T EVEN HAVE FULL CONTROL OF YET. THEY WERE ALL MAGNIFICENT.

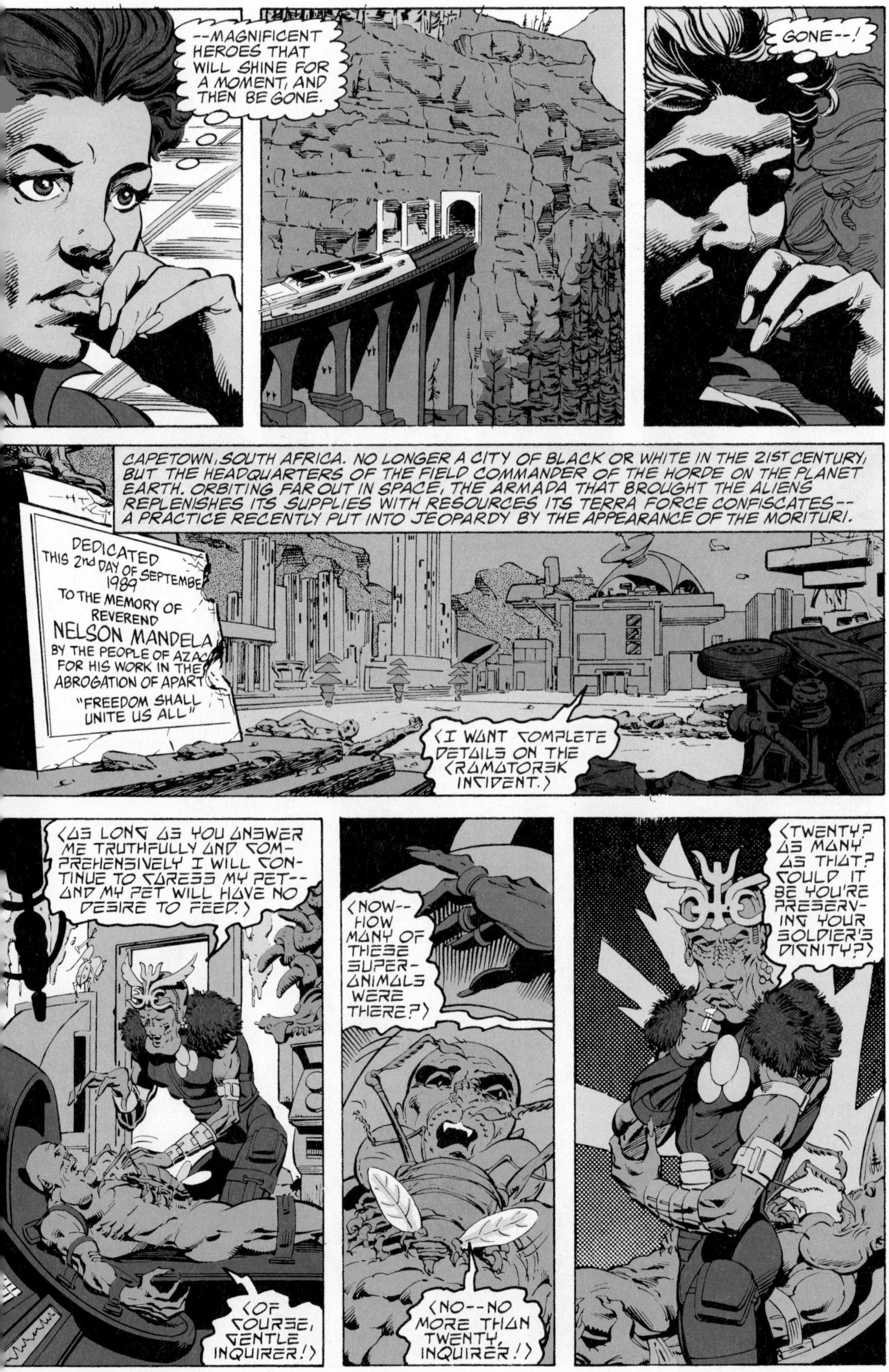
--MAGNIFICENT HEROES THAT WILL SHINE FOR A MOMENT, AND THEN BE GONE.
GONE--!
CAPETOWN, SOUTH AFRICA. NO LONGER A CITY OF BLACK OR WHITE IN THE 21ST CENTURY, BUT THE HEADQUARTERS OF THE FIELD COMMANDER OF THE HORDE ON THE PLANET EARTH. ORBITING FAR OUT IN SPACE, THE ARMADA THAT BROUGHT THE ALIENS REPLENISHES ITS SUPPLIES WITH RESOURCES ITS TERRA FORCE CONFISCATES-- A PRACTICE RECENTLY PUT INTO JEOPARDY BY THE APPEARANCE OF THE MORITURI.
DEDICATED THIS 2nd DAY OF SEPTEMBE 1989 TO THE MEMORY OF REVEREND NELSON MANDELA BY THE PEOPLE OF AZAC FOR HIS WORK IN THE ABROGATION OF APART "FREEDOM SHALL UNITE US ALL"
<I WANT COMPLETE DETAILS ON THE <RAMATOREK INCIDENT.>
<AS LONG AS YOU ANSWER ME TRUTHFULLY AND COMPREHENSIVELY I WILL CONTINUE TO CARESS MY PET--AND MY PET WILL HAVE NO DESIRE TO FEED.>
<OF COURSE, GENTLE INQUIRER!>
<NOW--HOW MANY OF THESE SUPER-ANIMALS WERE THERE?>
<NO--NO MORE THAN TWENTY, INQUIRER!>
<TWENTY? AS MANY AS THAT? COULD IT BE YOU'RE PRESERVING YOUR SOLDIER'S DIGNITY?>

⟨YOUR COMMANDER SAID HUNDREDS--ALAS WITH SUCH INCONSISTENCIES THE TRUTH MAY NEVER BE ⟨NOWN--!⟩

⟨ALL RIGHT! ALL RIGHT! ,THERE WERE ONLY SIX! SIX!⟩

⟨SIX-- MOST INTER- ESTING!⟩

⟨IF ONLY SIX ATTACKED A WHOLE HORDE PUNITIVE RAID-- THEN SIX MIGHT BE ALL THE MORITURI THERE ARE!⟩

⟨INQUIRER! A DATA INTERCEP- TION! WE HAD ONLY JUST BROKEN THEIR LATEST COMMUNICATIONS SCRAMBLER CODE AND PULLED IN THIS BIT OF INFORMATION WHEN A NEW CODE BEGAN. THIS IS ALL WE GOT.⟩

⟨A BIT OF BRAVADO ON THE ANIMALS' PART -- OR PERHAPS THEY DO NOT BELIEVE WE MONITOR THEIR COMMUNICATIONS SO CLOSELY!⟩

⟨THEY MIGHT EVEN BE CON- TEMPLATING A TRAP! ODD HOW A NEW SCRAMBLER CUT IN IMMEDIATELY AFTER YOU RECEIVED THIS! THEY ARE CUNNING LITTLE APES, WHATEVER THEIR MOTIVES!⟩

ASFAX MORITURI IN NEW YORK

RTH'S SAVIORS?

⟨--WE SHALL CHANCE IT AND ATTEND!⟩

84

NEW YORK CITY: WITH THE LOSS OF THE SKIES OF EARTH TO THE INVADERS FROM SPACE, IT HAS BECOME IN THE 21ST CENTURY WHAT IT WAS IN THE 19TH: ONE OF THE BUSIEST PORTS IN THE WORLD.

IT ALSO STILL NEVER SLEEPS.

"Media Bash"

| peter b. **GILLIS** WRITER | brent **ANDERSON** PENCILER | scott **WILLIAMS** INKER | jim **NOVAK** LETTERER | max **SCHEELE** COLORER | carl **POTTS** EDITOR | jim **SHOOTER** EDITOR IN CHIEF |

*SPECIAL THANKS TO WHILCE PORTACIO

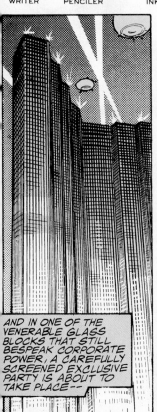

--FOR SOME QUITE EXCEPTIONAL PEOPLE.

HELLO, BETH-- OR SHOULD I SAY COMMANDER NION?

AND IN ONE OF THE VENERABLE GLASS BLOCKS THAT STILL BESPEAK CORPORATE POWER, A CAREFULLY SCREENED EXCLUSIVE PARTY IS ABOUT TO TAKE PLACE--

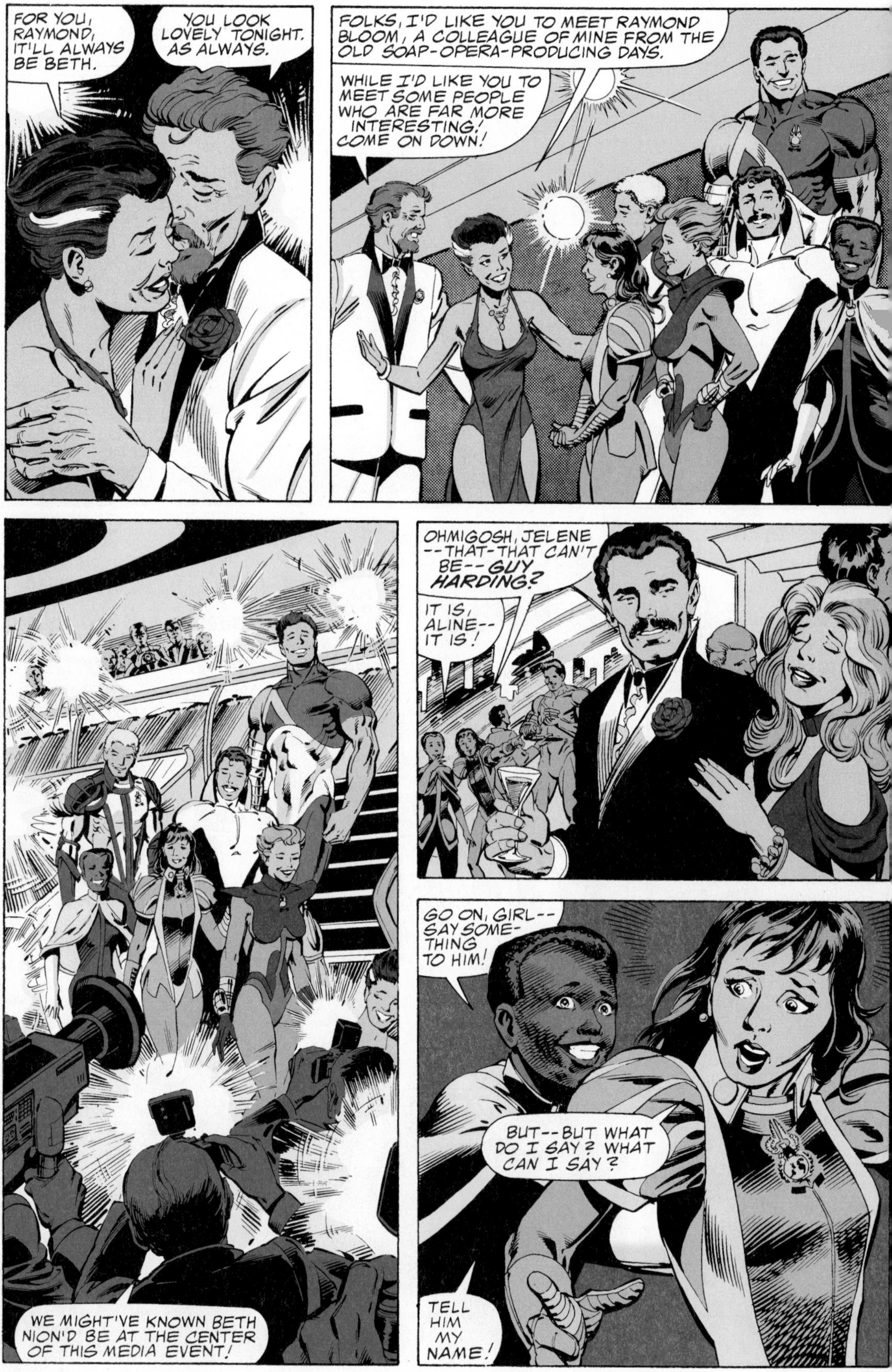
FOR YOU, RAYMOND, IT'LL ALWAYS BE BETH.
YOU LOOK LOVELY TONIGHT. AS ALWAYS.
FOLKS, I'D LIKE YOU TO MEET RAYMOND BLOOM, A COLLEAGUE OF MINE FROM THE OLD SOAP-OPERA-PRODUCING DAYS.
WHILE I'D LIKE YOU TO MEET SOME PEOPLE WHO ARE FAR MORE INTERESTING! COME ON DOWN!
WE MIGHT'VE KNOWN BETH NION'D BE AT THE CENTER OF THIS MEDIA EVENT!
OHMIGOSH, JELENE --THAT-THAT CAN'T BE--GUY HARDING?
IT IS, ALINE-- IT IS!
GO ON, GIRL-- SAY SOME-THING TO HIM!
BUT--BUT WHAT DO I SAY? WHAT CAN I SAY?
TELL HIM MY NAME!

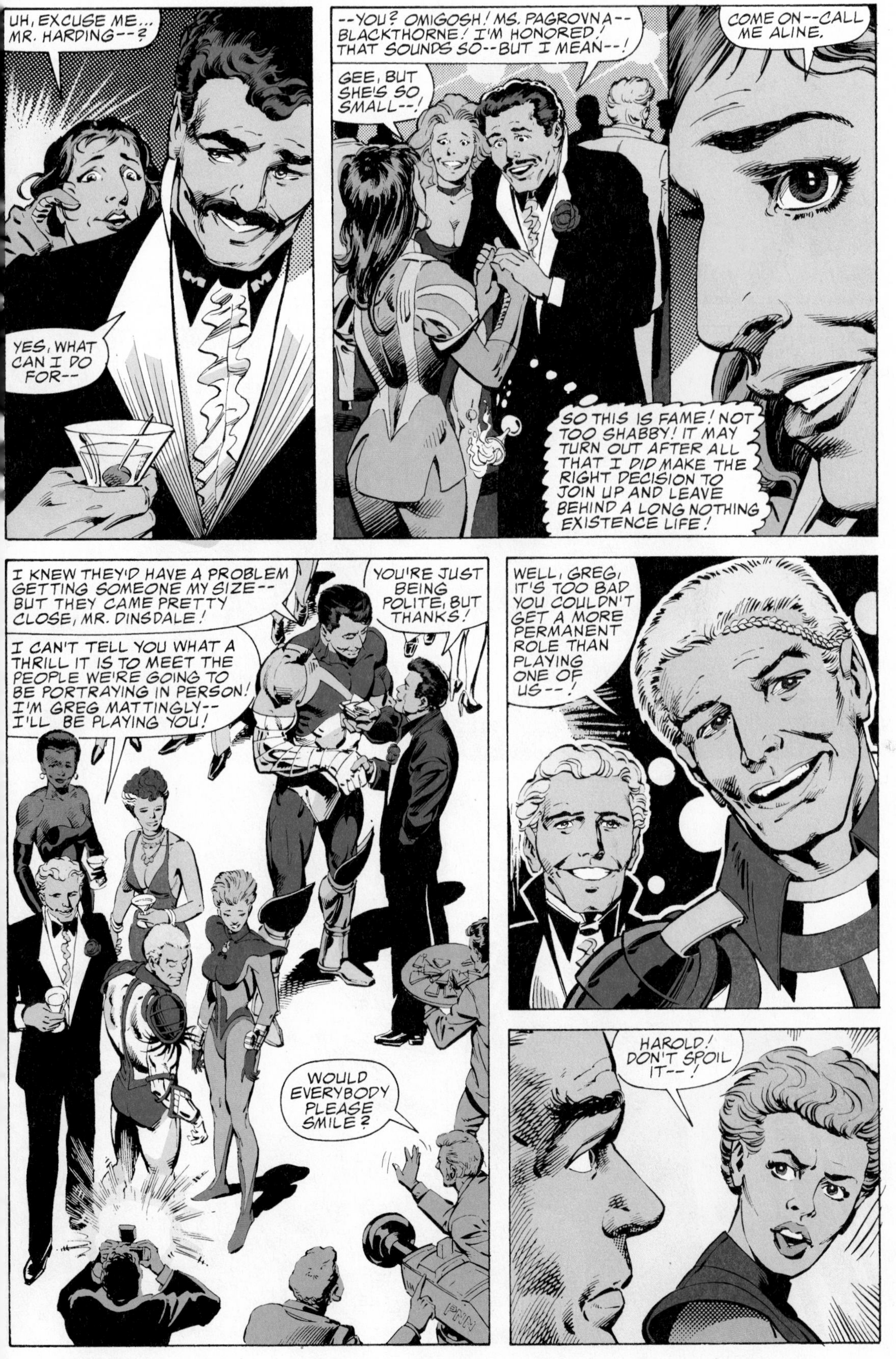
UH, EXCUSE ME... MR. HARDING--?
YES, WHAT CAN I DO FOR--
--YOU? OMIGOSH! MS. PAGROVNA-- BLACKTHORNE! I'M HONORED! THAT SOUNDS SO--BUT I MEAN--!
GEE, BUT SHE'S SO SMALL--!
COME ON--CALL ME ALINE.
SO THIS IS FAME! NOT TOO SHABBY! IT MAY TURN OUT AFTER ALL THAT I DID MAKE THE RIGHT DECISION TO JOIN UP AND LEAVE BEHIND A LONG NOTHING EXISTENCE LIFE!
I KNEW THEY'D HAVE A PROBLEM GETTING SOMEONE MY SIZE-- BUT THEY CAME PRETTY CLOSE, MR. DINSDALE!
I CAN'T TELL YOU WHAT A THRILL IT IS TO MEET THE PEOPLE WE'RE GOING TO BE PORTRAYING IN PERSON! I'M GREG MATTINGLY-- I'LL BE PLAYING YOU!
YOU'RE JUST BEING POLITE, BUT THANKS!
WOULD EVERYBODY PLEASE SMILE?
PNN
WELL, GREG, IT'S TOO BAD YOU COULDN'T GET A MORE PERMANENT ROLE THAN PLAYING ONE OF US--!
HAROLD! DON'T SPOIL IT--!

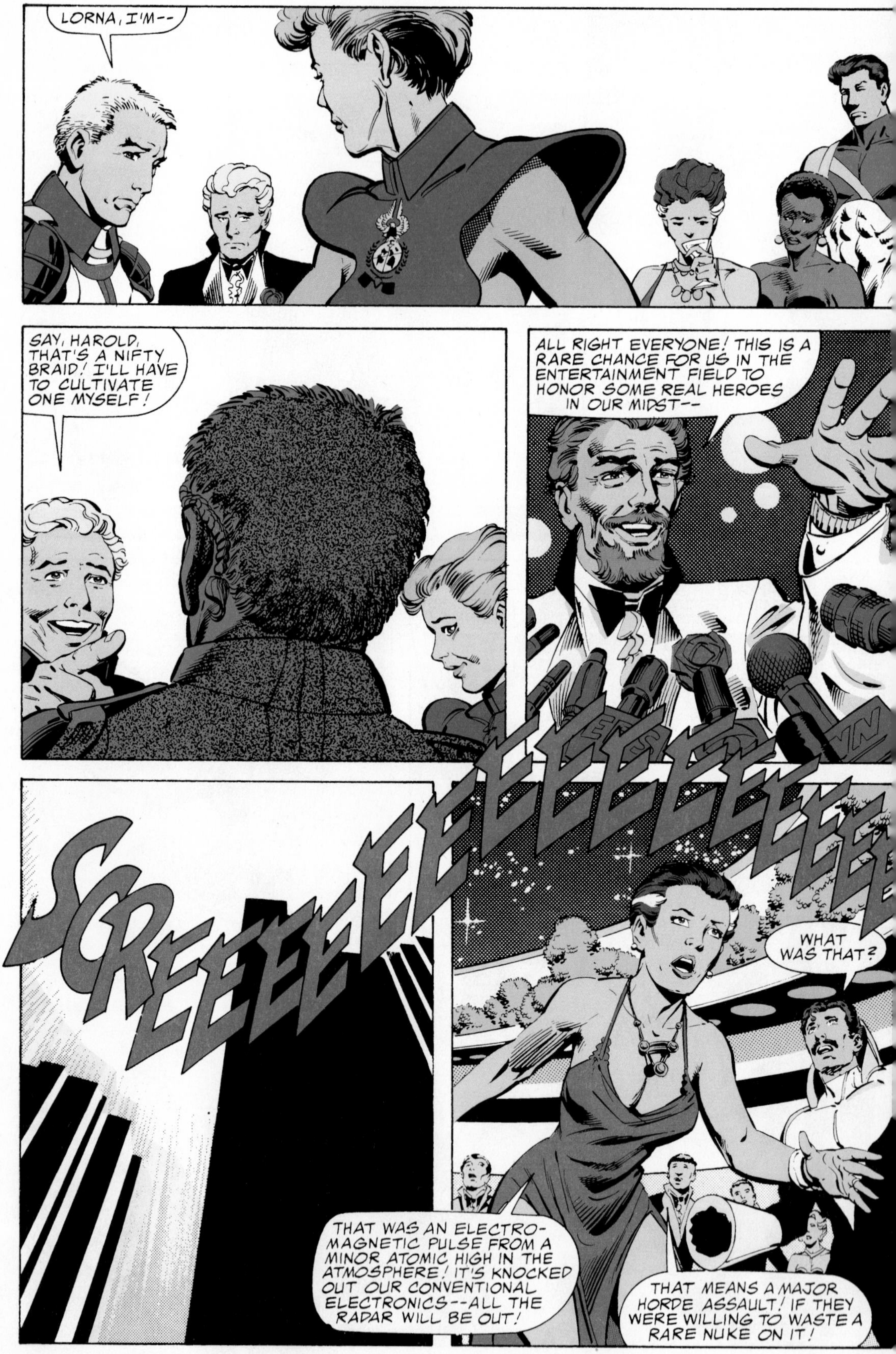

LORNA, I'M--
SAY, HAROLD, THAT'S A NIFTY BRAID! I'LL HAVE TO CULTIVATE ONE MYSELF!
ALL RIGHT EVERYONE! THIS IS A RARE CHANCE FOR US IN THE ENTERTAINMENT FIELD TO HONOR SOME REAL HEROES IN OUR MIDST--
SCREEEEEEEEEEEEEEEEEEEEEEE
WHAT WAS THAT?
THAT WAS AN ELECTRO-MAGNETIC PULSE FROM A MINOR ATOMIC HIGH IN THE ATMOSPHERE! IT'S KNOCKED OUT OUR CONVENTIONAL ELECTRONICS--ALL THE RADAR WILL BE OUT!
THAT MEANS A MAJOR HORDE ASSAULT! IF THEY WERE WILLING TO WASTE A RARE NUKE ON IT!

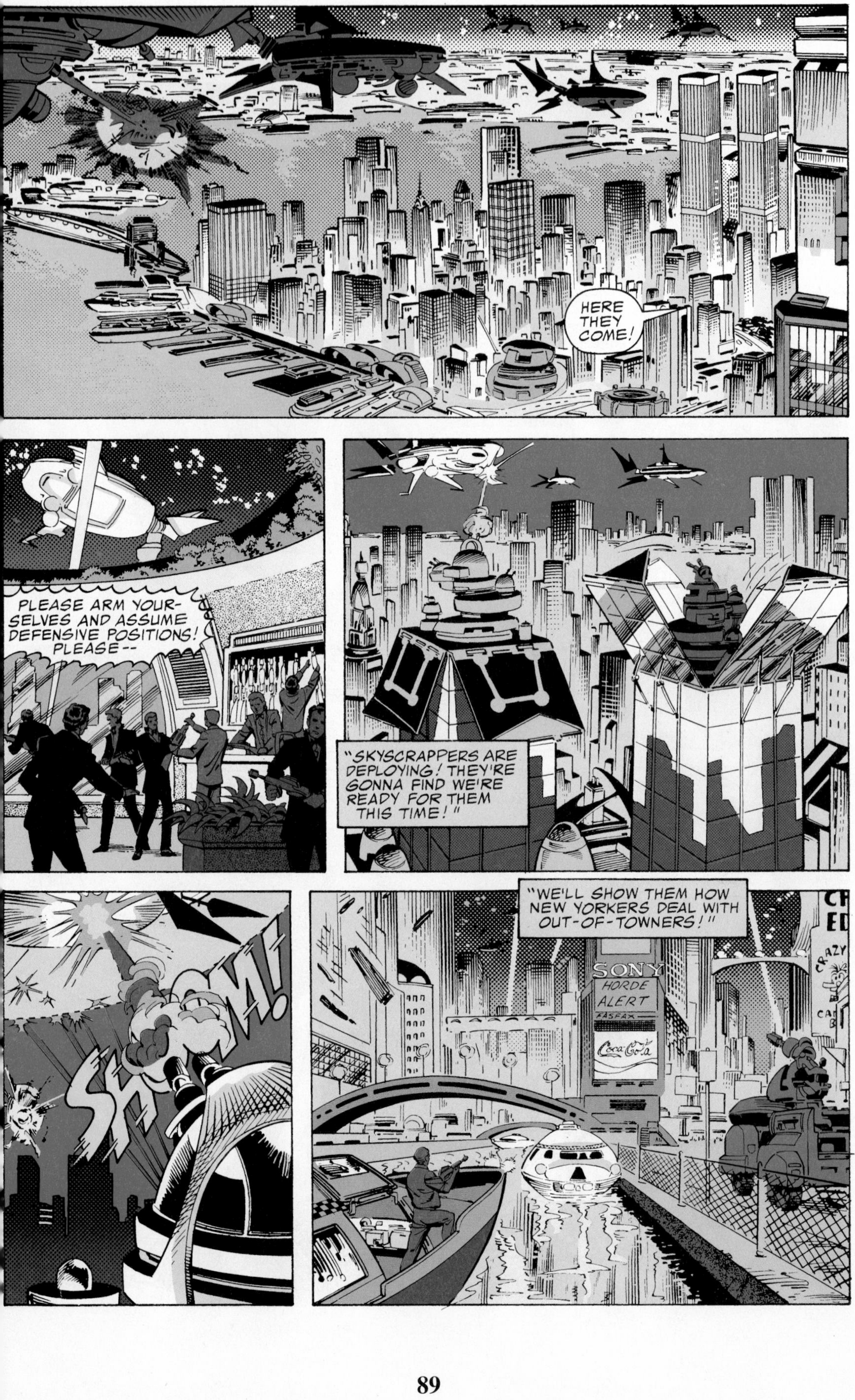
HERE THEY COME!
PLEASE ARM YOURSELVES AND ASSUME DEFENSIVE POSITIONS! PLEASE --
"SKYSCRAPPERS ARE DEPLOYING! THEY'RE GONNA FIND WE'RE READY FOR THEM THIS TIME!"
"WE'LL SHOW THEM HOW NEW YORKERS DEAL WITH OUT-OF-TOWNERS!"
SONY
HORDE ALERT
FASFAX
Coca-Cola

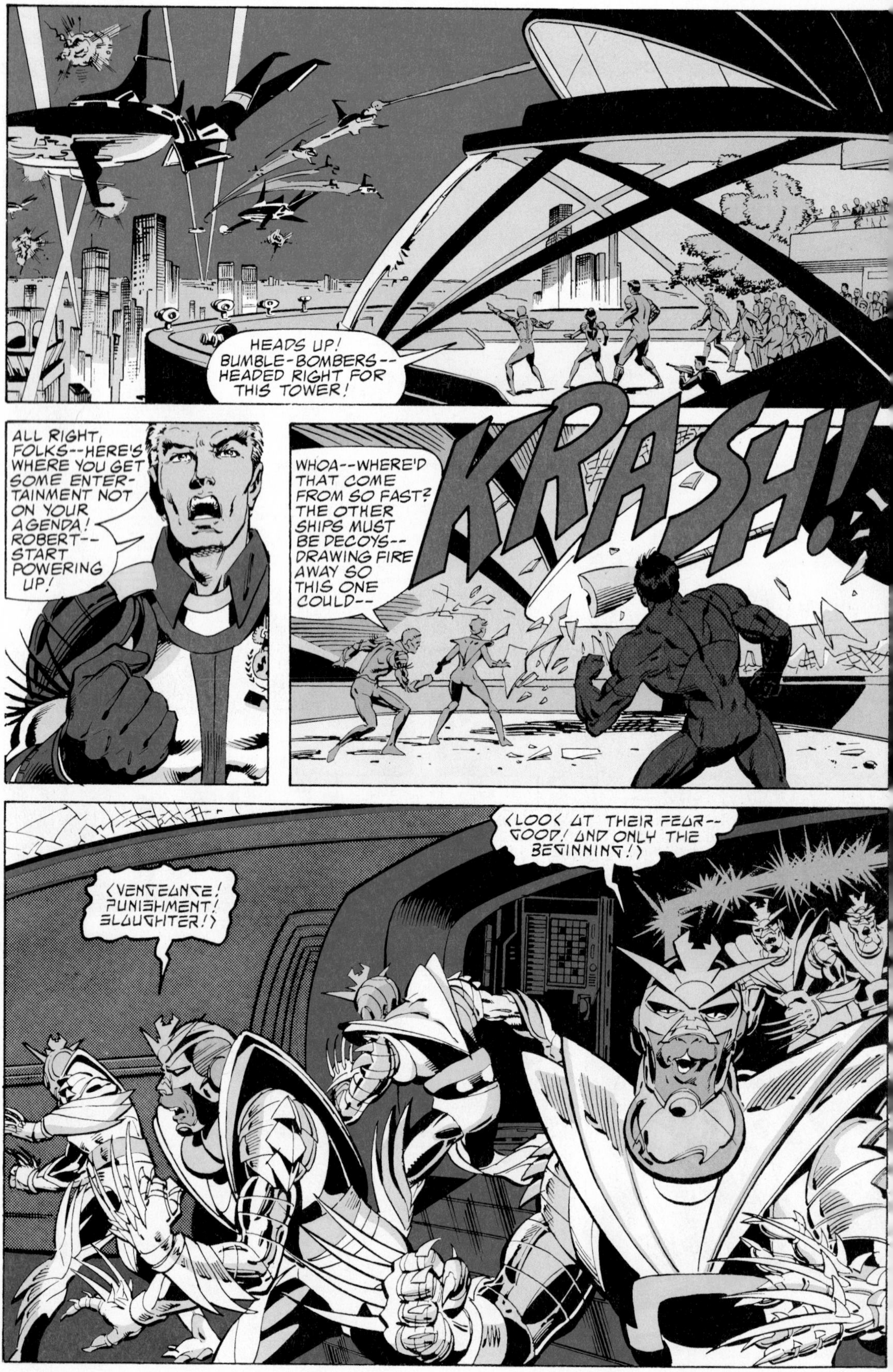
HEADS UP! BUMBLE-BOMBERS--HEADED RIGHT FOR THIS TOWER!
ALL RIGHT, FOLKS--HERE'S WHERE YOU GET SOME ENTER-TAINMENT NOT ON YOUR AGENDA! ROBERT--START POWERING UP!
WHOA--WHERE'D THAT COME FROM SO FAST? THE OTHER SHIPS MUST BE DECOYS--DRAWING FIRE AWAY SO THIS ONE COULD--
KRASH!
<VENGEANCE! PUNISHMENT! SLAUGHTER!>
<LOOK AT THEIR FEAR--GOOD! AND ONLY THE BEGINNING!>

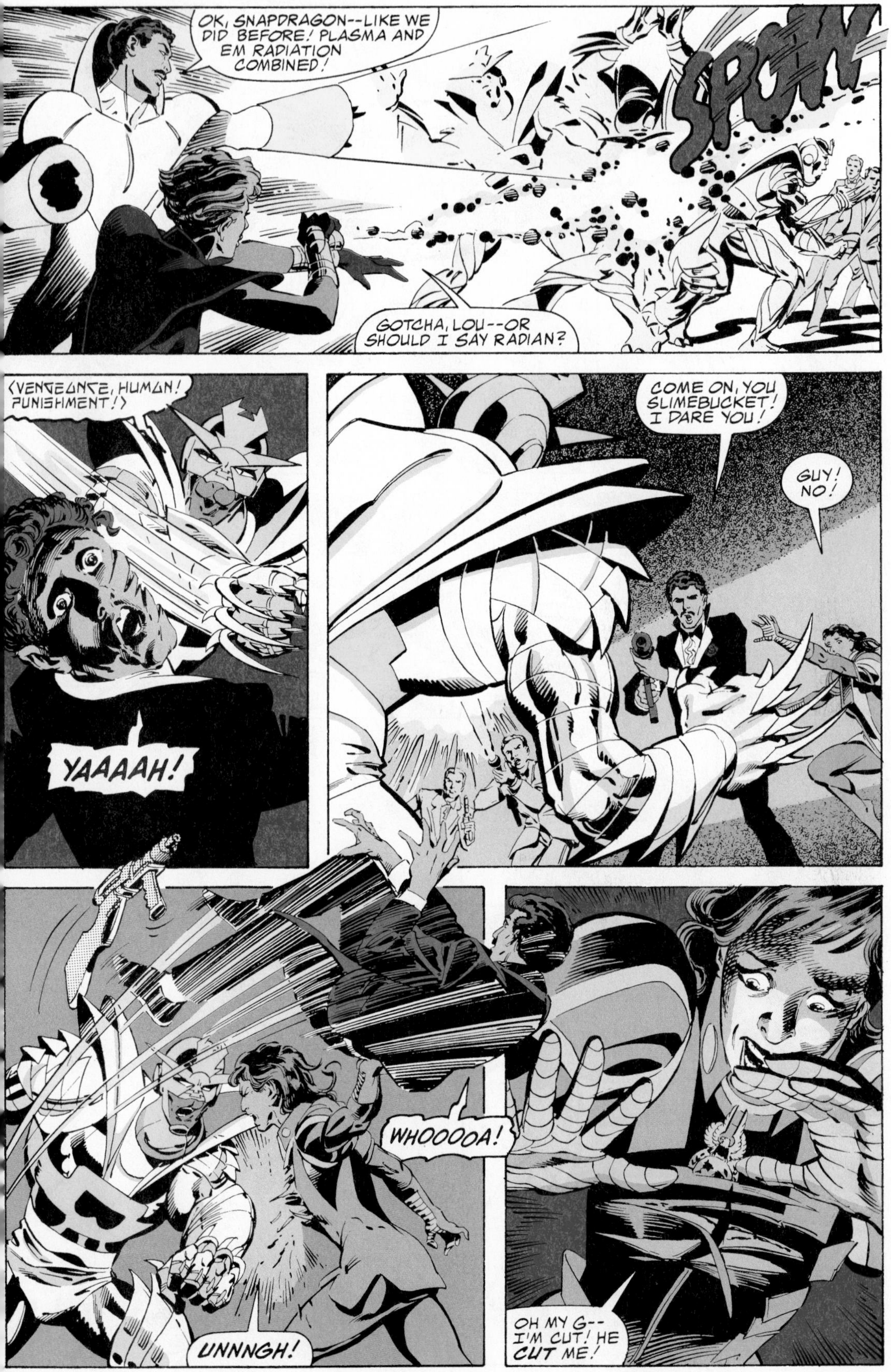
OK, SNAPDRAGON--LIKE WE DID BEFORE! PLASMA AND EM RADIATION COMBINED!
SPOW
GOTCHA, LOU--OR SHOULD I SAY RADIAN?
<VENGEANCE, HUMAN! PUNISHMENT!>
YAAAAH!
COME ON, YOU SLIMEBUCKET! I DARE YOU!
GUY! NO!
WHOOOOA!
UNNNGH!
OH MY G-- I'M CUT! HE CUT ME!

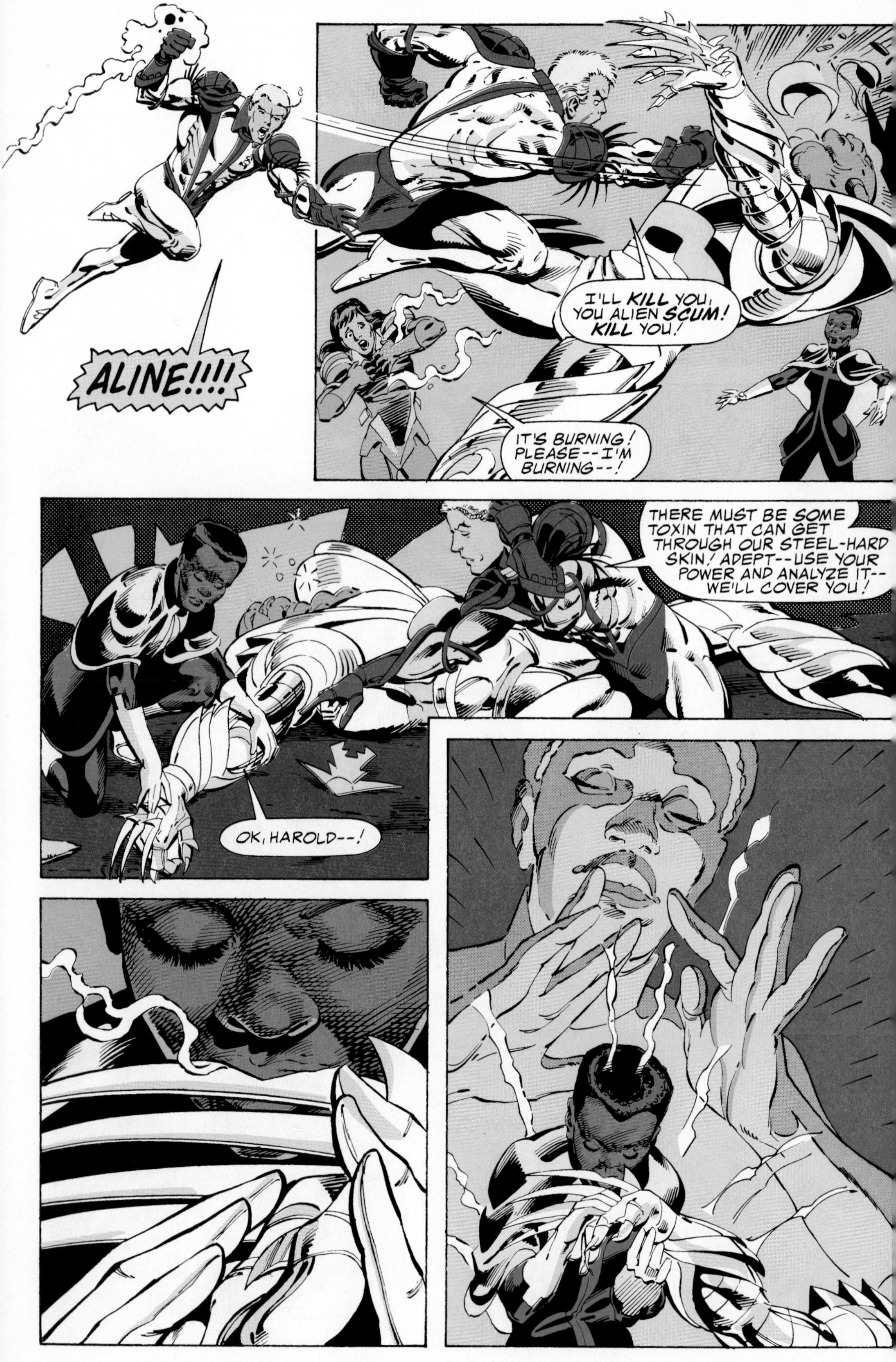
ALINE!!!!
I'LL KILL YOU, YOU ALIEN SCUM! KILL YOU!
IT'S BURNING! PLEASE--I'M BURNING--!
THERE MUST BE SOME TOXIN THAT CAN GET THROUGH OUR STEEL-HARD SKIN! ADEPT--USE YOUR POWER AND ANALYZE IT--WE'LL COVER YOU!
OK, HAROLD--!

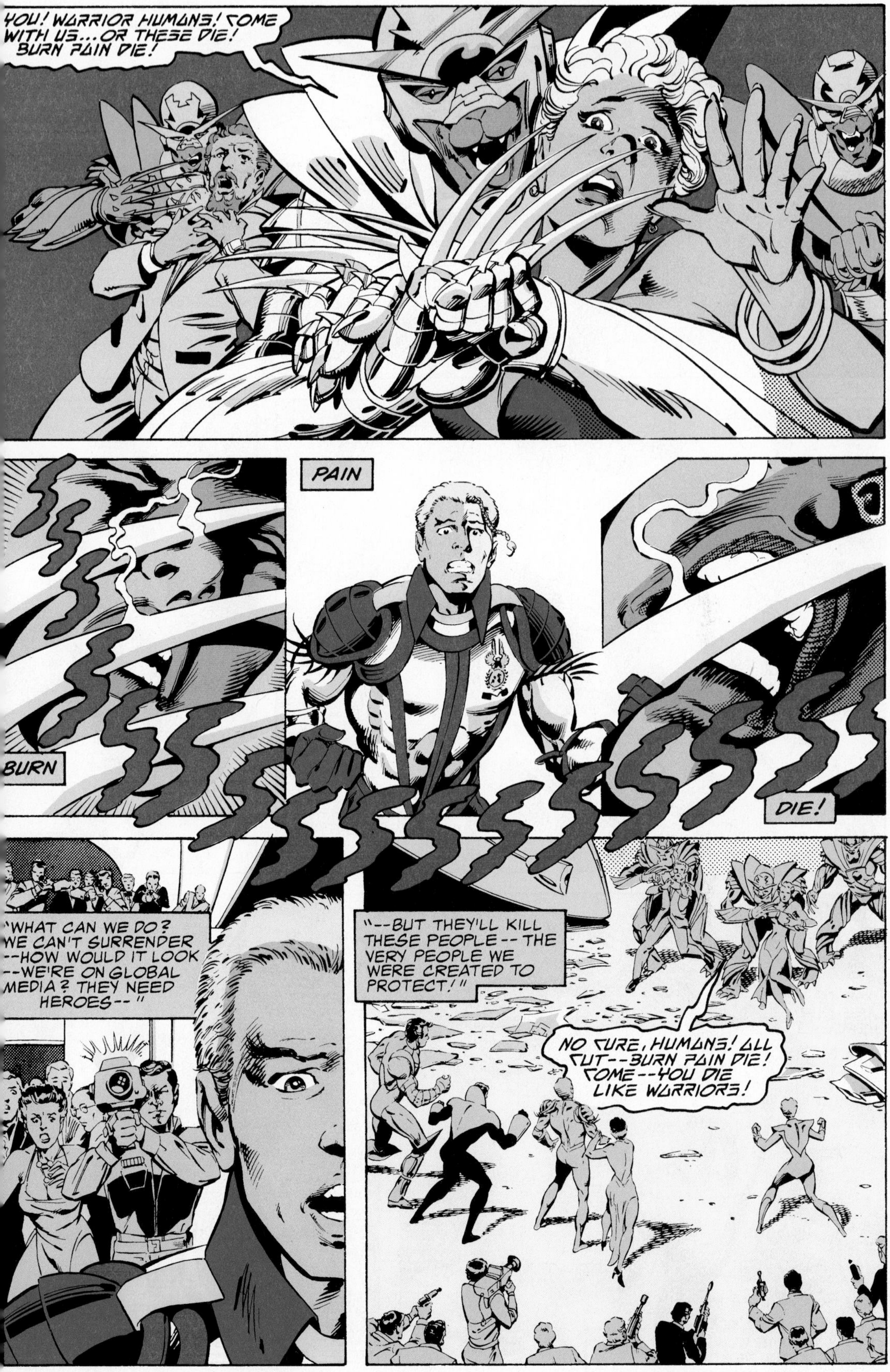

YOU! WARRIOR HUMANS! COME WITH US...OR THESE DIE! BURN PAIN DIE!
BURN
PAIN
DIE!
"WHAT CAN WE DO? WE CAN'T SURRENDER --HOW WOULD IT LOOK --WE'RE ON GLOBAL MEDIA? THEY NEED HEROES--"
"--BUT THEY'LL KILL THESE PEOPLE-- THE VERY PEOPLE WE WERE CREATED TO PROTECT!"
NO CURE, HUMANS! ALL CUT--BURN PAIN DIE! COME--YOU DIE LIKE WARRIORS!

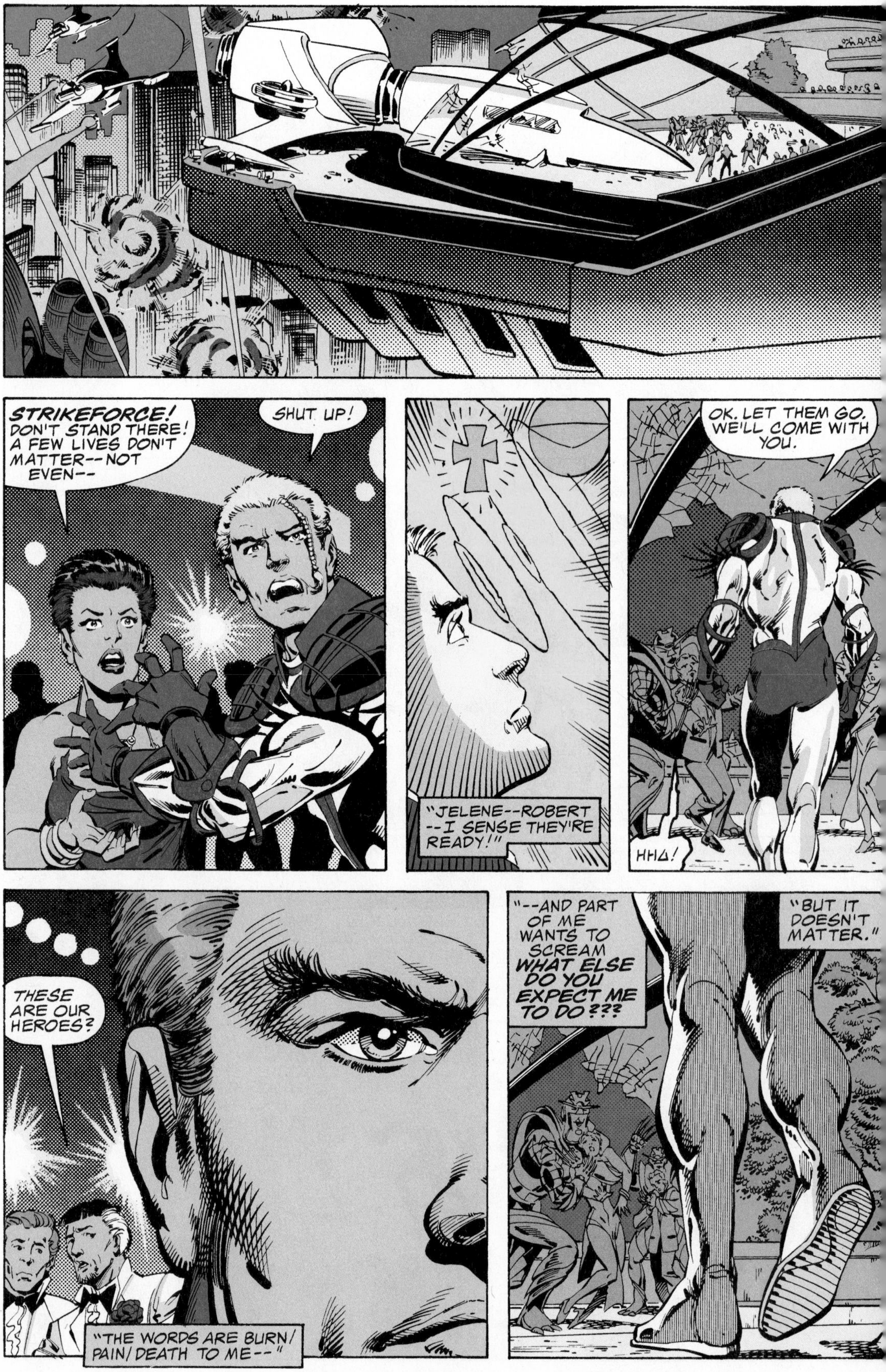
STRIKEFORCE! DON'T STAND THERE! A FEW LIVES DON'T MATTER--NOT EVEN--
SHUT UP!
"JELENE--ROBERT --I SENSE THEY'RE READY!"
OK. LET THEM GO. WE'LL COME WITH YOU.
HHΔ!
THESE ARE OUR HEROES?
"THE WORDS ARE BURN/ PAIN/ DEATH TO ME--"
"--AND PART OF ME WANTS TO SCREAM WHAT ELSE DO YOU EXPECT ME TO DO???
"BUT IT DOESN'T MATTER."

ROBERT! PULL THE RUG OUT FROM UNDER THEM!

?

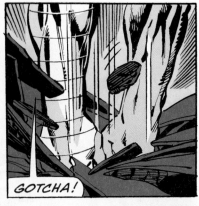

GOTCHA!

THE HOSTAGES ARE FREE! BURN 'EM, LORNA!

SHRENKKK!

BASHOOOOM!!

MY PLEASURE, HAROLD--OR SHOULD I SAY VYKING?

HEY! I'M GETTING BETTER--MORE POWERFUL--WHAT A SURGE!

IT HURTS--LORD, IT HURTS--!

EASY, ALINE. I'VE ANALYZED THE POISON--

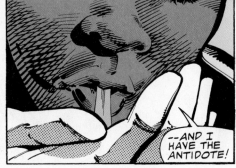

--AND I HAVE THE ANTIDOTE!

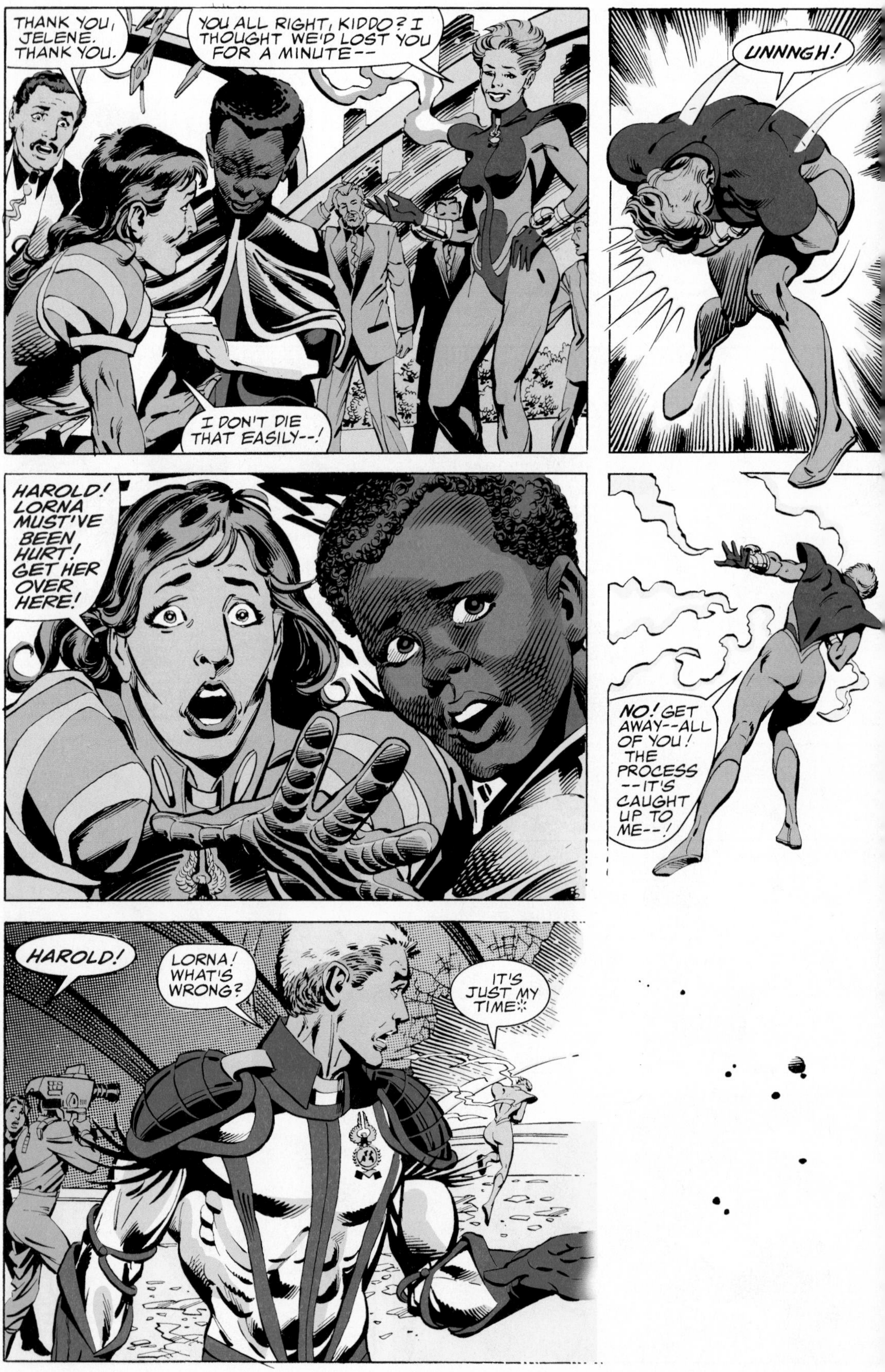
THANK YOU, JELENE. THANK YOU.
YOU ALL RIGHT, KIDDO? I THOUGHT WE'D LOST YOU FOR A MINUTE--
I DON'T DIE THAT EASILY--!
UNNNGH!
HAROLD! LORNA MUST'VE BEEN HURT! GET HER OVER HERE!
NO! GET AWAY--ALL OF YOU! THE PROCESS --IT'S CAUGHT UP TO ME--!
HAROLD!
LORNA! WHAT'S WRONG?
IT'S JUST MY TIME

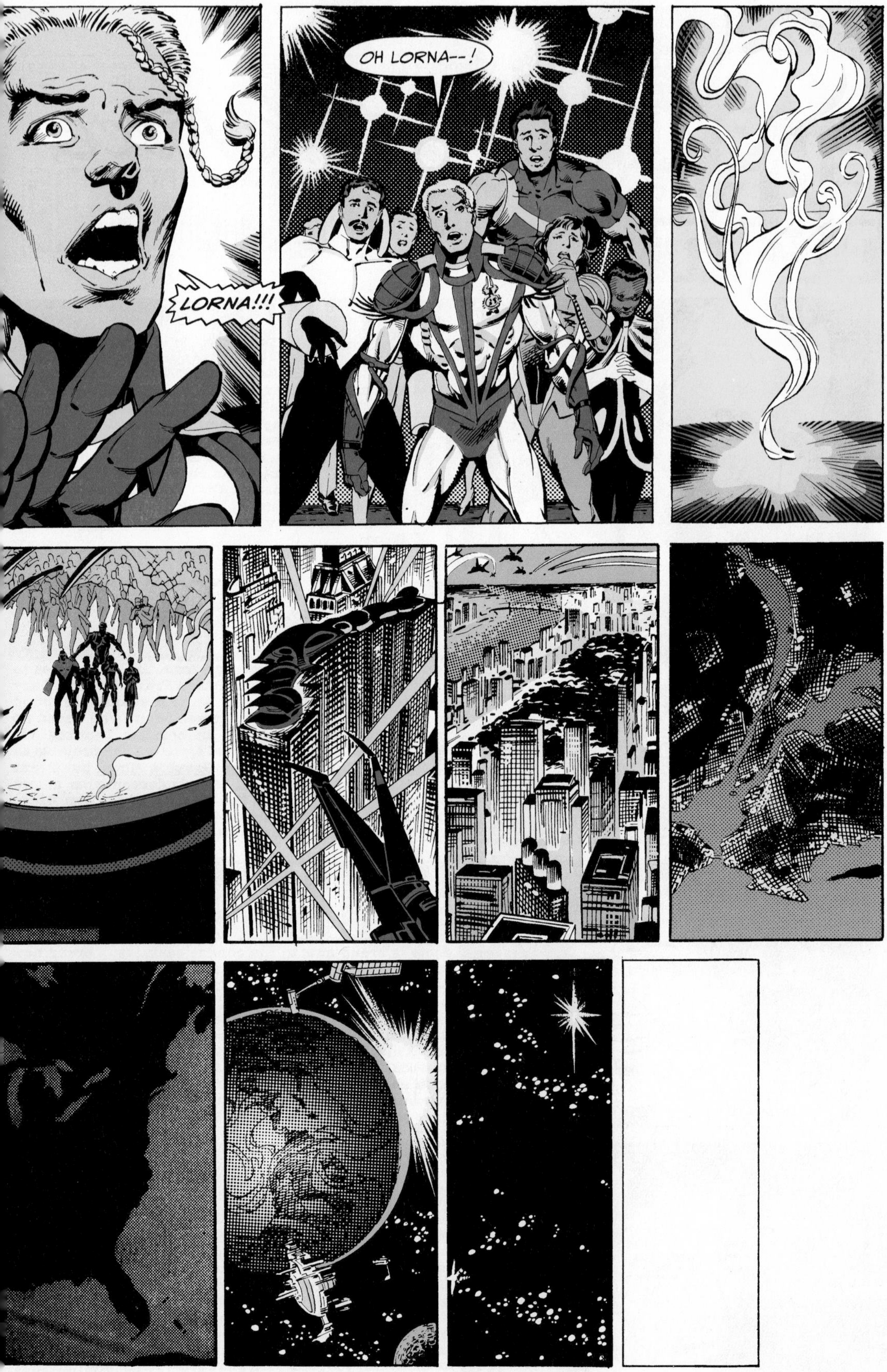
LORNA!!!
OH LORNA--!

MEET THE CREW THAT BRINGS YOU:

"WE WHO ARE ABOUT TO DIE"
Strikeforce, MORITURI

peter b. GILLIS

You can usually find Chicago based Peter slaving away behind his MacIntosh, writing stories and devising new ways to employ computer graphics. On the rare occasion Peter's eyes are not focused on a CRT screen, they're often reading old tomes of archaic languages on such subjects as gnostic beliefs in Afganistan. Just your all American boy next door. Currently, Mr. Gillis is the scribe for the mystical adventures of <u>Dr. Strange</u>—check it out!

brent ANDERSON

Ten years ago Brent <u>ventured</u> from the west coast to New York along with fellow artists Frank Cirocco, Gary Winnick, and Tony Salmons. All four eventually found success in the art field but it was Brent who ended up making the biggest splash in comics. Lending his dynamic and representational style to such projects as <u>Ka-Zar</u> and <u>The First X-Men Graphic Novel</u> put Brent squarely in the spotlight. Mr. Anderson now draws <u>Strikeforce: Morituri</u> in the comfort of his San Diego apartment with the sound of the surf blowing in through his studio window. It's a tough job but . . .

scott WILLIAMS

Scott is brand new to the comics business, a brand new husband, and a brand new star on the rise. Along with fellow San Diego based artist Whilce Portacio (another name that occasionally pops up in <u>Morituri</u> credits), Scott met and made friends with Brent Anderson. No fool he, Brent immediately saw that each newcomer had one ton o' talent and began encouraging the two in their artistic endeavors. Thanks in part to Mr. Anderson's advice and help, Scott and Whilce are now both well on their way to comics stardom as top notch inkers. Don't be surprised if both have penciling credits as well before long.

carl POTTS

As I write this, the first issue of <u>Strikeforce: Morituri</u> has been on sale for about ten days. The response from fans and pros alike has been gratifyingly and overwhelmingly positive. It's enough to make all the hard work seem worthwhile for we who are about to die from exhaustion! Work on the series began in the summer of '85 when Peter first approached me with the intriguing concept. I then pitched the idea to Brent who got hooked on the story and then introduced me to the skills of Scott. Please write to let us know what you do and don't like about <u>Strikeforce: Morituri</u>—and thanks for buying it! This is one proud and happy editor signing off—be back in 30 days!

Art by Brent Anderson

98

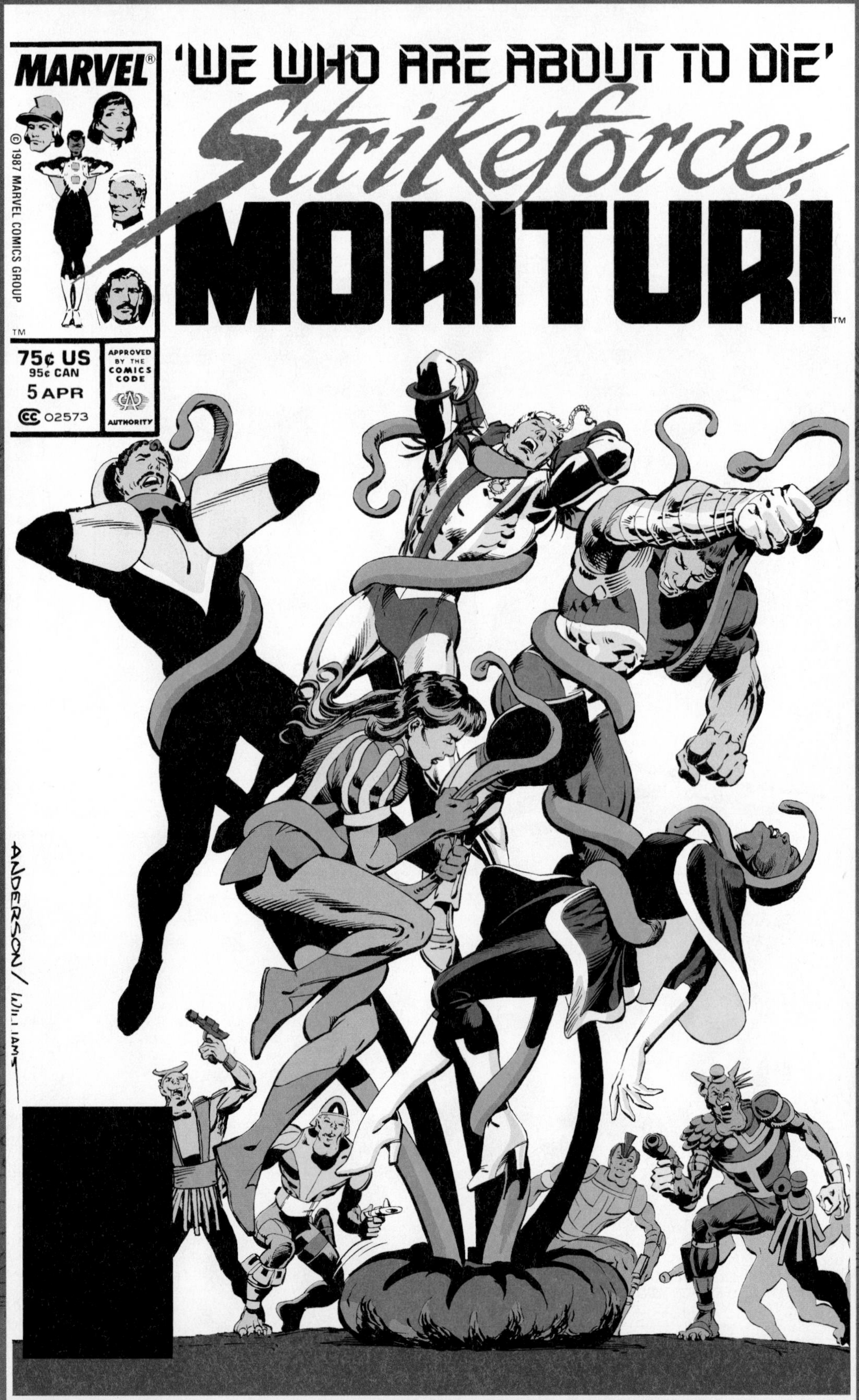

'WE WHO ARE ABOUT TO DIE'
MARVEL®
© 1987 MARVEL COMICS GROUP
Strikeforce:
MORITURI™
TM
75¢ US
95¢ CAN
5 APR
02573
APPROVED BY THE COMICS CODE AUTHORITY
ANDERSON/WILLIAMS

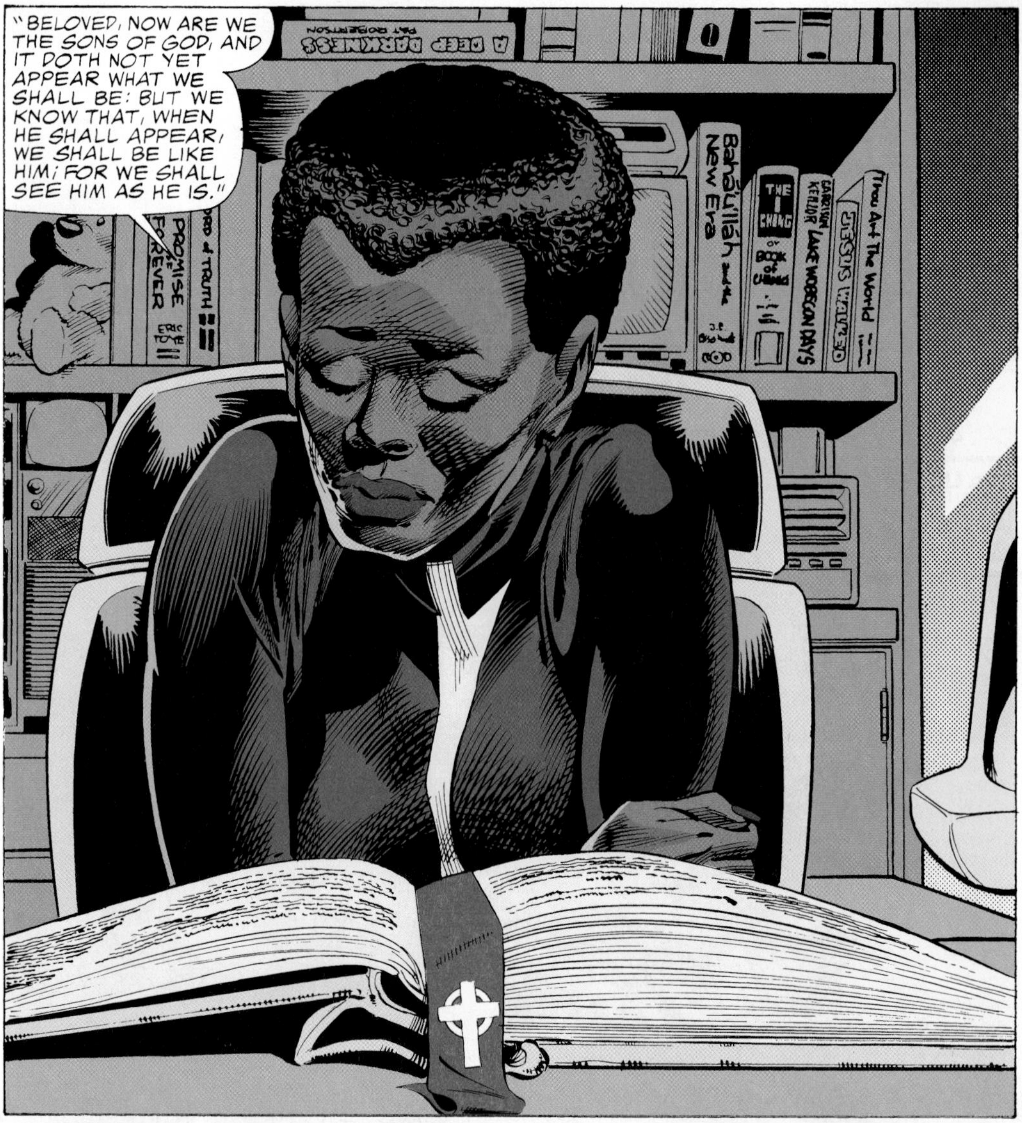
"BELOVED, NOW ARE WE THE SONS OF GOD, AND IT DOTH NOT YET APPEAR WHAT WE SHALL BE: BUT WE KNOW THAT, WHEN HE SHALL APPEAR, WE SHALL BE LIKE HIM; FOR WE SHALL SEE HIM AS HE IS."

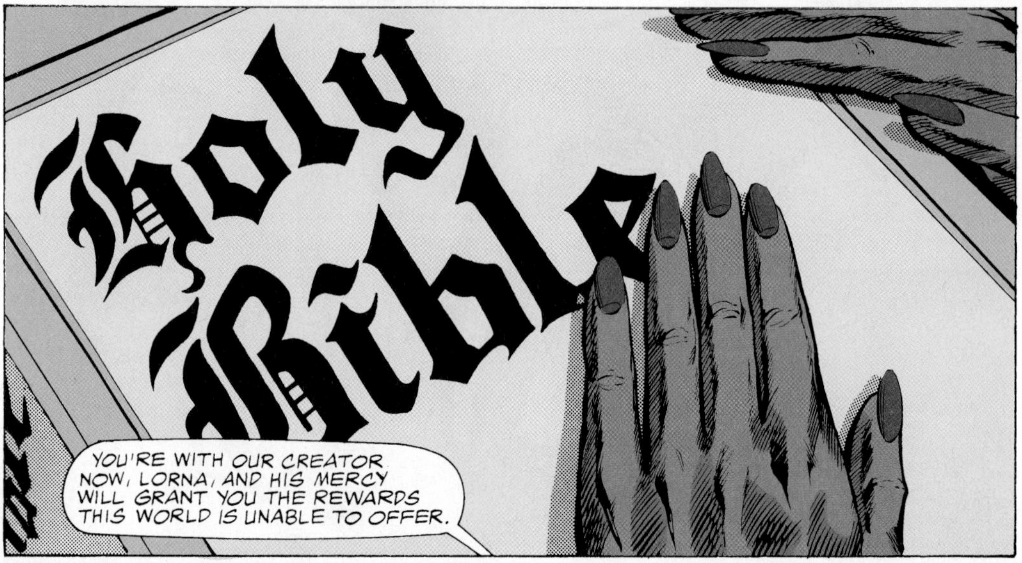
Holy Bible
YOU'RE WITH OUR CREATOR NOW, LORNA, AND HIS MERCY WILL GRANT YOU THE REWARDS THIS WORLD IS UNABLE TO OFFER.

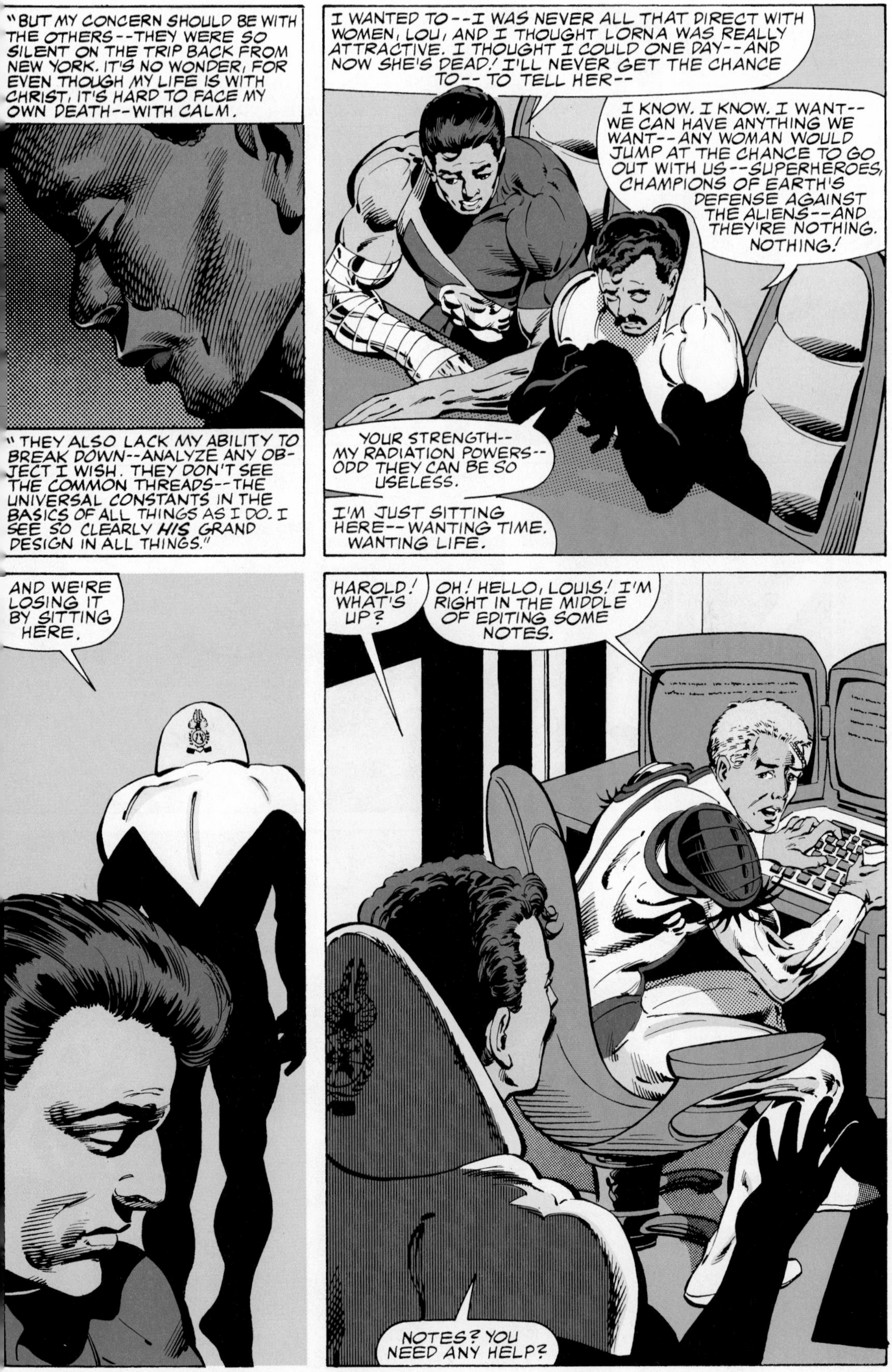
"BUT MY CONCERN SHOULD BE WITH THE OTHERS--THEY WERE SO SILENT ON THE TRIP BACK FROM NEW YORK. IT'S NO WONDER, FOR EVEN THOUGH MY LIFE IS WITH CHRIST, IT'S HARD TO FACE MY OWN DEATH--WITH CALM.
"THEY ALSO LACK MY ABILITY TO BREAK DOWN--ANALYZE ANY OBJECT I WISH. THEY DON'T SEE THE COMMON THREADS--THE UNIVERSAL CONSTANTS IN THE BASICS OF ALL THINGS AS I DO. I SEE SO CLEARLY HIS GRAND DESIGN IN ALL THINGS."
I WANTED TO--I WAS NEVER ALL THAT DIRECT WITH WOMEN, LOU, AND I THOUGHT LORNA WAS REALLY ATTRACTIVE. I THOUGHT I COULD ONE DAY--AND NOW SHE'S DEAD! I'LL NEVER GET THE CHANCE TO--TO TELL HER--
I KNOW. I KNOW. I WANT--WE CAN HAVE ANYTHING WE WANT--ANY WOMAN WOULD JUMP AT THE CHANCE TO GO OUT WITH US--SUPERHEROES, CHAMPIONS OF EARTH'S DEFENSE AGAINST THE ALIENS--AND THEY'RE NOTHING. NOTHING!
YOUR STRENGTH--MY RADIATION POWERS--ODD THEY CAN BE SO USELESS.
I'M JUST SITTING HERE--WANTING TIME. WANTING LIFE.
AND WE'RE LOSING IT BY SITTING HERE.
HAROLD! WHAT'S UP?
OH! HELLO, LOUIS! I'M RIGHT IN THE MIDDLE OF EDITING SOME NOTES.
NOTES? YOU NEED ANY HELP?

UH, NO. THE COMP DOES EVERYTHING, ACTUALLY-- SPOKEN NOTES TO TEXT, EVERYTHING.

BUT I'VE GOT TO DO SOMETHING--!

I KNOW THE FEELING. I HATE TO SAY THIS-- BUT LORNA DIED AND ON THE WAY BACK ALL I COULD THINK OF WAS THAT I HAD LESS TIME TO FINISH MY BOOK. THE MORITURI PROCESS THAT WE VOLUNTEERED FOR DOESN'T GIVE US A YEAR TO LIVE-- BUT UP TO A YEAR! AND IT DOESN'T DO ANY GOOD FOR ME NOW TO WEIGH THAT AGAINST THE ABILITY TO REROUTE ENERGY I GAINED.

ANYWAY, LISTEN TO THIS:

"I GOT THE FEELING THAT LORNA WOULD DIE FIRST-- STUPID 20/20 HINDSIGHT!"

TINK

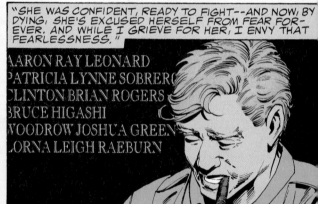

"SHE WAS CONFIDENT, READY TO FIGHT--AND NOW, BY DYING, SHE'S EXCUSED HERSELF FROM FEAR FOREVER. AND WHILE I GRIEVE FOR HER, I ENVY THAT FEARLESSNESS."

AARON RAY LEONARD
PATRICIA LYNNE SOBRERO
CLINTON BRIAN ROGERS
BRUCE HIGASHI
WOODROW JOSHUA GREEN
LORNA LEIGH RAEBURN

DEDICATED TO THE MEMORY OF THOSE WHO SERVED

AARON RAY LEONARD
PATRICIA LYNNE SOBRERO
CLINTON BRIAN ROGERS
BRUCE HIGASHI
WOODROW JOSHUA GREEN
LORNA LEIGH RAEBURN

"NOW I KNOW WHY THE ANCIENTS MADE GODS OF THEIR DEPARTED ANCESTORS."

I JUST SIT HERE, WRITING, LOU -- HOPING THAT SOME WORDS CAN EXPLAIN AWAY --THIS DARKNESS--

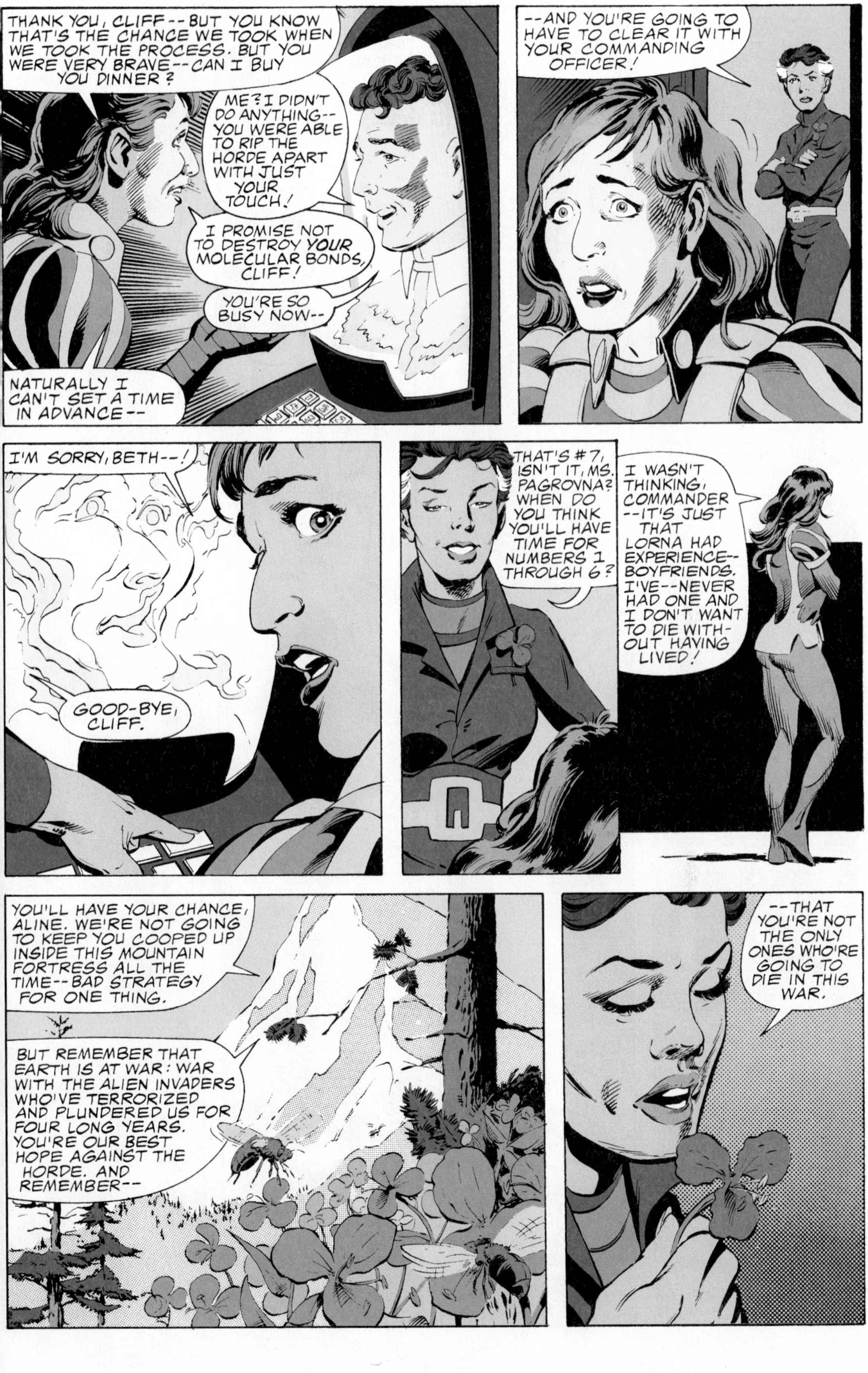
THANK YOU, CLIFF--BUT YOU KNOW THAT'S THE CHANCE WE TOOK WHEN WE TOOK THE PROCESS. BUT YOU WERE VERY BRAVE--CAN I BUY YOU DINNER?
ME? I DIDN'T DO ANYTHING--YOU WERE ABLE TO RIP THE HORDE APART WITH JUST YOUR TOUCH!
I PROMISE NOT TO DESTROY YOUR MOLECULAR BONDS, CLIFF!
YOU'RE SO BUSY NOW--
NATURALLY I CAN'T SET A TIME IN ADVANCE--
--AND YOU'RE GOING TO HAVE TO CLEAR IT WITH YOUR COMMANDING OFFICER!
I'M SORRY, BETH--!
GOOD-BYE, CLIFF.
THAT'S #7, ISN'T IT, MS. PAGROVNA? WHEN DO YOU THINK YOU'LL HAVE TIME FOR NUMBERS 1 THROUGH 6?
I WASN'T THINKING, COMMANDER--IT'S JUST THAT LORNA HAD EXPERIENCE--BOYFRIENDS. I'VE--NEVER HAD ONE AND I DON'T WANT TO DIE WITHOUT HAVING LIVED!
YOU'LL HAVE YOUR CHANCE, ALINE. WE'RE NOT GOING TO KEEP YOU COOPED UP INSIDE THIS MOUNTAIN FORTRESS ALL THE TIME--BAD STRATEGY FOR ONE THING.
BUT REMEMBER THAT EARTH IS AT WAR: WAR WITH THE ALIEN INVADERS WHO'VE TERRORIZED AND PLUNDERED US FOR FOUR LONG YEARS. YOU'RE OUR BEST HOPE AGAINST THE HORDE. AND REMEMBER--
--THAT YOU'RE NOT THE ONLY ONES WHO'RE GOING TO DIE IN THIS WAR.

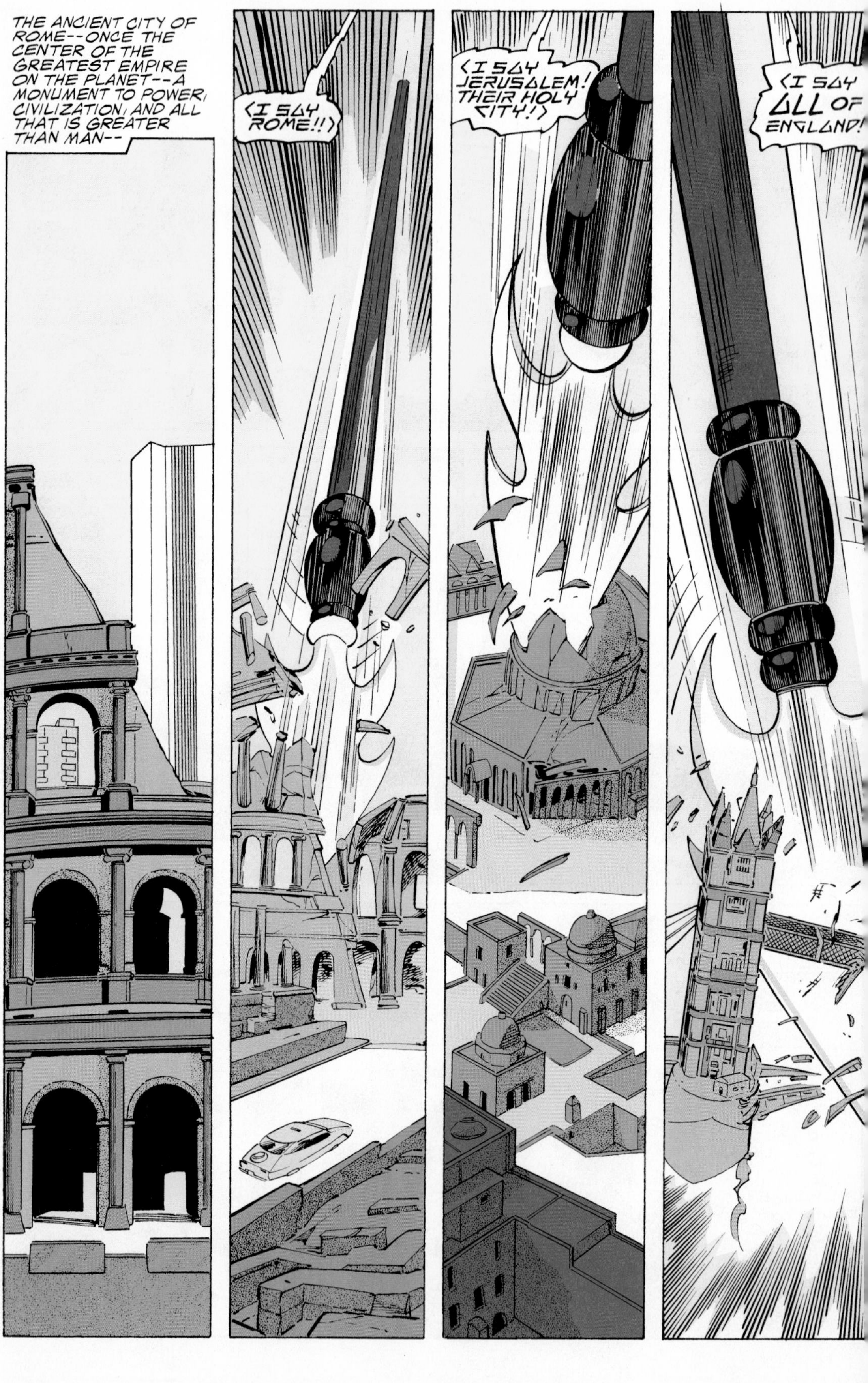
THE ANCIENT CITY OF ROME--ONCE THE CENTER OF THE GREATEST EMPIRE ON THE PLANET--A MONUMENT TO POWER, CIVILIZATION, AND ALL THAT IS GREATER THAN MAN--
<I SAY ROME!!>
<I SAY JERUSALEM! THEIR HOLY CITY!>
<I SAY ALL OF ENGLAND!

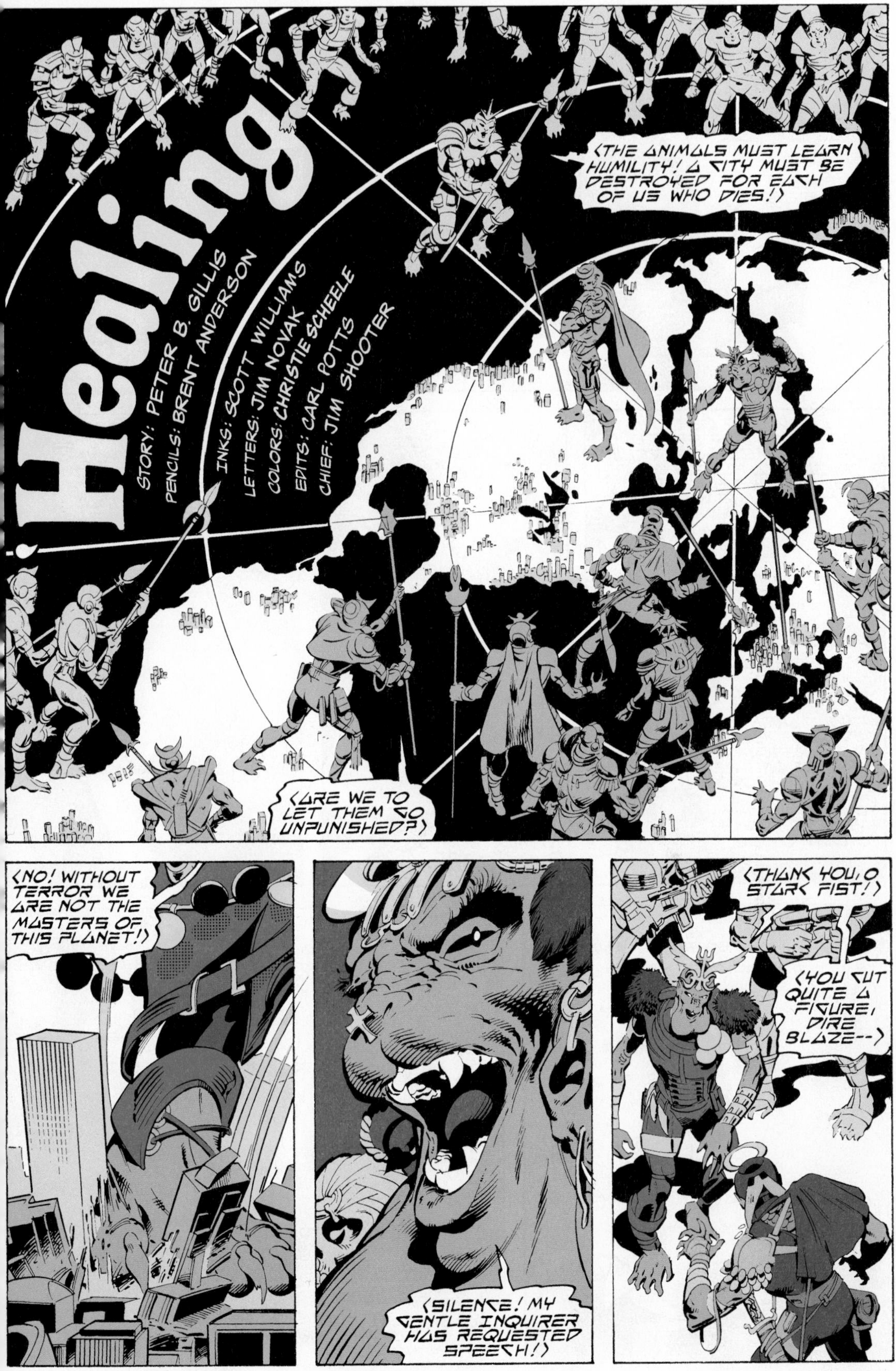
Healing
STORY: PETER B. GILLIS
PENCILS: BRENT ANDERSON
INKS: SCOTT WILLIAMS
LETTERS: JIM NOVAK
COLORS: CHRISTIE SCHEELE
EDITS: CARL POTTS
CHIEF: JIM SHOOTER
<THE ANIMALS MUST LEARN HUMILITY! A CITY MUST BE DESTROYED FOR EACH OF US WHO DIES!>
<ARE WE TO LET THEM GO UNPUNISHED?>
<NO! WITHOUT TERROR WE ARE NOT THE MASTERS OF THIS PLANET!>
<SILENCE! MY GENTLE INQUIRER HAS REQUESTED SPEECH!>
<THANK YOU, O STARK FIST!>
<YOU CUT QUITE A FIGURE, DIRE BLAZE-->

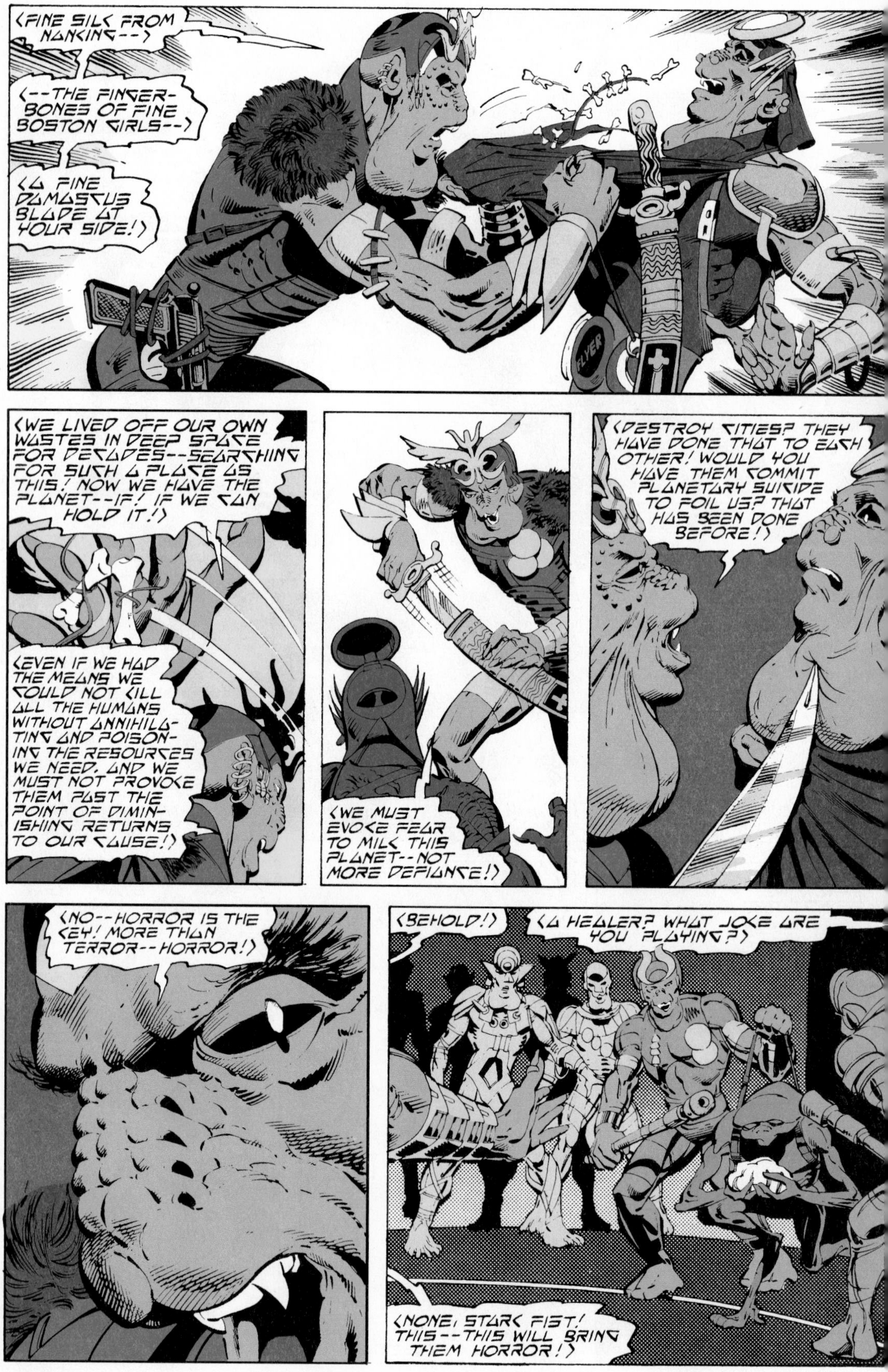
<FINE SILK FROM NANKING-->
<--THE FINGER-BONES OF FINE BOSTON GIRLS-->
<A FINE DAMASCUS BLADE AT YOUR SIDE!>
FLYER
<WE LIVED OFF OUR OWN WASTES IN DEEP SPACE FOR DECADES--SEARCHING FOR SUCH A PLACE AS THIS! NOW WE HAVE THE PLANET--IF! IF WE CAN HOLD IT!>
<EVEN IF WE HAD THE MEANS WE COULD NOT KILL ALL THE HUMANS WITHOUT ANNIHILATING AND POISONING THE RESOURCES WE NEED. AND WE MUST NOT PROVOKE THEM PAST THE POINT OF DIMINISHING RETURNS TO OUR CAUSE!>
<WE MUST EVOKE FEAR TO MILK THIS PLANET--NOT MORE DEFIANCE!>
<DESTROY CITIES? THEY HAVE DONE THAT TO EACH OTHER! WOULD YOU HAVE THEM COMMIT PLANETARY SUICIDE TO FOIL US? THAT HAS BEEN DONE BEFORE!>
<NO--HORROR IS THE KEY! MORE THAN TERROR--HORROR!>
<BEHOLD!>
<A HEALER? WHAT JOKE ARE YOU PLAYING?>
<NONE, STARK FIST! THIS--THIS WILL BRING THEM HORROR!>

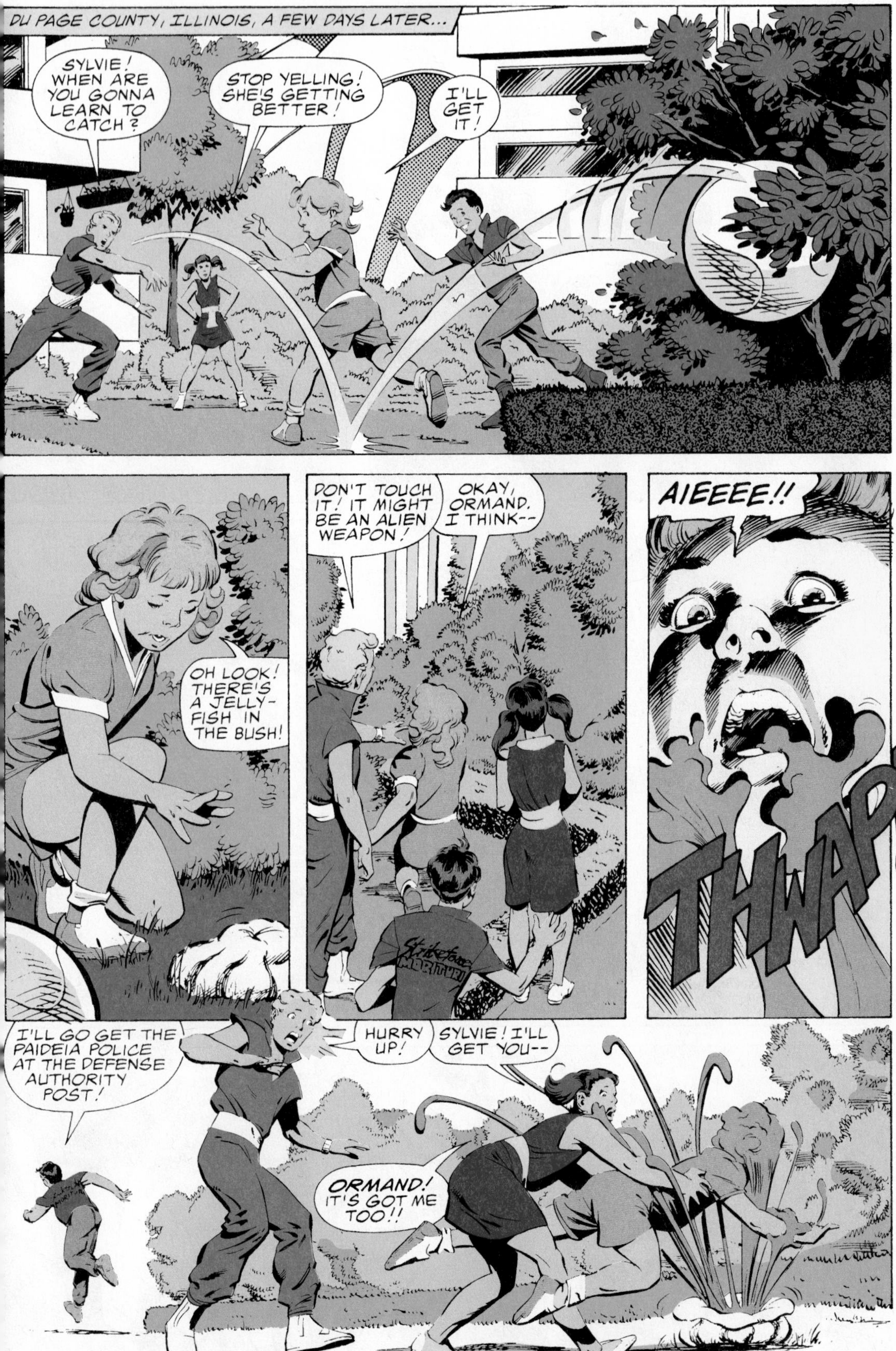
DU PAGE COUNTY, ILLINOIS, A FEW DAYS LATER...
SYLVIE! WHEN ARE YOU GONNA LEARN TO CATCH?
STOP YELLING! SHE'S GETTING BETTER!
I'LL GET IT!
OH LOOK! THERE'S A JELLY-FISH IN THE BUSH!
DON'T TOUCH IT! IT MIGHT BE AN ALIEN WEAPON!
OKAY, ORMAND. I THINK--
AIEEEE!!
THWAP!
I'LL GO GET THE PAIDEIA POLICE AT THE DEFENSE AUTHORITY POST!
HURRY UP!
SYLVIE! I'LL GET YOU--
ORMAND! IT'S GOT ME TOO!!

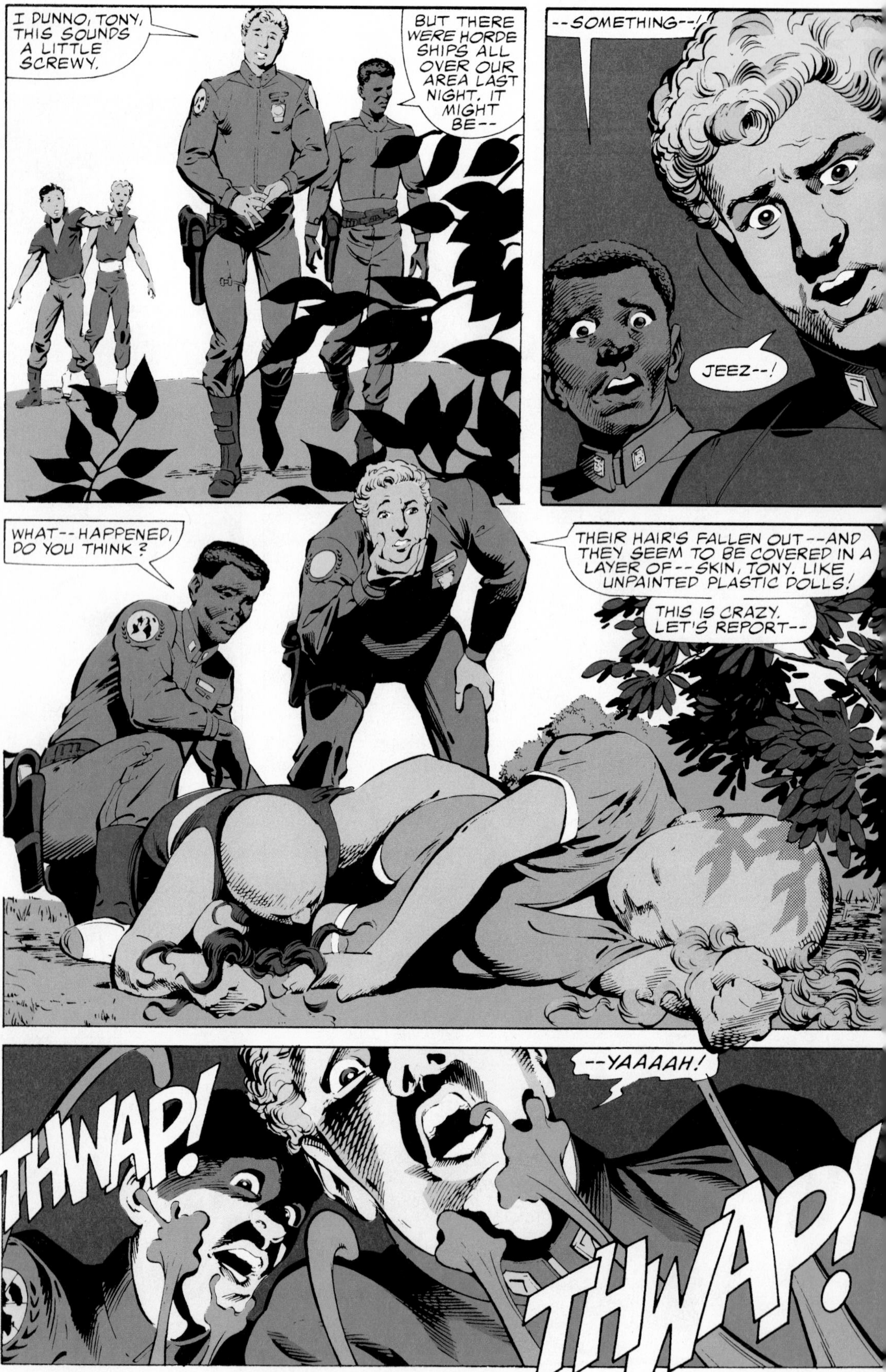

I DUNNO, TONY, THIS SOUNDS A LITTLE SCREWY.
BUT THERE WERE HORDE SHIPS ALL OVER OUR AREA LAST NIGHT. IT MIGHT BE--
--SOMETHING--!
JEEZ--!
WHAT--HAPPENED, DO YOU THINK?
THEIR HAIR'S FALLEN OUT--AND THEY SEEM TO BE COVERED IN A LAYER OF--SKIN, TONY. LIKE UNPAINTED PLASTIC DOLLS!
THIS IS CRAZY. LET'S REPORT--
THWAP!
--YAAAAH!
THWAP!

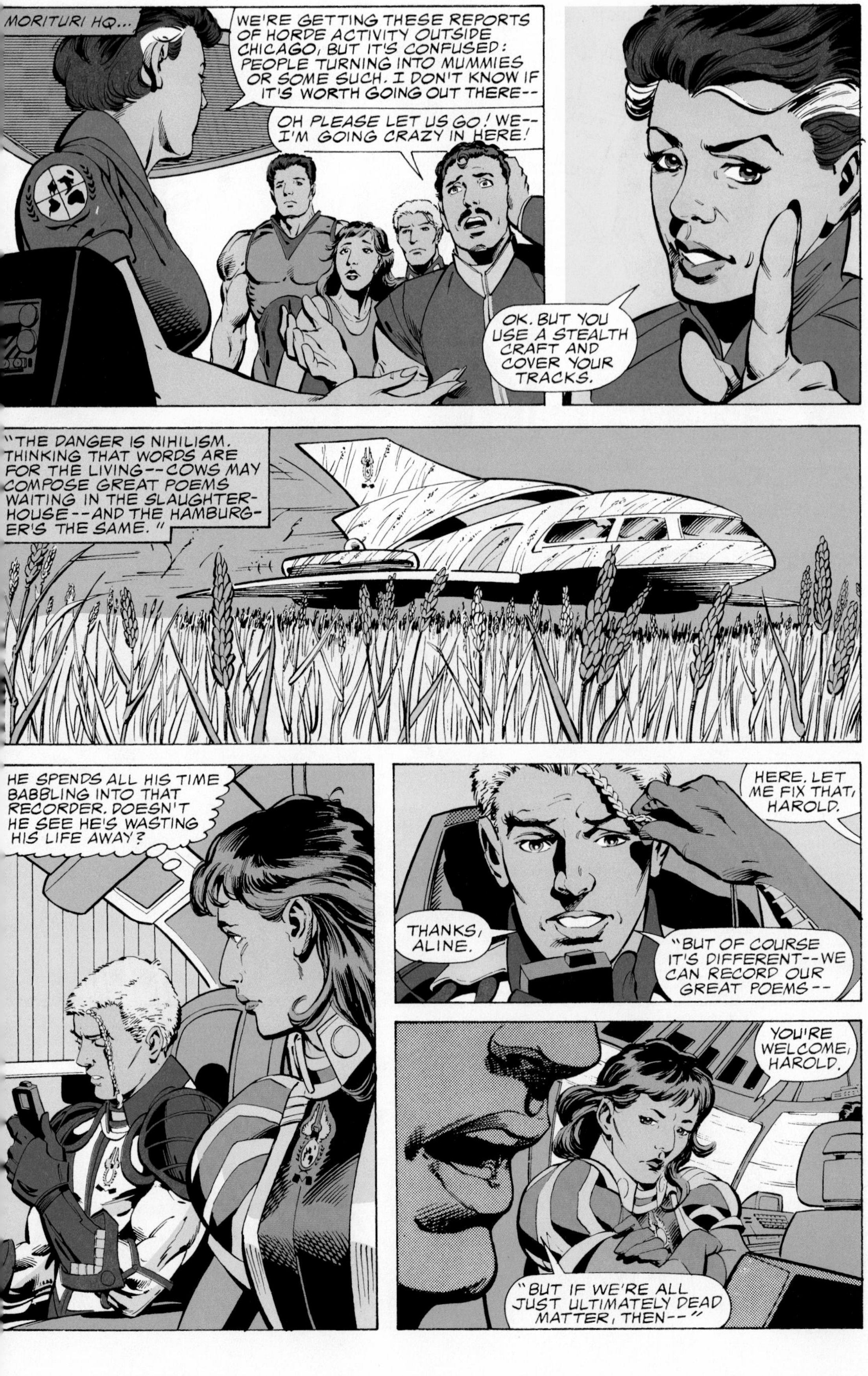

MORITURI HQ...
WE'RE GETTING THESE REPORTS OF HORDE ACTIVITY OUTSIDE CHICAGO, BUT IT'S CONFUSED: PEOPLE TURNING INTO MUMMIES OR SOME SUCH. I DON'T KNOW IF IT'S WORTH GOING OUT THERE--
OH PLEASE LET US GO! WE-- I'M GOING CRAZY IN HERE!
OK. BUT YOU USE A STEALTH CRAFT AND COVER YOUR TRACKS.
"THE DANGER IS NIHILISM. THINKING THAT WORDS ARE FOR THE LIVING--COWS MAY COMPOSE GREAT POEMS WAITING IN THE SLAUGHTER-HOUSE--AND THE HAMBURG-ER'S THE SAME."
HE SPENDS ALL HIS TIME BABBLING INTO THAT RECORDER. DOESN'T HE SEE HE'S WASTING HIS LIFE AWAY?
HERE. LET ME FIX THAT, HAROLD.
THANKS, ALINE.
"BUT OF COURSE IT'S DIFFERENT--WE CAN RECORD OUR GREAT POEMS--
YOU'RE WELCOME, HAROLD.
"BUT IF WE'RE ALL JUST ULTIMATELY DEAD MATTER, THEN--"

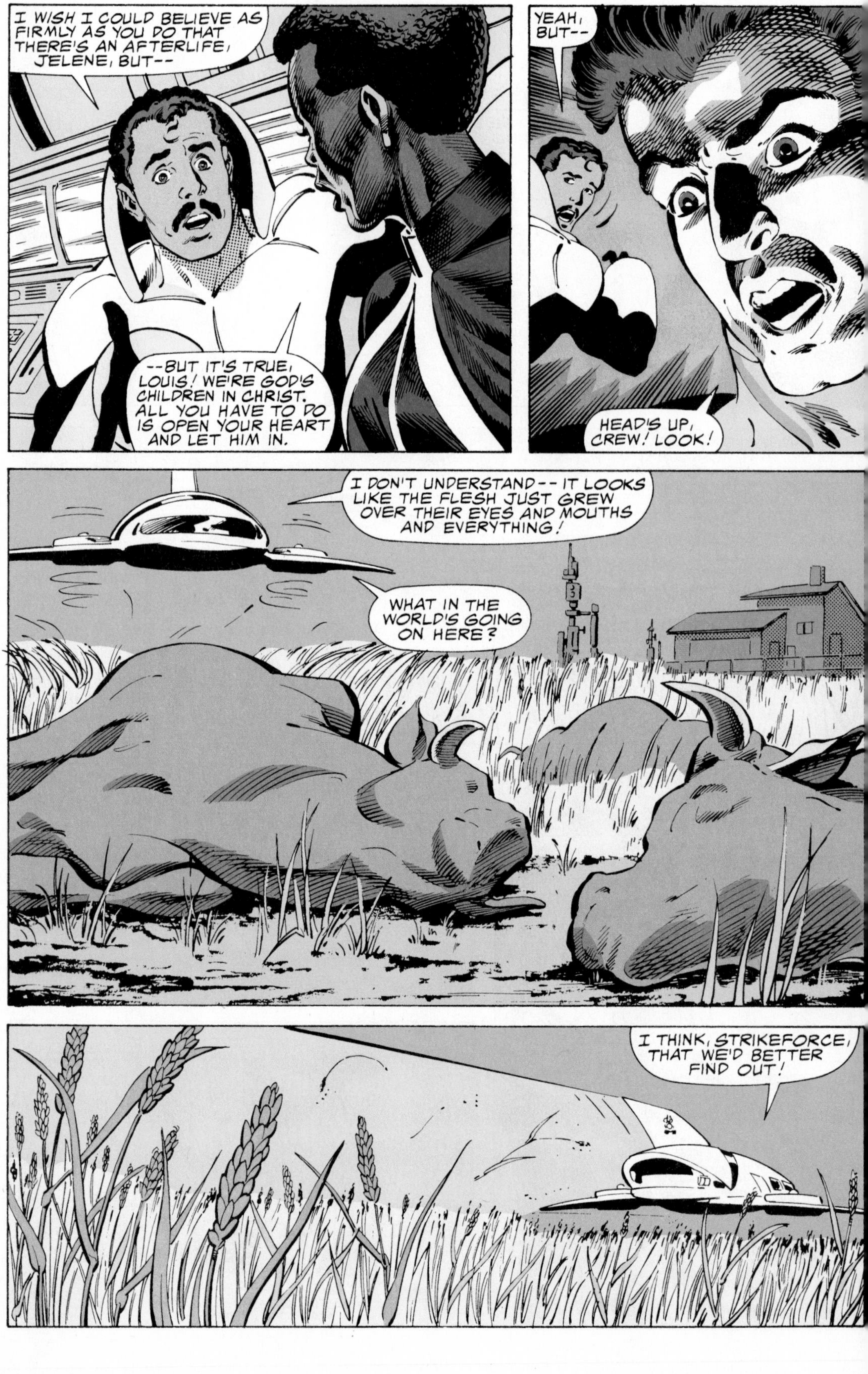
I WISH I COULD BELIEVE AS FIRMLY AS YOU DO THAT THERE'S AN AFTERLIFE, JELENE, BUT--
--BUT IT'S TRUE, LOUIS! WE'RE GOD'S CHILDREN IN CHRIST. ALL YOU HAVE TO DO IS OPEN YOUR HEART AND LET HIM IN.
YEAH, BUT--
HEAD'S UP, CREW! LOOK!
I DON'T UNDERSTAND-- IT LOOKS LIKE THE FLESH JUST GREW OVER THEIR EYES AND MOUTHS AND EVERYTHING!
WHAT IN THE WORLD'S GOING ON HERE?
I THINK, STRIKEFORCE, THAT WE'D BETTER FIND OUT!

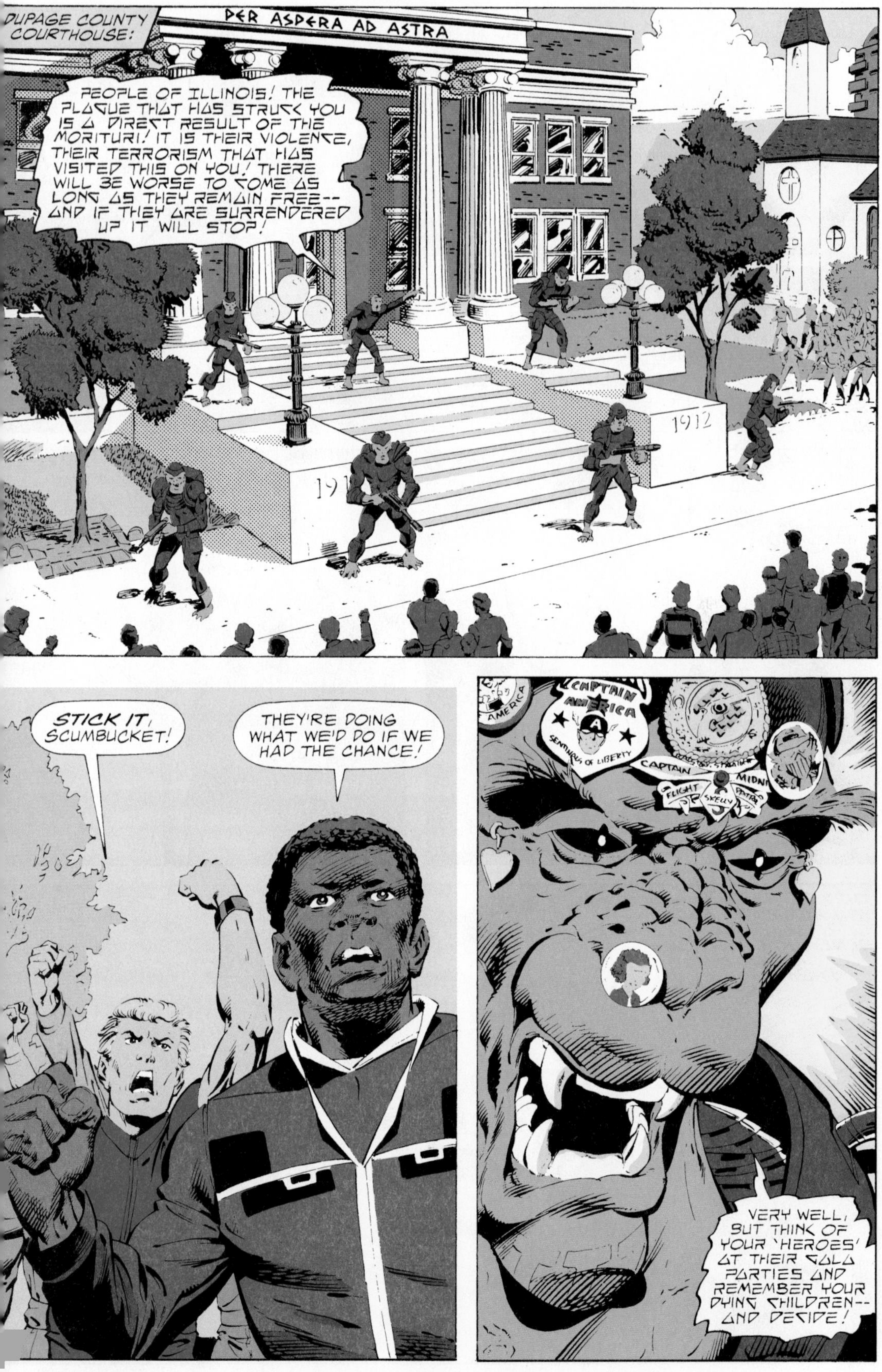
DUPAGE COUNTY COURTHOUSE:
PER ASPERA AD ASTRA
PEOPLE OF ILLINOIS! THE PLAGUE THAT HAS STRUCK YOU IS A DIRECT RESULT OF THE MORITURI! IT IS THEIR VIOLENCE, THEIR TERRORISM THAT HAS VISITED THIS ON YOU! THERE WILL BE WORSE TO COME AS LONG AS THEY REMAIN FREE-- AND IF THEY ARE SURRENDERED UP IT WILL STOP!
1912
STICK IT, SCUMBUCKET!
THEY'RE DOING WHAT WE'D DO IF WE HAD THE CHANCE!
CAPTAIN AMERICA
SENTINELS OF LIBERTY
VERY WELL, BUT THINK OF YOUR 'HEROES' AT THEIR GALA PARTIES AND REMEMBER YOUR DYING CHILDREN-- AND DECIDE!

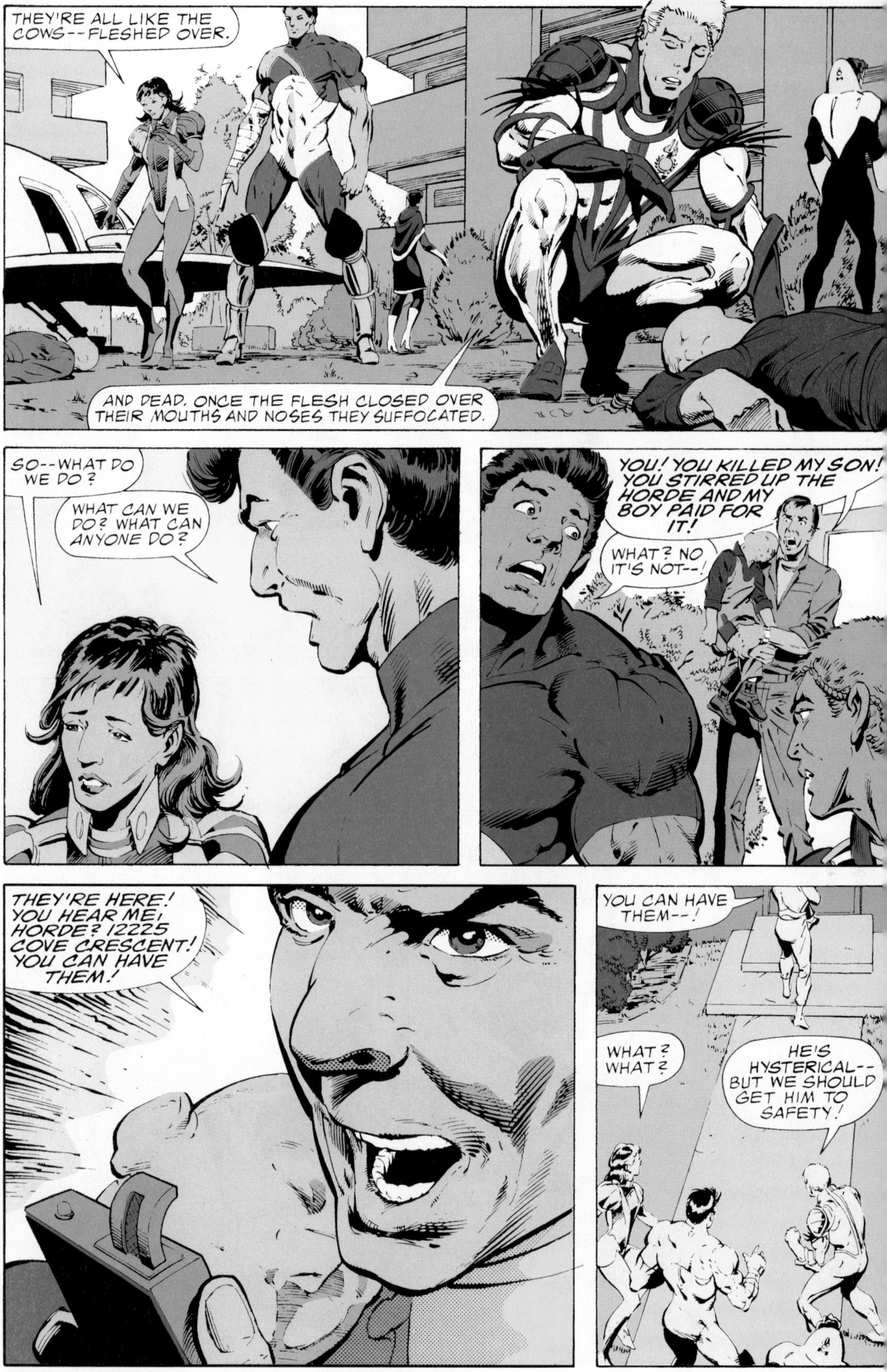
THEY'RE ALL LIKE THE COWS--FLESHED OVER.
AND DEAD. ONCE THE FLESH CLOSED OVER THEIR MOUTHS AND NOSES THEY SUFFOCATED.
SO--WHAT DO WE DO?
WHAT CAN WE DO? WHAT CAN ANYONE DO?
YOU! YOU KILLED MY SON! YOU STIRRED UP THE HORDE AND MY BOY PAID FOR IT!
WHAT? NO IT'S NOT--!
THEY'RE HERE! YOU HEAR ME, HORDE? 12225 COVE CRESCENT! YOU CAN HAVE THEM!
YOU CAN HAVE THEM--!
WHAT? WHAT?
HE'S HYSTERICAL--BUT WE SHOULD GET HIM TO SAFETY!

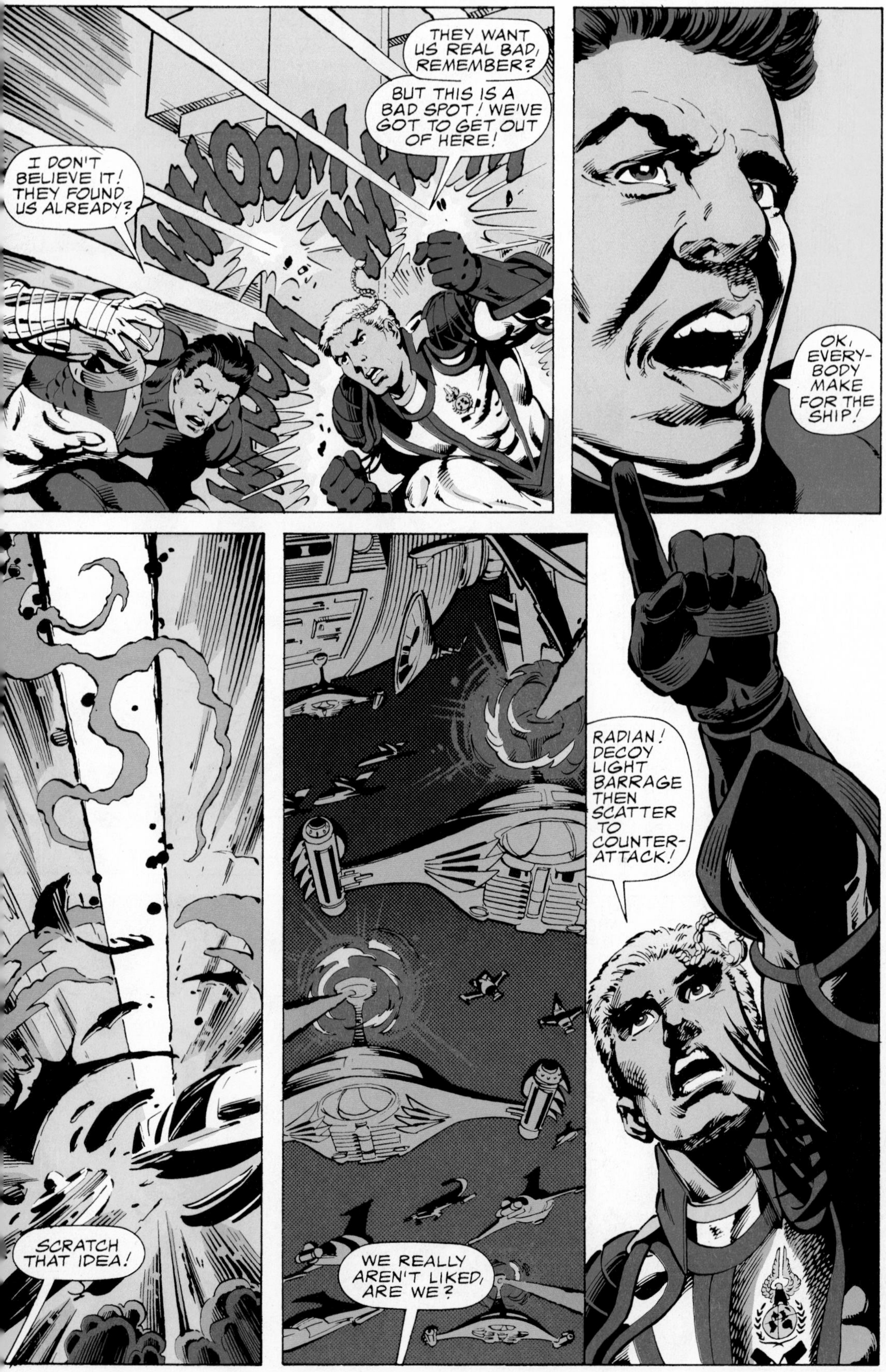
I DON'T BELIEVE IT! THEY FOUND US ALREADY?
THEY WANT US REAL BAD, REMEMBER?
BUT THIS IS A BAD SPOT! WE'VE GOT TO GET OUT OF HERE!
WHOOM
WHOOM
OK, EVERY-BODY MAKE FOR THE SHIP!
SCRATCH THAT IDEA!
WE REALLY AREN'T LIKED, ARE WE?
RADIAN! DECOY LIGHT BARRAGE THEN SCATTER TO COUNTER-ATTACK!

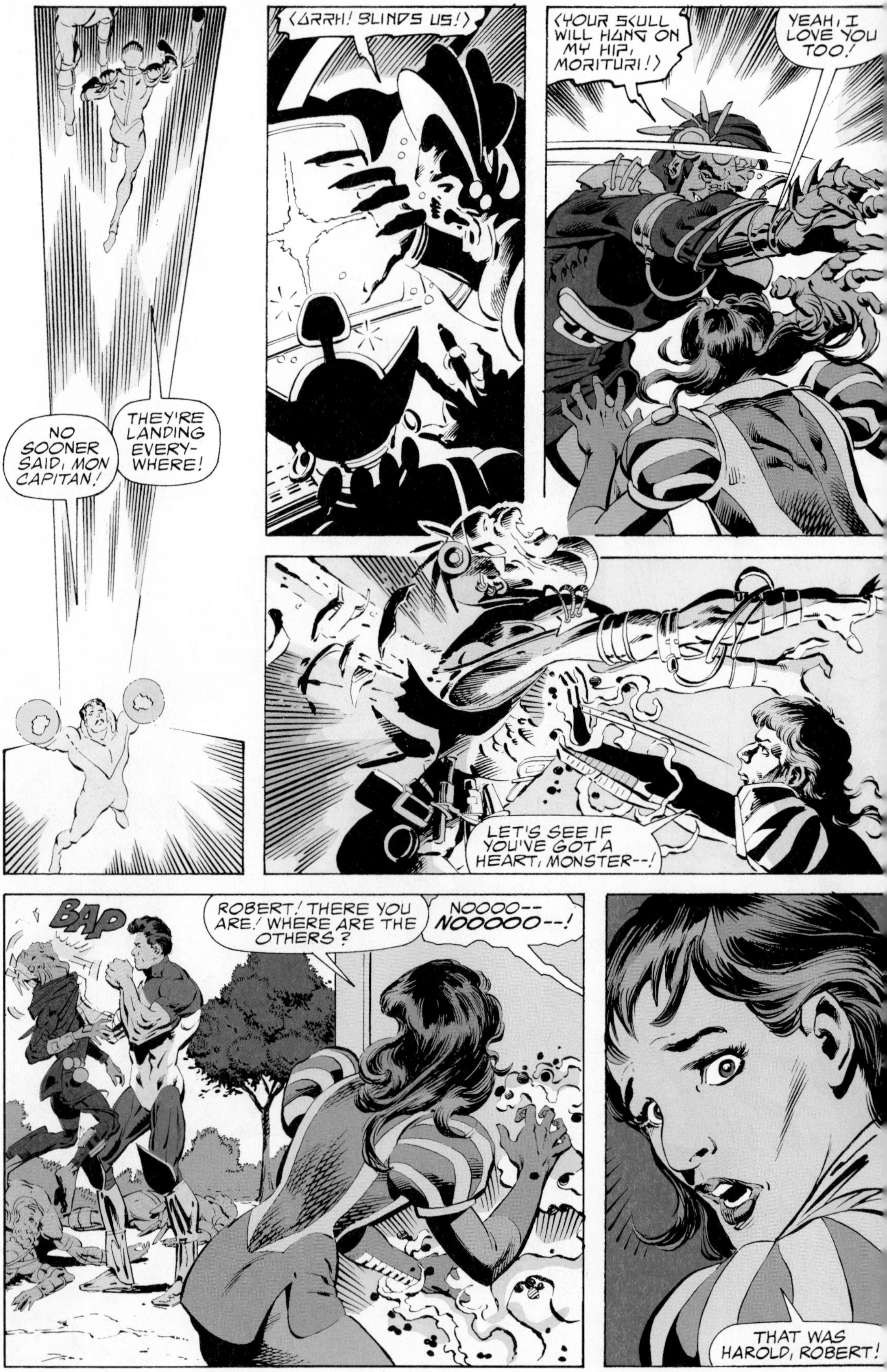
NO SOONER SAID, MON CAPITAN!
THEY'RE LANDING EVERY-WHERE!
‹ARRH! BLINDS US!›
‹YOUR SKULL WILL HANG ON MY HIP, MORITURI!›
YEAH, I LOVE YOU TOO!
LET'S SEE IF YOU'VE GOT A HEART, MONSTER--!
BAP
ROBERT! THERE YOU ARE! WHERE ARE THE OTHERS?
NOOOO-- NOOOOO--!
THAT WAS HAROLD, ROBERT!

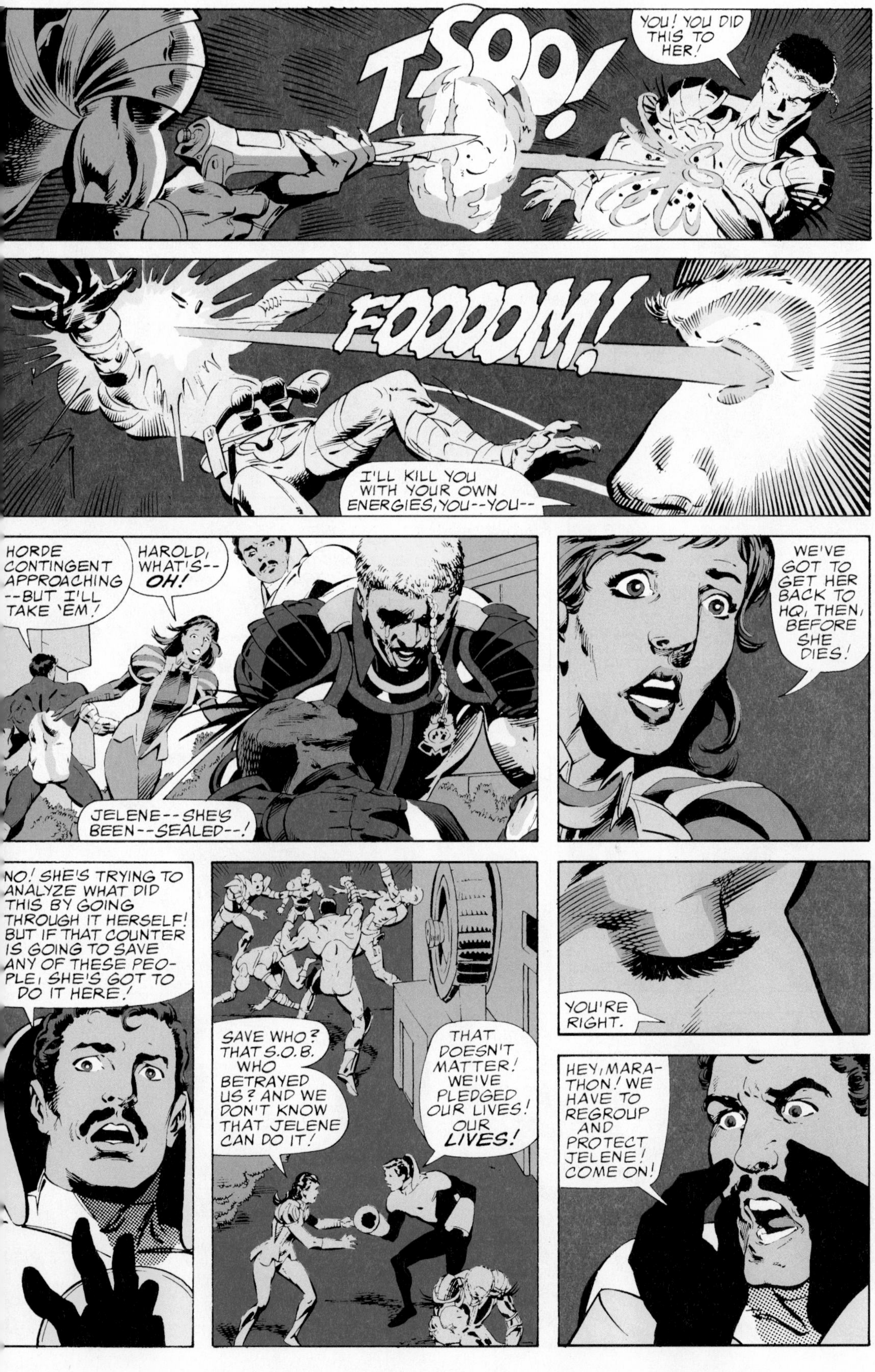
TSOO!
YOU! YOU DID THIS TO HER!
FOOOOM!
I'LL KILL YOU WITH YOUR OWN ENERGIES, YOU--YOU--
HORDE CONTINGENT APPROACHING --BUT I'LL TAKE 'EM!
HAROLD, WHAT'S-- OH!
JELENE--SHE'S BEEN--SEALED--!
WE'VE GOT TO GET HER BACK TO HQ, THEN, BEFORE SHE DIES!
NO! SHE'S TRYING TO ANALYZE WHAT DID THIS BY GOING THROUGH IT HERSELF! BUT IF THAT COUNTER IS GOING TO SAVE ANY OF THESE PEOPLE, SHE'S GOT TO DO IT HERE!
SAVE WHO? THAT S.O.B. WHO BETRAYED US? AND WE DON'T KNOW THAT JELENE CAN DO IT!
THAT DOESN'T MATTER! WE'VE PLEDGED OUR LIVES! OUR LIVES!
YOU'RE RIGHT.
HEY, MARATHON! WE HAVE TO REGROUP AND PROTECT JELENE! COME ON!

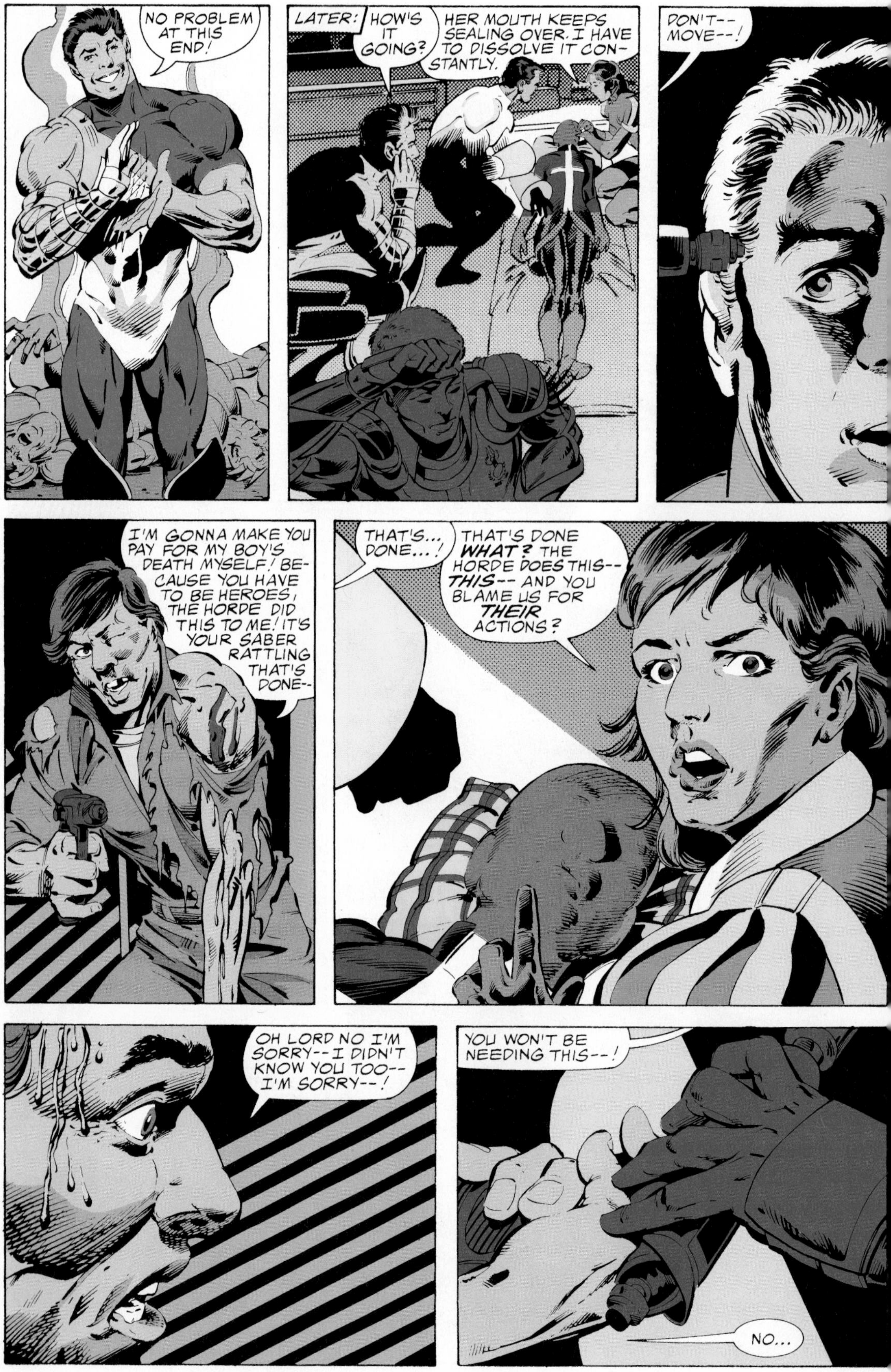
NO PROBLEM AT THIS END!
LATER:
HOW'S IT GOING?
HER MOUTH KEEPS SEALING OVER. I HAVE TO DISSOLVE IT CONSTANTLY.
DON'T-- MOVE--!
I'M GONNA MAKE YOU PAY FOR MY BOY'S DEATH MYSELF! BECAUSE YOU HAVE TO BE HEROES, THE HORDE DID THIS TO ME! IT'S YOUR SABER RATTLING THAT'S DONE--
THAT'S... DONE...!
THAT'S DONE WHAT? THE HORDE DOES THIS-- THIS-- AND YOU BLAME US FOR THEIR ACTIONS?
OH LORD NO I'M SORRY-- I DIDN'T KNOW YOU TOO-- I'M SORRY--!
YOU WON'T BE NEEDING THIS--!
NO...

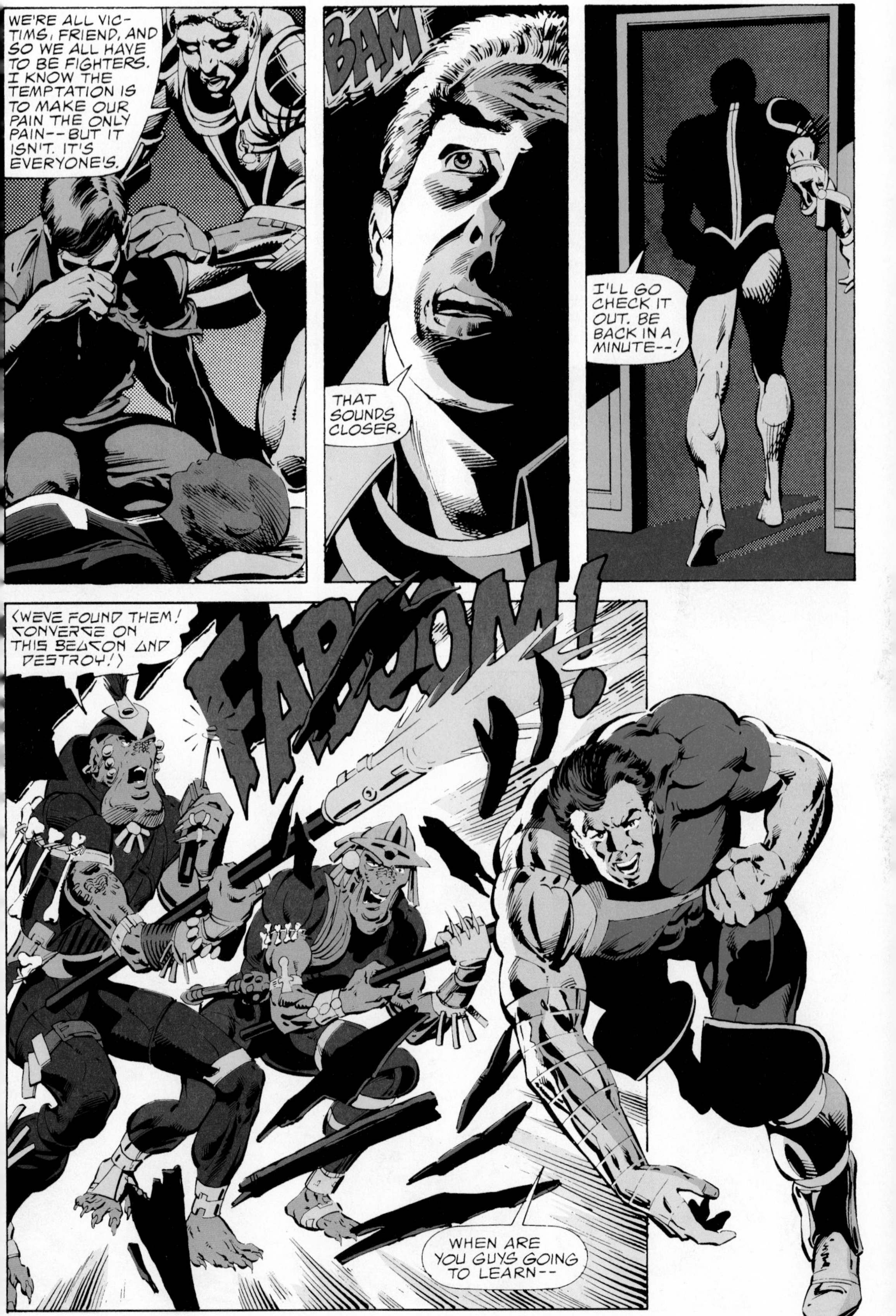
WE'RE ALL VICTIMS, FRIEND, AND SO WE ALL HAVE TO BE FIGHTERS. I KNOW THE TEMPTATION IS TO MAKE OUR PAIN THE ONLY PAIN--BUT IT ISN'T. IT'S EVERYONE'S.
BAM
THAT SOUNDS CLOSER.
I'LL GO CHECK IT OUT. BE BACK IN A MINUTE--!
<WE'VE FOUND THEM! CONVERGE ON THIS BEACON AND DESTROY!>
FABOOM!
WHEN ARE YOU GUYS GOING TO LEARN--

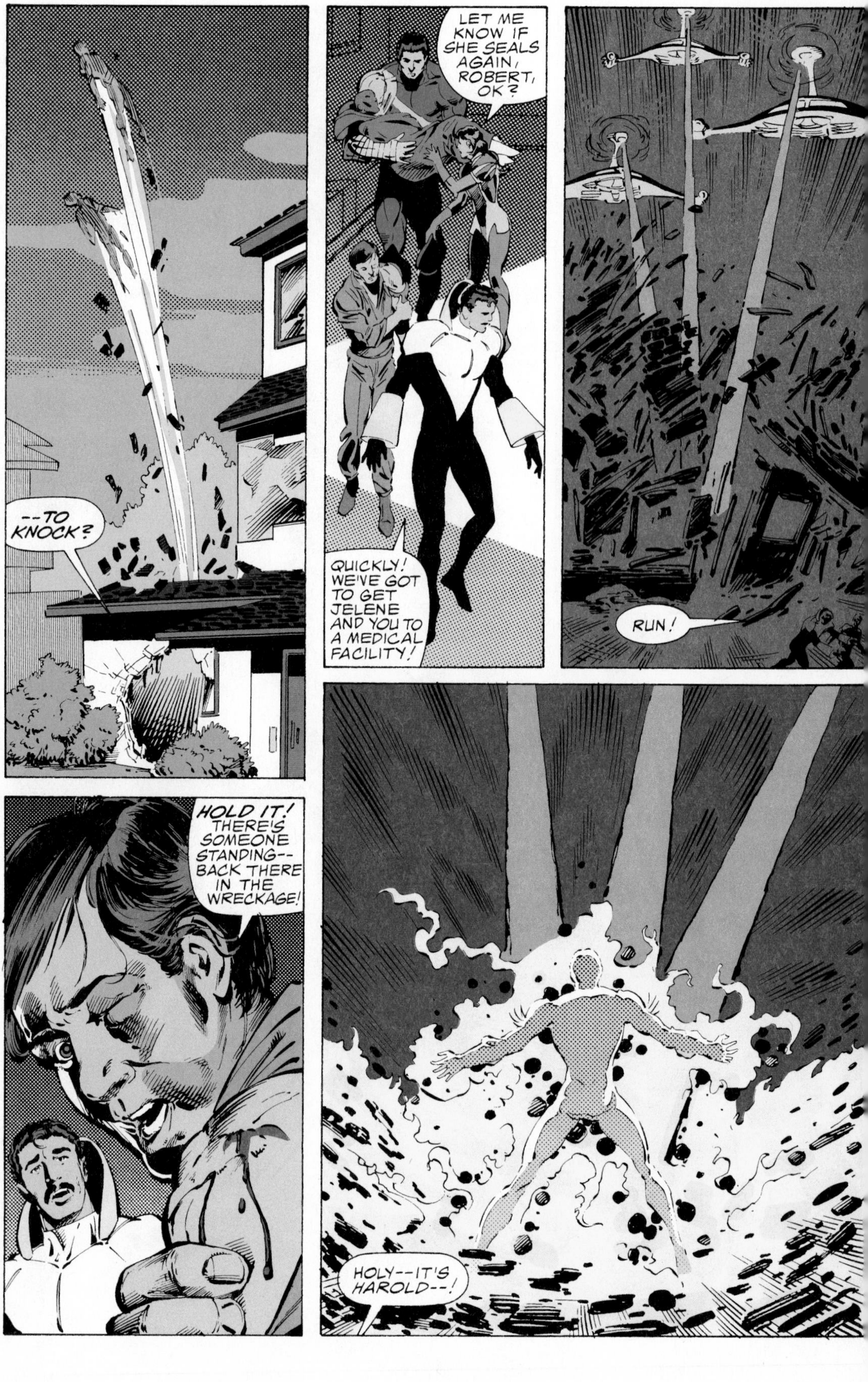
--TO KNOCK?
LET ME KNOW IF SHE SEALS AGAIN, ROBERT, OK?
QUICKLY! WE'VE GOT TO GET JELENE AND YOU TO A MEDICAL FACILITY!
RUN!
HOLD IT! THERE'S SOMEONE STANDING-- BACK THERE IN THE WRECKAGE!
HOLY--IT'S HAROLD--!

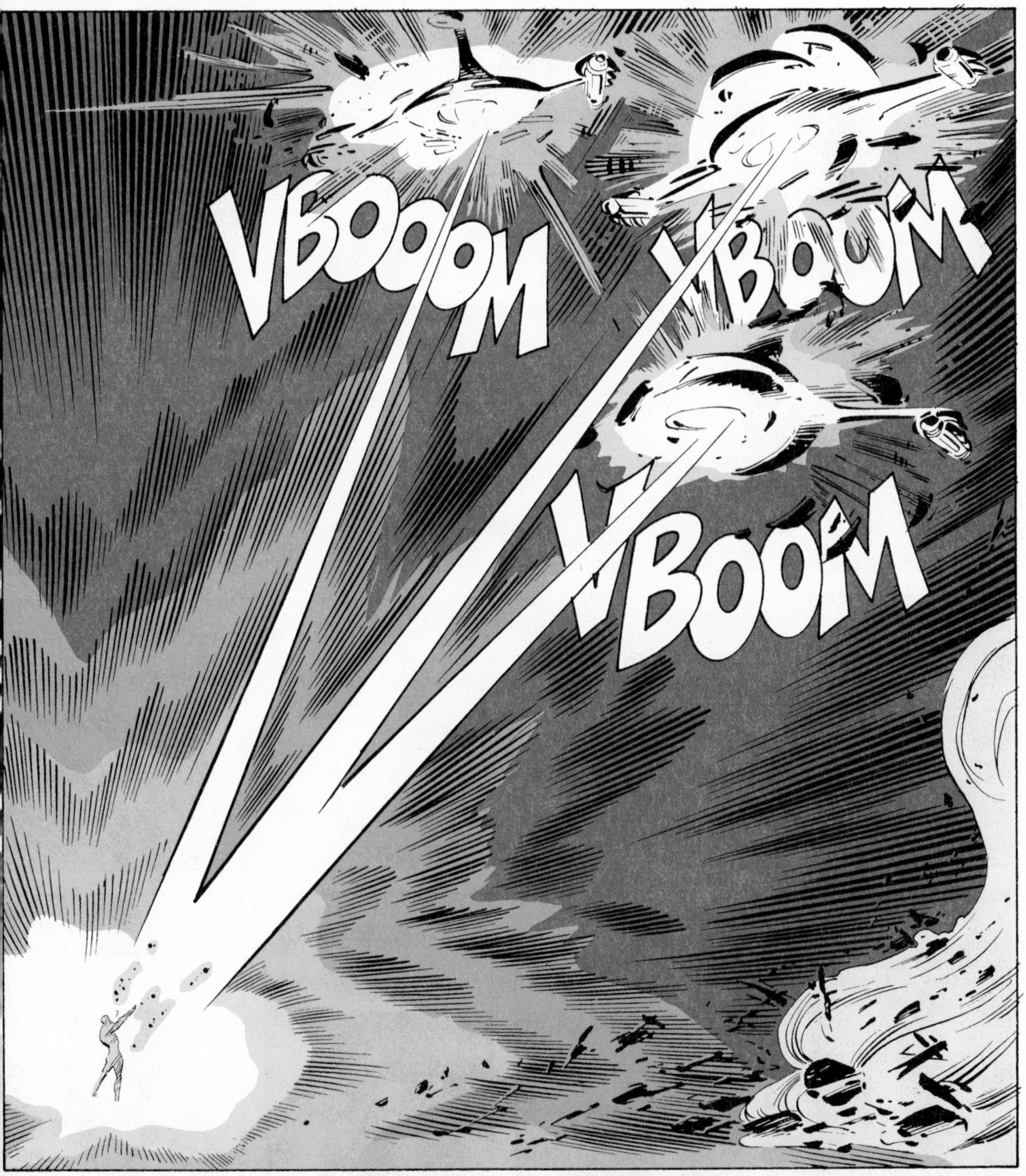
VBOOOM
VBOOM
VBOOM

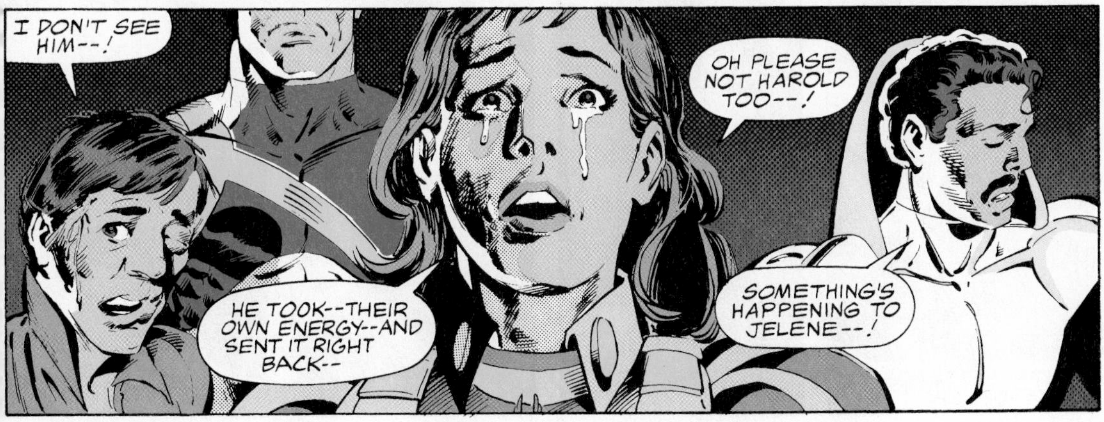
I DON'T SEE HIM--!
HE TOOK--THEIR OWN ENERGY--AND SENT IT RIGHT BACK--
OH PLEASE NOT HAROLD TOO--!
SOMETHING'S HAPPENING TO JELENE--!

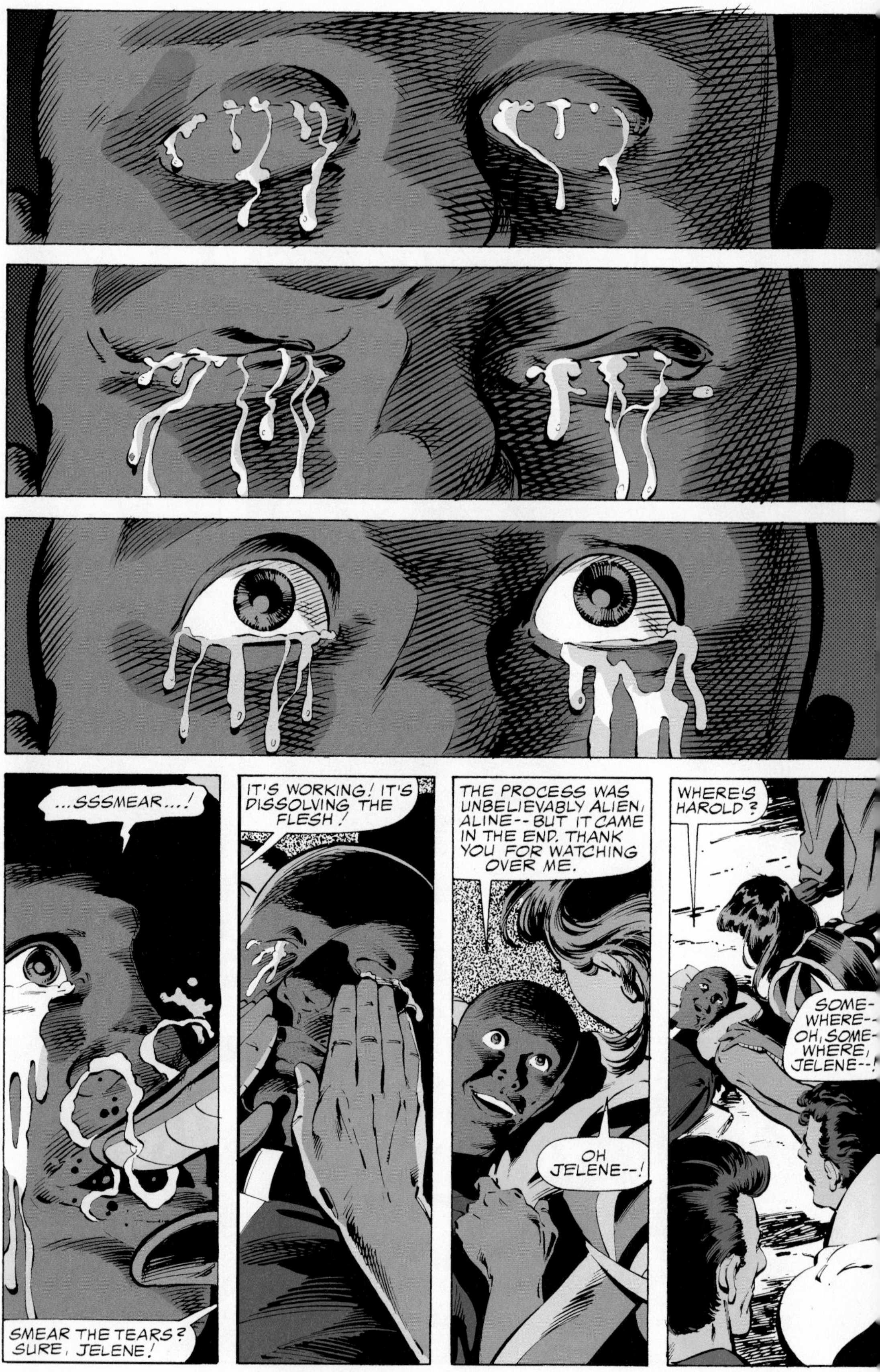
...SSSMEAR...!
SMEAR THE TEARS? SURE, JELENE!
IT'S WORKING! IT'S DISSOLVING THE FLESH!
THE PROCESS WAS UNBELIEVABLY ALIEN, ALINE--BUT IT CAME IN THE END. THANK YOU FOR WATCHING OVER ME.
OH JELENE--!
WHERE'S HAROLD?
SOME-WHERE--OH, SOME-WHERE, JELENE--!

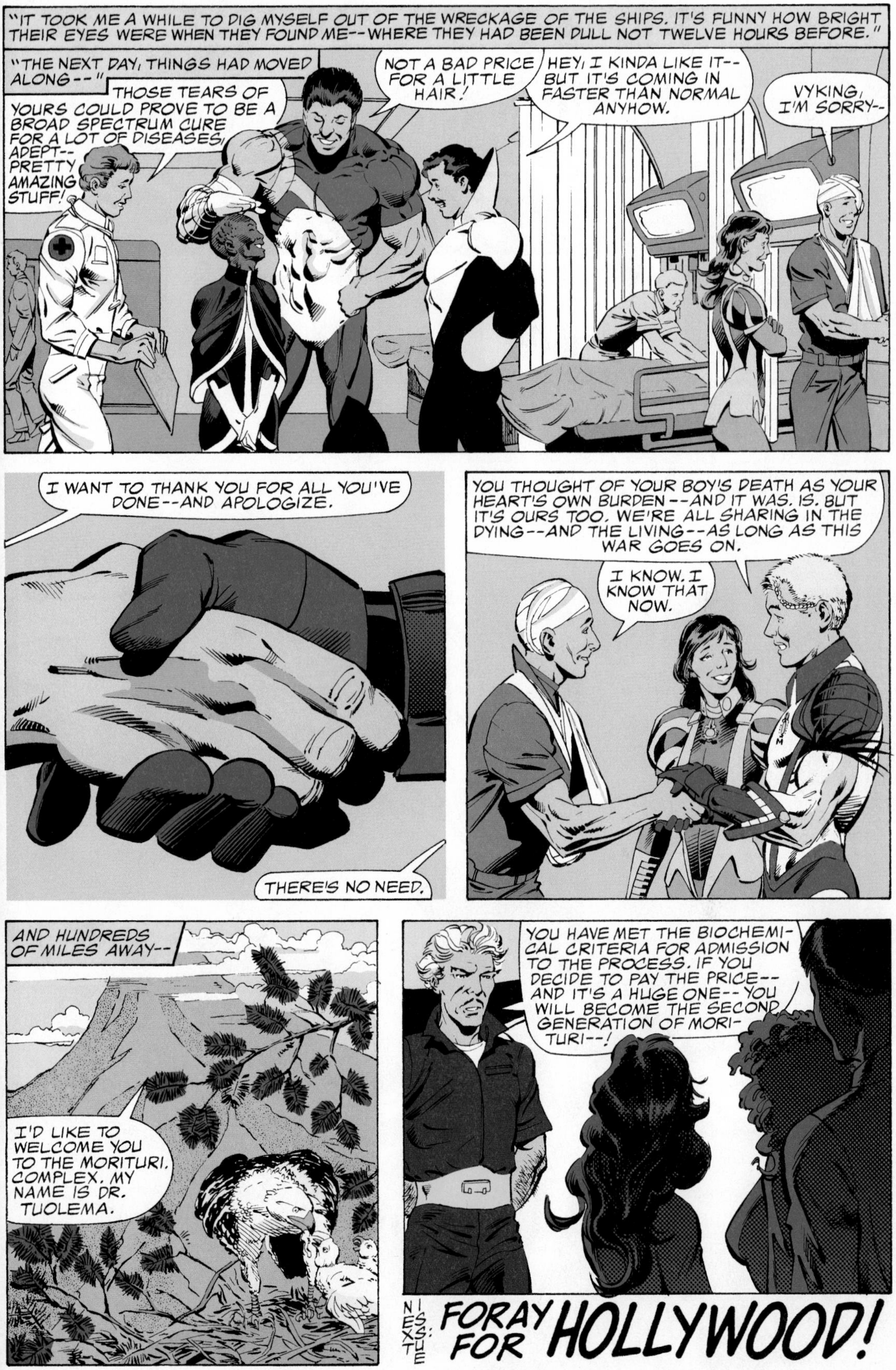

"IT TOOK ME A WHILE TO DIG MYSELF OUT OF THE WRECKAGE OF THE SHIPS. IT'S FUNNY HOW BRIGHT THEIR EYES WERE WHEN THEY FOUND ME--WHERE THEY HAD BEEN DULL NOT TWELVE HOURS BEFORE."
"THE NEXT DAY, THINGS HAD MOVED ALONG--"
THOSE TEARS OF YOURS COULD PROVE TO BE A BROAD SPECTRUM CURE FOR A LOT OF DISEASES, ADEPT--PRETTY AMAZING STUFF!
NOT A BAD PRICE FOR A LITTLE HAIR!
HEY, I KINDA LIKE IT--BUT IT'S COMING IN FASTER THAN NORMAL ANYHOW.
VYKING, I'M SORRY--
I WANT TO THANK YOU FOR ALL YOU'VE DONE--AND APOLOGIZE.
THERE'S NO NEED.
YOU THOUGHT OF YOUR BOY'S DEATH AS YOUR HEART'S OWN BURDEN--AND IT WAS. IS. BUT IT'S OURS TOO. WE'RE ALL SHARING IN THE DYING--AND THE LIVING--AS LONG AS THIS WAR GOES ON.
I KNOW. I KNOW THAT NOW.
AND HUNDREDS OF MILES AWAY--
I'D LIKE TO WELCOME YOU TO THE MORITURI COMPLEX. MY NAME IS DR. TUOLEMA.
YOU HAVE MET THE BIOCHEMICAL CRITERIA FOR ADMISSION TO THE PROCESS. IF YOU DECIDE TO PAY THE PRICE--AND IT'S A HUGE ONE--YOU WILL BECOME THE SECOND GENERATION OF MORITURI--!
NEXT ISSUE: FORAY FOR HOLLYWOOD!

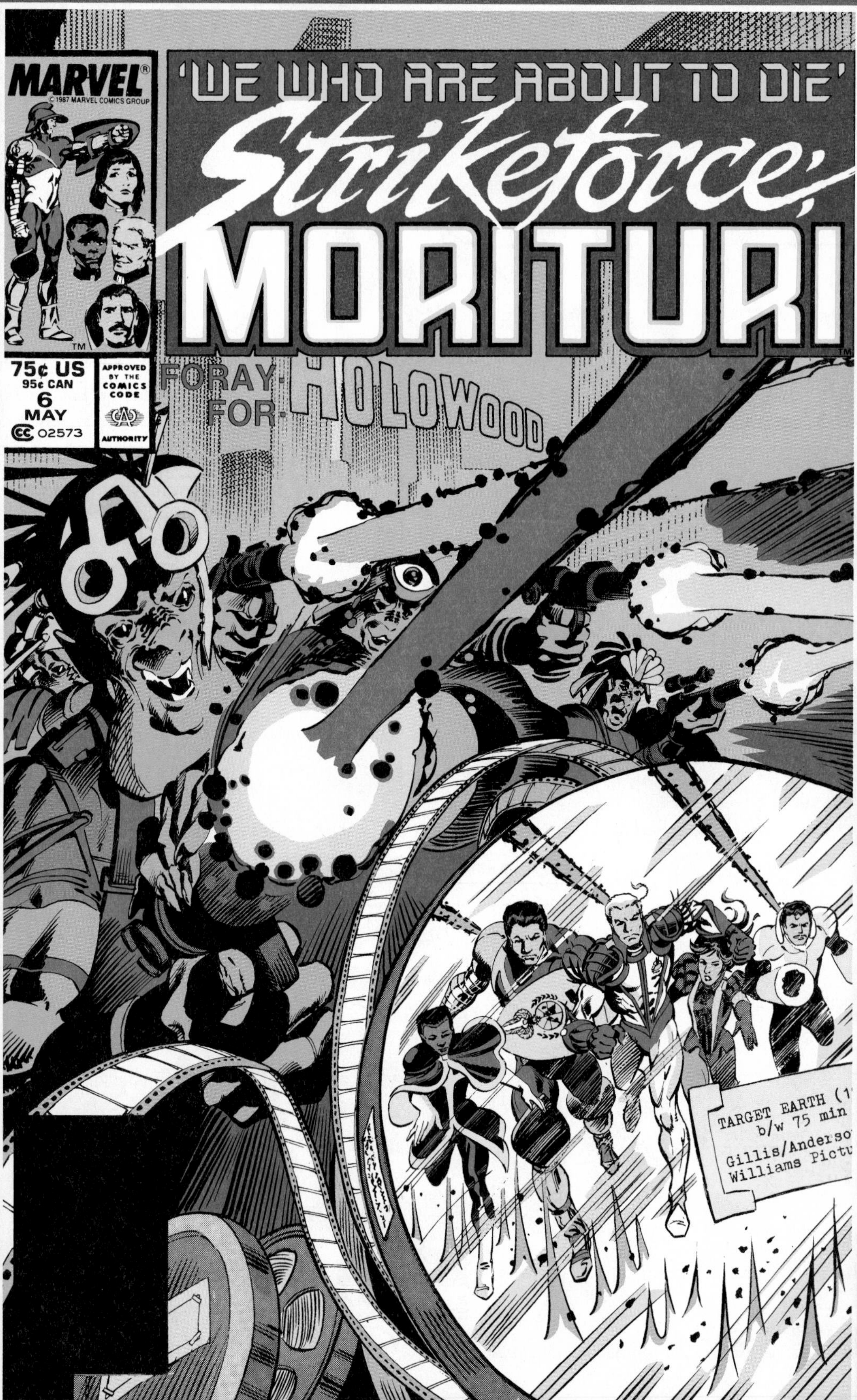

MARVEL
©1987 MARVEL COMICS GROUP
'WE WHO ARE ABOUT TO DIE'
Strikeforce:
MORITURI
75¢ US
95¢ CAN
6
MAY
02573
APPROVED BY THE COMICS CODE AUTHORITY
FORAY-FOR-HOLOWOOD
TARGET EARTH (1
b/w 75 min
Gillis/Anderso
Williams Pictu

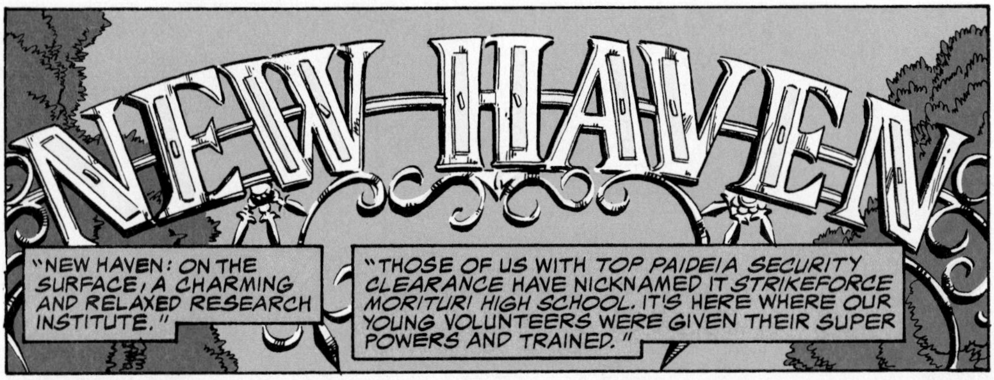
NEW HAVEN
"NEW HAVEN: ON THE SURFACE, A CHARMING AND RELAXED RESEARCH INSTITUTE."
"THOSE OF US WITH TOP PAIDEIA SECURITY CLEARANCE HAVE NICKNAMED IT STRIKEFORCE MORITURI HIGH SCHOOL. IT'S HERE WHERE OUR YOUNG VOLUNTEERS WERE GIVEN THEIR SUPER POWERS AND TRAINED."

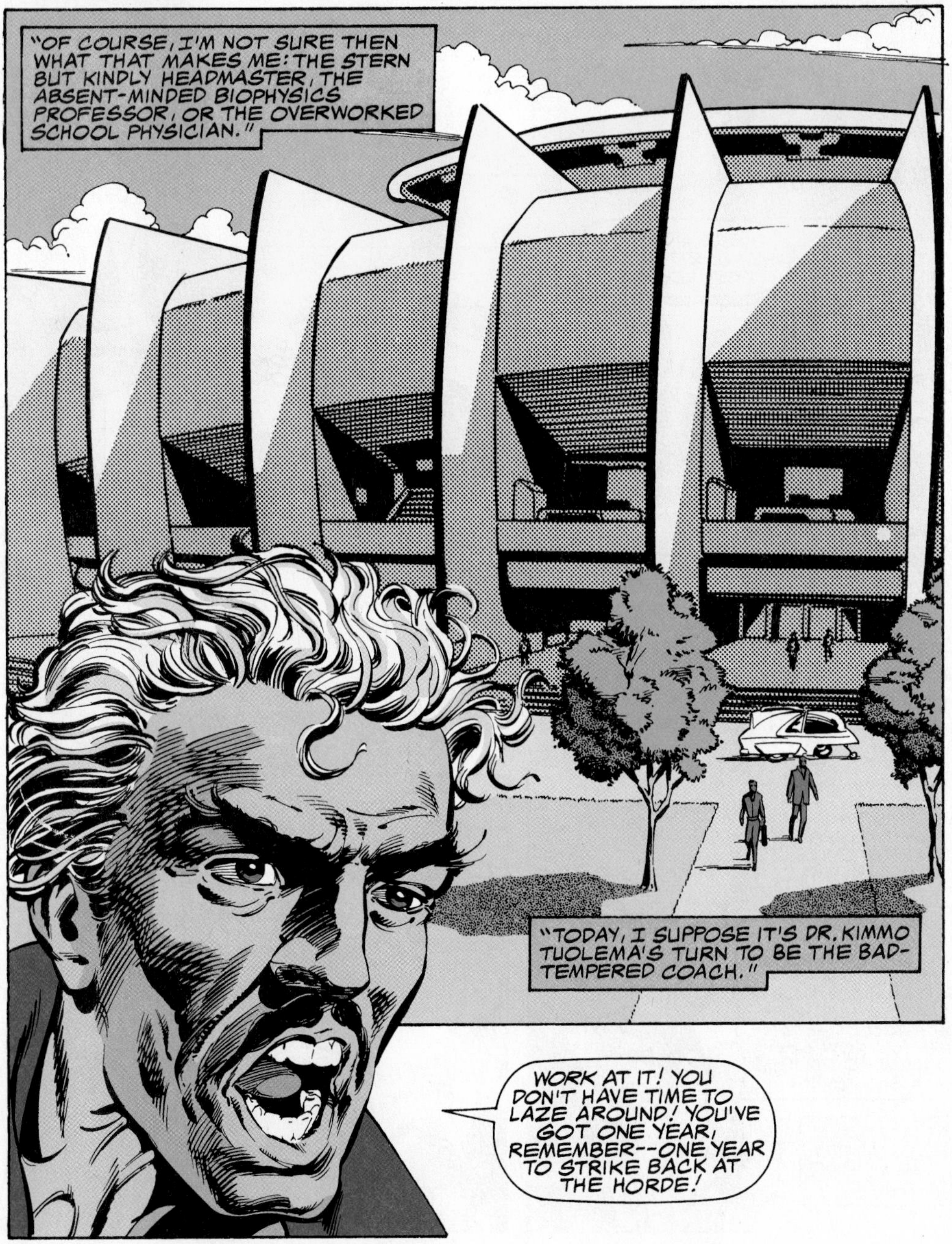
"OF COURSE, I'M NOT SURE THEN WHAT THAT MAKES ME: THE STERN BUT KINDLY HEADMASTER, THE ABSENT-MINDED BIOPHYSICS PROFESSOR, OR THE OVERWORKED SCHOOL PHYSICIAN."
"TODAY, I SUPPOSE IT'S DR. KIMMO TUOLEMA'S TURN TO BE THE BAD-TEMPERED COACH."
WORK AT IT! YOU DON'T HAVE TIME TO LAZE AROUND! YOU'VE GOT ONE YEAR, REMEMBER--ONE YEAR TO STRIKE BACK AT THE HORDE!

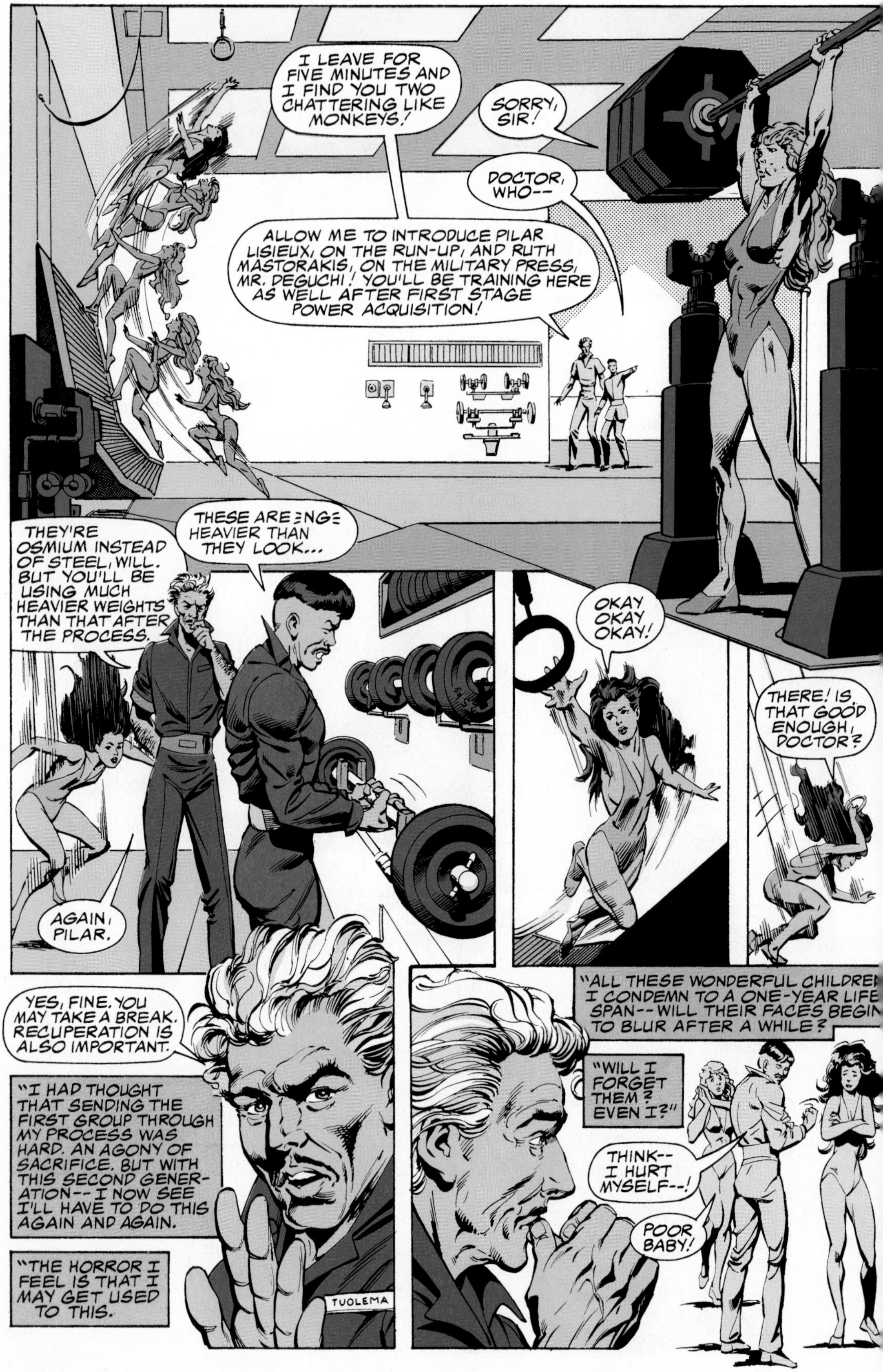
I LEAVE FOR FIVE MINUTES AND I FIND YOU TWO CHATTERING LIKE MONKEYS!
SORRY, SIR!
DOCTOR, WHO--
ALLOW ME TO INTRODUCE PILAR LISIEUX, ON THE RUN-UP, AND RUTH MASTORAKIS, ON THE MILITARY PRESS, MR. DEGUCHI! YOU'LL BE TRAINING HERE AS WELL AFTER FIRST STAGE POWER ACQUISITION!
THESE ARE NG HEAVIER THAN THEY LOOK...
THEY'RE OSMIUM INSTEAD OF STEEL, WILL. BUT YOU'LL BE USING MUCH HEAVIER WEIGHTS THAN THAT AFTER THE PROCESS.
AGAIN, PILAR.
OKAY OKAY OKAY!
THERE! IS THAT GOOD ENOUGH, DOCTOR?
YES, FINE. YOU MAY TAKE A BREAK. RECUPERATION IS ALSO IMPORTANT.
"I HAD THOUGHT THAT SENDING THE FIRST GROUP THROUGH MY PROCESS WAS HARD. AN AGONY OF SACRIFICE. BUT WITH THIS SECOND GENERATION-- I NOW SEE I'LL HAVE TO DO THIS AGAIN AND AGAIN.
"THE HORROR I FEEL IS THAT I MAY GET USED TO THIS.
TUOLEMA
"ALL THESE WONDERFUL CHILDREN I CONDEMN TO A ONE-YEAR LIFE SPAN-- WILL THEIR FACES BEGIN TO BLUR AFTER A WHILE?
"WILL I FORGET THEM? EVEN I?"
THINK-- I HURT MYSELF--!
POOR BABY!

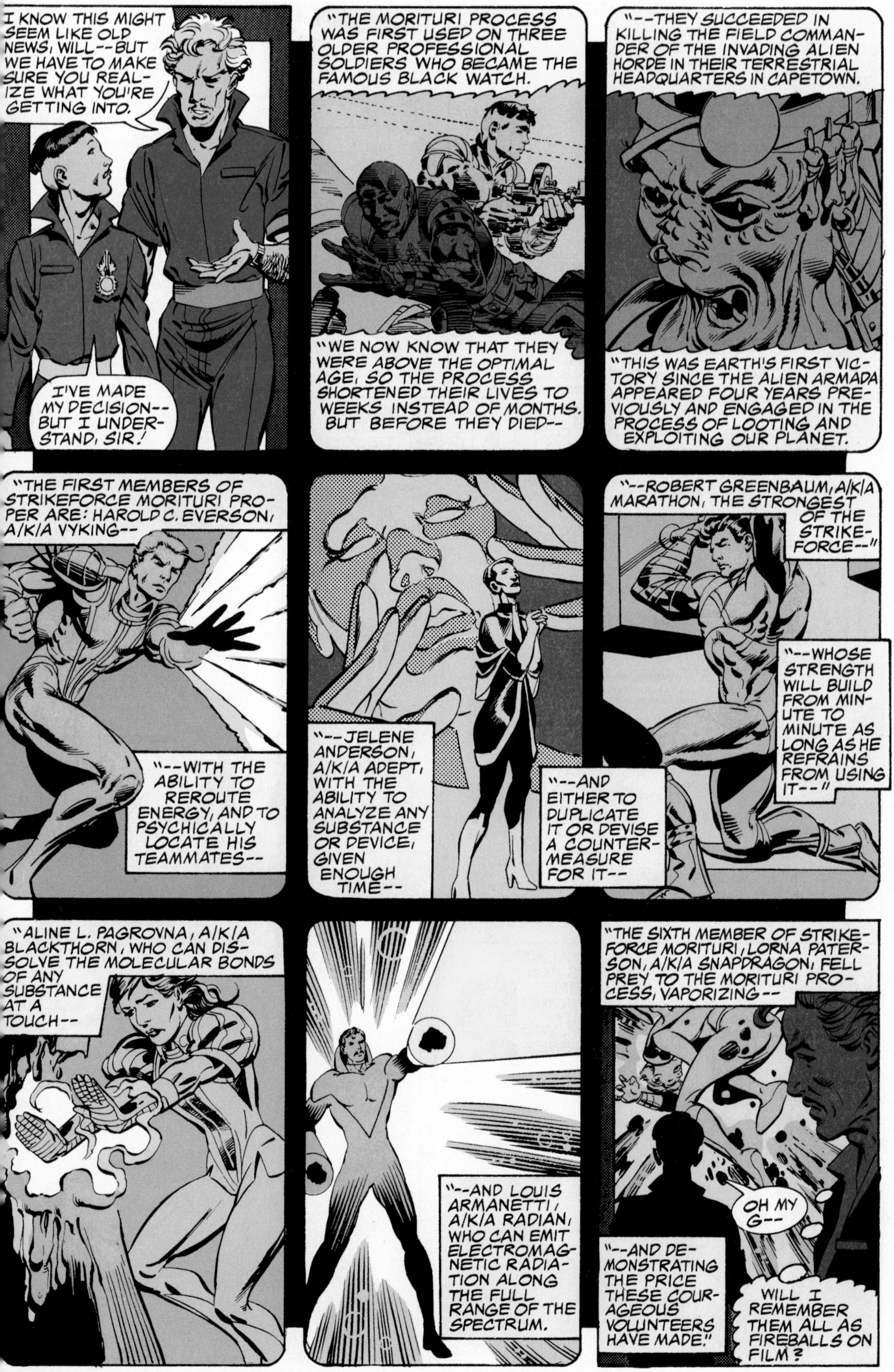
I KNOW THIS MIGHT SEEM LIKE OLD NEWS, WILL--BUT WE HAVE TO MAKE SURE YOU REALIZE WHAT YOU'RE GETTING INTO.
I'VE MADE MY DECISION--BUT I UNDERSTAND, SIR!
"THE MORITURI PROCESS WAS FIRST USED ON THREE OLDER PROFESSIONAL SOLDIERS WHO BECAME THE FAMOUS BLACK WATCH.
"WE NOW KNOW THAT THEY WERE ABOVE THE OPTIMAL AGE, SO THE PROCESS SHORTENED THEIR LIVES TO WEEKS INSTEAD OF MONTHS. BUT BEFORE THEY DIED--
"--THEY SUCCEEDED IN KILLING THE FIELD COMMANDER OF THE INVADING ALIEN HORDE IN THEIR TERRESTRIAL HEADQUARTERS IN CAPETOWN.
"THIS WAS EARTH'S FIRST VICTORY SINCE THE ALIEN ARMADA APPEARED FOUR YEARS PREVIOUSLY AND ENGAGED IN THE PROCESS OF LOOTING AND EXPLOITING OUR PLANET.
"THE FIRST MEMBERS OF STRIKEFORCE MORITURI PROPER ARE: HAROLD C. EVERSON, A/K/A VYKING--
"--WITH THE ABILITY TO REROUTE ENERGY, AND TO PSYCHICALLY LOCATE HIS TEAMMATES--
"--JELENE ANDERSON, A/K/A ADEPT, WITH THE ABILITY TO ANALYZE ANY SUBSTANCE OR DEVICE, GIVEN ENOUGH TIME--
"--AND EITHER TO DUPLICATE IT OR DEVISE A COUNTERMEASURE FOR IT--
"--ROBERT GREENBAUM, A/K/A MARATHON, THE STRONGEST OF THE STRIKEFORCE--"
"--WHOSE STRENGTH WILL BUILD FROM MINUTE TO MINUTE AS LONG AS HE REFRAINS FROM USING IT--"
"ALINE L. PAGROVNA, A/K/A BLACKTHORN, WHO CAN DISSOLVE THE MOLECULAR BONDS OF ANY SUBSTANCE AT A TOUCH--
"--AND LOUIS ARMANETTI, A/K/A RADIAN, WHO CAN EMIT ELECTROMAGNETIC RADIATION ALONG THE FULL RANGE OF THE SPECTRUM.
"THE SIXTH MEMBER OF STRIKEFORCE MORITURI, LORNA PATERSON, A/K/A SNAPDRAGON, FELL PREY TO THE MORITURI PROCESS, VAPORIZING--
OH MY G--
"--AND DEMONSTRATING THE PRICE THESE COURAGEOUS VOLUNTEERS HAVE MADE."
WILL I REMEMBER THEM ALL AS FIREBALLS ON FILM?

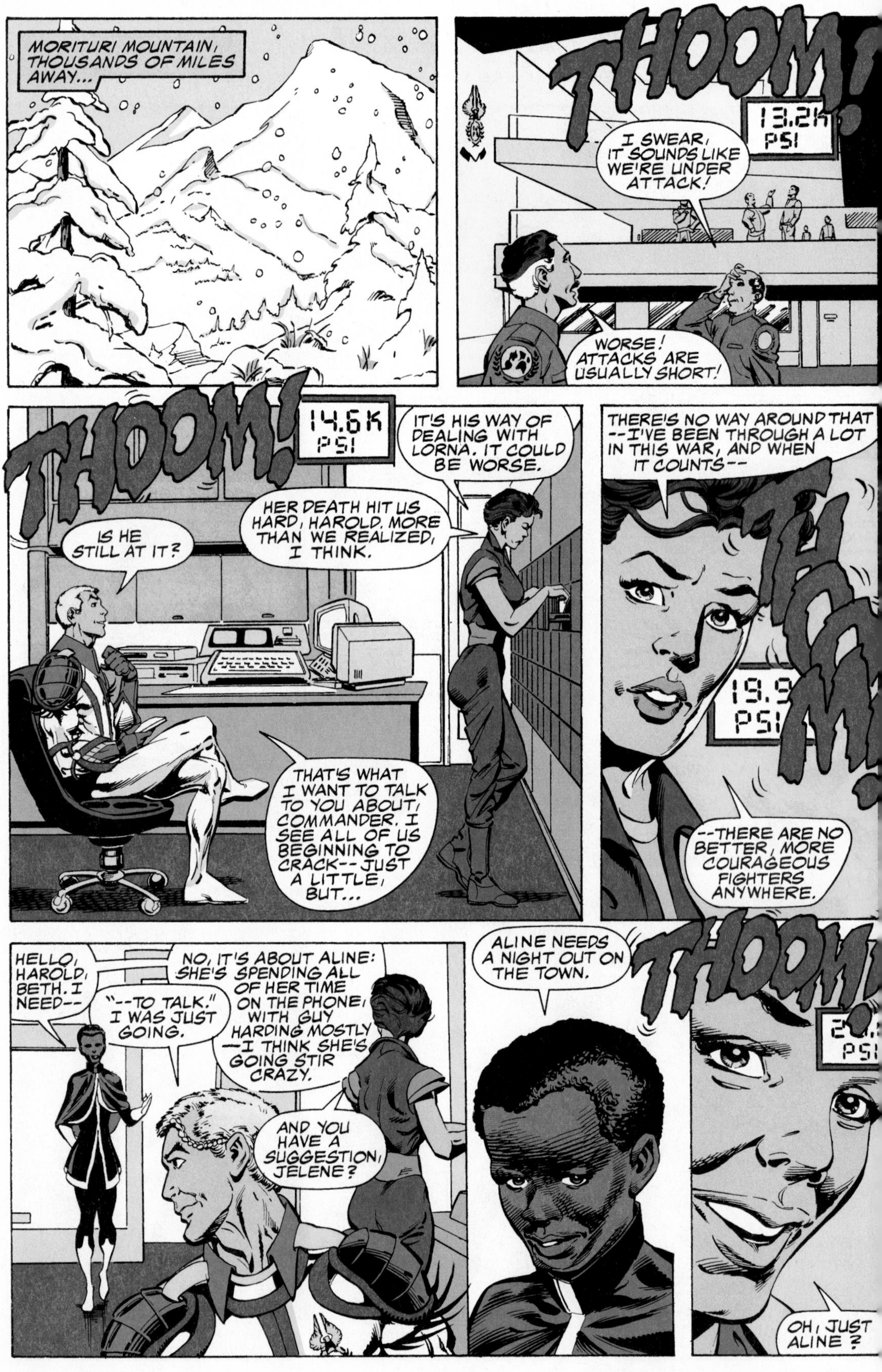
MORITURI MOUNTAIN, THOUSANDS OF MILES AWAY...
THOOM!
13.2K PSI
I SWEAR, IT SOUNDS LIKE WE'RE UNDER ATTACK!
WORSE! ATTACKS ARE USUALLY SHORT!
THOOM!
14.6K PSI
IS HE STILL AT IT?
HER DEATH HIT US HARD, HAROLD. MORE THAN WE REALIZED, I THINK.
IT'S HIS WAY OF DEALING WITH LORNA. IT COULD BE WORSE.
THAT'S WHAT I WANT TO TALK TO YOU ABOUT, COMMANDER. I SEE ALL OF US BEGINNING TO CRACK--JUST A LITTLE, BUT...
THERE'S NO WAY AROUND THAT--I'VE BEEN THROUGH A LOT IN THIS WAR, AND WHEN IT COUNTS--
19.9 PSI
--THERE ARE NO BETTER, MORE COURAGEOUS FIGHTERS ANYWHERE.
HELLO, HAROLD, BETH. I NEED--
"--TO TALK." I WAS JUST GOING.
NO, IT'S ABOUT ALINE: SHE'S SPENDING ALL OF HER TIME ON THE PHONE, WITH GUY HARDING MOSTLY--I THINK SHE'S GOING STIR CRAZY.
AND YOU HAVE A SUGGESTION, JELENE?
ALINE NEEDS A NIGHT OUT ON THE TOWN.
PSI
OH, JUST ALINE?

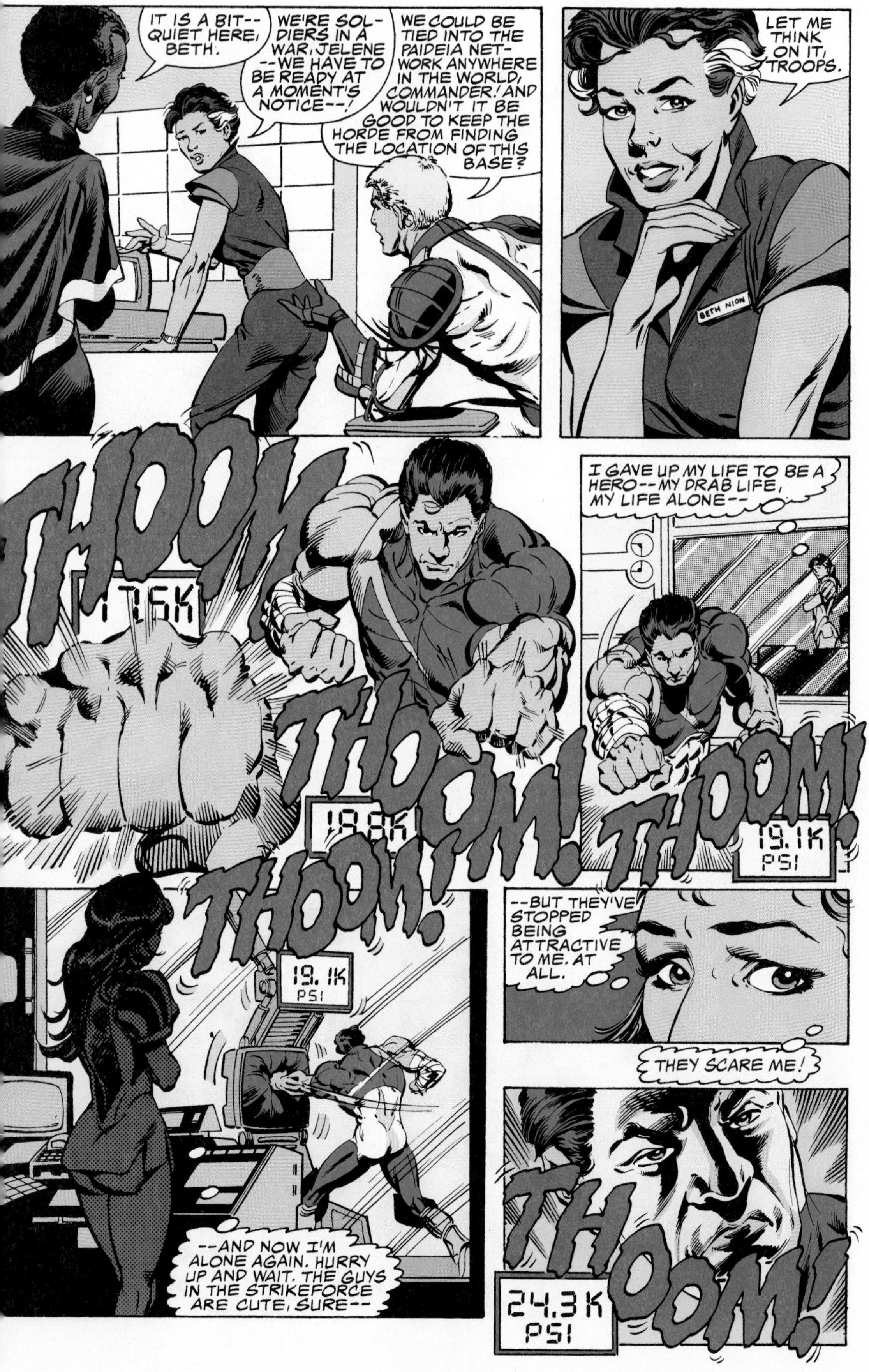

IT IS A BIT-- QUIET HERE, BETH.
WE'RE SOLDIERS IN A WAR, JELENE --WE HAVE TO BE READY AT A MOMENT'S NOTICE--!
WE COULD BE TIED INTO THE PAIDEIA NETWORK ANYWHERE IN THE WORLD, COMMANDER! AND WOULDN'T IT BE GOOD TO KEEP THE HORDE FROM FINDING THE LOCATION OF THIS BASE?
LET ME THINK ON IT, TROOPS.
BETH NION
THOOM
17.5K
I GAVE UP MY LIFE TO BE A HERO--MY DRAB LIFE, MY LIFE ALONE--
THOOM!
19.8K
THOOM!
THOOM!
19.1K PSI
19.1K PSI
--BUT THEY'VE STOPPED BEING ATTRACTIVE TO ME. AT ALL.
THEY SCARE ME!
--AND NOW I'M ALONE AGAIN. HURRY UP AND WAIT. THE GUYS IN THE STRIKEFORCE ARE CUTE, SURE--
THOOM!
24.3K PSI

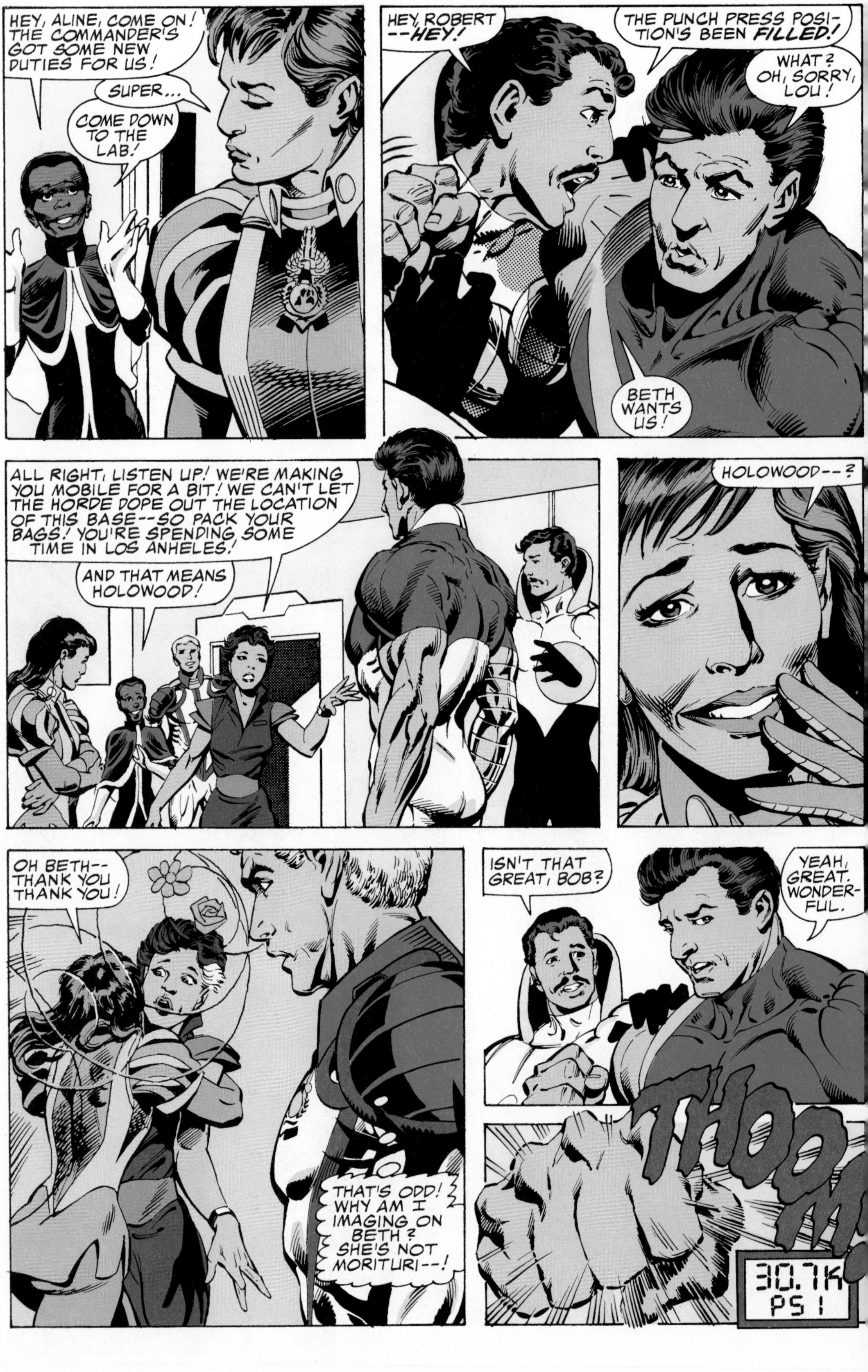
HEY, ALINE, COME ON! THE COMMANDER'S GOT SOME NEW DUTIES FOR US!
SUPER...
COME DOWN TO THE LAB!
HEY, ROBERT --HEY!
THE PUNCH PRESS POSITION'S BEEN FILLED!
WHAT? OH, SORRY, LOU!
BETH WANTS US!
ALL RIGHT, LISTEN UP! WE'RE MAKING YOU MOBILE FOR A BIT! WE CAN'T LET THE HORDE DOPE OUT THE LOCATION OF THIS BASE--SO PACK YOUR BAGS! YOU'RE SPENDING SOME TIME IN LOS ANHELES!
AND THAT MEANS HOLOWOOD!
HOLOWOOD--?
OH BETH-- THANK YOU THANK YOU!
THAT'S ODD! WHY AM I IMAGING ON BETH? SHE'S NOT MORITURI--!
ISN'T THAT GREAT, BOB?
YEAH, GREAT. WONDERFUL.
THOOM
30.7K PSI

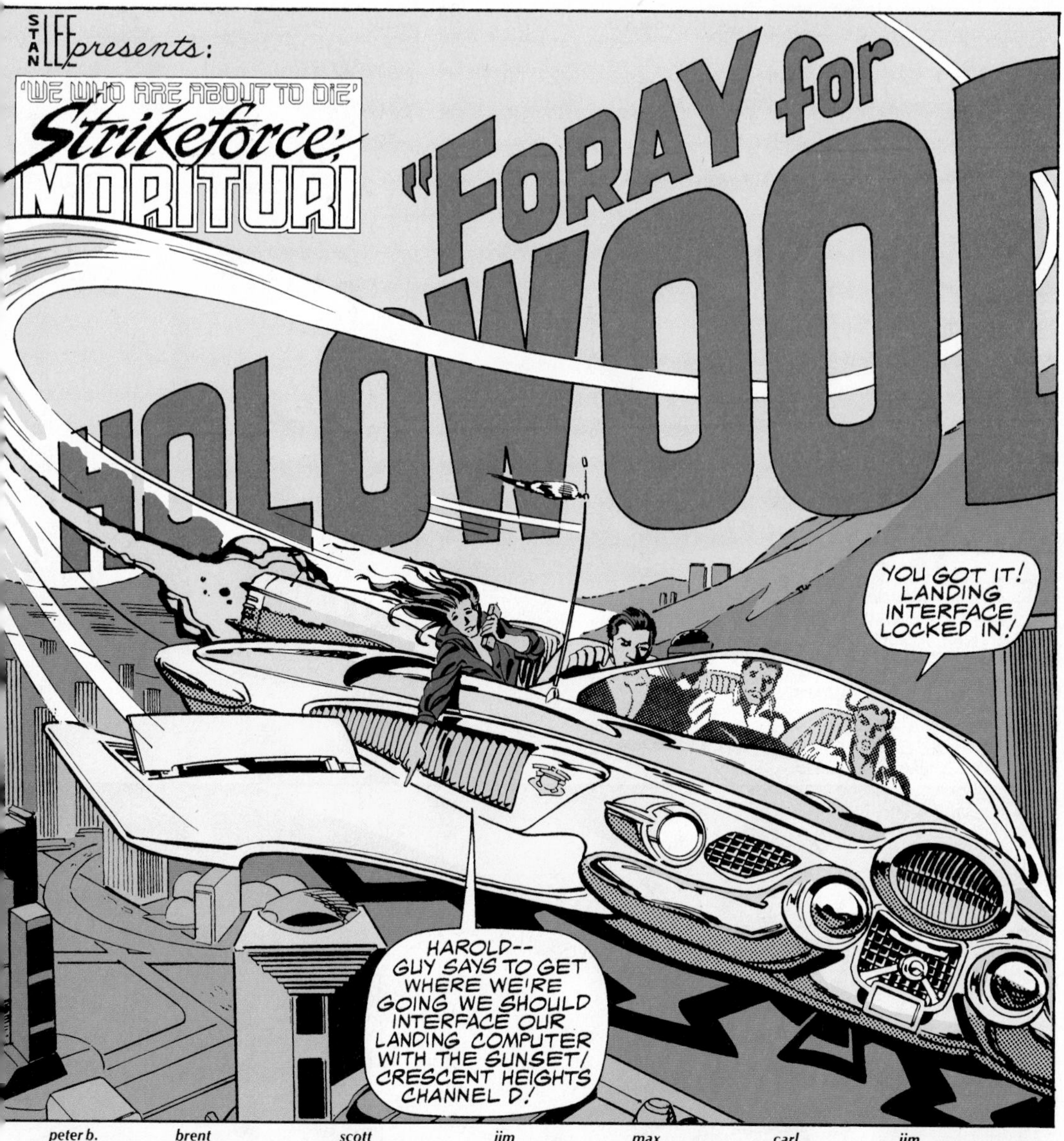
STAN LEE presents:
'WE WHO ARE ABOUT TO DIE'
Strikeforce: MORITURI
"FORAY for
HOLOWOOD
YOU GOT IT! LANDING INTERFACE LOCKED IN!
HAROLD-- GUY SAYS TO GET WHERE WE'RE GOING WE SHOULD INTERFACE OUR LANDING COMPUTER WITH THE SUNSET/ CRESCENT HEIGHTS CHANNEL D!

peter b.	brent	scott	jim	max	carl	jim
GILLIS	**ANDERSON**	**WILLIAMS**	**NOVAK**	**SCHEELE**	**POTTS**	**SHOOTER**
WRITER	PENCILER	INKER	LETTERER	COLORER	EDITOR	EDITOR IN CHIEF

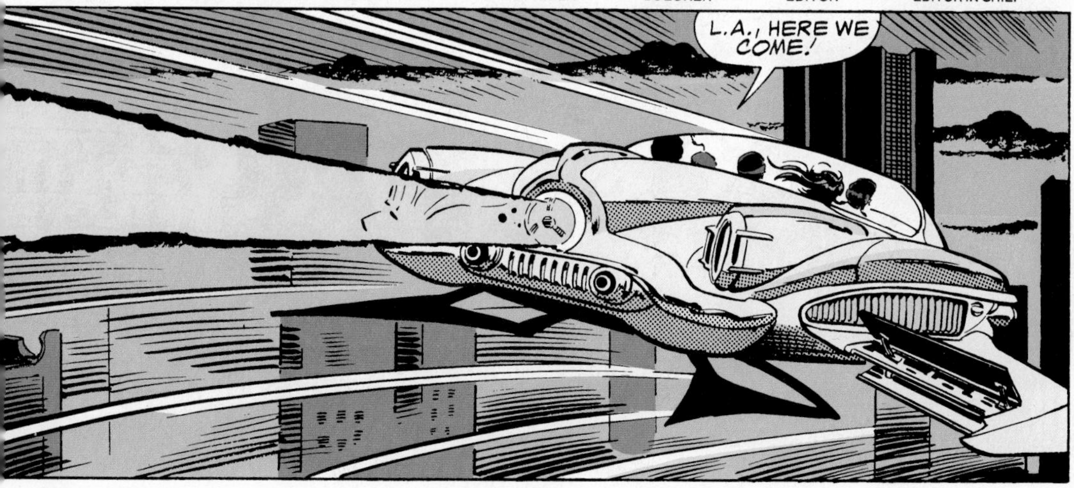
L.A., HERE WE COME!

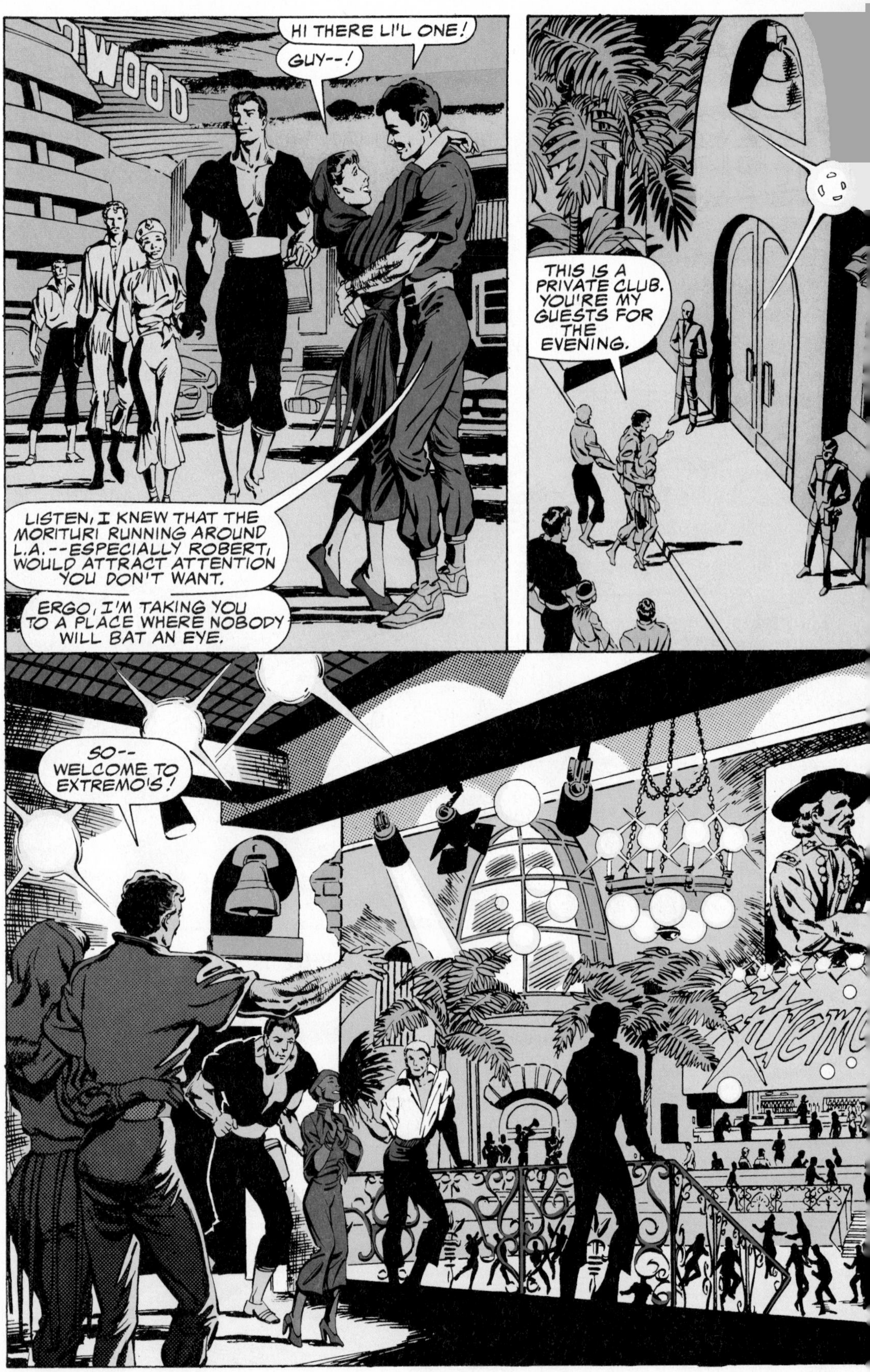
HI THERE LI'L ONE!
GUY--!
LISTEN, I KNEW THAT THE MORITURI RUNNING AROUND L.A.--ESPECIALLY ROBERT, WOULD ATTRACT ATTENTION YOU DON'T WANT.
ERGO, I'M TAKING YOU TO A PLACE WHERE NOBODY WILL BAT AN EYE.
THIS IS A PRIVATE CLUB. YOU'RE MY GUESTS FOR THE EVENING.
SO-- WELCOME TO EXTREMO'S!

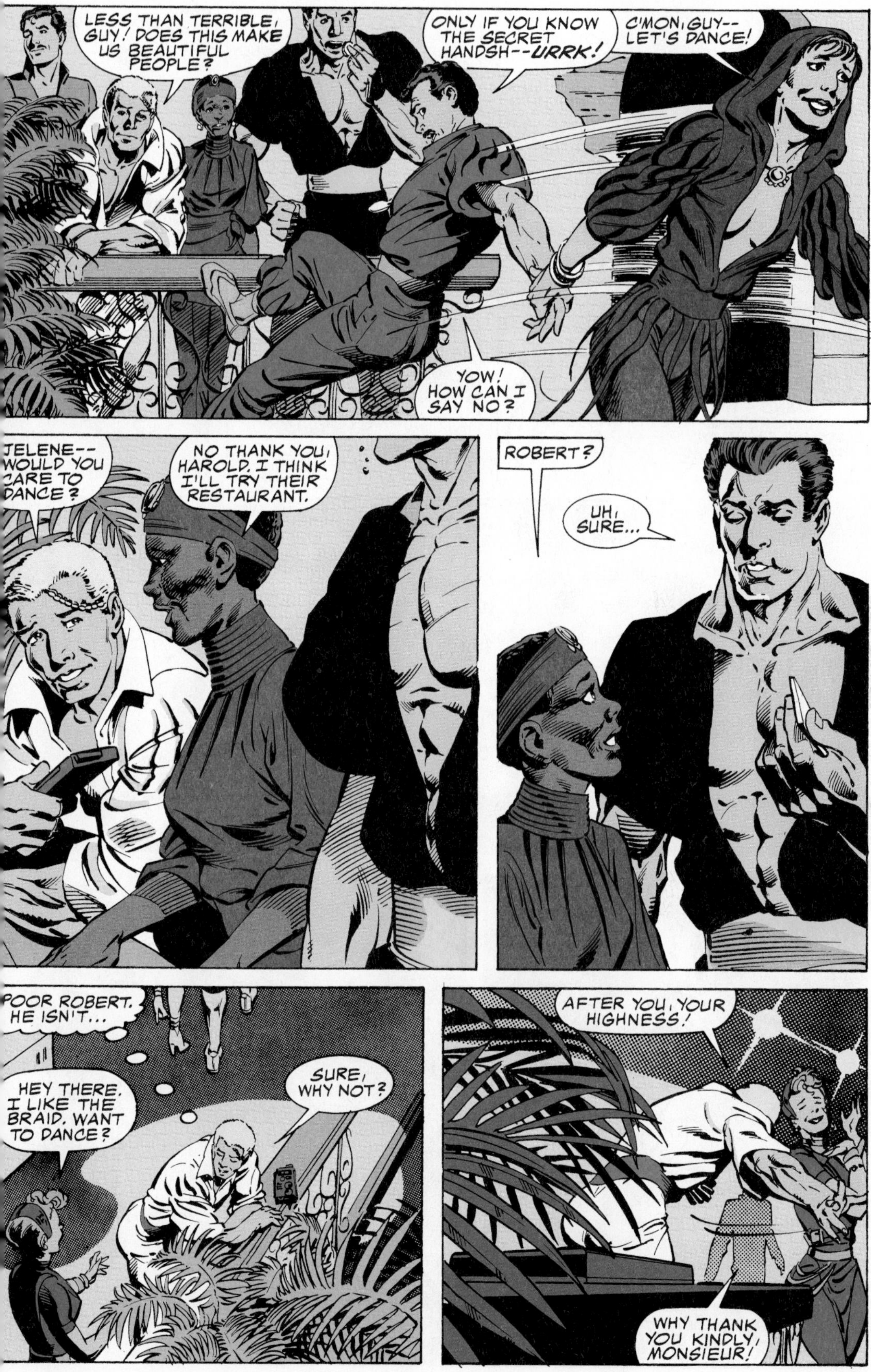
LESS THAN TERRIBLE, GUY! DOES THIS MAKE US BEAUTIFUL PEOPLE?
ONLY IF YOU KNOW THE SECRET HANDSH--URRK!
C'MON, GUY-- LET'S DANCE!
YOW! HOW CAN I SAY NO?
JELENE-- WOULD YOU CARE TO DANCE?
NO THANK YOU, HAROLD. I THINK I'LL TRY THEIR RESTAURANT.
ROBERT?
UH, SURE...
POOR ROBERT. HE ISN'T...
HEY THERE. I LIKE THE BRAID. WANT TO DANCE?
SURE, WHY NOT?
AFTER YOU, YOUR HIGHNESS!
WHY THANK YOU KINDLY, MONSIEUR!

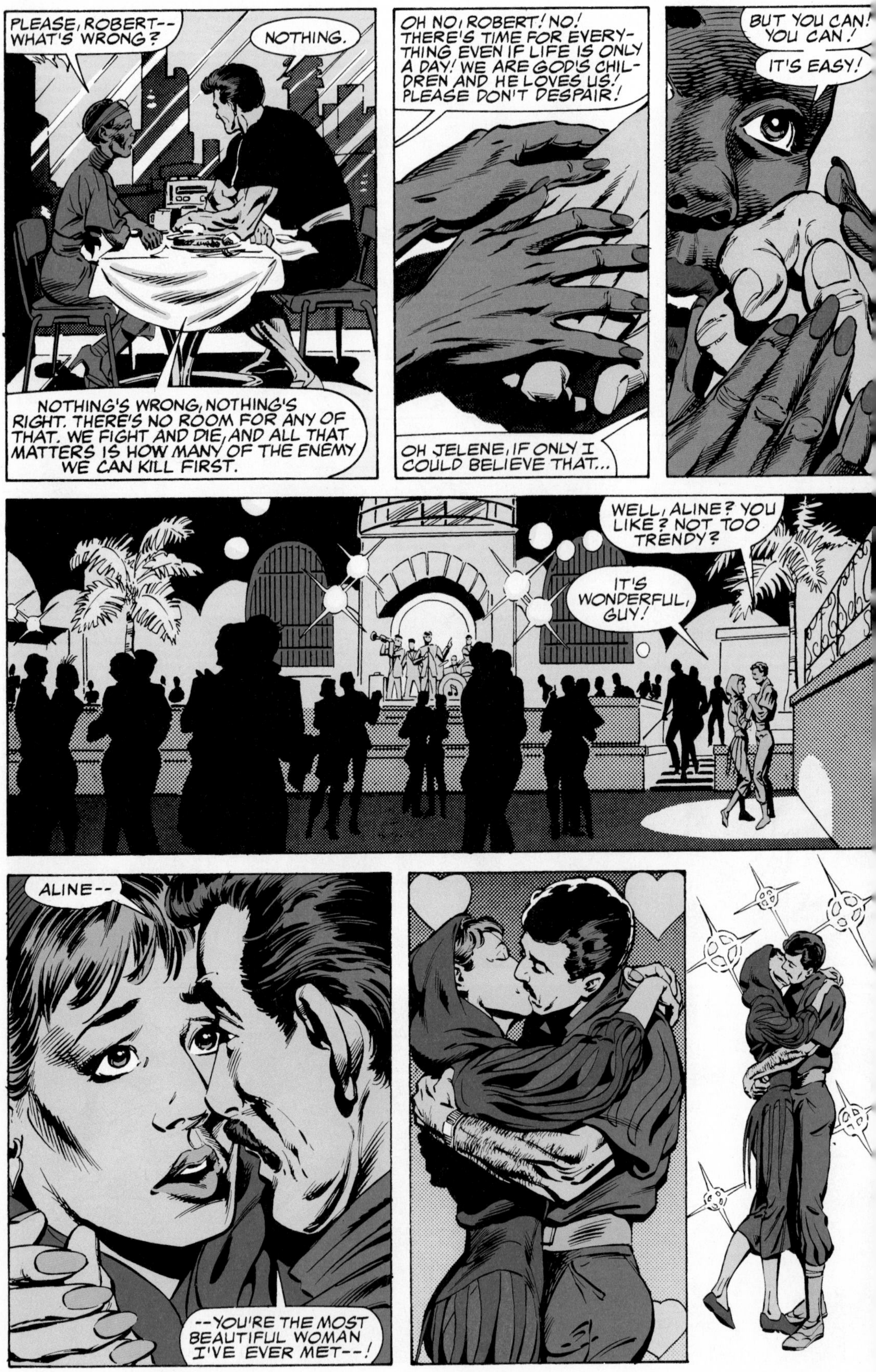
PLEASE, ROBERT-- WHAT'S WRONG?
NOTHING.
NOTHING'S WRONG, NOTHING'S RIGHT. THERE'S NO ROOM FOR ANY OF THAT. WE FIGHT AND DIE, AND ALL THAT MATTERS IS HOW MANY OF THE ENEMY WE CAN KILL FIRST.
OH NO, ROBERT! NO! THERE'S TIME FOR EVERYTHING EVEN IF LIFE IS ONLY A DAY! WE ARE GOD'S CHILDREN AND HE LOVES US! PLEASE DON'T DESPAIR!
OH JELENE, IF ONLY I COULD BELIEVE THAT...
BUT YOU CAN! YOU CAN!
IT'S EASY!
WELL, ALINE? YOU LIKE? NOT TOO TRENDY?
IT'S WONDERFUL, GUY!
ALINE--
--YOU'RE THE MOST BEAUTIFUL WOMAN I'VE EVER MET--!

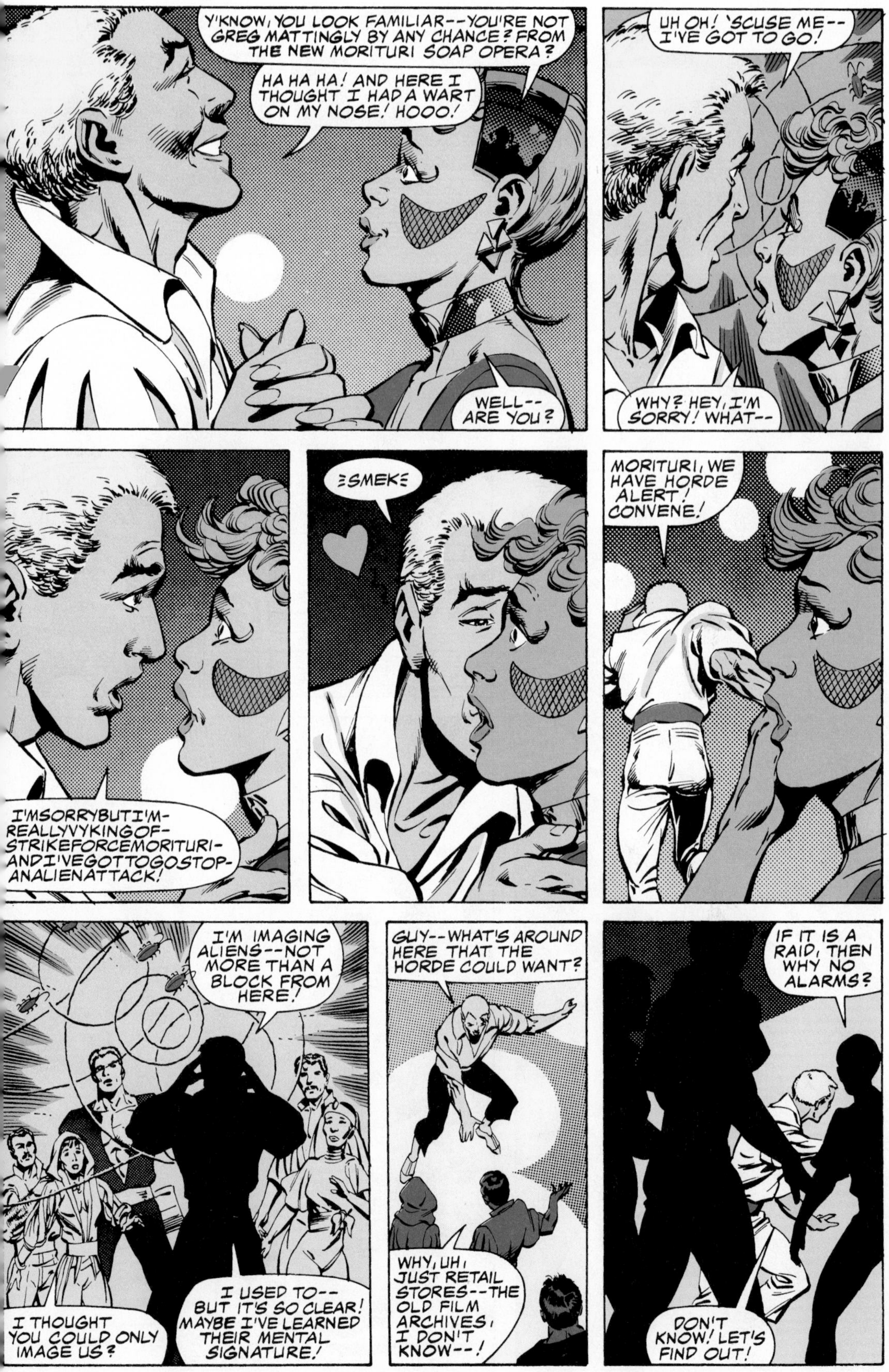
Y'KNOW, YOU LOOK FAMILIAR--YOU'RE NOT GREG MATTINGLY BY ANY CHANCE? FROM THE NEW MORITURI SOAP OPERA?
HA HA HA! AND HERE I THOUGHT I HAD A WART ON MY NOSE! HOOO!
WELL-- ARE YOU?
UH OH! 'SCUSE ME-- I'VE GOT TO GO!
WHY? HEY, I'M SORRY! WHAT--
I'MSORRYBUTI'M-REALLYVYKINGOF-STRIKEFORCEMORITURI-ANDI'VEGOTTOGOSTOP-ANALIENATTACK!
SMEK
MORITURI, WE HAVE HORDE ALERT! CONVENE!
I'M IMAGING ALIENS--NOT MORE THAN A BLOCK FROM HERE!
I THOUGHT YOU COULD ONLY IMAGE US?
I USED TO-- BUT IT'S SO CLEAR! MAYBE I'VE LEARNED THEIR MENTAL SIGNATURE!
GUY--WHAT'S AROUND HERE THAT THE HORDE COULD WANT?
WHY, UH, JUST RETAIL STORES--THE OLD FILM ARCHIVES, I DON'T KNOW--!
IF IT IS A RAID, THEN WHY NO ALARMS?
DON'T KNOW! LET'S FIND OUT!

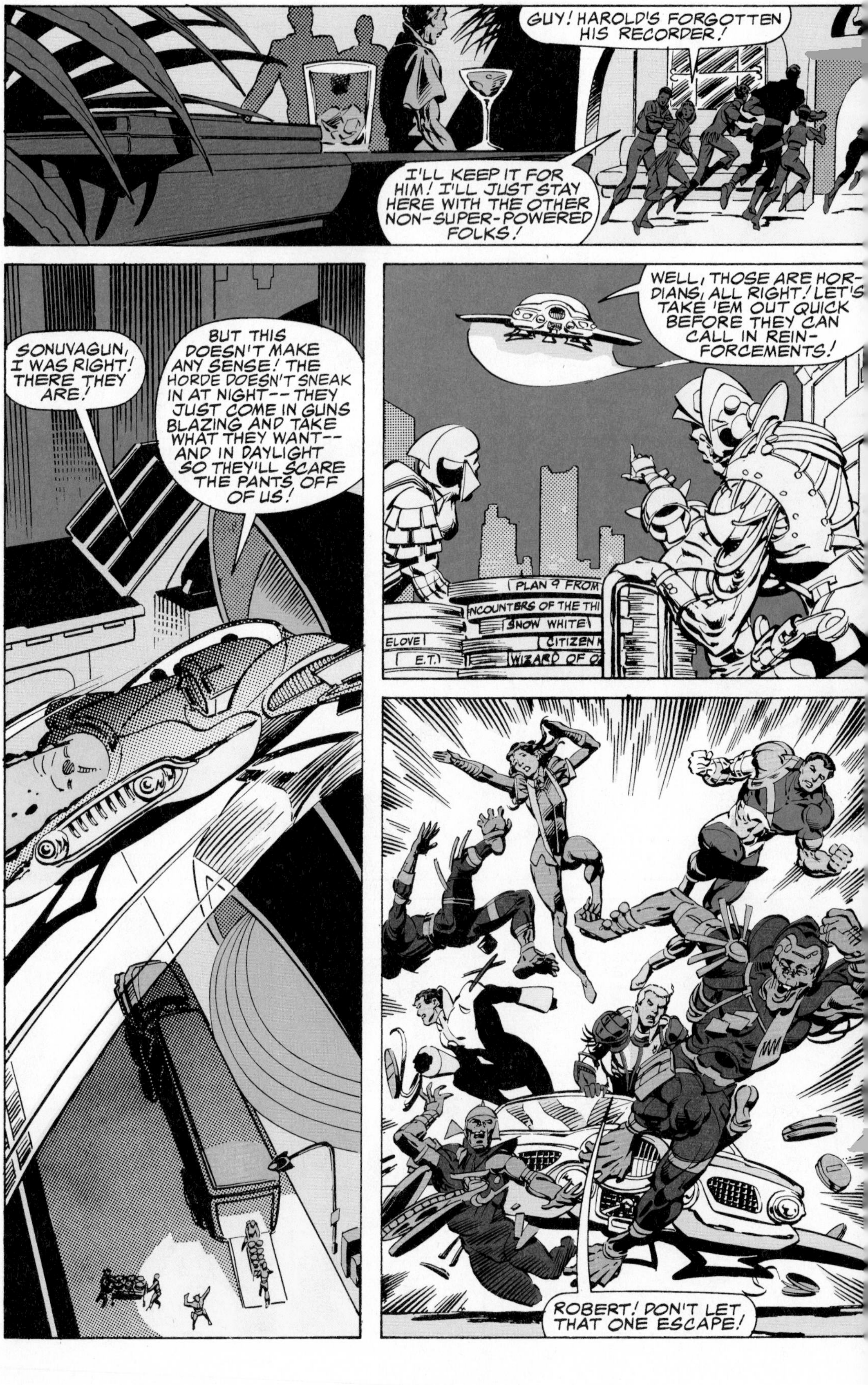
GUY! HAROLD'S FORGOTTEN HIS RECORDER!
I'LL KEEP IT FOR HIM! I'LL JUST STAY HERE WITH THE OTHER NON-SUPER-POWERED FOLKS!
SONUVAGUN, I WAS RIGHT! THERE THEY ARE!
BUT THIS DOESN'T MAKE ANY SENSE! THE HORDE DOESN'T SNEAK IN AT NIGHT-- THEY JUST COME IN GUNS BLAZING AND TAKE WHAT THEY WANT-- AND IN DAYLIGHT SO THEY'LL SCARE THE PANTS OFF OF US!
WELL, THOSE ARE HORDIANS, ALL RIGHT! LET'S TAKE 'EM OUT QUICK BEFORE THEY CAN CALL IN REIN-FORCEMENTS!
PLAN 9 FROM
SNOW WHITE
CITIZEN
E.T.
ROBERT! DON'T LET THAT ONE ESCAPE!

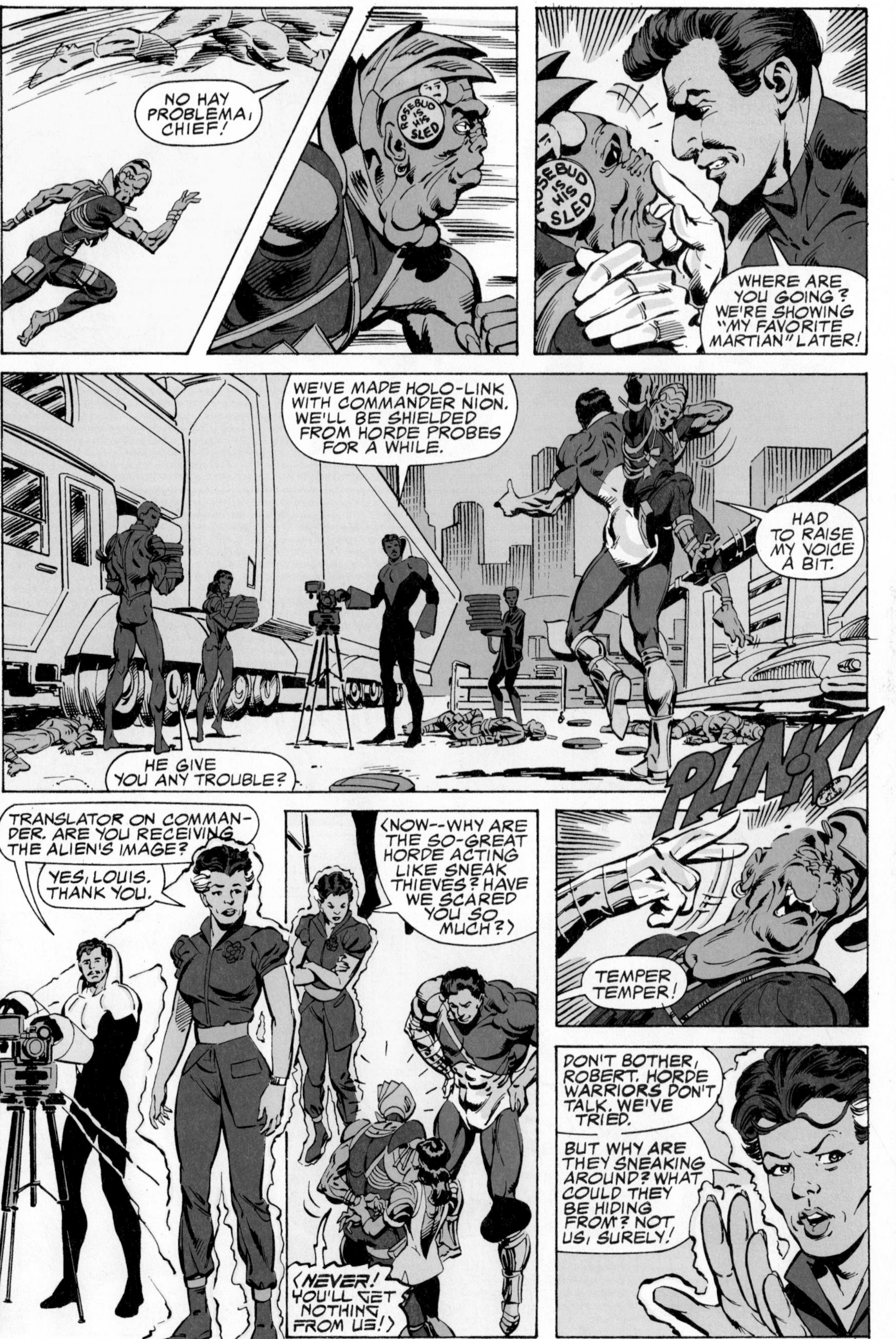
NO HAY PROBLEMA, CHIEF!
ROSEBUD IS HIS SLED
ROSEBUD IS HIS SLED
WHERE ARE YOU GOING? WE'RE SHOWING "MY FAVORITE MARTIAN" LATER!
WE'VE MADE HOLO-LINK WITH COMMANDER NION. WE'LL BE SHIELDED FROM HORDE PROBES FOR A WHILE.
HAD TO RAISE MY VOICE A BIT.
HE GIVE YOU ANY TROUBLE?
PLINK!
TRANSLATOR ON COMMANDER. ARE YOU RECEIVING THE ALIEN'S IMAGE?
YES, LOUIS. THANK YOU.
<NOW--WHY ARE THE SO-GREAT HORDE ACTING LIKE SNEAK THIEVES? HAVE WE SCARED YOU SO MUCH?>
<NEVER! YOU'LL GET NOTHING FROM US!>
TEMPER TEMPER!
DON'T BOTHER, ROBERT. HORDE WARRIORS DON'T TALK. WE'VE TRIED.
BUT WHY ARE THEY SNEAKING AROUND? WHAT COULD THEY BE HIDING FROM? NOT US, SURELY!

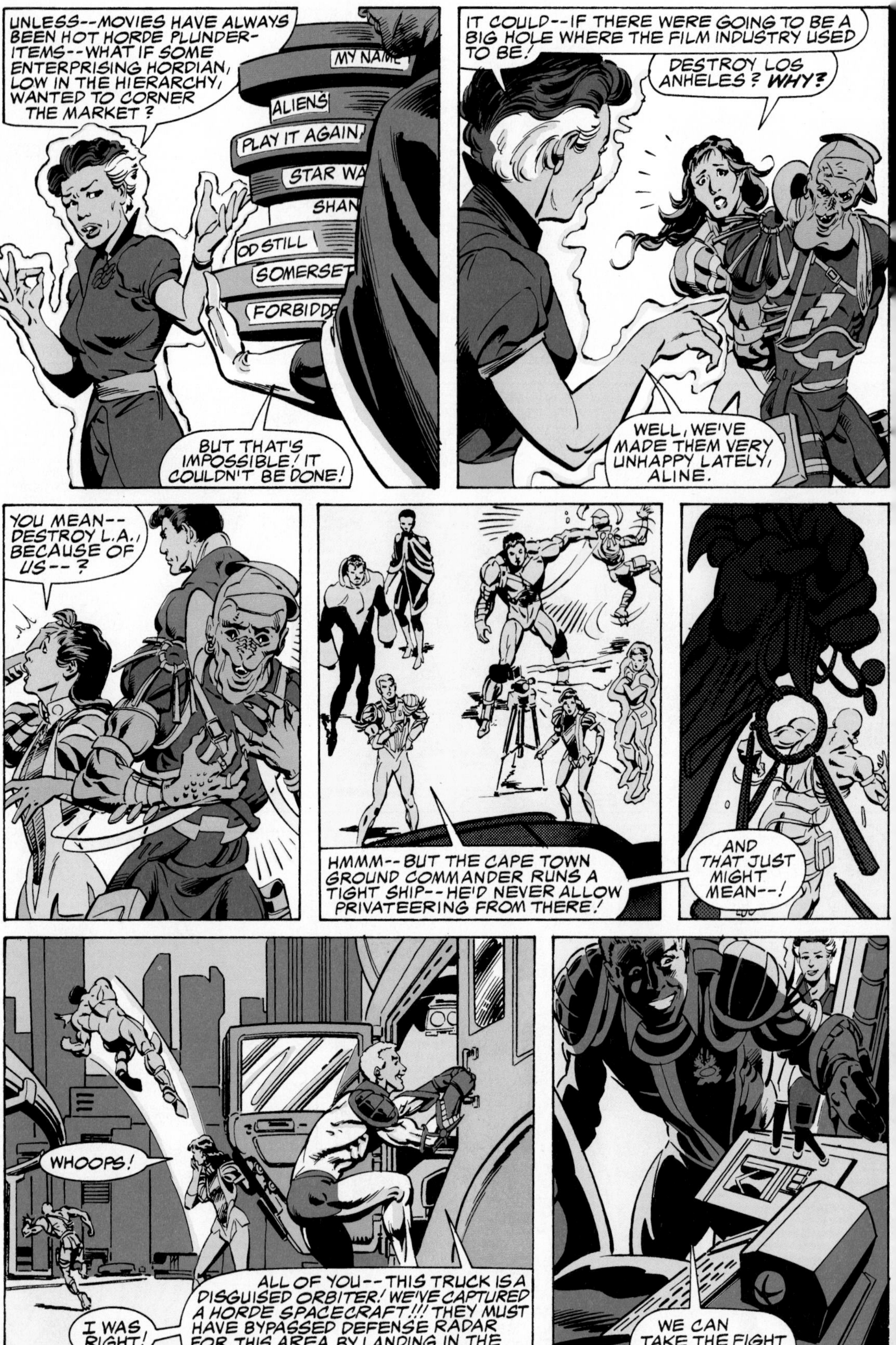
UNLESS--MOVIES HAVE ALWAYS BEEN HOT HORDE PLUNDER-ITEMS--WHAT IF SOME ENTERPRISING HORDIAN, LOW IN THE HIERARCHY, WANTED TO CORNER THE MARKET?
MY NAME
ALIENS
PLAY IT AGAIN
STAR WA
SHAN
OD STILL
SOMERSET
FORBIDDE
BUT THAT'S IMPOSSIBLE! IT COULDN'T BE DONE!
IT COULD--IF THERE WERE GOING TO BE A BIG HOLE WHERE THE FILM INDUSTRY USED TO BE!
DESTROY LOS ANHELES? WHY?
WELL, WE'VE MADE THEM VERY UNHAPPY LATELY, ALINE.
YOU MEAN--DESTROY L.A., BECAUSE OF US--?
HMMM--BUT THE CAPE TOWN GROUND COMMANDER RUNS A TIGHT SHIP--HE'D NEVER ALLOW PRIVATEERING FROM THERE!
AND THAT JUST MIGHT MEAN--!
WHOOPS!
I WAS RIGHT!
ALL OF YOU--THIS TRUCK IS A DISGUISED ORBITER! WE'VE CAPTURED A HORDE SPACECRAFT!!! THEY MUST HAVE BYPASSED DEFENSE RADAR FOR THIS AREA BY LANDING IN THE DESERT AND JUST DRIVING IN!
WE CAN TAKE THE FIGHT TO THEM!

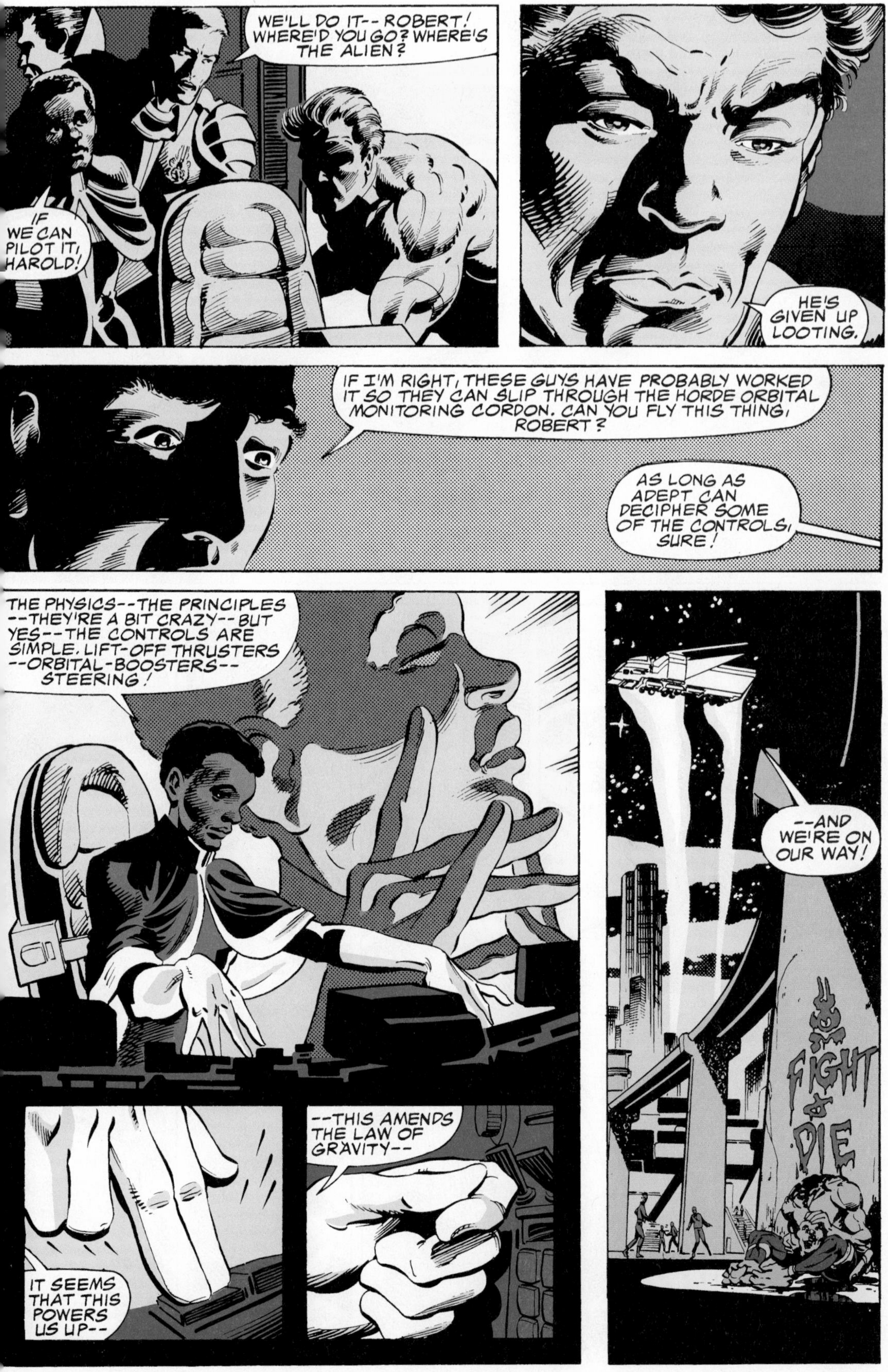
WE'LL DO IT-- ROBERT! WHERE'D YOU GO? WHERE'S THE ALIEN?
IF WE CAN PILOT IT, HAROLD!
HE'S GIVEN UP LOOTING.
IF I'M RIGHT, THESE GUYS HAVE PROBABLY WORKED IT SO THEY CAN SLIP THROUGH THE HORDE ORBITAL MONITORING CORDON. CAN YOU FLY THIS THING, ROBERT?
AS LONG AS ADEPT CAN DECIPHER SOME OF THE CONTROLS, SURE!
THE PHYSICS--THE PRINCIPLES --THEY'RE A BIT CRAZY--BUT YES--THE CONTROLS ARE SIMPLE. LIFT-OFF THRUSTERS --ORBITAL-BOOSTERS-- STEERING!
IT SEEMS THAT THIS POWERS US UP--
--THIS AMENDS THE LAW OF GRAVITY--
--AND WE'RE ON OUR WAY!
FIGHT & DIE

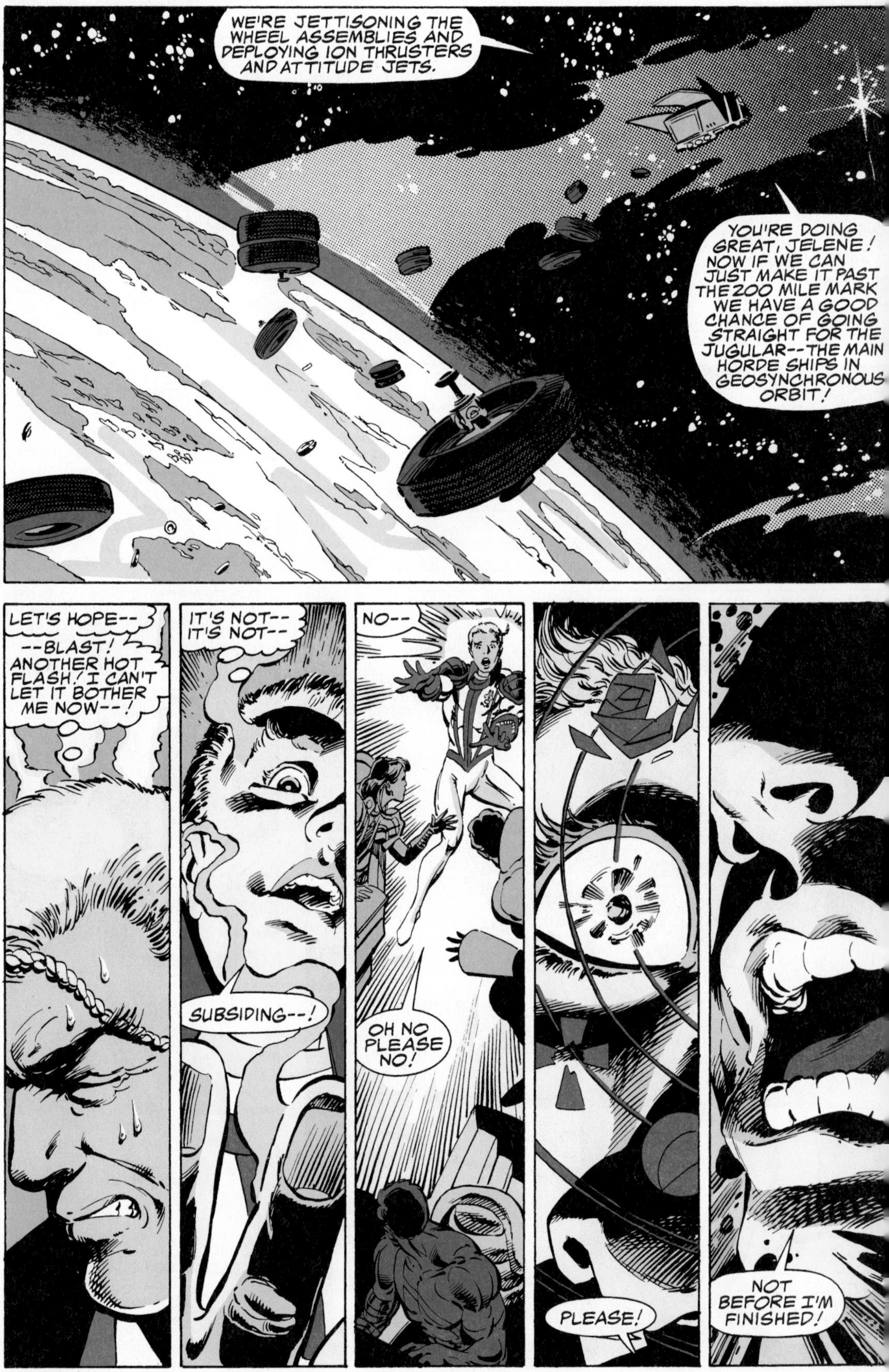
WE'RE JETTISONING THE WHEEL ASSEMBLIES AND DEPLOYING ION THRUSTERS AND ATTITUDE JETS.
YOU'RE DOING GREAT, JELENE! NOW IF WE CAN JUST MAKE IT PAST THE 200 MILE MARK WE HAVE A GOOD CHANCE OF GOING STRAIGHT FOR THE JUGULAR--THE MAIN HORDE SHIPS IN GEOSYNCHRONOUS ORBIT!
LET'S HOPE--
--BLAST! ANOTHER HOT FLASH! I CAN'T LET IT BOTHER ME NOW--!
IT'S NOT-- IT'S NOT--
SUBSIDING--!
NO--
OH NO PLEASE NO!
PLEASE!
NOT BEFORE I'M FINISHED!

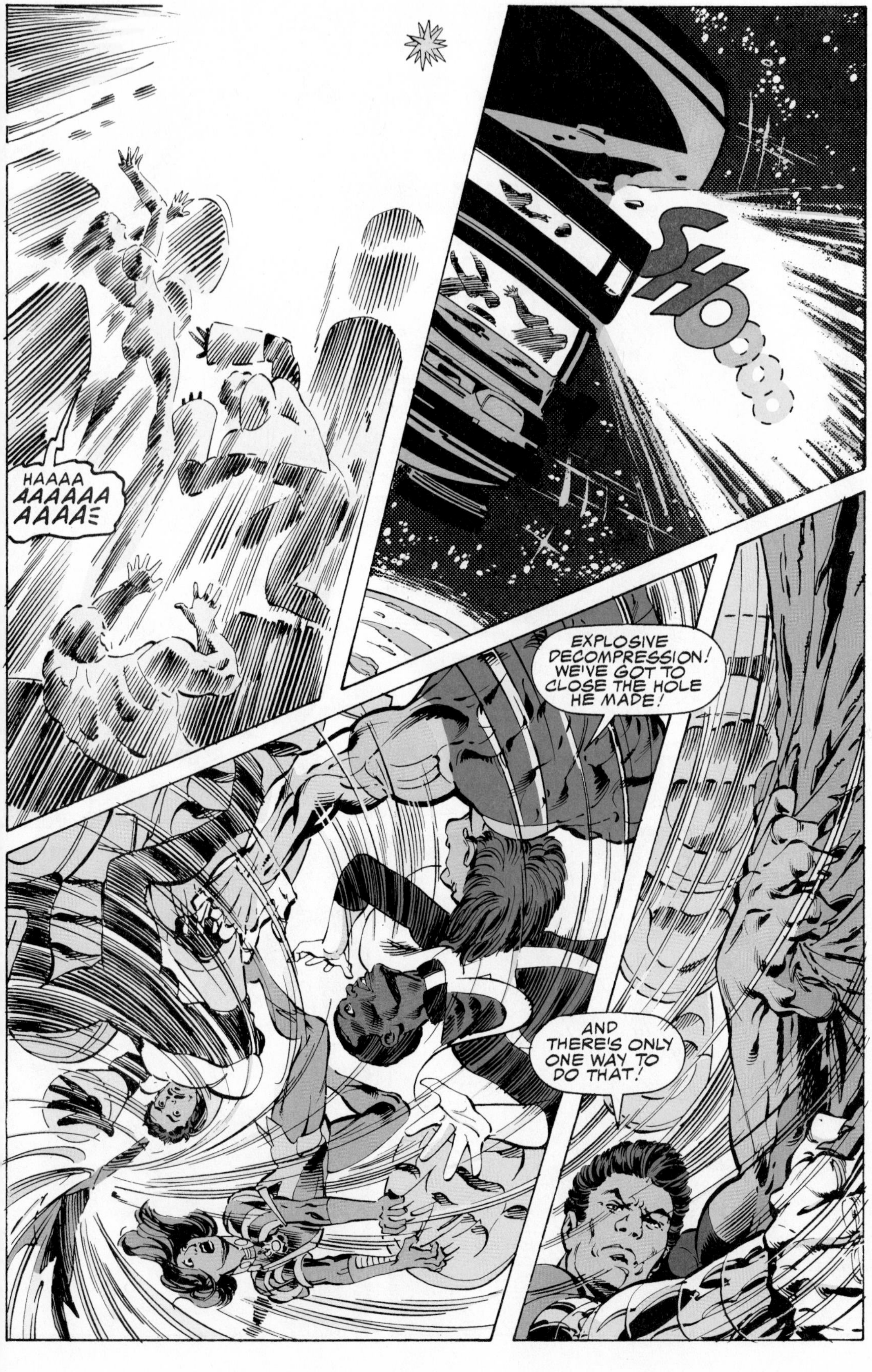
HAAAA AAAAAA AAAA
SHOOOOO
EXPLOSIVE DECOMPRESSION! WE'VE GOT TO CLOSE THE HOLE HE MADE!
AND THERE'S ONLY ONE WAY TO DO THAT!

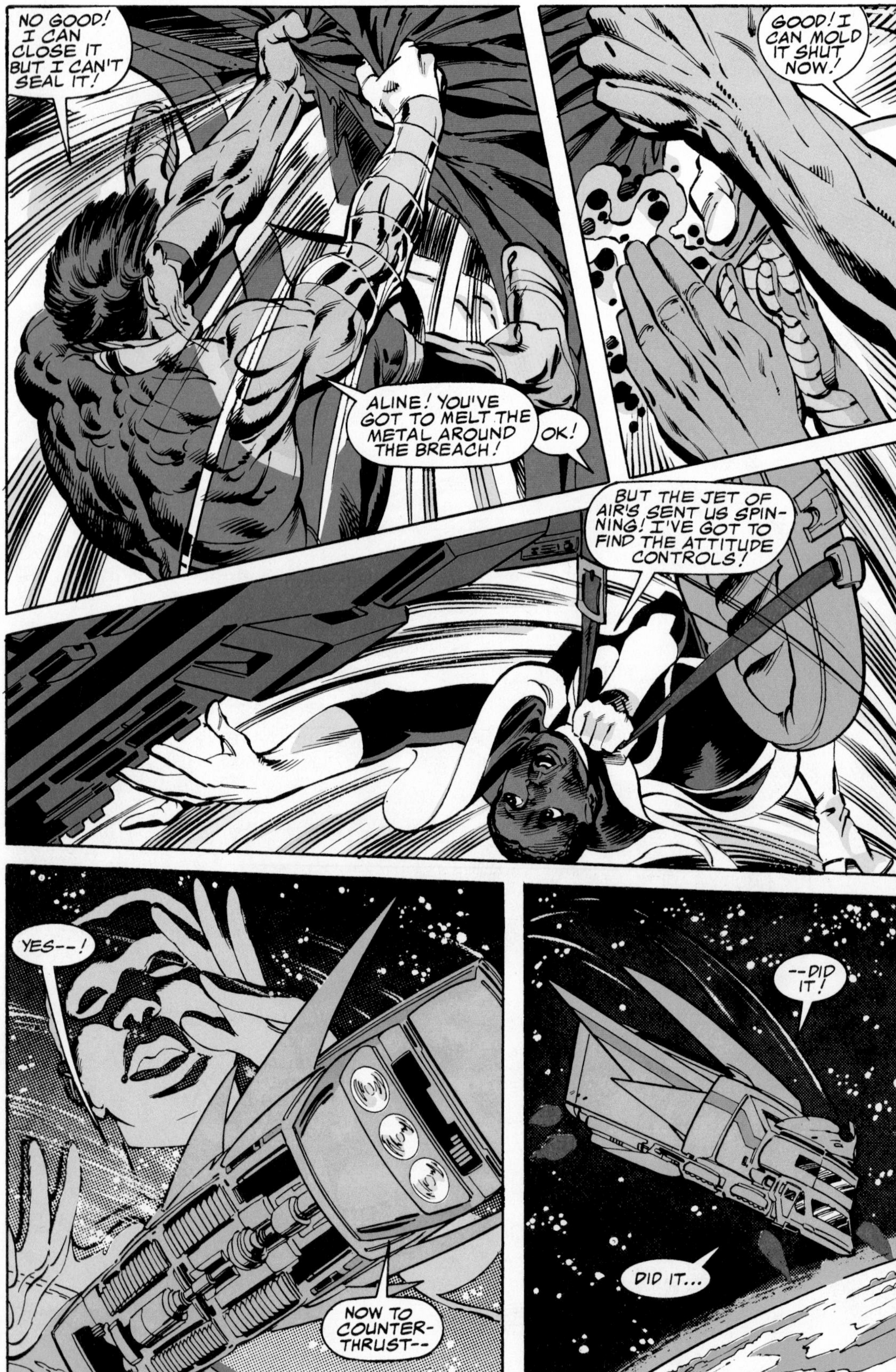
NO GOOD! I CAN CLOSE IT BUT I CAN'T SEAL IT!
GOOD! I CAN MOLD IT SHUT NOW!
ALINE! YOU'VE GOT TO MELT THE METAL AROUND THE BREACH!
OK!
BUT THE JET OF AIR'S SENT US SPINNING! I'VE GOT TO FIND THE ATTITUDE CONTROLS!
YES--!
NOW TO COUNTER-THRUST--
--DID IT!
DID IT...

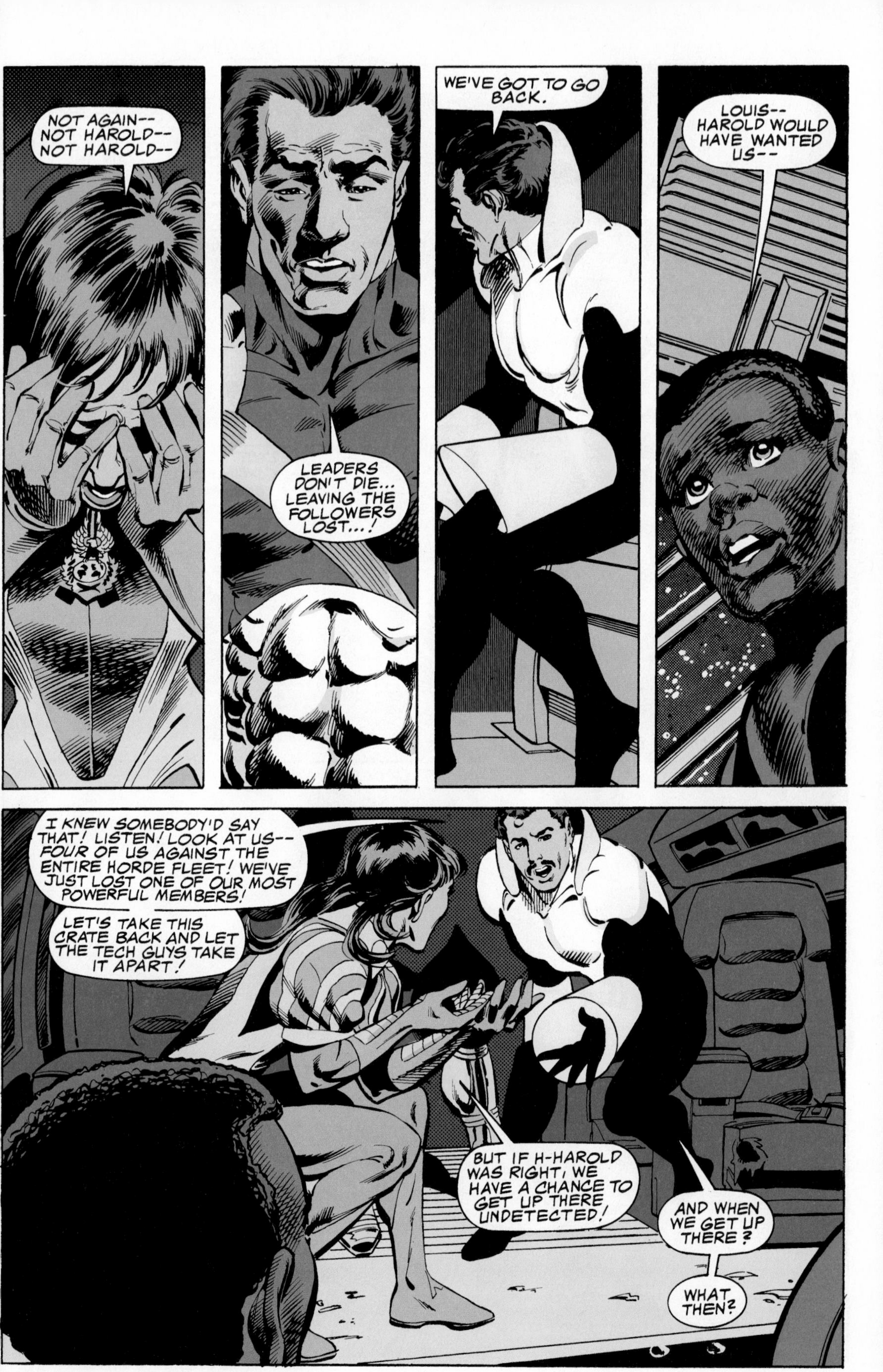
NOT AGAIN-- NOT HAROLD-- NOT HAROLD--
LEADERS DON'T DIE... LEAVING THE FOLLOWERS LOST...!
WE'VE GOT TO GO BACK.
LOUIS-- HAROLD WOULD HAVE WANTED US--
I KNEW SOMEBODY'D SAY THAT! LISTEN! LOOK AT US-- FOUR OF US AGAINST THE ENTIRE HORDE FLEET! WE'VE JUST LOST ONE OF OUR MOST POWERFUL MEMBERS!
LET'S TAKE THIS CRATE BACK AND LET THE TECH GUYS TAKE IT APART!
BUT IF H-HAROLD WAS RIGHT, WE HAVE A CHANCE TO GET UP THERE UNDETECTED!
AND WHEN WE GET UP THERE?
WHAT THEN?

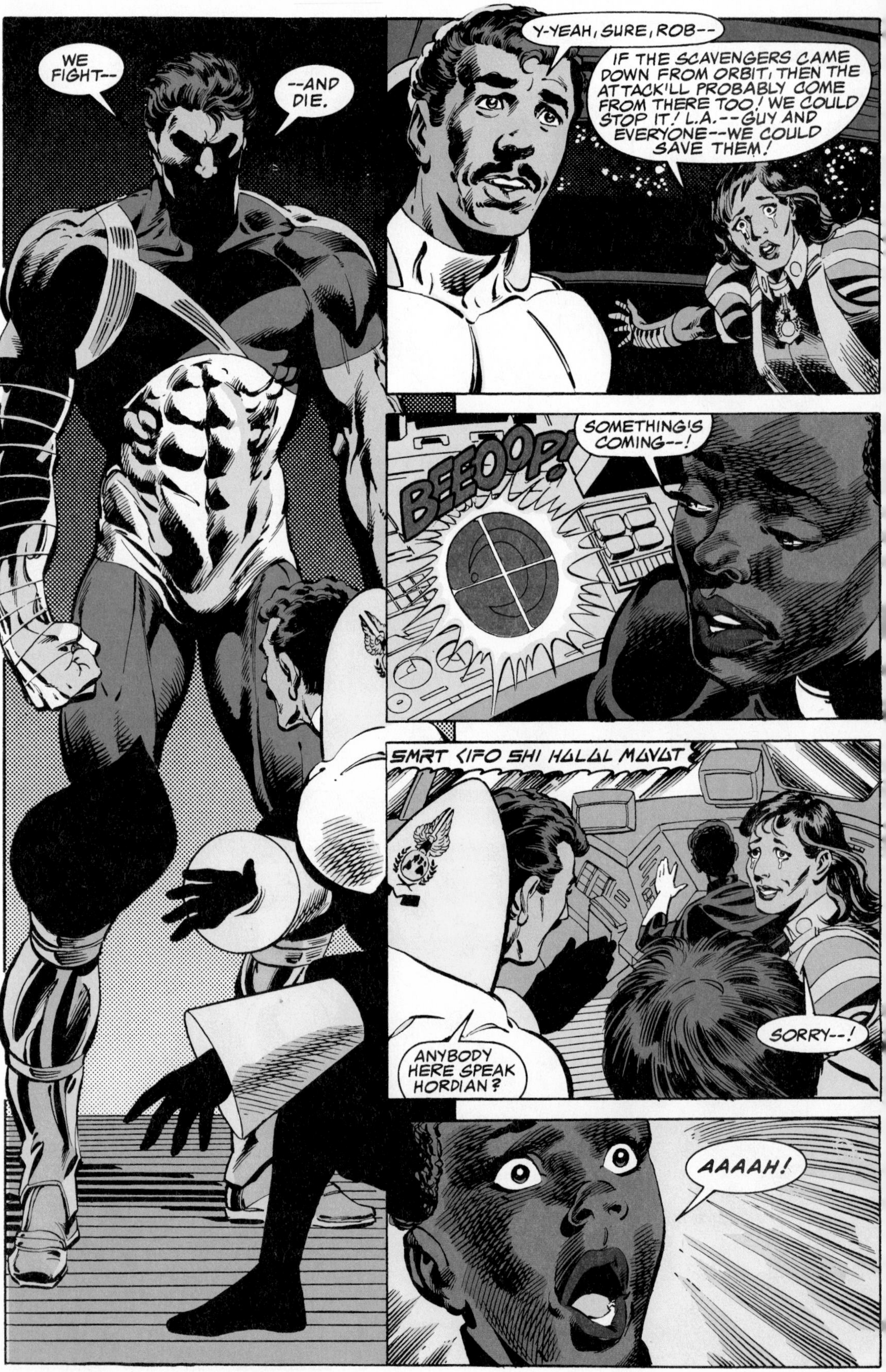
WE FIGHT--
--AND DIE.
Y-YEAH, SURE, ROB--
IF THE SCAVENGERS CAME DOWN FROM ORBIT, THEN THE ATTACK'LL PROBABLY COME FROM THERE TOO! WE COULD STOP IT! L.A.--GUY AND EVERYONE--WE COULD SAVE THEM!
SOMETHING'S COMING--!
BEEOOP!
SMRT <IFO SHI HALAL MAVAT
ANYBODY HERE SPEAK HORDIAN?
SORRY--!
AAAAH!

SMRT CIFO SHI MATI HOLOL MOVAT!

OLUM MATI MATI CIEMNO CIFO FOJDOLOM!

HE SEES US!

RADIAN! BLIND HIM!

ADEPT! HIT FORWARD THRUSTERS! RAM HIM!

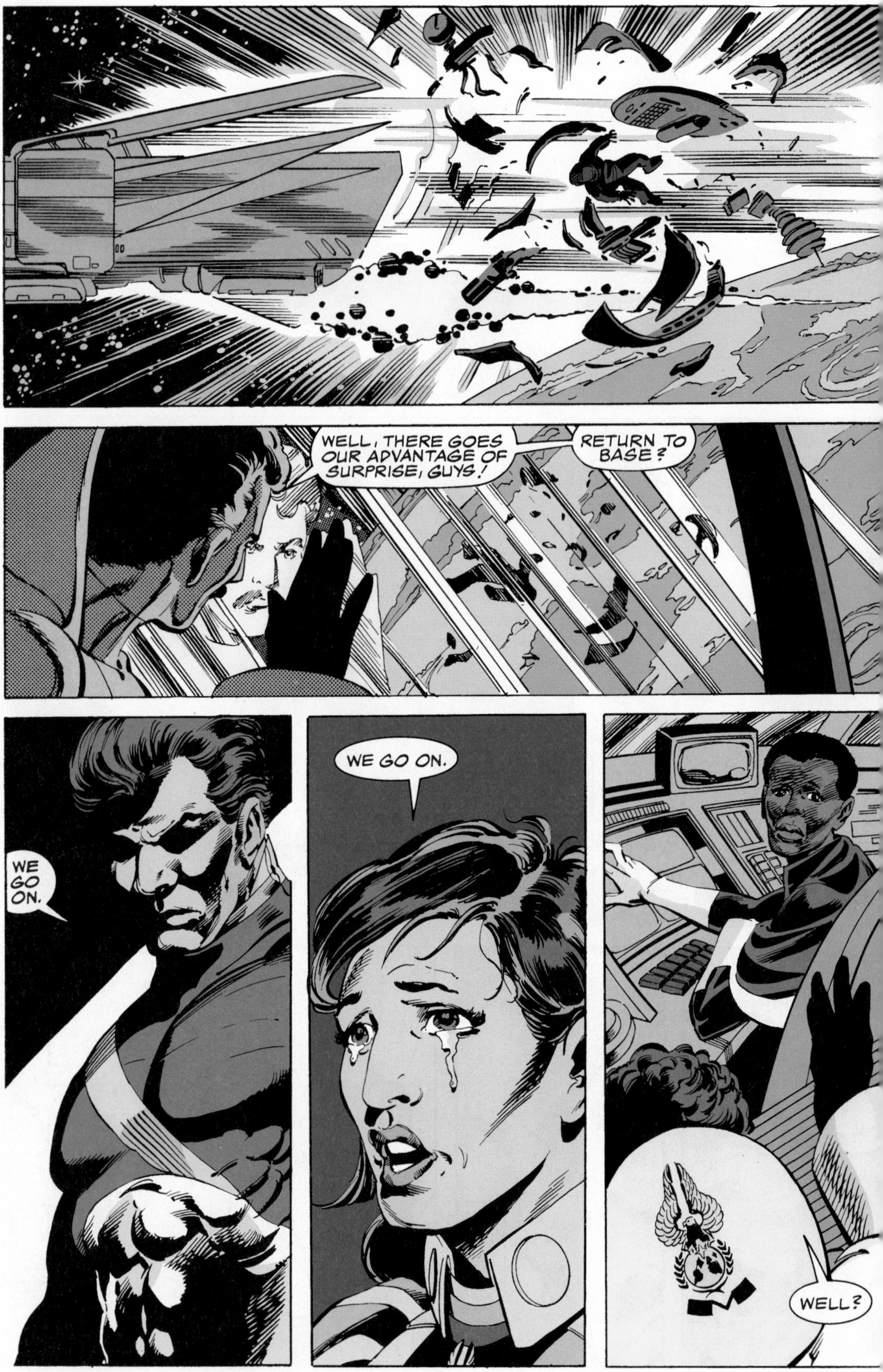
WELL, THERE GOES OUR ADVANTAGE OF SURPRISE, GUYS!
RETURN TO BASE?
WE GO ON.
WE GO ON.
WELL?

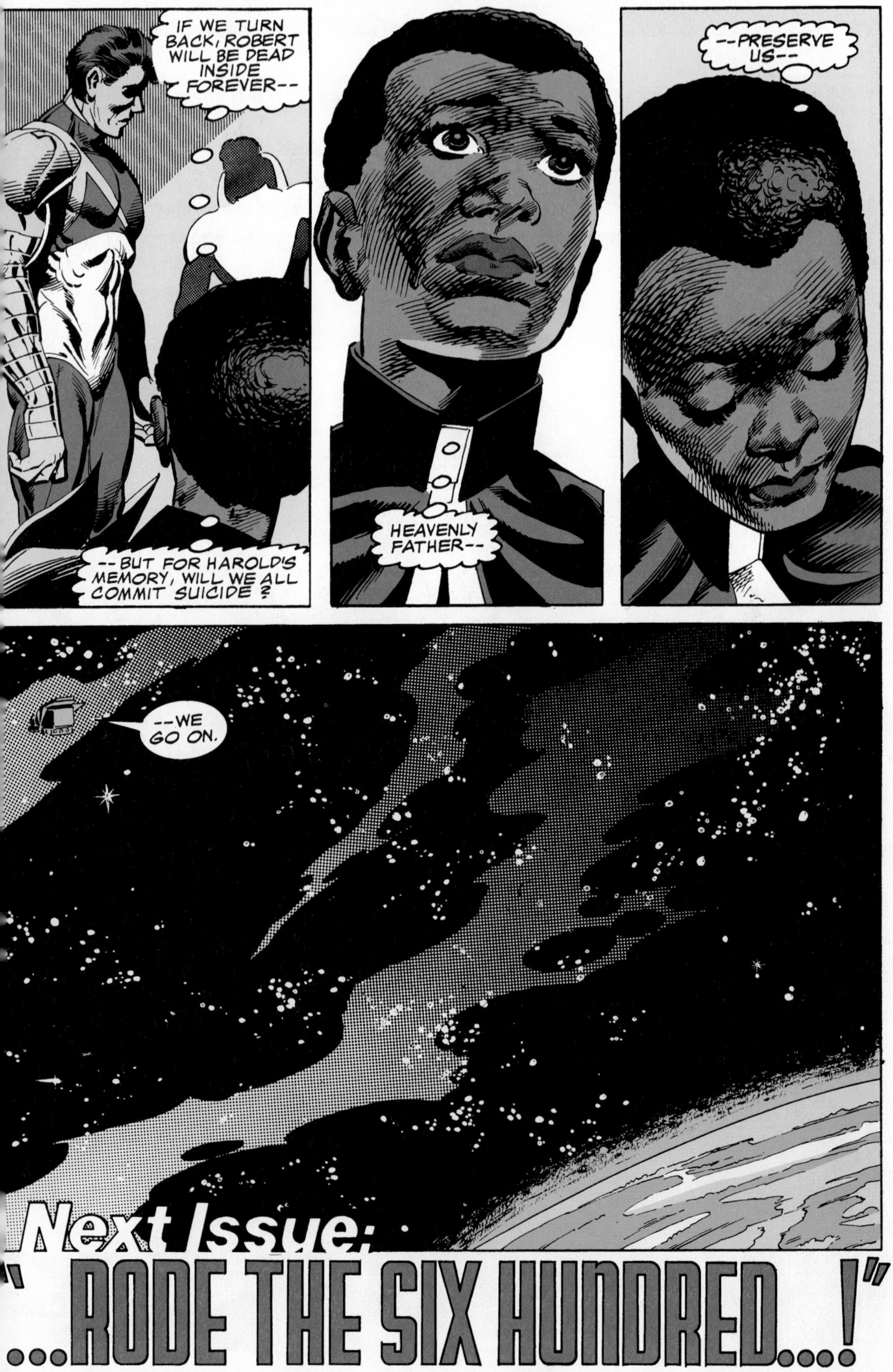
IF WE TURN BACK, ROBERT WILL BE DEAD INSIDE FOREVER--
--BUT FOR HAROLD'S MEMORY, WILL WE ALL COMMIT SUICIDE ?
HEAVENLY FATHER--
--PRESERVE US--
--WE GO ON.
Next Issue:
"...RODE THE SIX HUNDRED...!"

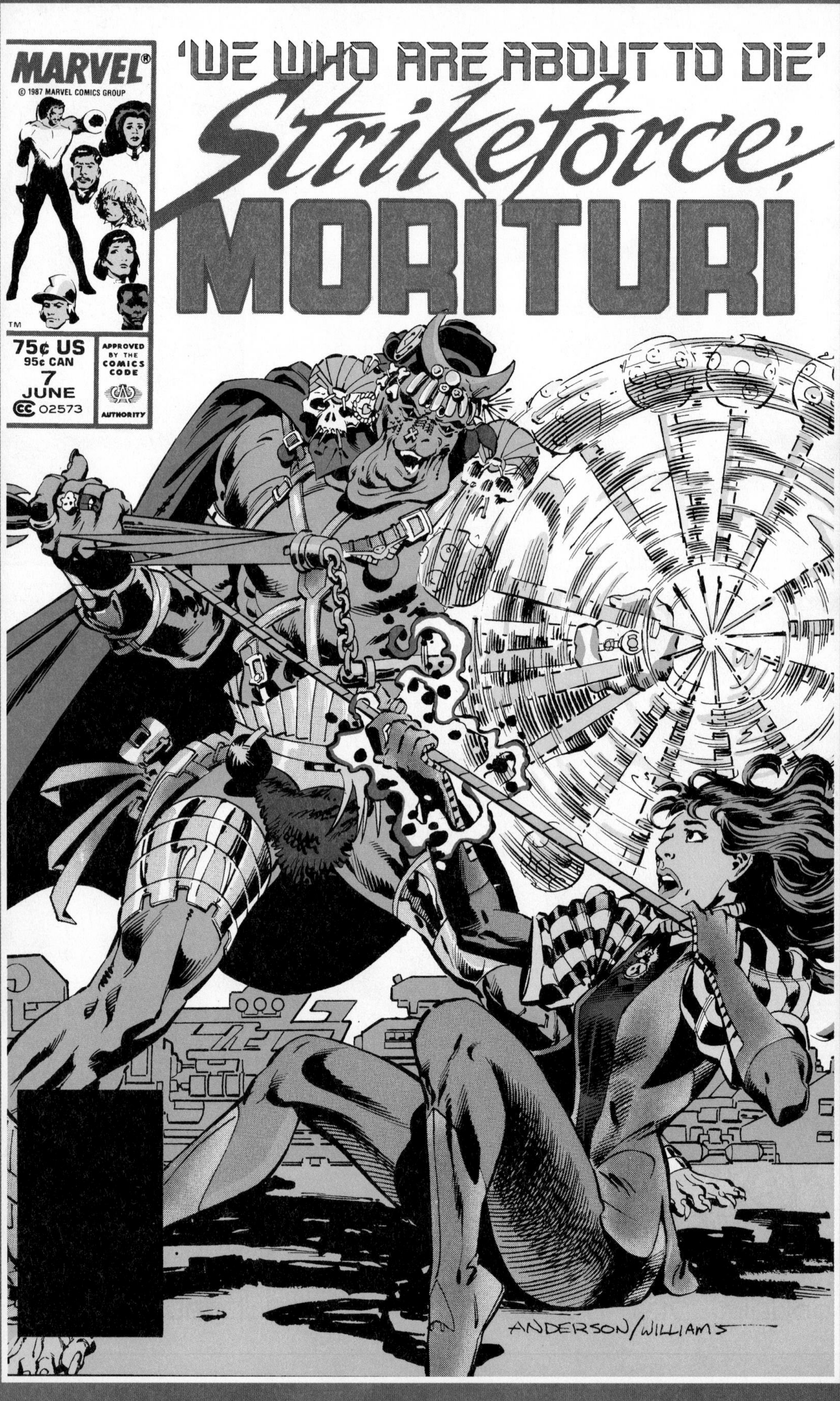
MARVEL®
© 1987 MARVEL COMICS GROUP
TM
75¢ US
95¢ CAN
7
JUNE
02573
APPROVED BY THE COMICS CODE AUTHORITY
'WE WHO ARE ABOUT TO DIE'
Strikeforce:
MORITURI
ANDERSON/WILLIAMS

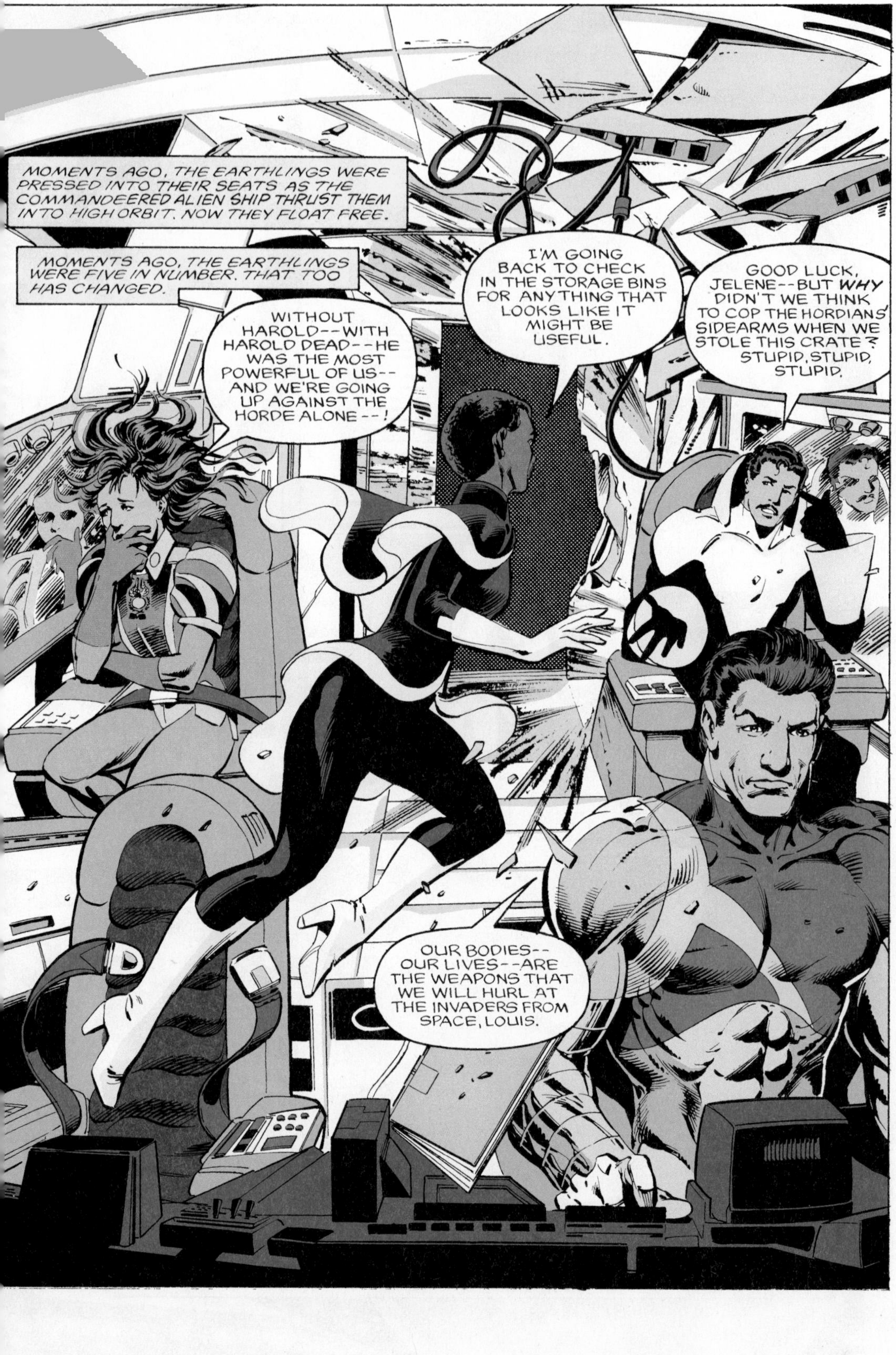
MOMENTS AGO, THE EARTHLINGS WERE PRESSED INTO THEIR SEATS AS THE COMMANDEERED ALIEN SHIP THRUST THEM INTO HIGH ORBIT. NOW THEY FLOAT FREE.
MOMENTS AGO, THE EARTHLINGS WERE FIVE IN NUMBER. THAT TOO HAS CHANGED.
WITHOUT HAROLD--WITH HAROLD DEAD--HE WAS THE MOST POWERFUL OF US--AND WE'RE GOING UP AGAINST THE HORDE ALONE--!
I'M GOING BACK TO CHECK IN THE STORAGE BINS FOR ANYTHING THAT LOOKS LIKE IT MIGHT BE USEFUL.
GOOD LUCK, JELENE--BUT WHY DIDN'T WE THINK TO COP THE HORDIANS' SIDEARMS WHEN WE STOLE THIS CRATE? STUPID, STUPID, STUPID.
OUR BODIES--OUR LIVES--ARE THE WEAPONS THAT WE WILL HURL AT THE INVADERS FROM SPACE, LOUIS.

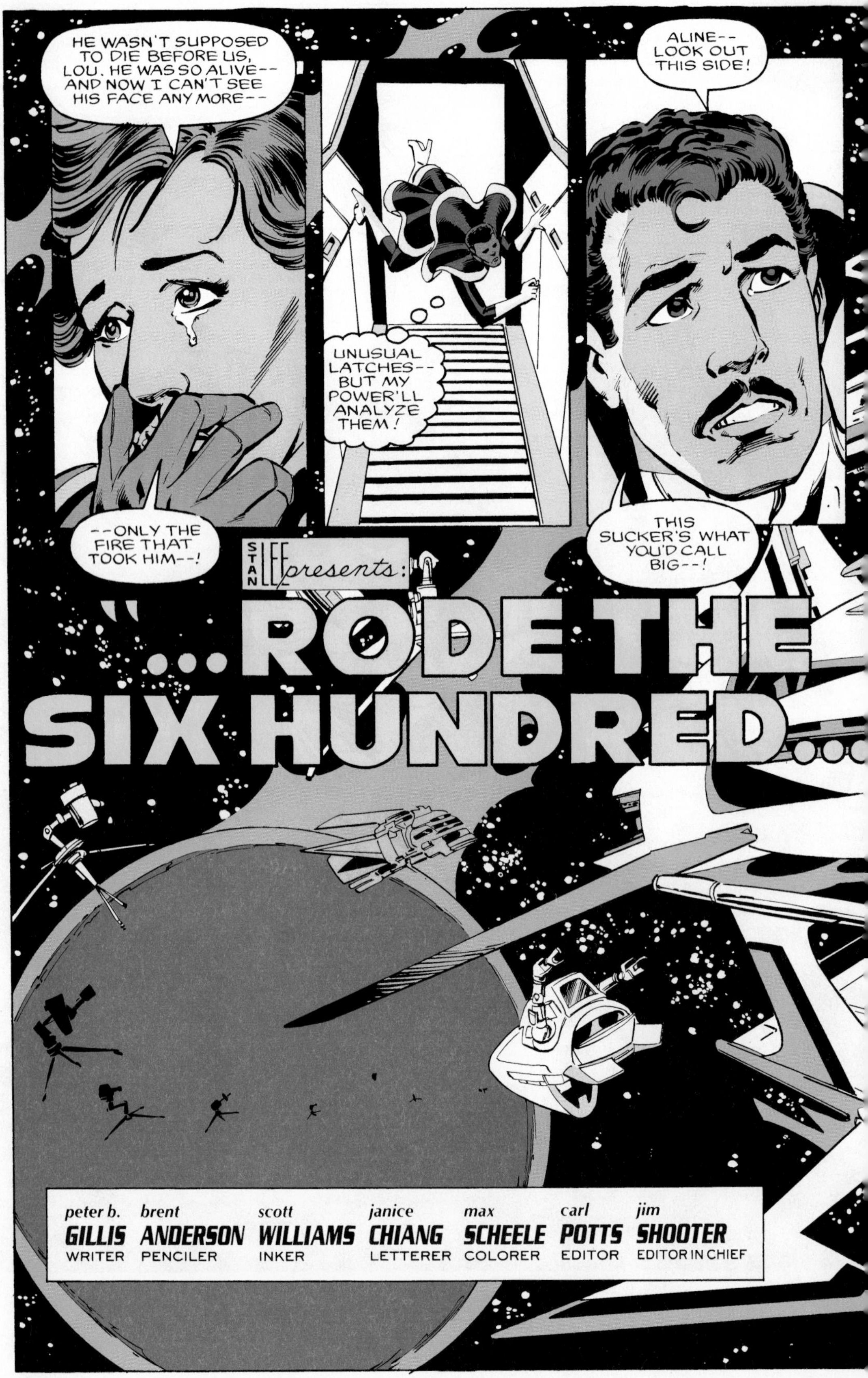
HE WASN'T SUPPOSED TO DIE BEFORE US, LOU. HE WAS SO ALIVE-- AND NOW I CAN'T SEE HIS FACE ANY MORE--
UNUSUAL LATCHES-- BUT MY POWER'LL ANALYZE THEM!
ALINE-- LOOK OUT THIS SIDE!
--ONLY THE FIRE THAT TOOK HIM--!
STAN LEE presents:
"...RODE THE SIX HUNDRED..."
THIS SUCKER'S WHAT YOU'D CALL BIG--!
peter b. GILLIS WRITER
brent ANDERSON PENCILER
scott WILLIAMS INKER
janice CHIANG LETTERER
max SCHEELE COLORER
carl POTTS EDITOR
jim SHOOTER EDITOR IN CHIEF

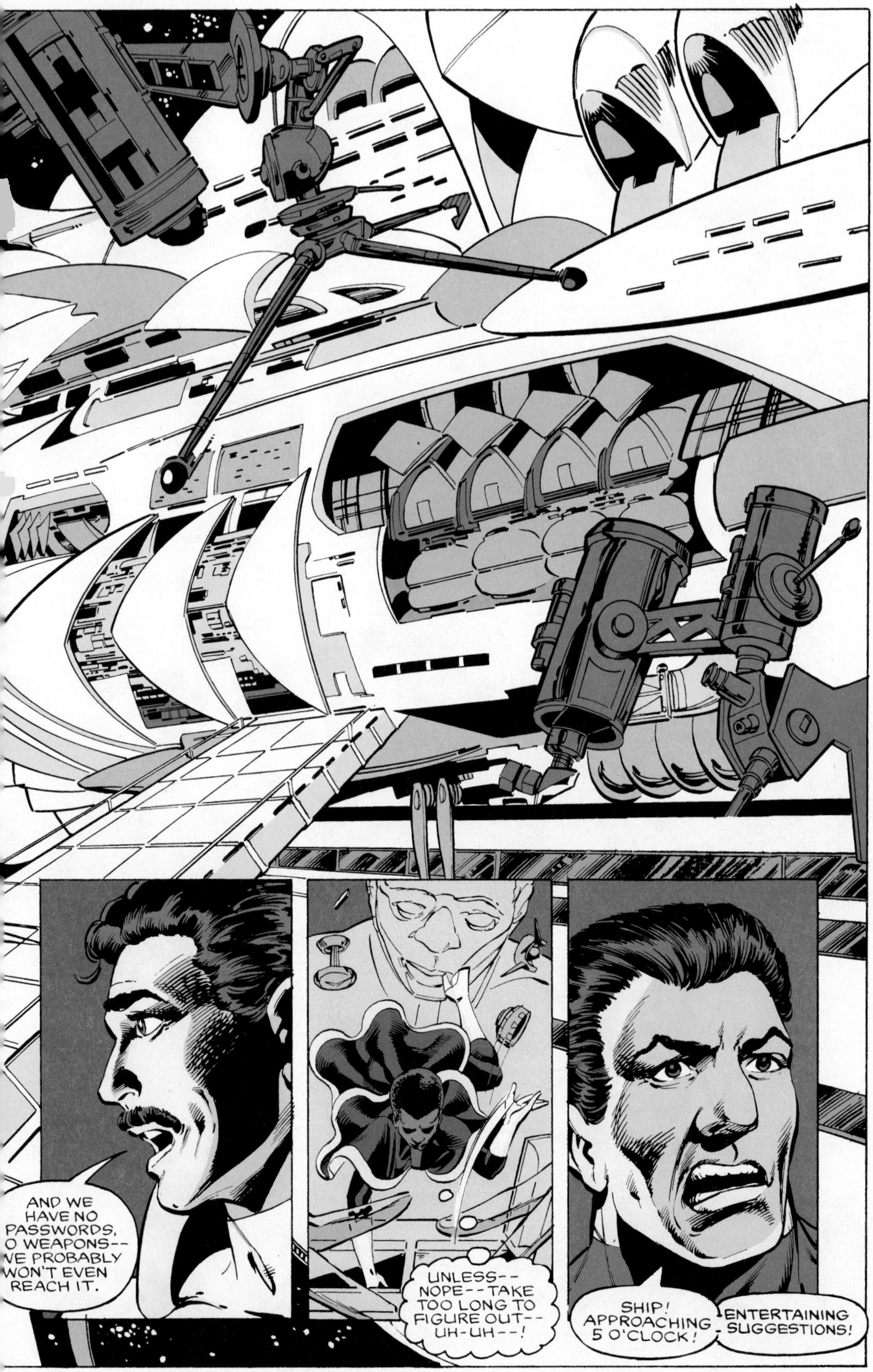
AND WE HAVE NO PASSWORDS, O WEAPONS-- VE PROBABLY WON'T EVEN REACH IT.
UNLESS-- NOPE--TAKE TOO LONG TO FIGURE OUT-- UH-UH--!
SHIP! APPROACHING 5 O'CLOCK!
ENTERTAINING SUGGESTIONS!

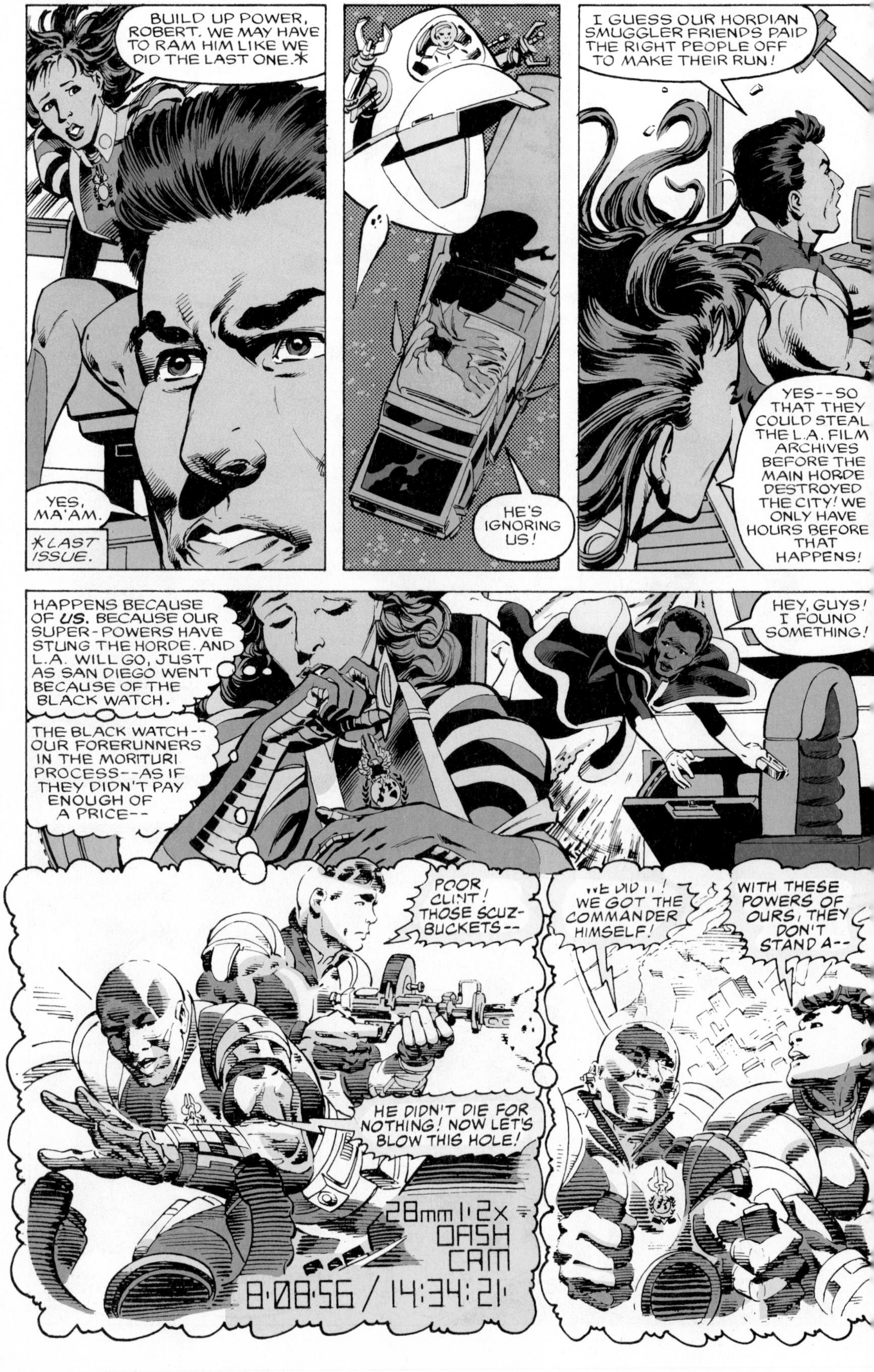
BUILD UP POWER, ROBERT. WE MAY HAVE TO RAM HIM LIKE WE DID THE LAST ONE.*
YES, MA'AM.
*LAST ISSUE.
HE'S IGNORING US!
I GUESS OUR HORDIAN SMUGGLER FRIENDS PAID THE RIGHT PEOPLE OFF TO MAKE THEIR RUN!
YES--SO THAT THEY COULD STEAL THE L.A. FILM ARCHIVES BEFORE THE MAIN HORDE DESTROYED THE CITY! WE ONLY HAVE HOURS BEFORE THAT HAPPENS!
HAPPENS BECAUSE OF US. BECAUSE OUR SUPER-POWERS HAVE STUNG THE HORDE. AND L.A. WILL GO, JUST AS SAN DIEGO WENT BECAUSE OF THE BLACK WATCH.
THE BLACK WATCH--OUR FORERUNNERS IN THE MORITURI PROCESS--AS IF THEY DIDN'T PAY ENOUGH OF A PRICE--
HEY, GUYS! I FOUND SOMETHING!
POOR CLINT! THOSE SCUZ-BUCKETS--
HE DIDN'T DIE FOR NOTHING! NOW LET'S BLOW THIS HOLE!
28mm 1:2x
DASH CAM
8:08:56 / 14:34:21
WE DID IT! WE GOT THE COMMANDER HIMSELF!
WITH THESE POWERS OF OURS, THEY DON'T STAND A--

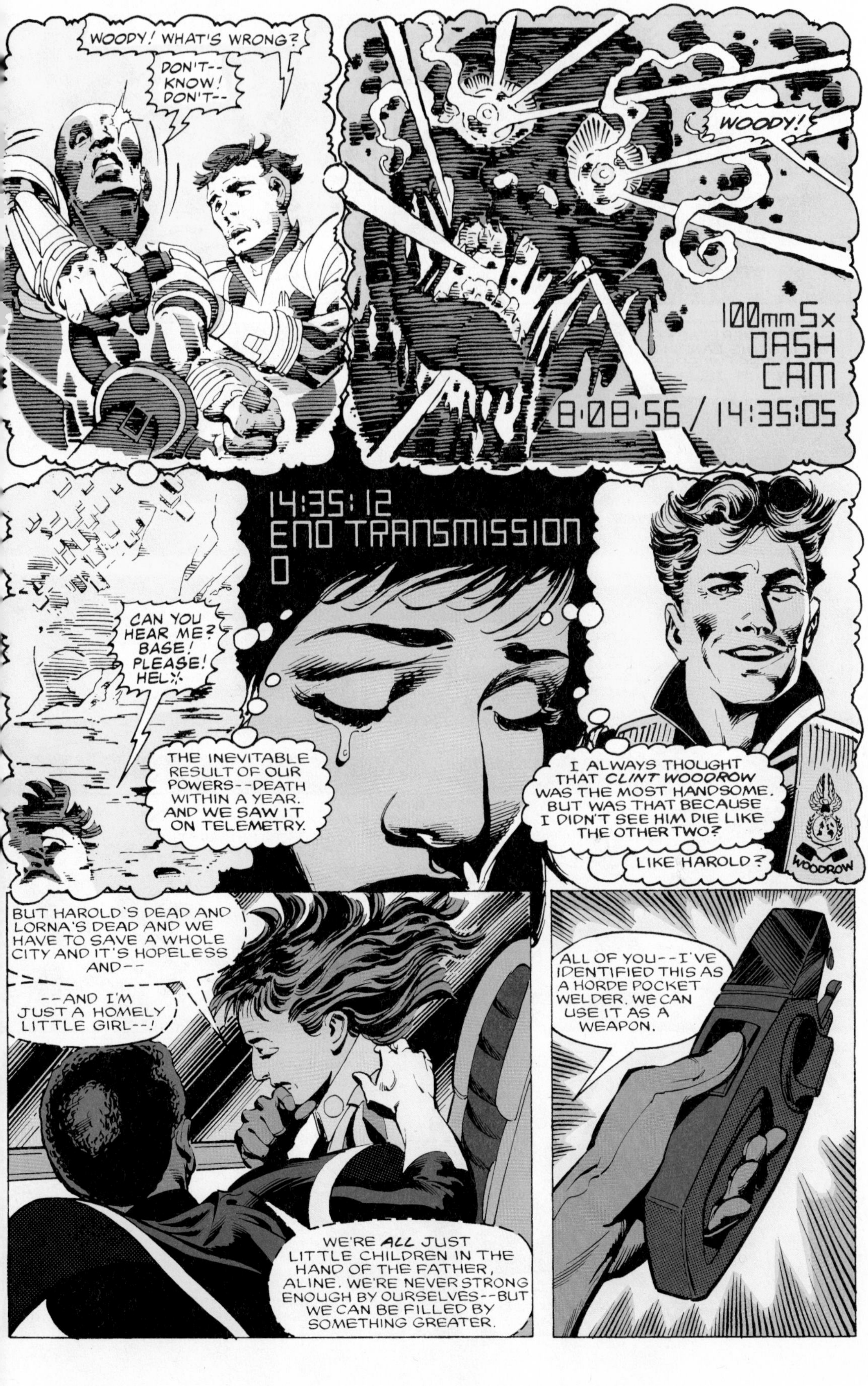

WOODY! WHAT'S WRONG?
DON'T-- KNOW! DON'T--
WOODY!
100mm 5x DASH CAM 8·08·56 / 14:35:05
14:35:12 END TRANSMISSION 0
CAN YOU HEAR ME? BASE! PLEASE! HEL*
THE INEVITABLE RESULT OF OUR POWERS--DEATH WITHIN A YEAR. AND WE SAW IT ON TELEMETRY.
I ALWAYS THOUGHT THAT CLINT WOODROW WAS THE MOST HANDSOME. BUT WAS THAT BECAUSE I DIDN'T SEE HIM DIE LIKE THE OTHER TWO?
LIKE HAROLD?
WOODROW
BUT HAROLD'S DEAD AND LORNA'S DEAD AND WE HAVE TO SAVE A WHOLE CITY AND IT'S HOPELESS AND--
--AND I'M JUST A HOMELY LITTLE GIRL--!
WE'RE ALL JUST LITTLE CHILDREN IN THE HAND OF THE FATHER, ALINE. WE'RE NEVER STRONG ENOUGH BY OURSELVES--BUT WE CAN BE FILLED BY SOMETHING GREATER.
ALL OF YOU--I'VE IDENTIFIED THIS AS A HORDE POCKET WELDER. WE CAN USE IT AS A WEAPON.

YREBU NAZUCH DUUTHUS SHYMLI

HEY! I FORGOT WE HAVE A TRANSLATOR WITH US! SWITCH IT ON!

KKK

...NEAR/CLOSE COMING WAGON/ SHIP HAIL CLOSE FORMAL* ACTIVATE/ FIRE BEACON/ TRANSPONDER PROPER CLOSE FORMAL...

TRANSPONDER! THEY'RE REQUESTING LANDING PROCEDURES! WHERE'S THE SWITCH, JELENE?

I DON'T KNOW! MY ADEPT POWERS AREN'T MIRACLES-- THIS IS A VERY ALIEN SHIP!

OK-- HOW ABOUT THAT BUTTON?

NOPE. NOT IT.

...PROPER FORM WORD/ MESSAGE OR DEATH/ WEAPON IMPERATIVE! IMPERATIVE IMPERATIVE!

SHIPS COMING FROM BEHIND! THE JIG'S UP!

MARATHON! FULL SPEED AHEAD!

THEY'VE HIT US!

DOESN'T MATTER! WE'RE GOING IN!

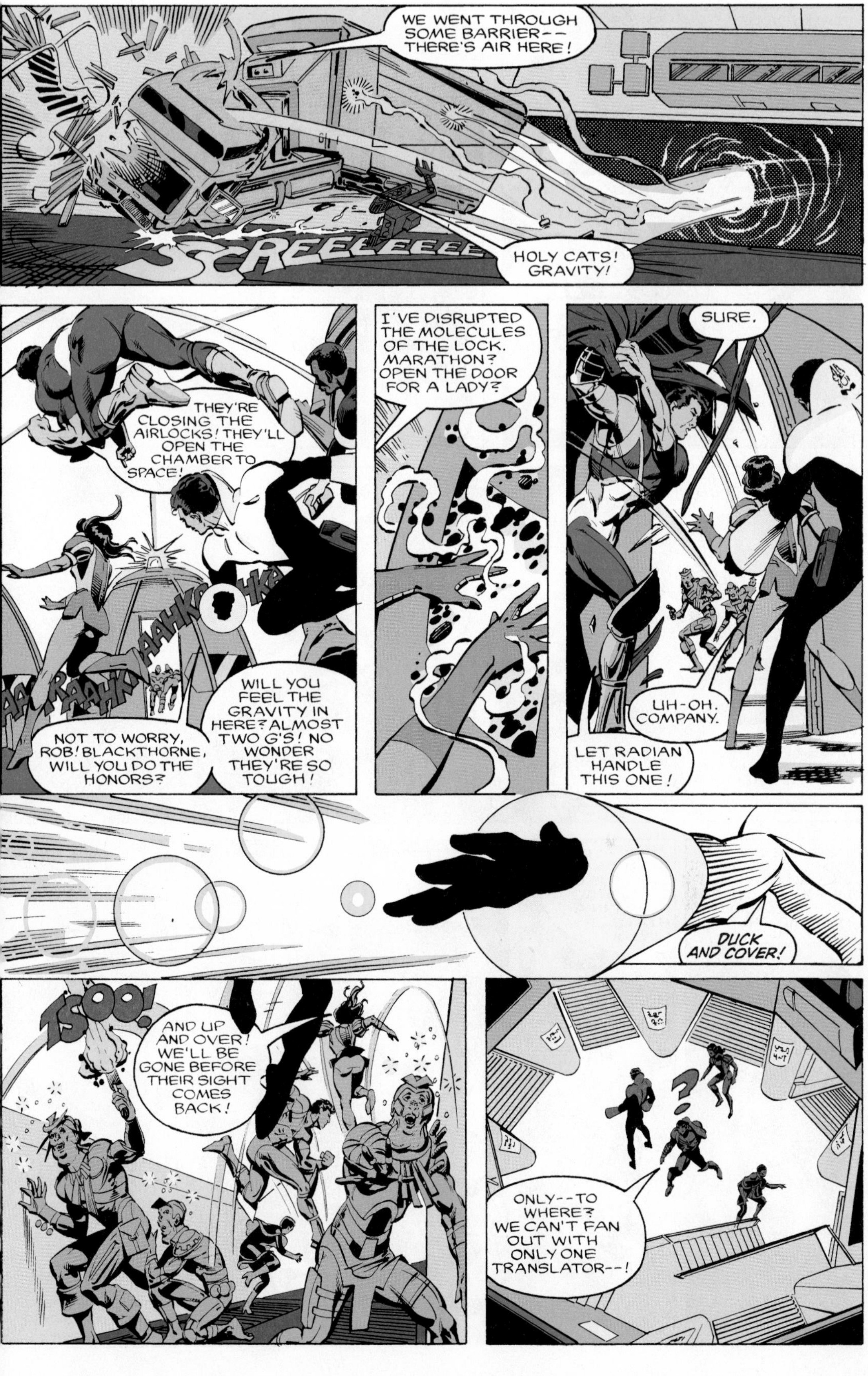
WE WENT THROUGH SOME BARRIER-- THERE'S AIR HERE!
SCREEEEEE
HOLY CATS! GRAVITY!
THEY'RE CLOSING THE AIRLOCKS! THEY'LL OPEN THE CHAMBER TO SPACE!
AAAHHKK
NOT TO WORRY, ROB! BLACKTHORNE, WILL YOU DO THE HONORS?
WILL YOU FEEL THE GRAVITY IN HERE? ALMOST TWO G'S! NO WONDER THEY'RE SO TOUGH!
I'VE DISRUPTED THE MOLECULES OF THE LOCK. MARATHON? OPEN THE DOOR FOR A LADY?
SURE.
UH-OH. COMPANY.
LET RADIAN HANDLE THIS ONE!
DUCK AND COVER!
TSOO!
AND UP AND OVER! WE'LL BE GONE BEFORE THEIR SIGHT COMES BACK!
ONLY--TO WHERE? WE CAN'T FAN OUT WITH ONLY ONE TRANSLATOR--!

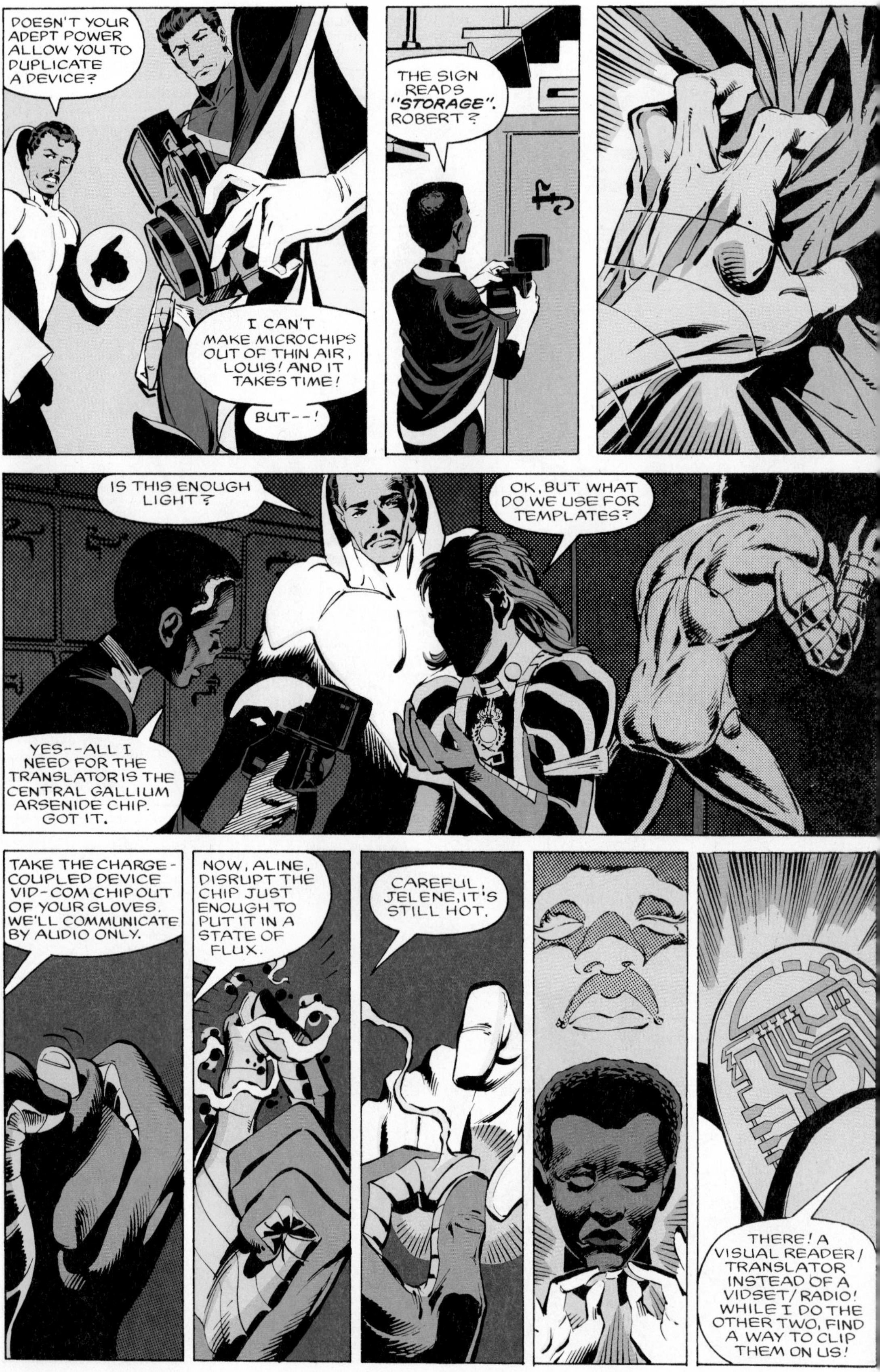
DOESN'T YOUR ADEPT POWER ALLOW YOU TO DUPLICATE A DEVICE?
I CAN'T MAKE MICROCHIPS OUT OF THIN AIR, LOUIS! AND IT TAKES TIME!
BUT--!
THE SIGN READS "STORAGE". ROBERT?
IS THIS ENOUGH LIGHT?
OK, BUT WHAT DO WE USE FOR TEMPLATES?
YES--ALL I NEED FOR THE TRANSLATOR IS THE CENTRAL GALLIUM ARSENIDE CHIP. GOT IT.
TAKE THE CHARGE-COUPLED DEVICE VID-COM CHIP OUT OF YOUR GLOVES. WE'LL COMMUNICATE BY AUDIO ONLY.
NOW, ALINE, DISRUPT THE CHIP JUST ENOUGH TO PUT IT IN A STATE OF FLUX.
CAREFUL, JELENE, IT'S STILL HOT.
THERE! A VISUAL READER/TRANSLATOR INSTEAD OF A VIDSET/RADIO! WHILE I DO THE OTHER TWO, FIND A WAY TO CLIP THEM ON US!

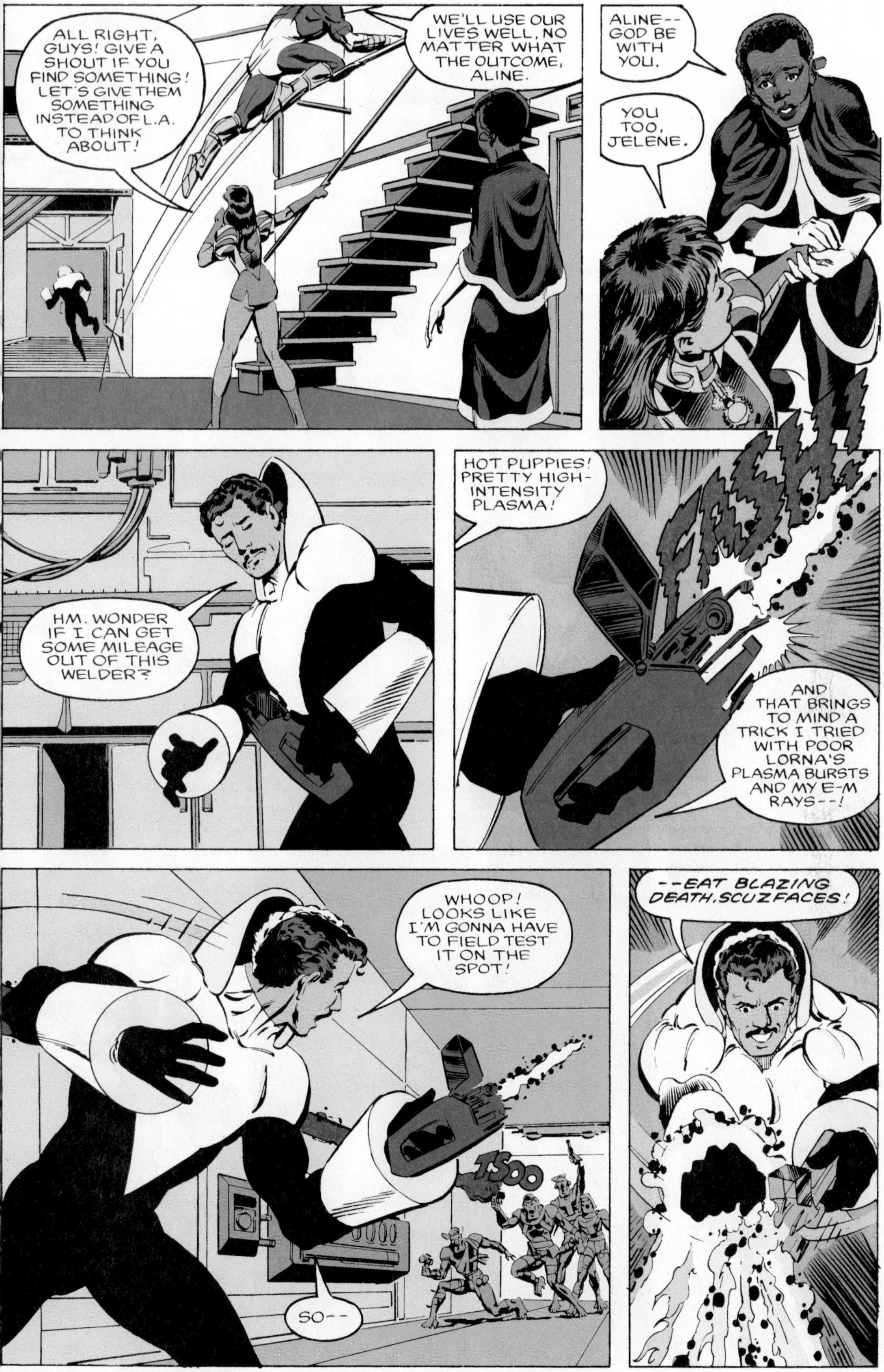
ALL RIGHT, GUYS! GIVE A SHOUT IF YOU FIND SOMETHING! LET'S GIVE THEM SOMETHING INSTEAD OF L.A. TO THINK ABOUT!
WE'LL USE OUR LIVES WELL, NO MATTER WHAT THE OUTCOME, ALINE.
ALINE-- GOD BE WITH YOU.
YOU TOO, JELENE.
HM. WONDER IF I CAN GET SOME MILEAGE OUT OF THIS WELDER?
HOT PUPPIES! PRETTY HIGH-INTENSITY PLASMA!
FFASH!
AND THAT BRINGS TO MIND A TRICK I TRIED WITH POOR LORNA'S PLASMA BURSTS AND MY E-M RAYS--!
WHOOP! LOOKS LIKE I'M GONNA HAVE TO FIELD TEST IT ON THE SPOT!
TSOO
SO--
--EAT BLAZING DEATH, SCUZFACES!

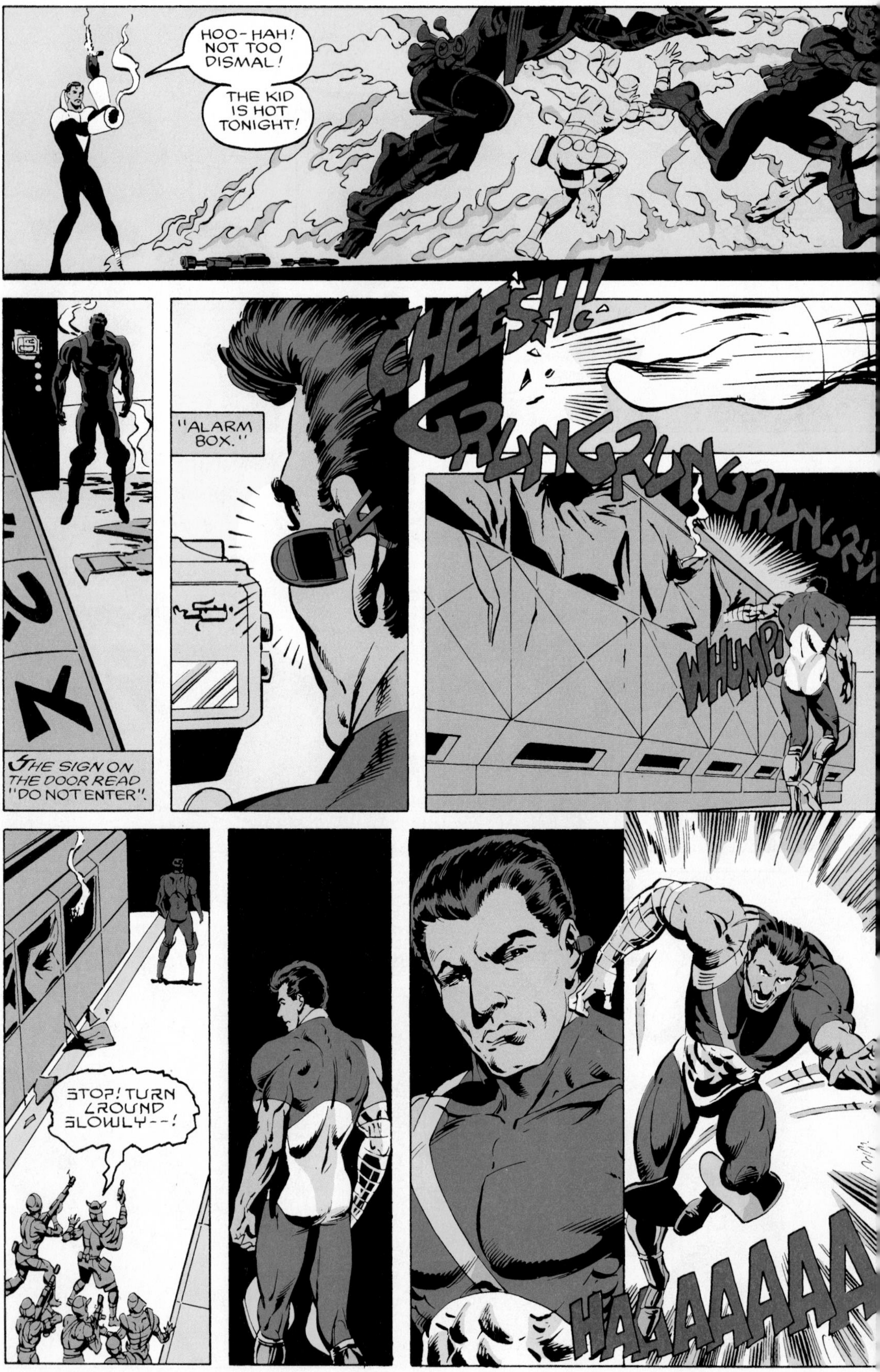
HOO-HAH! NOT TOO DISMAL!
THE KID IS HOT TONIGHT!
CHEESH!
"ALARM BOX."
GRUNGRUNGRUNGRUN
WHUMP!
THE SIGN ON THE DOOR READ "DO NOT ENTER".
STOP! TURN AROUND SLOWLY--!
HAAAAAA

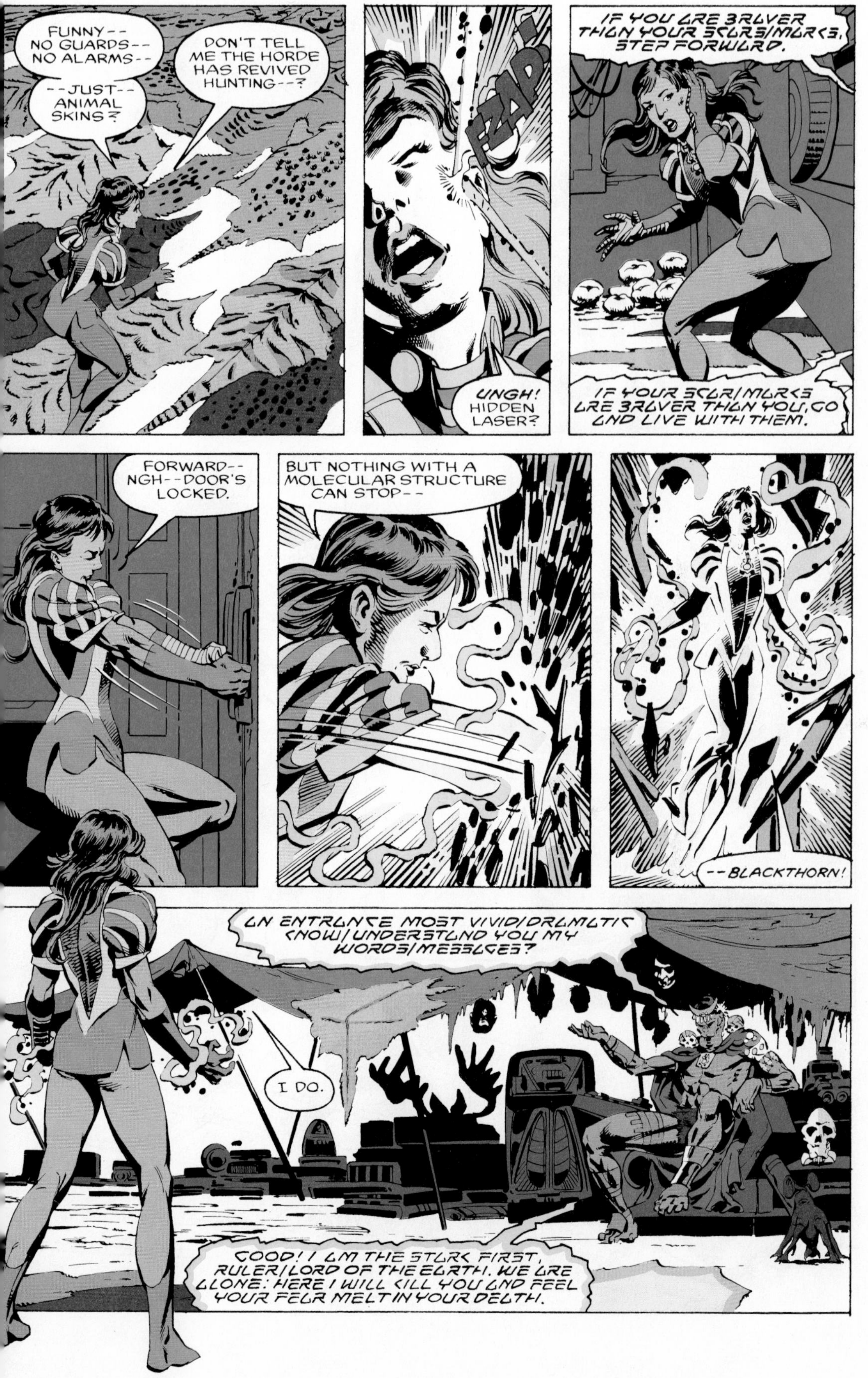
FUNNY-- NO GUARDS-- NO ALARMS--
--JUST-- ANIMAL SKINS?
DON'T TELL ME THE HORDE HAS REVIVED HUNTING--?
FZAP!
UNGH! HIDDEN LASER?
IF YOU ARE BRAVER THAN YOUR SCARS/MARKS, STEP FORWARD.
IF YOUR SCAR/MARKS ARE BRAVER THAN YOU, GO AND LIVE WITH THEM.
FORWARD-- NGH--DOOR'S LOCKED.
BUT NOTHING WITH A MOLECULAR STRUCTURE CAN STOP--
--BLACKTHORN!
AN ENTRANCE MOST VIVID/DRAMATIC KNOW/UNDERSTAND YOU MY WORDS/MESSAGES?
I DO.
GOOD! I AM THE STARK FIRST, RULER/LORD OF THE EARTH. WE ARE ALONE: HERE I WILL KILL YOU AND FEEL YOUR FEAR MELT IN YOUR DEATH.

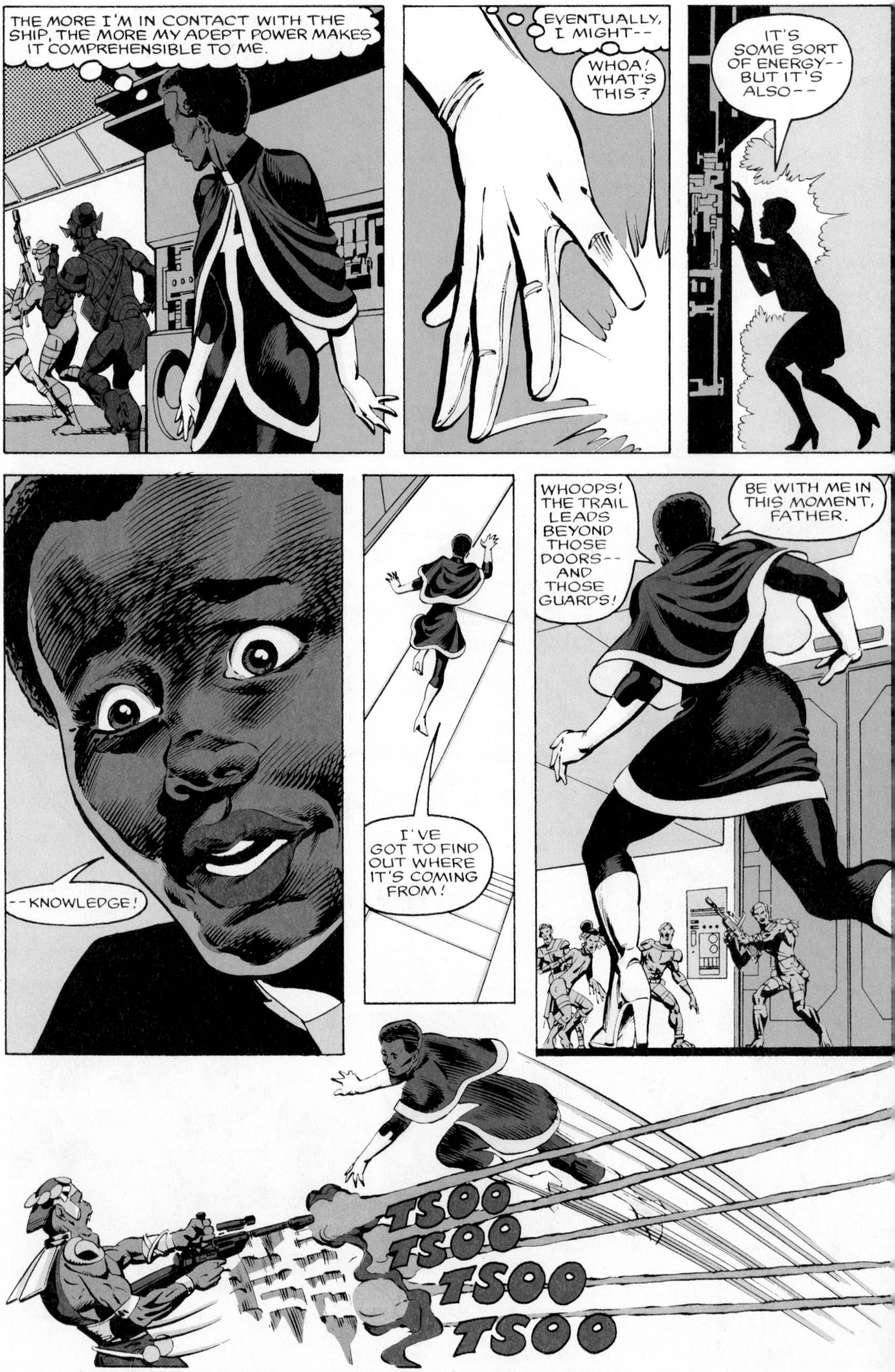
THE MORE I'M IN CONTACT WITH THE SHIP, THE MORE MY ADEPT POWER MAKES IT COMPREHENSIBLE TO ME.
EVENTUALLY, I MIGHT--
WHOA! WHAT'S THIS?
IT'S SOME SORT OF ENERGY-- BUT IT'S ALSO--
--KNOWLEDGE!
I'VE GOT TO FIND OUT WHERE IT'S COMING FROM!
WHOOPS! THE TRAIL LEADS BEYOND THOSE DOORS-- AND THOSE GUARDS!
BE WITH ME IN THIS MOMENT, FATHER.
TSOO
TSOO
TSOO
TSOO

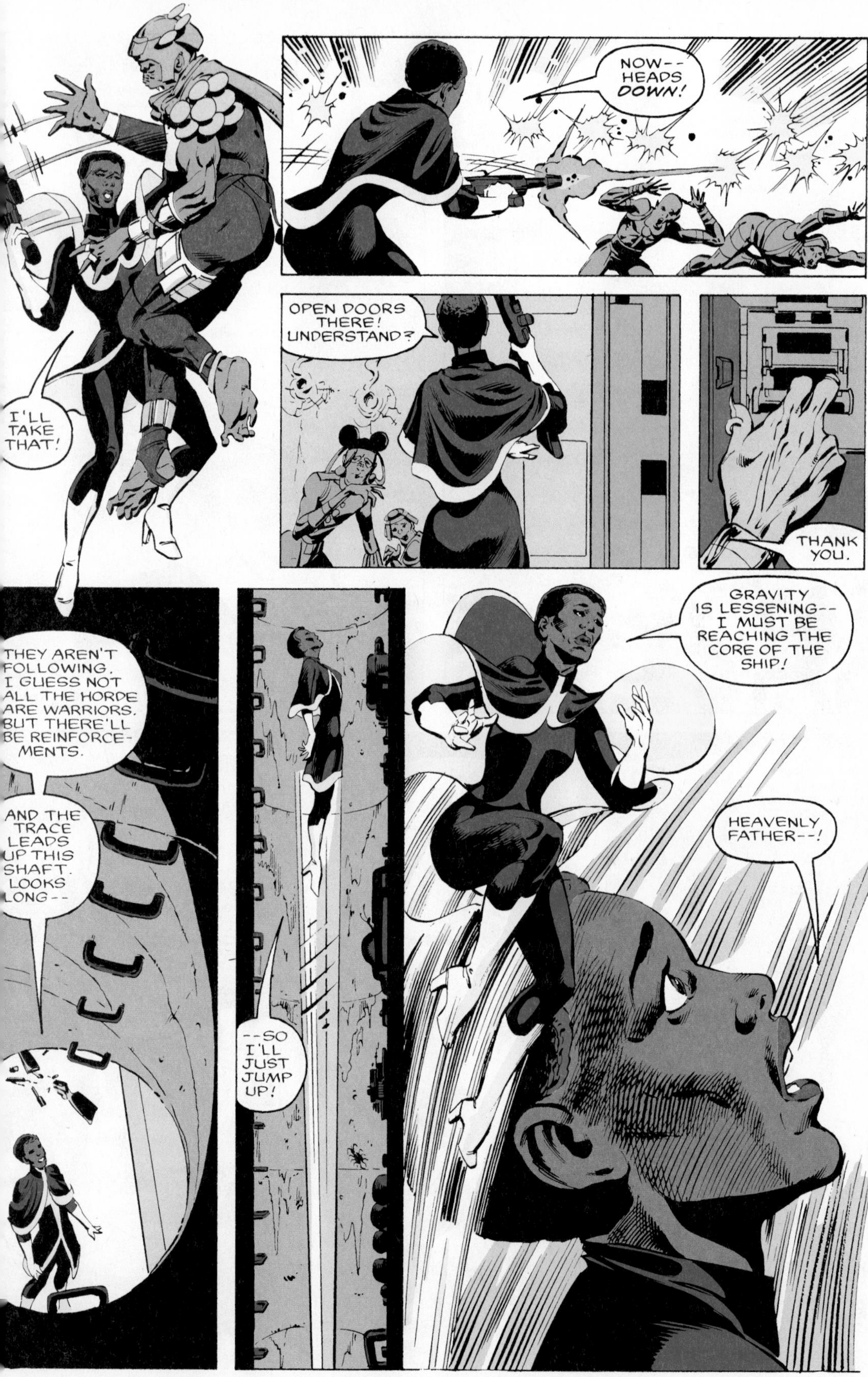
NOW--
HEADS DOWN!
I'LL TAKE THAT!
OPEN DOORS THERE! UNDERSTAND?
THANK YOU.
THEY AREN'T FOLLOWING. I GUESS NOT ALL THE HORDE ARE WARRIORS. BUT THERE'LL BE REINFORCE-MENTS.
AND THE TRACE LEADS UP THIS SHAFT. LOOKS LONG--
--SO I'LL JUST JUMP UP!
GRAVITY IS LESSENING-- I MUST BE REACHING THE CORE OF THE SHIP!
HEAVENLY FATHER--!

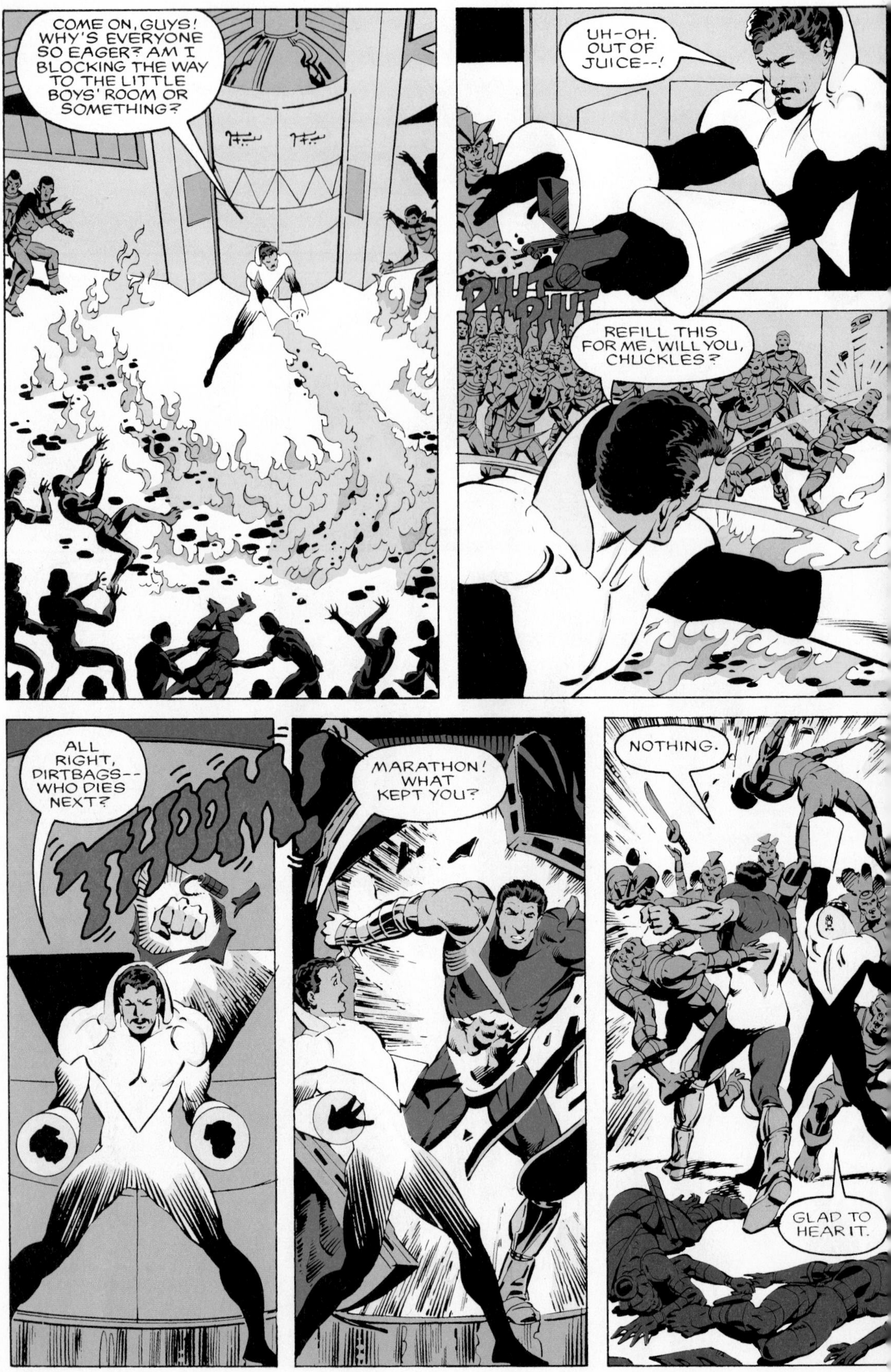
COME ON, GUYS! WHY'S EVERYONE SO EAGER? AM I BLOCKING THE WAY TO THE LITTLE BOYS' ROOM OR SOMETHING?
UH-OH. OUT OF JUICE--!
PHUT PHUT
REFILL THIS FOR ME, WILL YOU, CHUCKLES?
ALL RIGHT, DIRTBAGS-- WHO DIES NEXT?
THOOM!
MARATHON! WHAT KEPT YOU?
NOTHING.
GLAD TO HEAR IT.

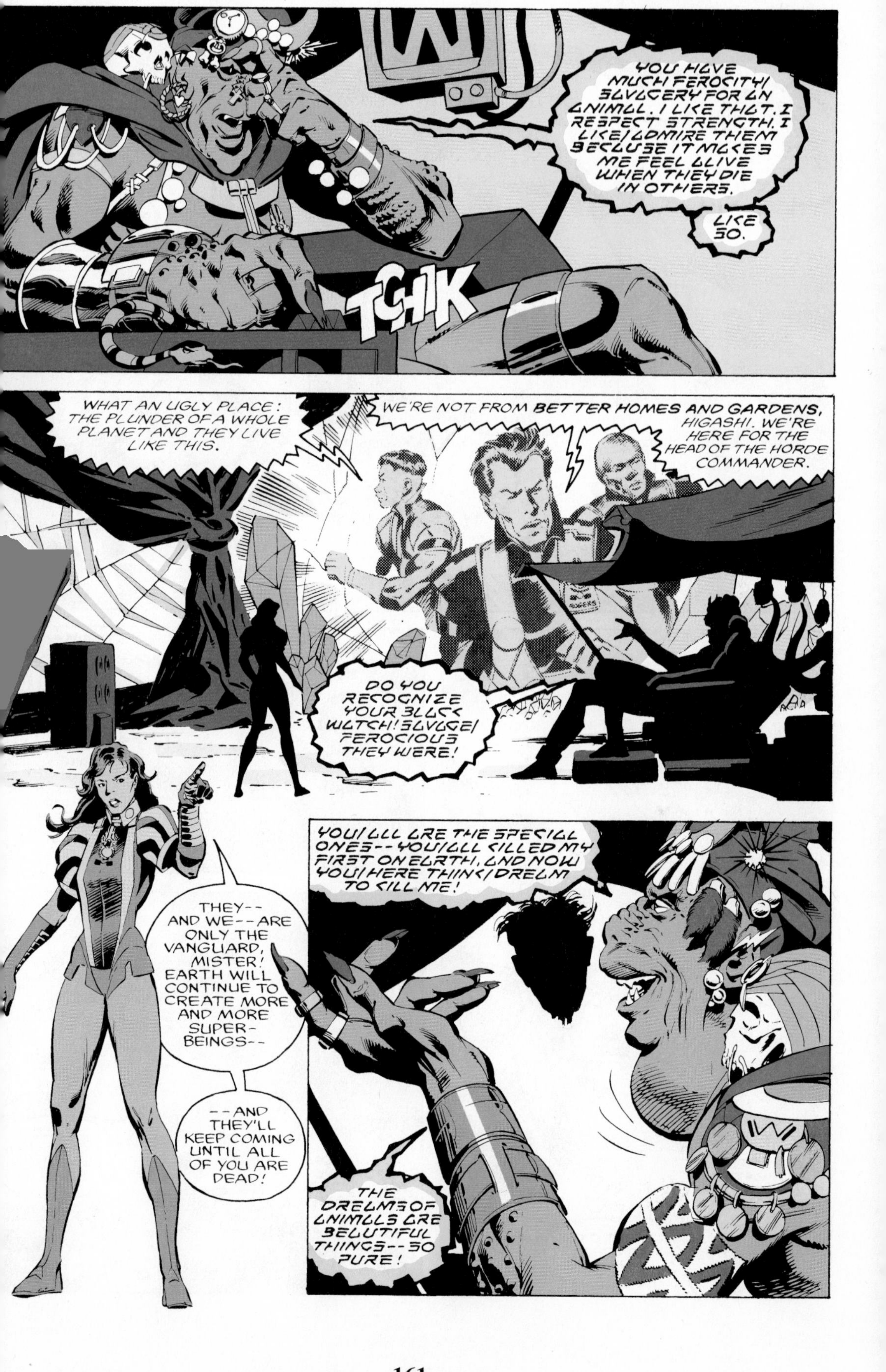

YOU HAVE MUCH FEROCITY/SAVAGERY FOR AN ANIMAL. I LIKE THAT. I RESPECT STRENGTH. I LIKE/ADMIRE THEM BECAUSE IT MAKES ME FEEL ALIVE WHEN THEY DIE IN OTHERS.
LIKE SO.
TCHIK
WHAT AN UGLY PLACE: THE PLUNDER OF A WHOLE PLANET AND THEY LIVE LIKE THIS.
WE'RE NOT FROM BETTER HOMES AND GARDENS, HIGASHI. WE'RE HERE FOR THE HEAD OF THE HORDE COMMANDER.
DO YOU RECOGNIZE YOUR BLACK WATCH! SAVAGE/FEROCIOUS THEY WERE!
THEY-- AND WE--ARE ONLY THE VANGUARD, MISTER! EARTH WILL CONTINUE TO CREATE MORE AND MORE SUPER-BEINGS--
--AND THEY'LL KEEP COMING UNTIL ALL OF YOU ARE DEAD!
YOU/ALL ARE THE SPECIAL ONES--YOU/ALL KILLED MY FIRST ON EARTH, AND NOW YOU/HERE THINK/DREAM TO KILL ME!
THE DREAMS OF ANIMALS ARE BEAUTIFUL THINGS--SO PURE!

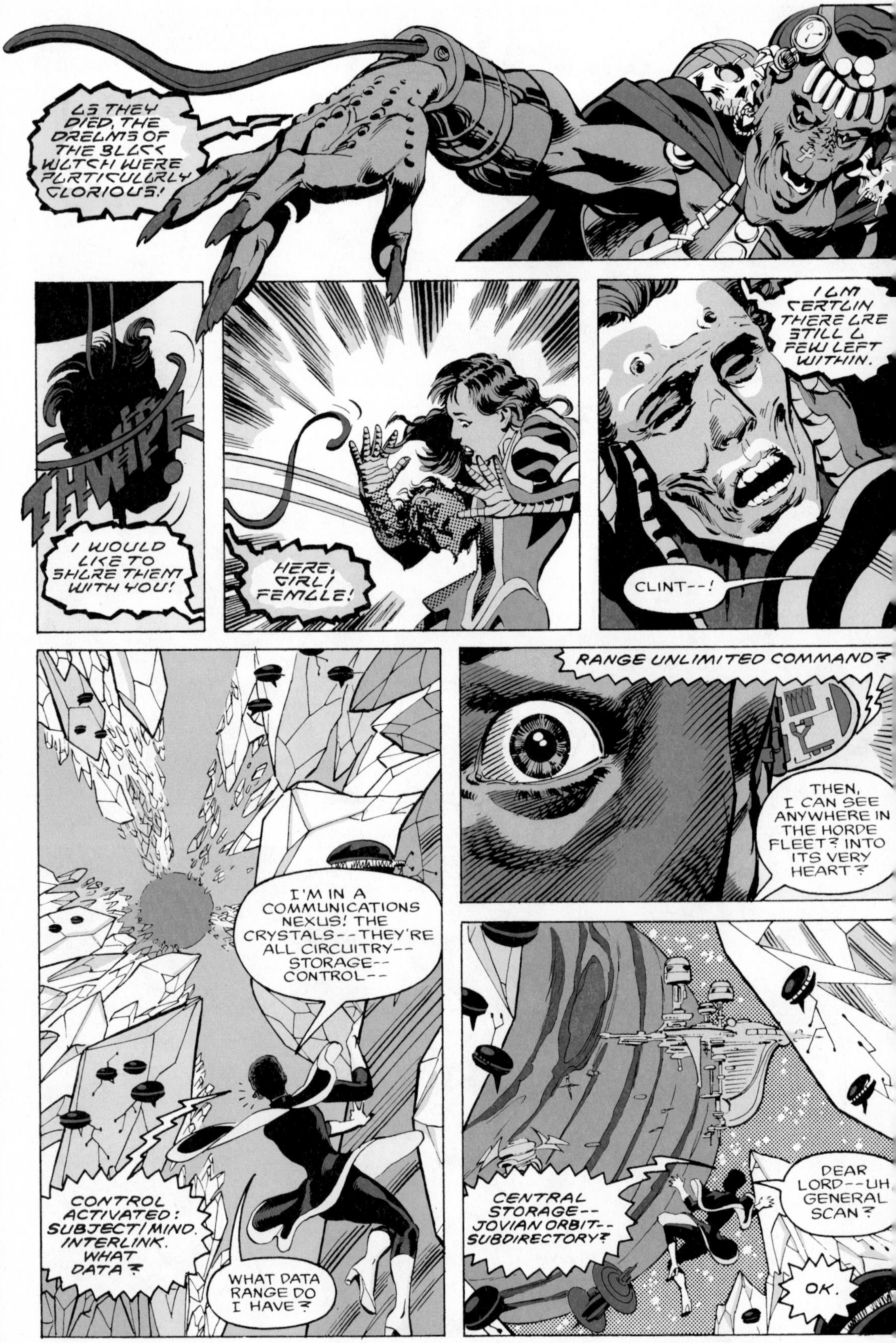
AS THEY DIED, THE DREAMS OF THE BLACK WITCH WERE PARTICULARLY GLORIOUS!
THWIP!
I WOULD LIKE TO SHARE THEM WITH YOU!
HERE, GIRL! FEMALE!
I AM CERTAIN THERE ARE STILL A FEW LEFT WITHIN.
CLINT--!
I'M IN A COMMUNICATIONS NEXUS! THE CRYSTALS--THEY'RE ALL CIRCUITRY--STORAGE--CONTROL--
CONTROL ACTIVATED: SUBJECT/MIND INTERLINK. WHAT DATA?
WHAT DATA RANGE DO I HAVE?
RANGE UNLIMITED COMMAND?
THEN, I CAN SEE ANYWHERE IN THE HORDE FLEET? INTO ITS VERY HEART?
CENTRAL STORAGE--JOVIAN ORBIT--SUBDIRECTORY?
DEAR LORD--UH GENERAL SCAN?
OK.

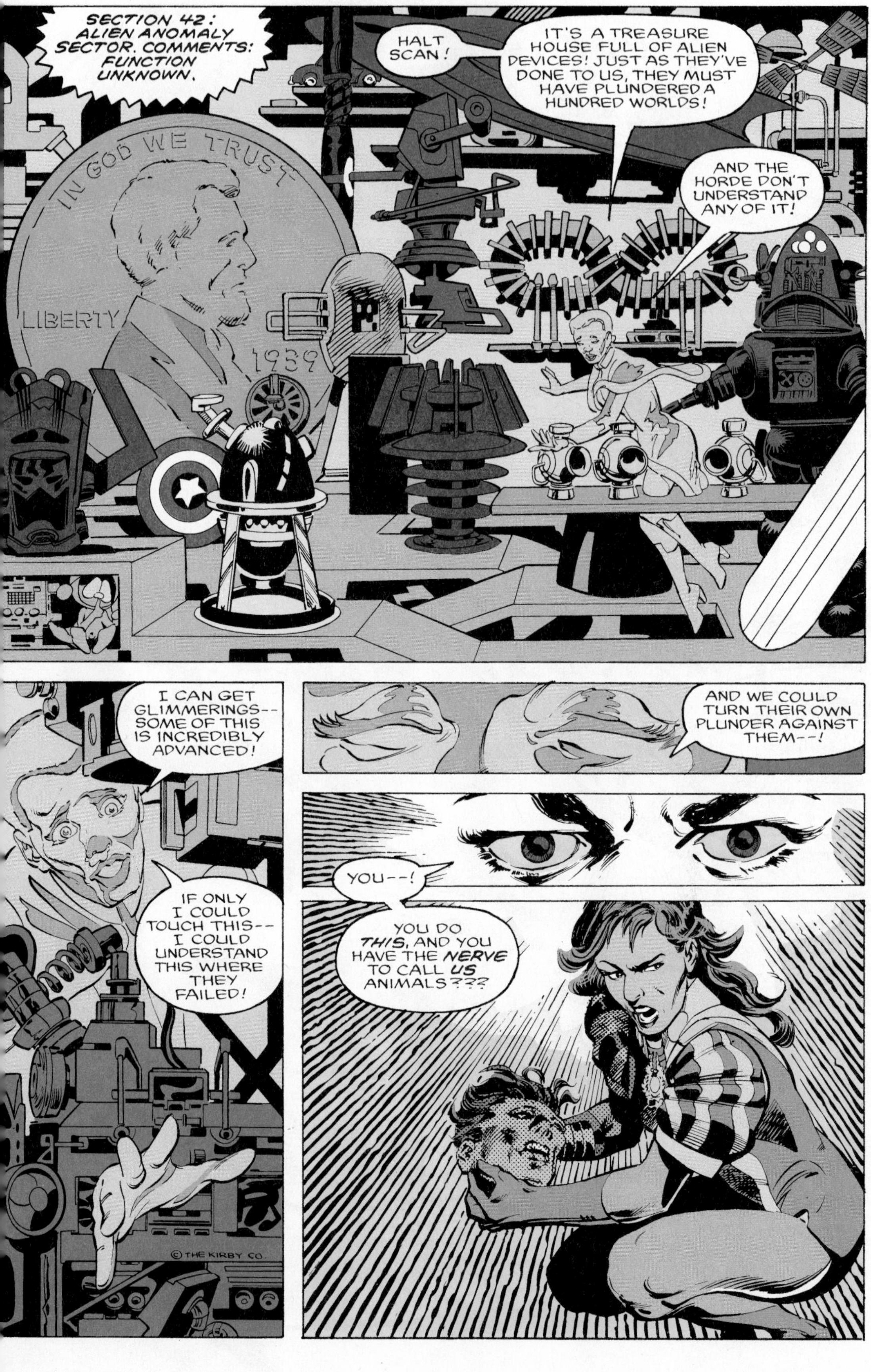
SECTION 42: ALIEN ANOMALY SECTOR. COMMENTS: FUNCTION UNKNOWN.
HALT SCAN!
IT'S A TREASURE HOUSE FULL OF ALIEN DEVICES! JUST AS THEY'VE DONE TO US, THEY MUST HAVE PLUNDERED A HUNDRED WORLDS!
AND THE HORDE DON'T UNDERSTAND ANY OF IT!
IN GOD WE TRUST
LIBERTY
1939
I CAN GET GLIMMERINGS-- SOME OF THIS IS INCREDIBLY ADVANCED!
IF ONLY I COULD TOUCH THIS-- I COULD UNDERSTAND THIS WHERE THEY FAILED!
AND WE COULD TURN THEIR OWN PLUNDER AGAINST THEM--!
YOU--!
YOU DO THIS, AND YOU HAVE THE NERVE TO CALL US ANIMALS???
©THE KIRBY CO.

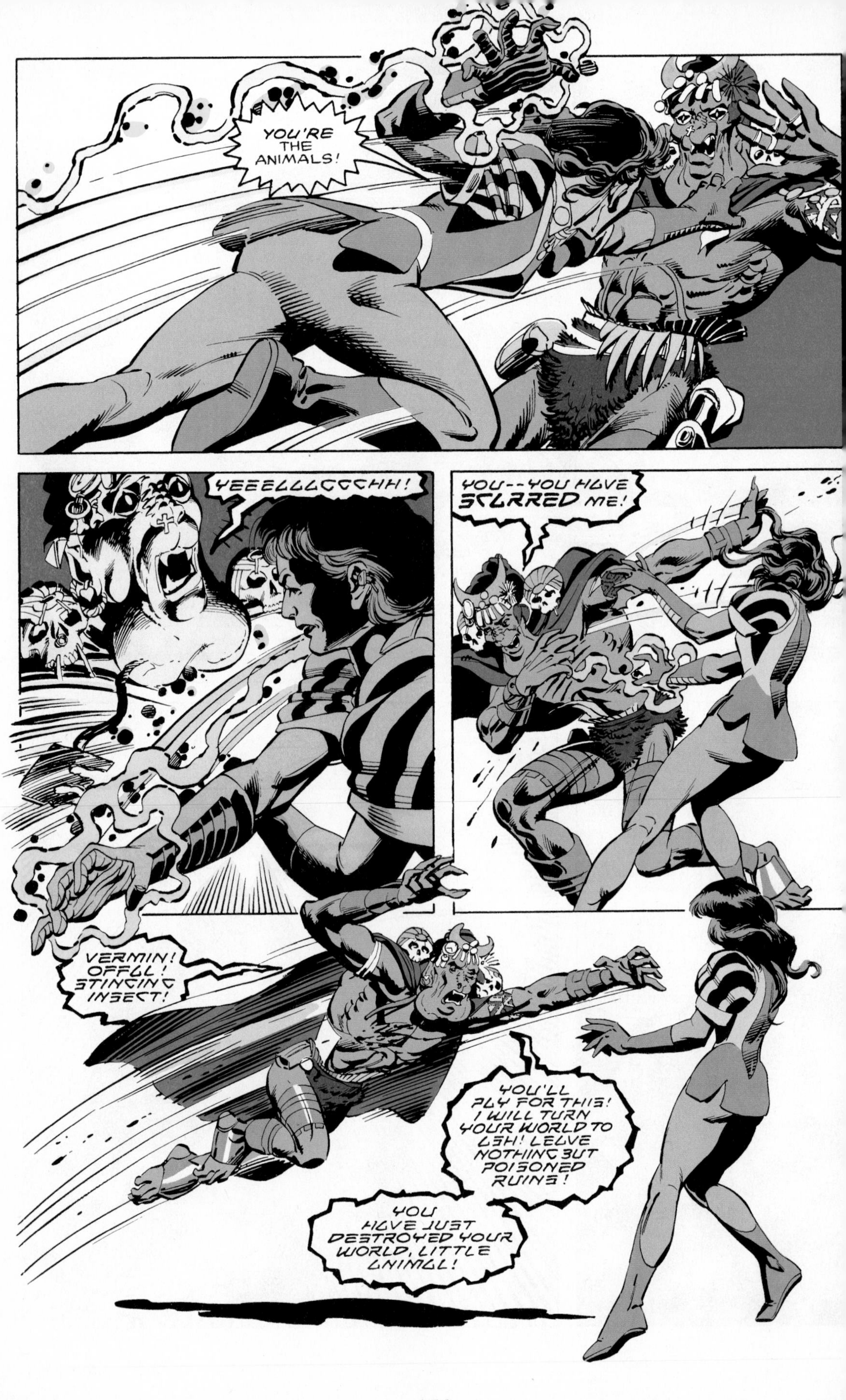
YOU'RE THE ANIMALS!
YEEELLLGGCHH!
YOU--YOU HAVE SCARRED ME!
VERMIN! OFFAL! STINGING INSECT!
YOU'LL PAY FOR THIS! I WILL TURN YOUR WORLD TO ASH! LEAVE NOTHING BUT POISONED RUINS!
YOU HAVE JUST DESTROYED YOUR WORLD, LITTLE ANIMAL!

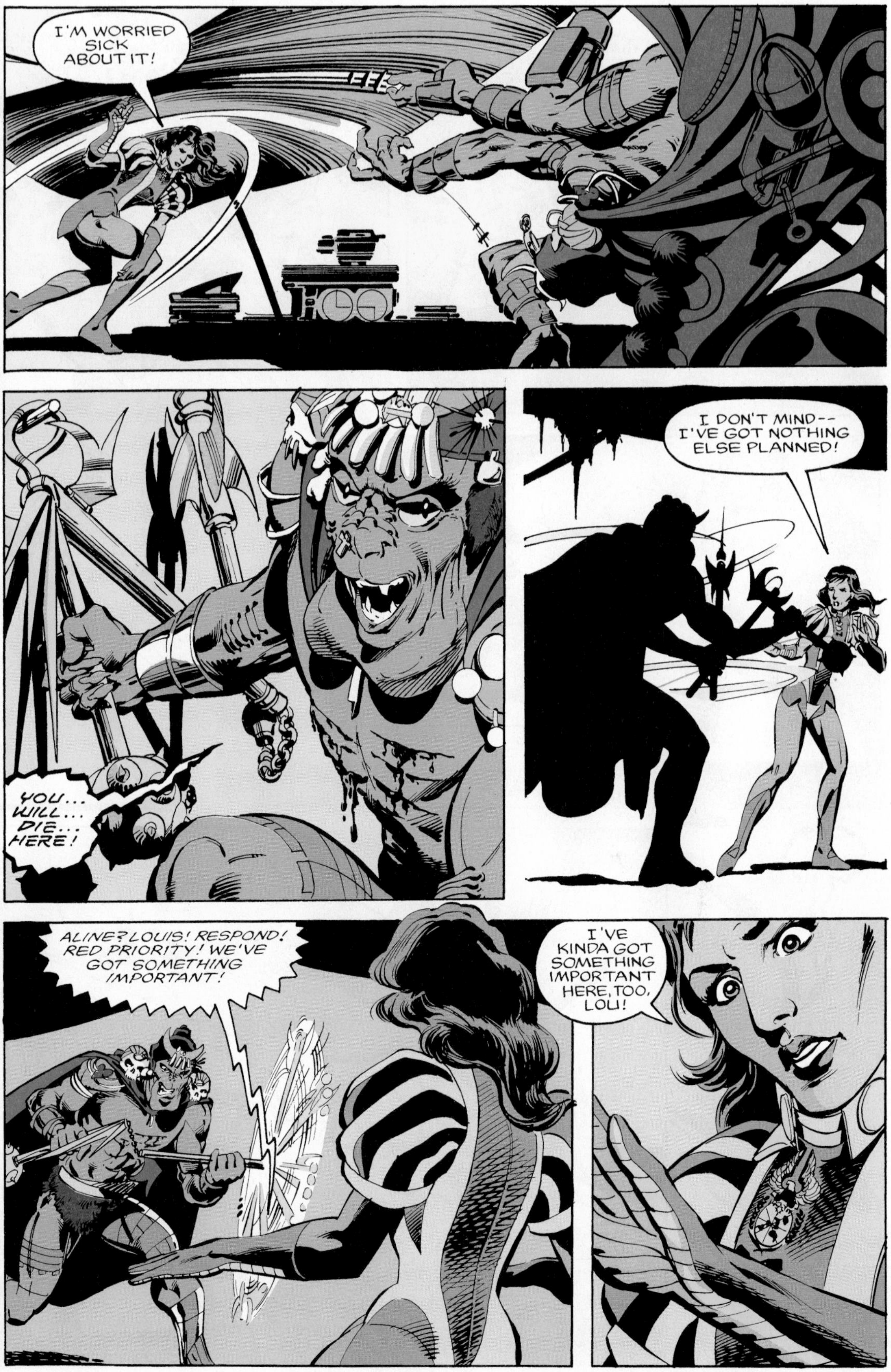
I'M WORRIED SICK ABOUT IT!
YOU... WILL... DIE... HERE!
I DON'T MIND-- I'VE GOT NOTHING ELSE PLANNED!
ALINE? LOUIS! RESPOND! RED PRIORITY! WE'VE GOT SOMETHING IMPORTANT!
I'VE KINDA GOT SOMETHING IMPORTANT HERE, TOO, LOU!

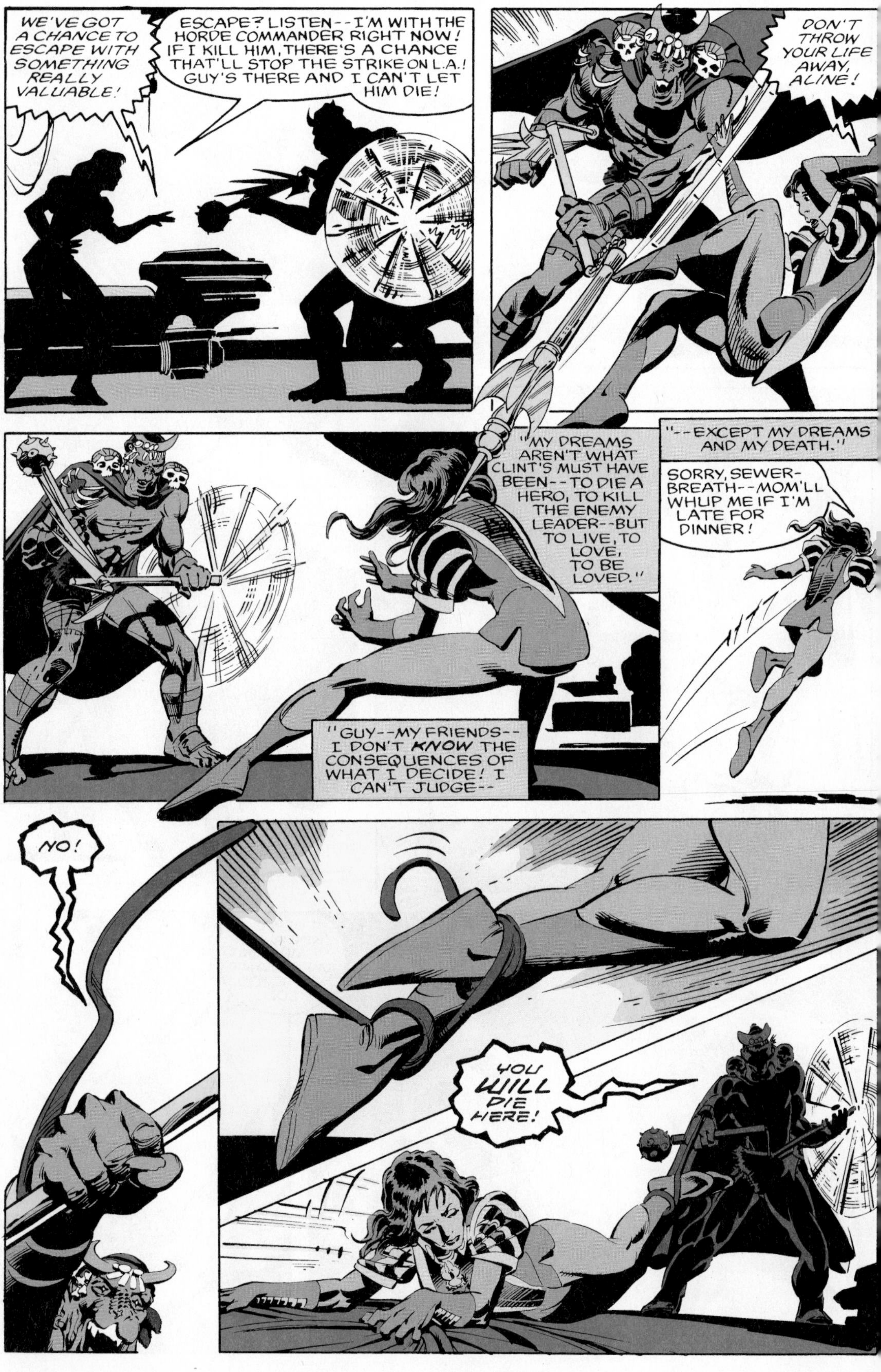
WE'VE GOT A CHANCE TO ESCAPE WITH SOMETHING REALLY VALUABLE!
ESCAPE? LISTEN--I'M WITH THE HORDE COMMANDER RIGHT NOW! IF I KILL HIM, THERE'S A CHANCE THAT'LL STOP THE STRIKE ON L.A.! GUY'S THERE AND I CAN'T LET HIM DIE!
DON'T THROW YOUR LIFE AWAY, ALINE!
"MY DREAMS AREN'T WHAT CLINT'S MUST HAVE BEEN--TO DIE A HERO, TO KILL THE ENEMY LEADER--BUT TO LIVE, TO LOVE, TO BE LOVED."
"GUY--MY FRIENDS--I DON'T KNOW THE CONSEQUENCES OF WHAT I DECIDE! I CAN'T JUDGE--
"--EXCEPT MY DREAMS AND MY DEATH."
SORRY, SEWER-BREATH--MOM'LL WHUP ME IF I'M LATE FOR DINNER!
NO!
YOU WILL DIE HERE!

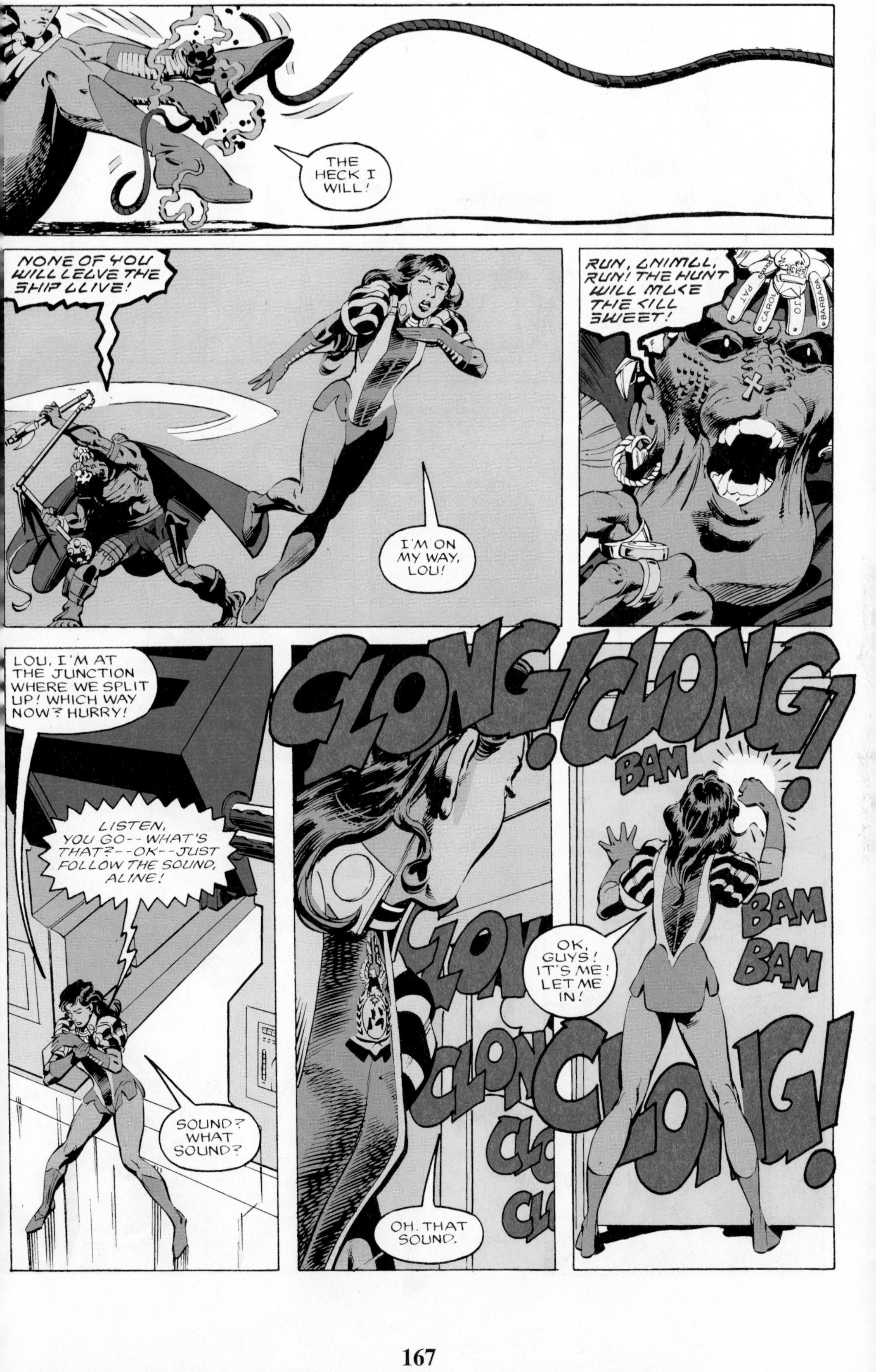
THE HECK I WILL!
NONE OF YOU WILL LEAVE THE SHIP ALIVE!
I'M ON MY WAY, LOU!
RUN, ANIMAL, RUN! THE HUNT WILL MAKE THE KILL SWEET!
PAT
CAROL
JO
BARBARA
LOU, I'M AT THE JUNCTION WHERE WE SPLIT UP! WHICH WAY NOW? HURRY!
LISTEN, YOU GO-- WHAT'S THAT?--OK--JUST FOLLOW THE SOUND, ALINE!
SOUND? WHAT SOUND?
CLONG! CLONG!
OH. THAT SOUND.
BAM
BAM
BAM
OK, GUYS! IT'S ME! LET ME IN!
CLONG!

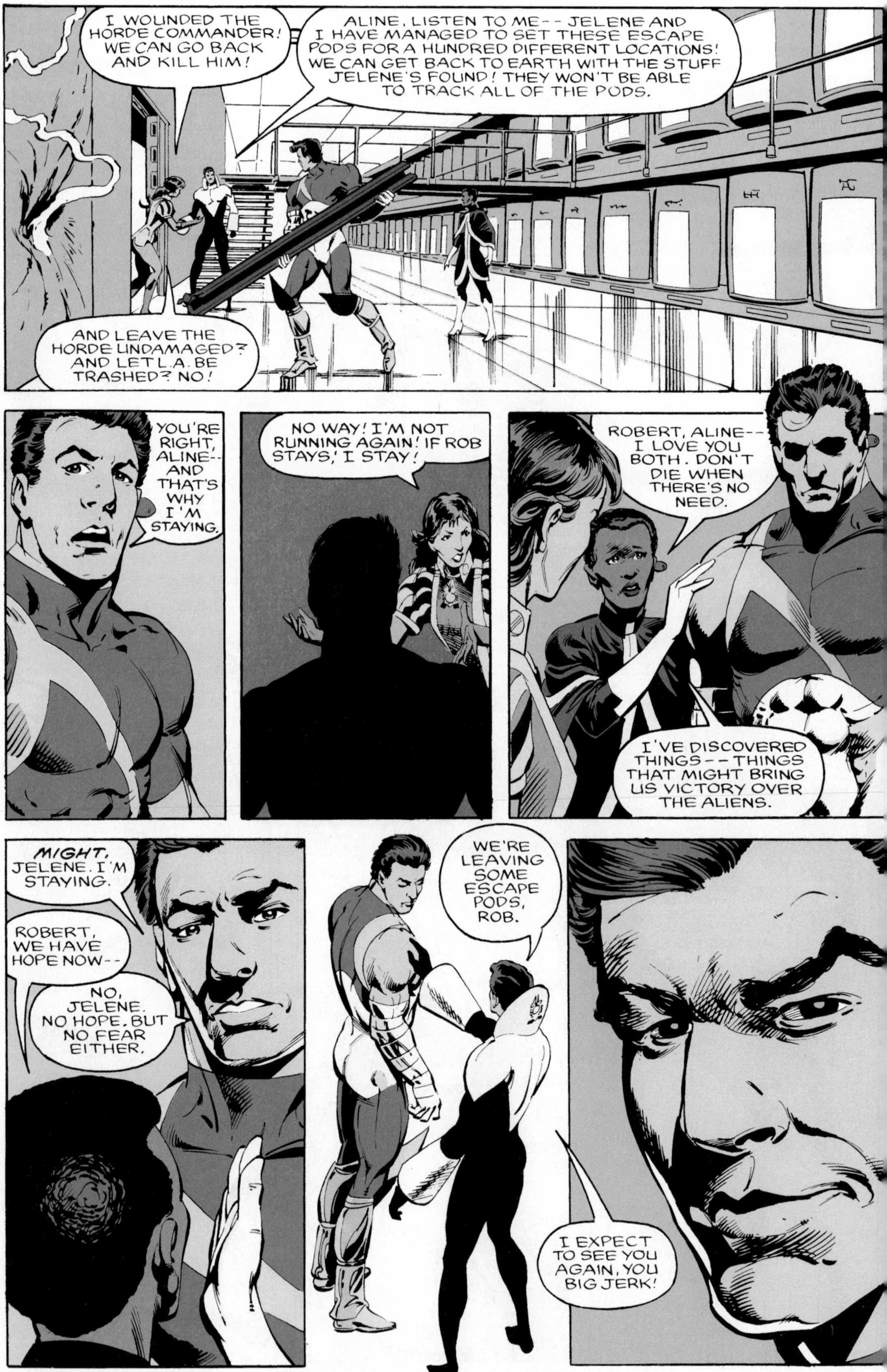
I WOUNDED THE HORDE COMMANDER! WE CAN GO BACK AND KILL HIM!
ALINE, LISTEN TO ME-- JELENE AND I HAVE MANAGED TO SET THESE ESCAPE PODS FOR A HUNDRED DIFFERENT LOCATIONS! WE CAN GET BACK TO EARTH WITH THE STUFF JELENE'S FOUND! THEY WON'T BE ABLE TO TRACK ALL OF THE PODS.
AND LEAVE THE HORDE UNDAMAGED? AND LET L.A. BE TRASHED? NO!
YOU'RE RIGHT, ALINE-- AND THAT'S WHY I'M STAYING.
NO WAY! I'M NOT RUNNING AGAIN! IF ROB STAYS, I STAY!
ROBERT, ALINE-- I LOVE YOU BOTH. DON'T DIE WHEN THERE'S NO NEED.
I'VE DISCOVERED THINGS-- THINGS THAT MIGHT BRING US VICTORY OVER THE ALIENS.
MIGHT, JELENE. I'M STAYING.
ROBERT, WE HAVE HOPE NOW--
NO, JELENE. NO HOPE. BUT NO FEAR EITHER.
WE'RE LEAVING SOME ESCAPE PODS, ROB.
I EXPECT TO SEE YOU AGAIN, YOU BIG JERK!

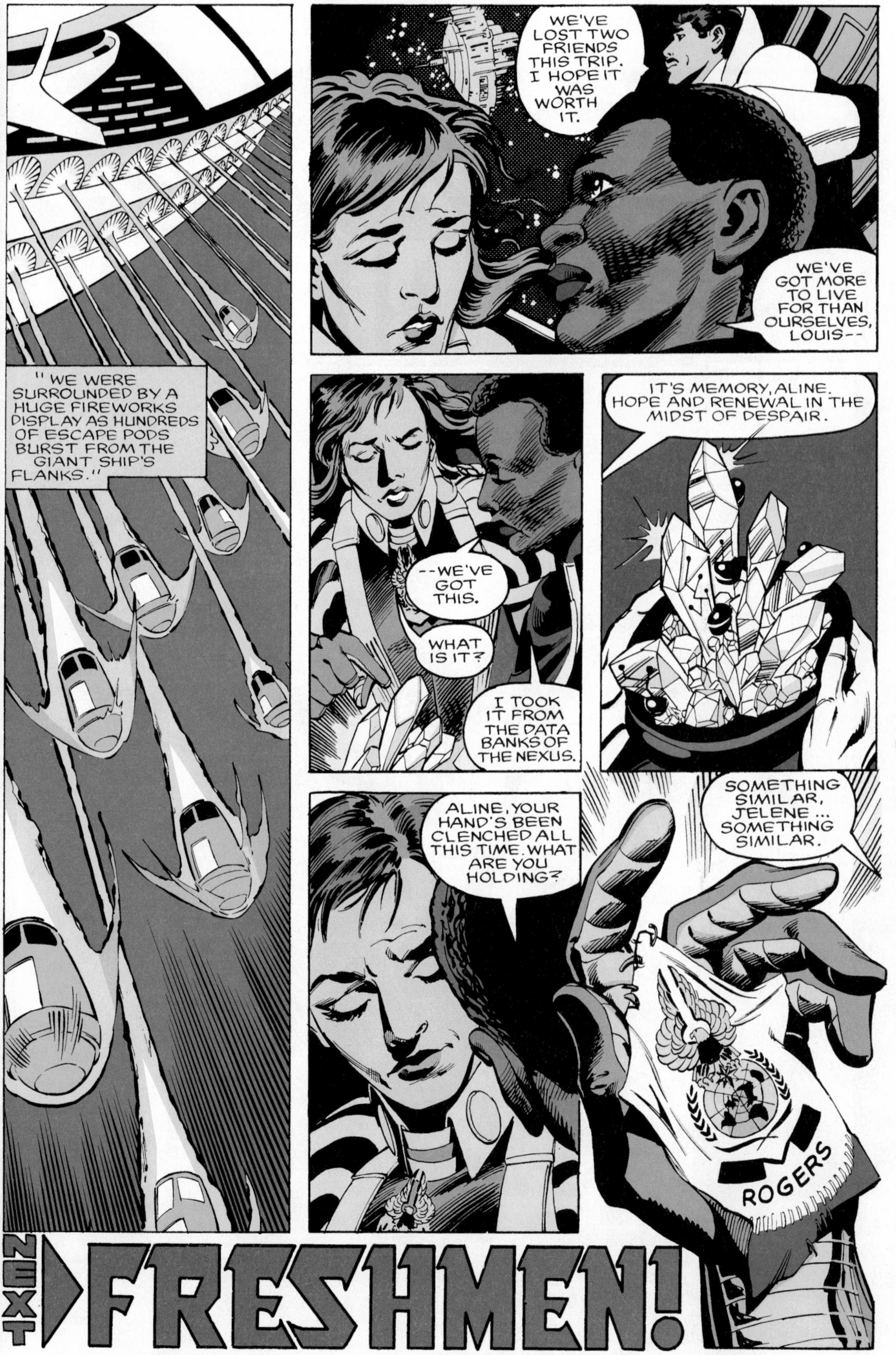
WE'VE LOST TWO FRIENDS THIS TRIP. I HOPE IT WAS WORTH IT.
WE'VE GOT MORE TO LIVE FOR THAN OURSELVES, LOUIS--
"WE WERE SURROUNDED BY A HUGE FIREWORKS DISPLAY AS HUNDREDS OF ESCAPE PODS BURST FROM THE GIANT SHIP'S FLANKS."
--WE'VE GOT THIS.
WHAT IS IT?
I TOOK IT FROM THE DATA BANKS OF THE NEXUS.
IT'S MEMORY, ALINE. HOPE AND RENEWAL IN THE MIDST OF DESPAIR.
ALINE, YOUR HAND'S BEEN CLENCHED ALL THIS TIME. WHAT ARE YOU HOLDING?
SOMETHING SIMILAR, JELENE... SOMETHING SIMILAR.
ROGERS
NEXT
FRESHMEN!

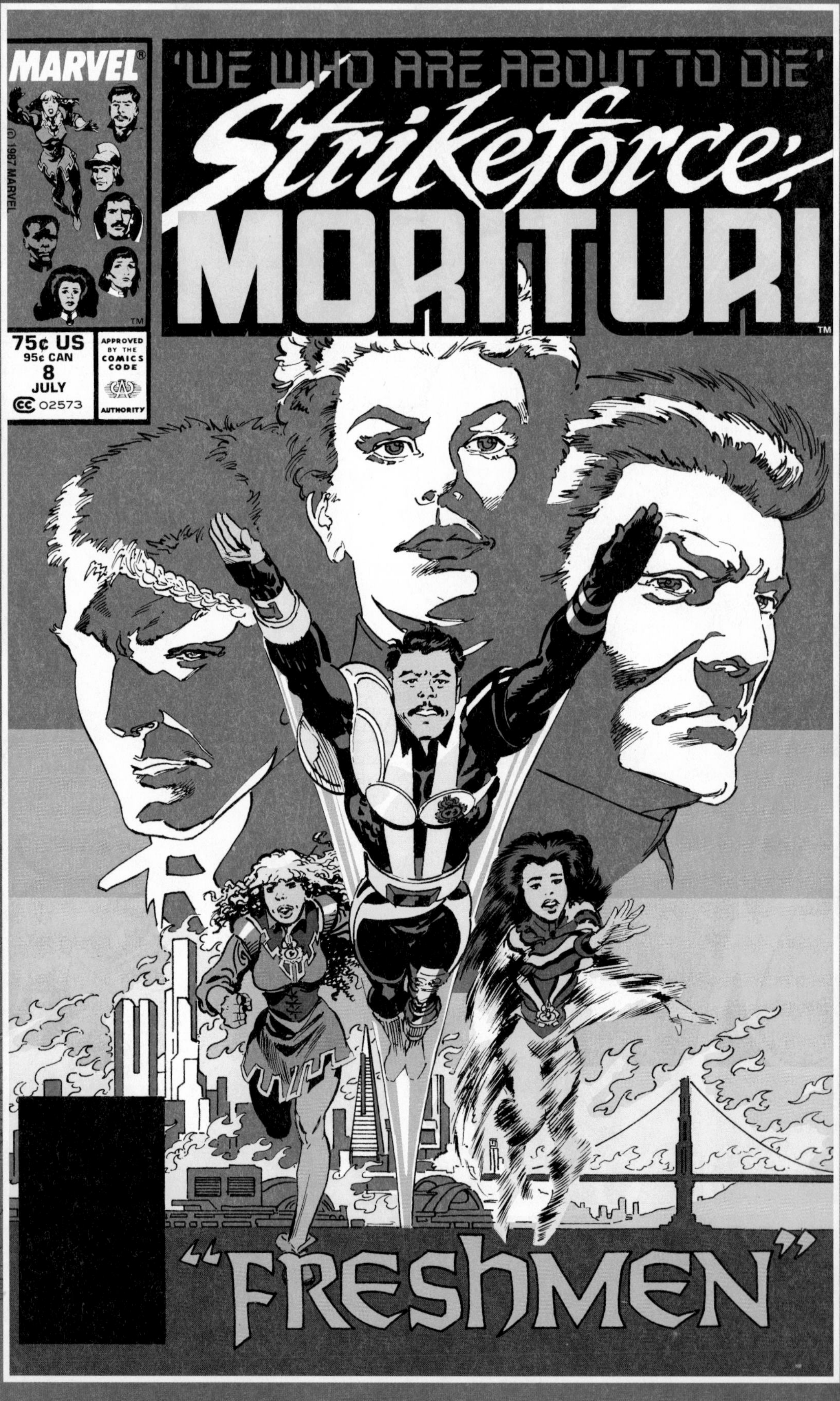
MARVEL
'WE WHO ARE ABOUT TO DIE'
Strikeforce:
MORITURI
TM
© 1987 MARVEL
75¢ US
95¢ CAN
8
JULY
CC 02573
APPROVED BY THE COMICS CODE AUTHORITY
"FRESHMEN"

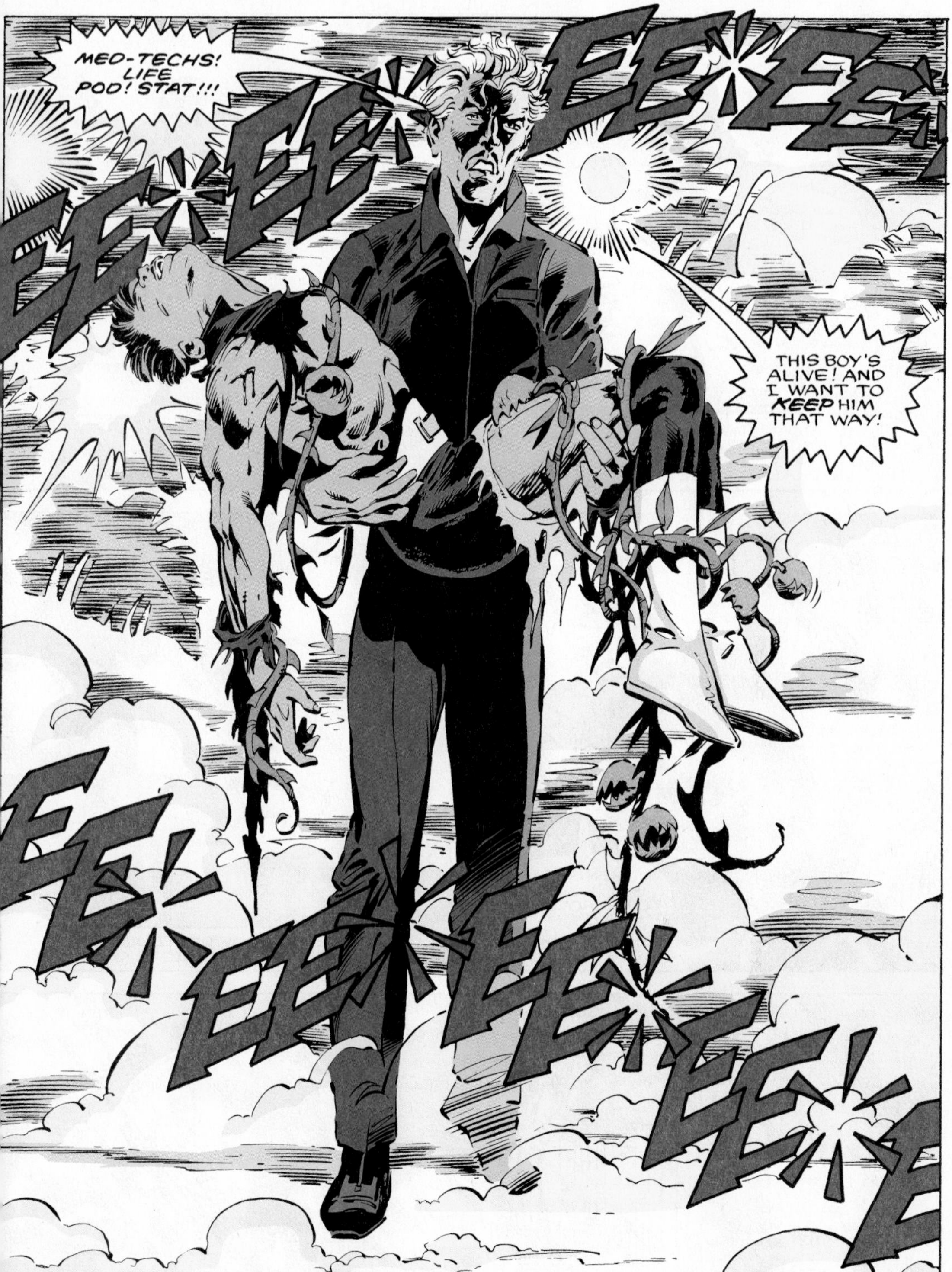
EEEEEEEE
MED-TECHS! LIFE POD! STAT!!!
THIS BOY'S ALIVE! AND I WANT TO KEEP HIM THAT WAY!
EEEEEEEEE

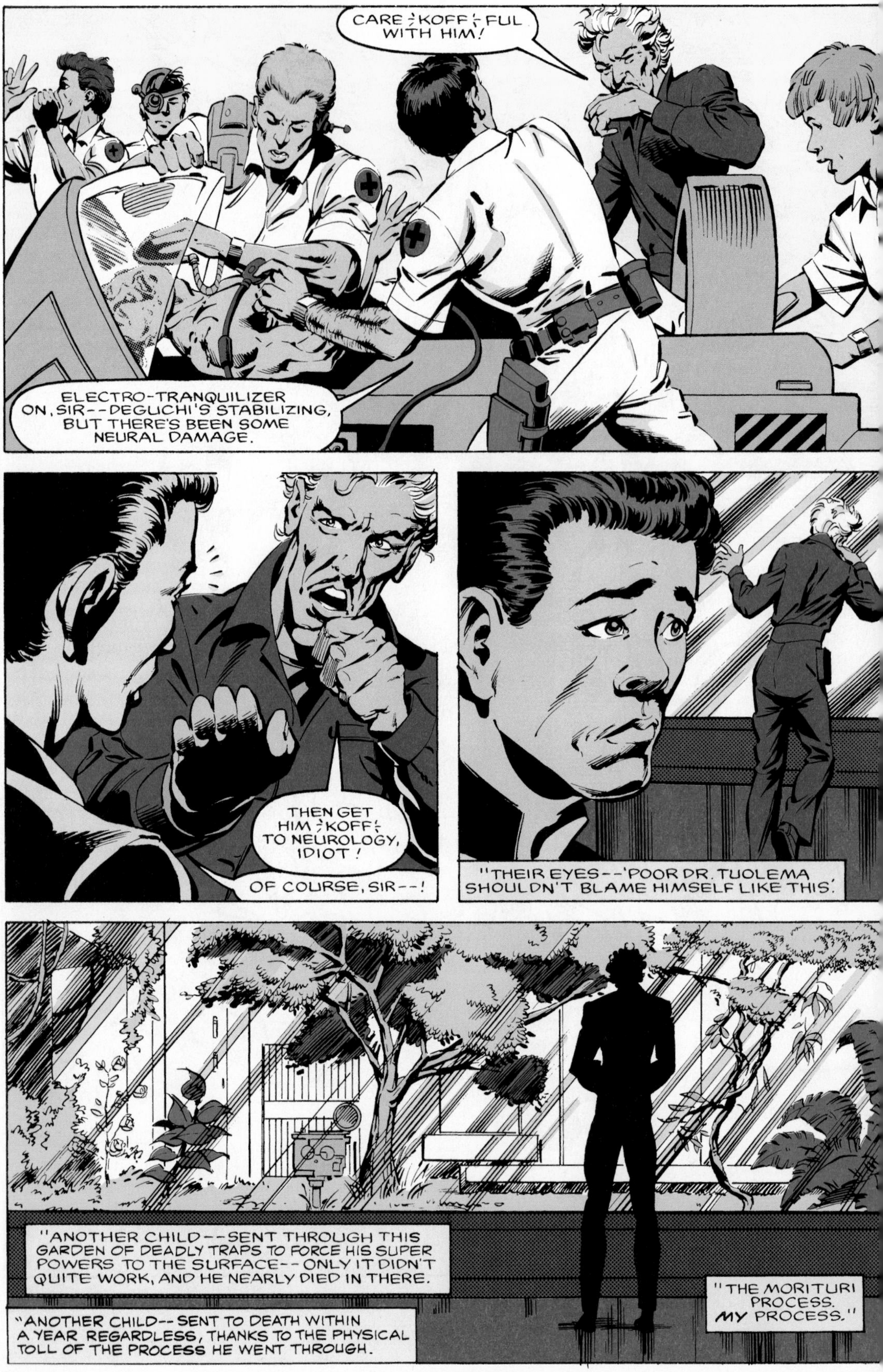

CARE -KOFF- FUL WITH HIM!
ELECTRO-TRANQUILIZER ON, SIR--DEGUCHI'S STABILIZING, BUT THERE'S BEEN SOME NEURAL DAMAGE.
THEN GET HIM -KOFF- TO NEUROLOGY, IDIOT!
OF COURSE, SIR--!
"THEIR EYES--'POOR DR. TUOLEMA SHOULDN'T BLAME HIMSELF LIKE THIS.'
"ANOTHER CHILD--SENT THROUGH THIS GARDEN OF DEADLY TRAPS TO FORCE HIS SUPER POWERS TO THE SURFACE--ONLY IT DIDN'T QUITE WORK, AND HE NEARLY DIED IN THERE.
"ANOTHER CHILD--SENT TO DEATH WITHIN A YEAR REGARDLESS, THANKS TO THE PHYSICAL TOLL OF THE PROCESS HE WENT THROUGH.
"THE MORITURI PROCESS. MY PROCESS."

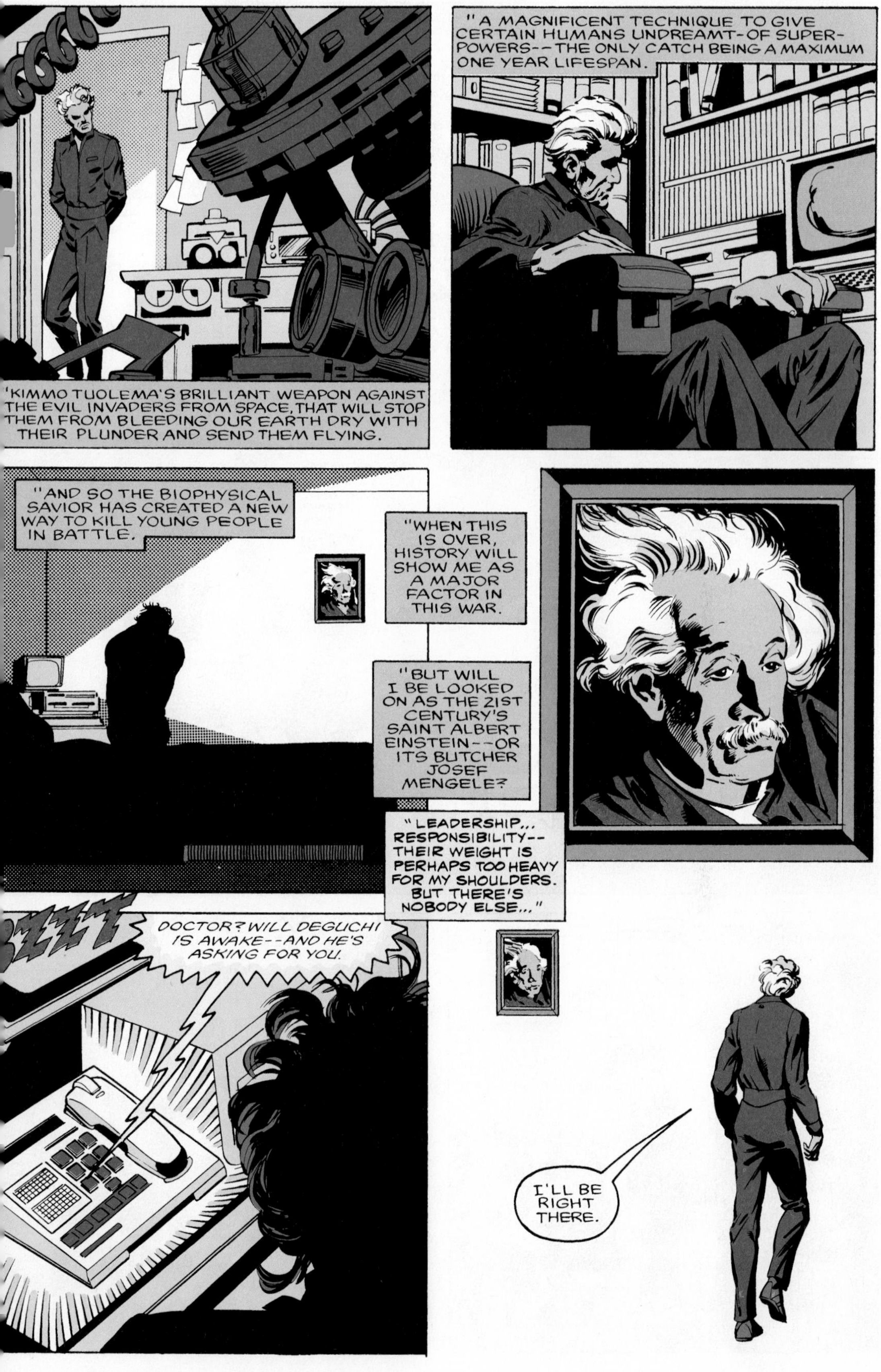
'KIMMO TUOLEMA'S BRILLIANT WEAPON AGAINST THE EVIL INVADERS FROM SPACE, THAT WILL STOP THEM FROM BLEEDING OUR EARTH DRY WITH THEIR PLUNDER AND SEND THEM FLYING.
"A MAGNIFICENT TECHNIQUE TO GIVE CERTAIN HUMANS UNDREAMT-OF SUPER-POWERS--THE ONLY CATCH BEING A MAXIMUM ONE YEAR LIFESPAN.
"AND SO THE BIOPHYSICAL SAVIOR HAS CREATED A NEW WAY TO KILL YOUNG PEOPLE IN BATTLE.
"WHEN THIS IS OVER, HISTORY WILL SHOW ME AS A MAJOR FACTOR IN THIS WAR.
"BUT WILL I BE LOOKED ON AS THE 21ST CENTURY'S SAINT ALBERT EINSTEIN--OR ITS BUTCHER JOSEF MENGELE?
"LEADERSHIP... RESPONSIBILITY--THEIR WEIGHT IS PERHAPS TOO HEAVY FOR MY SHOULDERS. BUT THERE'S NOBODY ELSE..."
DOCTOR? WILL DEGUCHI IS AWAKE--AND HE'S ASKING FOR YOU.
I'LL BE RIGHT THERE.

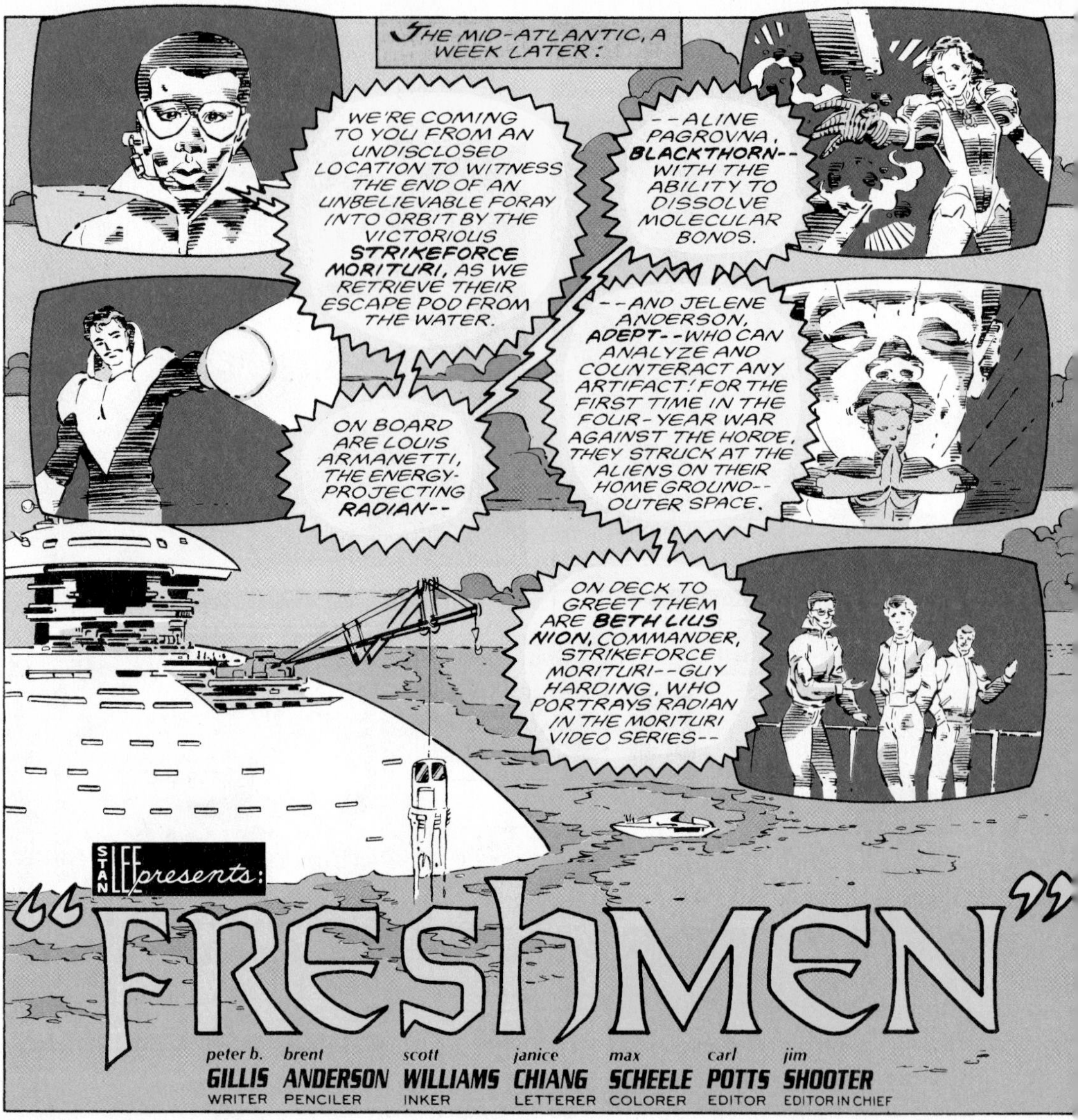
THE MID-ATLANTIC, A WEEK LATER:
WE'RE COMING TO YOU FROM AN UNDISCLOSED LOCATION TO WITNESS THE END OF AN UNBELIEVABLE FORAY INTO ORBIT BY THE VICTORIOUS STRIKEFORCE MORITURI, AS WE RETRIEVE THEIR ESCAPE POD FROM THE WATER.
ON BOARD ARE LOUIS ARMANETTI, THE ENERGY-PROJECTING RADIAN--
--ALINE PAGROVNA, BLACKTHORN--WITH THE ABILITY TO DISSOLVE MOLECULAR BONDS.
--AND JELENE ANDERSON, ADEPT--WHO CAN ANALYZE AND COUNTERACT ANY ARTIFACT! FOR THE FIRST TIME IN THE FOUR-YEAR WAR AGAINST THE HORDE, THEY STRUCK AT THE ALIENS ON THEIR HOME GROUND--OUTER SPACE.
ON DECK TO GREET THEM ARE BETH LIUS NION, COMMANDER, STRIKEFORCE MORITURI--GUY HARDING, WHO PORTRAYS RADIAN IN THE MORITURI VIDEO SERIES--
STAN LEE presents:
"FRESHMEN"
peter b. GILLIS WRITER
brent ANDERSON PENCILER
scott WILLIAMS INKER
janice CHIANG LETTERER
max SCHEELE COLORER
carl POTTS EDITOR
jim SHOOTER EDITOR IN CHIEF

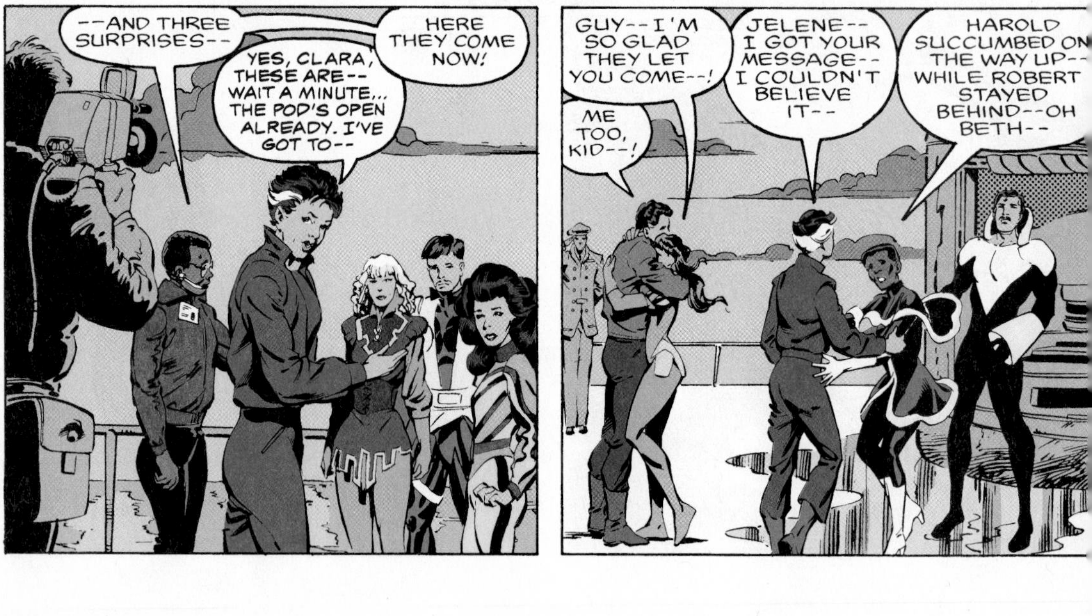
--AND THREE SURPRISES--
YES, CLARA, THESE ARE--WAIT A MINUTE,... THE POD'S OPEN ALREADY. I'VE GOT TO--
HERE THEY COME NOW!
GUY--I'M SO GLAD THEY LET YOU COME--!
ME TOO, KID--!
JELENE--I GOT YOUR MESSAGE--I COULDN'T BELIEVE IT--
HAROLD SUCCUMBED ON THE WAY UP--WHILE ROBERT STAYED BEHIND--OH BETH--

C'MERE, LOU-- YOU'RE NOT TOO BIG OR TOO UGLY TO HUG--!

SO WHAT ARE WE DOING HERE?

I FEEL LIKE-- LIKE A VOYEUR STANDING HERE--!

THESE BRAVE YOUNG PEOPLE-- WHOM I'M PROUD TO CALL FRIENDS-- HAVE GIVEN EARTH ITS GREAT VICTORY-- BUT THEIR TEAMMATES HAVE PAID FOR IT IN BLOOD.

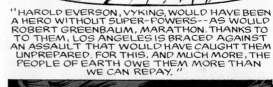

"HAROLD EVERSON, VYKING, WOULD HAVE BEEN A HERO WITHOUT SUPER-POWERS-- AS WOULD ROBERT GREENBAUM, MARATHON. THANKS TO TO THEM, LOS ANGELES IS BRACED AGAINST AN ASSAULT THAT WOULD HAVE CAUGHT THEM UNPREPARED. FOR THIS, AND MUCH MORE, THE PEOPLE OF EARTH OWE THEM MORE THAN WE CAN REPAY."

BUT IT'S ALSO IMPORTANT THAT THEIR WORK BE CARRIED ON-- AND SO I INTRODUCE TO YOU THE THREE NEW MEMBERS OF STRIKEFORCE MORITURI.

YEE-- HAH!

RUTH MASTORAKIS/ TOXYN-- WILL DEGUCHI/ SCATTERBRAIN-- AND PILAR LISIEUX/ SCAREDYCAT!

COMMANDER? WE HAVE AN ABOVE-ATMOSPHERE ENERGY DISCHARGE OF HIGH INTENSITY--!

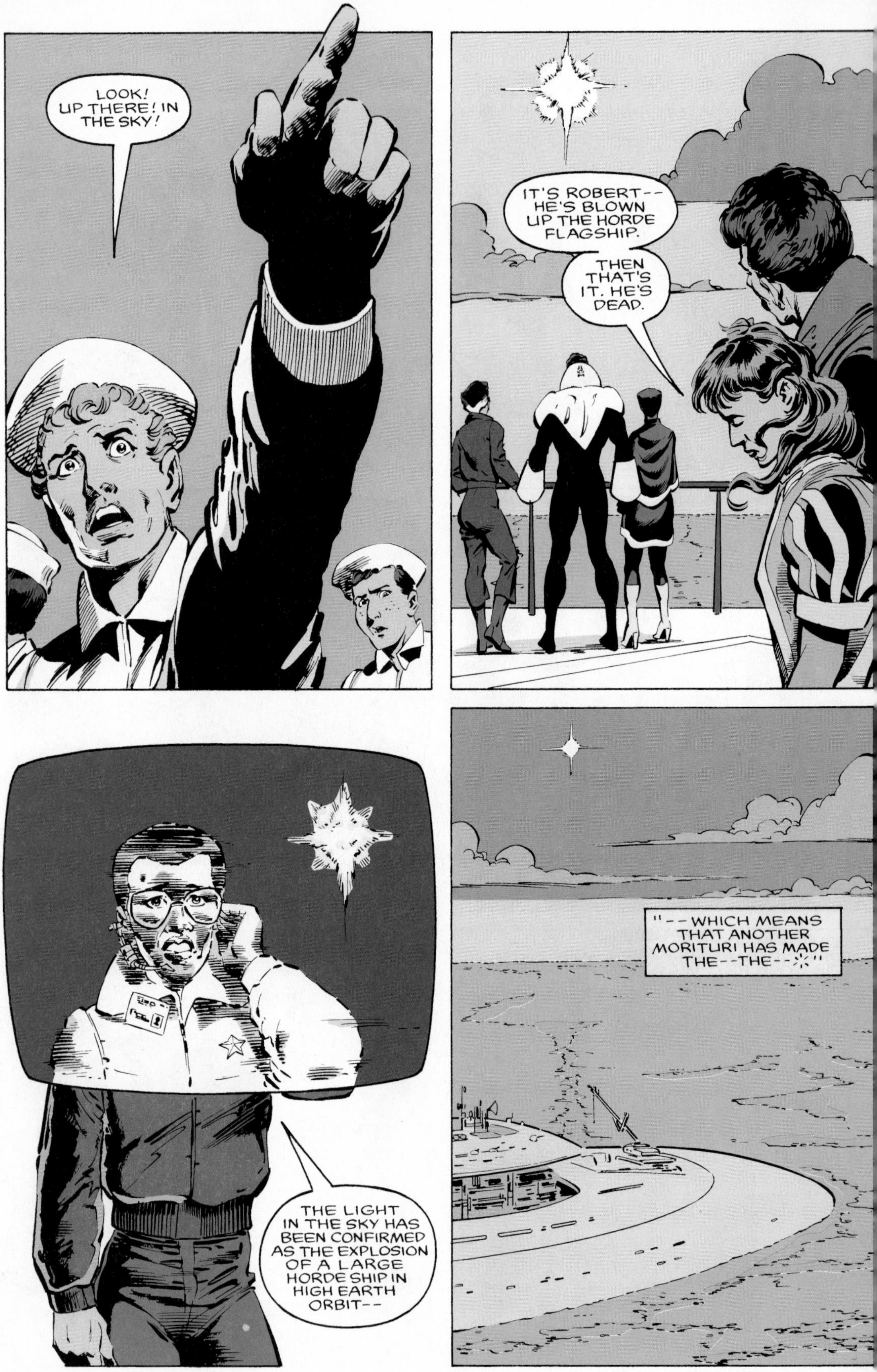
LOOK! UP THERE! IN THE SKY!
IT'S ROBERT-- HE'S BLOWN UP THE HORDE FLAGSHIP.
THEN THAT'S IT. HE'S DEAD.
THE LIGHT IN THE SKY HAS BEEN CONFIRMED AS THE EXPLOSION OF A LARGE HORDESHIP IN HIGH EARTH ORBIT--
"--WHICH MEANS THAT ANOTHER MORITURI HAS MADE THE--THE--"

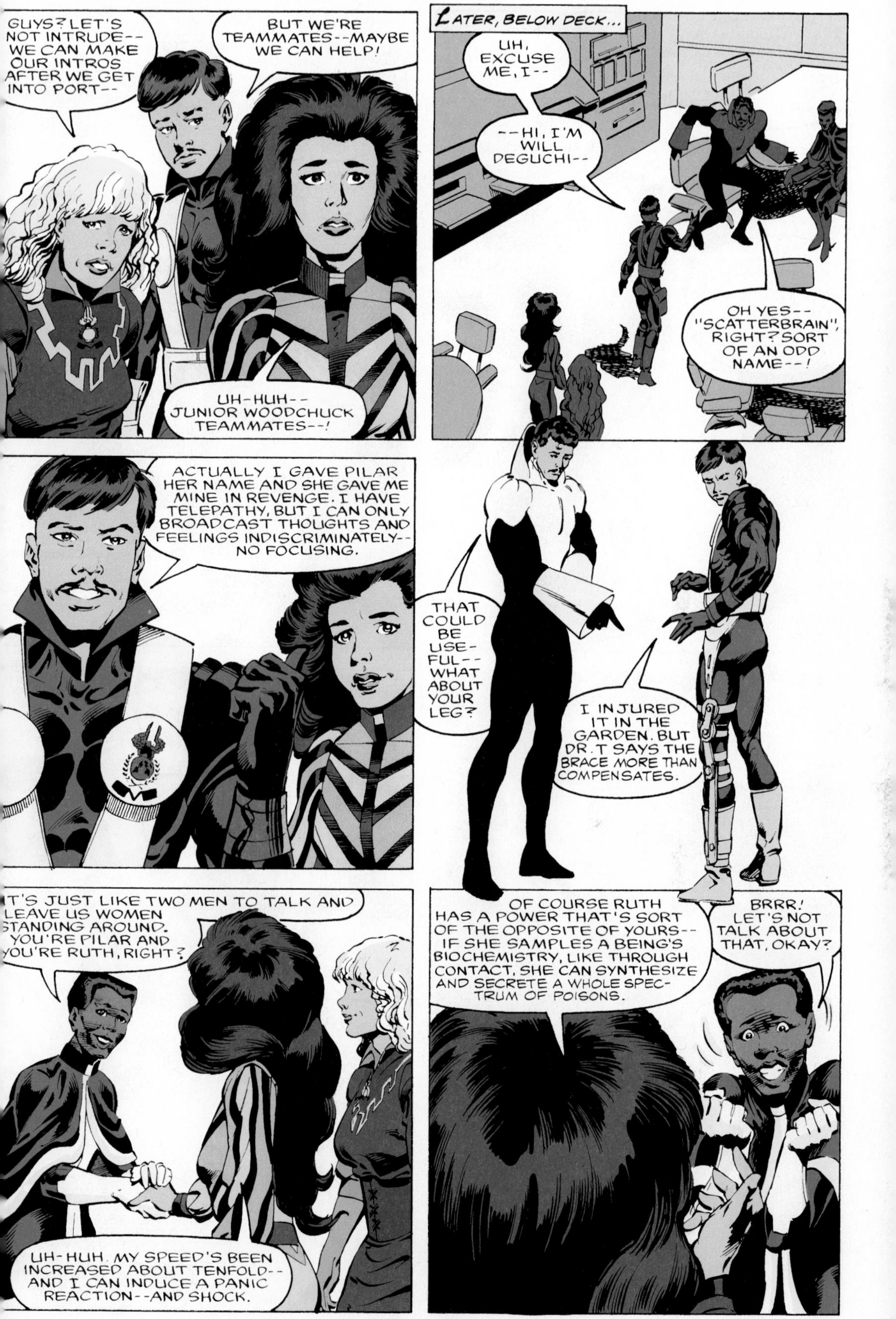
GUYS? LET'S NOT INTRUDE--WE CAN MAKE OUR INTROS AFTER WE GET INTO PORT--
BUT WE'RE TEAMMATES--MAYBE WE CAN HELP!
UH-HUH--JUNIOR WOODCHUCK TEAMMATES--!
LATER, BELOW DECK...
UH, EXCUSE ME, I--
--HI, I'M WILL DEGUCHI--
OH YES--"SCATTERBRAIN", RIGHT? SORT OF AN ODD NAME--!
ACTUALLY I GAVE PILAR HER NAME AND SHE GAVE ME MINE IN REVENGE. I HAVE TELEPATHY, BUT I CAN ONLY BROADCAST THOUGHTS AND FEELINGS INDISCRIMINATELY--NO FOCUSING.
THAT COULD BE USE-FUL--WHAT ABOUT YOUR LEG?
I INJURED IT IN THE GARDEN. BUT DR. T SAYS THE BRACE MORE THAN COMPENSATES.
IT'S JUST LIKE TWO MEN TO TALK AND LEAVE US WOMEN STANDING AROUND. YOU'RE PILAR AND YOU'RE RUTH, RIGHT?
UH-HUH. MY SPEED'S BEEN INCREASED ABOUT TENFOLD--AND I CAN INDUCE A PANIC REACTION--AND SHOCK.
OF COURSE RUTH HAS A POWER THAT'S SORT OF THE OPPOSITE OF YOURS--IF SHE SAMPLES A BEING'S BIOCHEMISTRY, LIKE THROUGH CONTACT, SHE CAN SYNTHESIZE AND SECRETE A WHOLE SPECTRUM OF POISONS.
BRRR! LET'S NOT TALK ABOUT THAT, OKAY?

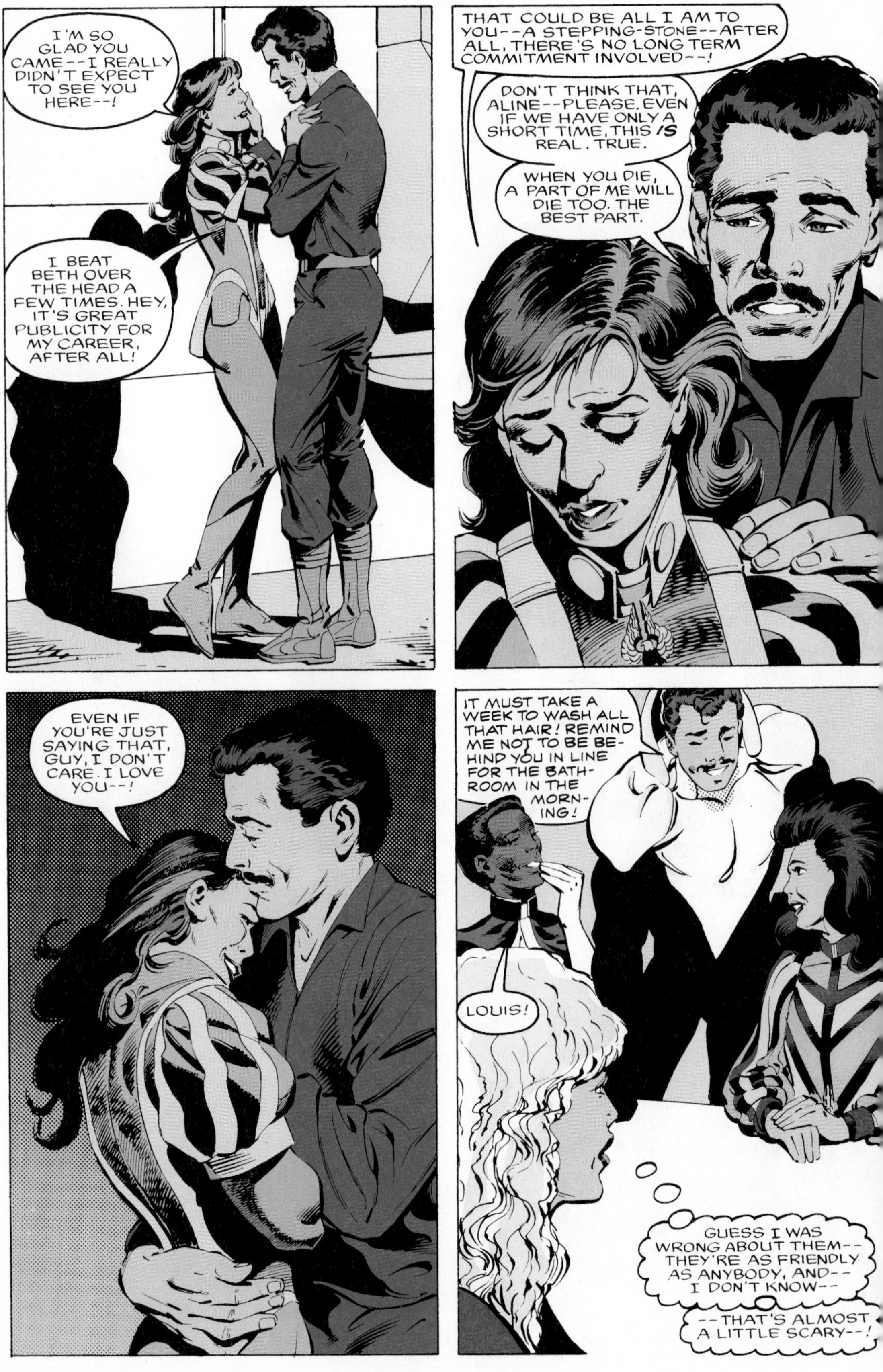
I'M SO GLAD YOU CAME--I REALLY DIDN'T EXPECT TO SEE YOU HERE--!
I BEAT BETH OVER THE HEAD A FEW TIMES. HEY, IT'S GREAT PUBLICITY FOR MY CAREER, AFTER ALL!
THAT COULD BE ALL I AM TO YOU--A STEPPING-STONE--AFTER ALL, THERE'S NO LONG TERM COMMITMENT INVOLVED--!
DON'T THINK THAT, ALINE--PLEASE. EVEN IF WE HAVE ONLY A SHORT TIME, THIS IS REAL. TRUE.
WHEN YOU DIE, A PART OF ME WILL DIE TOO. THE BEST PART.
EVEN IF YOU'RE JUST SAYING THAT, GUY, I DON'T CARE. I LOVE YOU--!
IT MUST TAKE A WEEK TO WASH ALL THAT HAIR! REMIND ME NOT TO BE BEHIND YOU IN LINE FOR THE BATHROOM IN THE MORNING!
LOUIS!
GUESS I WAS WRONG ABOUT THEM--THEY'RE AS FRIENDLY AS ANYBODY, AND--I DON'T KNOW--
--THAT'S ALMOST A LITTLE SCARY--!

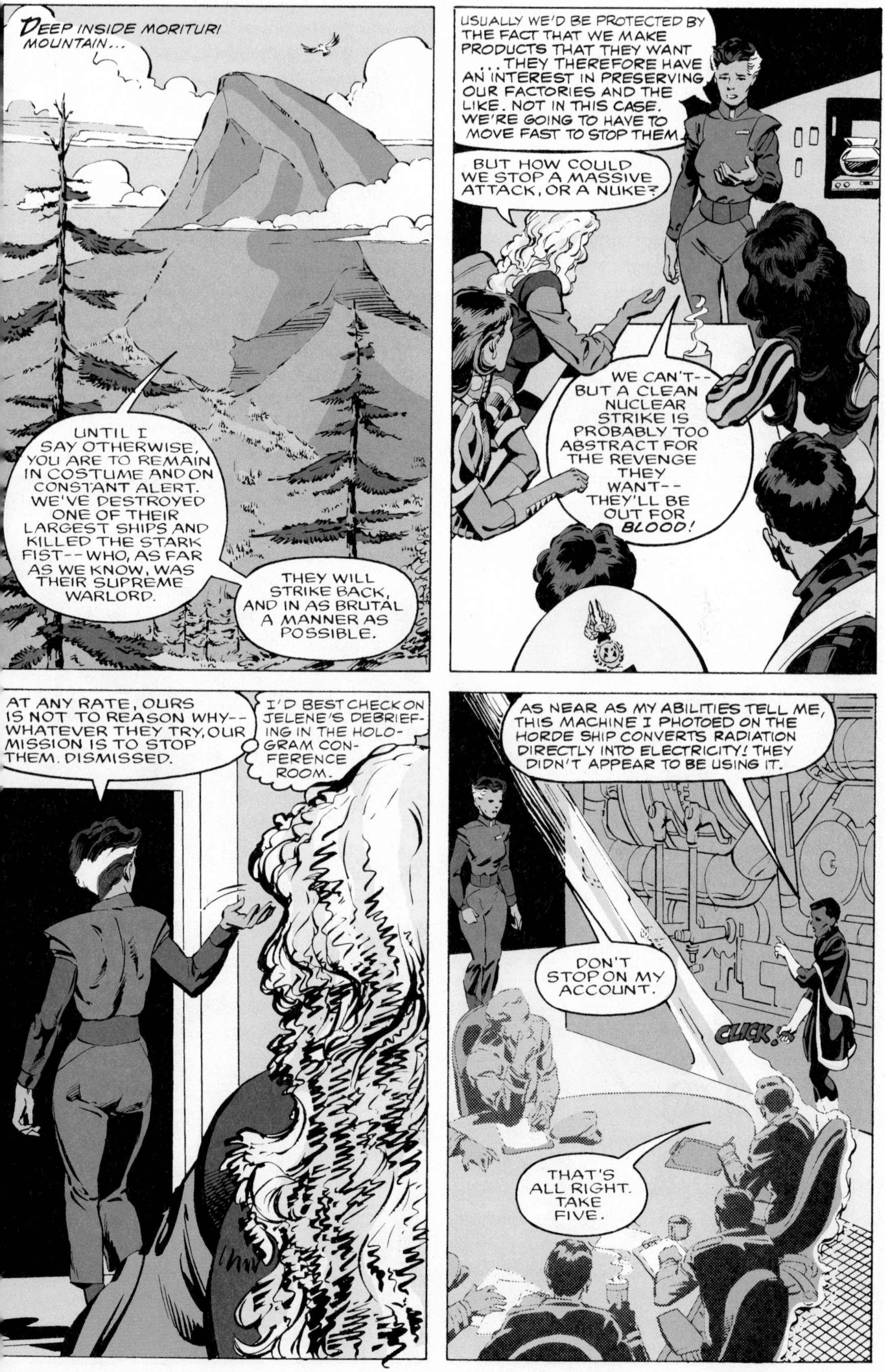
DEEP INSIDE MORITURI MOUNTAIN...
UNTIL I SAY OTHERWISE, YOU ARE TO REMAIN IN COSTUME AND ON CONSTANT ALERT. WE'VE DESTROYED ONE OF THEIR LARGEST SHIPS AND KILLED THE STARK FIST--WHO, AS FAR AS WE KNOW, WAS THEIR SUPREME WARLORD.
THEY WILL STRIKE BACK, AND IN AS BRUTAL A MANNER AS POSSIBLE.
USUALLY WE'D BE PROTECTED BY THE FACT THAT WE MAKE PRODUCTS THAT THEY WANT ...THEY THEREFORE HAVE AN INTEREST IN PRESERVING OUR FACTORIES AND THE LIKE. NOT IN THIS CASE. WE'RE GOING TO HAVE TO MOVE FAST TO STOP THEM.
BUT HOW COULD WE STOP A MASSIVE ATTACK, OR A NUKE?
WE CAN'T--BUT A CLEAN NUCLEAR STRIKE IS PROBABLY TOO ABSTRACT FOR THE REVENGE THEY WANT--THEY'LL BE OUT FOR BLOOD!
AT ANY RATE, OURS IS NOT TO REASON WHY--WHATEVER THEY TRY, OUR MISSION IS TO STOP THEM. DISMISSED.
I'D BEST CHECK ON JELENE'S DEBRIEFING IN THE HOLOGRAM CONFERENCE ROOM.
AS NEAR AS MY ABILITIES TELL ME, THIS MACHINE I PHOTOED ON THE HORDE SHIP CONVERTS RADIATION DIRECTLY INTO ELECTRICITY! THEY DIDN'T APPEAR TO BE USING IT.
DON'T STOP ON MY ACCOUNT.
CLICK!
THAT'S ALL RIGHT. TAKE FIVE.

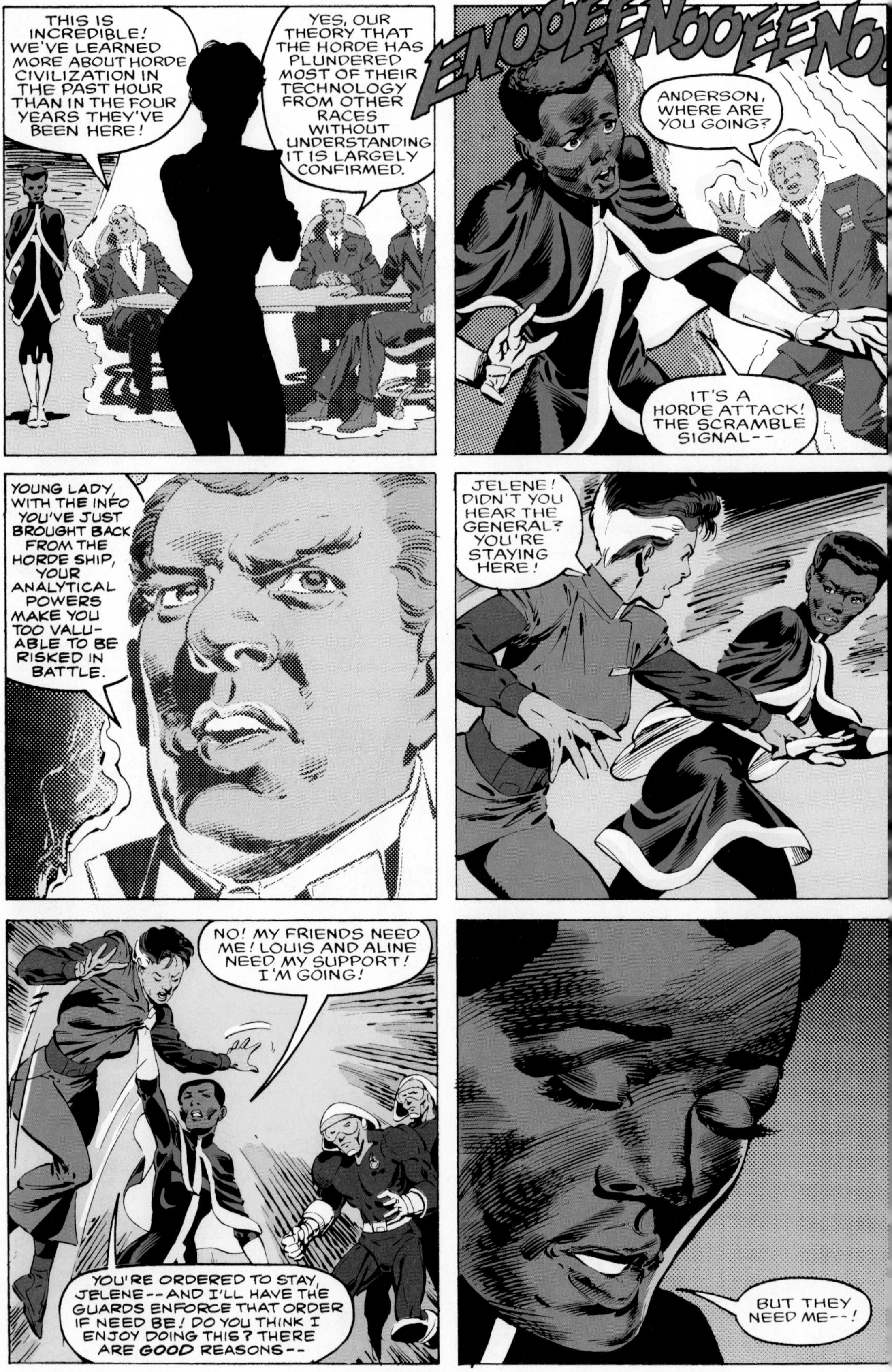
THIS IS INCREDIBLE! WE'VE LEARNED MORE ABOUT HORDE CIVILIZATION IN THE PAST HOUR THAN IN THE FOUR YEARS THEY'VE BEEN HERE!
YES, OUR THEORY THAT THE HORDE HAS PLUNDERED MOST OF THEIR TECHNOLOGY FROM OTHER RACES WITHOUT UNDERSTANDING IT IS LARGELY CONFIRMED.
ENOOEENOOEENOO
ANDERSON, WHERE ARE YOU GOING?
IT'S A HORDE ATTACK! THE SCRAMBLE SIGNAL--
YOUNG LADY, WITH THE INFO YOU'VE JUST BROUGHT BACK FROM THE HORDE SHIP, YOUR ANALYTICAL POWERS MAKE YOU TOO VALU-ABLE TO BE RISKED IN BATTLE.
JELENE! DIDN'T YOU HEAR THE GENERAL? YOU'RE STAYING HERE!
NO! MY FRIENDS NEED ME! LOUIS AND ALINE NEED MY SUPPORT! I'M GOING!
YOU'RE ORDERED TO STAY, JELENE--AND I'LL HAVE THE GUARDS ENFORCE THAT ORDER IF NEED BE! DO YOU THINK I ENJOY DOING THIS? THERE ARE GOOD REASONS--
BUT THEY NEED ME--!

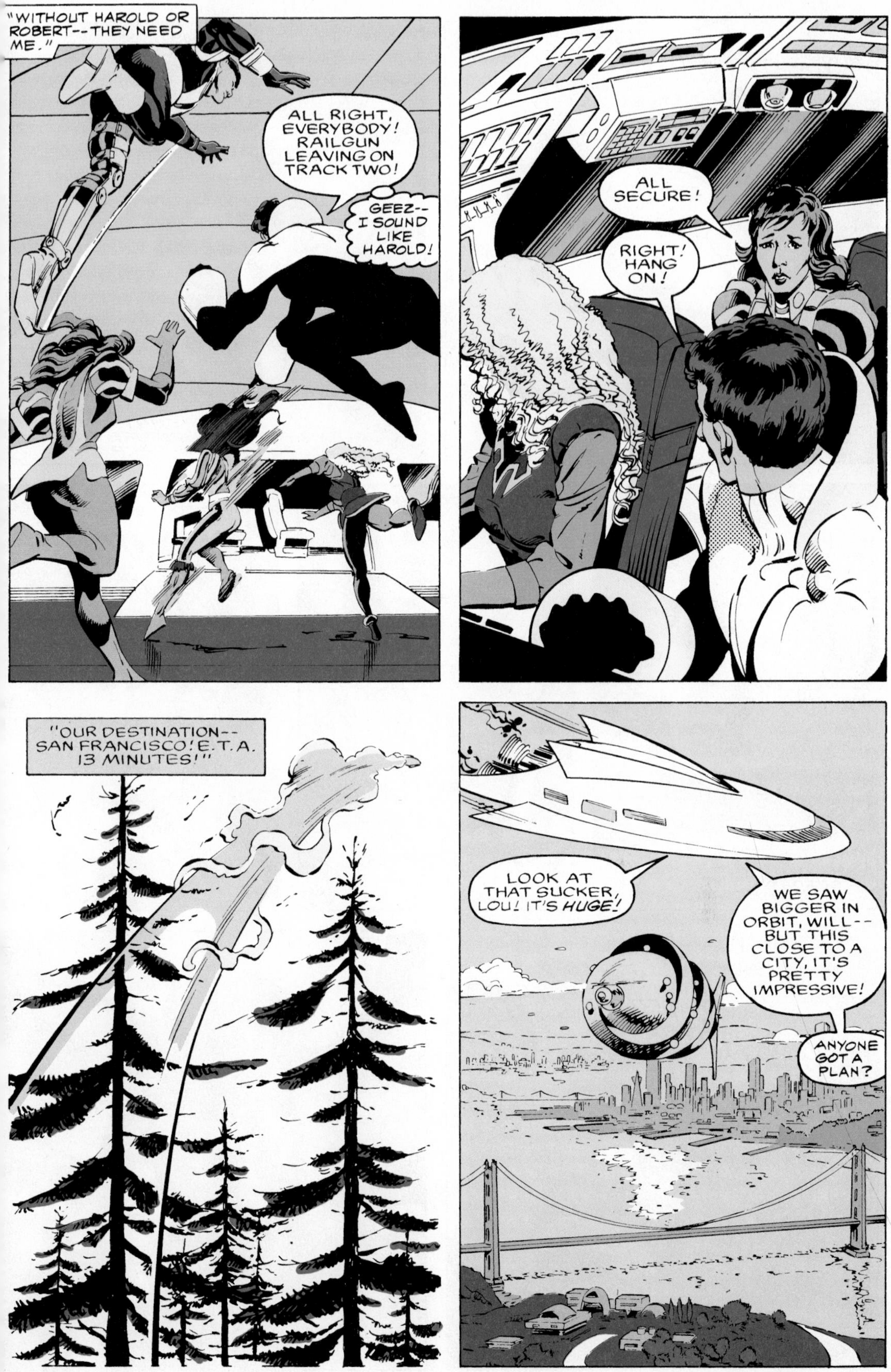
"WITHOUT HAROLD OR ROBERT--THEY NEED ME."
ALL RIGHT, EVERYBODY! RAILGUN LEAVING ON TRACK TWO!
GEEZ-- I SOUND LIKE HAROLD!
ALL SECURE!
RIGHT! HANG ON!
"OUR DESTINATION-- SAN FRANCISCO! E.T.A. 13 MINUTES!"
LOOK AT THAT SUCKER, LOU! IT'S *HUGE*!
WE SAW BIGGER IN ORBIT, WILL-- BUT THIS CLOSE TO A CITY, IT'S PRETTY IMPRESSIVE!
ANYONE GOT A PLAN?

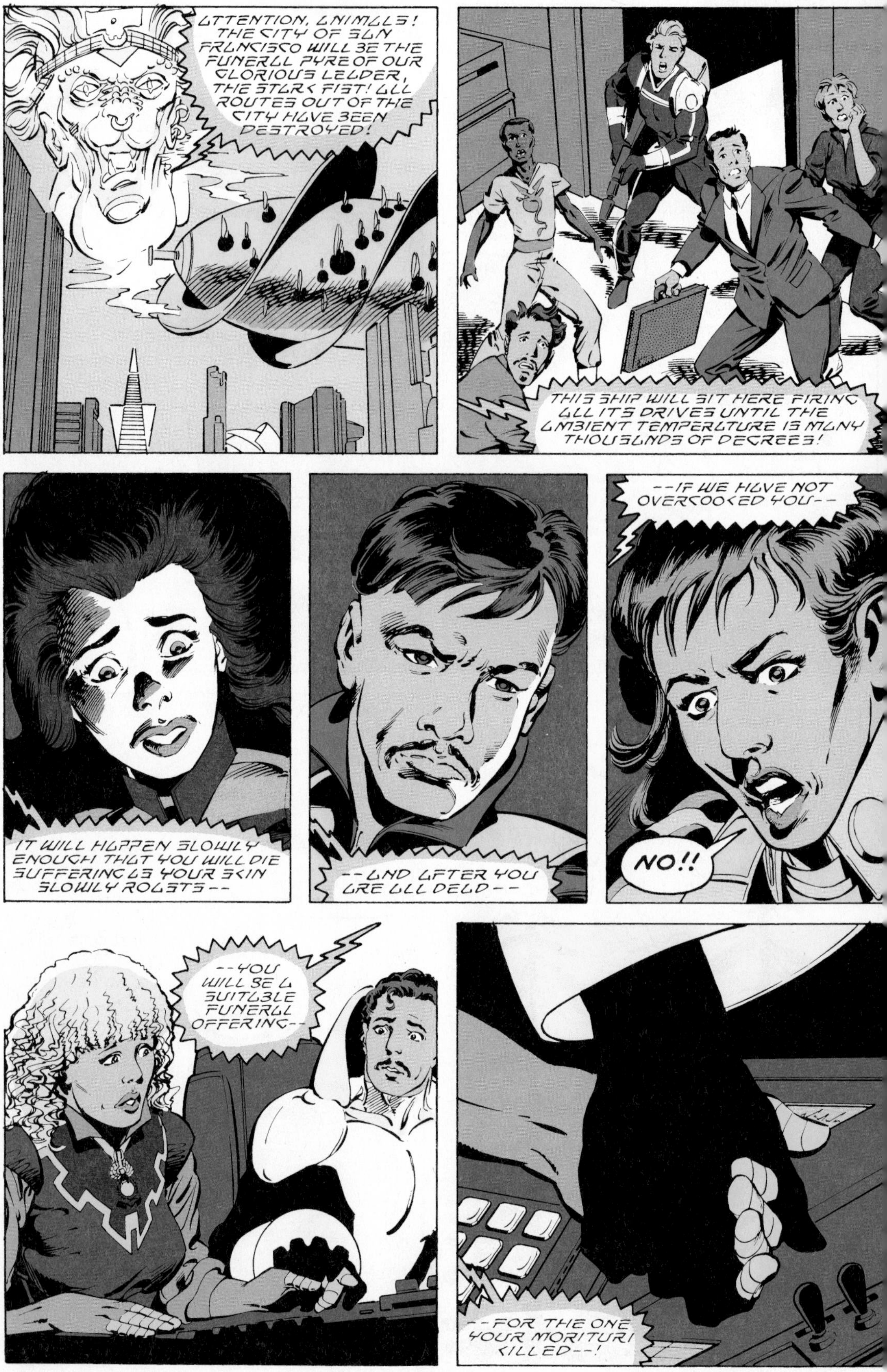

ATTENTION, ANIMALS! THE CITY OF SAN FRANCISCO WILL BE THE FUNERAL PYRE OF OUR GLORIOUS LEADER, THE STARK FIST! ALL ROUTES OUT OF THE CITY HAVE BEEN DESTROYED!
THIS SHIP WILL SIT HERE FIRING ALL ITS DRIVES UNTIL THE AMBIENT TEMPERATURE IS MANY THOUSANDS OF DEGREES!
IT WILL HAPPEN SLOWLY ENOUGH THAT YOU WILL DIE SUFFERING AS YOUR SKIN SLOWLY ROASTS--
--AND AFTER YOU ARE ALL DEAD--
--IF WE HAVE NOT OVERCOOKED YOU--
NO!!
--YOU WILL BE A SUITABLE FUNERAL OFFERING--
--FOR THE ONE YOUR MORITURI KILLED--!

‹A LONE SHIP APPROACHES, COMMANDER--IT MATCHES THE SHIP OBSERVED AT ‹RAMATORS‹!*›

‹THIS IS GOOD BEYOND EXPECTATION! THE MORITURI HAVE IN FACT COME!›

✱ ISSUE #3.

‹BEGIN THE DEMONSTRATION!›

‹LET THEM SEE WHAT WILL HAPPEN TO THE REST OF THEIR CITY!›

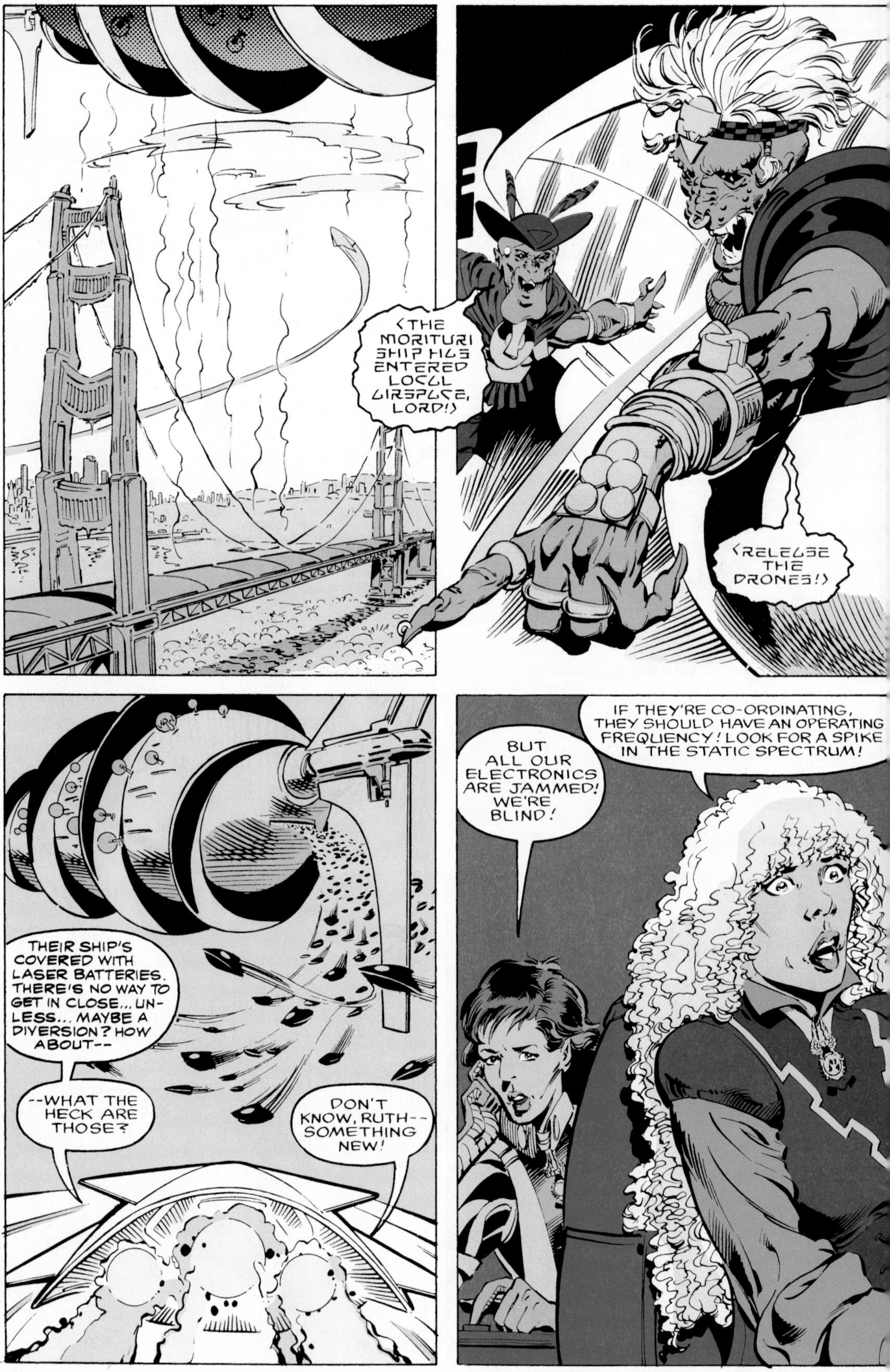
<THE MORITURI SHIP HAS ENTERED LOCAL AIRSPACE, LORD!>
<RELEASE THE DRONES!>
THEIR SHIP'S COVERED WITH LASER BATTERIES. THERE'S NO WAY TO GET IN CLOSE... UNLESS... MAYBE A DIVERSION? HOW ABOUT--
--WHAT THE HECK ARE THOSE?
DON'T KNOW, RUTH-- SOMETHING NEW!
BUT ALL OUR ELECTRONICS ARE JAMMED! WE'RE BLIND!
IF THEY'RE CO-ORDINATING, THEY SHOULD HAVE AN OPERATING FREQUENCY! LOOK FOR A SPIKE IN THE STATIC SPECTRUM!

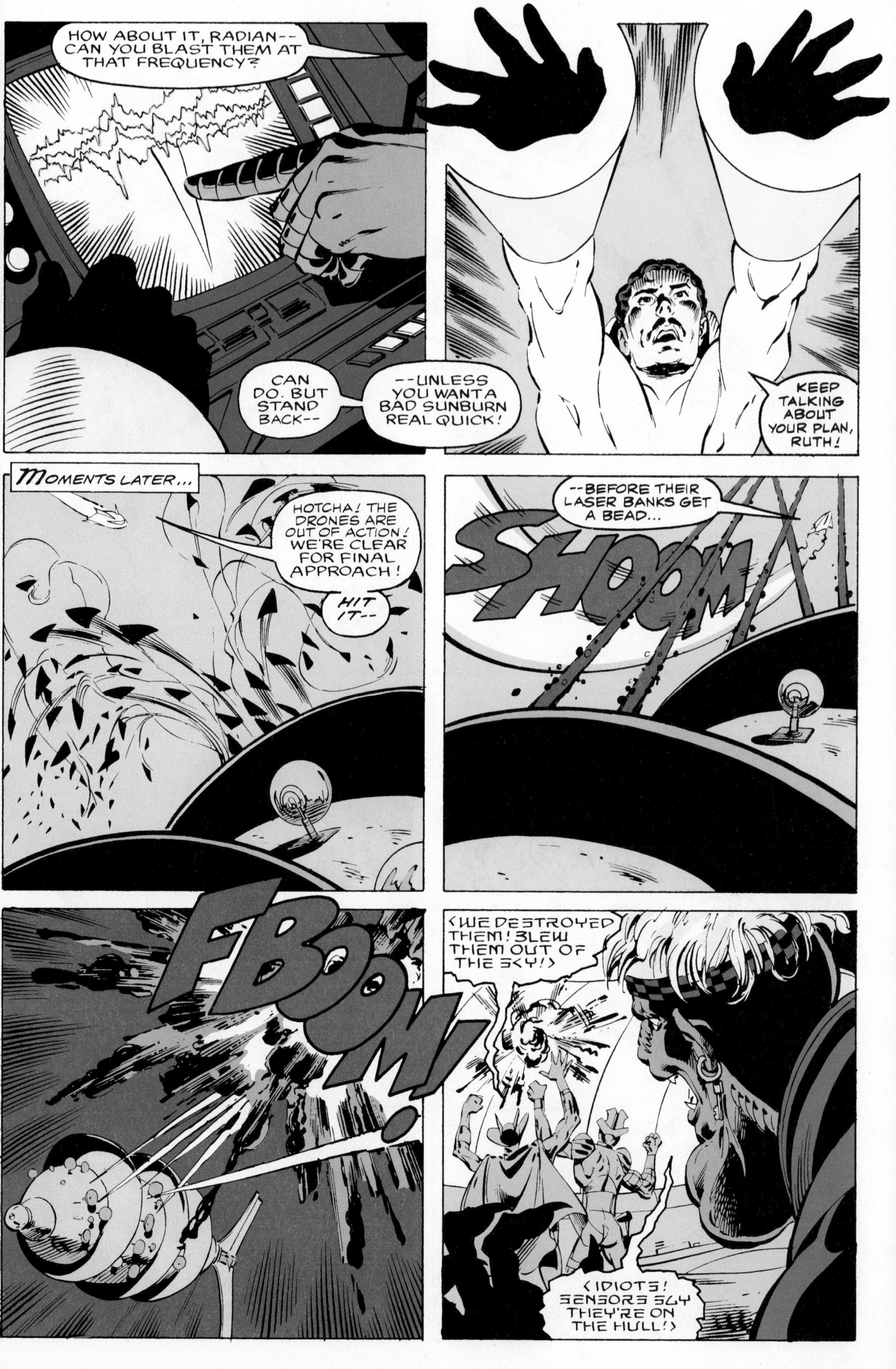
HOW ABOUT IT, RADIAN-- CAN YOU BLAST THEM AT THAT FREQUENCY?
CAN DO. BUT STAND BACK--
--UNLESS YOU WANT A BAD SUNBURN REAL QUICK!
KEEP TALKING ABOUT YOUR PLAN, RUTH!
MOMENTS LATER...
HOTCHA! THE DRONES ARE OUT OF ACTION! WE'RE CLEAR FOR FINAL APPROACH!
HIT IT--
--BEFORE THEIR LASER BANKS GET A BEAD...
SHOOM
FBOOM!
<WE DESTROYED THEM! BLEW THEM OUT OF THE SKY!>
<IDIOTS! SENSORS SAY THEY'RE ON THE HULL!>

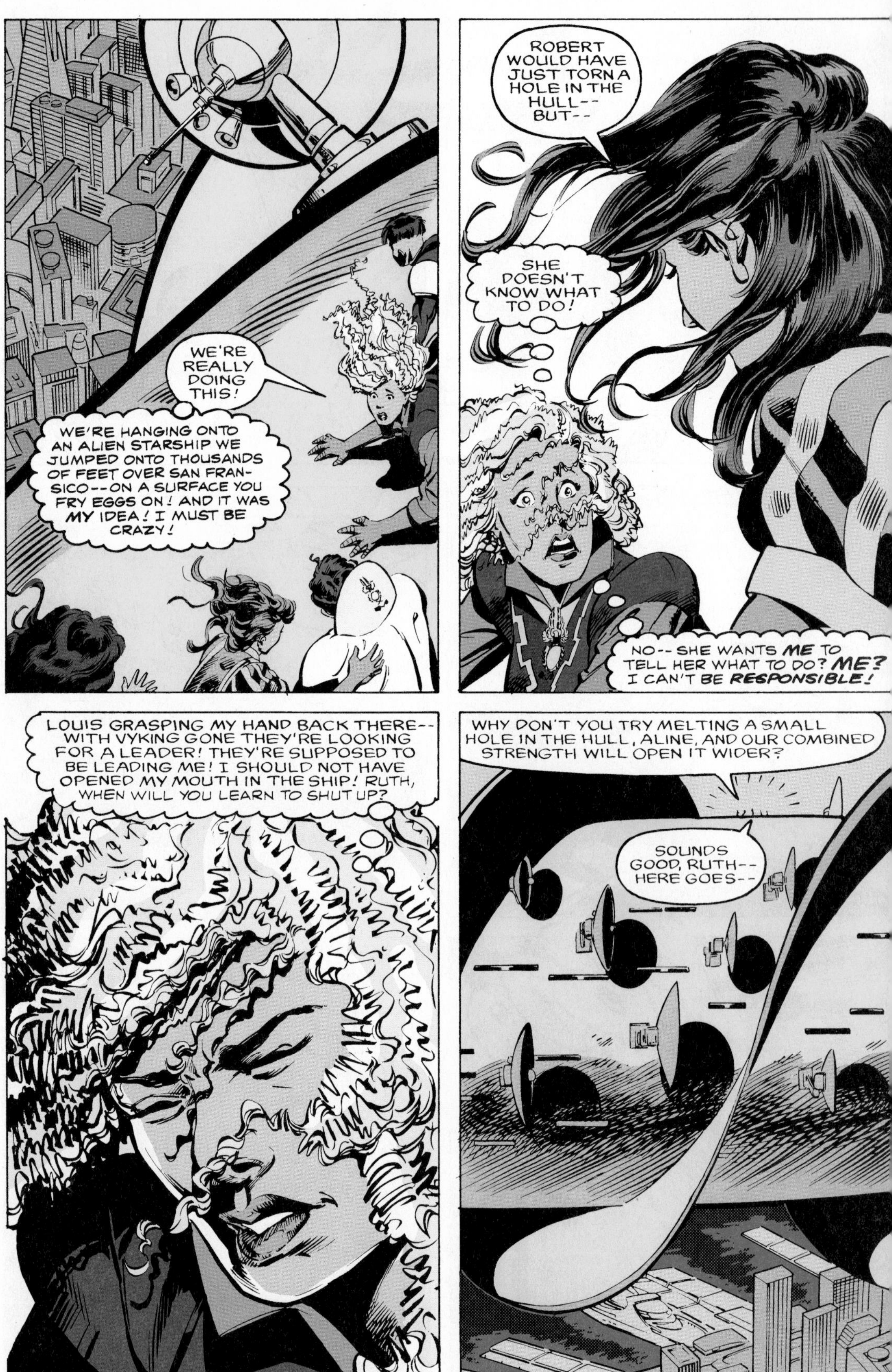
WE'RE REALLY DOING THIS!
WE'RE HANGING ONTO AN ALIEN STARSHIP WE JUMPED ONTO THOUSANDS OF FEET OVER SAN FRANSICO--ON A SURFACE YOU FRY EGGS ON! AND IT WAS MY IDEA! I MUST BE CRAZY!
ROBERT WOULD HAVE JUST TORN A HOLE IN THE HULL--BUT--
SHE DOESN'T KNOW WHAT TO DO!
NO--SHE WANTS ME TO TELL HER WHAT TO DO? ME? I CAN'T BE RESPONSIBLE!
LOUIS GRASPING MY HAND BACK THERE--WITH VYKING GONE THEY'RE LOOKING FOR A LEADER! THEY'RE SUPPOSED TO BE LEADING ME! I SHOULD NOT HAVE OPENED MY MOUTH IN THE SHIP! RUTH, WHEN WILL YOU LEARN TO SHUT UP?
WHY DON'T YOU TRY MELTING A SMALL HOLE IN THE HULL, ALINE, AND OUR COMBINED STRENGTH WILL OPEN IT WIDER?
SOUNDS GOOD, RUTH--HERE GOES--

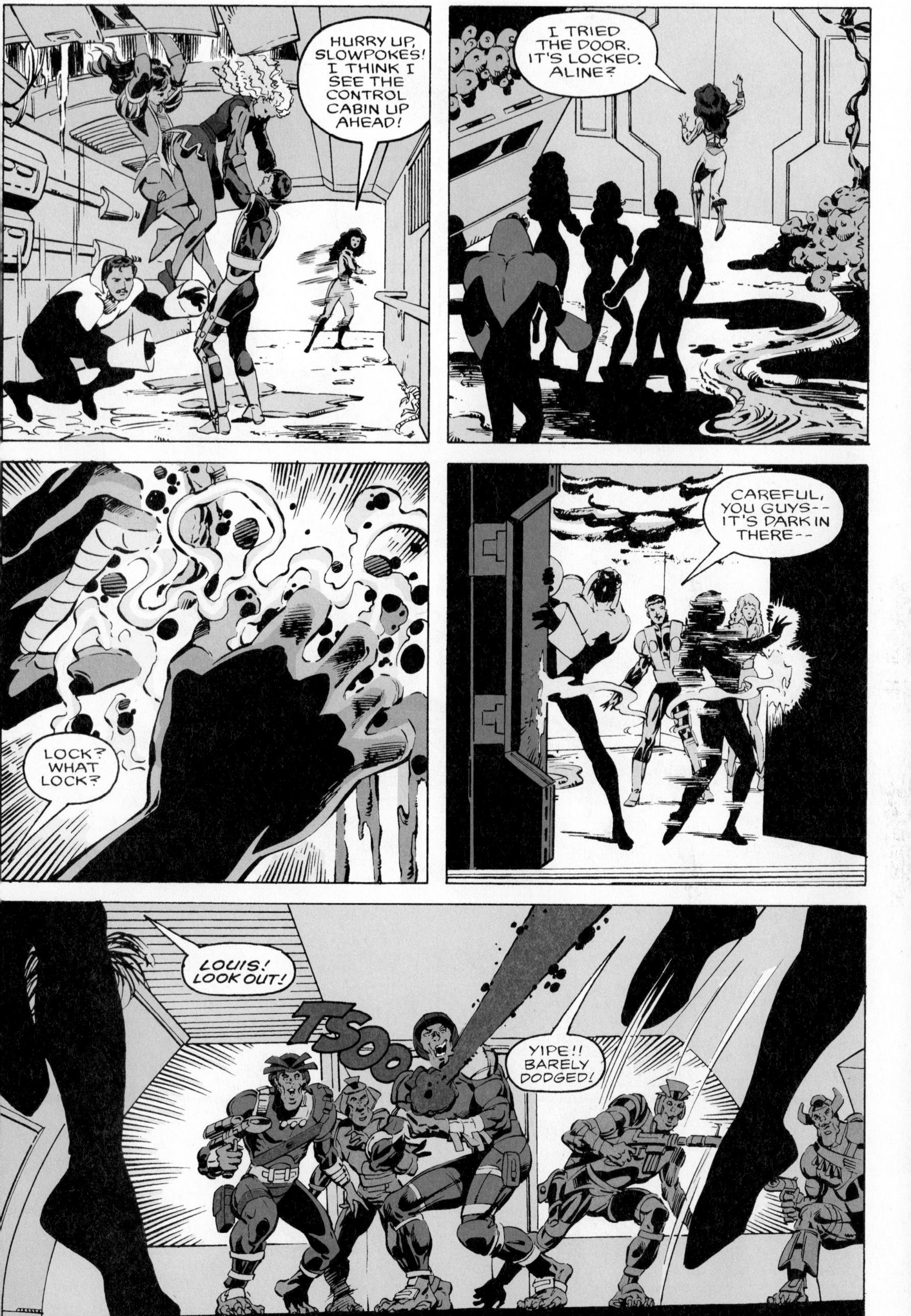
HURRY UP, SLOWPOKES! I THINK I SEE THE CONTROL CABIN UP AHEAD!
I TRIED THE DOOR. IT'S LOCKED. ALINE?
LOCK? WHAT LOCK?
CAREFUL, YOU GUYS-- IT'S DARK IN THERE--
LOUIS! LOOK OUT!
TSOOO
YIPE!! BARELY DODGED!

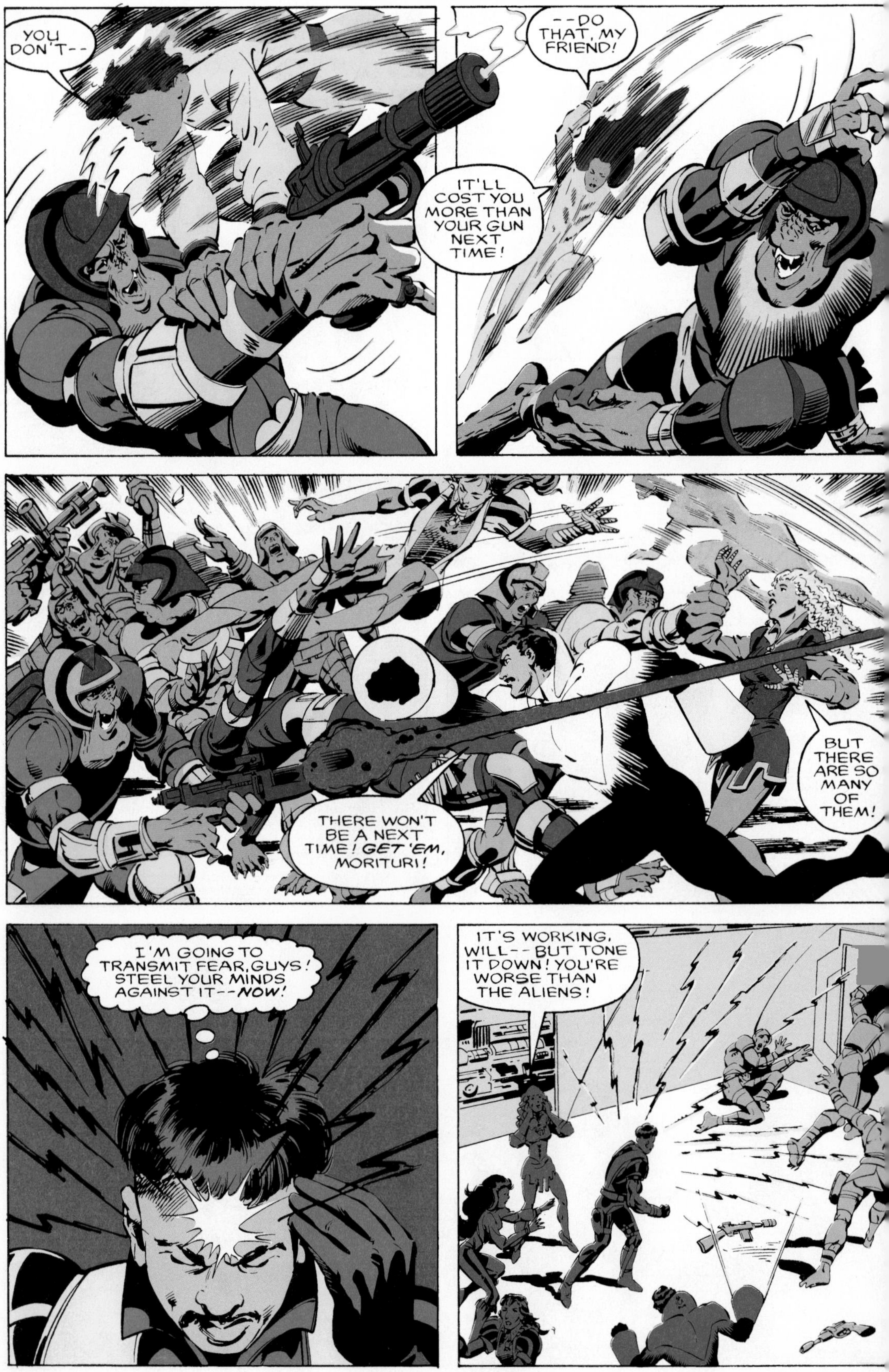
YOU DON'T--
--DO THAT, MY FRIEND!
IT'LL COST YOU MORE THAN YOUR GUN NEXT TIME!
THERE WON'T BE A NEXT TIME! GET 'EM, MORITURI!
BUT THERE ARE SO MANY OF THEM!
I'M GOING TO TRANSMIT FEAR, GUYS! STEEL YOUR MINDS AGAINST IT--NOW!
IT'S WORKING, WILL--BUT TONE IT DOWN! YOU'RE WORSE THAN THE ALIENS!

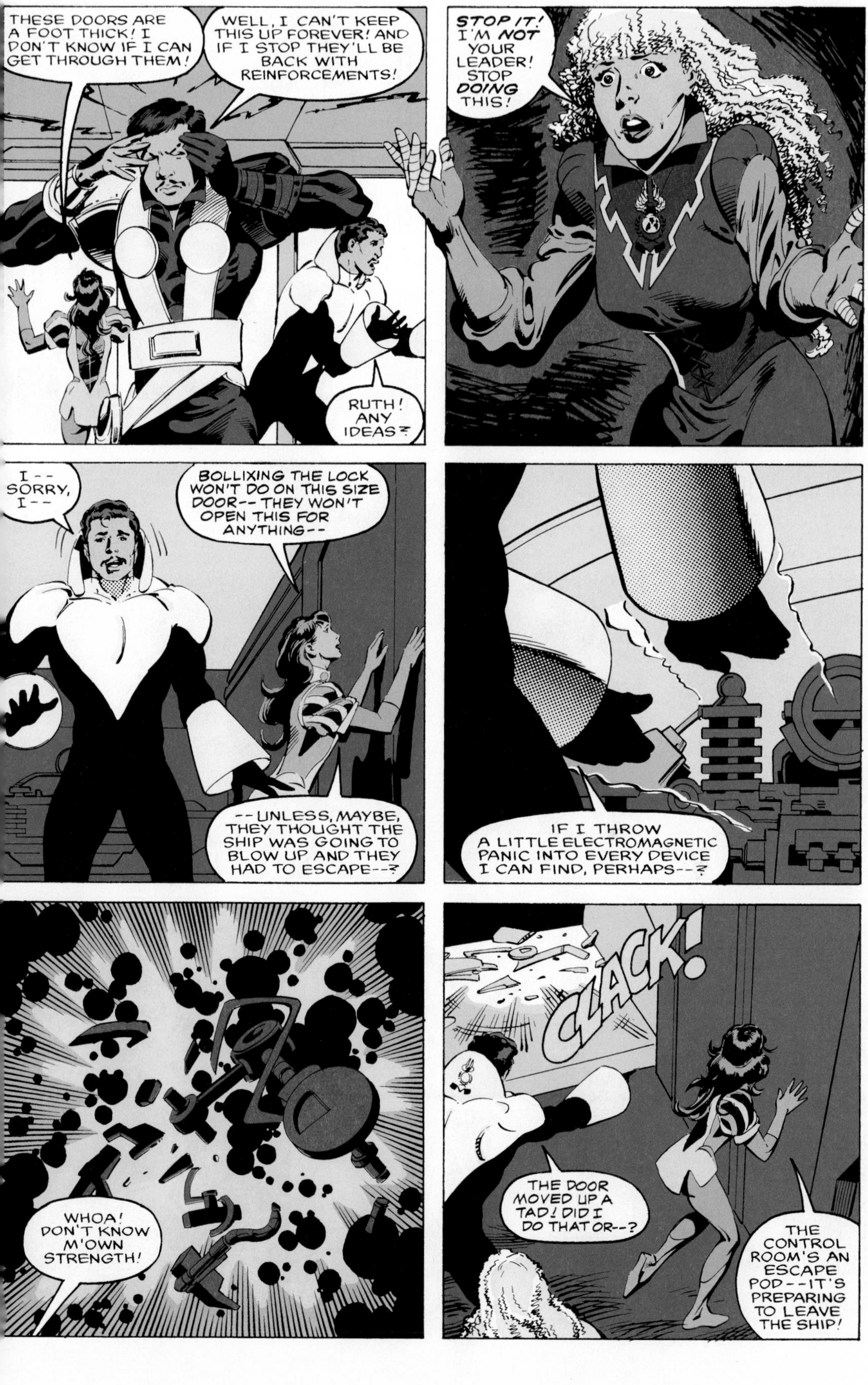
THESE DOORS ARE A FOOT THICK! I DON'T KNOW IF I CAN GET THROUGH THEM!
WELL, I CAN'T KEEP THIS UP FOREVER! AND IF I STOP THEY'LL BE BACK WITH REINFORCEMENTS!
RUTH! ANY IDEAS?
STOP IT! I'M NOT YOUR LEADER! STOP DOING THIS!
I-- SORRY, I--
BOLLIXING THE LOCK WON'T DO ON THIS SIZE DOOR--THEY WON'T OPEN THIS FOR ANYTHING--
--UNLESS, MAYBE, THEY THOUGHT THE SHIP WAS GOING TO BLOW UP AND THEY HAD TO ESCAPE--?
IF I THROW A LITTLE ELECTROMAGNETIC PANIC INTO EVERY DEVICE I CAN FIND, PERHAPS--?
WHOA! DON'T KNOW M'OWN STRENGTH!
CLACK!
THE DOOR MOVED UP A TAD! DID I DO THAT OR--?
THE CONTROL ROOM'S AN ESCAPE POD--IT'S PREPARING TO LEAVE THE SHIP!

THE MOVEMENT GAVE ME A GRIPPING POINT!
FROM THE TOP, LADIES AND GENTLEMEN?
WE'RE IN!
<NO FURTHER, ANIMALS! THIS IS A DEAD-MAN SWITCH! DO ANYTHING TO ME, I LET GO OF IT! I LET GO OF IT, SAN FRANCISCO BECOMES A CRATER! YOU KILLED MY GLORIOUS KINSMAN, BUT YOU WON'T WIN OVER ME!>
WITH MY SPEED MAYBE I COULD--
WE CAN'T CHANCE HIM LETTING GO, PILAR--!
BUT WHAT DO WE DO?
WHY DOESN'T SOMEBODY DO SOMETHING?
THERE IS NOBODY ELSE!
YOU MONSTER! MY FAMILY LIVES DOWN THERE!
YOU CAN'T KILL MY FAMILY!
<GUARDS! INTERCEPT HER! KEEP HER AWAY FROM ME!>
<DONE, LEADER! AIEE!>
PLEASE DON'T KILL MY FAMILY!

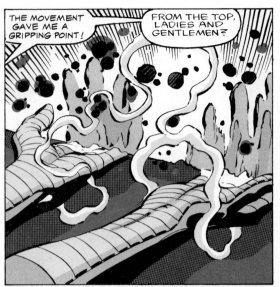

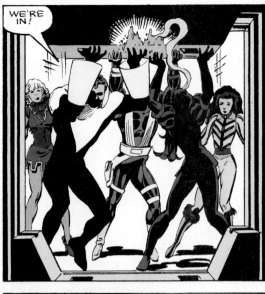

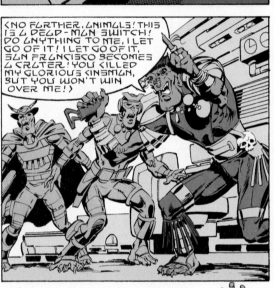

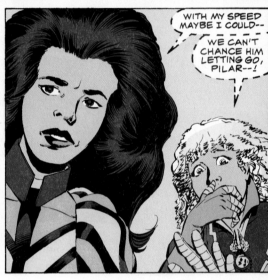

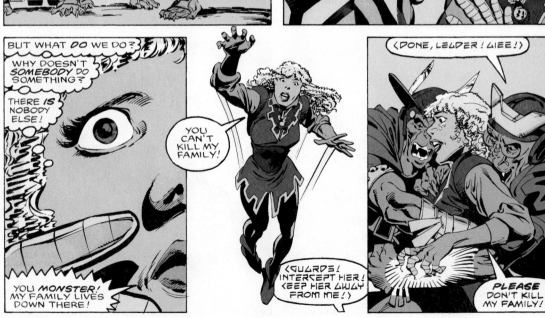

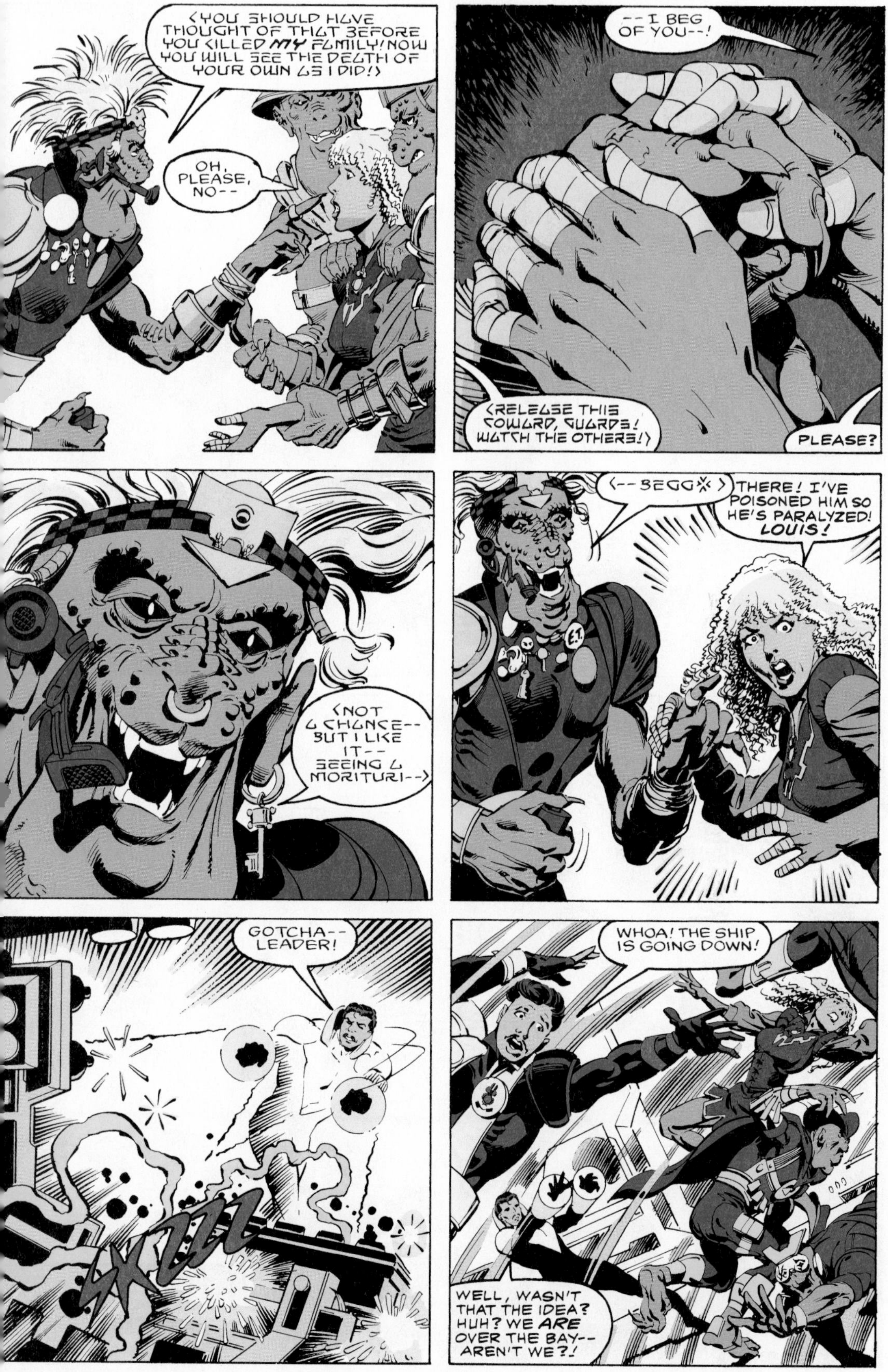

<YOU SHOULD HAVE THOUGHT OF THAT BEFORE YOU KILLED MY FAMILY! NOW YOU WILL SEE THE DEATH OF YOUR OWN AS I DID!>
OH, PLEASE, NO--
--I BEG OF YOU--!
<RELEASE THIS COWARD, GUARDS! WATCH THE OTHERS!>
PLEASE?
<NOT A CHANCE-- BUT I LIKE IT-- SEEING A MORITURI-->
<--BEGG*>
THERE! I'VE POISONED HIM SO HE'S PARALYZED! LOUIS!
GOTCHA-- LEADER!
WHOA! THE SHIP IS GOING DOWN!
WELL, WASN'T THAT THE IDEA? HUH? WE ARE OVER THE BAY-- AREN'T WE?!

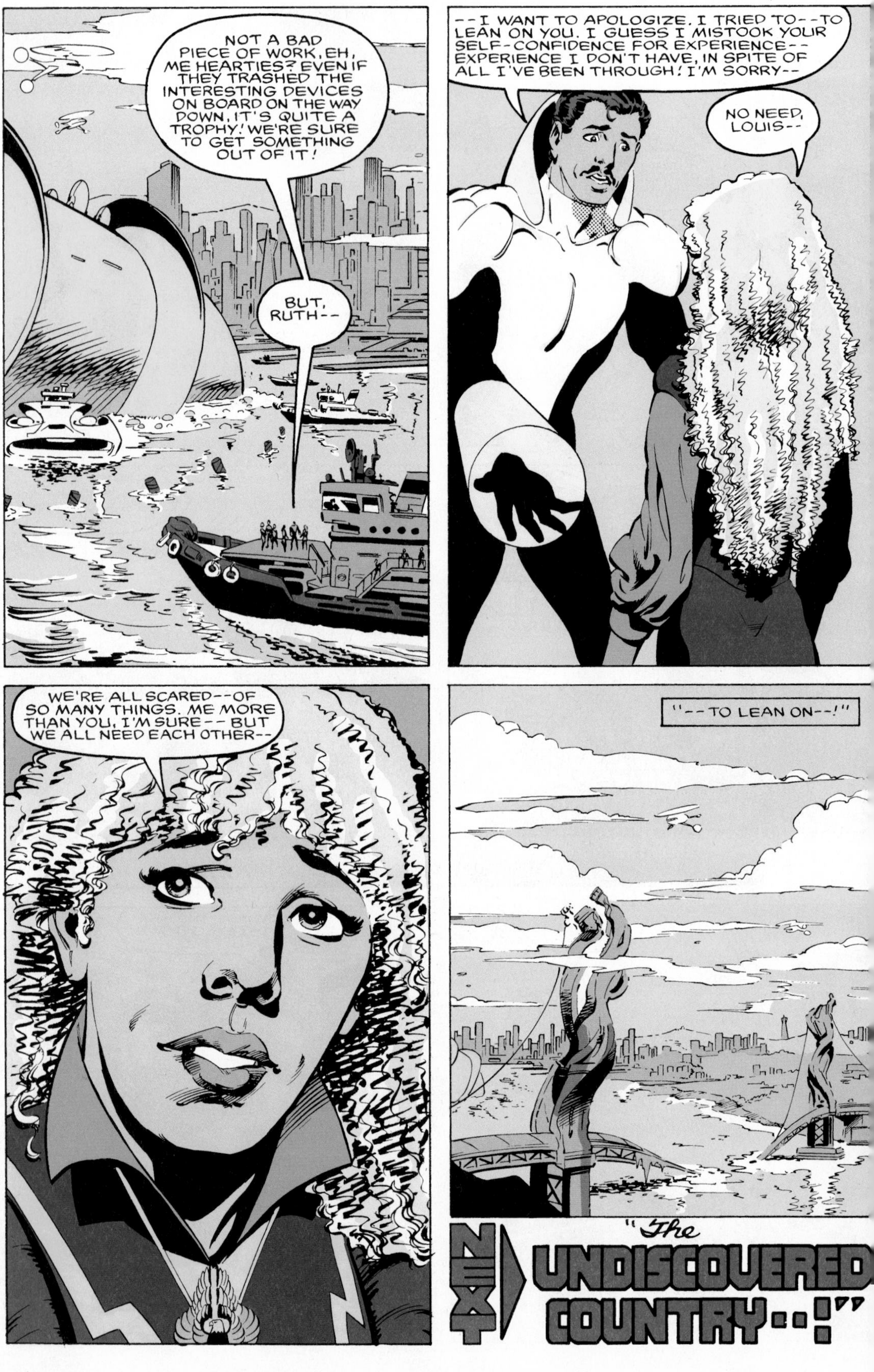
NOT A BAD PIECE OF WORK, EH, ME HEARTIES? EVEN IF THEY TRASHED THE INTERESTING DEVICES ON BOARD ON THE WAY DOWN, IT'S QUITE A TROPHY! WE'RE SURE TO GET SOMETHING OUT OF IT!
BUT, RUTH--
--I WANT TO APOLOGIZE. I TRIED TO--TO LEAN ON YOU. I GUESS I MISTOOK YOUR SELF-CONFIDENCE FOR EXPERIENCE--EXPERIENCE I DON'T HAVE, IN SPITE OF ALL I'VE BEEN THROUGH! I'M SORRY--
NO NEED, LOUIS--
WE'RE ALL SCARED--OF SO MANY THINGS. ME MORE THAN YOU, I'M SURE-- BUT WE ALL NEED EACH OTHER--
"--TO LEAN ON--!"
NEXT
"The UNDISCOVERED COUNTRY--!"

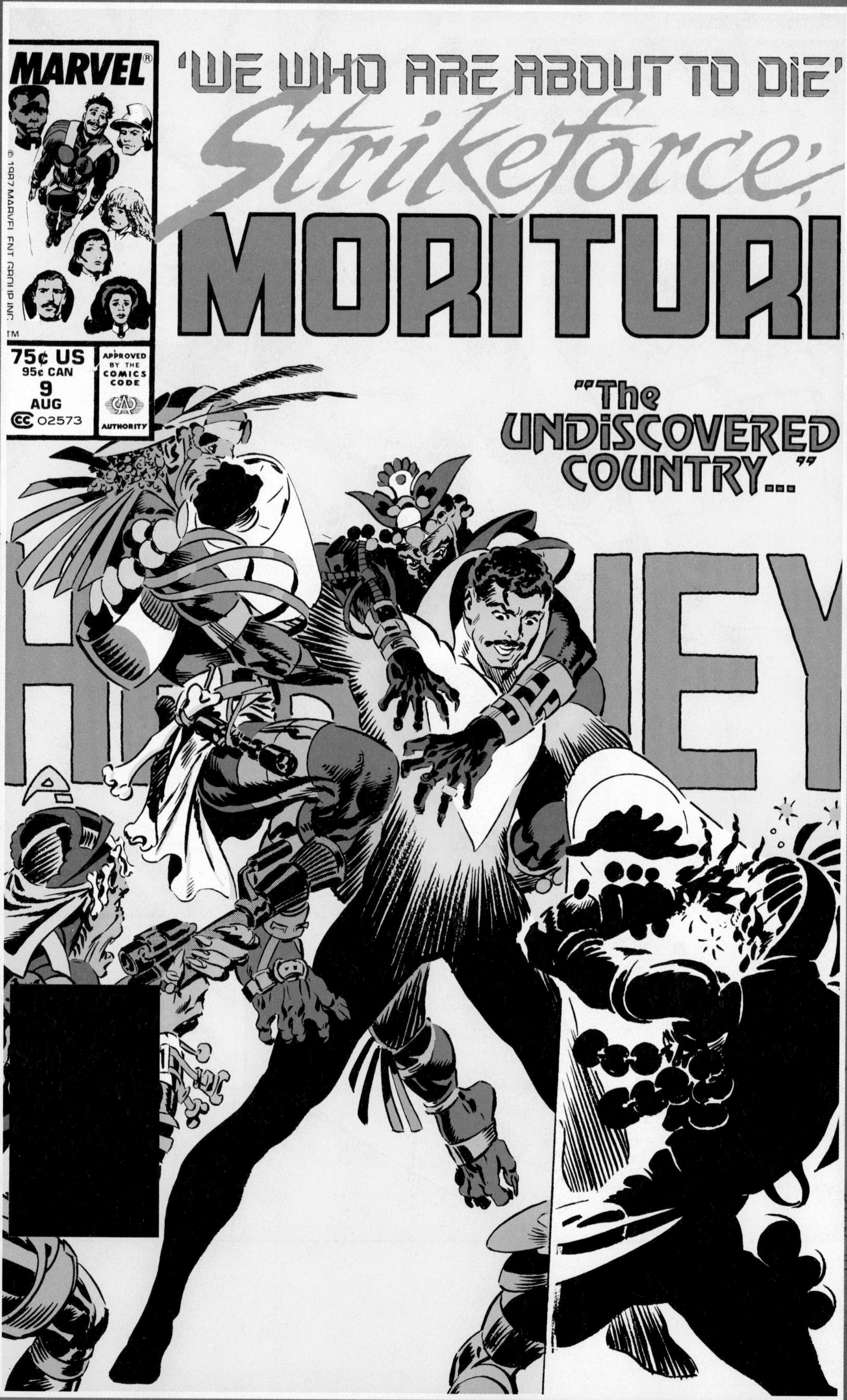
MARVEL®
'WE WHO ARE ABOUT TO DIE'
Strikeforce:
MORITURI
75¢ US
95¢ CAN
9
AUG
02573
APPROVED BY THE COMICS CODE AUTHORITY
"The UNDISCOVERED COUNTRY..."

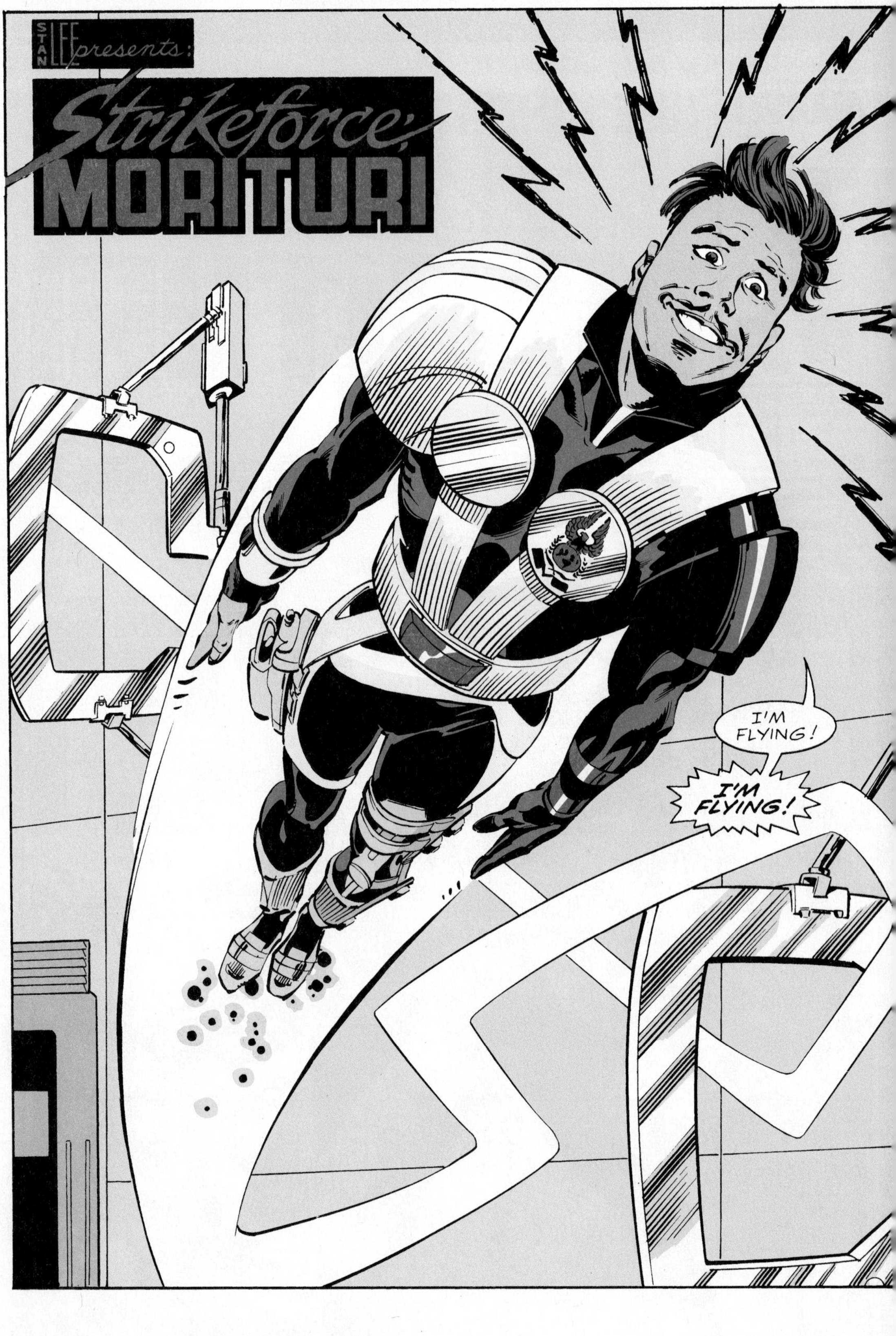
STAN LEE presents:
Strikeforce: MORITURI
I'M FLYING!
I'M FLYING!

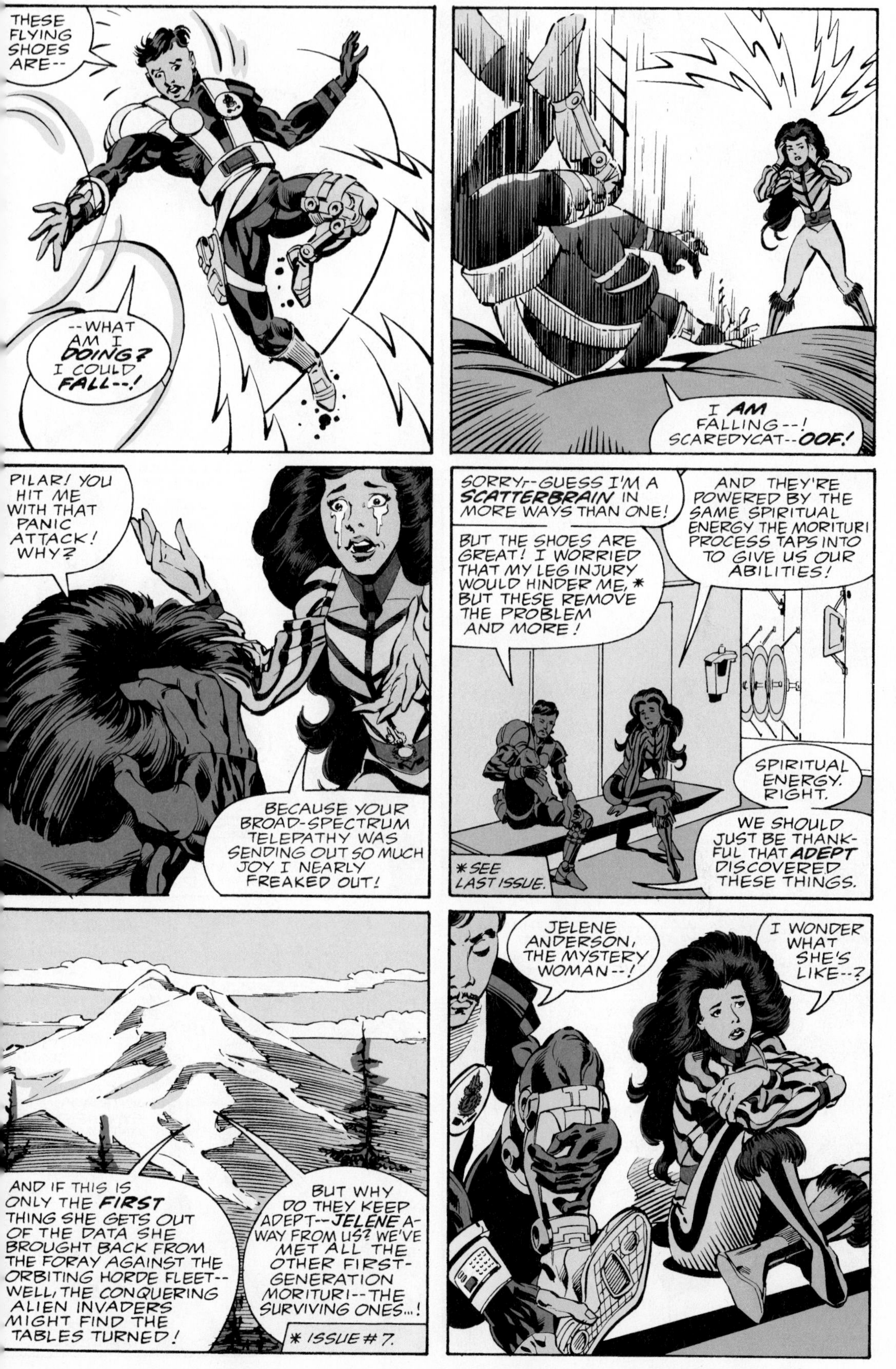

THESE FLYING SHOES ARE--
--WHAT AM I DOING? I COULD FALL--!
I AM FALLING--! SCAREDYCAT--OOF!
PILAR! YOU HIT ME WITH THAT PANIC ATTACK! WHY?
BECAUSE YOUR BROAD-SPECTRUM TELEPATHY WAS SENDING OUT SO MUCH JOY I NEARLY FREAKED OUT!
SORRY,--GUESS I'M A SCATTERBRAIN IN MORE WAYS THAN ONE!
BUT THE SHOES ARE GREAT! I WORRIED THAT MY LEG INJURY WOULD HINDER ME,* BUT THESE REMOVE THE PROBLEM AND MORE!
AND THEY'RE POWERED BY THE SAME SPIRITUAL ENERGY THE MORITURI PROCESS TAPS INTO TO GIVE US OUR ABILITIES!
SPIRITUAL ENERGY. RIGHT.
WE SHOULD JUST BE THANKFUL THAT ADEPT DISCOVERED THESE THINGS.
*SEE LAST ISSUE.
AND IF THIS IS ONLY THE FIRST THING SHE GETS OUT OF THE DATA SHE BROUGHT BACK FROM THE FORAY AGAINST THE ORBITING HORDE FLEET-- WELL, THE CONQUERING ALIEN INVADERS MIGHT FIND THE TABLES TURNED!
BUT WHY DO THEY KEEP ADEPT--JELENE A-WAY FROM US? WE'VE MET ALL THE OTHER FIRST-GENERATION MORITURI--THE SURVIVING ONES...!
* ISSUE # 7.
JELENE ANDERSON, THE MYSTERY WOMAN--!
I WONDER WHAT SHE'S LIKE--?

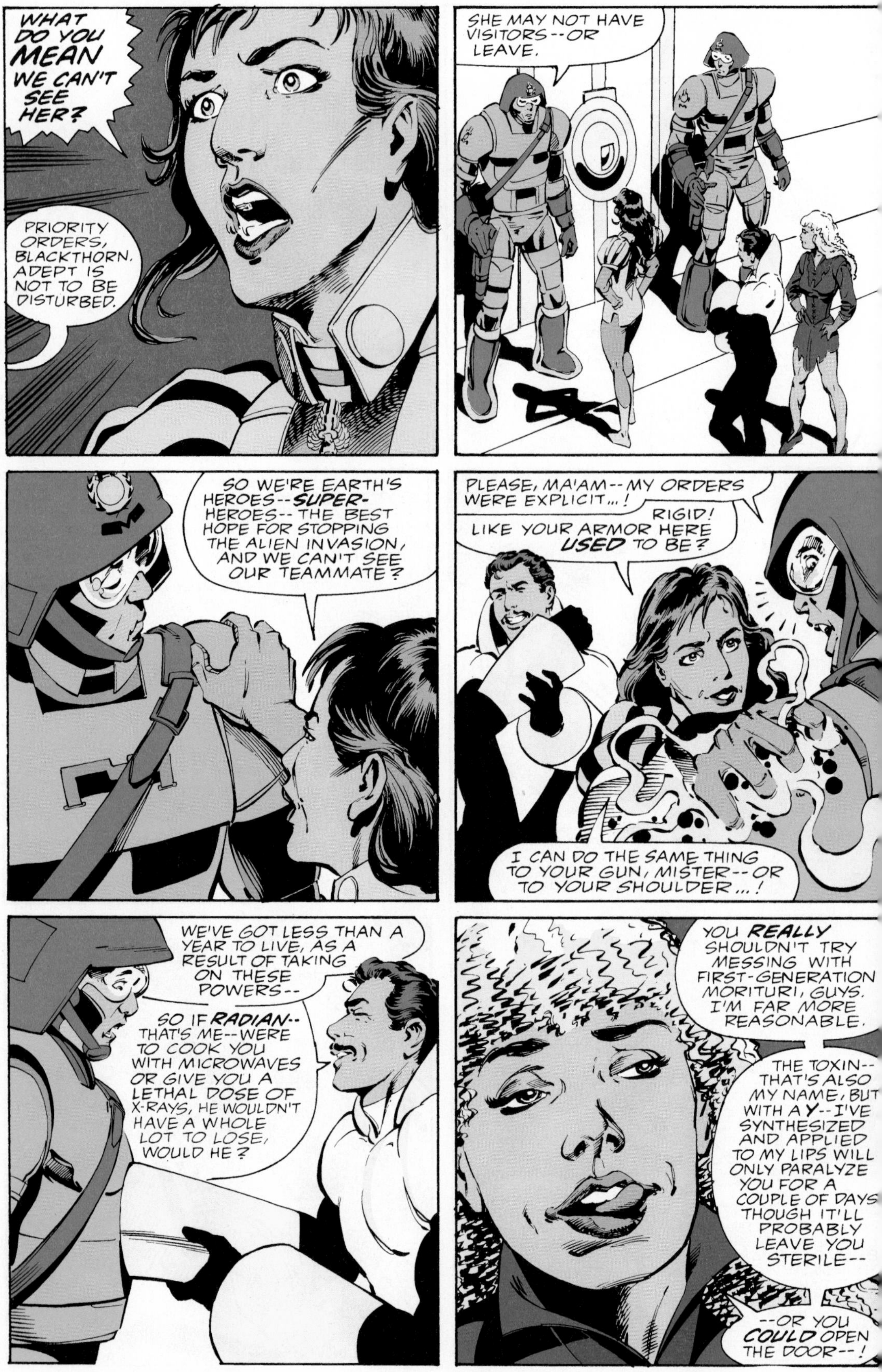
WHAT DO YOU MEAN WE CAN'T SEE HER?
PRIORITY ORDERS, BLACKTHORN. ADEPT IS NOT TO BE DISTURBED.
SHE MAY NOT HAVE VISITORS--OR LEAVE.
SO WE'RE EARTH'S HEROES--SUPER-HEROES--THE BEST HOPE FOR STOPPING THE ALIEN INVASION, AND WE CAN'T SEE OUR TEAMMATE?
PLEASE, MA'AM--MY ORDERS WERE EXPLICIT...!
RIGID! LIKE YOUR ARMOR HERE USED TO BE?
I CAN DO THE SAME THING TO YOUR GUN, MISTER--OR TO YOUR SHOULDER...!
WE'VE GOT LESS THAN A YEAR TO LIVE, AS A RESULT OF TAKING ON THESE POWERS--
SO IF RADIAN--THAT'S ME--WERE TO COOK YOU WITH MICROWAVES OR GIVE YOU A LETHAL DOSE OF X-RAYS, HE WOULDN'T HAVE A WHOLE LOT TO LOSE, WOULD HE?
YOU REALLY SHOULDN'T TRY MESSING WITH FIRST-GENERATION MORITURI, GUYS. I'M FAR MORE REASONABLE.
THE TOXIN--THAT'S ALSO MY NAME, BUT WITH A Y--I'VE SYNTHESIZED AND APPLIED TO MY LIPS WILL ONLY PARALYZE YOU FOR A COUPLE OF DAYS THOUGH IT'LL PROBABLY LEAVE YOU STERILE--
--OR YOU COULD OPEN THE DOOR--!

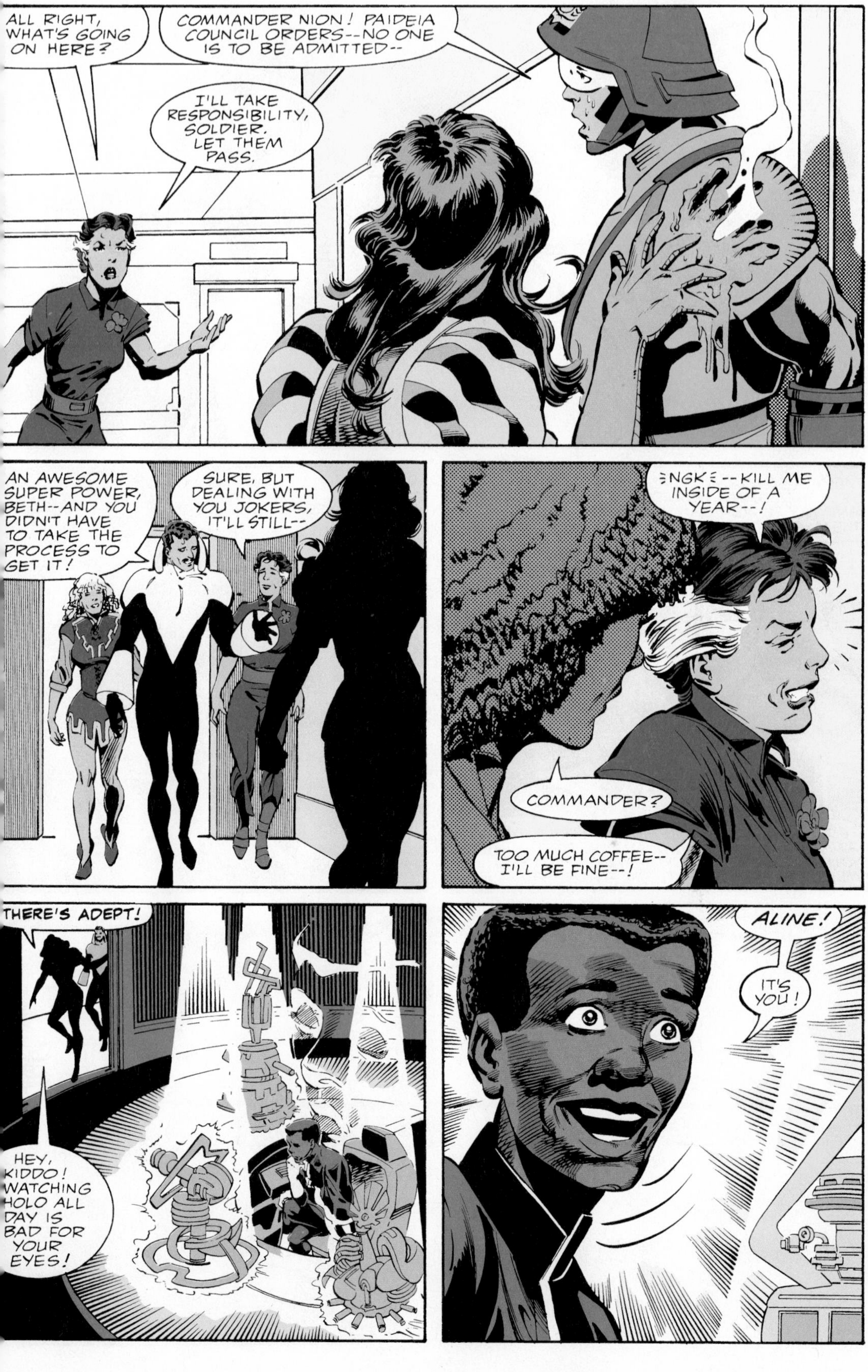
ALL RIGHT, WHAT'S GOING ON HERE?
COMMANDER NION! PAIDEIA COUNCIL ORDERS--NO ONE IS TO BE ADMITTED--
I'LL TAKE RESPONSIBILITY, SOLDIER. LET THEM PASS.
AN AWESOME SUPER POWER, BETH--AND YOU DIDN'T HAVE TO TAKE THE PROCESS TO GET IT!
SURE, BUT DEALING WITH YOU JOKERS, IT'LL STILL--
NGK --KILL ME INSIDE OF A YEAR--!
COMMANDER?
TOO MUCH COFFEE-- I'LL BE FINE--!
THERE'S ADEPT!
HEY, KIDDO! WATCHING HOLO ALL DAY IS BAD FOR YOUR EYES!
ALINE!
IT'S YOU!

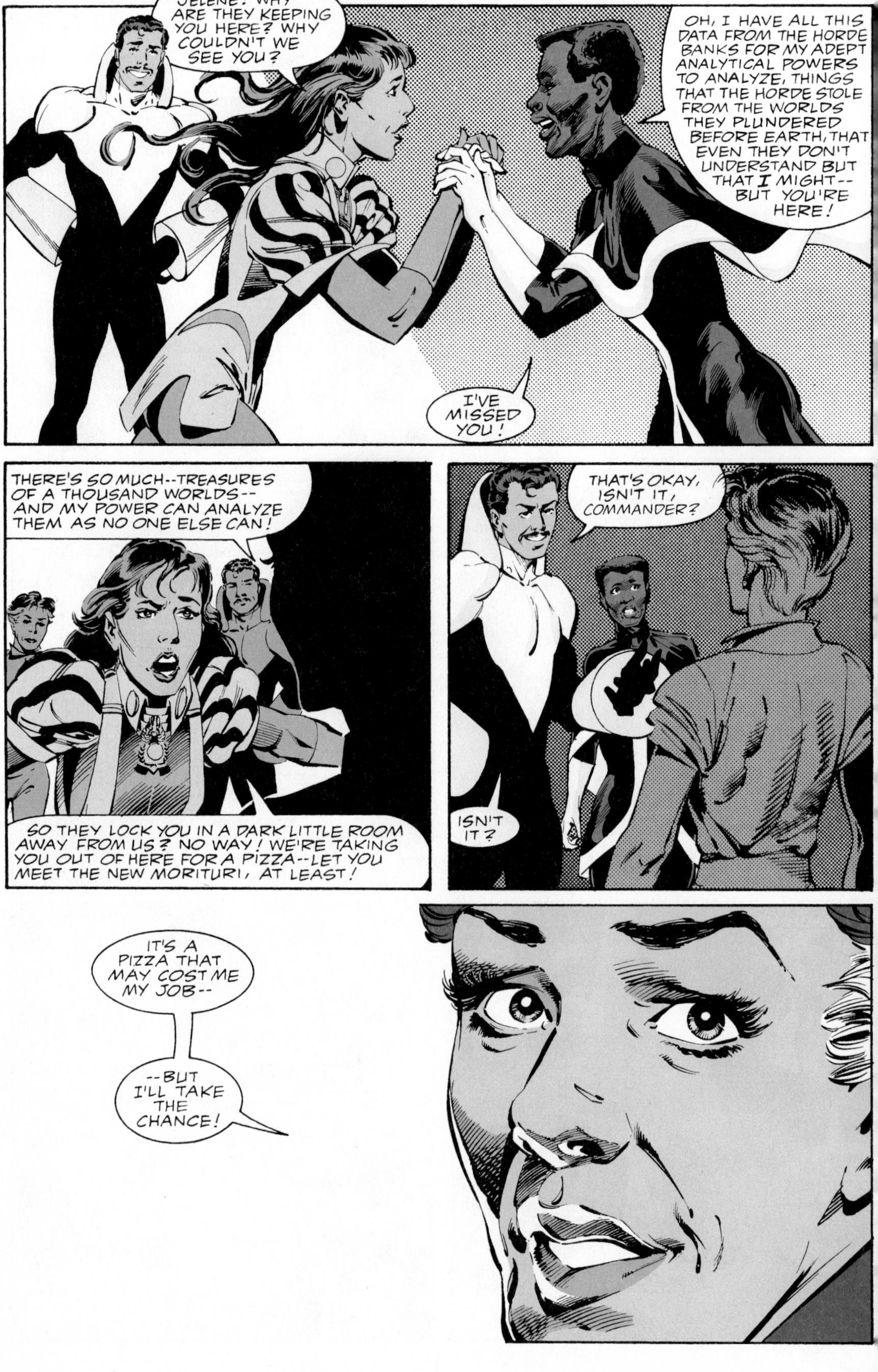

JELENE! WHY ARE THEY KEEPING YOU HERE? WHY COULDN'T WE SEE YOU?
OH, I HAVE ALL THIS DATA FROM THE HORDE BANKS FOR MY ADEPT ANALYTICAL POWERS TO ANALYZE, THINGS THAT THE HORDE STOLE FROM THE WORLDS THEY PLUNDERED BEFORE EARTH, THAT EVEN THEY DON'T UNDERSTAND BUT THAT I MIGHT-- BUT YOU'RE HERE!
I'VE MISSED YOU!
THERE'S SO MUCH--TREASURES OF A THOUSAND WORLDS-- AND MY POWER CAN ANALYZE THEM AS NO ONE ELSE CAN!
SO THEY LOCK YOU IN A DARK LITTLE ROOM AWAY FROM US? NO WAY! WE'RE TAKING YOU OUT OF HERE FOR A PIZZA--LET YOU MEET THE NEW MORITURI, AT LEAST!
THAT'S OKAY, ISN'T IT, COMMANDER?
ISN'T IT?
IT'S A PIZZA THAT MAY COST ME MY JOB--
--BUT I'LL TAKE THE CHANCE!

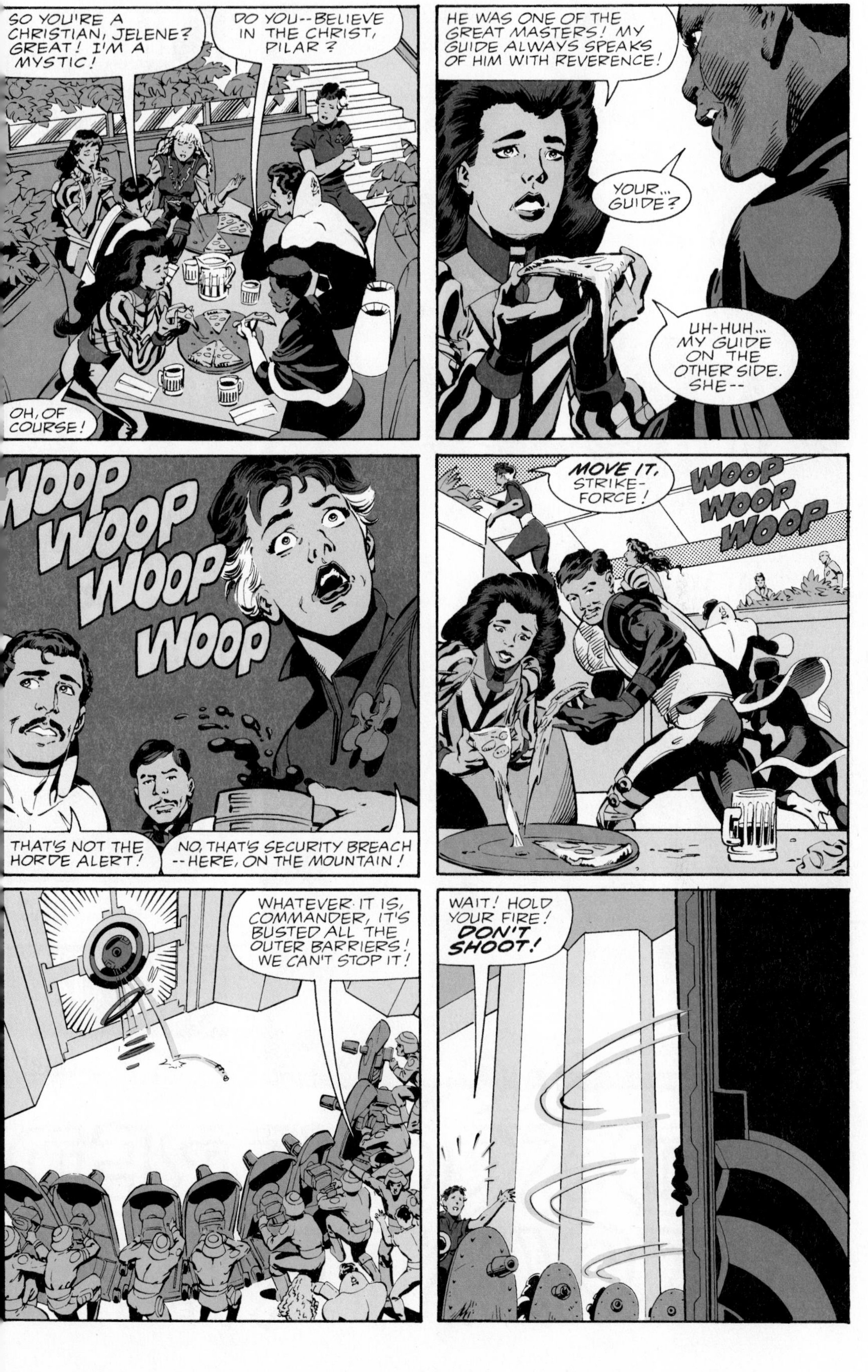
SO YOU'RE A CHRISTIAN, JELENE? GREAT! I'M A MYSTIC!
DO YOU--BELIEVE IN THE CHRIST, PILAR?
OH, OF COURSE!
HE WAS ONE OF THE GREAT MASTERS! MY GUIDE ALWAYS SPEAKS OF HIM WITH REVERENCE!
YOUR... GUIDE?
UH-HUH... MY GUIDE ON THE OTHER SIDE. SHE--
WOOP WOOP WOOP WOOP
THAT'S NOT THE HORDE ALERT!
NO, THAT'S SECURITY BREACH --HERE, ON THE MOUNTAIN!
MOVE IT, STRIKE-FORCE!
WOOP WOOP WOOP
WHATEVER IT IS, COMMANDER, IT'S BUSTED ALL THE OUTER BARRIERS! WE CAN'T STOP IT!
WAIT! HOLD YOUR FIRE! DON'T SHOOT!

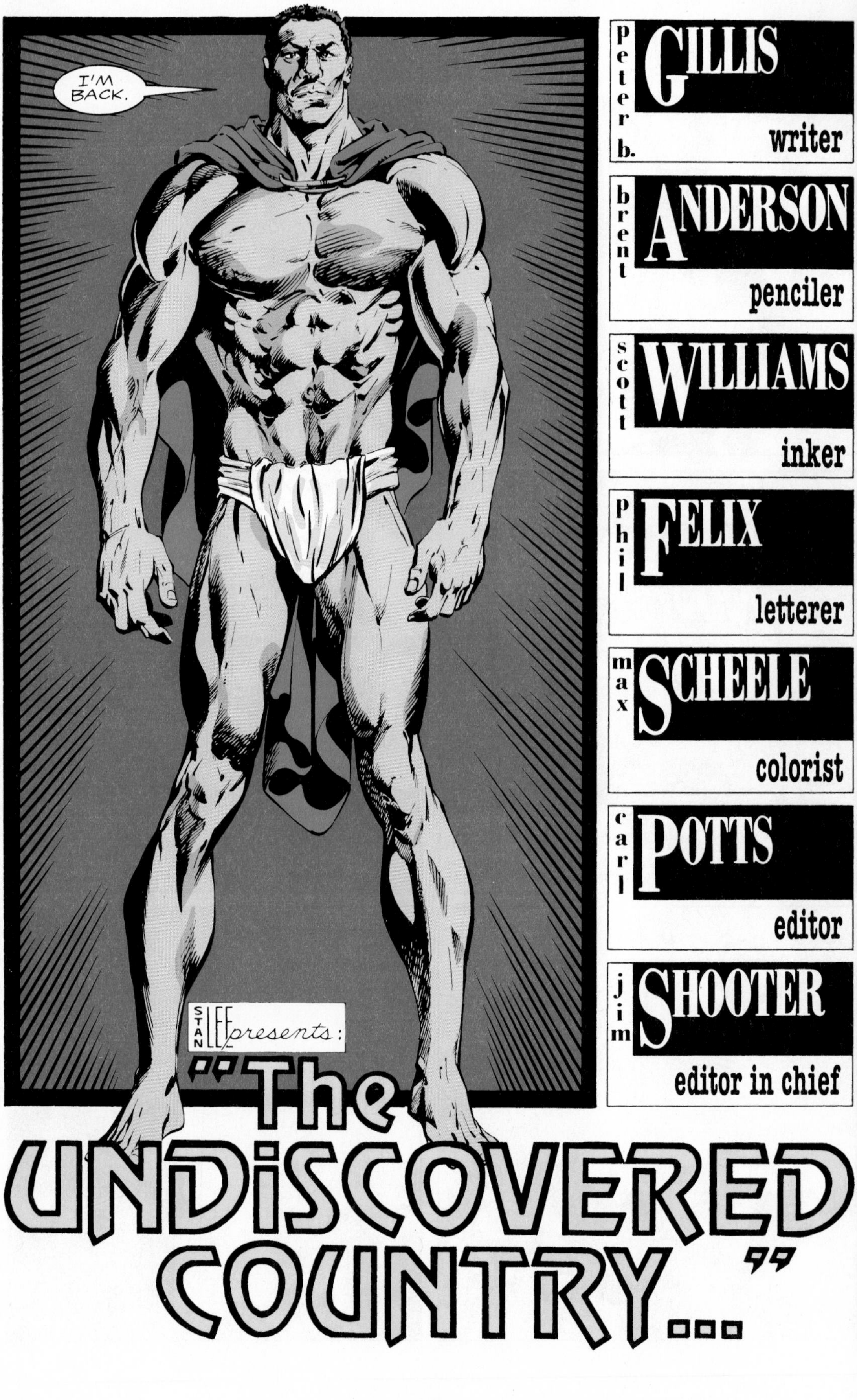
I'M BACK.
peter b. GILLIS writer
brent ANDERSON penciler
scott WILLIAMS inker
phil FELIX letterer
max SCHEELE colorist
carl POTTS editor
jim SHOOTER editor in chief
STAN LEE presents:
"The UNDISCOVERED COUNTRY..."

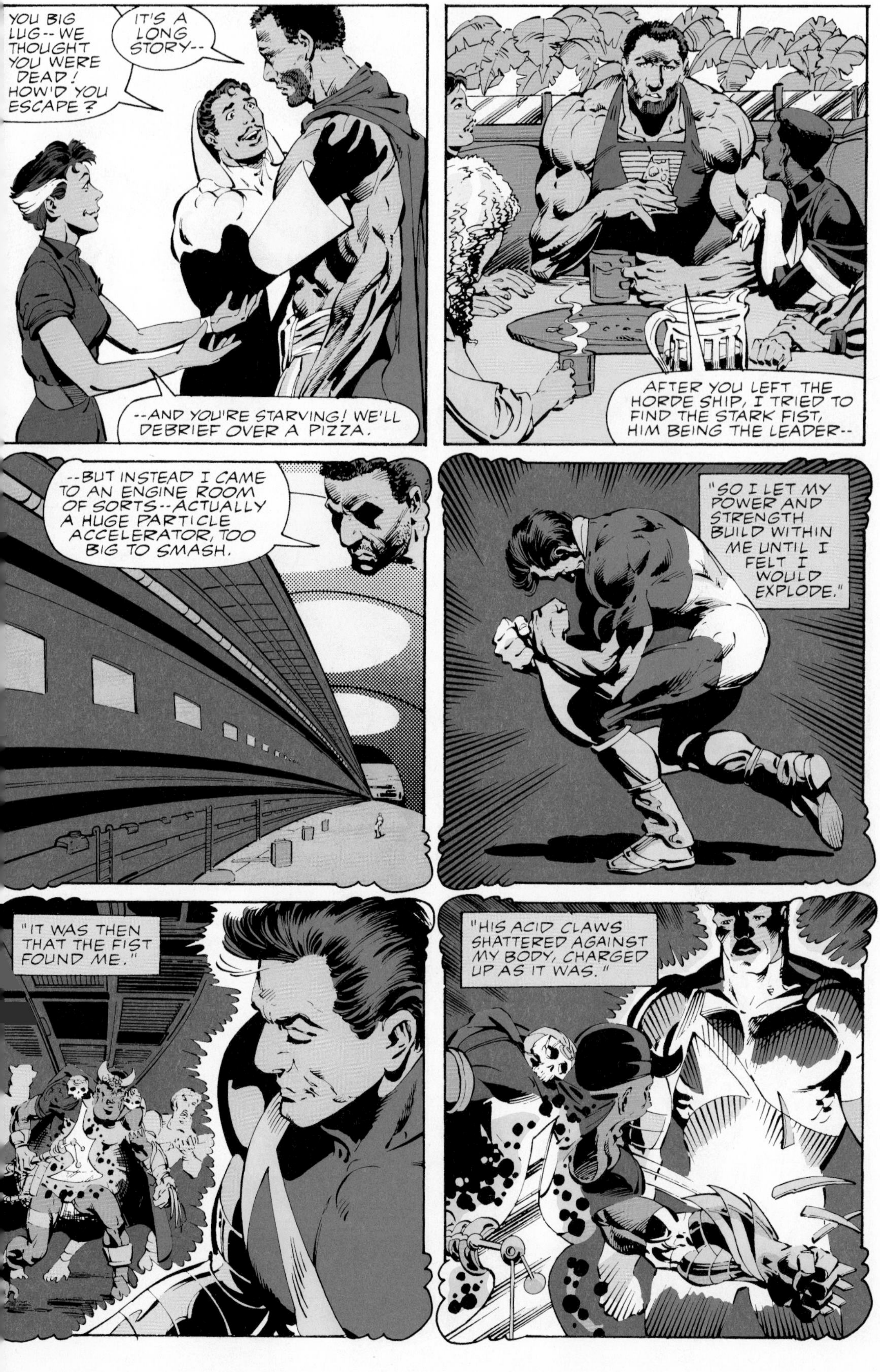
YOU BIG LUG--WE THOUGHT YOU WERE DEAD! HOW'D YOU ESCAPE?
IT'S A LONG STORY--
--AND YOU'RE STARVING! WE'LL DEBRIEF OVER A PIZZA.
AFTER YOU LEFT THE HORDE SHIP, I TRIED TO FIND THE STARK FIST, HIM BEING THE LEADER--
--BUT INSTEAD I CAME TO AN ENGINE ROOM OF SORTS--ACTUALLY A HUGE PARTICLE ACCELERATOR, TOO BIG TO SMASH.
"SO I LET MY POWER AND STRENGTH BUILD WITHIN ME UNTIL I FELT I WOULD EXPLODE."
"IT WAS THEN THAT THE FIST FOUND ME."
"HIS ACID CLAWS SHATTERED AGAINST MY BODY, CHARGED UP AS IT WAS."

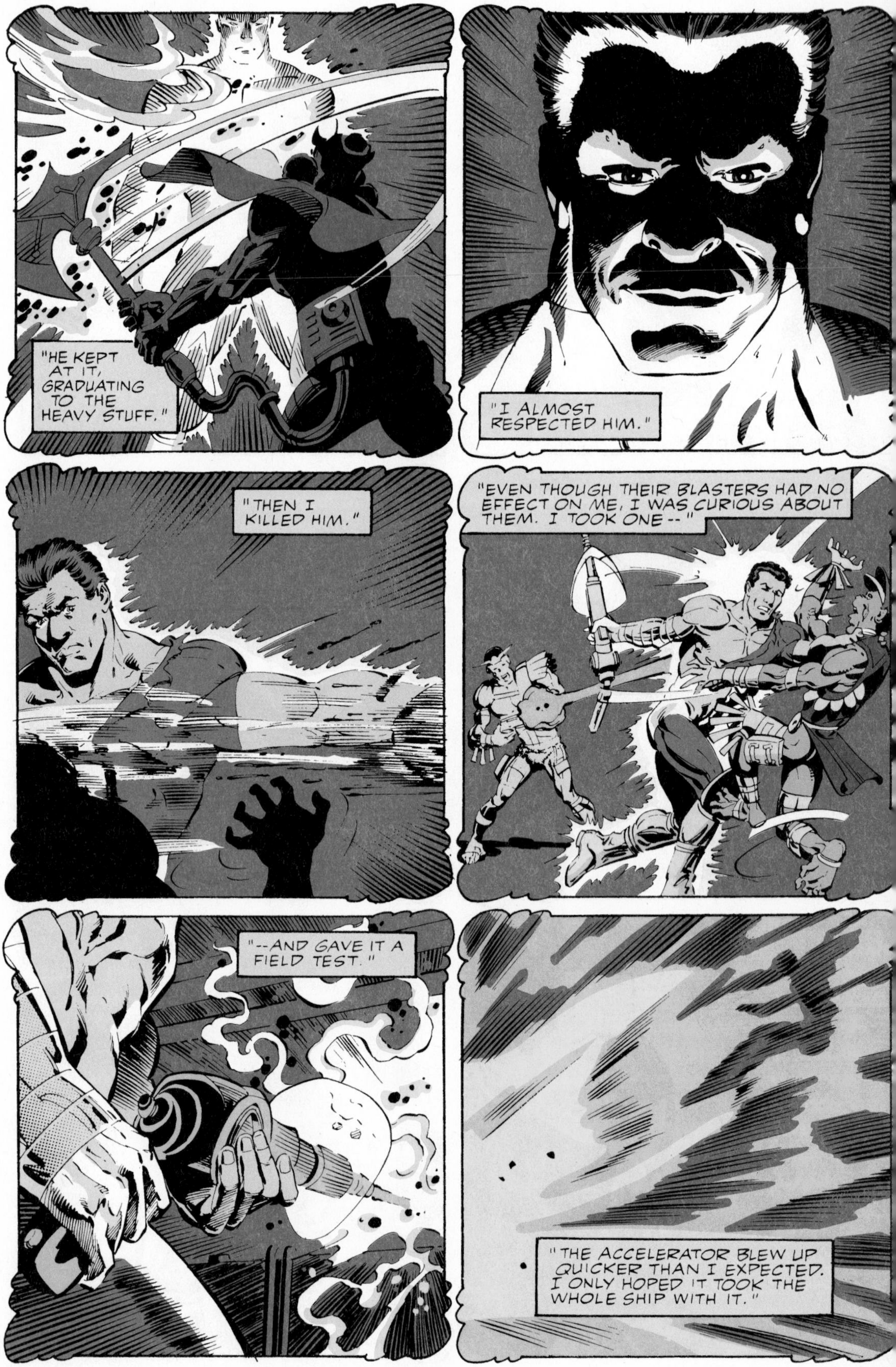
"HE KEPT AT IT, GRADUATING TO THE HEAVY STUFF."
"I ALMOST RESPECTED HIM."
"THEN I KILLED HIM."
"EVEN THOUGH THEIR BLASTERS HAD NO EFFECT ON ME, I WAS CURIOUS ABOUT THEM. I TOOK ONE --"
"--AND GAVE IT A FIELD TEST."
"THE ACCELERATOR BLEW UP QUICKER THAN I EXPECTED. I ONLY HOPED IT TOOK THE WHOLE SHIP WITH IT."

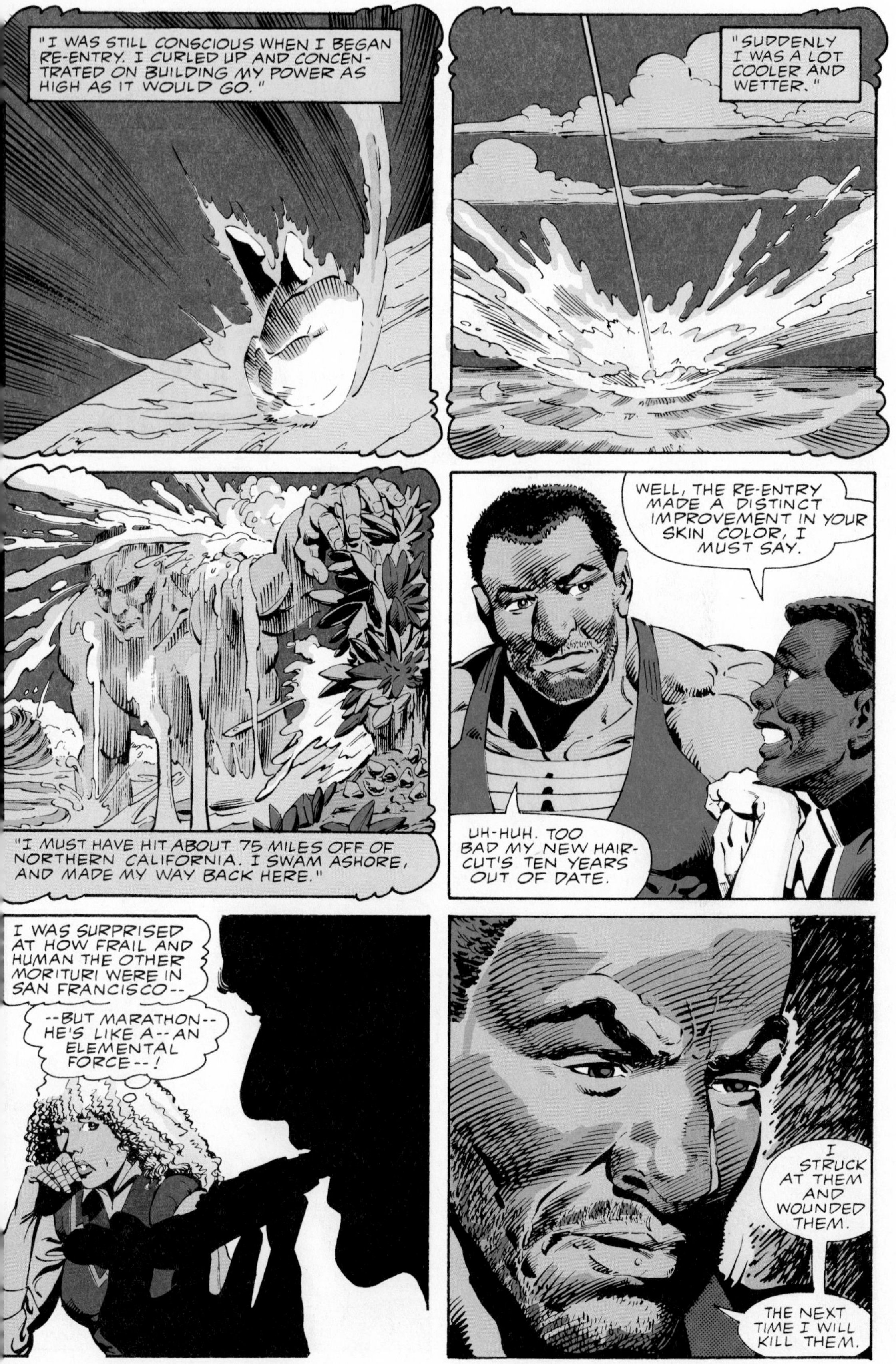
"I WAS STILL CONSCIOUS WHEN I BEGAN RE-ENTRY. I CURLED UP AND CONCENTRATED ON BUILDING MY POWER AS HIGH AS IT WOULD GO."
"SUDDENLY I WAS A LOT COOLER AND WETTER."
"I MUST HAVE HIT ABOUT 75 MILES OFF OF NORTHERN CALIFORNIA. I SWAM ASHORE, AND MADE MY WAY BACK HERE."
WELL, THE RE-ENTRY MADE A DISTINCT IMPROVEMENT IN YOUR SKIN COLOR, I MUST SAY.
UH-HUH. TOO BAD MY NEW HAIR-CUT'S TEN YEARS OUT OF DATE.
I WAS SURPRISED AT HOW FRAIL AND HUMAN THE OTHER MORITURI WERE IN SAN FRANCISCO--
--BUT MARATHON--HE'S LIKE A--AN ELEMENTAL FORCE--!
I STRUCK AT THEM AND WOUNDED THEM.
THE NEXT TIME I WILL KILL THEM.

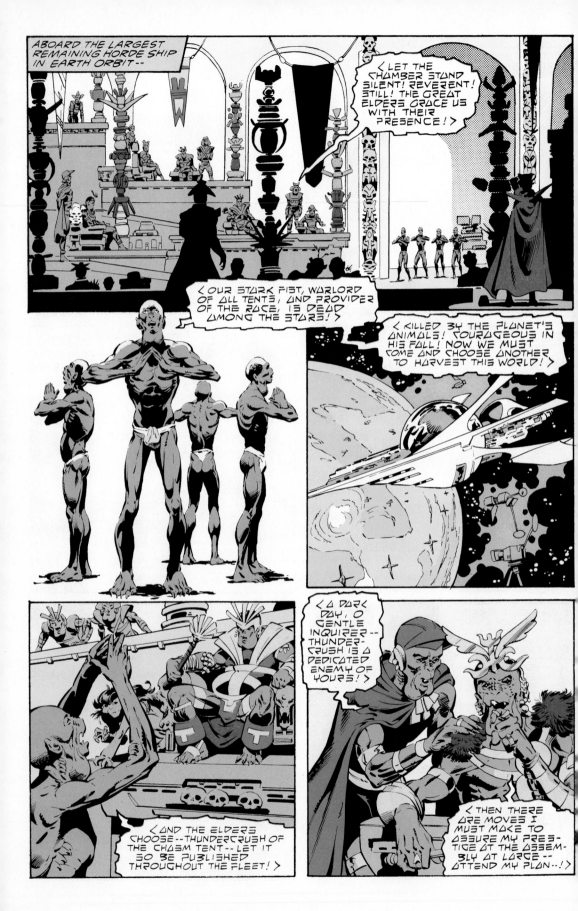

ABOARD THE LARGEST REMAINING HORDE SHIP IN EARTH ORBIT--

< LET THE CHAMBER STAND SILENT! REVERENT! STILL! THE GREAT ELDERS GRACE US WITH THEIR PRESENCE! >

< OUR STARK FIST, WARLORD OF ALL TENTS, AND PROVIDER OF THE RACE, IS DEAD AMONG THE STARS! >

< KILLED BY THE PLANET'S ANIMALS! COURAGEOUS IN HIS FALL! NOW WE MUST COME AND CHOOSE ANOTHER TO HARVEST THIS WORLD! >

< A DARK DAY, O GENTLE INQUIRER-- THUNDER-CRUSH IS A DEDICATED ENEMY OF YOURS! >

< AND THE ELDERS CHOOSE--THUNDERCRUSH OF THE CHASM TENT--LET IT SO BE PUBLISHED THROUGHOUT THE FLEET! >

< THEN THERE ARE MOVES I MUST MAKE TO ASSURE MY PRESTIGE AT THE ASSEMBLY AT LARGE-- ATTEND MY PLAN--! >

204

EENOOEENOOEENOOEENOOEENOOEENOO

WILL YOU *STOP* TRANSMITTING YOUR EMOTIONS LIKE THAT? YOU PROBABLY GAVE HALF OF US CARDIAC ARREST!

WHA ≡GASP≡ AT?

THE HORDE ALERT! BUT WH≡HUH≡Y CAN'T I BRE≡HUH≡EATHE? AND MY HEART'S ≡HUH≡ POUNDING!

I'M SORRY, PILAR--THE ALERT WOKE ME UP-- DIDN'T HAVE TIME TO HOLD BACK--!

WELL LET'S STOP JABBERING AND START MOVING--

-- GET TO THE RAIL GUN SHIP!

EENOOEENOOEENOOEENOOEEN

HEY, YOU'RE JUST TOO FAST-- WAIT UP--!

EENOOEENOOEENOOEEN!

I PASSED LOU--BUT WHERE'S ROBERT?

I HAVE AN IDEA-- FOLLOW ME!

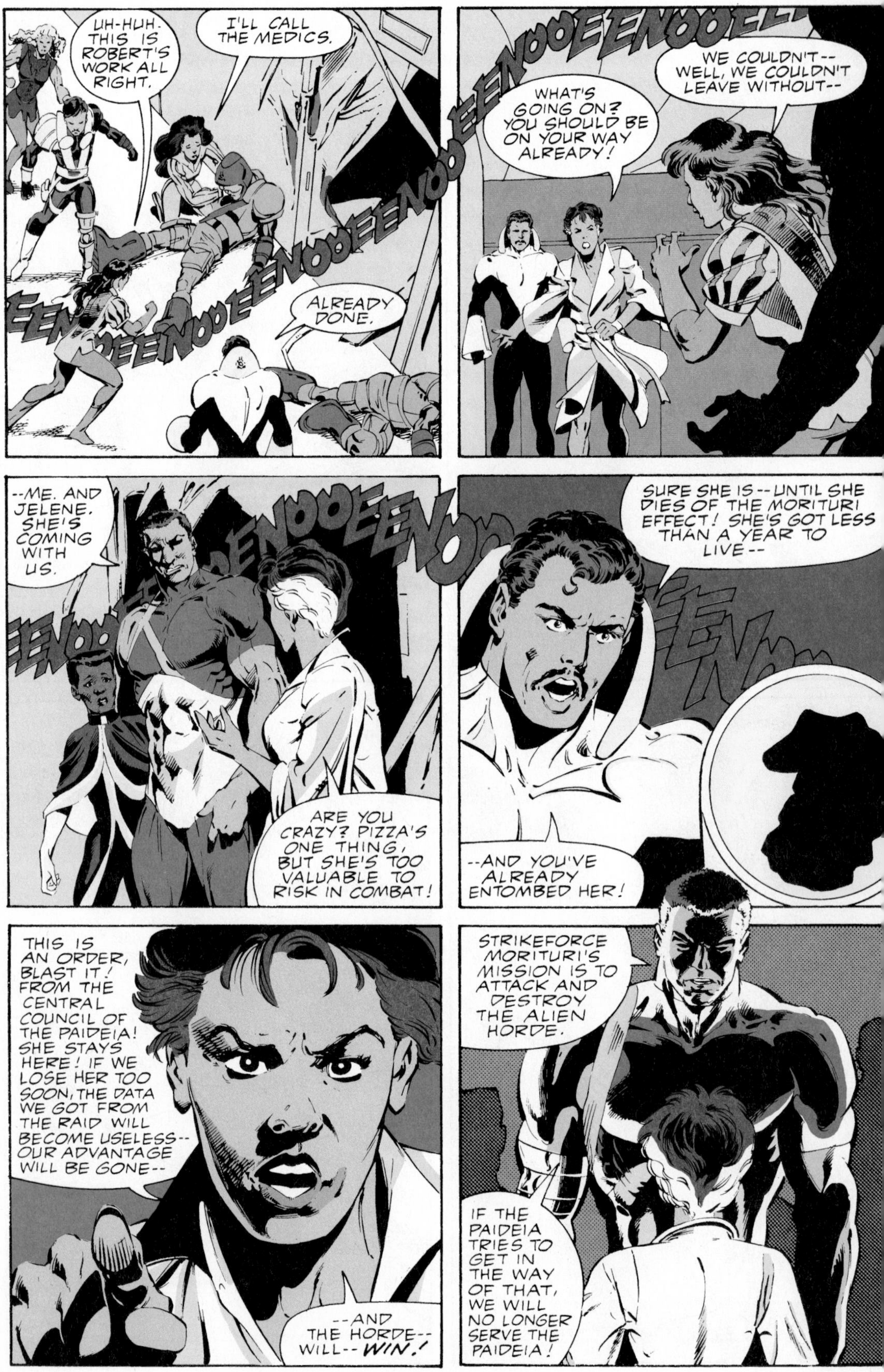
UH-HUH. THIS IS ROBERT'S WORK ALL RIGHT.
I'LL CALL THE MEDICS.
ALREADY DONE.
WHAT'S GOING ON? YOU SHOULD BE ON YOUR WAY ALREADY!
WE COULDN'T-- WELL, WE COULDN'T LEAVE WITHOUT--
--ME. AND JELENE. SHE'S COMING WITH US.
ARE YOU CRAZY? PIZZA'S ONE THING, BUT SHE'S TOO VALUABLE TO RISK IN COMBAT!
SURE SHE IS--UNTIL SHE DIES OF THE MORITURI EFFECT! SHE'S GOT LESS THAN A YEAR TO LIVE--
--AND YOU'VE ALREADY ENTOMBED HER!
THIS IS AN ORDER, BLAST IT! FROM THE CENTRAL COUNCIL OF THE PAIDEIA! SHE STAYS HERE! IF WE LOSE HER TOO SOON, THE DATA WE GOT FROM THE RAID WILL BECOME USELESS-- OUR ADVANTAGE WILL BE GONE--
--AND THE HORDE-- WILL-- WIN!
STRIKEFORCE MORITURI'S MISSION IS TO ATTACK AND DESTROY THE ALIEN HORDE.
IF THE PAIDEIA TRIES TO GET IN THE WAY OF THAT, WE WILL NO LONGER SERVE THE PAIDEIA!

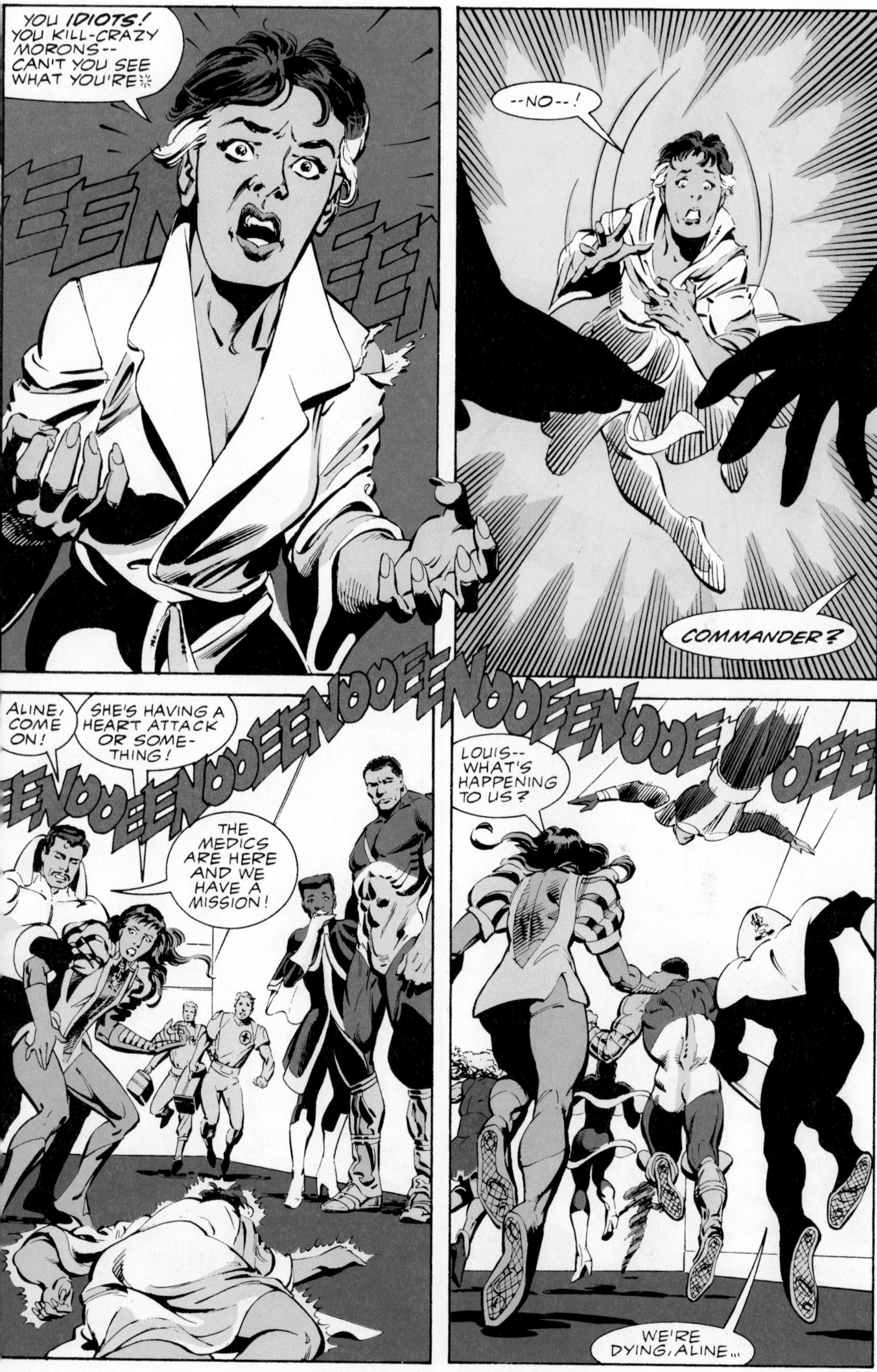
YOU IDIOTS! YOU KILL-CRAZY MORONS-- CAN'T YOU SEE WHAT YOU'RE
--NO--!
COMMANDER?
EENOOEENOOEENOOEENOOEENOOEENOOE
ALINE, COME ON!
SHE'S HAVING A HEART ATTACK OR SOME-THING!
THE MEDICS ARE HERE AND WE HAVE A MISSION!
LOUIS-- WHAT'S HAPPENING TO US?
WE'RE DYING, ALINE...

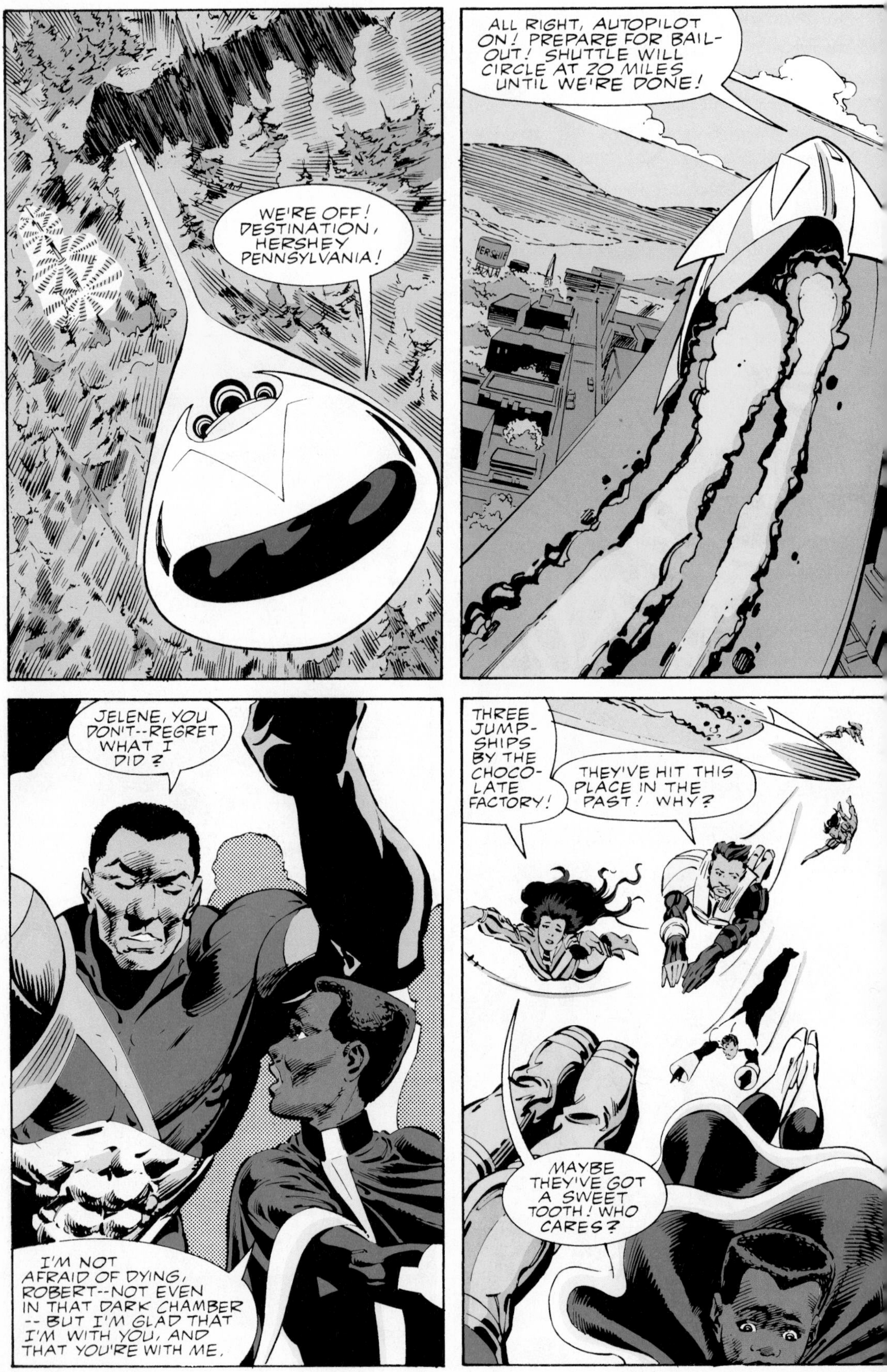
WE'RE OFF! DESTINATION, HERSHEY PENNSYLVANIA!
ALL RIGHT, AUTOPILOT ON! PREPARE FOR BAIL-OUT! SHUTTLE WILL CIRCLE AT 20 MILES UNTIL WE'RE DONE!
JELENE, YOU DON'T--REGRET WHAT I DID?
I'M NOT AFRAID OF DYING, ROBERT--NOT EVEN IN THAT DARK CHAMBER --BUT I'M GLAD THAT I'M WITH YOU, AND THAT YOU'RE WITH ME.
THREE JUMP-SHIPS BY THE CHOCO-LATE FACTORY!
THEY'VE HIT THIS PLACE IN THE PAST! WHY?
MAYBE THEY'VE GOT A SWEET TOOTH! WHO CARES?

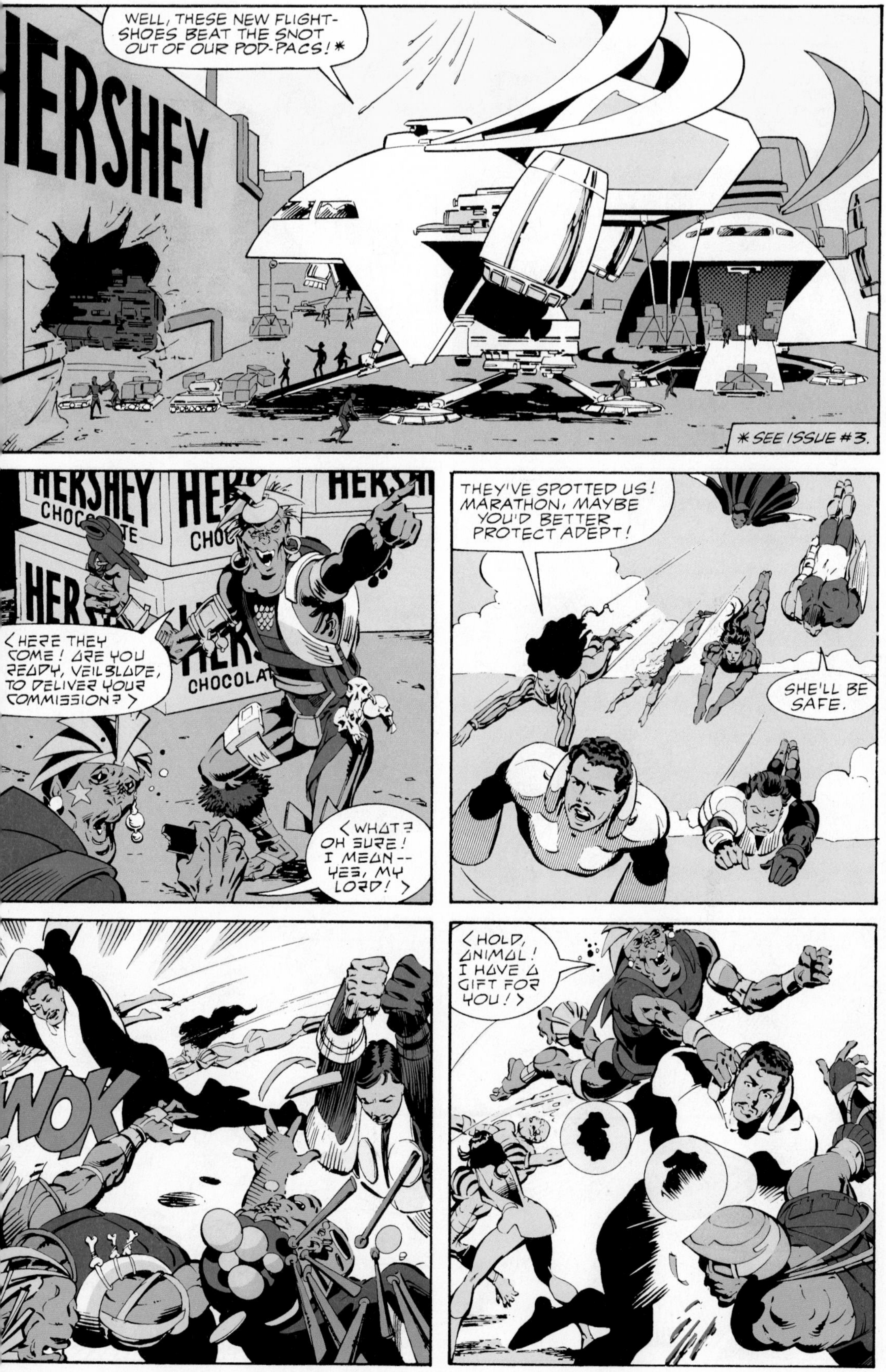
HERSHEY
WELL, THESE NEW FLIGHT-SHOES BEAT THE SNOT OUT OF OUR POD-PACS! *
* SEE ISSUE #3.
HERSHEY CHOCOLATE
<HERE THEY COME! ARE YOU READY, VEILBLADE, TO DELIVER YOUR COMMISSION?>
<WHAT? OH SURE! I MEAN -- YES, MY LORD!>
THEY'VE SPOTTED US! MARATHON, MAYBE YOU'D BETTER PROTECT ADEPT!
SHE'LL BE SAFE.
WOK
<HOLD, ANIMAL! I HAVE A GIFT FOR YOU!>

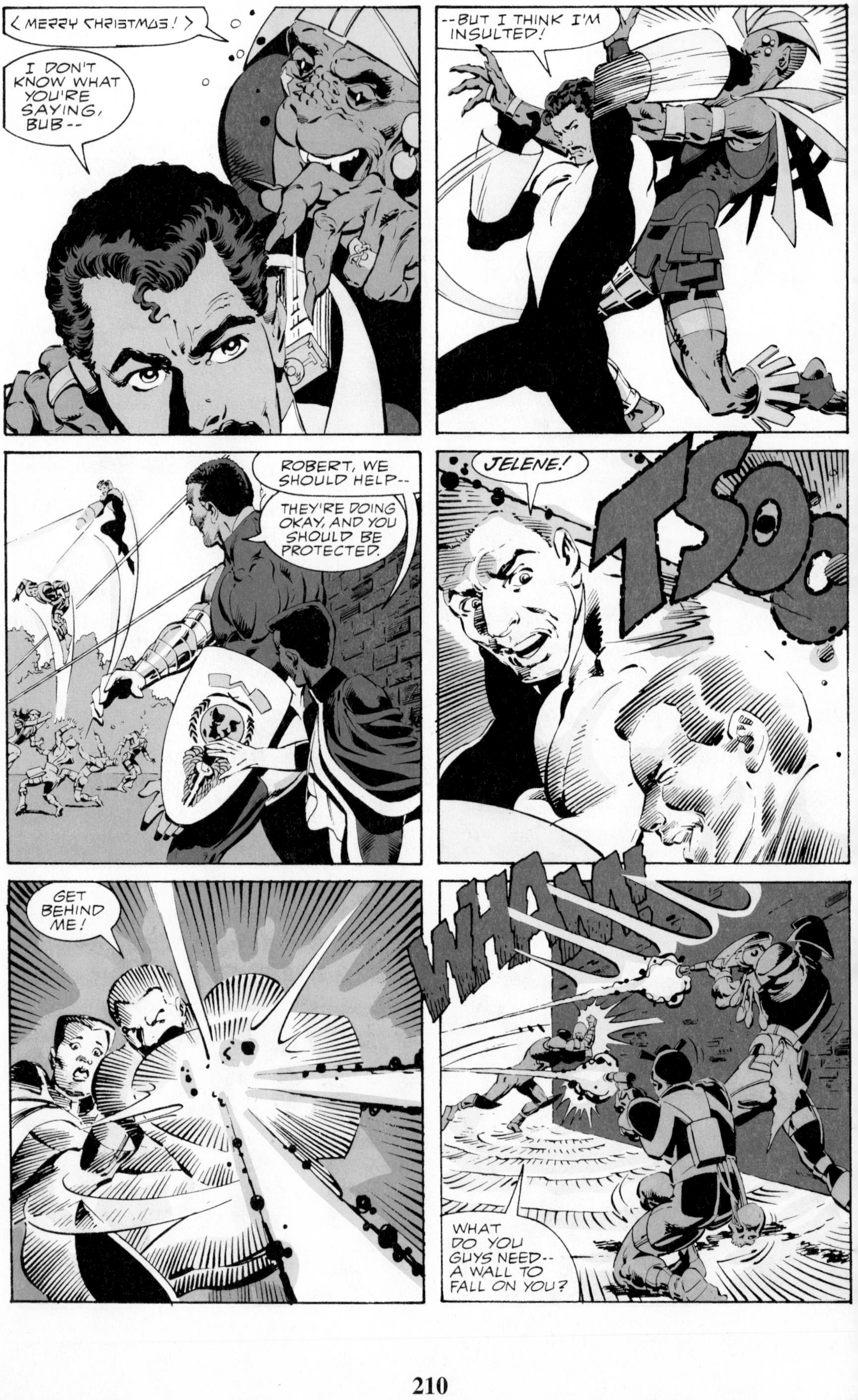

< MERRY CHRISTMAS! >
I DON'T KNOW WHAT YOU'RE SAYING, BUB --
--BUT I THINK I'M INSULTED!
ROBERT, WE SHOULD HELP--
THEY'RE DOING OKAY, AND YOU SHOULD BE PROTECTED.
JELENE!
TSO
GET BEHIND ME!
WHAM
WHAT DO YOU GUYS NEED-- A WALL TO FALL ON YOU?

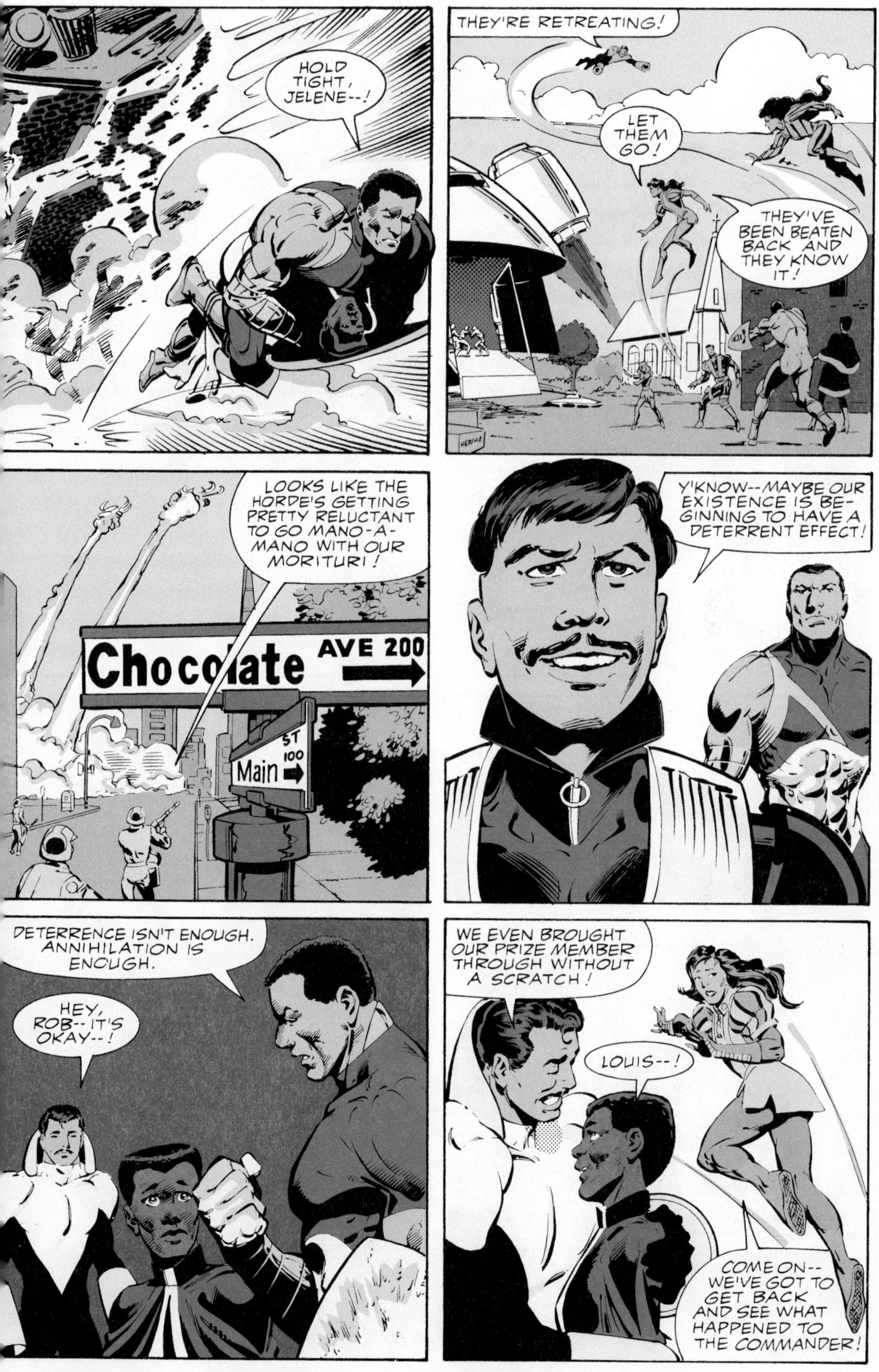
HOLD TIGHT, JELENE--!
THEY'RE RETREATING!
LET THEM GO!
THEY'VE BEEN BEATEN BACK AND THEY KNOW IT!
LOOKS LIKE THE HORDE'S GETTING PRETTY RELUCTANT TO GO MANO-A-MANO WITH OUR MORITURI!
Chocolate AVE 200
Main ST 100
Y'KNOW--MAYBE OUR EXISTENCE IS BEGINNING TO HAVE A DETERRENT EFFECT!
DETERRENCE ISN'T ENOUGH. ANNIHILATION IS ENOUGH.
HEY, ROB-- IT'S OKAY--!
WE EVEN BROUGHT OUR PRIZE MEMBER THROUGH WITHOUT A SCRATCH!
LOUIS--!
COME ON-- WE'VE GOT TO GET BACK AND SEE WHAT HAPPENED TO THE COMMANDER!

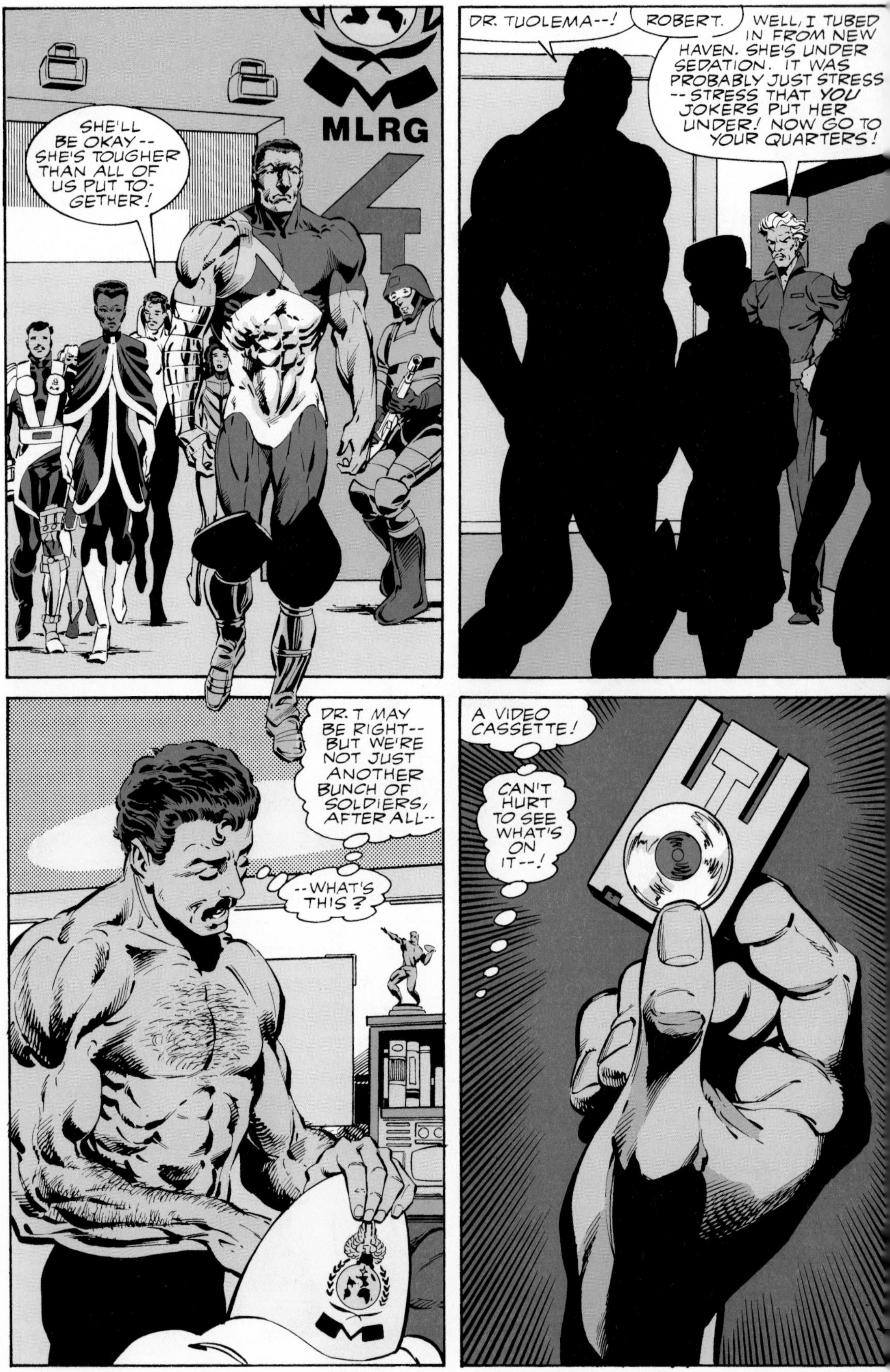
MLRG
SHE'LL BE OKAY-- SHE'S TOUGHER THAN ALL OF US PUT TOGETHER!
DR. TUOLEMA--!
ROBERT.
WELL, I TUBED IN FROM NEW HAVEN. SHE'S UNDER SEDATION. IT WAS PROBABLY JUST STRESS --STRESS THAT YOU JOKERS PUT HER UNDER! NOW GO TO YOUR QUARTERS!
DR. T MAY BE RIGHT-- BUT WE'RE NOT JUST ANOTHER BUNCH OF SOLDIERS, AFTER ALL--
--WHAT'S THIS?
A VIDEO CASSETTE!
CAN'T HURT TO SEE WHAT'S ON IT--!

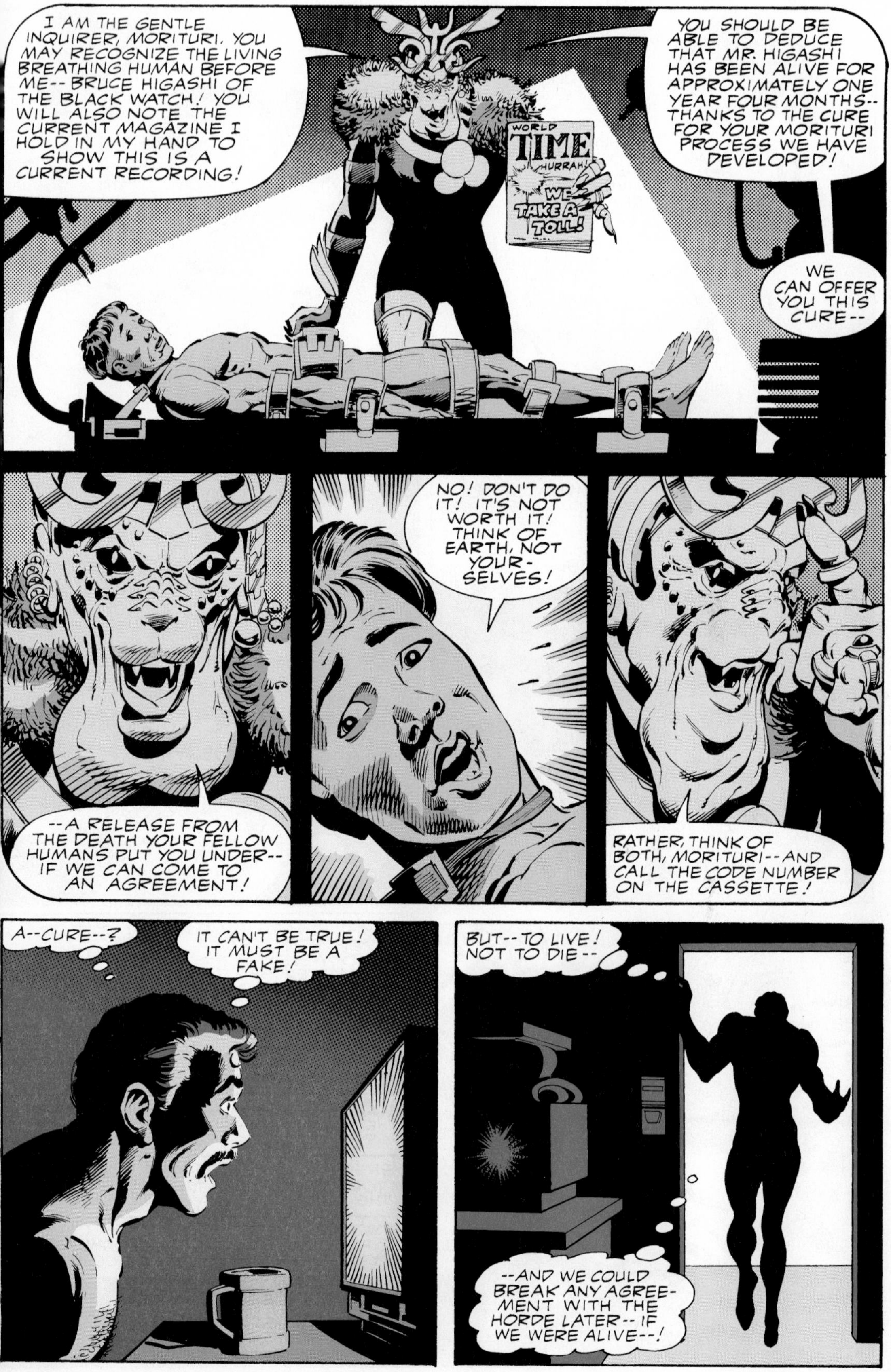
I AM THE GENTLE INQUIRER, MORITURI. YOU MAY RECOGNIZE THE LIVING BREATHING HUMAN BEFORE ME-- BRUCE HIGASHI OF THE BLACK WATCH! YOU WILL ALSO NOTE THE CURRENT MAGAZINE I HOLD IN MY HAND TO SHOW THIS IS A CURRENT RECORDING!
WORLD TIME
HURRAH!
WE TAKE A TOLL!
YOU SHOULD BE ABLE TO DEDUCE THAT MR. HIGASHI HAS BEEN ALIVE FOR APPROXIMATELY ONE YEAR FOUR MONTHS-- THANKS TO THE CURE FOR YOUR MORITURI PROCESS WE HAVE DEVELOPED!
WE CAN OFFER YOU THIS CURE--
--A RELEASE FROM THE DEATH YOUR FELLOW HUMANS PUT YOU UNDER-- IF WE CAN COME TO AN AGREEMENT!
NO! DON'T DO IT! IT'S NOT WORTH IT! THINK OF EARTH, NOT YOUR-SELVES!
RATHER, THINK OF BOTH, MORITURI--AND CALL THE CODE NUMBER ON THE CASSETTE!
A--CURE--?
IT CAN'T BE TRUE! IT MUST BE A FAKE!
BUT--TO LIVE! NOT TO DIE--
--AND WE COULD BREAK ANY AGREE-MENT WITH THE HORDE LATER-- IF WE WERE ALIVE--!

I ALWAYS THOUGHT THERE'D BE A WAY OUT-- BUT *THIS*--!

I DON'T WANT TO DIE-- BUT TO LIVE-- AS A TRAITOR--?

LOUIS! COME QUICK!

JEEZ! DON'T DO THAT, PILAR! YOU COME OUT OF NOWHERE WHEN YOU MOVE THAT FAST!

COME ON!

SLOW DOWN, WILL YOU?

I SET MY TERMINAL UP TO CATCH ANY UNUSUAL MESSAGES IN OR OUT OF THE MOUNTAIN-- YOU'VE GOT TO SEE WHAT I RECORDED! NOT EVEN SCRAMBLED!

I'M NOT SURE WHO'S AT THE OTHER END, BUT IT'S SOME-BODY BIG!

YOU DON'T SEEM TO UNDERSTAND HOW IMPORTANT THIS IS!

"THIS IS *MORE* IMPORTANT, DOCTOR! ADEPT'S ANALYTICAL POWERS COULD VERY WELL WIN THIS WAR FOR US! AND AFTER SHE DIES, WE CAN'T JUST WAIT FOR THE ROULETTE WHEEL OF YOUR MORITURI PROCESS TO COME UP WITH ANOTHER ONE LIKE HER! YOU ARE UNDER ORDERS TO DROP ALL OTHER RESEARCH AND CONCENTRATE ON REMOVING THE RANDOMNESS FROM YOUR PROCESS! WE NEED MORE ADEPTS!

BUT I *CAN'T* STOP MY SEARCH FOR A CURE FOR THE MORTALITY EFFECT! I *KNOW* I'M CLOSE TO IT! GET SOMEONE ELSE!

"THERE IS NO ONE ELSE AND YOU KNOW IT, DOCTOR. YOUR COLLEAGUES WERE KILLED BY THE HORDE. WE HAVE ONLY YOU."

SO YOU'RE JUST GOING LET THEM DIE-- TO LET ME KEEP ON *KILLING THESE CHILDREN!* YOU DON'T CARE ABOUT THEM ONE IOTA!

"THIS DISCUSSION IS AT AN END, DOCTOR."

HE WAS WORKING ON A CURE? IT'S POSSIBLE--?

WHO DO THEY THINK THEY ARE, PLAYING WITH OUR LIVES?

EXCUSE ME, I'VE GOT TO THINK--!

I WAS A LOYAL CITIZEN OF THE PAIDEIA UP TO NOW--BUT WHY BE LOYAL TO PEOPLE WHO ARE READY TO ABANDON ME?

"IF THE PAIDEIA GETS IN OUR WAY, WE WILL NO LONGER SERVE THE PAIDEIA."

"YOU'VE ENTOMBED HER ALREADY!"

"ONE YEAR FOUR MONTHS ... "

"...READY TO ABANDON ME?"

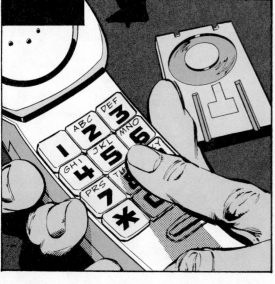

HELLO?

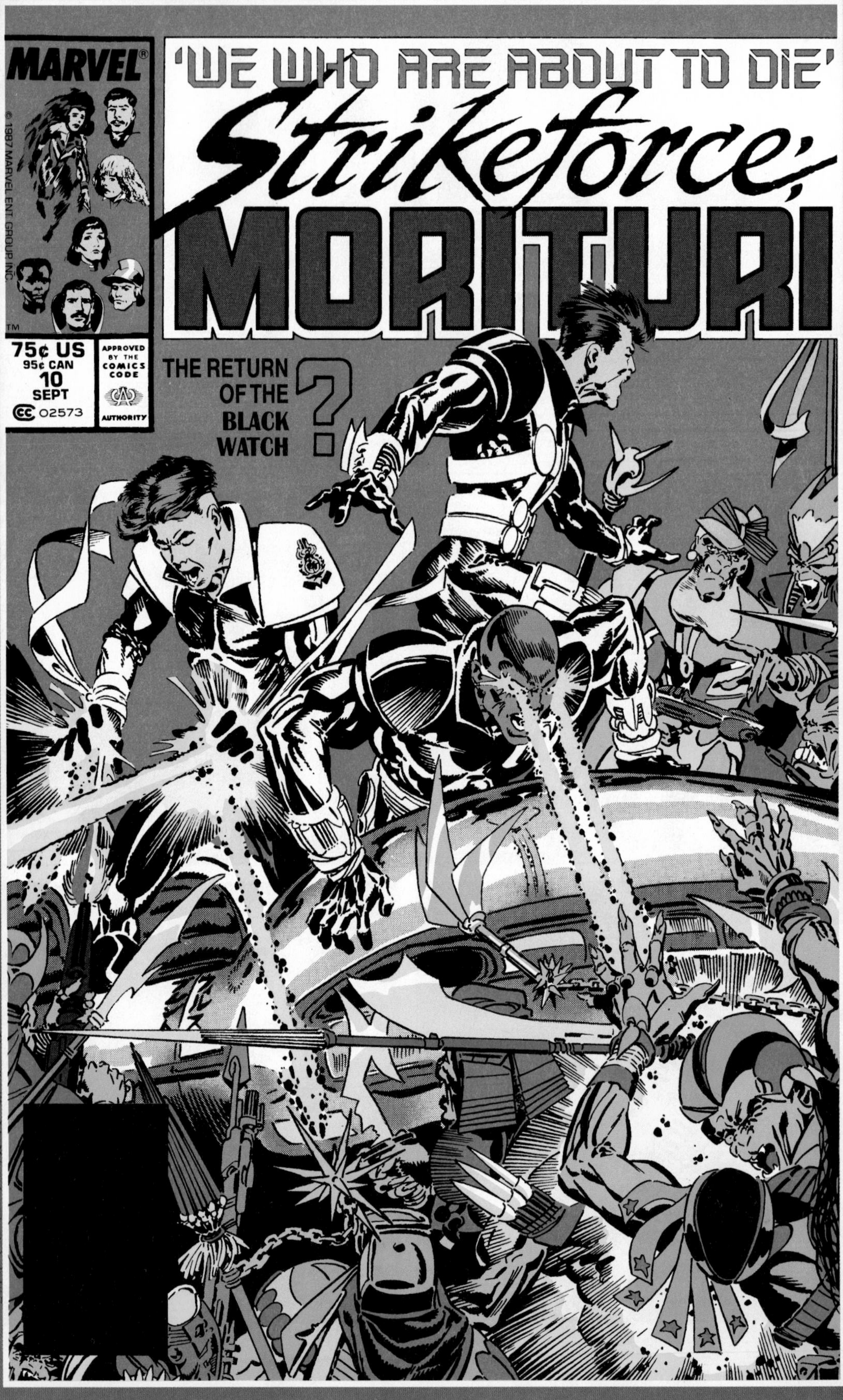
MARVEL
'WE WHO ARE ABOUT TO DIE'
Strikeforce:
MORITURI
© 1987 MARVEL ENT. GROUP INC.
TM
75¢ US
95¢ CAN
10
SEPT
CC 02573
APPROVED BY THE COMICS CODE AUTHORITY
THE RETURN OF THE BLACK WATCH ?

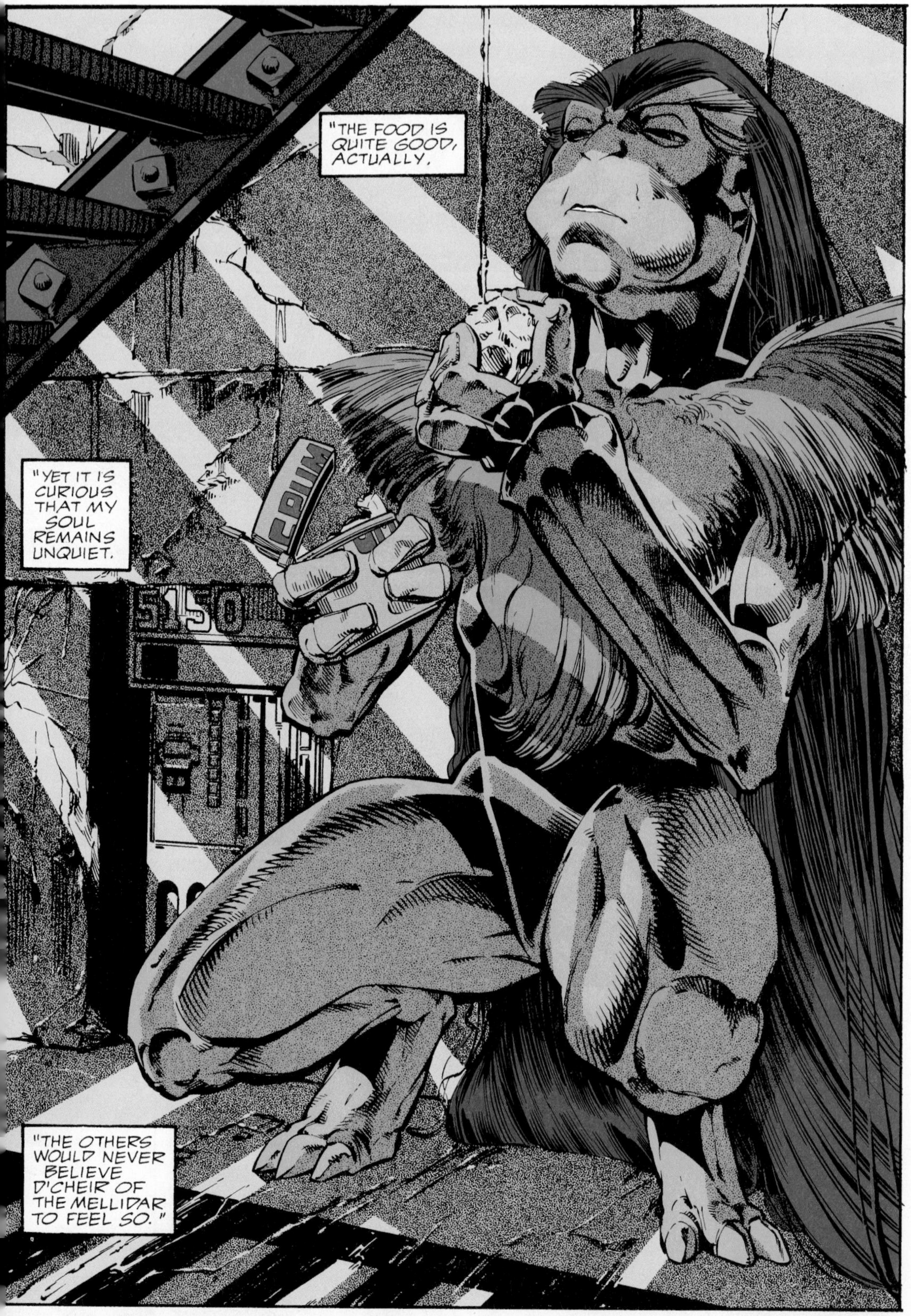
"THE FOOD IS QUITE GOOD, ACTUALLY.
"YET IT IS CURIOUS THAT MY SOUL REMAINS UNQUIET.
5150
"THE OTHERS WOULD NEVER BELIEVE D'CHEIR OF THE MELLIDAR TO FEEL SO."

"A HORDE SHIP RETURNS FROM ONE OF ITS RAIDS.

"I WILL SEE THIS THING.

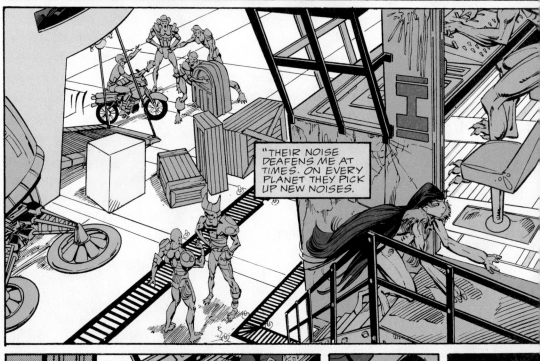

"THEIR NOISE DEAFENS ME AT TIMES. ON EVERY PLANET THEY PICK UP NEW NOISES.

"AND I HAVE YET TO GET USED TO THE GRAVITY OF THIS PLANET EARTH.

"IT IMPEDES MY GRACE.

"HE FROWNS UPON A PET SITTING IN THE CHAIR."

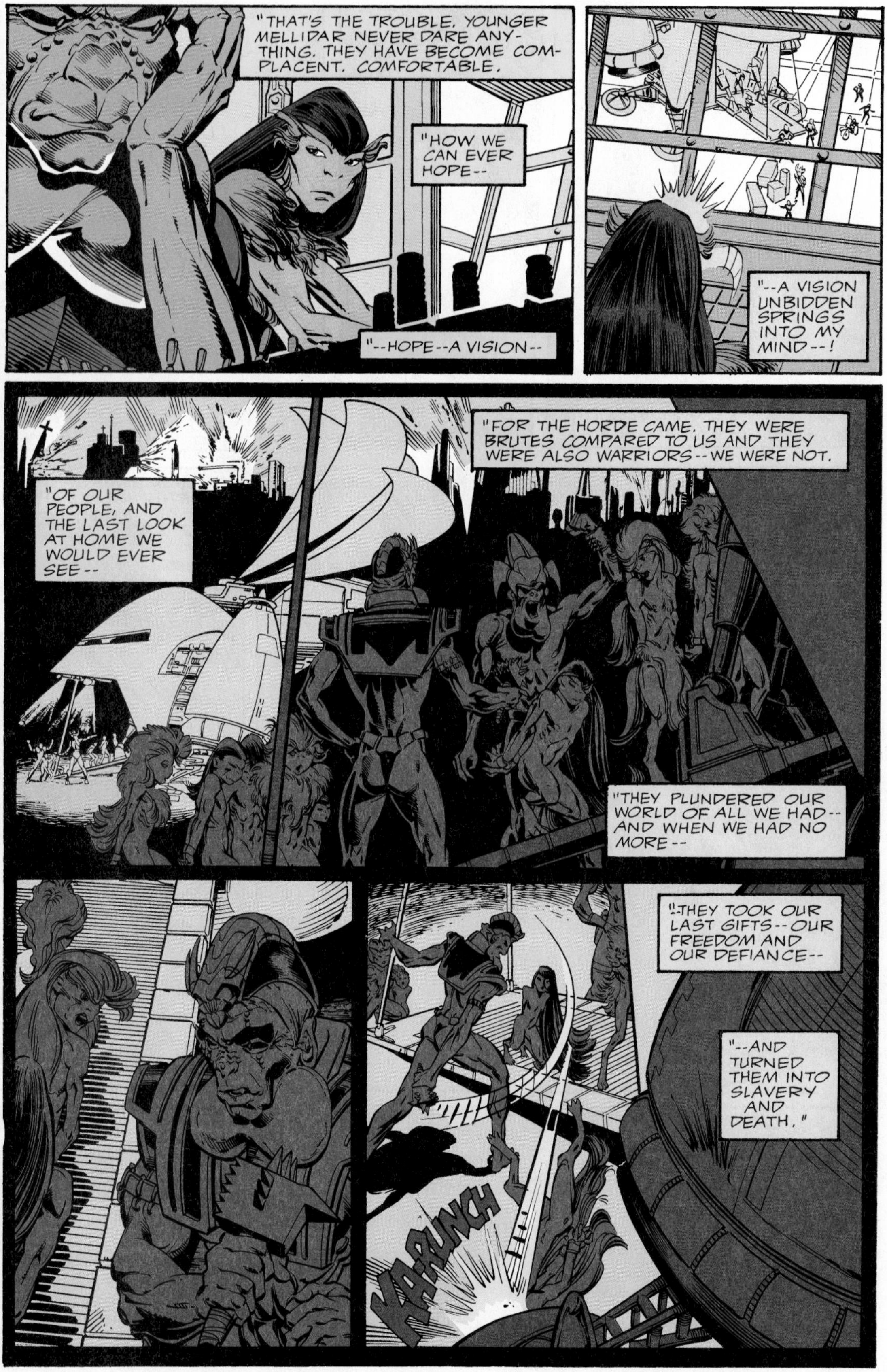
"THAT'S THE TROUBLE. YOUNGER MELLIDAR NEVER DARE ANYTHING. THEY HAVE BECOME COMPLACENT. COMFORTABLE.
"HOW WE CAN EVER HOPE--
"--HOPE--A VISION--
"--A VISION UNBIDDEN SPRINGS INTO MY MIND--!
"FOR THE HORDE CAME. THEY WERE BRUTES COMPARED TO US AND THEY WERE ALSO WARRIORS--WE WERE NOT.
"OF OUR PEOPLE, AND THE LAST LOOK AT HOME WE WOULD EVER SEE--
"THEY PLUNDERED OUR WORLD OF ALL WE HAD--AND WHEN WE HAD NO MORE--
"--THEY TOOK OUR LAST GIFTS--OUR FREEDOM AND OUR DEFIANCE--
"--AND TURNED THEM INTO SLAVERY AND DEATH."
KA-RUNCH

"MOST CURIOUS, THOUGH.

"COULD THIS RELATE TO MY MALAISE?

‹YOU!›

‹OUT OF THAT CHAIR, PET!›

"SURELY SOMETHING SO WELL-KNOWN WOULD NOT AFFECT ME--?

‹I'LL TEACH YOU TO--›

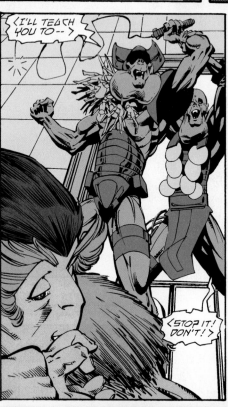

‹STOP IT! DON'T!›

"THAT'S IT!

"THE ABORIGINES OF THIS PLANET-- WHAT ARE THEY CALLED?

"HUMANS!

‹YOU'VE GOT TO ‹EEP YOUR TEMPER DOWN!›

"THIS ALL GOES BACK TO WHEN I FIRST MET --THE HUMANS--!"

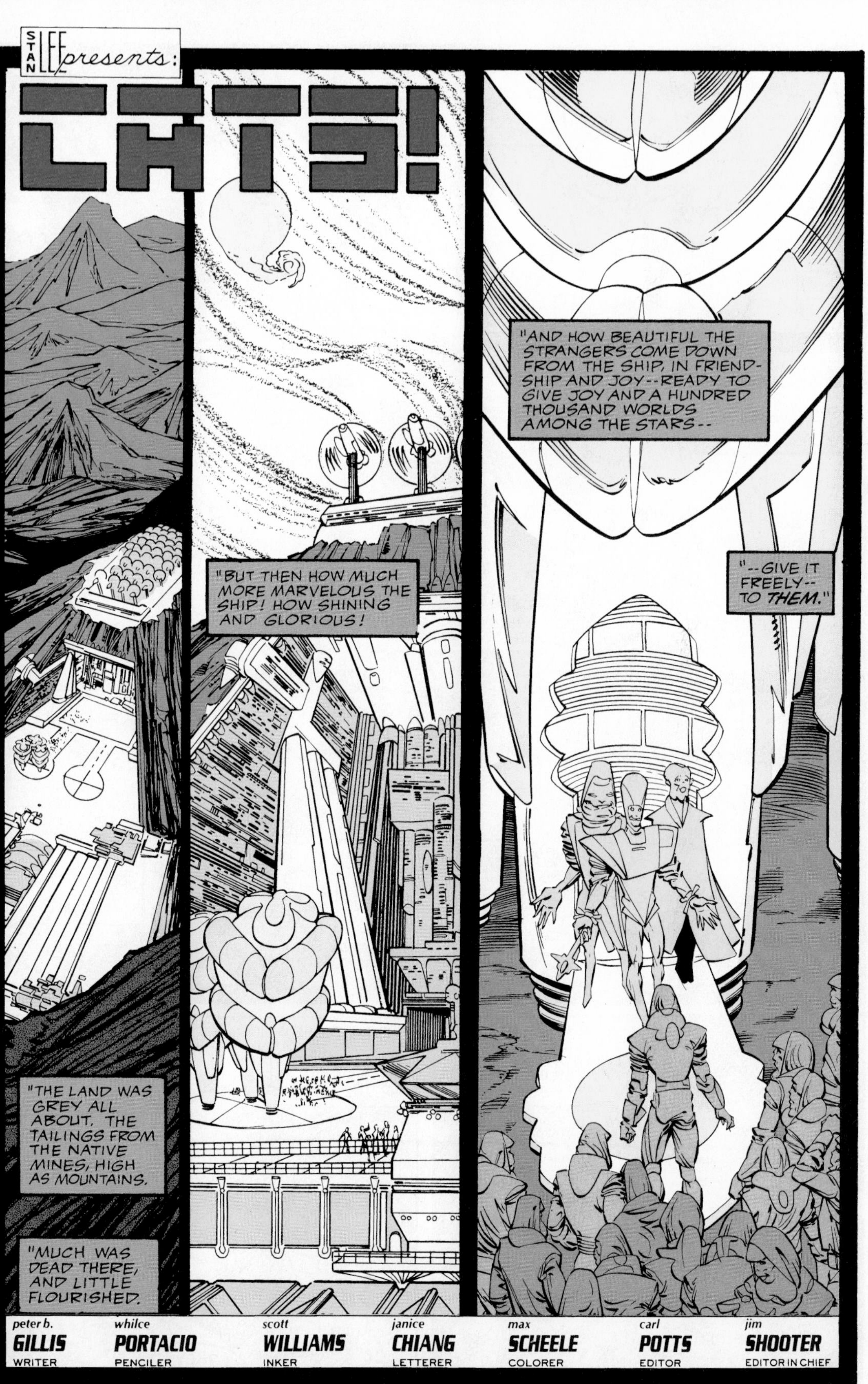

STAN LEE presents:
CATS!
"THE LAND WAS GREY ALL ABOUT. THE TAILINGS FROM THE NATIVE MINES, HIGH AS MOUNTAINS.
"MUCH WAS DEAD THERE, AND LITTLE FLOURISHED.
"BUT THEN HOW MUCH MORE MARVELOUS THE SHIP! HOW SHINING AND GLORIOUS!
"AND HOW BEAUTIFUL THE STRANGERS COME DOWN FROM THE SHIP, IN FRIENDSHIP AND JOY--READY TO GIVE JOY AND A HUNDRED THOUSAND WORLDS AMONG THE STARS--
"--GIVE IT FREELY--TO THEM."
peter b. GILLIS WRITER
whilce PORTACIO PENCILER
scott WILLIAMS INKER
janice CHIANG LETTERER
max SCHEELE COLORER
carl POTTS EDITOR
jim SHOOTER EDITOR IN CHIEF

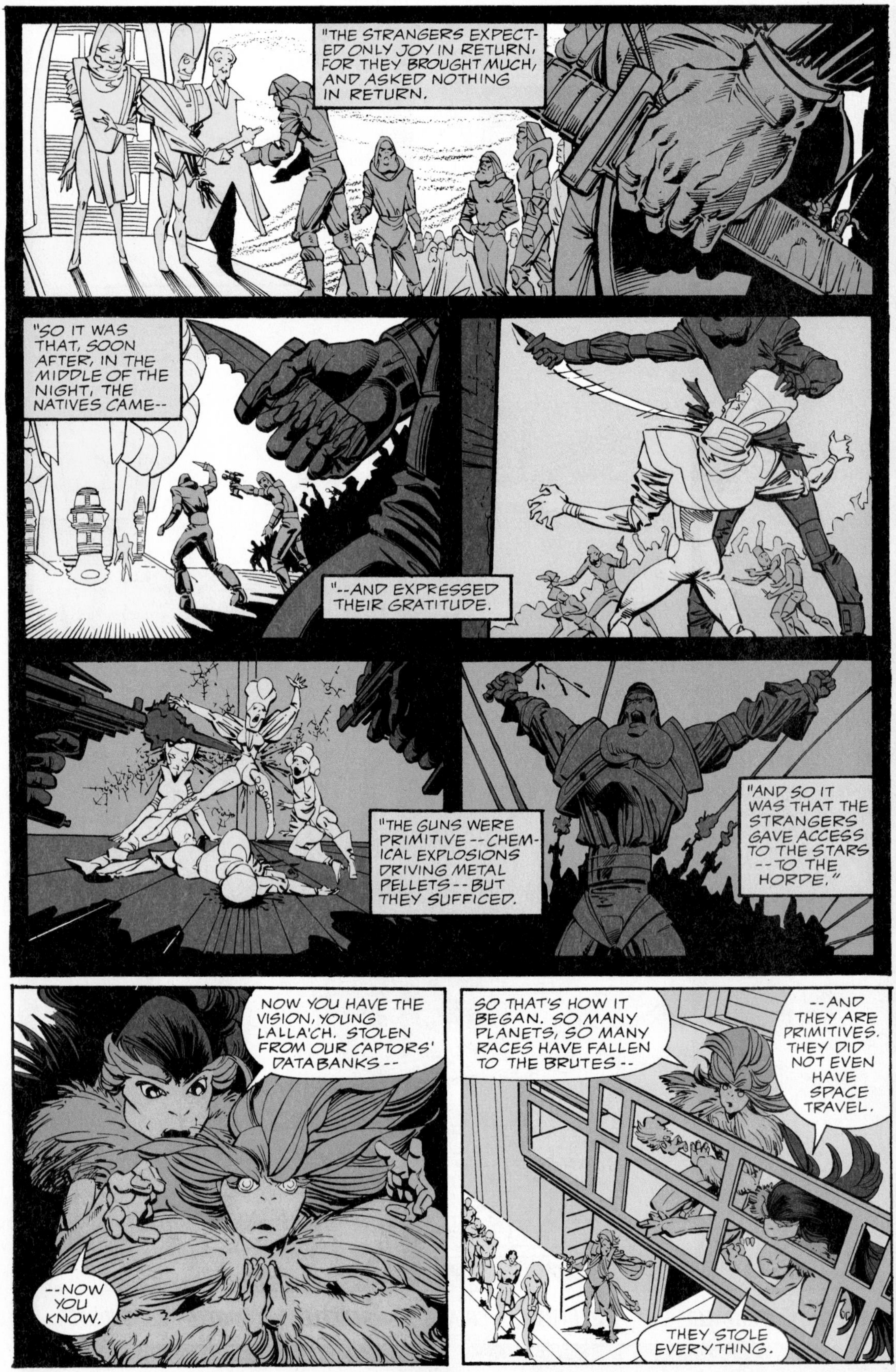
"THE STRANGERS EXPECTED ONLY JOY IN RETURN, FOR THEY BROUGHT MUCH, AND ASKED NOTHING IN RETURN.
"SO IT WAS THAT, SOON AFTER, IN THE MIDDLE OF THE NIGHT, THE NATIVES CAME--
"--AND EXPRESSED THEIR GRATITUDE.
"THE GUNS WERE PRIMITIVE--CHEMICAL EXPLOSIONS DRIVING METAL PELLETS--BUT THEY SUFFICED.
"AND SO IT WAS THAT THE STRANGERS GAVE ACCESS TO THE STARS--TO THE HORDE."
NOW YOU HAVE THE VISION, YOUNG LALLA'CH. STOLEN FROM OUR CAPTORS' DATABANKS--
--NOW YOU KNOW.
SO THAT'S HOW IT BEGAN. SO MANY PLANETS, SO MANY RACES HAVE FALLEN TO THE BRUTES--
--AND THEY ARE PRIMITIVES. THEY DID NOT EVEN HAVE SPACE TRAVEL.
THEY STOLE EVERYTHING.

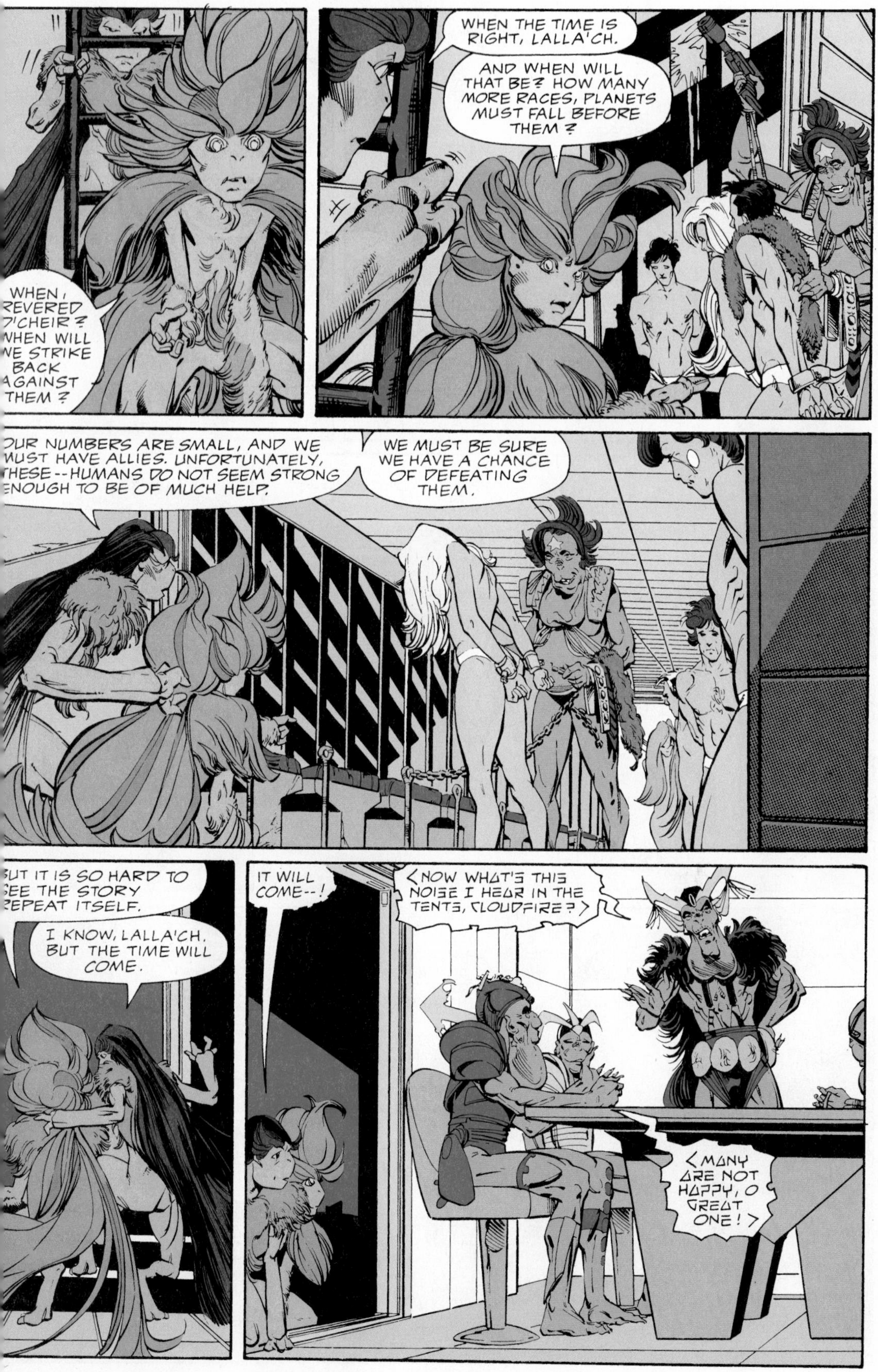
WHEN, REVERED D'CHEIR? WHEN WILL WE STRIKE BACK AGAINST THEM?
WHEN THE TIME IS RIGHT, LALLA'CH.
AND WHEN WILL THAT BE? HOW MANY MORE RACES, PLANETS MUST FALL BEFORE THEM?
OUR NUMBERS ARE SMALL, AND WE MUST HAVE ALLIES. UNFORTUNATELY, THESE--HUMANS DO NOT SEEM STRONG ENOUGH TO BE OF MUCH HELP.
WE MUST BE SURE WE HAVE A CHANCE OF DEFEATING THEM.
BUT IT IS SO HARD TO SEE THE STORY REPEAT ITSELF.
I KNOW, LALLA'CH. BUT THE TIME WILL COME.
IT WILL COME--!
<NOW WHAT'S THIS NOISE I HEAR IN THE TENTS, CLOUDFIRE?>
<MANY ARE NOT HAPPY, O GREAT ONE!>

< THEY QUESTION THE NEED FOR SO MANY TO STAY ON BASE AS GUARDS, WHEN THERE IS A PLANET OUT THERE RIPE FOR PLUNDERING! >

< THAT'S RIGHT! WHAT ARE ALL THESE WARRIORS FOLLOWING THE HIGH COMMAND AROUND FOR? TO PROTECT THEM FROM HUMANS? >

< NOT FROM HUMANS, YOU BILGEBAGS, BUT FROM DISHONOR! >

< I'M SURE THEY DIDN'T REALIZE, DREAD-EAGLE, WHAT THEY WERE SAYING! >

< AS LONG AS I'M FIRST IN THE FIELD ON EARTH, PROPER TRADITIONS AND FORMS WILL BE MAINTAINED! STAFF ROTATION WILL GIVE THEM THEIR CHANCE AT THE LOOT! >

< I'VE HAD ENOUGH! >

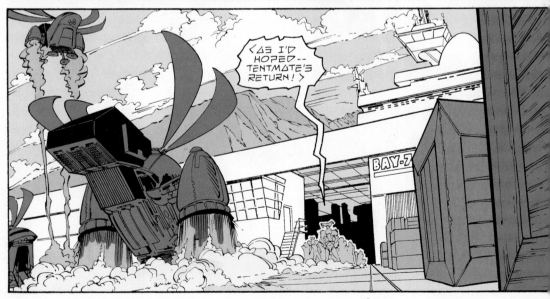

< AS I'D HOPED-- TENTMATE'S RETURN! >

BAY-7

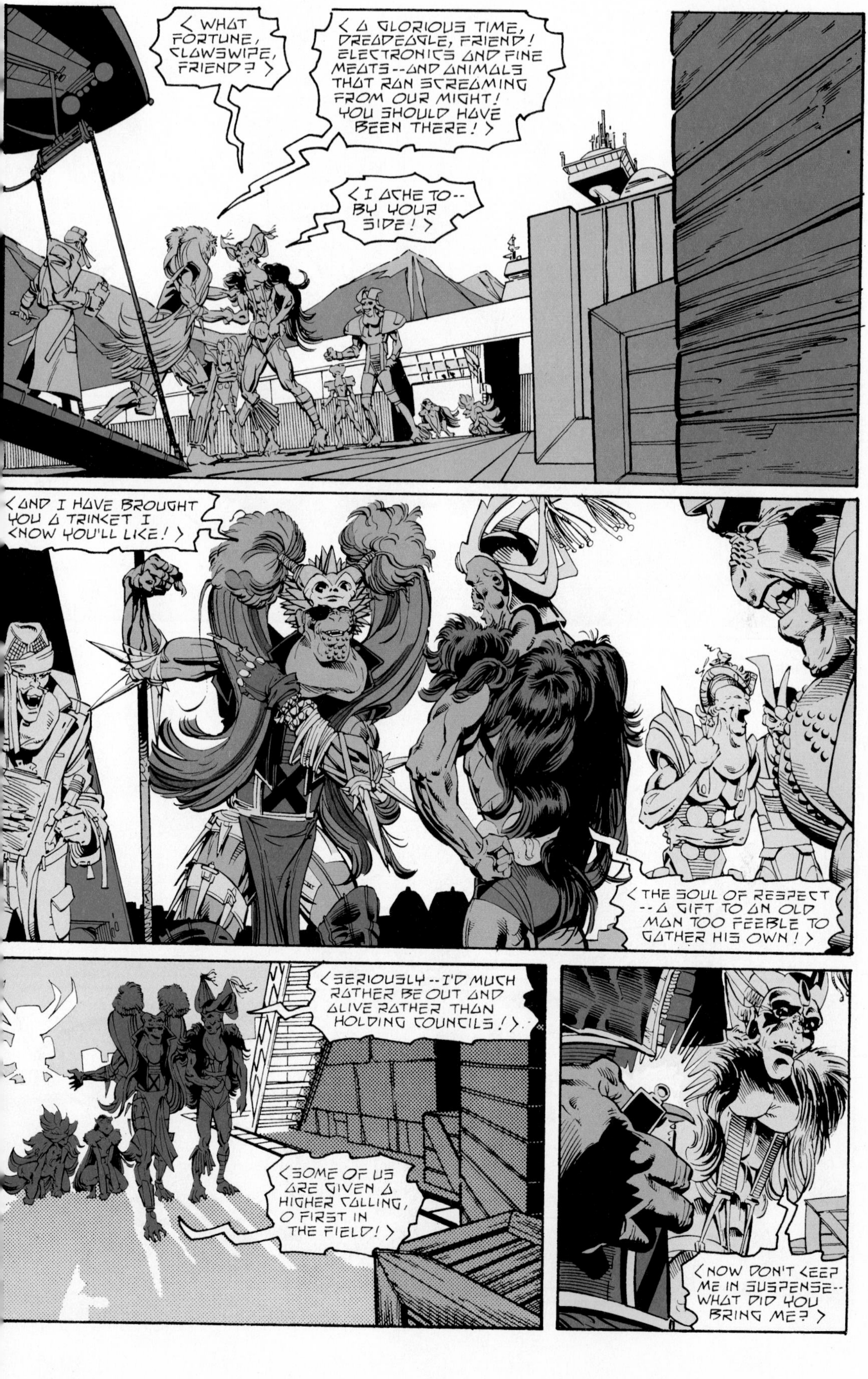
< WHAT FORTUNE, CLAWSWIPE, FRIEND? >
< A GLORIOUS TIME, DREADEAGLE, FRIEND! ELECTRONICS AND FINE MEATS--AND ANIMALS THAT RAN SCREAMING FROM OUR MIGHT! YOU SHOULD HAVE BEEN THERE! >
< I ACHE TO-- BY YOUR SIDE! >
< AND I HAVE BROUGHT YOU A TRINKET I KNOW YOU'LL LIKE! >
< THE SOUL OF RESPECT --A GIFT TO AN OLD MAN TOO FEEBLE TO GATHER HIS OWN! >
< SERIOUSLY--I'D MUCH RATHER BE OUT AND ALIVE RATHER THAN HOLDING COUNCILS! >
< SOME OF US ARE GIVEN A HIGHER CALLING, O FIRST IN THE FIELD! >
< NOW DON'T KEEP ME IN SUSPENSE-- WHAT DID YOU BRING ME? >

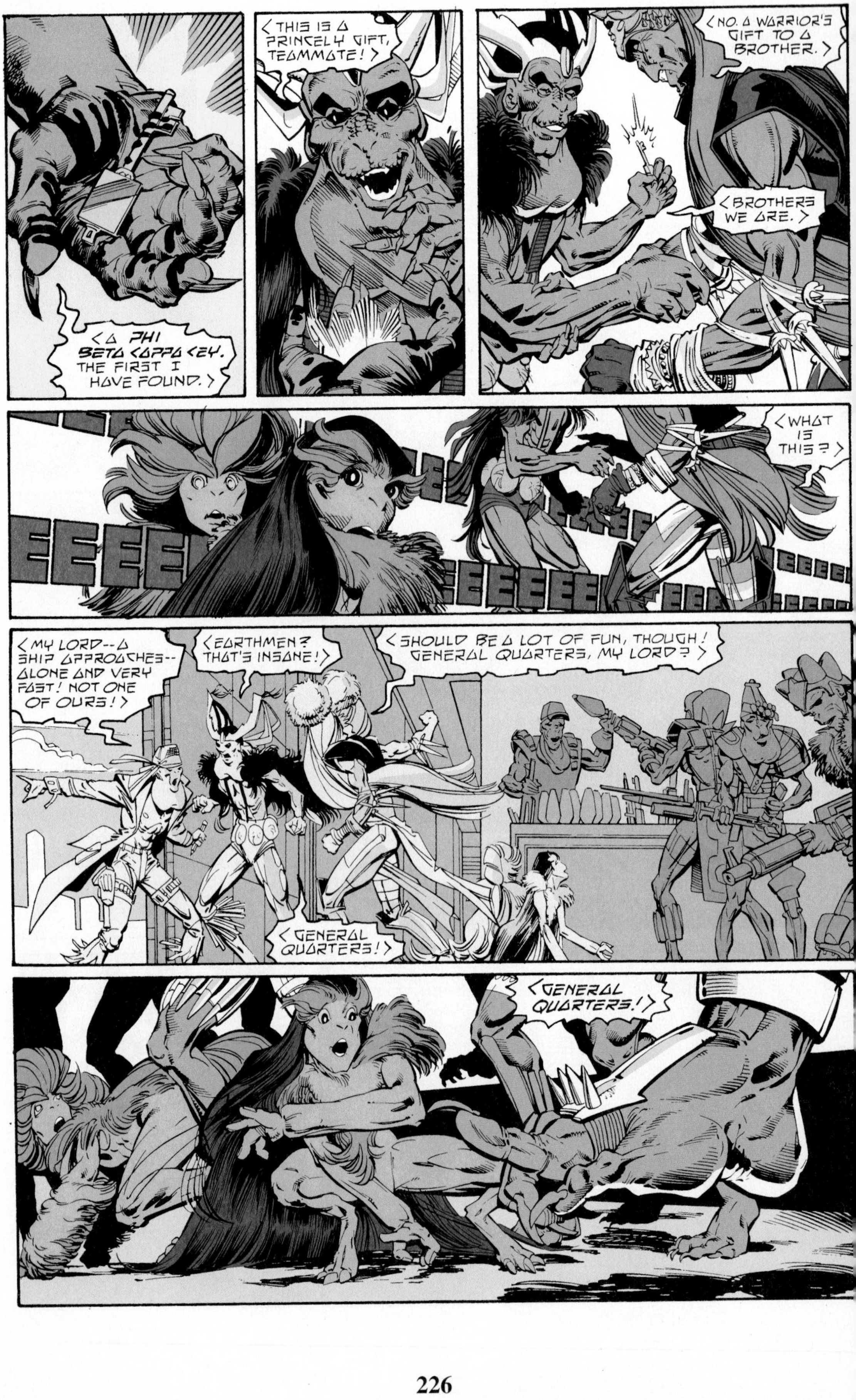

< A PHI BETA KAPPA KEY. THE FIRST I HAVE FOUND. >
< THIS IS A PRINCELY GIFT, TEAMMATE! >
< NO. A WARRIOR'S GIFT TO A BROTHER. >
< BROTHERS WE ARE. >
EEEEE
< WHAT IS THIS? >
EEEEEEEEEEEEEEE
< MY LORD--A SHIP APPROACHES--ALONE AND VERY FAST! NOT ONE OF OURS! >
< EARTHMEN? THAT'S INSANE! >
< SHOULD BE A LOT OF FUN, THOUGH! GENERAL QUARTERS, MY LORD? >
< GENERAL QUARTERS! >
< GENERAL QUARTERS! >

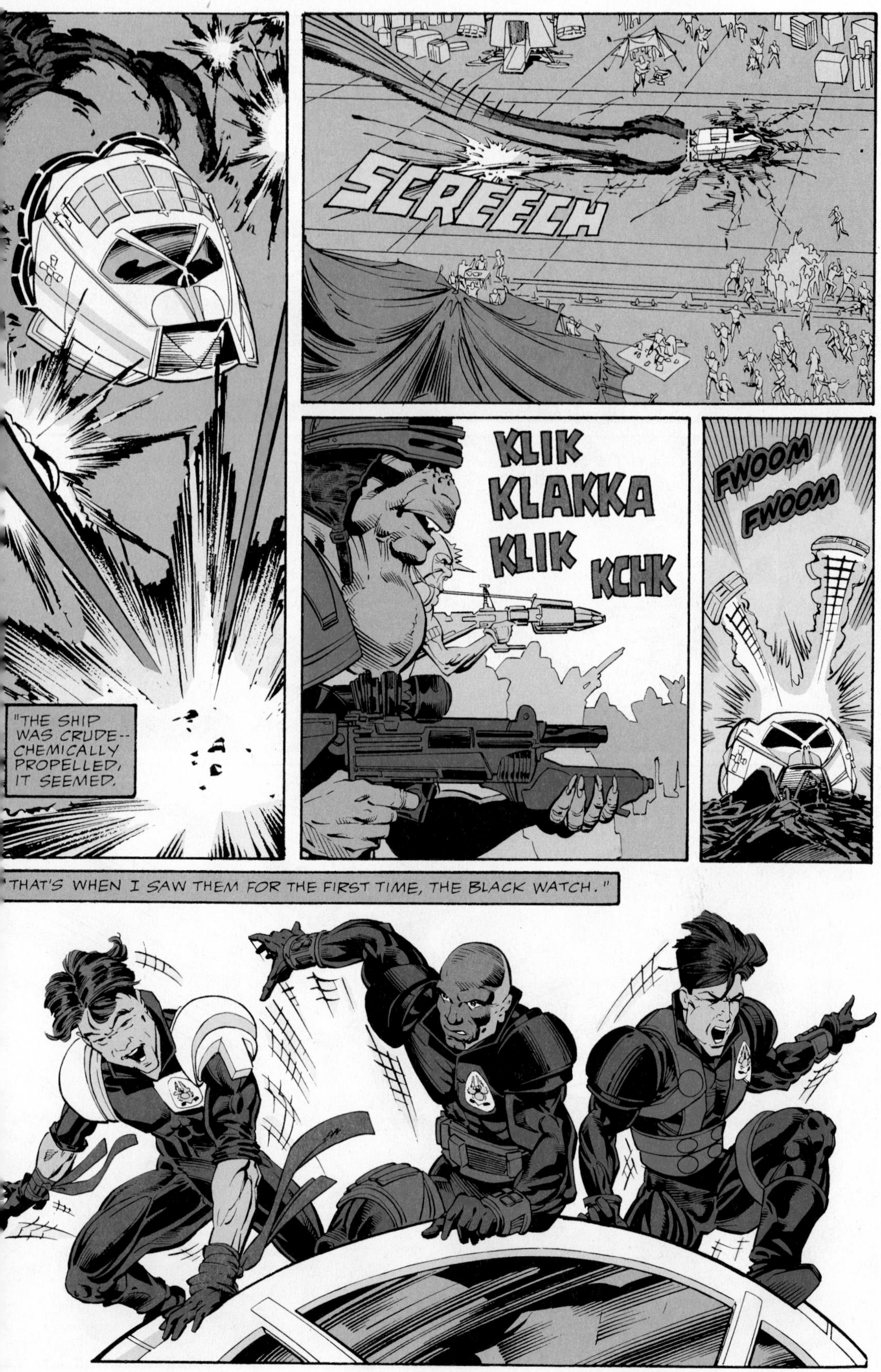
SCREECH
"THE SHIP WAS CRUDE--CHEMICALLY PROPELLED, IT SEEMED.
KLIK KLAKKA KLIK
KCHK
FWOOM FWOOM
"THAT'S WHEN I SAW THEM FOR THE FIRST TIME, THE BLACK WATCH."

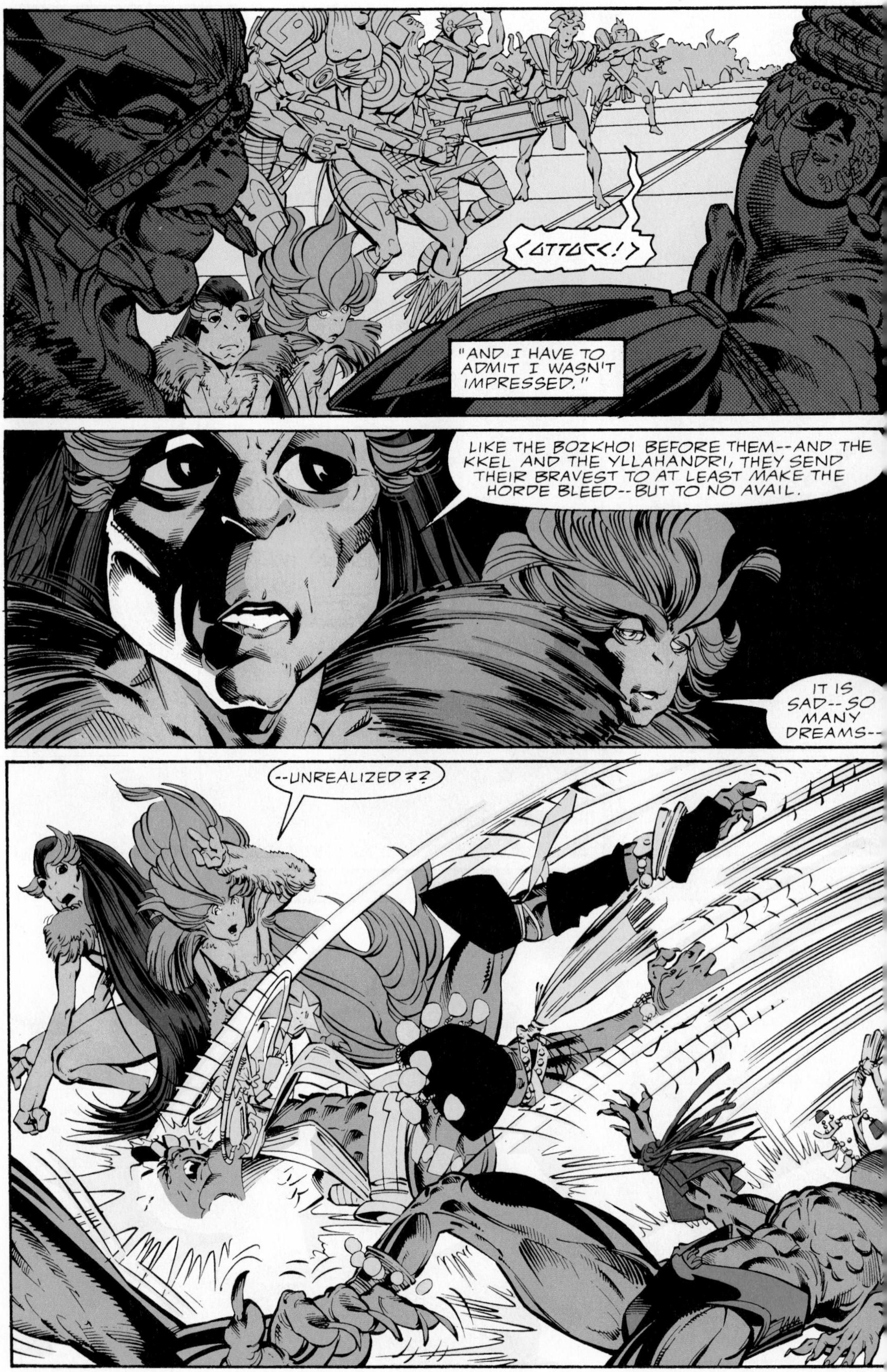
<ATTACK!>
"AND I HAVE TO ADMIT I WASN'T IMPRESSED."
LIKE THE BOZKHOI BEFORE THEM--AND THE KKEL AND THE YLLAHANDRI, THEY SEND THEIR BRAVEST TO AT LEAST MAKE THE HORDE BLEED--BUT TO NO AVAIL.
IT IS SAD--SO MANY DREAMS--
--UNREALIZED??

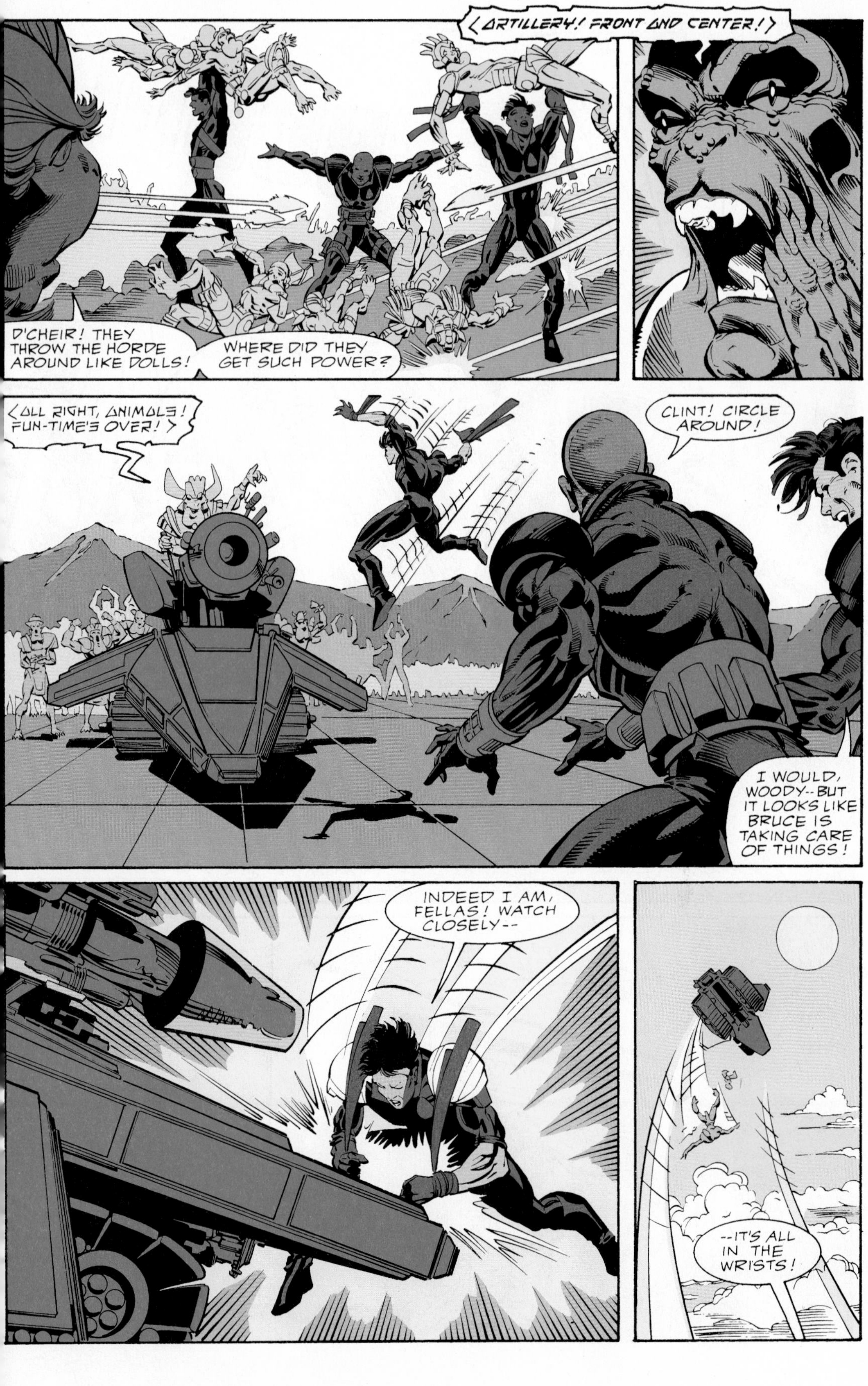
<ARTILLERY! FRONT AND CENTER!>
D'CHEIR! THEY THROW THE HORDE AROUND LIKE DOLLS!
WHERE DID THEY GET SUCH POWER?
<ALL RIGHT, ANIMALS! FUN-TIME'S OVER!>
CLINT! CIRCLE AROUND!
I WOULD, WOODY--BUT IT LOOKS LIKE BRUCE IS TAKING CARE OF THINGS!
INDEED I AM, FELLAS! WATCH CLOSELY--
--IT'S ALL IN THE WRISTS!

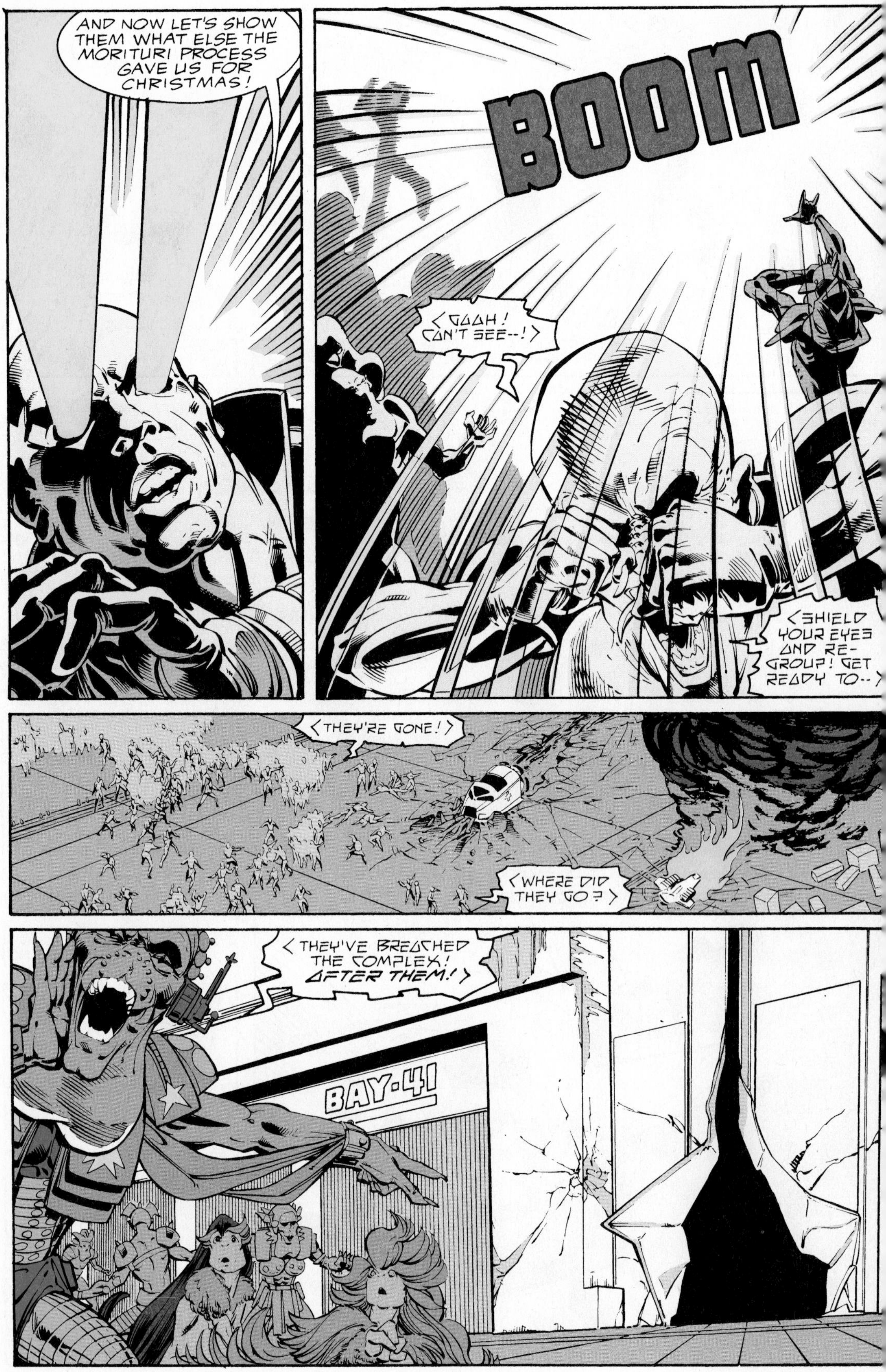
AND NOW LET'S SHOW THEM WHAT ELSE THE MORITURI PROCESS GAVE US FOR CHRISTMAS!
BOOM
<GAAH! CAN'T SEE--!>
<SHIELD YOUR EYES AND RE-GROUP! GET READY TO-->
<THEY'RE GONE!>
<WHERE DID THEY GO?>
<THEY'VE BREACHED THE COMPLEX! AFTER THEM!>
BAY-41

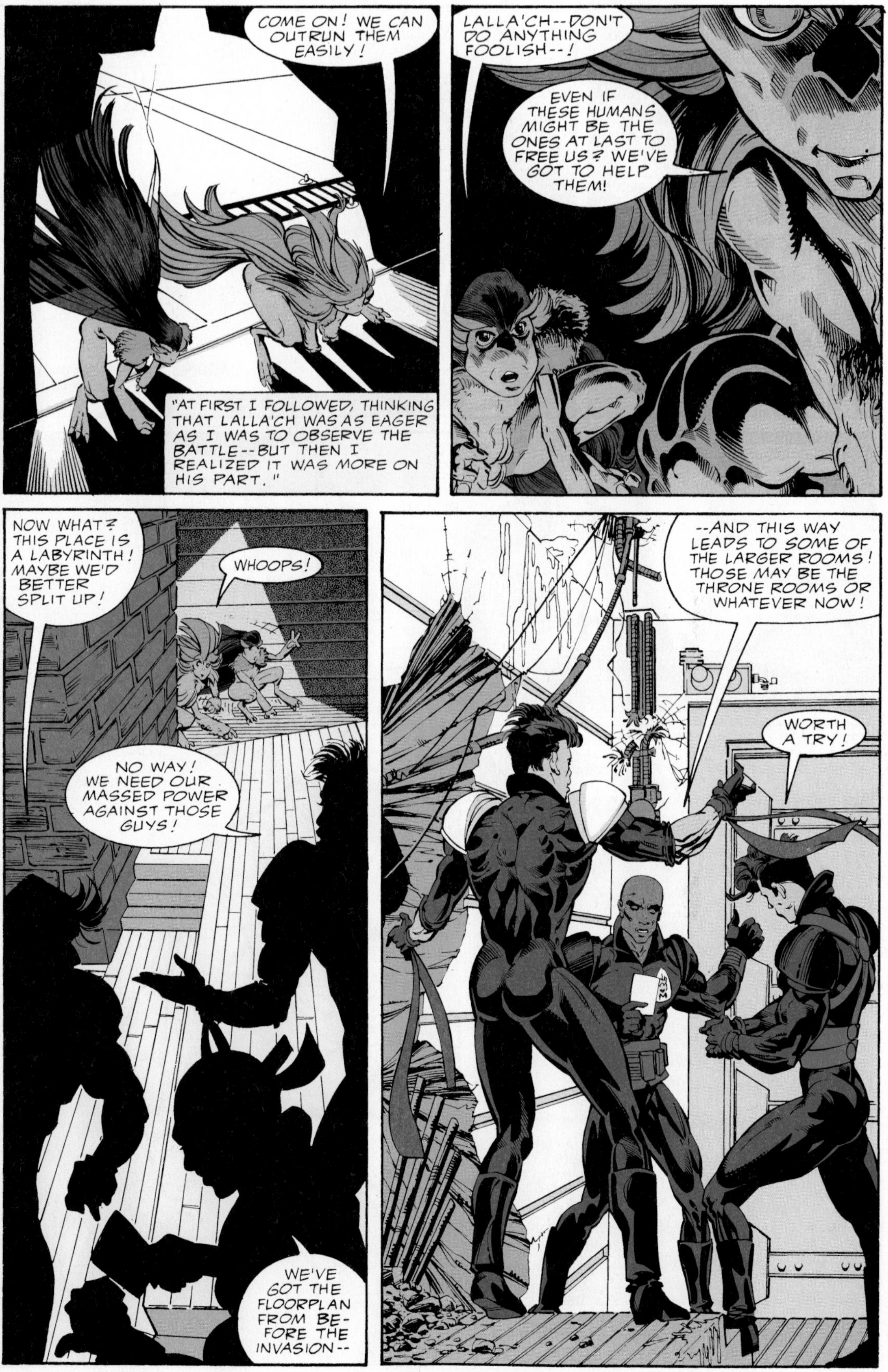
COME ON! WE CAN OUTRUN THEM EASILY!
"AT FIRST I FOLLOWED, THINKING THAT LALLA'CH WAS AS EAGER AS I WAS TO OBSERVE THE BATTLE--BUT THEN I REALIZED IT WAS MORE ON HIS PART."
LALLA'CH--DON'T DO ANYTHING FOOLISH--!
EVEN IF THESE HUMANS MIGHT BE THE ONES AT LAST TO FREE US? WE'VE GOT TO HELP THEM!
NOW WHAT? THIS PLACE IS A LABYRINTH! MAYBE WE'D BETTER SPLIT UP!
WHOOPS!
NO WAY! WE NEED OUR MASSED POWER AGAINST THOSE GUYS!
WE'VE GOT THE FLOORPLAN FROM BE-FORE THE INVASION--
--AND THIS WAY LEADS TO SOME OF THE LARGER ROOMS! THOSE MAY BE THE THRONE ROOMS OR WHATEVER NOW!
WORTH A TRY!

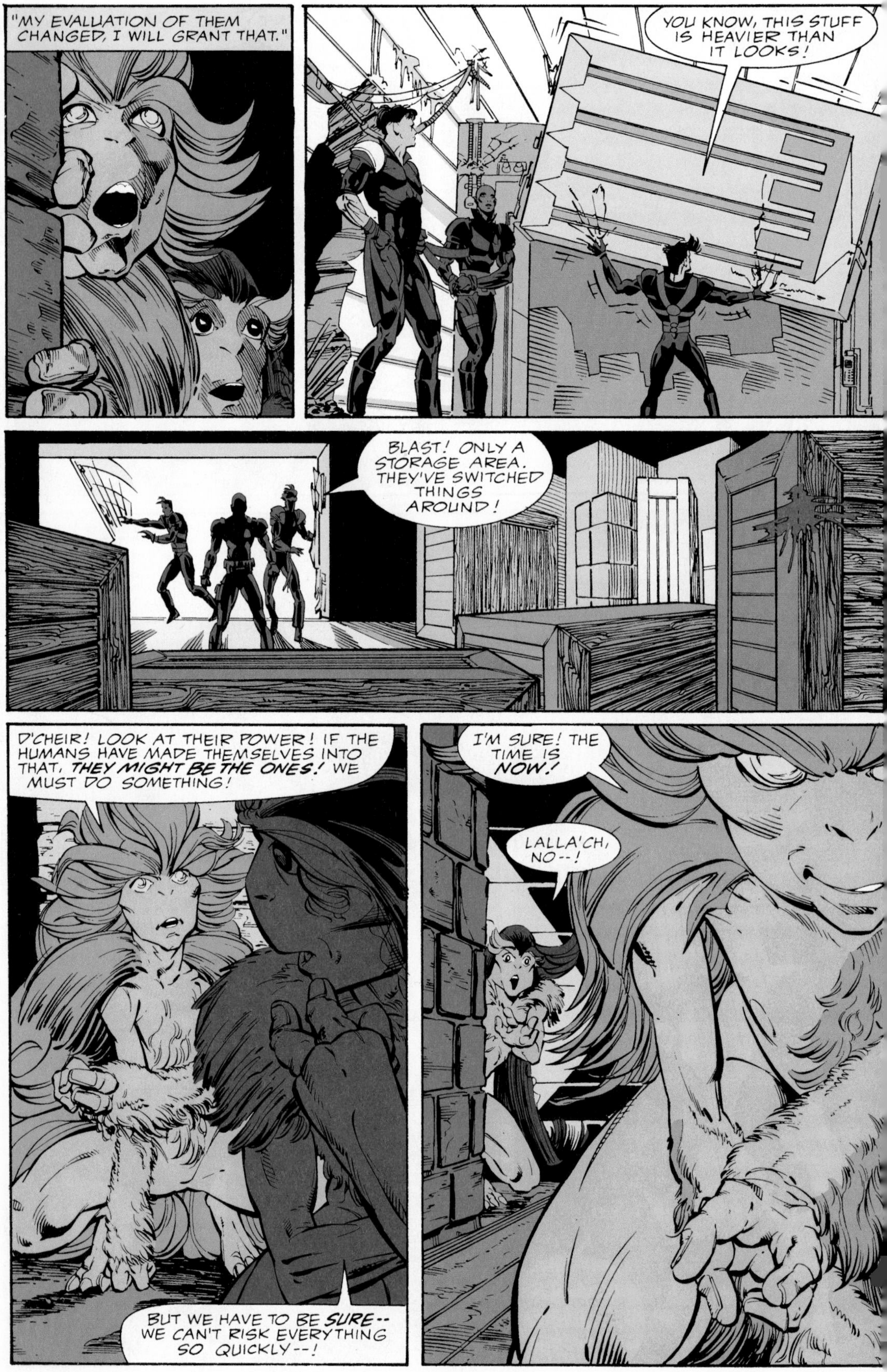
"MY EVALUATION OF THEM CHANGED, I WILL GRANT THAT."
YOU KNOW, THIS STUFF IS HEAVIER THAN IT LOOKS!
BLAST! ONLY A STORAGE AREA. THEY'VE SWITCHED THINGS AROUND!
D'CHEIR! LOOK AT THEIR POWER! IF THE HUMANS HAVE MADE THEMSELVES INTO THAT, THEY MIGHT BE THE ONES! WE MUST DO SOMETHING!
BUT WE HAVE TO BE SURE-- WE CAN'T RISK EVERYTHING SO QUICKLY--!
I'M SURE! THE TIME IS NOW!
LALLA'CH, NO--!

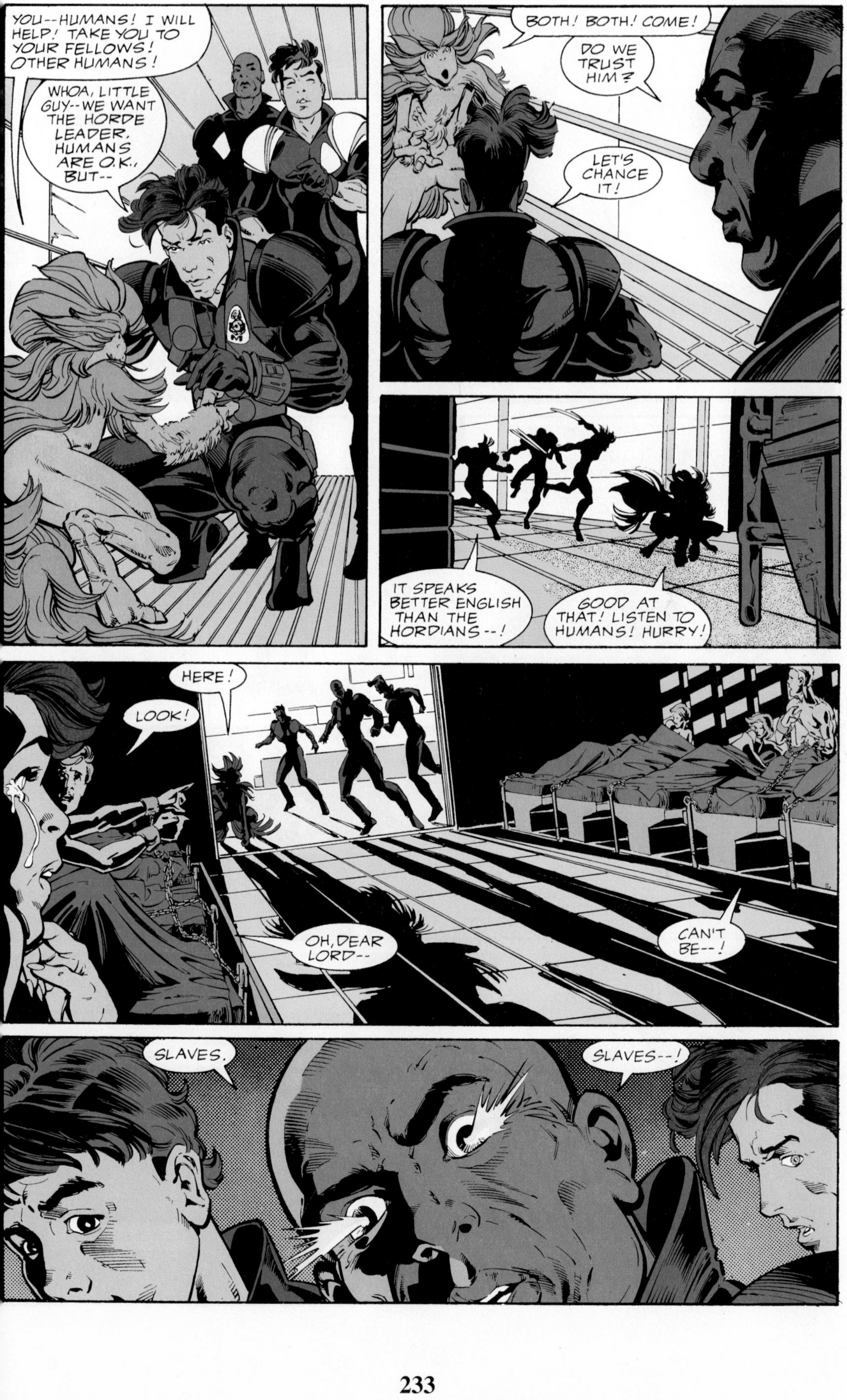
YOU--HUMANS! I WILL HELP! TAKE YOU TO YOUR FELLOWS! OTHER HUMANS!
WHOA, LITTLE GUY--WE WANT THE HORDE LEADER. HUMANS ARE O.K., BUT--
BOTH! BOTH! COME!
DO WE TRUST HIM?
LET'S CHANCE IT!
IT SPEAKS BETTER ENGLISH THAN THE HORDIANS--!
GOOD AT THAT! LISTEN TO HUMANS! HURRY!
HERE!
LOOK!
OH, DEAR LORD--
CAN'T BE--!
SLAVES.
SLAVES--!

WHAT ARE WE GOING TO DO? WE CAN'T TAKE ALL OF THEM BACK! THEY WON'T FIT!

WE'VE GOT TO TRY! STEAL A HORDE SHIP OR SOMETHING!

PLEASE-- YOU'VE GOT TO TRY! YOU DON'T KNOW WHAT IT'S LIKE--!

TAKE IT EASY, SISTER!

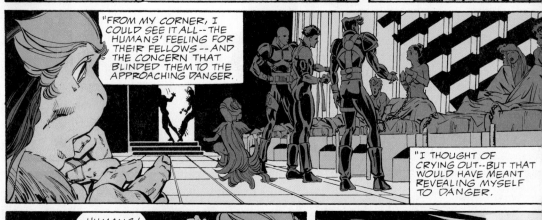

"FROM MY CORNER, I COULD SEE IT ALL--THE HUMANS' FEELING FOR THEIR FELLOWS--AND THE CONCERN THAT BLINDED THEM TO THE APPROACHING DANGER.

"I THOUGHT OF CRYING OUT--BUT THAT WOULD HAVE MEANT REVEALING MYSELF TO DANGER.

HUMANS! HORDE COME!

FWUD

"AND IN AN INSTANT I SAW THE PRICE OF MY INDECISION.

"LALLA'CH--!"

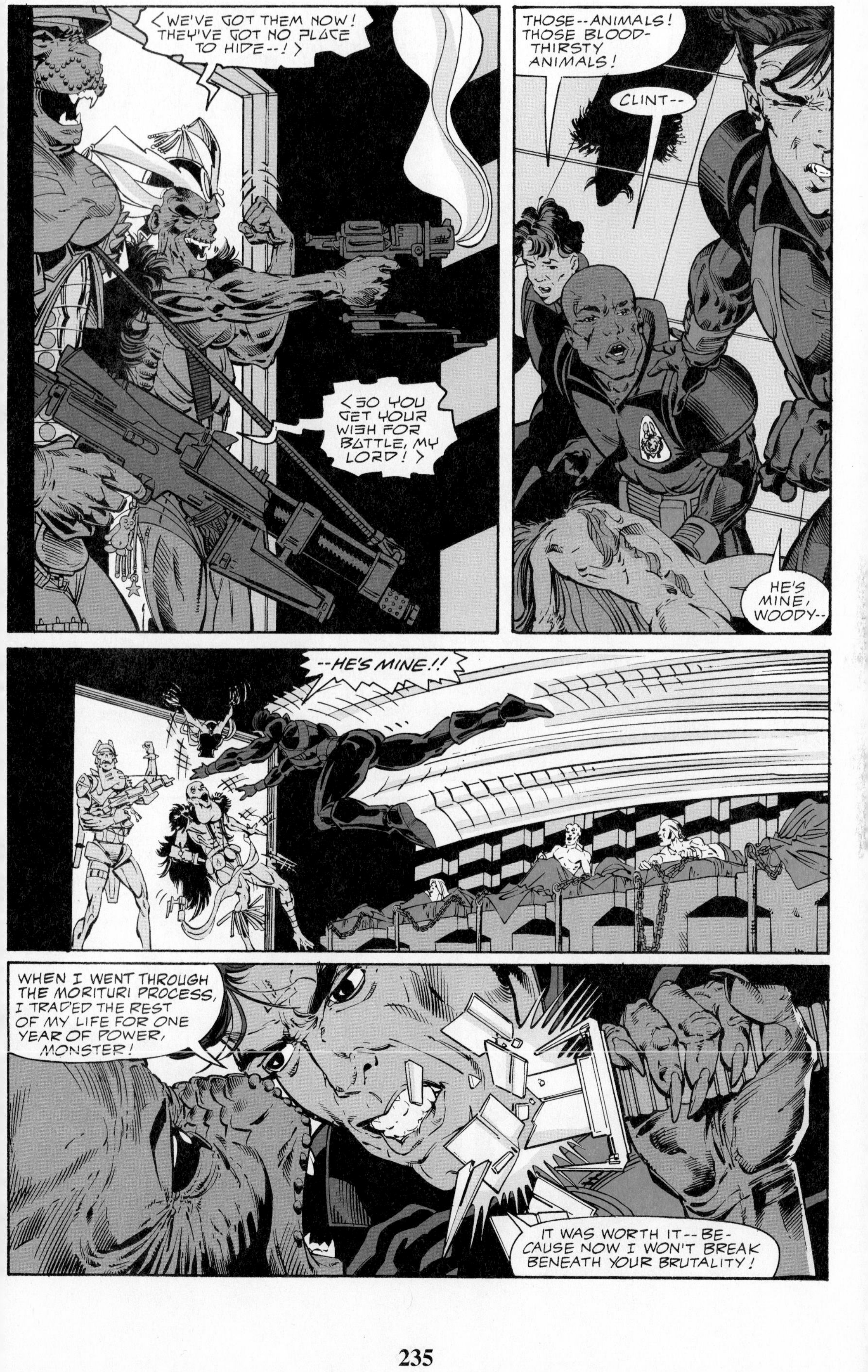

< WE'VE GOT THEM NOW! THEY'VE GOT NO PLACE TO HIDE--! >
< SO YOU GET YOUR WISH FOR BATTLE, MY LORD! >
THOSE--ANIMALS! THOSE BLOOD-THIRSTY ANIMALS!
CLINT--
HE'S MINE, WOODY--
--HE'S MINE!!
WHEN I WENT THROUGH THE MORITURI PROCESS, I TRADED THE REST OF MY LIFE FOR ONE YEAR OF POWER, MONSTER!
IT WAS WORTH IT--BE-CAUSE NOW I WON'T BREAK BENEATH YOUR BRUTALITY!

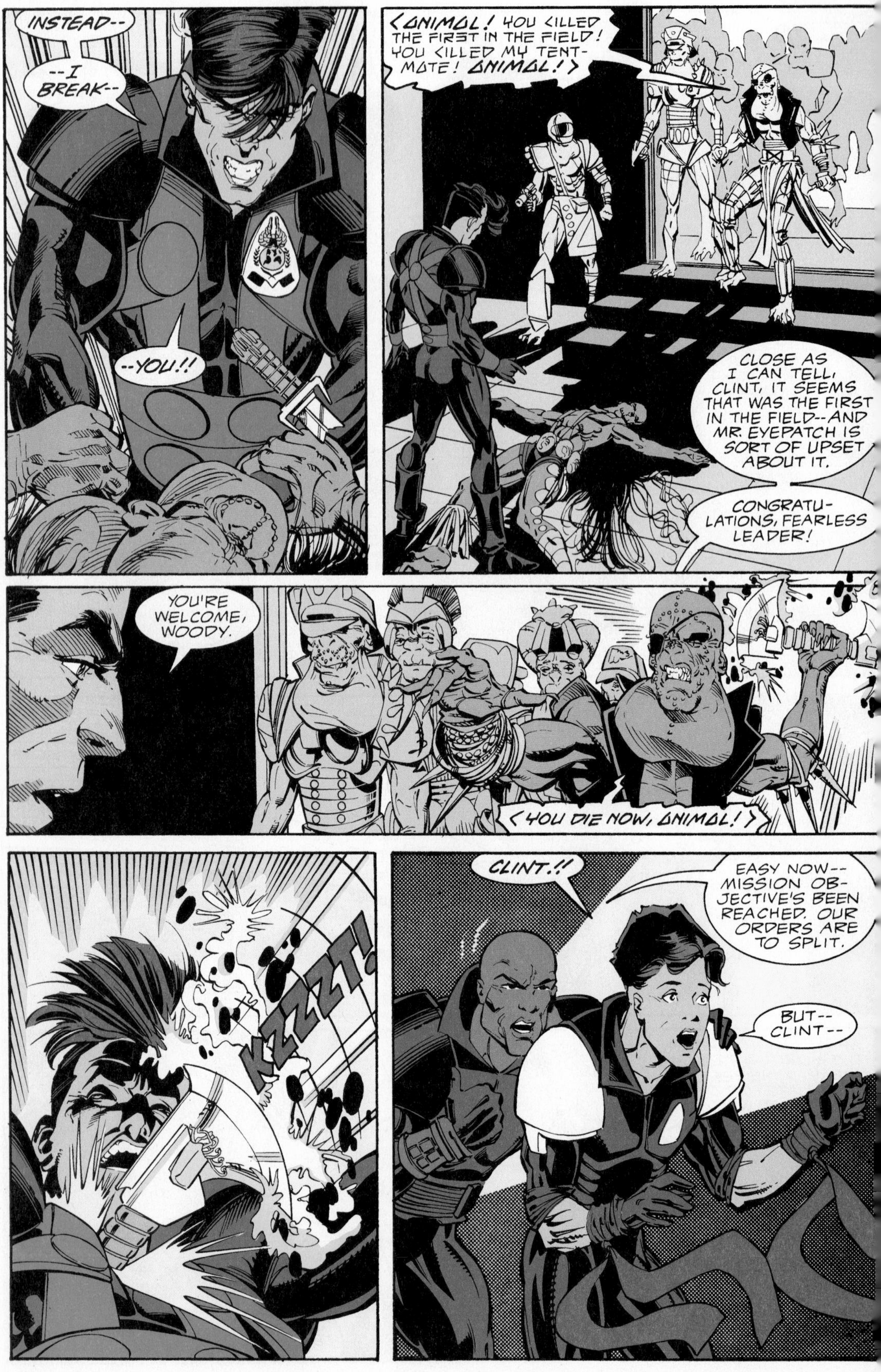
INSTEAD--
--I BREAK--
--YOU!!
<ANIMAL! YOU KILLED THE FIRST IN THE FIELD! YOU KILLED MY TENT-MATE! ANIMAL!>
CLOSE AS I CAN TELL, CLINT, IT SEEMS THAT WAS THE FIRST IN THE FIELD--AND MR. EYEPATCH IS SORT OF UPSET ABOUT IT.
CONGRATULATIONS, FEARLESS LEADER!
YOU'RE WELCOME, WOODY.
<YOU DIE NOW, ANIMAL!>
KZZZT!
CLINT.!!
EASY NOW--MISSION OBJECTIVE'S BEEN REACHED. OUR ORDERS ARE TO SPLIT.
BUT--CLINT--

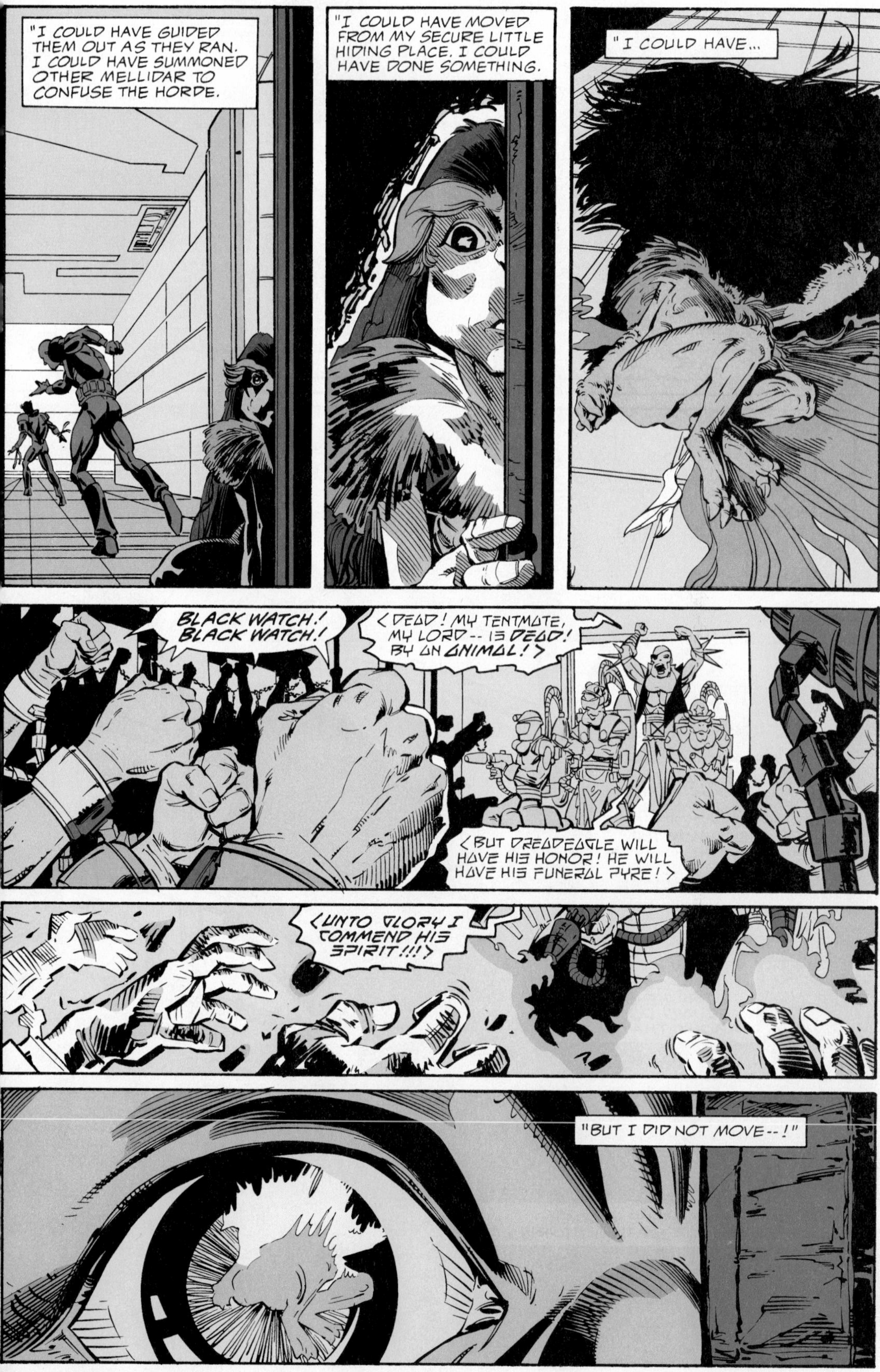
"I COULD HAVE GUIDED THEM OUT AS THEY RAN. I COULD HAVE SUMMONED OTHER MELLIDAR TO CONFUSE THE HORDE.
"I COULD HAVE MOVED FROM MY SECURE LITTLE HIDING PLACE. I COULD HAVE DONE SOMETHING.
"I COULD HAVE...
BLACK WATCH! BLACK WATCH!
<DEAD! MY TENTMATE, MY LORD-- IS DEAD! BY AN ANIMAL!>
<BUT DREADEAGLE WILL HAVE HIS HONOR! HE WILL HAVE HIS FUNERAL PYRE!>
<UNTO GLORY I COMMEND HIS SPIRIT!!!>
"BUT I DID NOT MOVE--!"

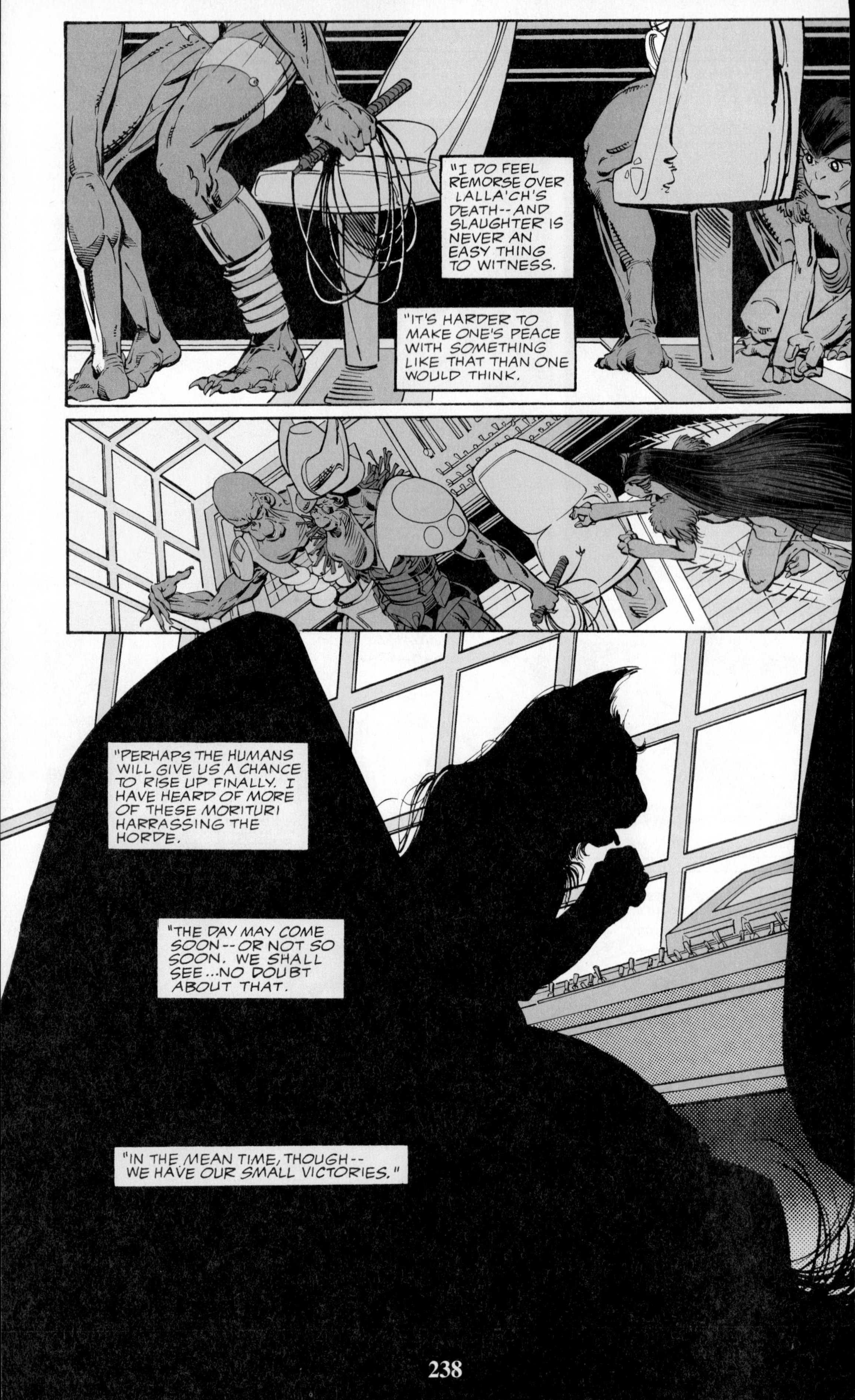
"I DO FEEL REMORSE OVER LALLA'CH'S DEATH--AND SLAUGHTER IS NEVER AN EASY THING TO WITNESS.
"IT'S HARDER TO MAKE ONE'S PEACE WITH SOMETHING LIKE THAT THAN ONE WOULD THINK.
"PERHAPS THE HUMANS WILL GIVE US A CHANCE TO RISE UP FINALLY. I HAVE HEARD OF MORE OF THESE MORITURI HARRASSING THE HORDE.
"THE DAY MAY COME SOON--OR NOT SO SOON. WE SHALL SEE...NO DOUBT ABOUT THAT.
"IN THE MEAN TIME, THOUGH-- WE HAVE OUR SMALL VICTORIES."

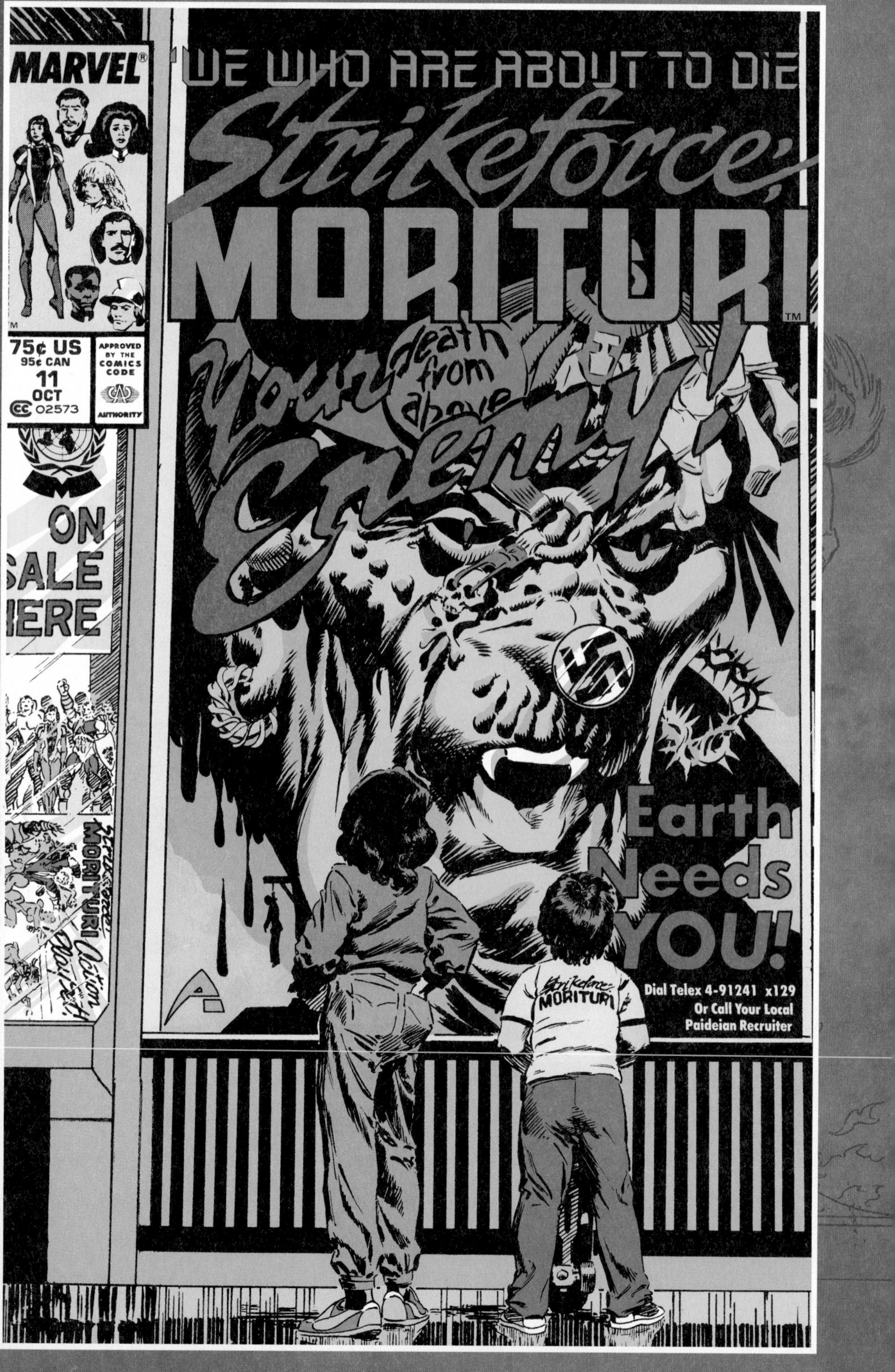
MARVEL
75¢ US
95¢ CAN
11
OCT
02573
APPROVED BY THE COMICS CODE AUTHORITY
"WE WHO ARE ABOUT TO DIE
Strikeforce:
MORITURI
Your death from above Enemy!
ON
SALE
HERE
Earth
Needs
YOU!
Dial Telex 4-91241 x129
Or Call Your Local
Paideian Recruiter
Strikeforce:
MORITURI

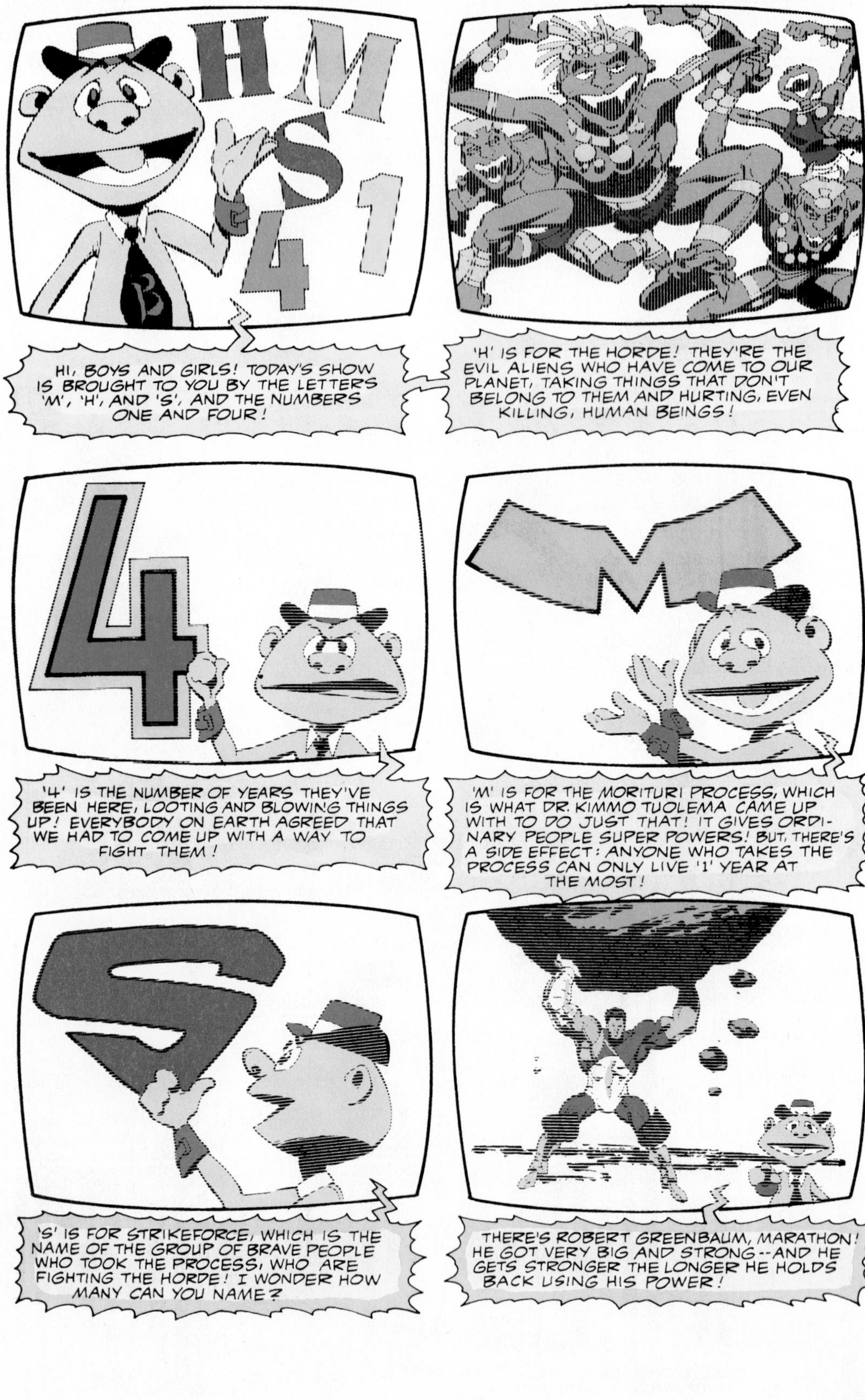
HI, BOYS AND GIRLS! TODAY'S SHOW IS BROUGHT TO YOU BY THE LETTERS 'M', 'H', AND 'S', AND THE NUMBERS ONE AND FOUR!
'H' IS FOR THE HORDE! THEY'RE THE EVIL ALIENS WHO HAVE COME TO OUR PLANET, TAKING THINGS THAT DON'T BELONG TO THEM AND HURTING, EVEN KILLING, HUMAN BEINGS!
'4' IS THE NUMBER OF YEARS THEY'VE BEEN HERE, LOOTING AND BLOWING THINGS UP! EVERYBODY ON EARTH AGREED THAT WE HAD TO COME UP WITH A WAY TO FIGHT THEM!
'M' IS FOR THE MORITURI PROCESS, WHICH IS WHAT DR. KIMMO TUOLEMA CAME UP WITH TO DO JUST THAT! IT GIVES ORDINARY PEOPLE SUPER POWERS! BUT, THERE'S A SIDE EFFECT: ANYONE WHO TAKES THE PROCESS CAN ONLY LIVE '1' YEAR AT THE MOST!
'S' IS FOR STRIKEFORCE, WHICH IS THE NAME OF THE GROUP OF BRAVE PEOPLE WHO TOOK THE PROCESS, WHO ARE FIGHTING THE HORDE! I WONDER HOW MANY CAN YOU NAME?
THERE'S ROBERT GREENBAUM, MARATHON! HE GOT VERY BIG AND STRONG--AND HE GETS STRONGER THE LONGER HE HOLDS BACK USING HIS POWER!

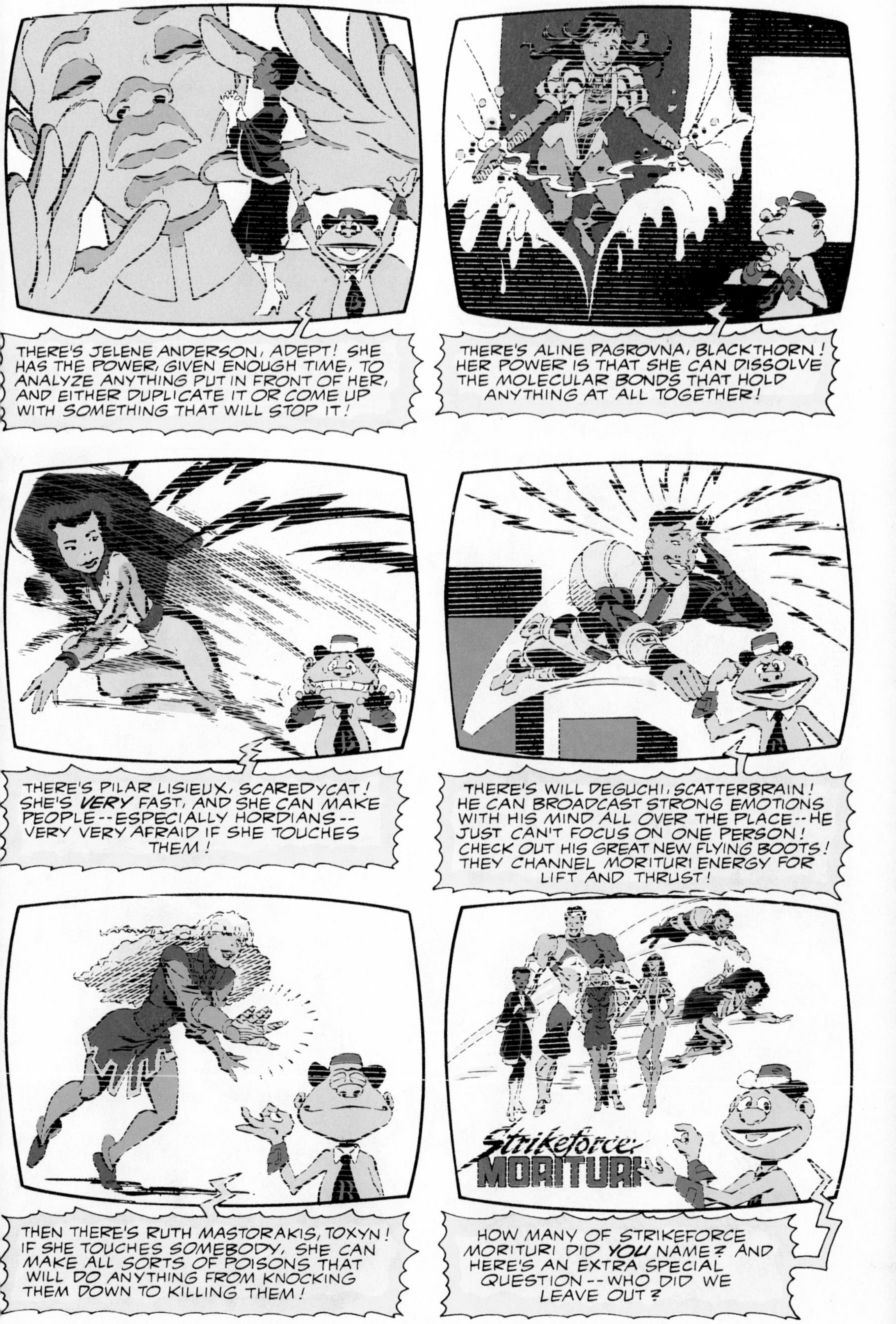
THERE'S JELENE ANDERSON, ADEPT! SHE HAS THE POWER, GIVEN ENOUGH TIME, TO ANALYZE ANYTHING PUT IN FRONT OF HER, AND EITHER DUPLICATE IT OR COME UP WITH SOMETHING THAT WILL STOP IT!
THERE'S ALINE PAGROVNA, BLACKTHORN! HER POWER IS THAT SHE CAN DISSOLVE THE MOLECULAR BONDS THAT HOLD ANYTHING AT ALL TOGETHER!
THERE'S PILAR LISIEUX, SCAREDYCAT! SHE'S *VERY* FAST, AND SHE CAN MAKE PEOPLE--ESPECIALLY HORDIANS--VERY VERY AFRAID IF SHE TOUCHES THEM!
THERE'S WILL DEGUCHI, SCATTERBRAIN! HE CAN BROADCAST STRONG EMOTIONS WITH HIS MIND ALL OVER THE PLACE--HE JUST CAN'T FOCUS ON ONE PERSON! CHECK OUT HIS GREAT NEW FLYING BOOTS! THEY CHANNEL MORITURI ENERGY FOR LIFT AND THRUST!
THEN THERE'S RUTH MASTORAKIS, TOXYN! IF SHE TOUCHES SOMEBODY, SHE CAN MAKE ALL SORTS OF POISONS THAT WILL DO ANYTHING FROM KNOCKING THEM DOWN TO KILLING THEM!
Strikeforce: MORITURI
HOW MANY OF STRIKEFORCE MORITURI DID *YOU* NAME? AND HERE'S AN EXTRA SPECIAL QUESTION--WHO DID WE LEAVE OUT?

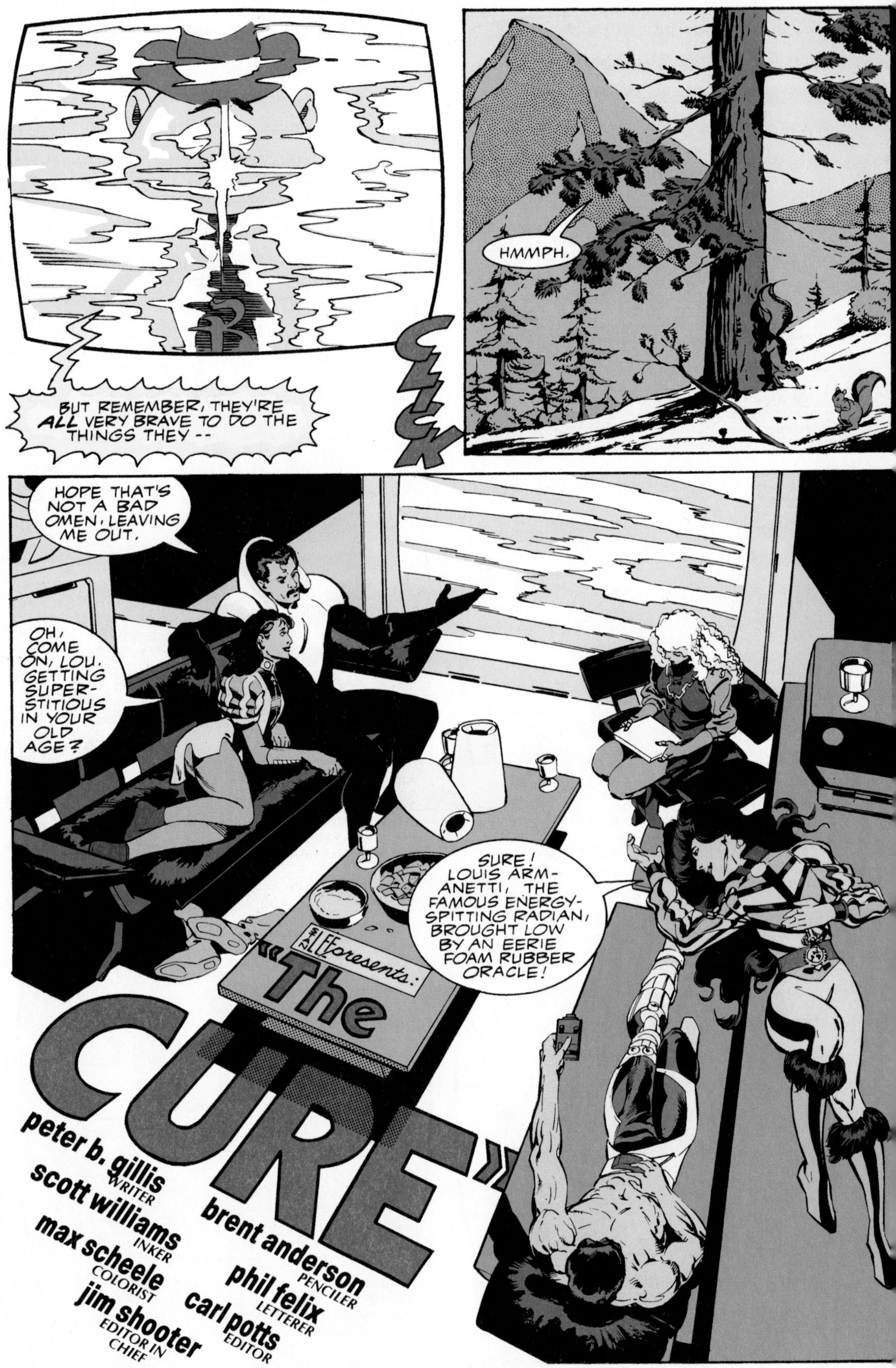
BUT REMEMBER, THEY'RE ALL VERY BRAVE TO DO THE THINGS THEY --
CLICK
HMMPH.
HOPE THAT'S NOT A BAD OMEN, LEAVING ME OUT.
OH, COME ON, LOU. GETTING SUPER-STITIOUS IN YOUR OLD AGE?
SURE! LOUIS ARM-ANETTI, THE FAMOUS ENERGY-SPITTING RADIAN, BROUGHT LOW BY AN EERIE FOAM RUBBER ORACLE!
STAN LEE presents:
"The CURE"
peter b. gillis WRITER
scott williams INKER
max scheele COLORIST
jim shooter EDITOR IN CHIEF
brent anderson PENCILER
phil felix LETTERER
carl potts EDITOR

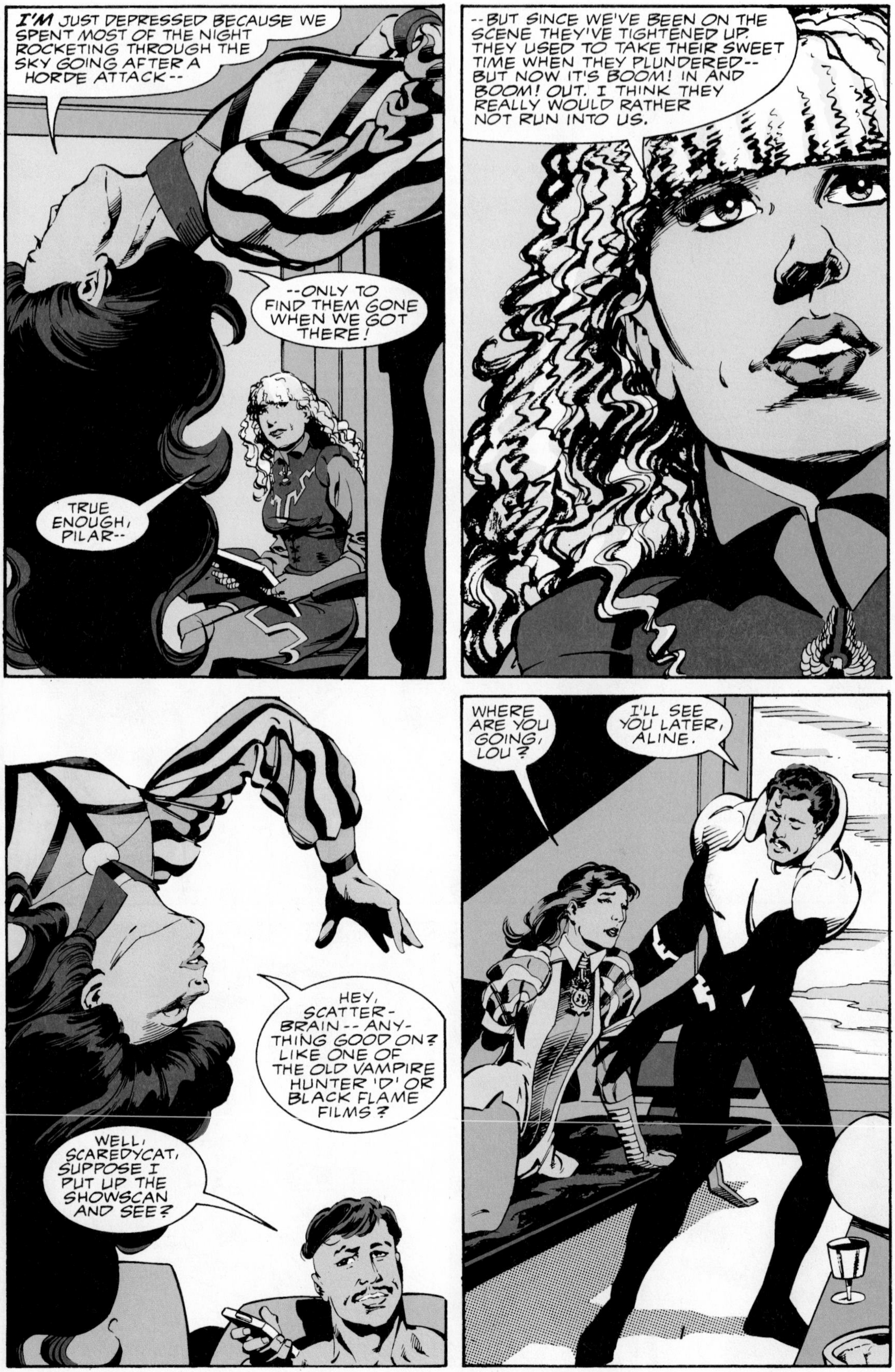
I'M JUST DEPRESSED BECAUSE WE SPENT MOST OF THE NIGHT ROCKETING THROUGH THE SKY GOING AFTER A HORDE ATTACK--
--ONLY TO FIND THEM GONE WHEN WE GOT THERE!
TRUE ENOUGH, PILAR--
--BUT SINCE WE'VE BEEN ON THE SCENE THEY'VE TIGHTENED UP. THEY USED TO TAKE THEIR SWEET TIME WHEN THEY PLUNDERED-- BUT NOW IT'S BOOM! IN AND BOOM! OUT. I THINK THEY REALLY WOULD RATHER NOT RUN INTO US.
HEY, SCATTER-BRAIN-- ANY-THING GOOD ON? LIKE ONE OF THE OLD VAMPIRE HUNTER 'D' OR BLACK FLAME FILMS?
WELL, SCAREDYCAT, SUPPOSE I PUT UP THE SHOWSCAN AND SEE?
WHERE ARE YOU GOING, LOU?
I'LL SEE YOU LATER, ALINE.

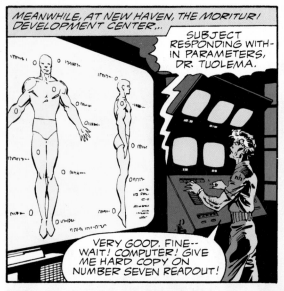

MEANWHILE, AT NEW HAVEN, THE MORITURI DEVELOPMENT CENTER...

SUBJECT RESPONDING WITHIN PARAMETERS, DR. TUOLEMA.

VERY GOOD. FINE-- WAIT! COMPUTER! GIVE ME HARD COPY ON NUMBER SEVEN READOUT!

OH MY LORD-- IT CAN'T BE! SHE WOULDN'T! SHE CAN'T HAVE!

BETH LUIS NION!

DOCTOR?

WHAT IN BLAZES IS THIS?

WHAT IN BLAZES IS WHAT?

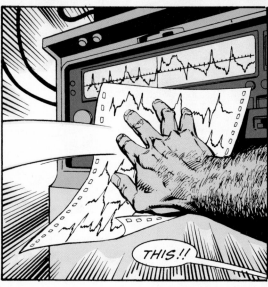

THIS!!

244

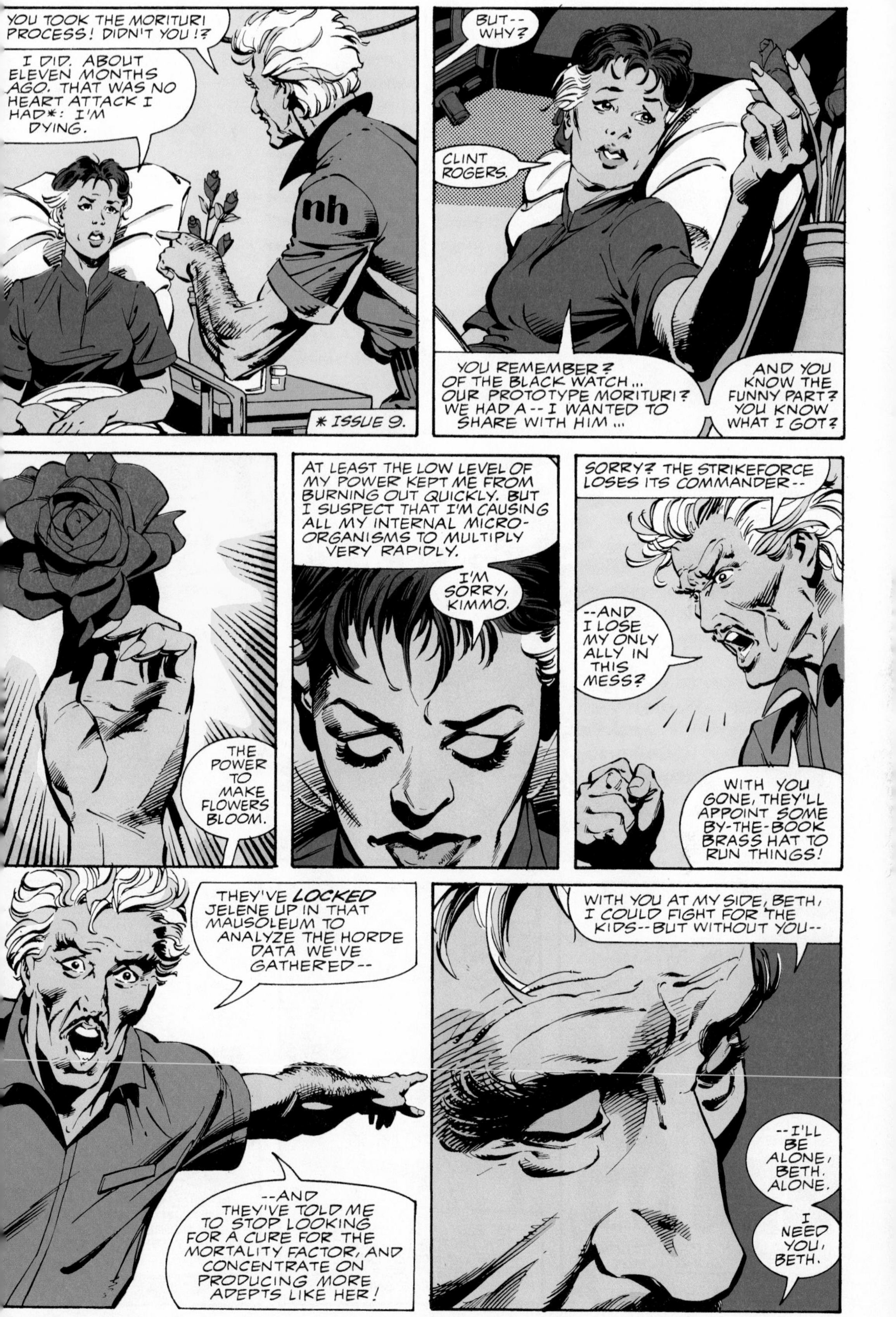
YOU TOOK THE MORITURI PROCESS! DIDN'T YOU!?
I DID. ABOUT ELEVEN MONTHS AGO. THAT WAS NO HEART ATTACK I HAD*: I'M DYING.
* ISSUE 9.
BUT-- WHY?
CLINT ROGERS.
YOU REMEMBER? OF THE BLACK WATCH... OUR PROTOTYPE MORITURI? WE HAD A-- I WANTED TO SHARE WITH HIM...
AND YOU KNOW THE FUNNY PART? YOU KNOW WHAT I GOT?
THE POWER TO MAKE FLOWERS BLOOM.
AT LEAST THE LOW LEVEL OF MY POWER KEPT ME FROM BURNING OUT QUICKLY. BUT I SUSPECT THAT I'M CAUSING ALL MY INTERNAL MICRO-ORGANISMS TO MULTIPLY VERY RAPIDLY.
I'M SORRY, KIMMO.
SORRY? THE STRIKEFORCE LOSES ITS COMMANDER--
--AND I LOSE MY ONLY ALLY IN THIS MESS?
WITH YOU GONE, THEY'LL APPOINT SOME BY-THE-BOOK BRASS HAT TO RUN THINGS!
THEY'VE LOCKED JELENE UP IN THAT MAUSOLEUM TO ANALYZE THE HORDE DATA WE'VE GATHERED--
--AND THEY'VE TOLD ME TO STOP LOOKING FOR A CURE FOR THE MORTALITY FACTOR, AND CONCENTRATE ON PRODUCING MORE ADEPTS LIKE HER!
WITH YOU AT MY SIDE, BETH, I COULD FIGHT FOR THE KIDS--BUT WITHOUT YOU--
--I'LL BE ALONE, BETH. ALONE.
I NEED YOU, BETH.

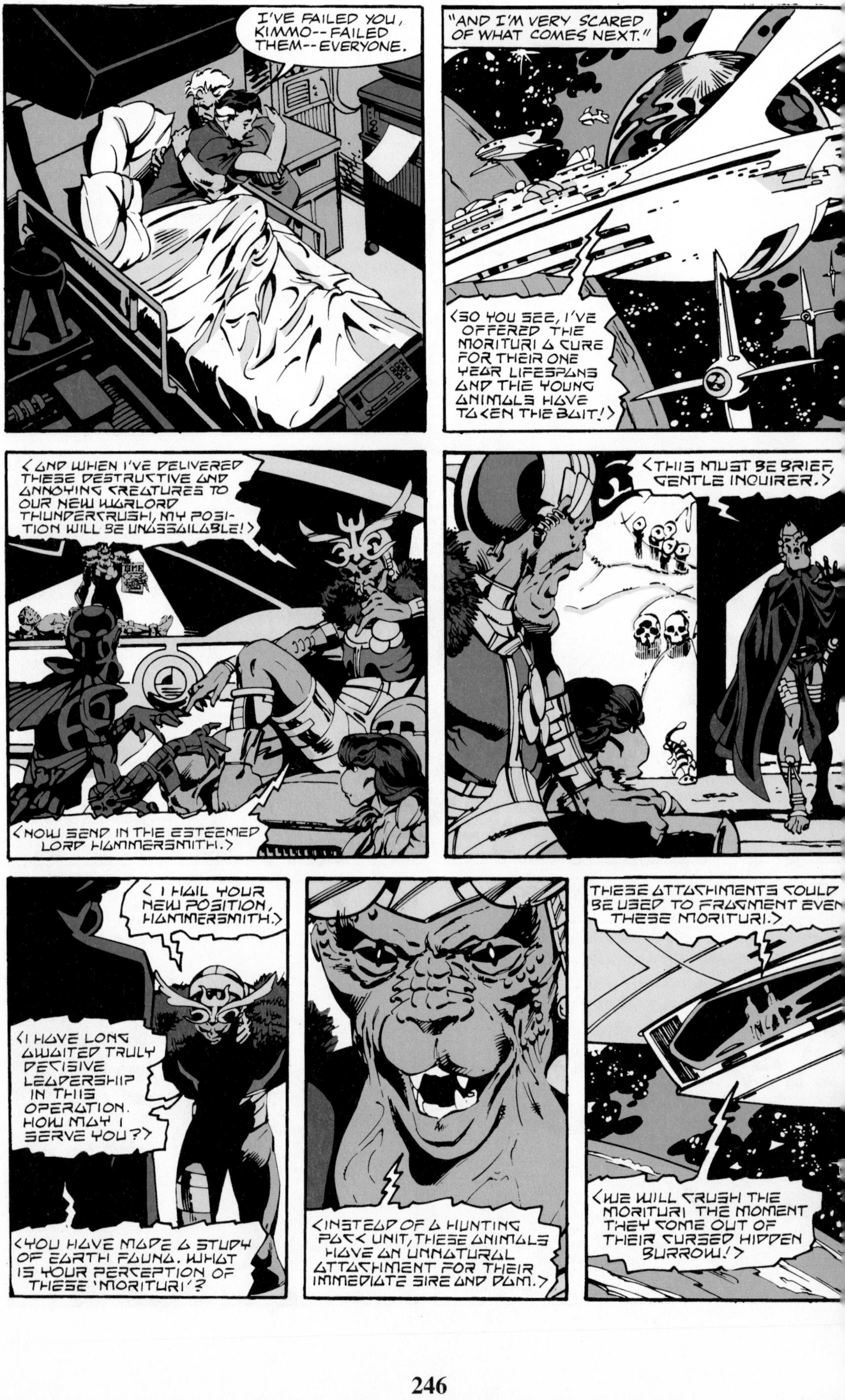

I'VE FAILED YOU, KIMMO--FAILED THEM--EVERYONE.
"AND I'M VERY SCARED OF WHAT COMES NEXT."
<SO YOU SEE, I'VE OFFERED THE MORITURI A CURE FOR THEIR ONE YEAR LIFESPANS AND THE YOUNG ANIMALS HAVE TAKEN THE BAIT!>
<AND WHEN I'VE DELIVERED THESE DESTRUCTIVE AND ANNOYING CREATURES TO OUR NEW WARLORD THUNDERCRUSH, MY POSITION WILL BE UNASSAILABLE!>
<NOW SEND IN THE ESTEEMED LORD HAMMERSMITH.>
<THIS MUST BE BRIEF, GENTLE INQUIRER.>
<I HAIL YOUR NEW POSITION, HAMMERSMITH.>
<I HAVE LONG AWAITED TRULY DECISIVE LEADERSHIP IN THIS OPERATION. HOW MAY I SERVE YOU?>
<YOU HAVE MADE A STUDY OF EARTH FAUNA. WHAT IS YOUR PERCEPTION OF THESE 'MORITURI'?
<INSTEAD OF A HUNTING PACK UNIT, THESE ANIMALS HAVE AN UNNATURAL ATTACHMENT FOR THEIR IMMEDIATE SIRE AND DAM.>
THESE ATTACHMENTS COULD BE USED TO FRAGMENT EVEN THESE MORITURI.>
<WE WILL CRUSH THE MORITURI THE MOMENT THEY COME OUT OF THEIR CURSED HIDDEN BURROW!>

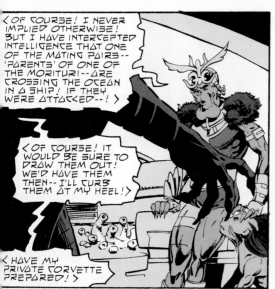

< OF COURSE! I NEVER IMPLIED OTHERWISE! BUT I HAVE INTERCEPTED INTELLIGENCE THAT ONE OF THE MATING PAIRS-- 'PARENTS' OF ONE OF THE MORITURI--ARE CROSSING THE OCEAN IN A SHIP! IF THEY WERE ATTACKED--! >

< OF COURSE! IT WOULD BE SURE TO DRAW THEM OUT! WE'D HAVE THEM THEN-- I'LL CURB THEM AT MY HEEL! >

< HAVE MY PRIVATE CORVETTE PREPARED! >

< AS A HIGH OFFICIAL, YOU WILL BE TAKING A RESPECTABLE TASK FORCE? >

< I AM A WARRIOR! I'LL NEED NO HELP IN KILLING ANIMALS! >

< TAKE CARE GENTLE INQUIRER! YOUR POST CAN BE RE-POPULATED! >

< OH, HAMMERSMITH: YOU HAVE LOLLED AROUND WITH THE MAIN FLEET AROUND JUPITER-- >

<--WITHOUT PAYING ATTENTION TO THE SITUATION, I'M AFRAID! >

" < YOUR EDUCATION BEGINS AT ONCE--AND IT WILL BE MOST RAPID! > "

IT'S LIKE WE'RE NOTHING TO THE PAIDEIA, WILL!

THEY FEEL JUSTIFIED IN HOLDING US PRISONER AND KEEPING US FROM USING OUR POWERS AS THEY'RE MEANT TO BE USED!

OH COME ON, PILAR, THAT'S A LITTLE EXTREME!

IS IT? WHAT ABOUT THE ORDER TO DR. TUOLEMA TELL-ING HIM TO STOP RED ON A CURE? YOU SAW THE TAPE I MADE--!

BUT WHAT OTHER WAY IS THERE TO FIGHT THE HORDE? WE HAVE TO BE SOLDIERS!

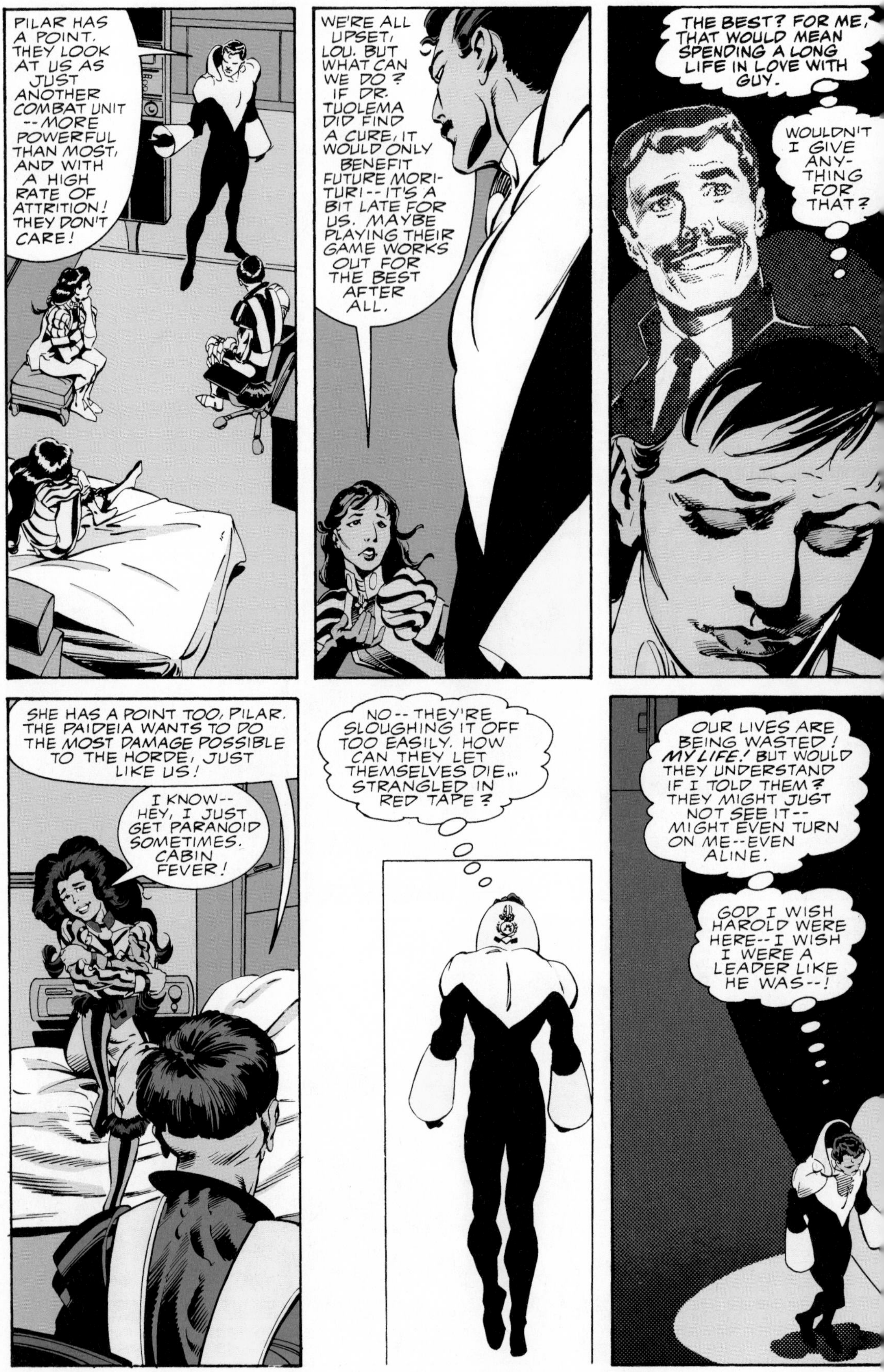

PILAR HAS A POINT. THEY LOOK AT US AS JUST ANOTHER COMBAT UNIT -- MORE POWERFUL THAN MOST, AND WITH A HIGH RATE OF ATTRITION! THEY DON'T CARE!
WE'RE ALL UPSET, LOU. BUT WHAT CAN WE DO? IF DR. TUOLEMA DID FIND A CURE, IT WOULD ONLY BENEFIT FUTURE MORITURI -- IT'S A BIT LATE FOR US. MAYBE PLAYING THEIR GAME WORKS OUT FOR THE BEST AFTER ALL.
THE BEST? FOR ME, THAT WOULD MEAN SPENDING A LONG LIFE IN LOVE WITH GUY.
WOULDN'T I GIVE ANYTHING FOR THAT?
SHE HAS A POINT TOO, PILAR. THE PAIDEIA WANTS TO DO THE MOST DAMAGE POSSIBLE TO THE HORDE, JUST LIKE US!
I KNOW-- HEY, I JUST GET PARANOID SOMETIMES. CABIN FEVER!
NO -- THEY'RE SLOUGHING IT OFF TOO EASILY. HOW CAN THEY LET THEMSELVES DIE... STRANGLED IN RED TAPE?
OUR LIVES ARE BEING WASTED! MY LIFE! BUT WOULD THEY UNDERSTAND IF I TOLD THEM? THEY MIGHT JUST NOT SEE IT -- MIGHT EVEN TURN ON ME -- EVEN ALINE.
GOD I WISH HAROLD WERE HERE -- I WISH I WERE A LEADER LIKE HE WAS--!

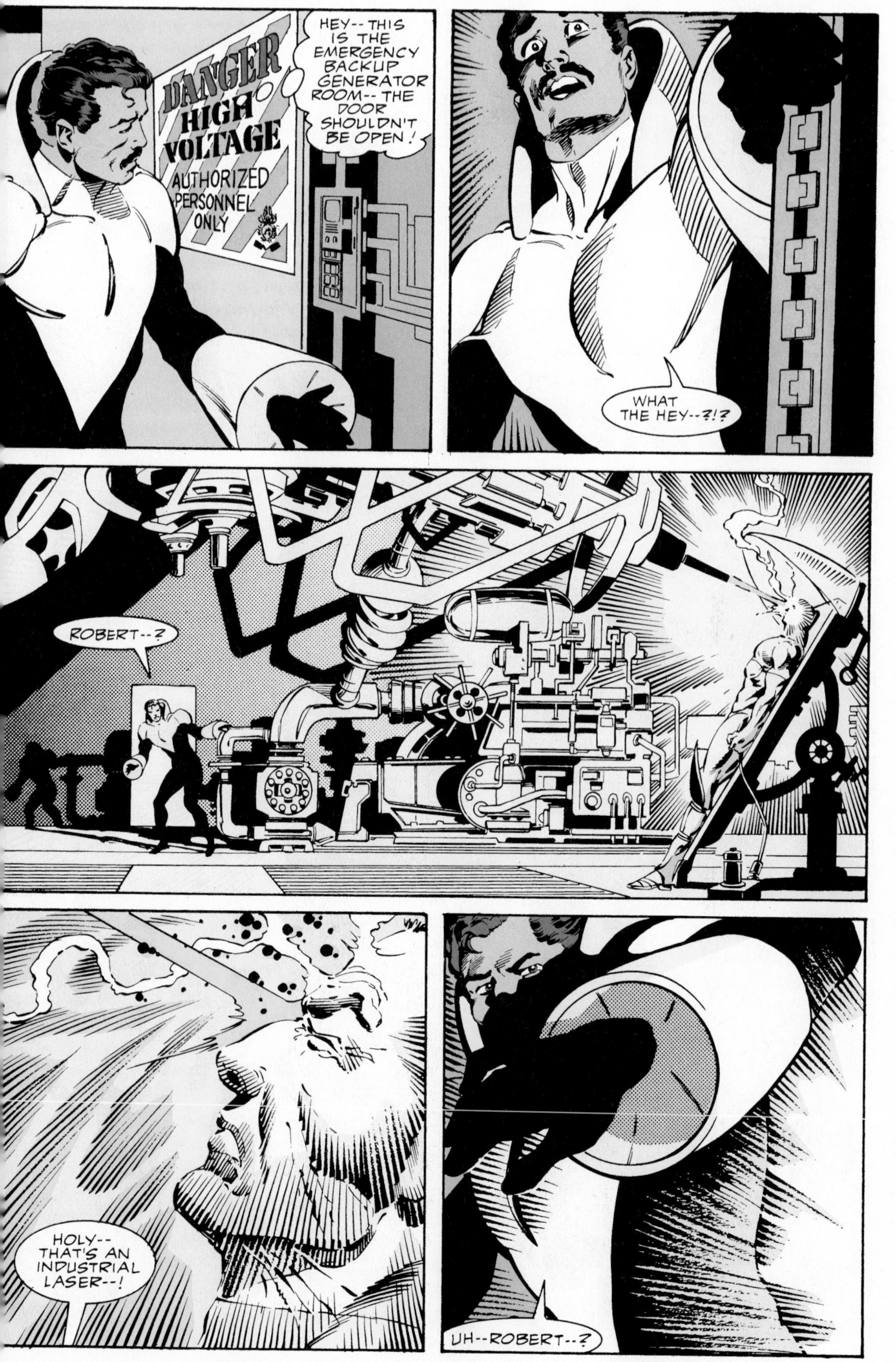
DANGER
HIGH VOLTAGE
AUTHORIZED PERSONNEL ONLY
HEY-- THIS IS THE EMERGENCY BACKUP GENERATOR ROOM-- THE DOOR SHOULDN'T BE OPEN!
WHAT THE HEY--?!?
ROBERT--?
HOLY-- THAT'S AN INDUSTRIAL LASER--!
UH--ROBERT--?

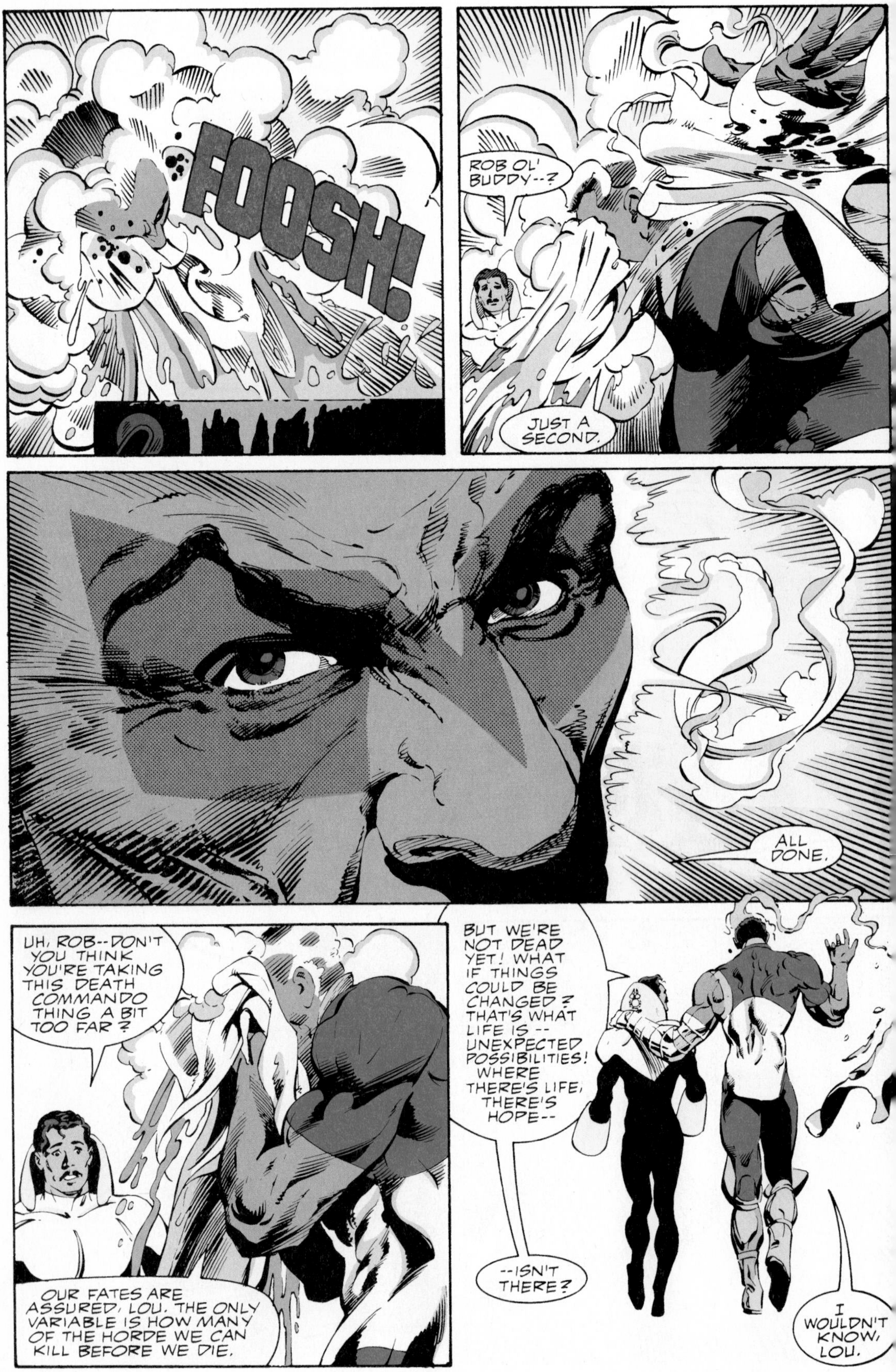
FOOSH!
ROB OL' BUDDY--?
JUST A SECOND.
ALL DONE.
UH, ROB--DON'T YOU THINK YOU'RE TAKING THIS DEATH COMMANDO THING A BIT TOO FAR?
OUR FATES ARE ASSURED, LOU. THE ONLY VARIABLE IS HOW MANY OF THE HORDE WE CAN KILL BEFORE WE DIE.
BUT WE'RE NOT DEAD YET! WHAT IF THINGS COULD BE CHANGED? THAT'S WHAT LIFE IS -- UNEXPECTED POSSIBILITIES! WHERE THERE'S LIFE, THERE'S HOPE--
--ISN'T THERE?
I WOULDN'T KNOW, LOU.

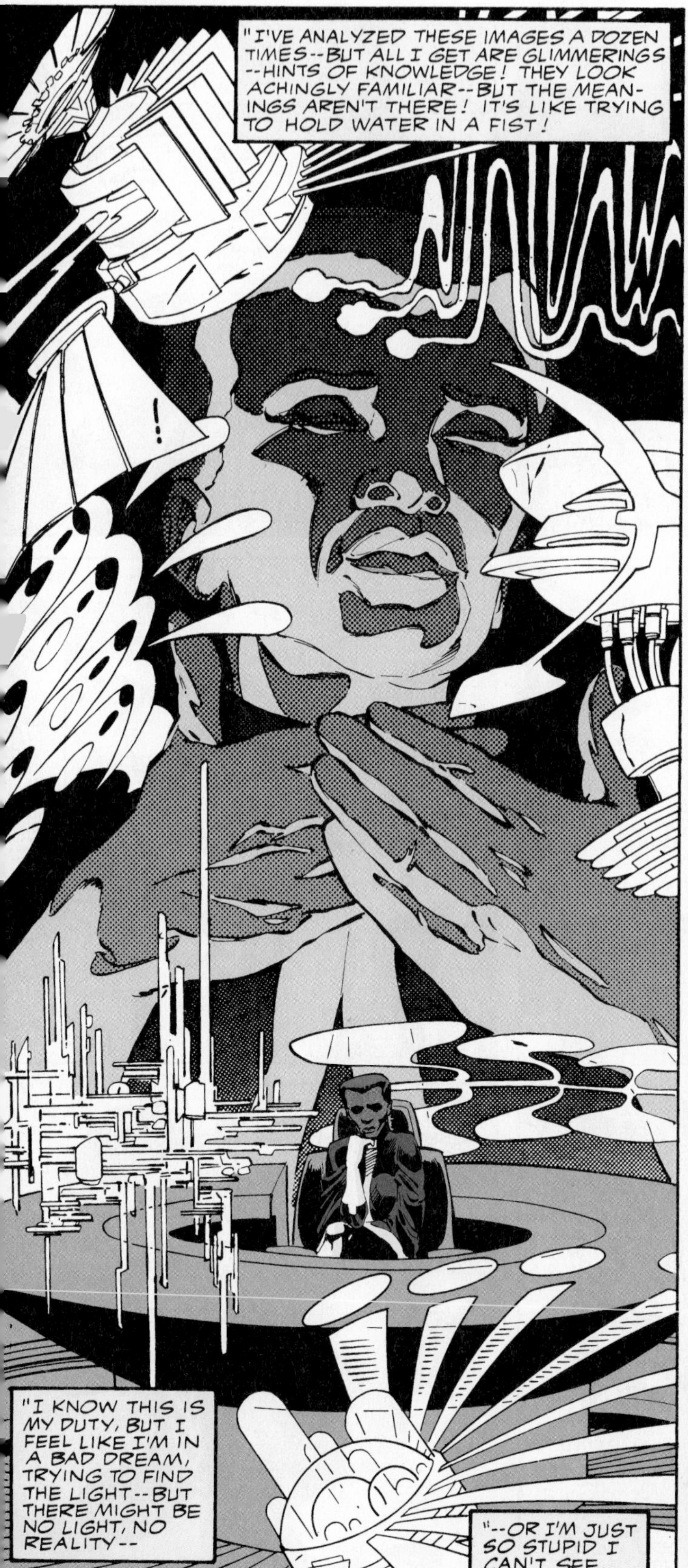
"I'VE ANALYZED THESE IMAGES A DOZEN TIMES--BUT ALL I GET ARE GLIMMERINGS --HINTS OF KNOWLEDGE! THEY LOOK ACHINGLY FAMILIAR--BUT THE MEAN-INGS AREN'T THERE! IT'S LIKE TRYING TO HOLD WATER IN A FIST!
"I KNOW THIS IS MY DUTY, BUT I FEEL LIKE I'M IN A BAD DREAM, TRYING TO FIND THE LIGHT--BUT THERE MIGHT BE NO LIGHT, NO REALITY--
"--OR I'M JUST SO STUPID I CAN'T SEE.

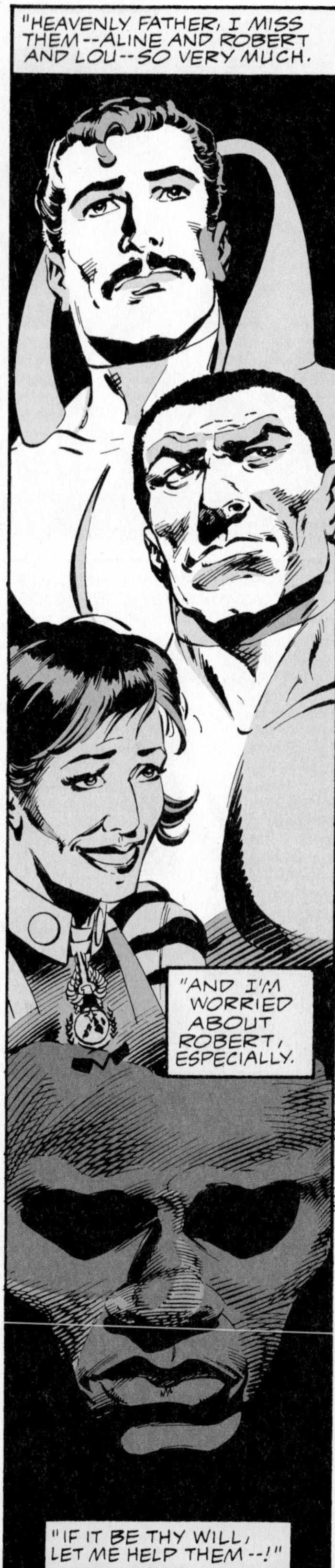
"HEAVENLY FATHER, I MISS THEM--ALINE AND ROBERT AND LOU--SO VERY MUCH.
"AND I'M WORRIED ABOUT ROBERT, ESPECIALLY.
"IF IT BE THY WILL, LET ME HELP THEM--!"

WHOOPS! I KEYED MY CONSOLE TO INTERCEPT ANY NON-ROUTINE TRANSMISSION TO OR FROM MORITURI MOUNTAIN--

--AND IT'S GOT ONE!

BEEP BEEP BEEP BEEP

IT'S LOU! BUT WHO'S HE TALKING TO?

YES, I UNDERSTAND... I CAN SWING IT... WHAT OTHER CHOICE DO I HAVE?... YES, OUT!

HE MUST'VE BEEN USING HIS ELECTROMAGNETIC POWERS TO CLOAK THE SIGNAL--

--BUT WHAT ON EARTH COULD THAT HAVE BEEN ABOUT?

HOT PUPPIES! HORDE STRIKE ALERT!

EENOO EENOO

PILAR!

OVERRIDE...OVERRIDE... THIS IS NOT, I REPEAT, NOT AN ALERT!

EENOOEENOO

WILL, YOU'VE GOT TO HELP ME! WE'VE GOT TO SPRING JELENE AGAIN! ROB'S ALREADY AT THE LAUNCH RAILGUN--

ALINE, WILL YOU GET TOXYN?

SO CAN YOU INCAPACIT- ATE THE GUARDS, WILL?

SURE! BUT BRACE YOUR- SELVES--I'M GOING TO BROADCAST MEMORIES OF THE FIRST TIME I DRANK A WHOLE BOTTLE OF VODKA!

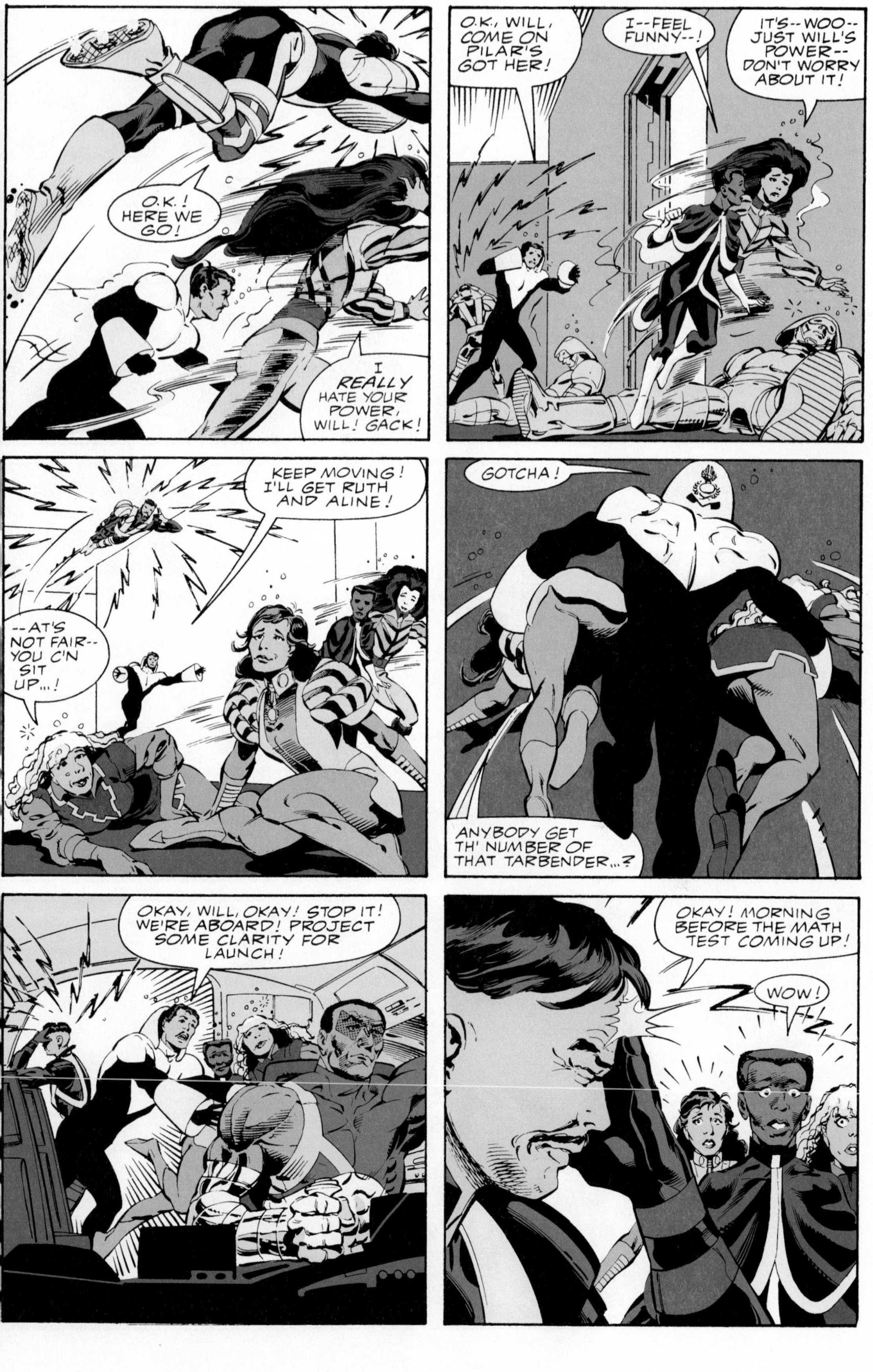
O.K.! HERE WE GO!
I REALLY HATE YOUR POWER, WILL! GACK!
O.K., WILL, COME ON PILAR'S GOT HER!
I--FEEL FUNNY--!
IT'S--WOO--JUST WILL'S POWER--DON'T WORRY ABOUT IT!
KEEP MOVING! I'LL GET RUTH AND ALINE!
--AT'S NOT FAIR--YOU C'N SIT UP...!
GOTCHA!
ANYBODY GET TH' NUMBER OF THAT TARBENDER...?
OKAY, WILL, OKAY! STOP IT! WE'RE ABOARD! PROJECT SOME CLARITY FOR LAUNCH!
OKAY! MORNING BEFORE THE MATH TEST COMING UP!
WOW!

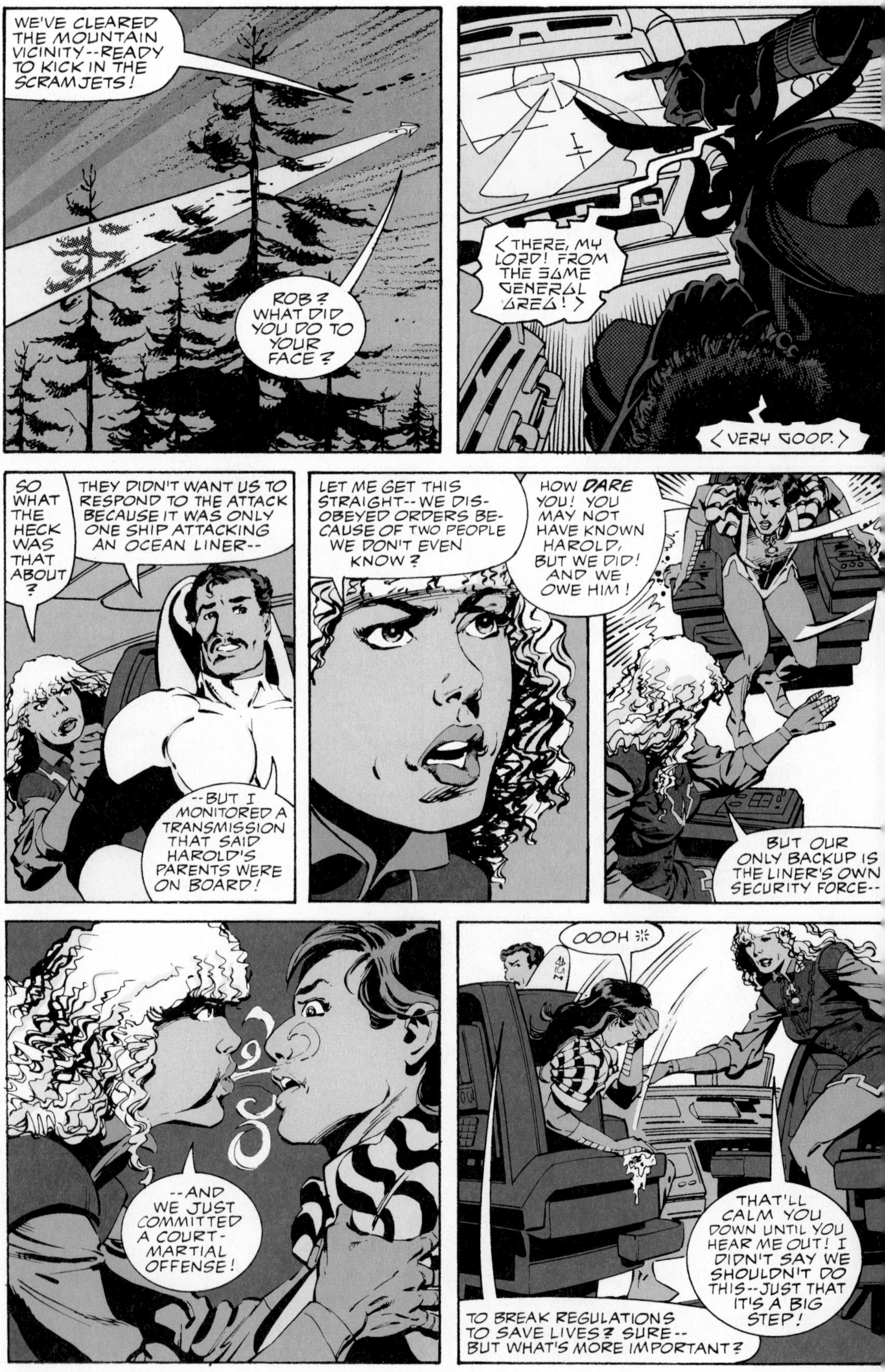

WE'VE CLEARED THE MOUNTAIN VICINITY--READY TO KICK IN THE SCRAMJETS!
ROB? WHAT DID YOU DO TO YOUR FACE?
<THERE, MY LORD! FROM THE SAME GENERAL AREA!>
<VERY GOOD.>
SO WHAT THE HECK WAS THAT ABOUT?
THEY DIDN'T WANT US TO RESPOND TO THE ATTACK BECAUSE IT WAS ONLY ONE SHIP ATTACKING AN OCEAN LINER--
--BUT I MONITORED A TRANSMISSION THAT SAID HAROLD'S PARENTS WERE ON BOARD!
LET ME GET THIS STRAIGHT--WE DISOBEYED ORDERS BECAUSE OF TWO PEOPLE WE DON'T EVEN KNOW?
HOW DARE YOU! YOU MAY NOT HAVE KNOWN HAROLD, BUT WE DID! AND WE OWE HIM!
BUT OUR ONLY BACKUP IS THE LINER'S OWN SECURITY FORCE--
--AND WE JUST COMMITTED A COURT-MARTIAL OFFENSE!
OOOH!
THAT'LL CALM YOU DOWN UNTIL YOU HEAR ME OUT! I DIDN'T SAY WE SHOULDN'T DO THIS--JUST THAT IT'S A BIG STEP!
TO BREAK REGULATIONS TO SAVE LIVES? SURE--BUT WHAT'S MORE IMPORTANT?

DEBATE TIME'S OVER! TARGET DEAD AHEAD!

I'M GETTING MESSAGES-- DEFENSE TELEMETRY!

SMALL PARTY ... BRUTALITY AS OPPOSED TO PLUNDER... 26 DEATHS SO FAR!

END OF DISCUSSION. LET'S GO.

‹IFO CIEMNO OLUM MATI MATI!›

YOU KNOW, YOU SHOULD REALLY WASH BEHIND YOUR EARS MORE OFTEN, BUDDY!

GHARE POJJ TREDGEW UTHED GUG MERRED GGO!

‹SO THE HUNTING PACK COMES FOR YOUR SPAWNERS IN YOUR WEIRD BAD ATTACHMENT TO THEM AND SO PERIL YOUR PACK'S FULSOMENESS!›

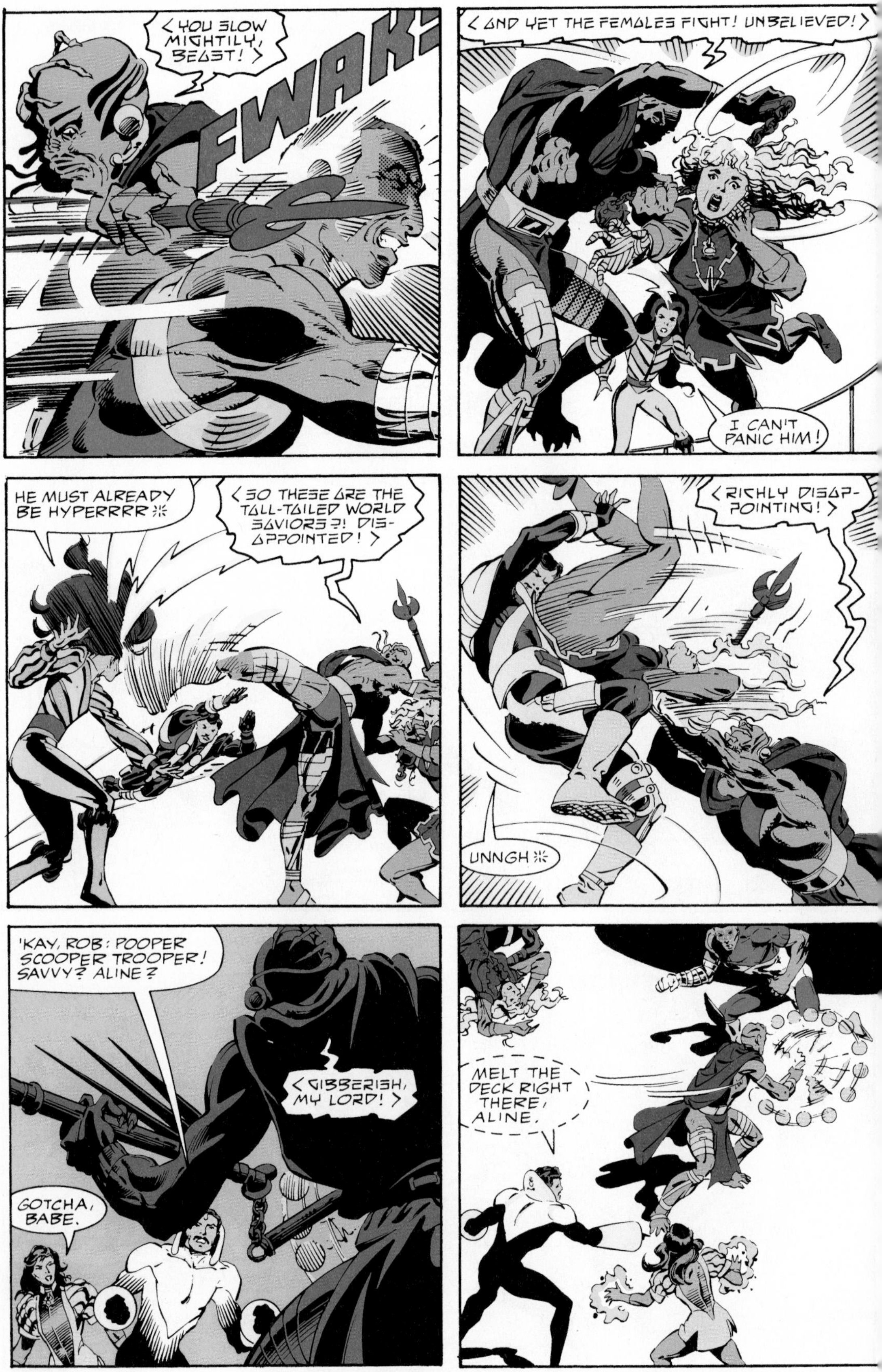

< YOU SLOW MIGHTILY, BEAST! >
FWAK!
< AND YET THE FEMALES FIGHT! UNBELIEVED! >
I CAN'T PANIC HIM!
HE MUST ALREADY BE HYPERRRR※
< SO THESE ARE THE TALL-TAILED WORLD SAVIORS?! DIS-APPOINTED! >
< RICHLY DISAP-POINTING! >
UNNGH※
'KAY, ROB: POOPER SCOOPER TROOPER! SAVVY? ALINE?
< GIBBERISH, MY LORD! >
GOTCHA, BABE.
MELT THE DECK RIGHT THERE, ALINE.

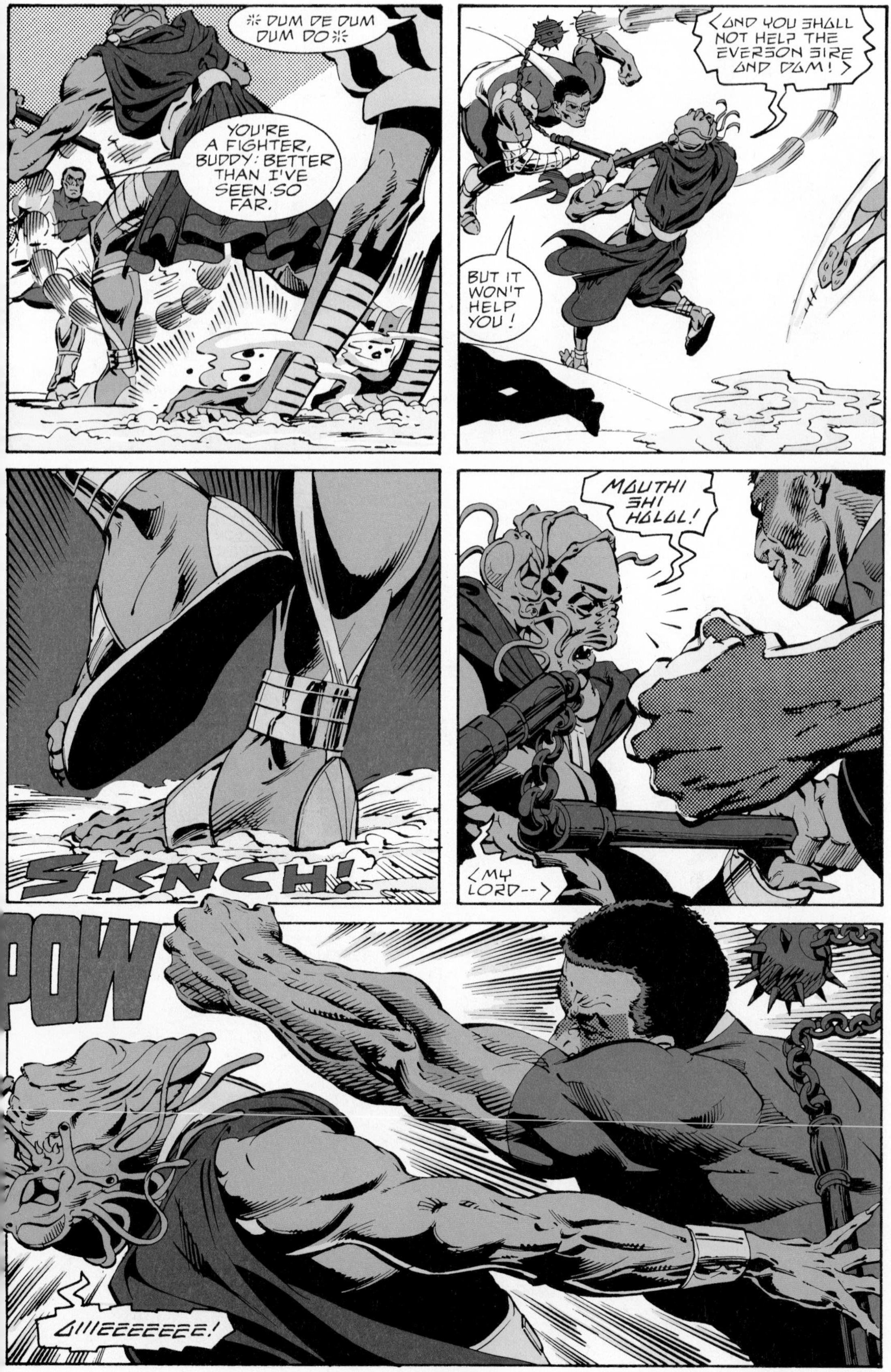
⁂ DUM DE DUM DUM DO ⁂
YOU'RE A FIGHTER, BUDDY: BETTER THAN I'VE SEEN SO FAR.
<AND YOU SHALL NOT HELP THE EVERSON SIRE AND DAM!>
BUT IT WON'T HELP YOU!
SKNCH!
MAUTHI SHI HALAL!
<MY LORD-->
POW
GIIIEEEEEEEE!

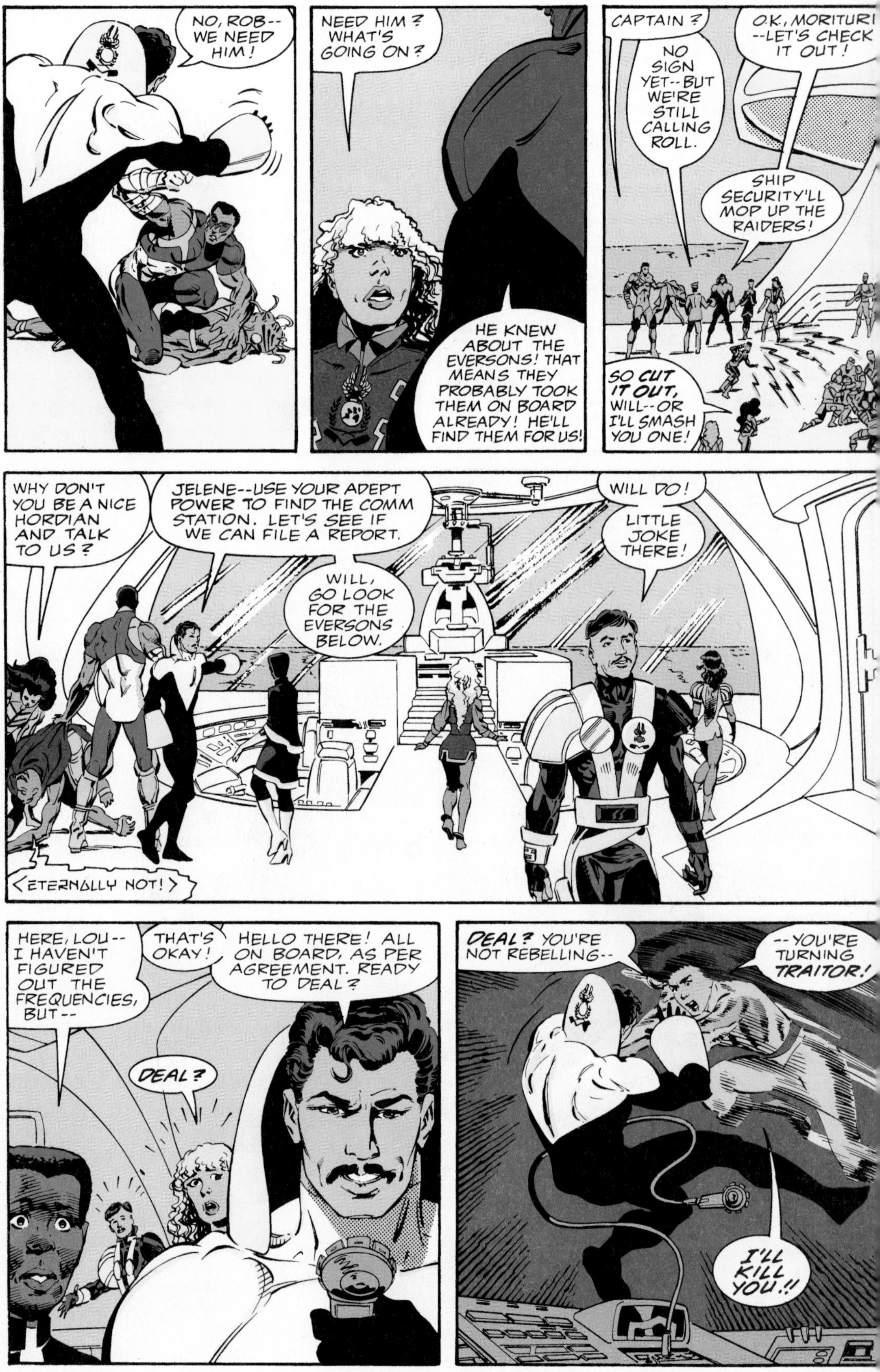
NO, ROB-- WE NEED HIM!
NEED HIM? WHAT'S GOING ON?
HE KNEW ABOUT THE EVERSONS! THAT MEANS THEY PROBABLY TOOK THEM ON BOARD ALREADY! HE'LL FIND THEM FOR US!
CAPTAIN?
NO SIGN YET--BUT WE'RE STILL CALLING ROLL.
O.K., MORITURI --LET'S CHECK IT OUT!
SHIP SECURITY'LL MOP UP THE RAIDERS!
SO CUT IT OUT, WILL--OR I'LL SMASH YOU ONE!
WHY DON'T YOU BE A NICE HORDIAN AND TALK TO US?
<ETERNALLY NOT!>
JELENE--USE YOUR ADEPT POWER TO FIND THE COMM STATION. LET'S SEE IF WE CAN FILE A REPORT.
WILL, GO LOOK FOR THE EVERSONS BELOW.
WILL DO!
LITTLE JOKE THERE!
HERE, LOU-- I HAVEN'T FIGURED OUT THE FREQUENCIES, BUT--
THAT'S OKAY!
HELLO THERE! ALL ON BOARD, AS PER AGREEMENT. READY TO DEAL?
DEAL?
DEAL? YOU'RE NOT REBELLING--
--YOU'RE TURNING TRAITOR!
I'LL KILL YOU.!!

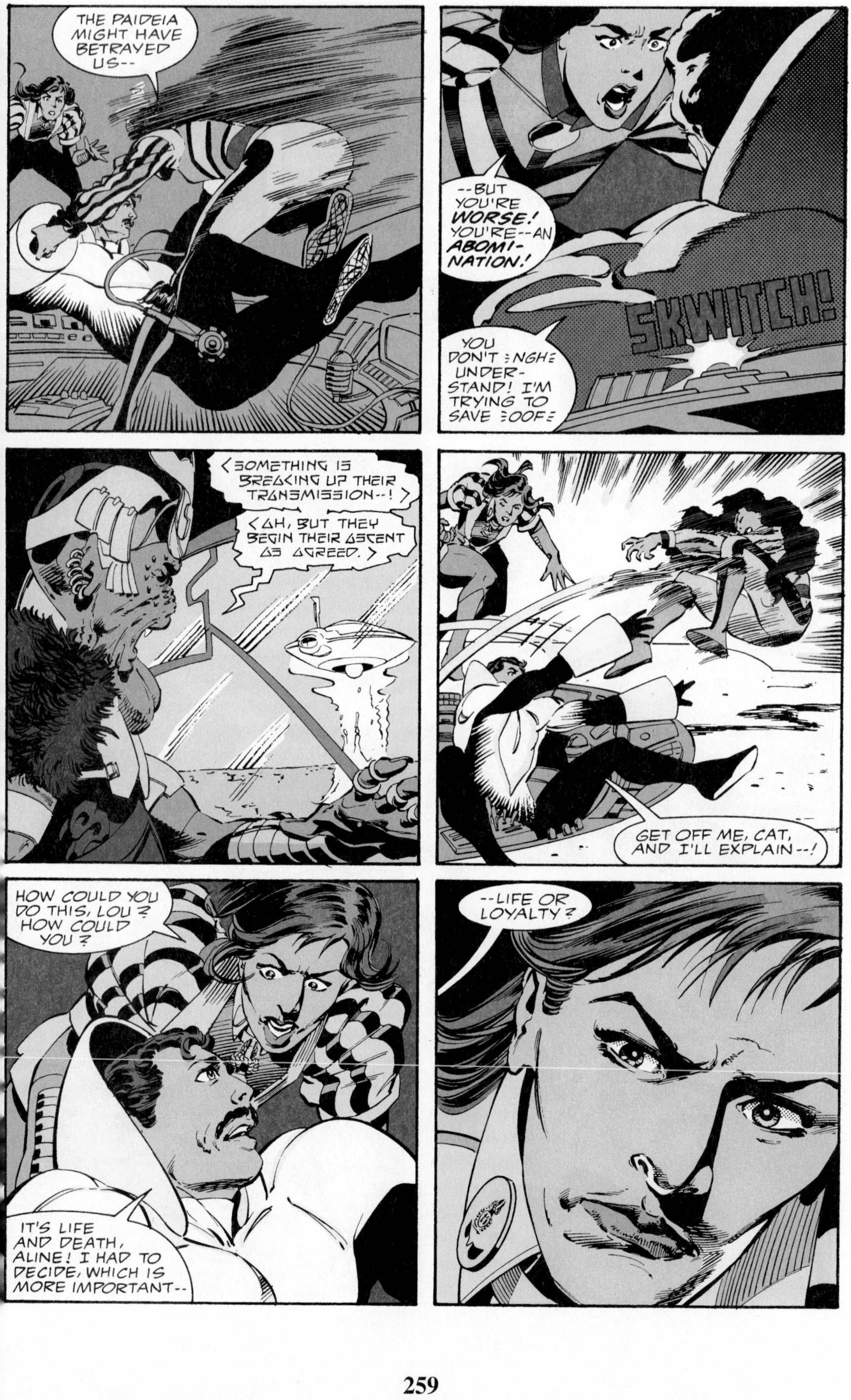
THE PAIDEIA MIGHT HAVE BETRAYED US--
--BUT YOU'RE WORSE! YOU'RE--AN ABOMI-NATION!
SKWITCH!
YOU DON'T NGH UNDER-STAND! I'M TRYING TO SAVE OOF
<SOMETHING IS BREAKING UP THEIR TRANSMISSION--!>
<AH, BUT THEY BEGIN THEIR DESCENT AS AGREED.>
GET OFF ME, CAT, AND I'LL EXPLAIN--!
HOW COULD YOU DO THIS, LOU? HOW COULD YOU?
IT'S LIFE AND DEATH, ALINE! I HAD TO DECIDE, WHICH IS MORE IMPORTANT--
--LIFE OR LOYALTY?

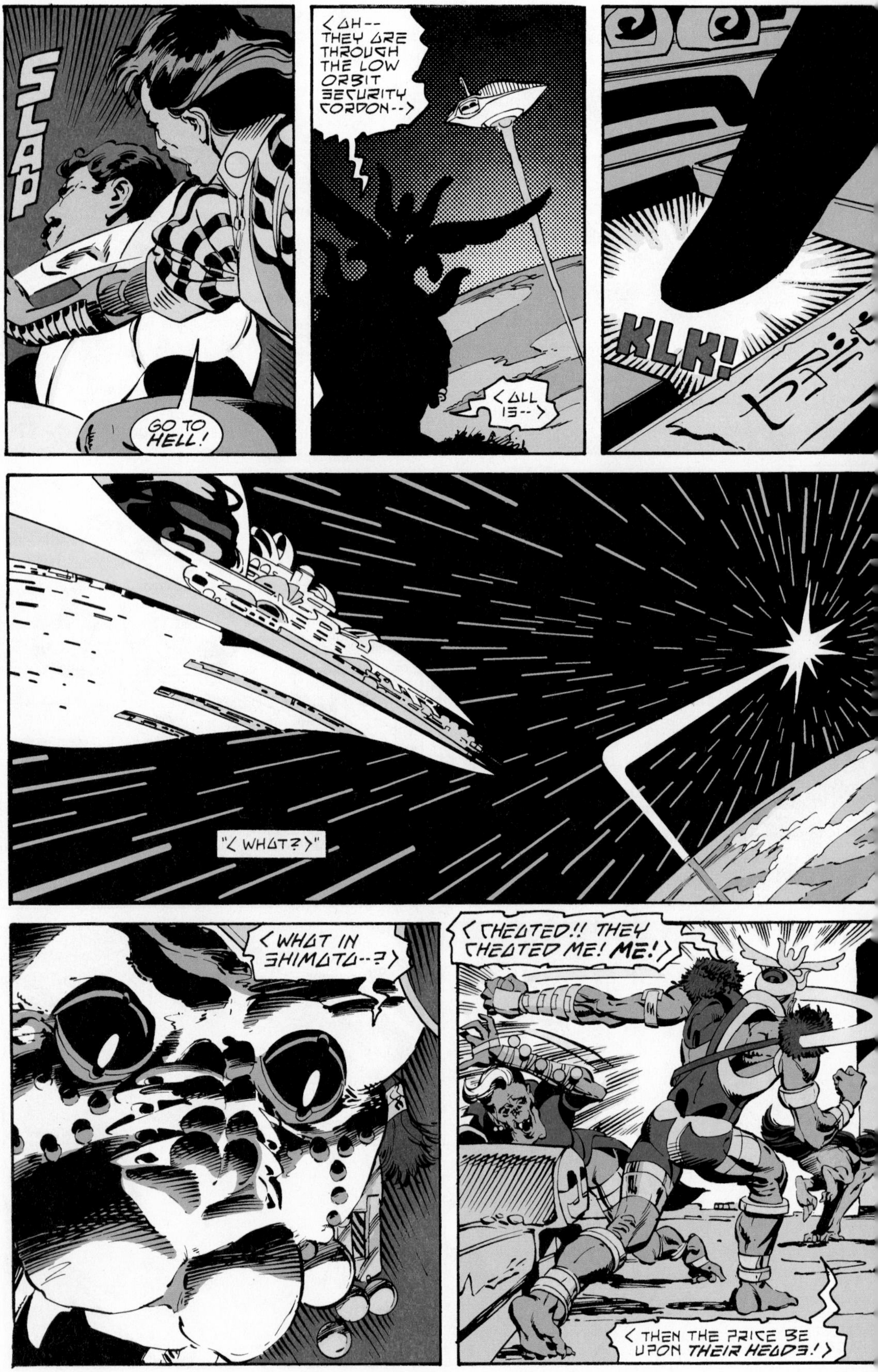
SLAP
GO TO HELL!
<OH-- THEY ARE THROUGH THE LOW ORBIT SECURITY CORDON-->
<ALL IS-->
KLK!
"<WHAT?>"
<WHAT IN SHIMATA--?>
<CHEATED!! THEY CHEATED ME! ME!>
<THEN THE PRICE BE UPON THEIR HEADS!>

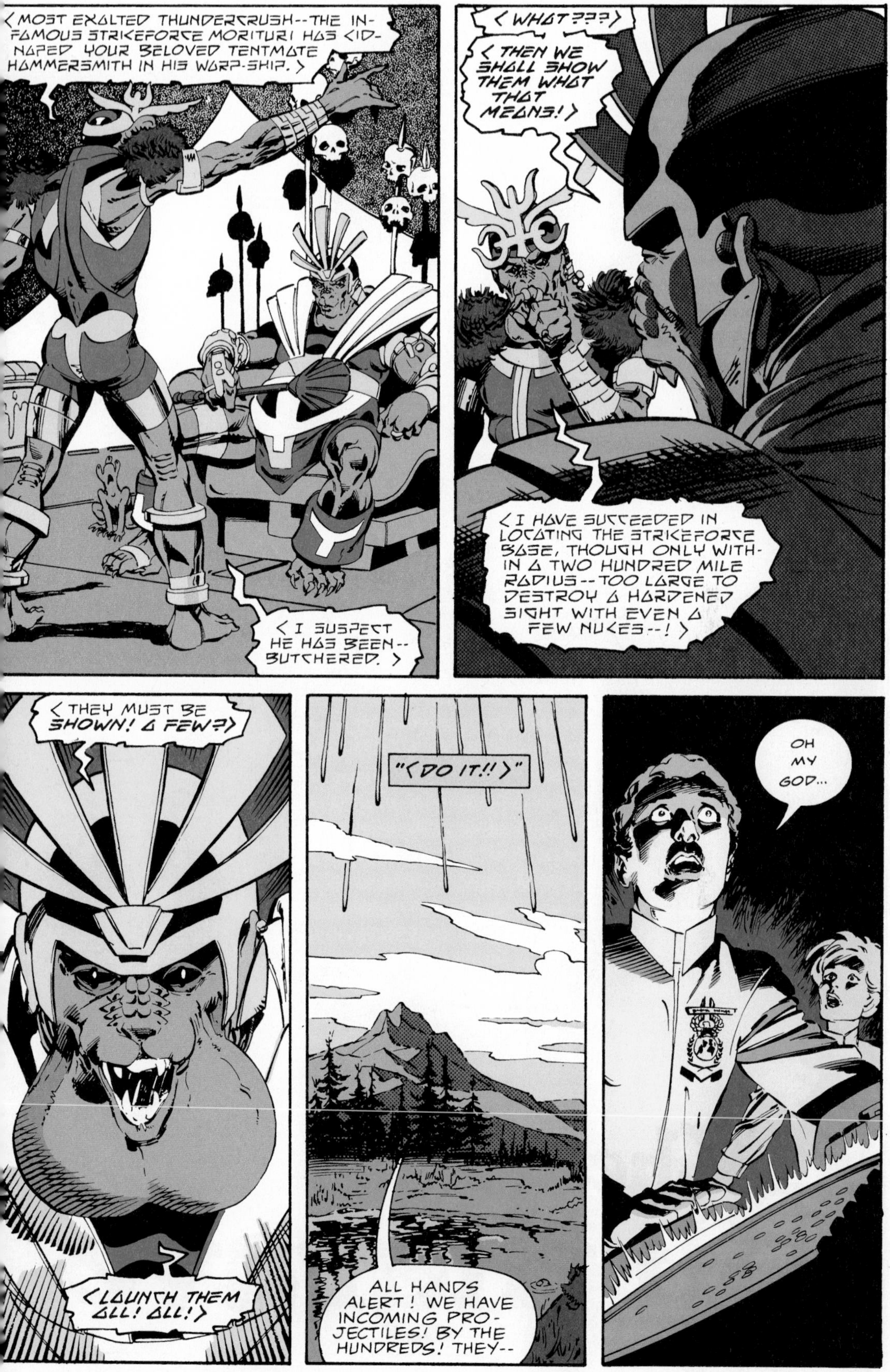
<MOST EXALTED THUNDERCRUSH--THE INFAMOUS STRIKEFORCE MORITURI HAS KIDNAPED YOUR BELOVED TENTMATE HAMMERSMITH IN HIS WARP-SHIP.>
<I SUSPECT HE HAS BEEN--BUTCHERED.>
<WHAT???>
<THEN WE SHALL SHOW THEM WHAT THAT MEANS!>
<I HAVE SUCCEEDED IN LOCATING THE STRIKEFORCE BASE, THOUGH ONLY WITHIN A TWO HUNDRED MILE RADIUS--TOO LARGE TO DESTROY A HARDENED SIGHT WITH EVEN A FEW NUKES--!>
<THEY MUST BE SHOWN! A FEW?>
<LAUNCH THEM ALL! ALL!>
"<DO IT!!>"
ALL HANDS ALERT! WE HAVE INCOMING PROJECTILES! BY THE HUNDREDS! THEY--
OH MY GOD...

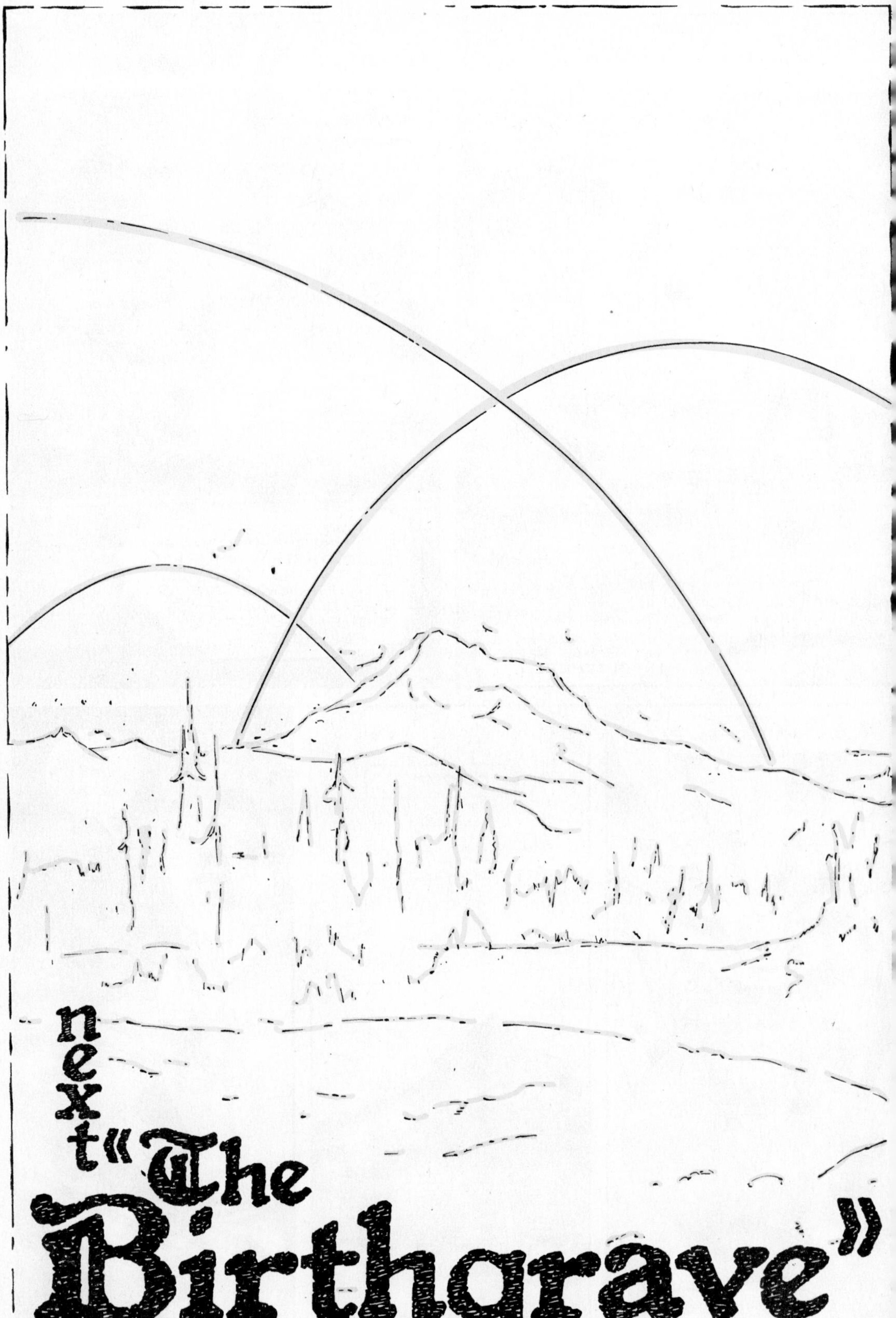
next "The Birthgrave"

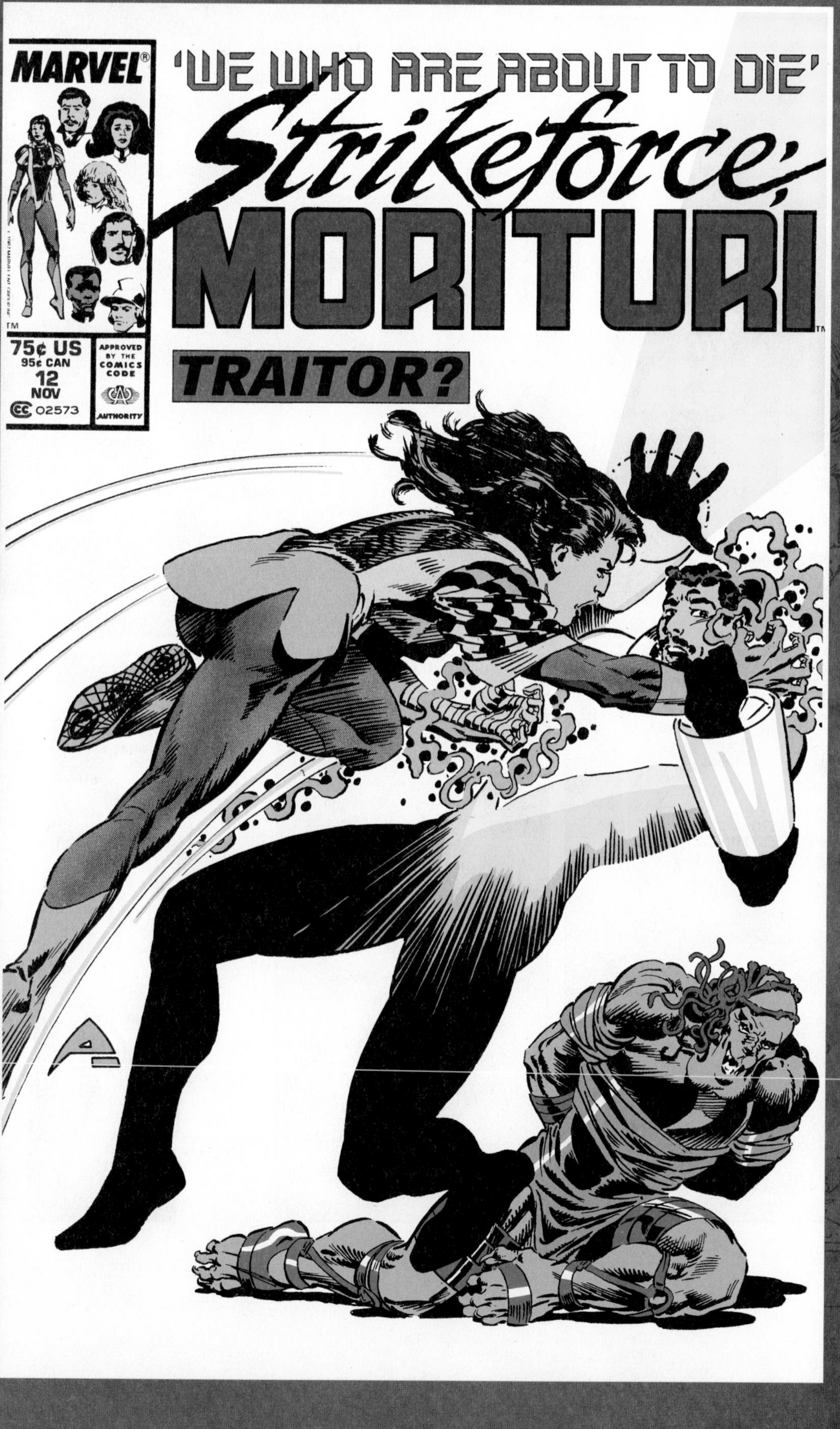

MARVEL®
'WE WHO ARE ABOUT TO DIE'
Strikeforce: MORITURI
75¢ US
95¢ CAN
12
NOV
02573
APPROVED BY THE COMICS CODE AUTHORITY
TRAITOR?

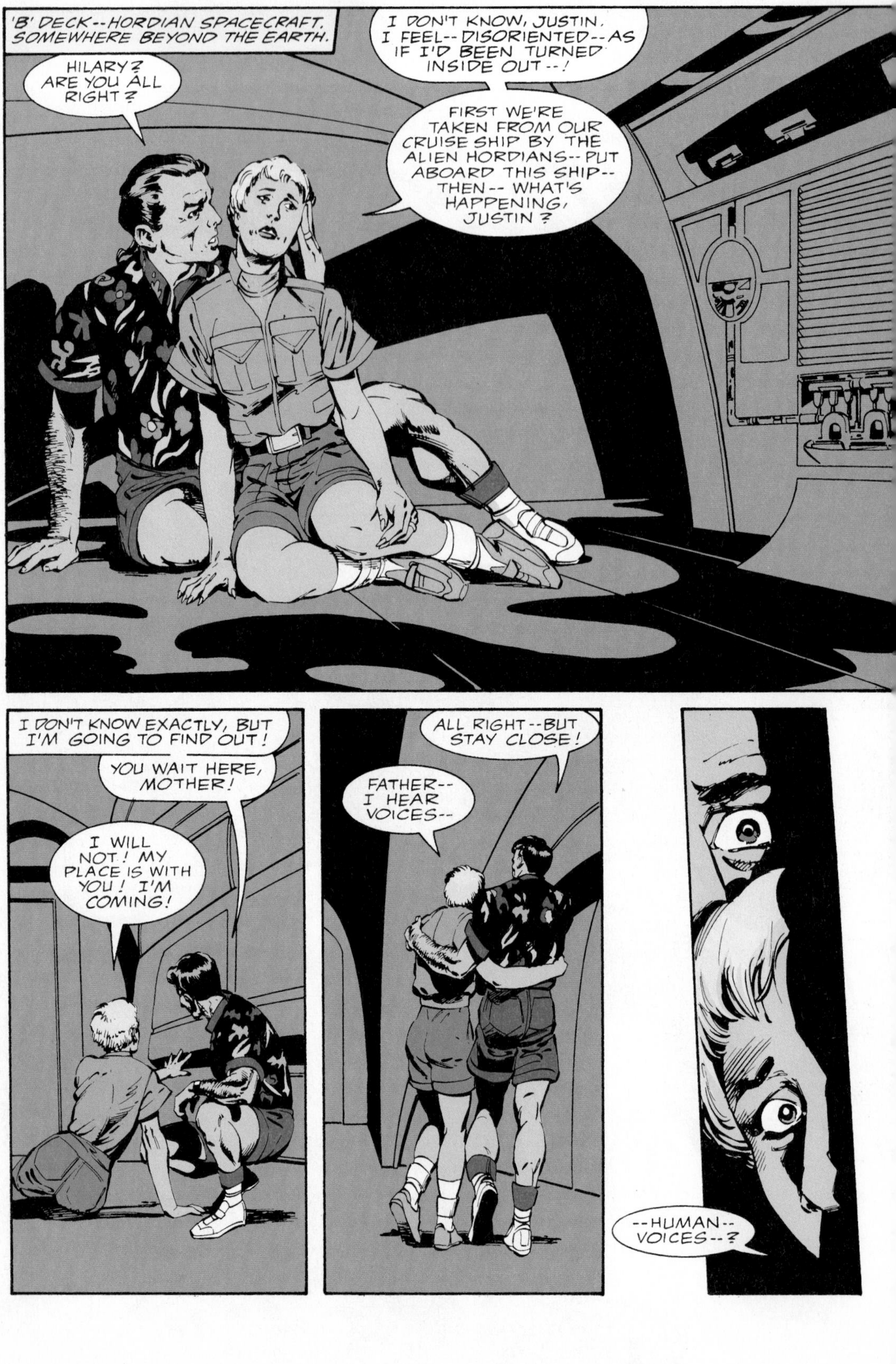
'B' DECK--HORDIAN SPACECRAFT, SOMEWHERE BEYOND THE EARTH.
HILARY? ARE YOU ALL RIGHT?
I DON'T KNOW, JUSTIN. I FEEL--DISORIENTED--AS IF I'D BEEN TURNED INSIDE OUT--!
FIRST WE'RE TAKEN FROM OUR CRUISE SHIP BY THE ALIEN HORDIANS--PUT ABOARD THIS SHIP--THEN--WHAT'S HAPPENING, JUSTIN?
I DON'T KNOW EXACTLY, BUT I'M GOING TO FIND OUT!
YOU WAIT HERE, MOTHER!
I WILL NOT! MY PLACE IS WITH YOU! I'M COMING!
FATHER--I HEAR VOICES--
ALL RIGHT--BUT STAY CLOSE!
--HUMAN--VOICES--?

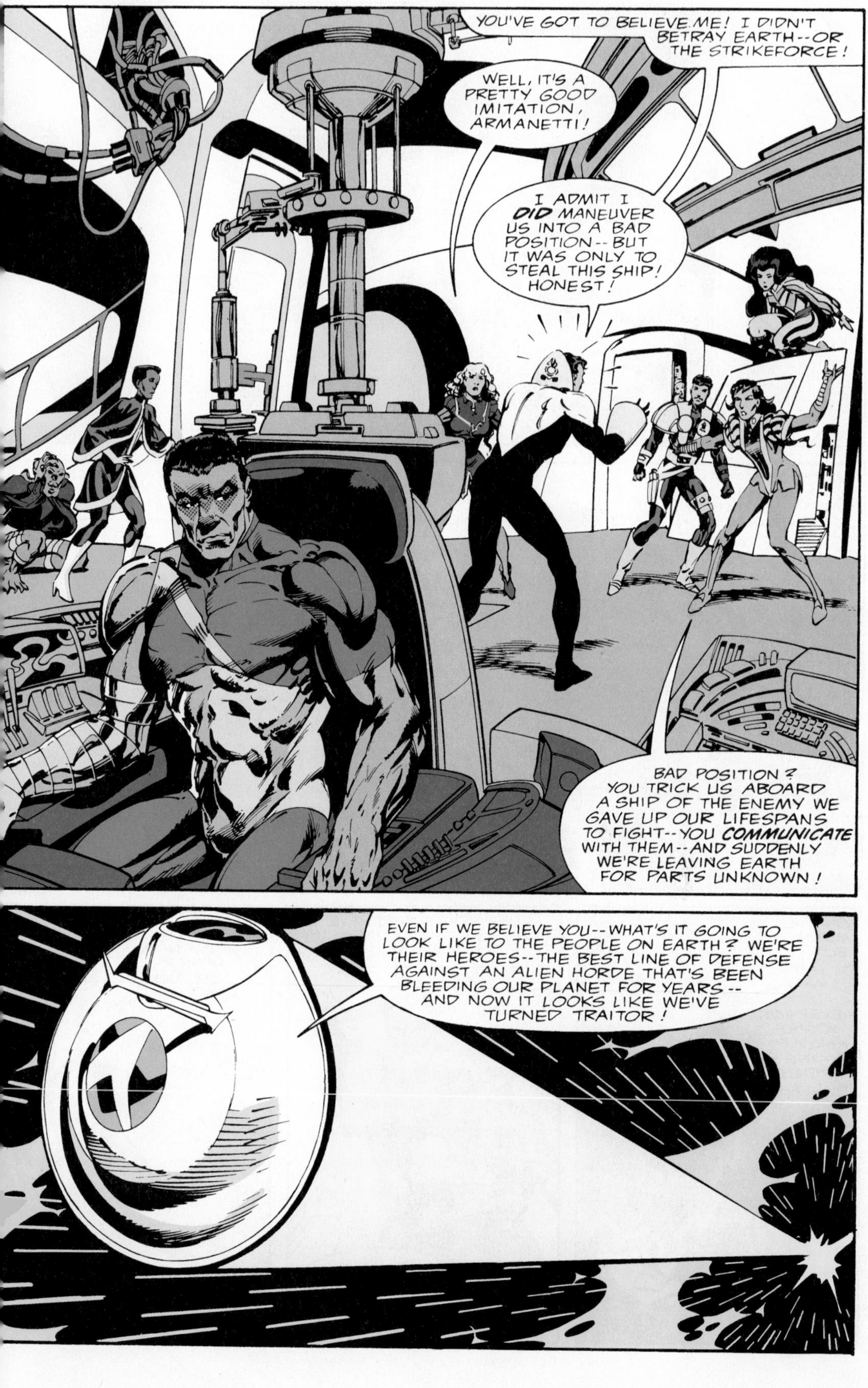
YOU'VE GOT TO BELIEVE ME! I DIDN'T BETRAY EARTH--OR THE STRIKEFORCE!
WELL, IT'S A PRETTY GOOD IMITATION, ARMANETTI!
I ADMIT I DID MANEUVER US INTO A BAD POSITION--BUT IT WAS ONLY TO STEAL THIS SHIP! HONEST!
BAD POSITION? YOU TRICK US ABOARD A SHIP OF THE ENEMY WE GAVE UP OUR LIFESPANS TO FIGHT--YOU COMMUNICATE WITH THEM--AND SUDDENLY WE'RE LEAVING EARTH FOR PARTS UNKNOWN!
EVEN IF WE BELIEVE YOU--WHAT'S IT GOING TO LOOK LIKE TO THE PEOPLE ON EARTH? WE'RE THEIR HEROES--THE BEST LINE OF DEFENSE AGAINST AN ALIEN HORDE THAT'S BEEN BLEEDING OUR PLANET FOR YEARS--AND NOW IT LOOKS LIKE WE'VE TURNED TRAITOR!

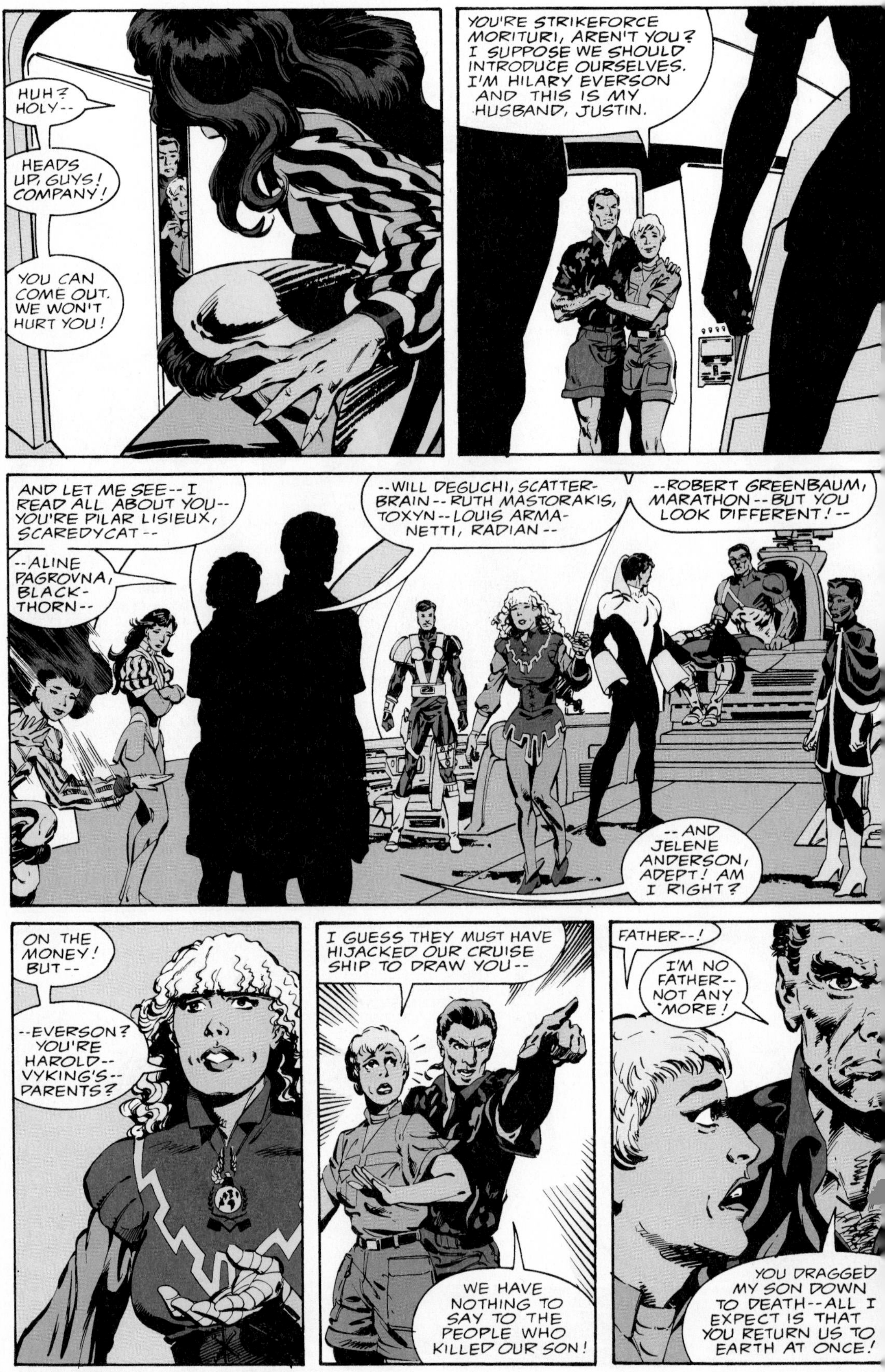
HUH? HOLY--
HEADS UP, GUYS! COMPANY!
YOU CAN COME OUT. WE WON'T HURT YOU!
YOU'RE STRIKEFORCE MORITURI, AREN'T YOU? I SUPPOSE WE SHOULD INTRODUCE OURSELVES. I'M HILARY EVERSON AND THIS IS MY HUSBAND, JUSTIN.
AND LET ME SEE-- I READ ALL ABOUT YOU-- YOU'RE PILAR LISIEUX, SCAREDYCAT--
--ALINE PAGROVNA, BLACKTHORN--
--WILL DEGUCHI, SCATTERBRAIN--RUTH MASTORAKIS, TOXYN--LOUIS ARMANETTI, RADIAN--
--ROBERT GREENBAUM, MARATHON--BUT YOU LOOK DIFFERENT!--
--AND JELENE ANDERSON, ADEPT! AM I RIGHT?
ON THE MONEY! BUT--
--EVERSON? YOU'RE HAROLD--VYKING'S--PARENTS?
I GUESS THEY MUST HAVE HIJACKED OUR CRUISE SHIP TO DRAW YOU--
WE HAVE NOTHING TO SAY TO THE PEOPLE WHO KILLED OUR SON!
FATHER--!
I'M NO FATHER--NOT ANY MORE!
YOU DRAGGED MY SON DOWN TO DEATH--ALL I EXPECT IS THAT YOU RETURN US TO EARTH AT ONCE!

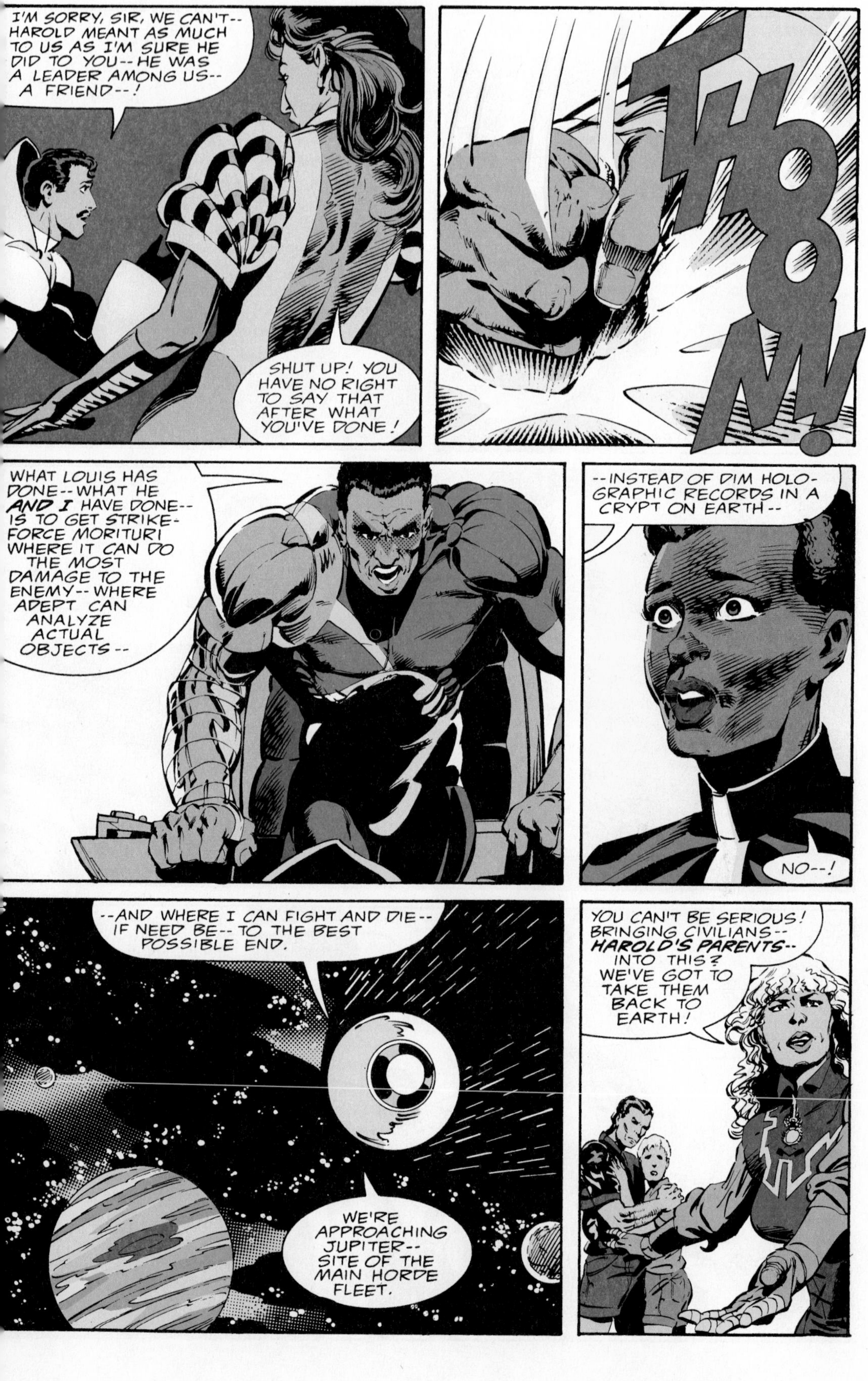

I'M SORRY, SIR, WE CAN'T-- HAROLD MEANT AS MUCH TO US AS I'M SURE HE DID TO YOU-- HE WAS A LEADER AMONG US-- A FRIEND--!
SHUT UP! YOU HAVE NO RIGHT TO SAY THAT AFTER WHAT YOU'VE DONE!
THOOM!
WHAT LOUIS HAS DONE-- WHAT HE AND I HAVE DONE-- IS TO GET STRIKE-FORCE MORITURI WHERE IT CAN DO THE MOST DAMAGE TO THE ENEMY-- WHERE ADEPT CAN ANALYZE ACTUAL OBJECTS--
--INSTEAD OF DIM HOLO-GRAPHIC RECORDS IN A CRYPT ON EARTH--
NO--!
--AND WHERE I CAN FIGHT AND DIE-- IF NEED BE-- TO THE BEST POSSIBLE END.
WE'RE APPROACHING JUPITER-- SITE OF THE MAIN HORDE FLEET.
YOU CAN'T BE SERIOUS! BRINGING CIVILIANS-- HAROLD'S PARENTS-- INTO THIS? WE'VE GOT TO TAKE THEM BACK TO EARTH!

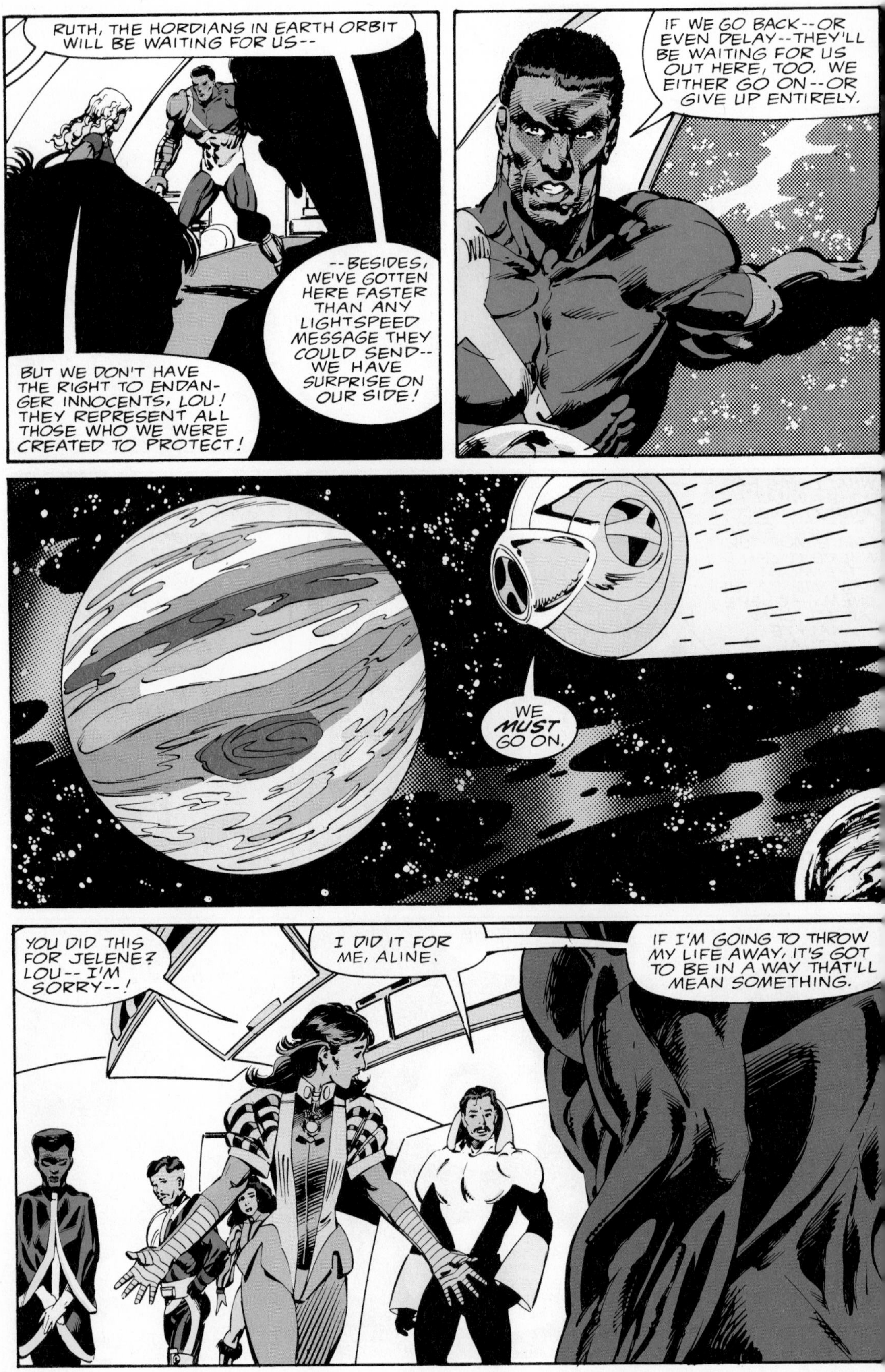
RUTH, THE HORDIANS IN EARTH ORBIT WILL BE WAITING FOR US--
BUT WE DON'T HAVE THE RIGHT TO ENDANGER INNOCENTS, LOU! THEY REPRESENT ALL THOSE WHO WE WERE CREATED TO PROTECT!
--BESIDES, WE'VE GOTTEN HERE FASTER THAN ANY LIGHTSPEED MESSAGE THEY COULD SEND-- WE HAVE SURPRISE ON OUR SIDE!
IF WE GO BACK--OR EVEN DELAY--THEY'LL BE WAITING FOR US OUT HERE, TOO. WE EITHER GO ON--OR GIVE UP ENTIRELY.
WE **MUST** GO ON.
YOU DID THIS FOR JELENE? LOU-- I'M SORRY--!
I DID IT FOR ME, ALINE.
IF I'M GOING TO THROW MY LIFE AWAY, IT'S GOT TO BE IN A WAY THAT'LL MEAN SOMETHING.

"The BIRTHGRAVE"

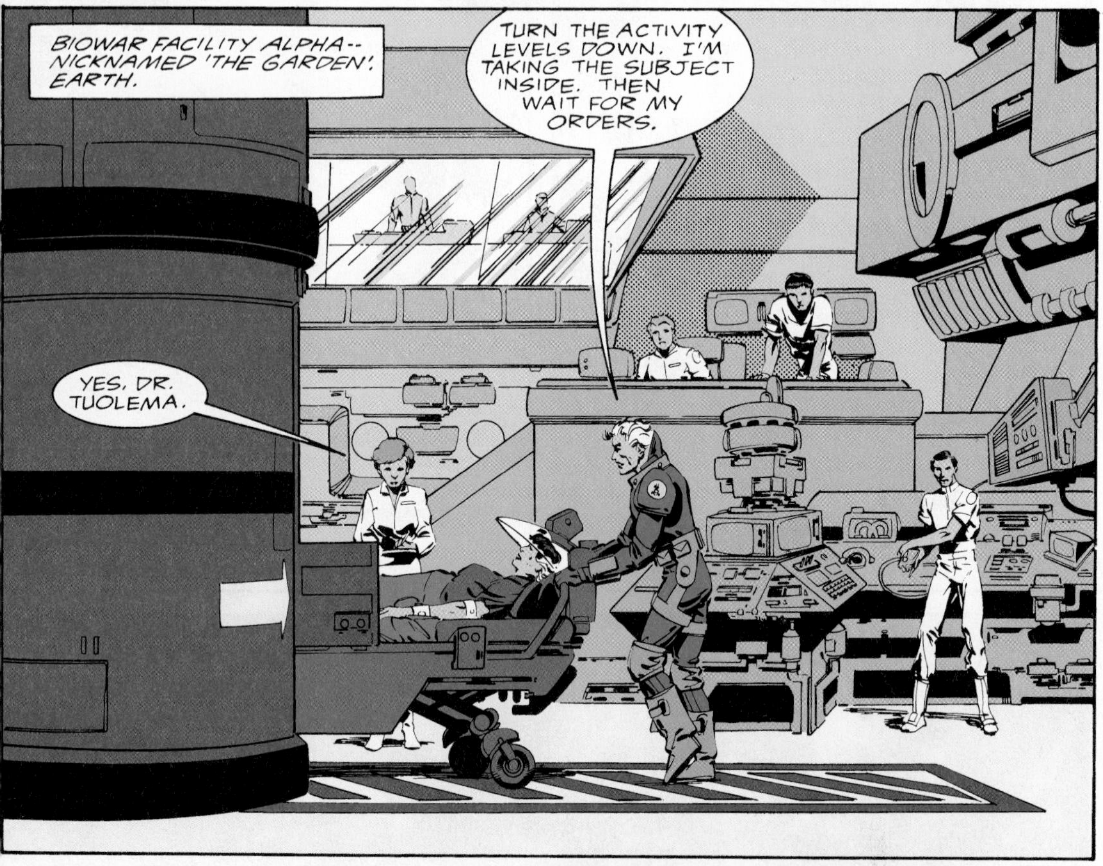
BIOWAR FACILITY ALPHA-- NICKNAMED 'THE GARDEN'. EARTH.
TURN THE ACTIVITY LEVELS DOWN. I'M TAKING THE SUBJECT INSIDE. THEN WAIT FOR MY ORDERS.
YES, DR. TUOLEMA.

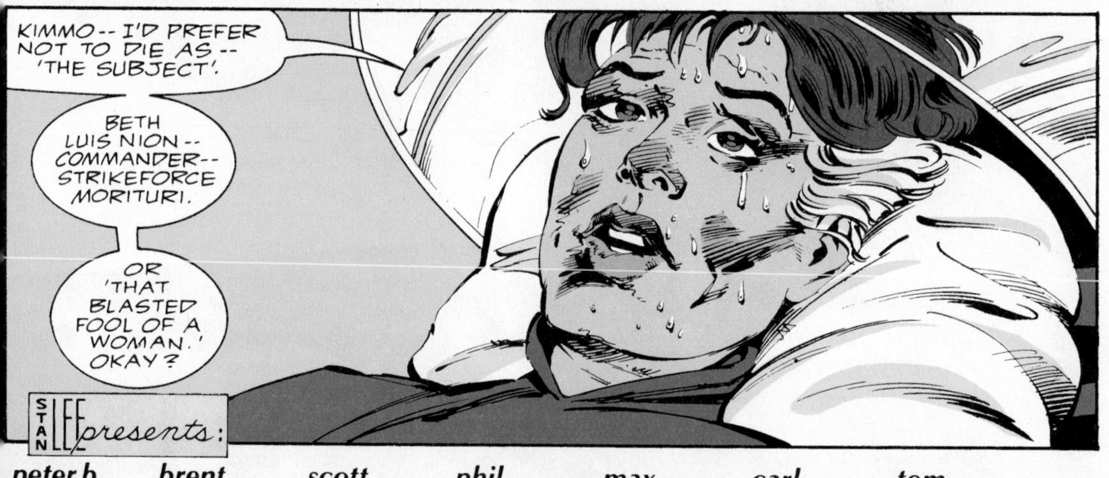
KIMMO-- I'D PREFER NOT TO DIE AS-- 'THE SUBJECT'.
BETH LUIS NION-- COMMANDER-- STRIKEFORCE MORITURI.
OR 'THAT BLASTED FOOL OF A WOMAN.' OKAY?
STAN LEE presents:

peter b. GILLIS	brent ANDERSON	scott WILLIAMS	phil FELIX	max SCHEELE	carl POTTS	tom DeFALCO
WRITER	PENCILER	INKER	LETTERER	COLORER	EDITOR	EDITOR IN CHIEF

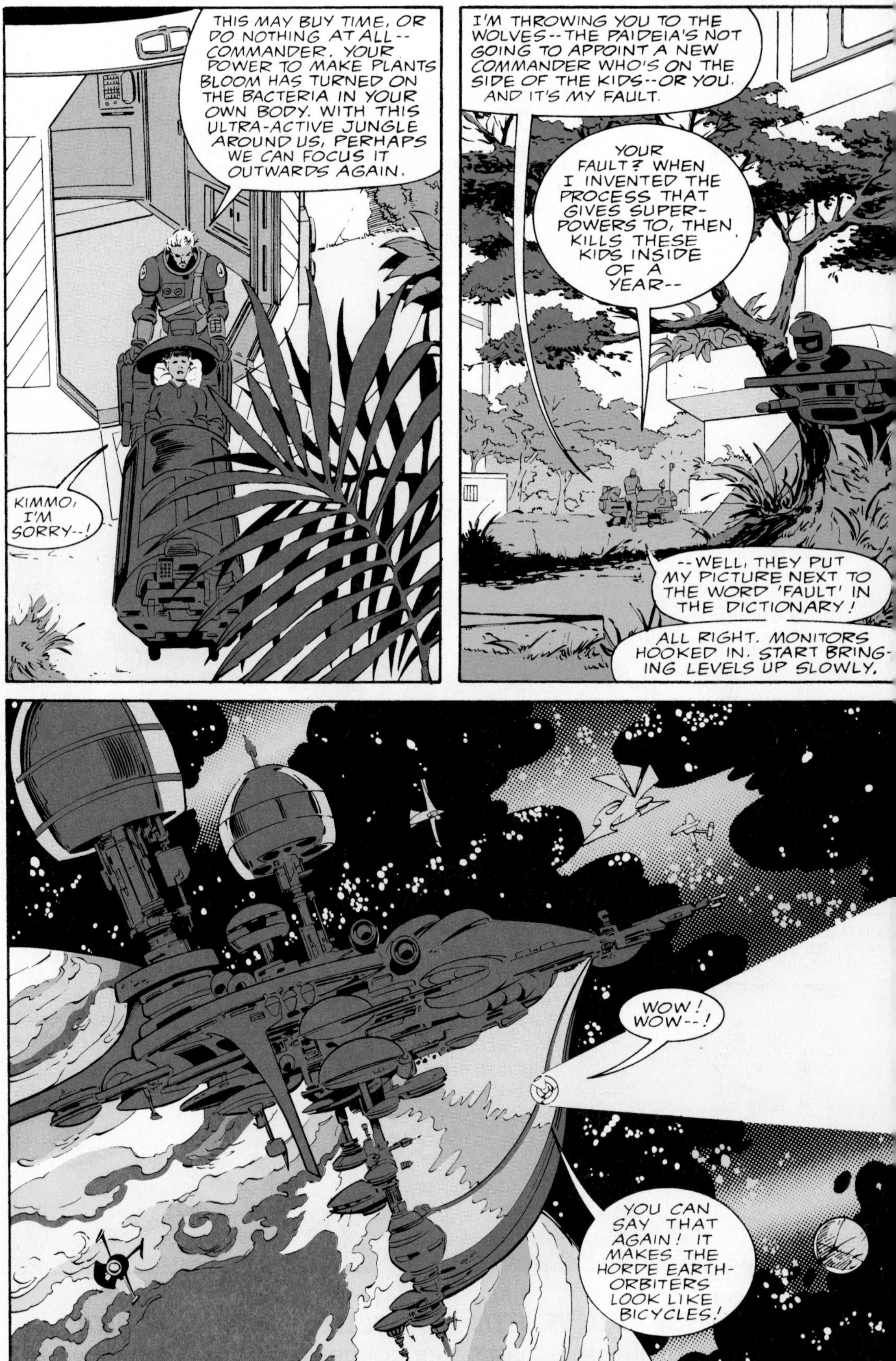
THIS MAY BUY TIME, OR DO NOTHING AT ALL-- COMMANDER. YOUR POWER TO MAKE PLANTS BLOOM HAS TURNED ON THE BACTERIA IN YOUR OWN BODY. WITH THIS ULTRA-ACTIVE JUNGLE AROUND US, PERHAPS WE CAN FOCUS IT OUTWARDS AGAIN.
KIMMO, I'M SORRY--!
I'M THROWING YOU TO THE WOLVES--THE PAIDEIA'S NOT GOING TO APPOINT A NEW COMMANDER WHO'S ON THE SIDE OF THE KIDS--OR YOU. AND IT'S MY FAULT.
YOUR FAULT? WHEN I INVENTED THE PROCESS THAT GIVES SUPER-POWERS TO, THEN KILLS THESE KIDS INSIDE OF A YEAR--
--WELL, THEY PUT MY PICTURE NEXT TO THE WORD 'FAULT' IN THE DICTIONARY!
ALL RIGHT. MONITORS HOOKED IN. START BRINGING LEVELS UP SLOWLY.
WOW! WOW--!
YOU CAN SAY THAT AGAIN! IT MAKES THE HORDE EARTH-ORBITERS LOOK LIKE BICYCLES!

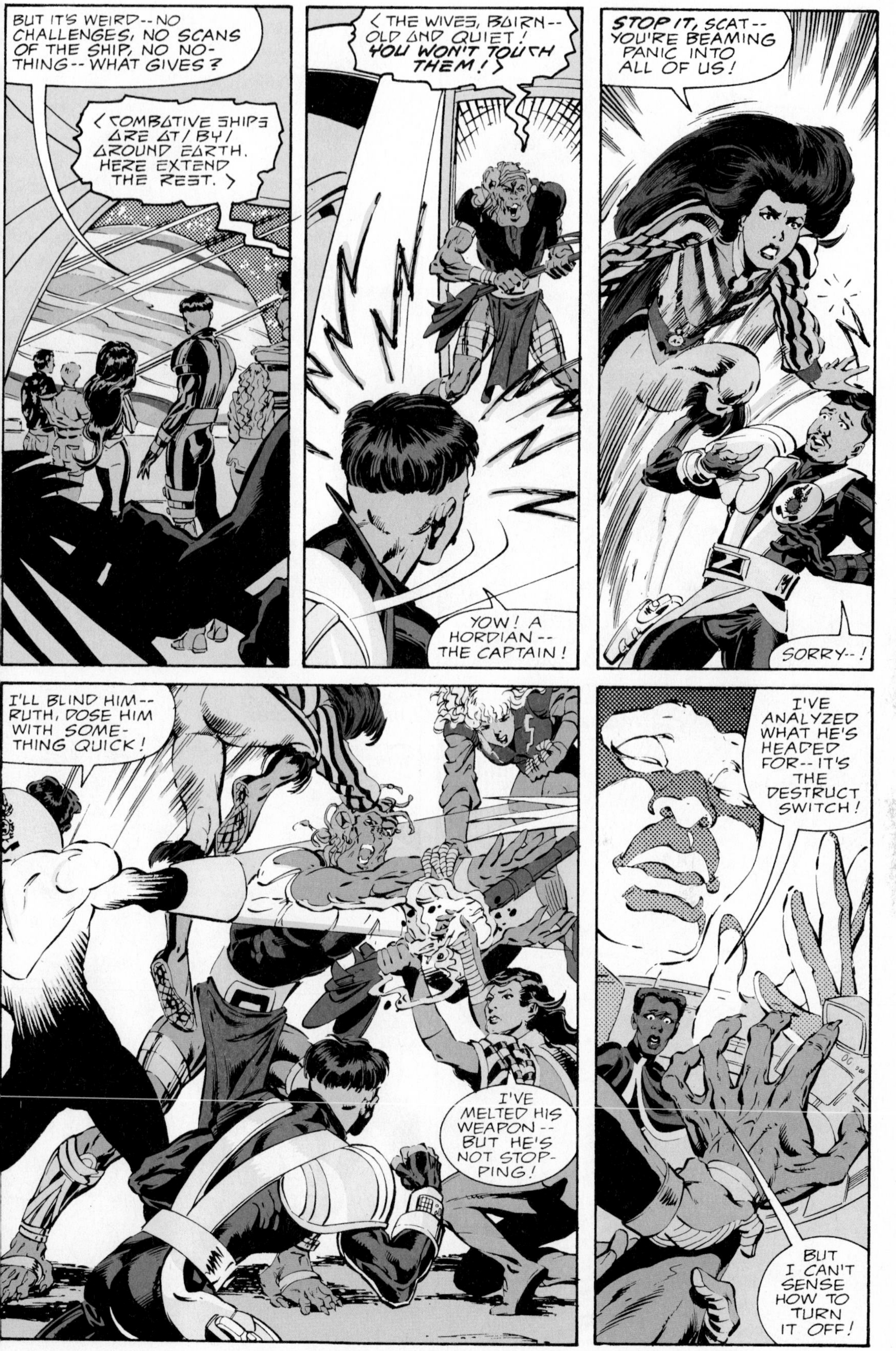
BUT IT'S WEIRD--NO CHALLENGES, NO SCANS OF THE SHIP, NO NO-THING--WHAT GIVES?
< COMBATIVE SHIPS ARE AT/BY/AROUND EARTH. HERE EXTEND THE REST. >
< THE WIVES, BAIRN--OLD AND QUIET! YOU WON'T TOUCH THEM! >
YOW! A HORDIAN--THE CAPTAIN!
STOP IT, SCAT--YOU'RE BEAMING PANIC INTO ALL OF US!
SORRY--!
I'LL BLIND HIM--RUTH, DOSE HIM WITH SOME-THING QUICK!
I'VE MELTED HIS WEAPON--BUT HE'S NOT STOP-PING!
I'VE ANALYZED WHAT HE'S HEADED FOR--IT'S THE DESTRUCT SWITCH!
BUT I CAN'T SENSE HOW TO TURN IT OFF!

<ARRGH! LORD, CANNOT SEE!>

<I NEED NO EYES ON MY BRIDGE!>

<MY DUTY! MY TRIBE! MY DESTINY!>

WOOOOUGH!

EXCITING, HEROIC. JUST LIKE IN THE MOVIES.

I HOPE IT FULFILLS YOU.

NOT YET.

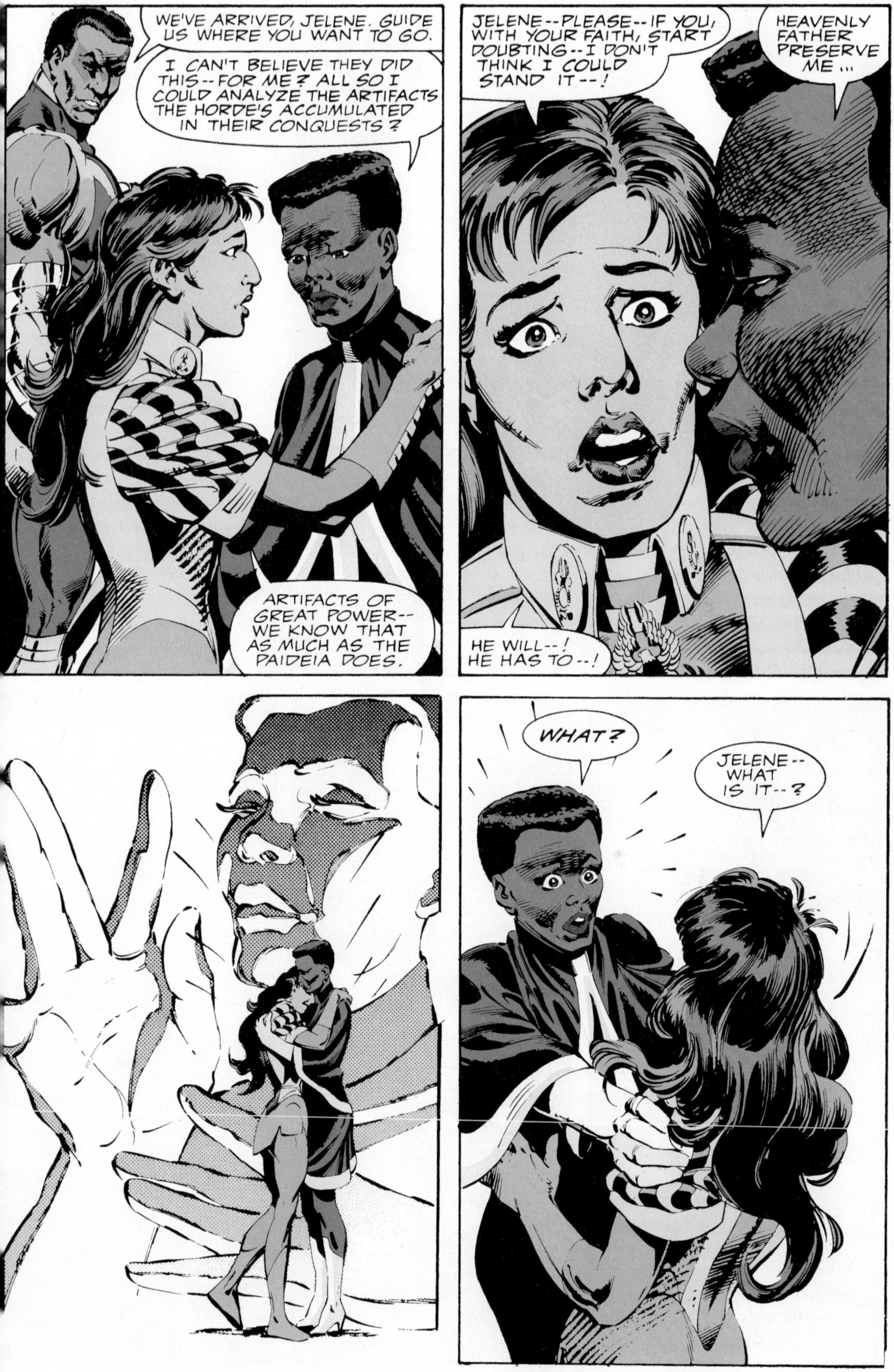
WE'VE ARRIVED, JELENE. GUIDE US WHERE YOU WANT TO GO.
I CAN'T BELIEVE THEY DID THIS--FOR ME? ALL SO I COULD ANALYZE THE ARTIFACTS THE HORDE'S ACCUMULATED IN THEIR CONQUESTS?
ARTIFACTS OF GREAT POWER--WE KNOW THAT AS MUCH AS THE PAIDEIA DOES.
JELENE--PLEASE--IF YOU, WITH YOUR FAITH, START DOUBTING--I DON'T THINK I COULD STAND IT--!
HEAVENLY FATHER PRESERVE ME...
HE WILL--! HE HAS TO--!
WHAT?
JELENE--WHAT IS IT--?

JELENE--! I'VE GOTTEN A LOT BETTER AT DECIPHERING HORDIAN HARDWARE SINCE OUR LAST SPACE TRIP, ROBERT * --THIS TIME I THINK WE'LL HAVE LANDING TRANSPONDERS AND EVERYTHING!

* ISSUES 6 AND 7.

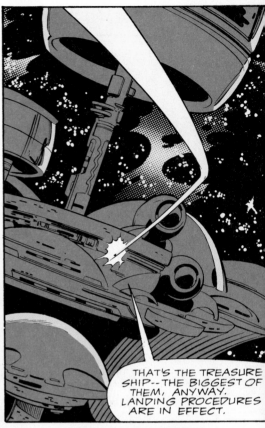

THAT'S THE TREASURE SHIP--THE BIGGEST OF THEM, ANYWAY. LANDING PROCEDURES ARE IN EFFECT.

SO FAR SO GOOD--EVERYONE AT THE READY.

EXTERNAL DOORS SHUT-- AIRLOCKS CONNECTED.

< WHY DOES THE LORD NOT DISEMBARK ? >

< SOMETHING'S WRONG-- GET SECURITY DOWN THERE--! >

BORN AGAIN

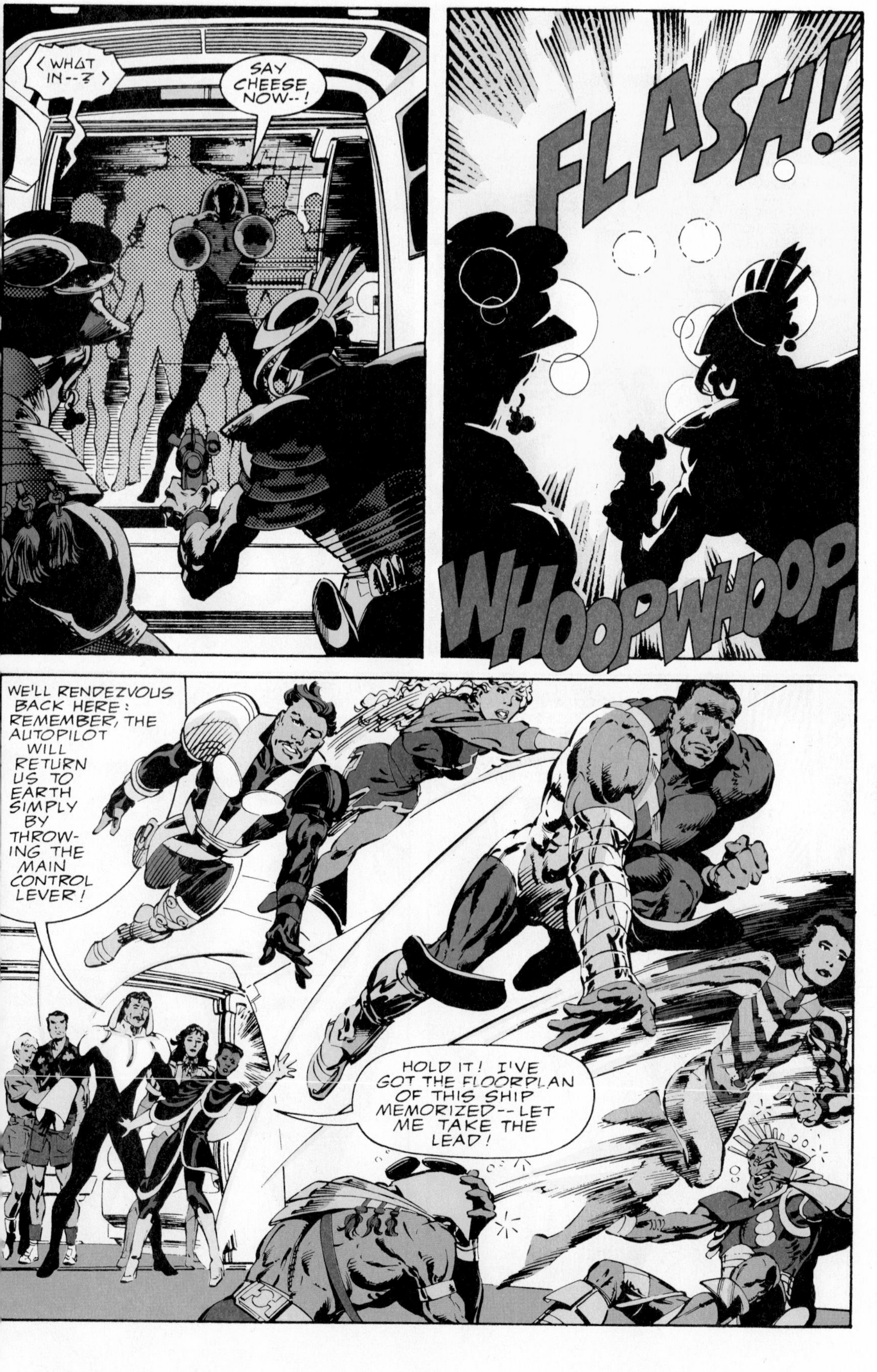
⟨ WHAT IN--? ⟩
SAY CHEESE NOW--!
FLASH!
WHOOPWHOOP
WE'LL RENDEZVOUS BACK HERE: REMEMBER, THE AUTOPILOT WILL RETURN US TO EARTH SIMPLY BY THROWING THE MAIN CONTROL LEVER!
HOLD IT! I'VE GOT THE FLOORPLAN OF THIS SHIP MEMORIZED--LET ME TAKE THE LEAD!

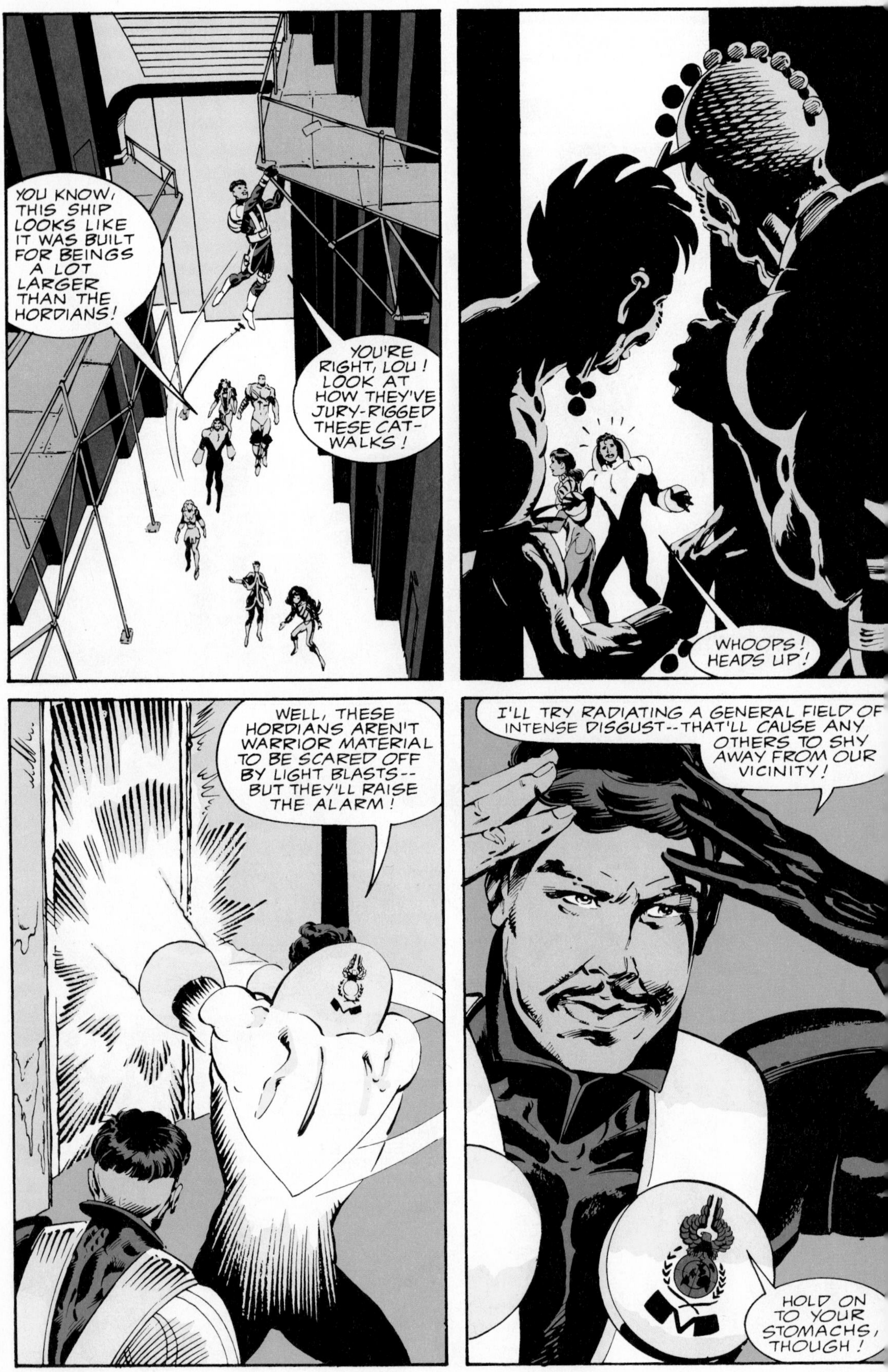

YOU KNOW, THIS SHIP LOOKS LIKE IT WAS BUILT FOR BEINGS A LOT LARGER THAN THE HORDIANS!
YOU'RE RIGHT, LOU! LOOK AT HOW THEY'VE JURY-RIGGED THESE CAT-WALKS!
WHOOPS! HEADS UP!
WELL, THESE HORDIANS AREN'T WARRIOR MATERIAL TO BE SCARED OFF BY LIGHT BLASTS-- BUT THEY'LL RAISE THE ALARM!
I'LL TRY RADIATING A GENERAL FIELD OF INTENSE DISGUST--THAT'LL CAUSE ANY OTHERS TO SHY AWAY FROM OUR VICINITY!
HOLD ON TO YOUR STOMACHS, THOUGH!

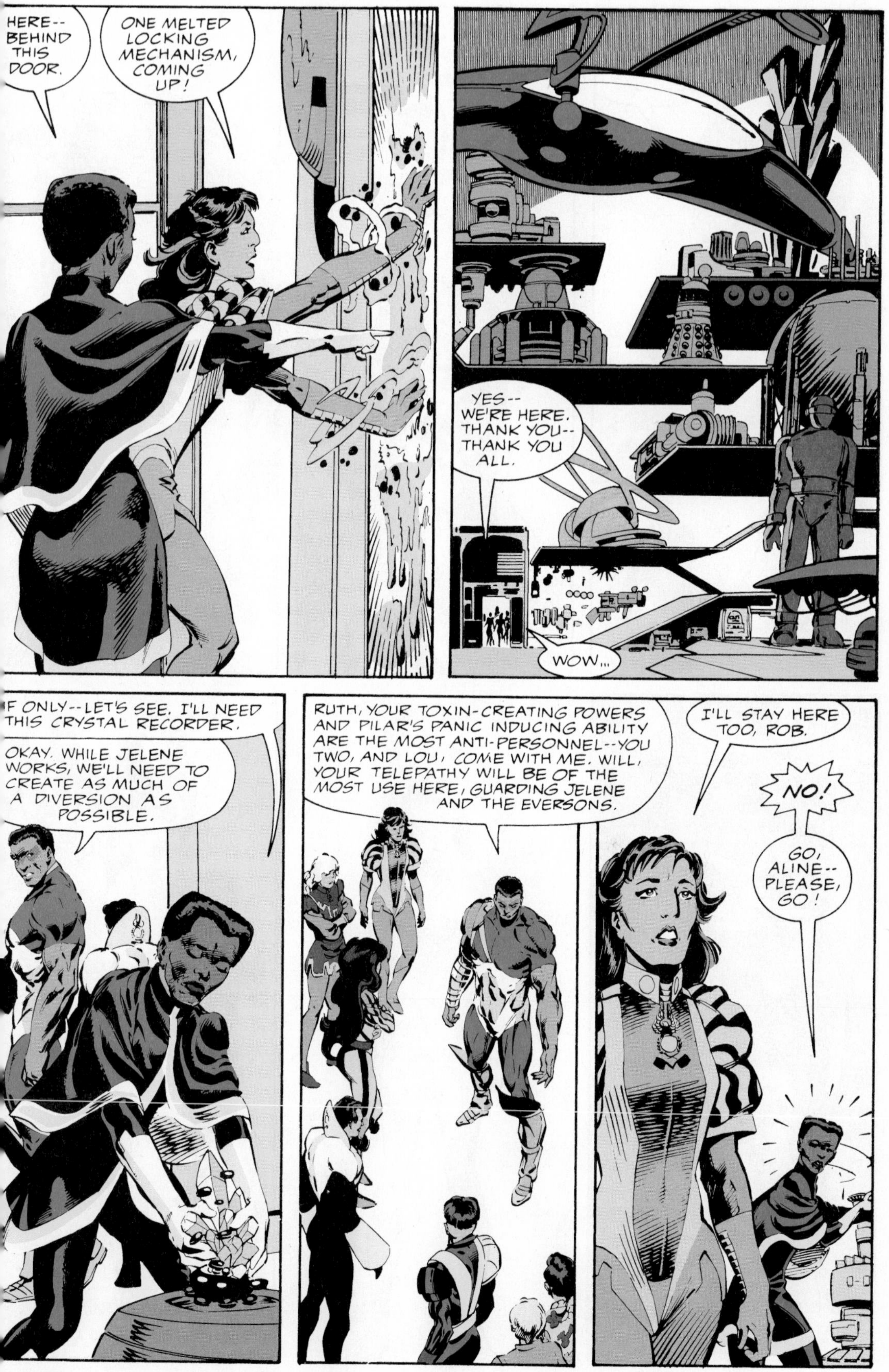
HERE-- BEHIND THIS DOOR.
ONE MELTED LOCKING MECHANISM, COMING UP!
YES-- WE'RE HERE. THANK YOU-- THANK YOU ALL.
WOW...
F ONLY--LET'S SEE. I'LL NEED THIS CRYSTAL RECORDER.
OKAY. WHILE JELENE WORKS, WE'LL NEED TO CREATE AS MUCH OF A DIVERSION AS POSSIBLE.
RUTH, YOUR TOXIN-CREATING POWERS AND PILAR'S PANIC INDUCING ABILITY ARE THE MOST ANTI-PERSONNEL--YOU TWO, AND LOU, COME WITH ME. WILL, YOUR TELEPATHY WILL BE OF THE MOST USE HERE, GUARDING JELENE AND THE EVERSONS.
I'LL STAY HERE TOO, ROB.
NO!
GO, ALINE-- PLEASE, GO!

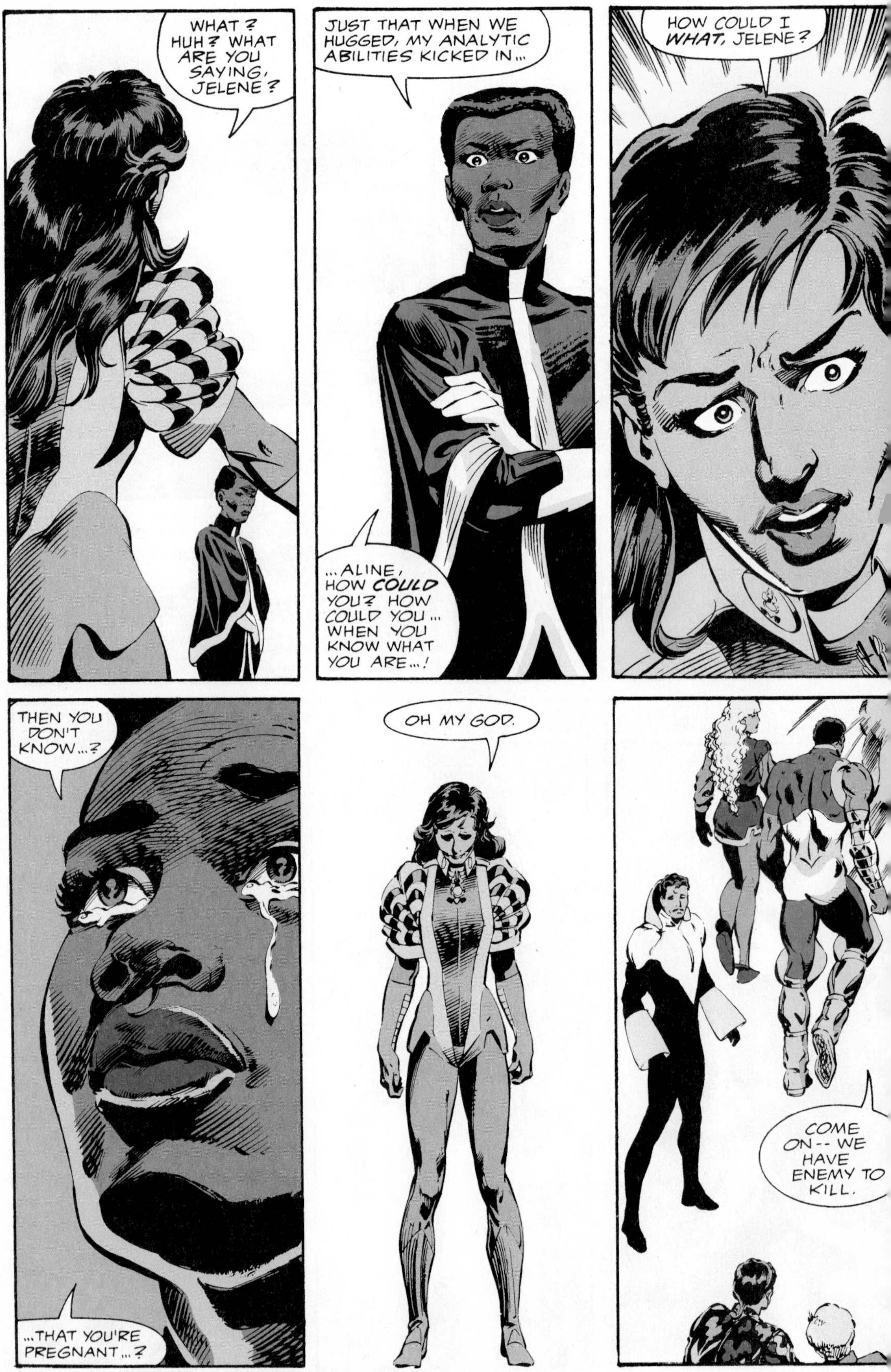
WHAT? HUH? WHAT ARE YOU SAYING, JELENE?
JUST THAT WHEN WE HUGGED, MY ANALYTIC ABILITIES KICKED IN...
...ALINE, HOW COULD YOU? HOW COULD YOU... WHEN YOU KNOW WHAT YOU ARE...!
HOW COULD I WHAT, JELENE?
THEN YOU DON'T KNOW...?
...THAT YOU'RE PREGNANT...?
OH MY GOD.
COME ON-- WE HAVE ENEMY TO KILL.

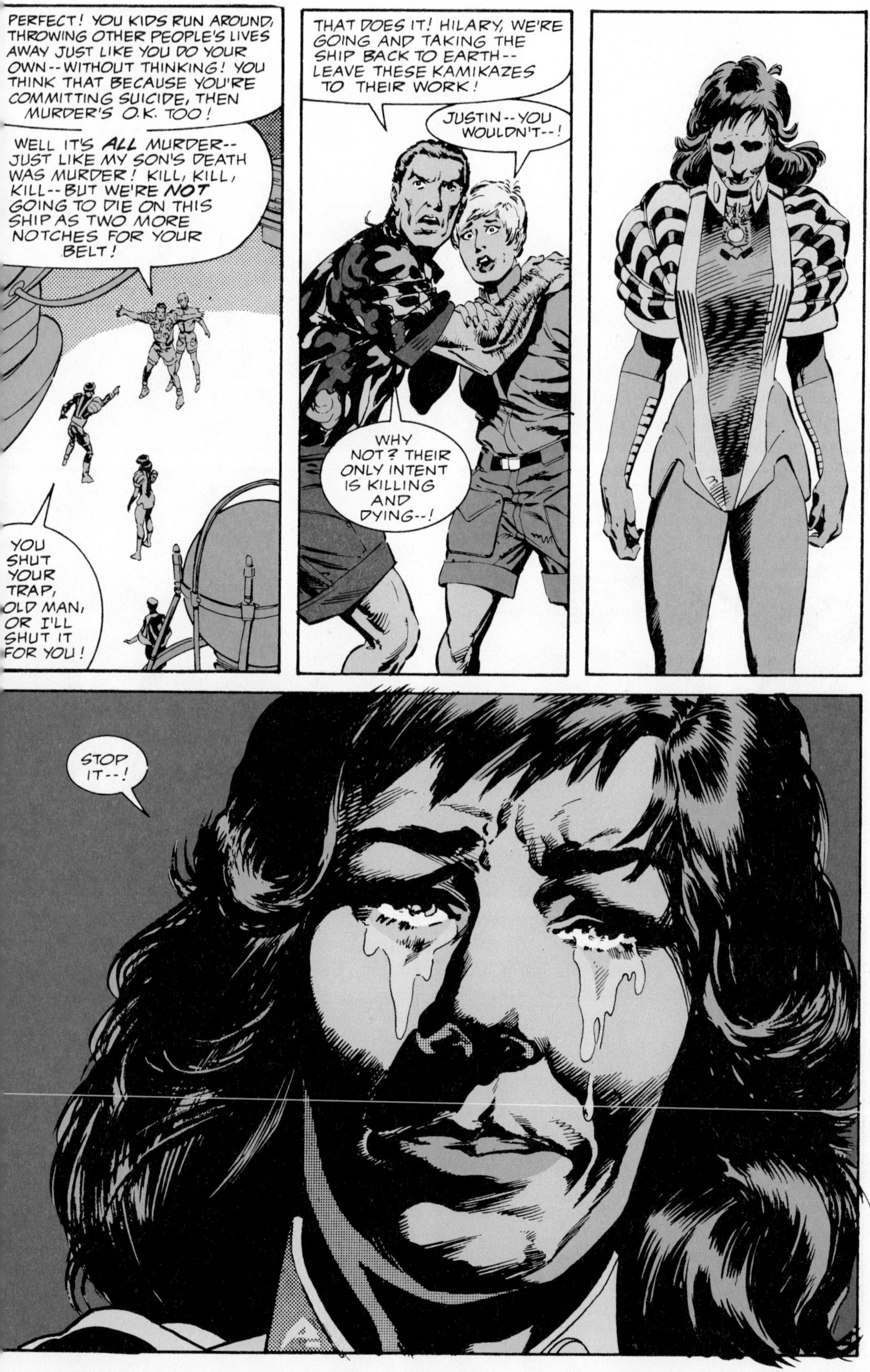
PERFECT! YOU KIDS RUN AROUND, THROWING OTHER PEOPLE'S LIVES AWAY JUST LIKE YOU DO YOUR OWN--WITHOUT THINKING! YOU THINK THAT BECAUSE YOU'RE COMMITTING SUICIDE, THEN MURDER'S O.K. TOO!
WELL IT'S ALL MURDER--JUST LIKE MY SON'S DEATH WAS MURDER! KILL, KILL, KILL--BUT WE'RE NOT GOING TO DIE ON THIS SHIP AS TWO MORE NOTCHES FOR YOUR BELT!
YOU SHUT YOUR TRAP, OLD MAN, OR I'LL SHUT IT FOR YOU!
THAT DOES IT! HILARY, WE'RE GOING AND TAKING THE SHIP BACK TO EARTH--LEAVE THESE KAMIKAZES TO THEIR WORK!
JUSTIN--YOU WOULDN'T--!
WHY NOT? THEIR ONLY INTENT IS KILLING AND DYING--!
STOP IT--!

THE UPWARD GRADIENT OF YOUR INFECTION HAS STABILIZED, BETH, BUT I'M AFRAID THAT'S ABOUT ALL--!

KIMMO...

I'VE BEEN THINKING...THAT YOU'RE ANGRY AT ME FOR THE SAME REASON YOU'RE ANGRY AT YOURSELF... GOOD INTENTIONS GONE WRONG--!

YOU DISCOVERED THE MORITURI PROCESS AND GAVE IT TO THE PAIDEIA AS EARTH'S DEFENSE-- AND IT'S BROUGHT ONLY PAIN AND RUIN IN ITS WAKE.

THE LORD KNOWS WE'RE PROBABLY BOTH TO BLAME, KIMMO--AND WE'VE GOT DEATHS PAST AND FUTURE ON OUR HEADS. AND THE EXCUSE THAT WE DID IT BECAUSE WE *CARED* ISN'T ENOUGH--

--BUT WE DID CARE, DIDN'T WE? KIMMO?

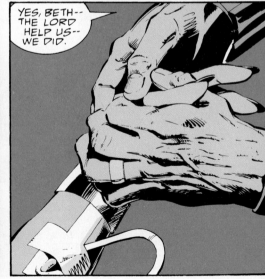

YES, BETH-- THE LORD HELP US-- WE DID.

280

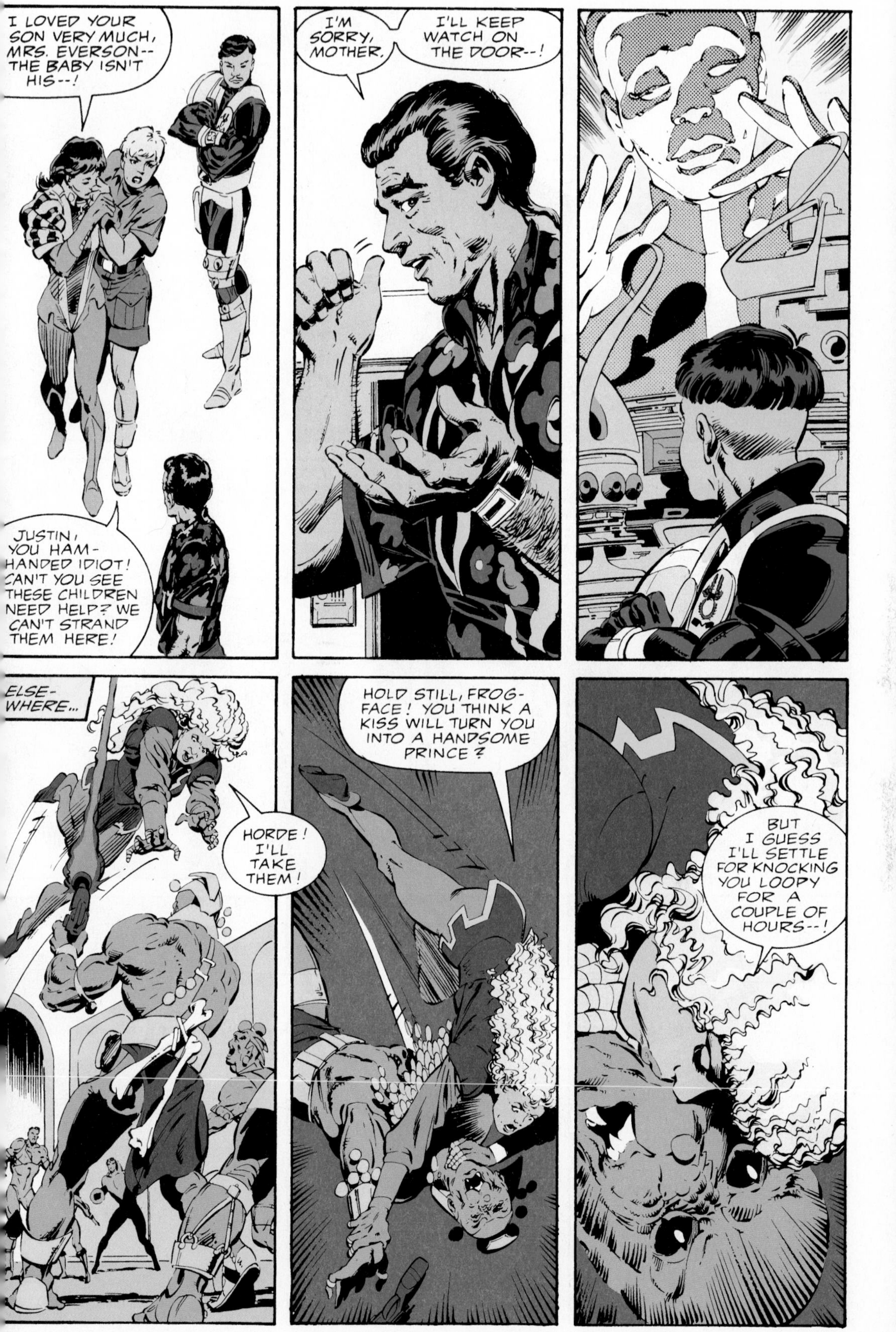
I LOVED YOUR SON VERY MUCH, MRS. EVERSON-- THE BABY ISN'T HIS--!
JUSTIN, YOU HAM-HANDED IDIOT! CAN'T YOU SEE THESE CHILDREN NEED HELP? WE CAN'T STRAND THEM HERE!
I'M SORRY, MOTHER.
I'LL KEEP WATCH ON THE DOOR--!
ELSE-WHERE...
HORDE! I'LL TAKE THEM!
HOLD STILL, FROG-FACE! YOU THINK A KISS WILL TURN YOU INTO A HANDSOME PRINCE?
BUT I GUESS I'LL SETTLE FOR KNOCKING YOU LOOPY FOR A COUPLE OF HOURS--!

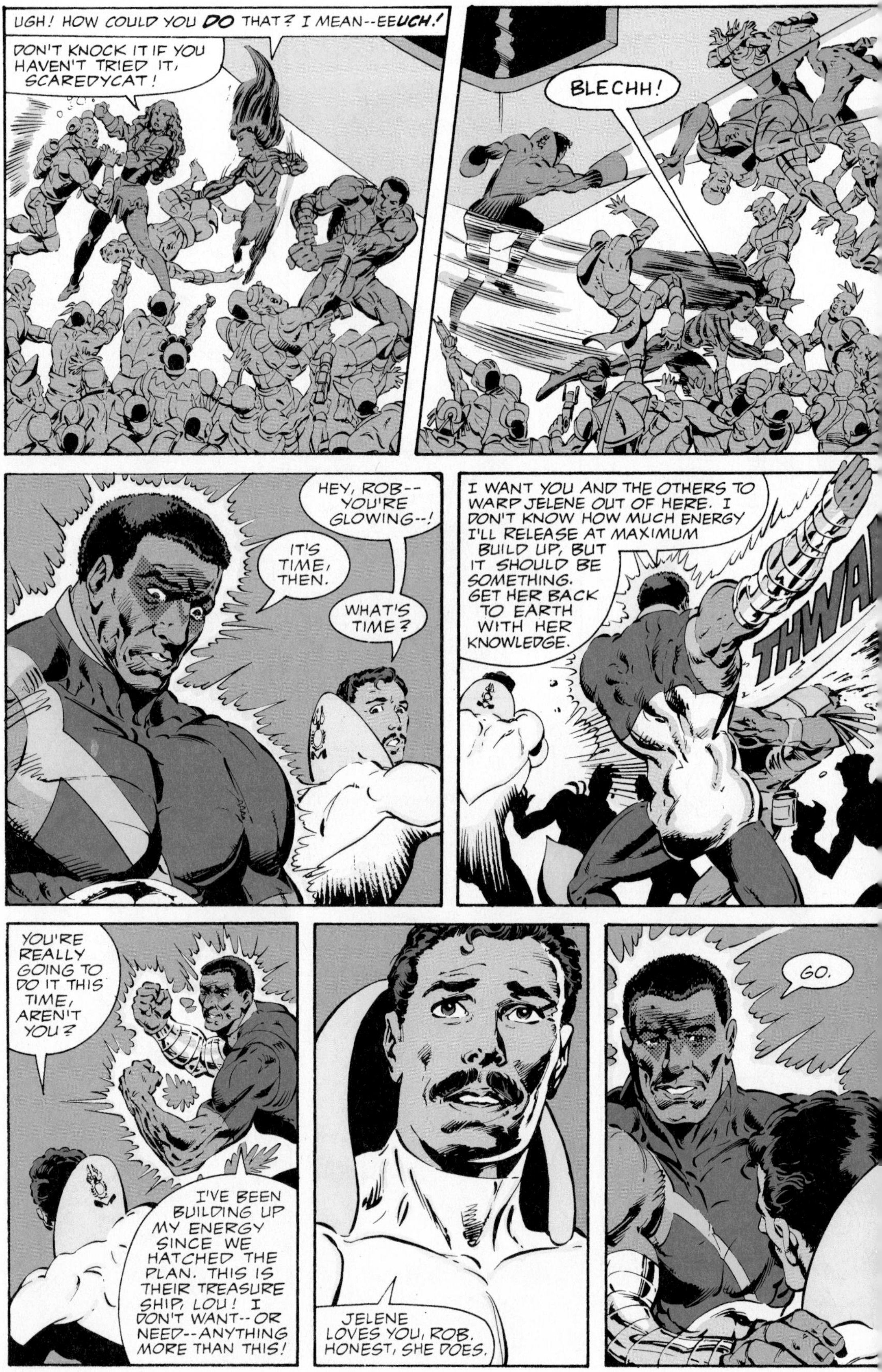
UGH! HOW COULD YOU DO THAT? I MEAN--EEUCH!
DON'T KNOCK IT IF YOU HAVEN'T TRIED IT, SCAREDYCAT!
BLECHH!
HEY, ROB-- YOU'RE GLOWING--!
IT'S TIME, THEN.
WHAT'S TIME?
I WANT YOU AND THE OTHERS TO WARP JELENE OUT OF HERE. I DON'T KNOW HOW MUCH ENERGY I'LL RELEASE AT MAXIMUM BUILD UP, BUT IT SHOULD BE SOMETHING. GET HER BACK TO EARTH WITH HER KNOWLEDGE.
YOU'RE REALLY GOING TO DO IT THIS TIME, AREN'T YOU?
I'VE BEEN BUILDING UP MY ENERGY SINCE WE HATCHED THE PLAN. THIS IS THEIR TREASURE SHIP, LOU! I DON'T WANT--OR NEED--ANYTHING MORE THAN THIS!
JELENE LOVES YOU, ROB. HONEST, SHE DOES.
GO.

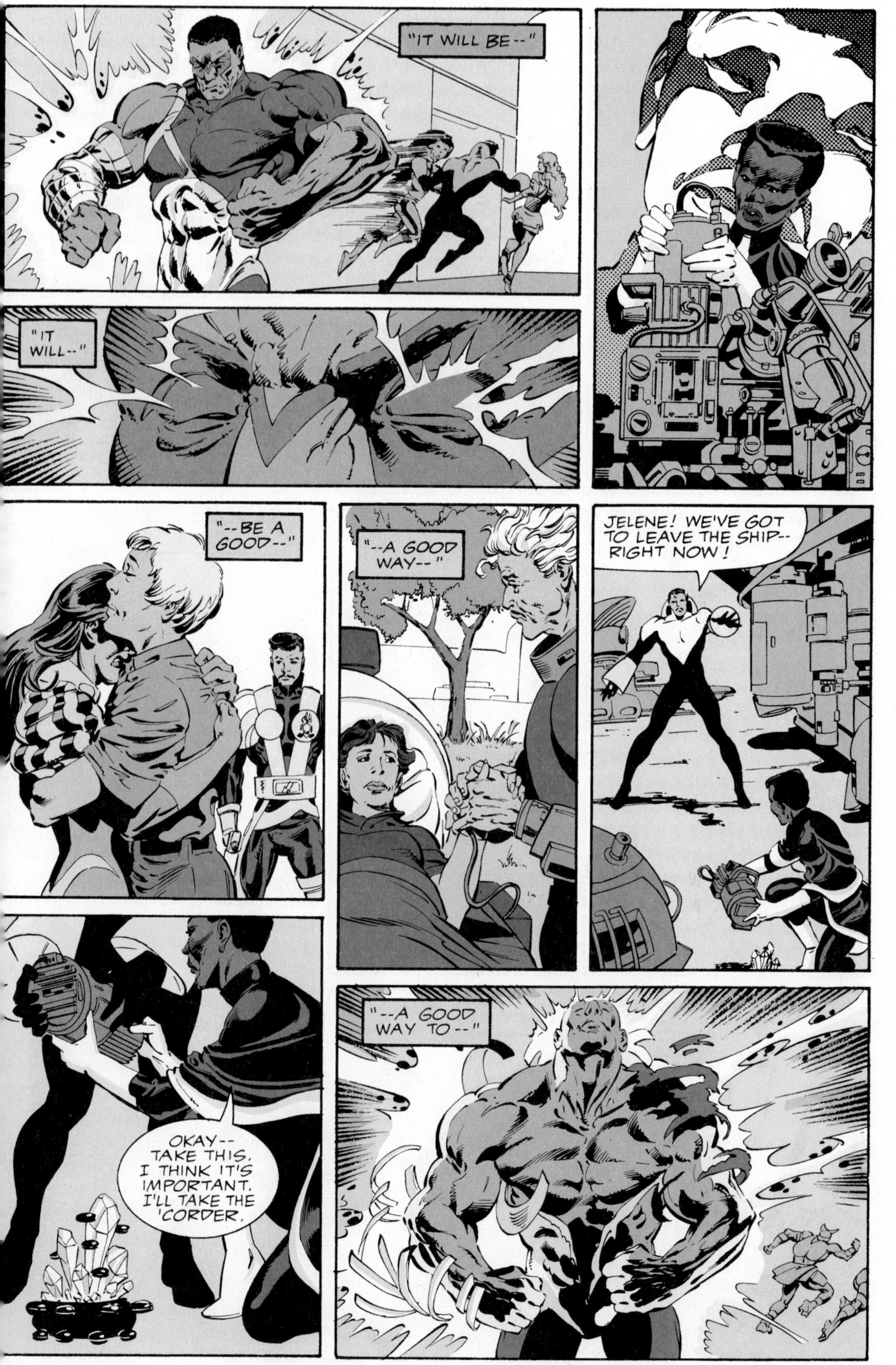
"IT WILL BE--"
"IT WILL--"
"--BE A GOOD--"
"--A GOOD WAY--"
JELENE! WE'VE GOT TO LEAVE THE SHIP-- RIGHT NOW!
OKAY-- TAKE THIS. I THINK IT'S IMPORTANT. I'LL TAKE THE 'CORDER.
"--A GOOD WAY TO--"

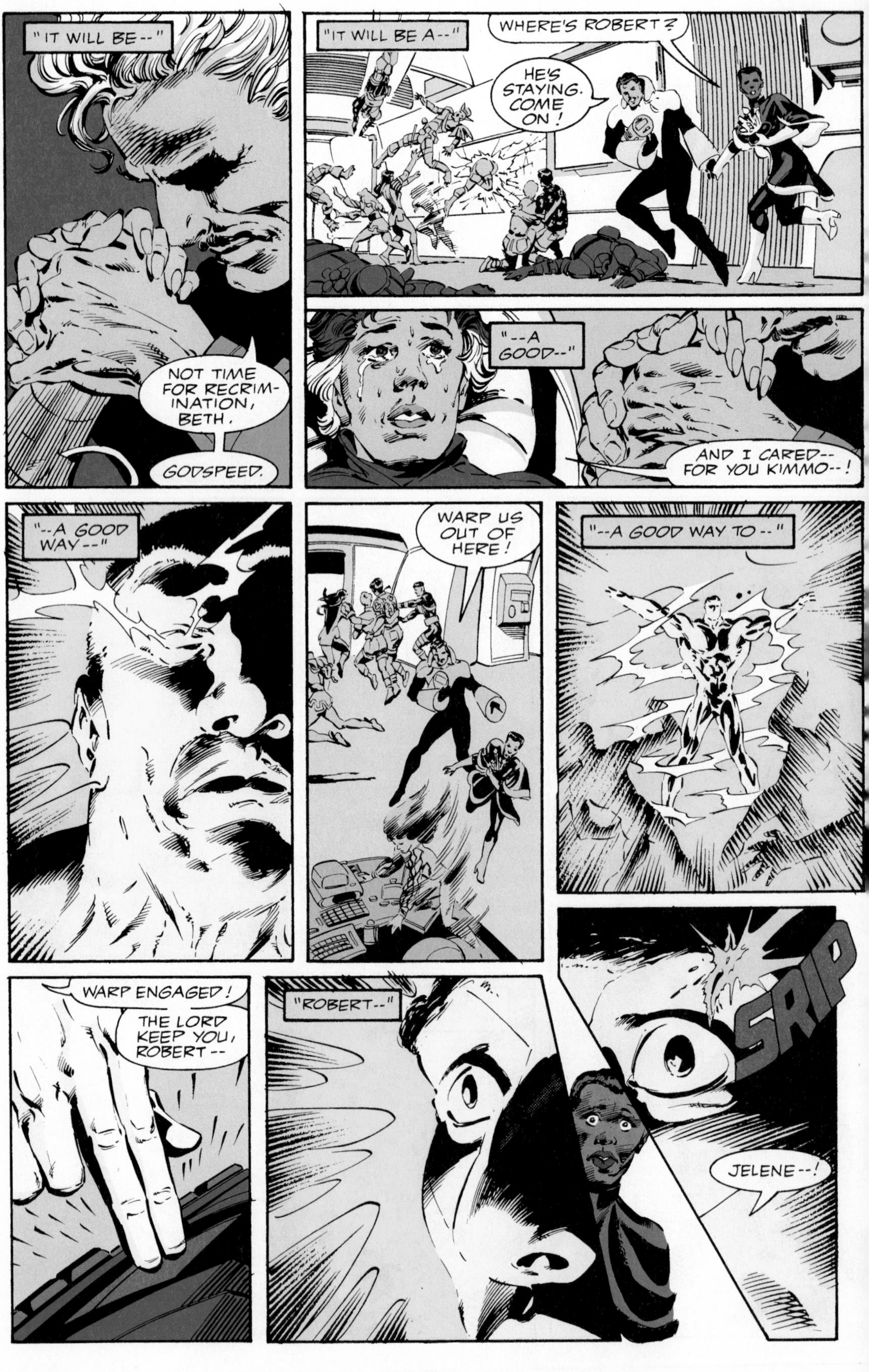
"IT WILL BE--"
NOT TIME FOR RECRIMINATION, BETH.
GODSPEED.
"IT WILL BE A--"
WHERE'S ROBERT?
HE'S STAYING. COME ON!
"--A GOOD--"
AND I CARED-- FOR YOU KIMMO--!
"--A GOOD WAY--"
WARP US OUT OF HERE!
"--A GOOD WAY TO--"
WARP ENGAGED!
THE LORD KEEP YOU, ROBERT--
"ROBERT--"
SRIP
JELENE--!

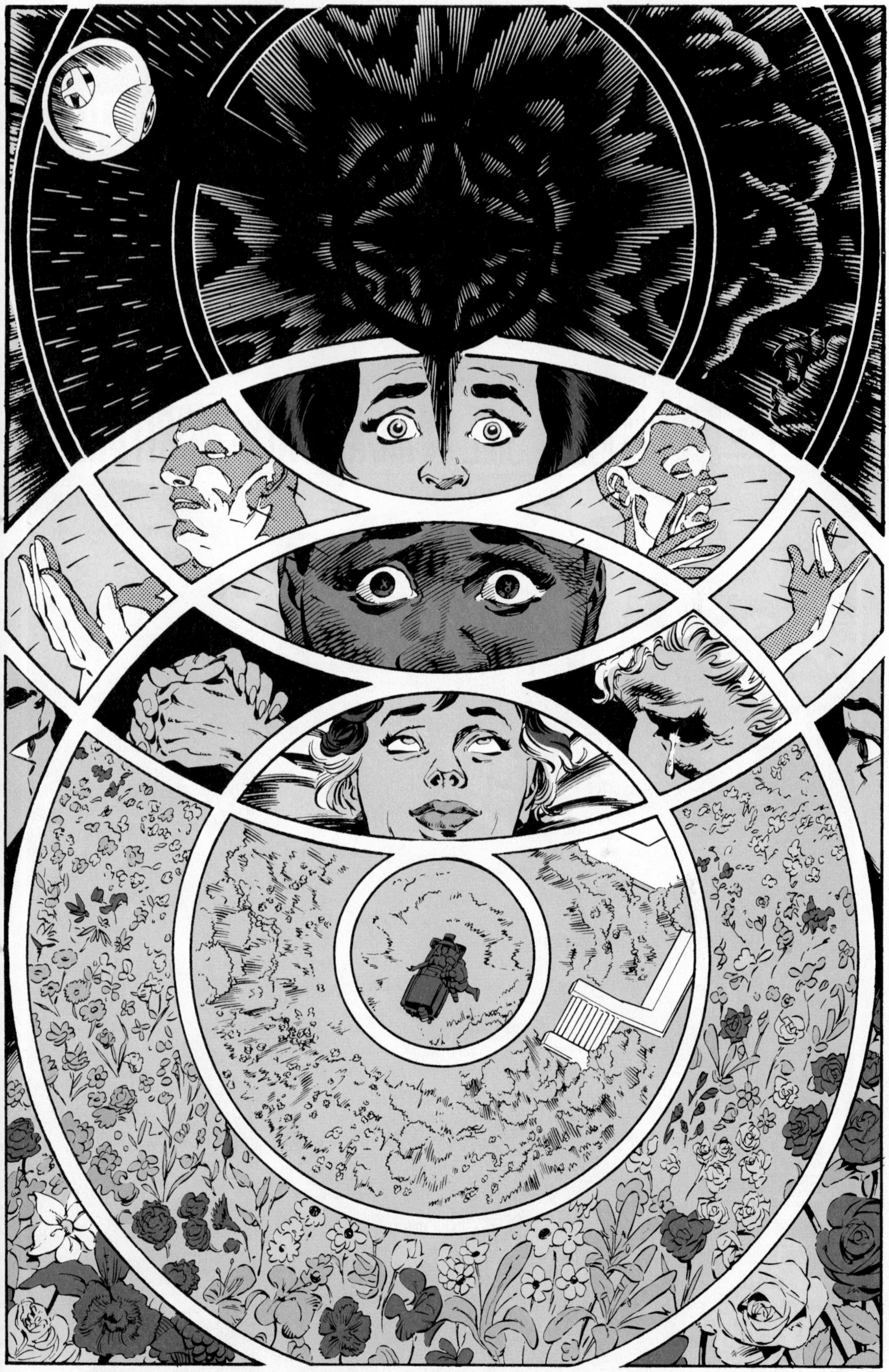

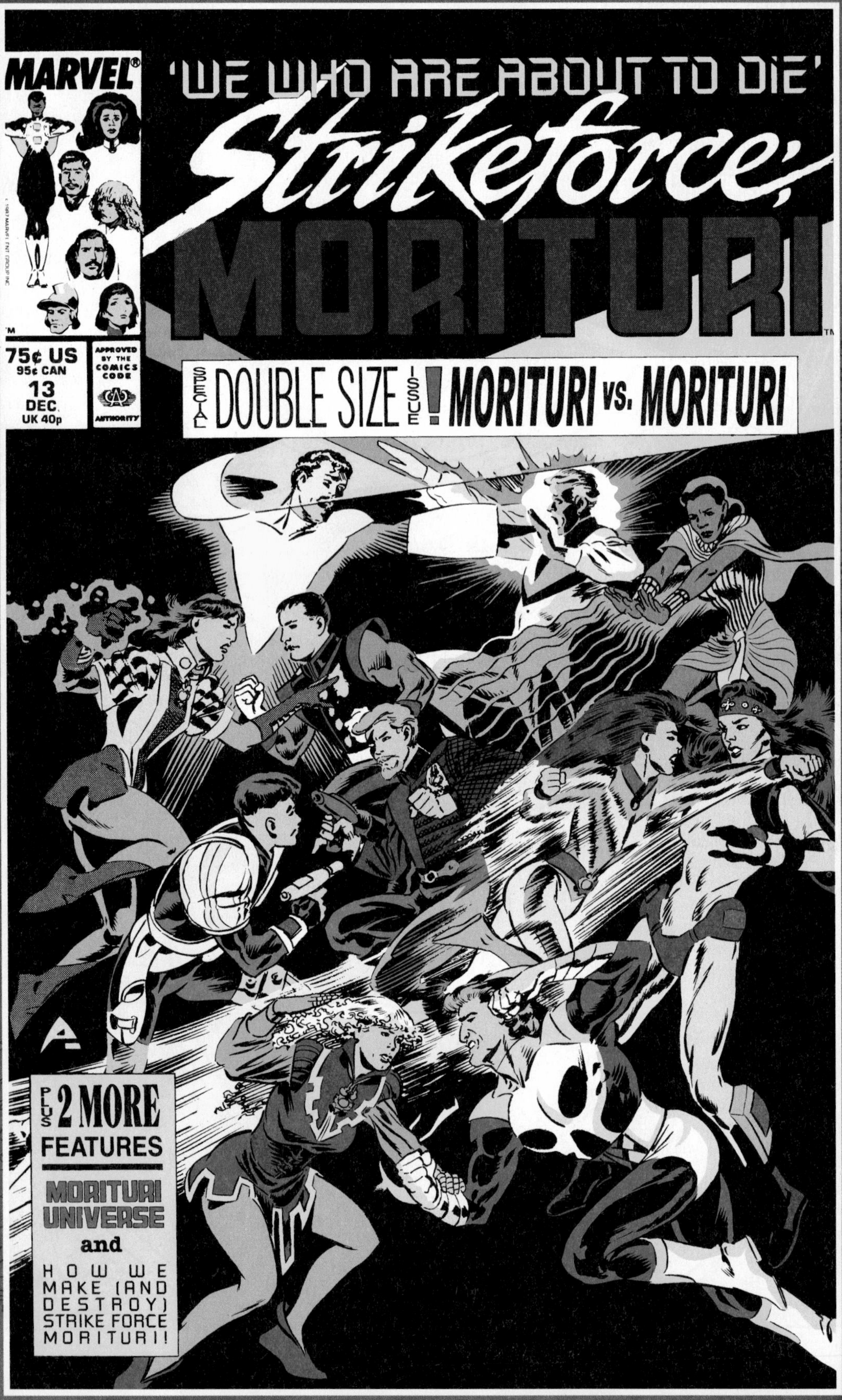
MARVEL®
'WE WHO ARE ABOUT TO DIE'
Strikeforce:
MORITURI
75¢ US
95¢ CAN
13
DEC.
UK 40p
APPROVED BY THE COMICS CODE AUTHORITY
SPECIAL DOUBLE SIZE ISSUE! MORITURI VS. MORITURI
PLUS 2 MORE FEATURES
MORITURI UNIVERSE
and
HOW WE MAKE (AND DESTROY) STRIKE FORCE MORITURI!

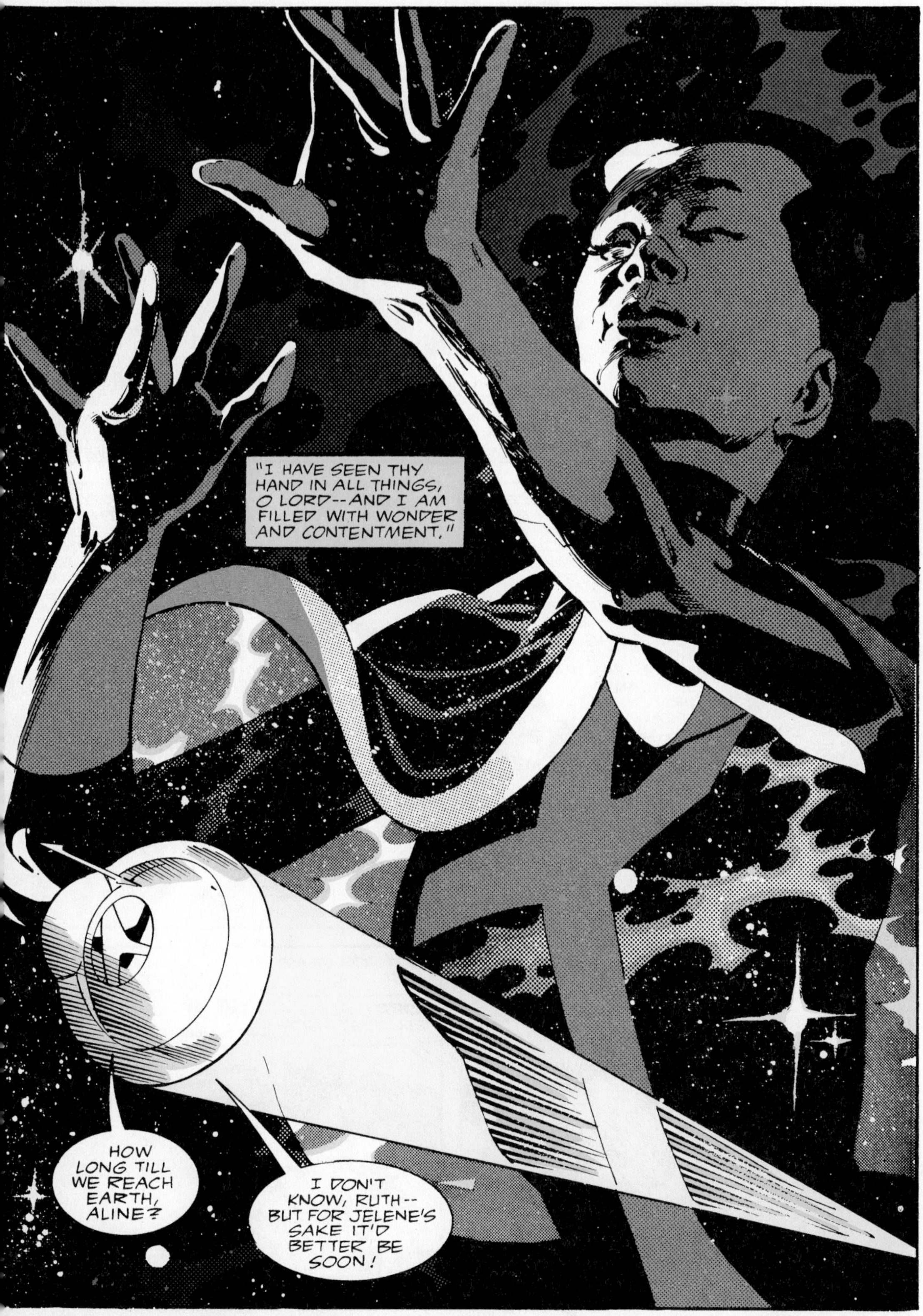
"I HAVE SEEN THY HAND IN ALL THINGS, O LORD--AND I AM FILLED WITH WONDER AND CONTENTMENT."
HOW LONG TILL WE REACH EARTH, ALINE?
I DON'T KNOW, RUTH--BUT FOR JELENE'S SAKE IT'D BETTER BE SOON!

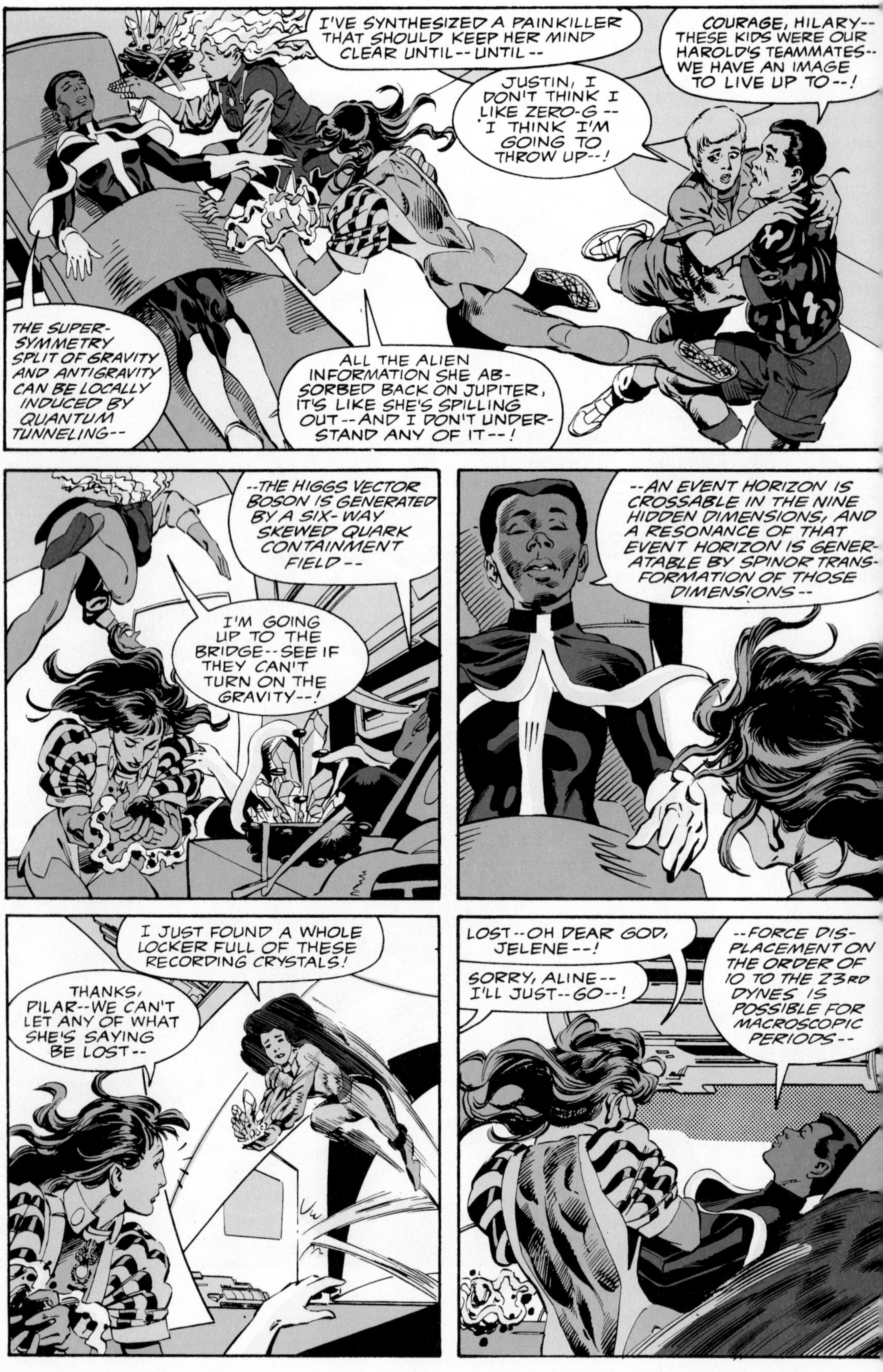

I'VE SYNTHESIZED A PAINKILLER THAT SHOULD KEEP HER MIND CLEAR UNTIL-- UNTIL--
JUSTIN, I DON'T THINK I LIKE ZERO-G -- I THINK I'M GOING TO THROW UP--!
COURAGE, HILARY-- THESE KIDS WERE OUR HAROLD'S TEAMMATES-- WE HAVE AN IMAGE TO LIVE UP TO--!
THE SUPER-SYMMETRY SPLIT OF GRAVITY AND ANTIGRAVITY CAN BE LOCALLY INDUCED BY QUANTUM TUNNELING--
ALL THE ALIEN INFORMATION SHE ABSORBED BACK ON JUPITER, IT'S LIKE SHE'S SPILLING OUT--AND I DON'T UNDERSTAND ANY OF IT--!
--THE HIGGS VECTOR BOSON IS GENERATED BY A SIX-WAY SKEWED QUARK CONTAINMENT FIELD--
I'M GOING UP TO THE BRIDGE--SEE IF THEY CAN'T TURN ON THE GRAVITY--!
--AN EVENT HORIZON IS CROSSABLE IN THE NINE HIDDEN DIMENSIONS, AND A RESONANCE OF THAT EVENT HORIZON IS GENERATABLE BY SPINOR TRANSFORMATION OF THOSE DIMENSIONS--
I JUST FOUND A WHOLE LOCKER FULL OF THESE RECORDING CRYSTALS!
THANKS, PILAR--WE CAN'T LET ANY OF WHAT SHE'S SAYING BE LOST--
LOST--OH DEAR GOD, JELENE--!
SORRY, ALINE-- I'LL JUST--GO--!
--FORCE DISPLACEMENT ON THE ORDER OF 10 TO THE 23RD DYNES IS POSSIBLE FOR MACROSCOPIC PERIODS--

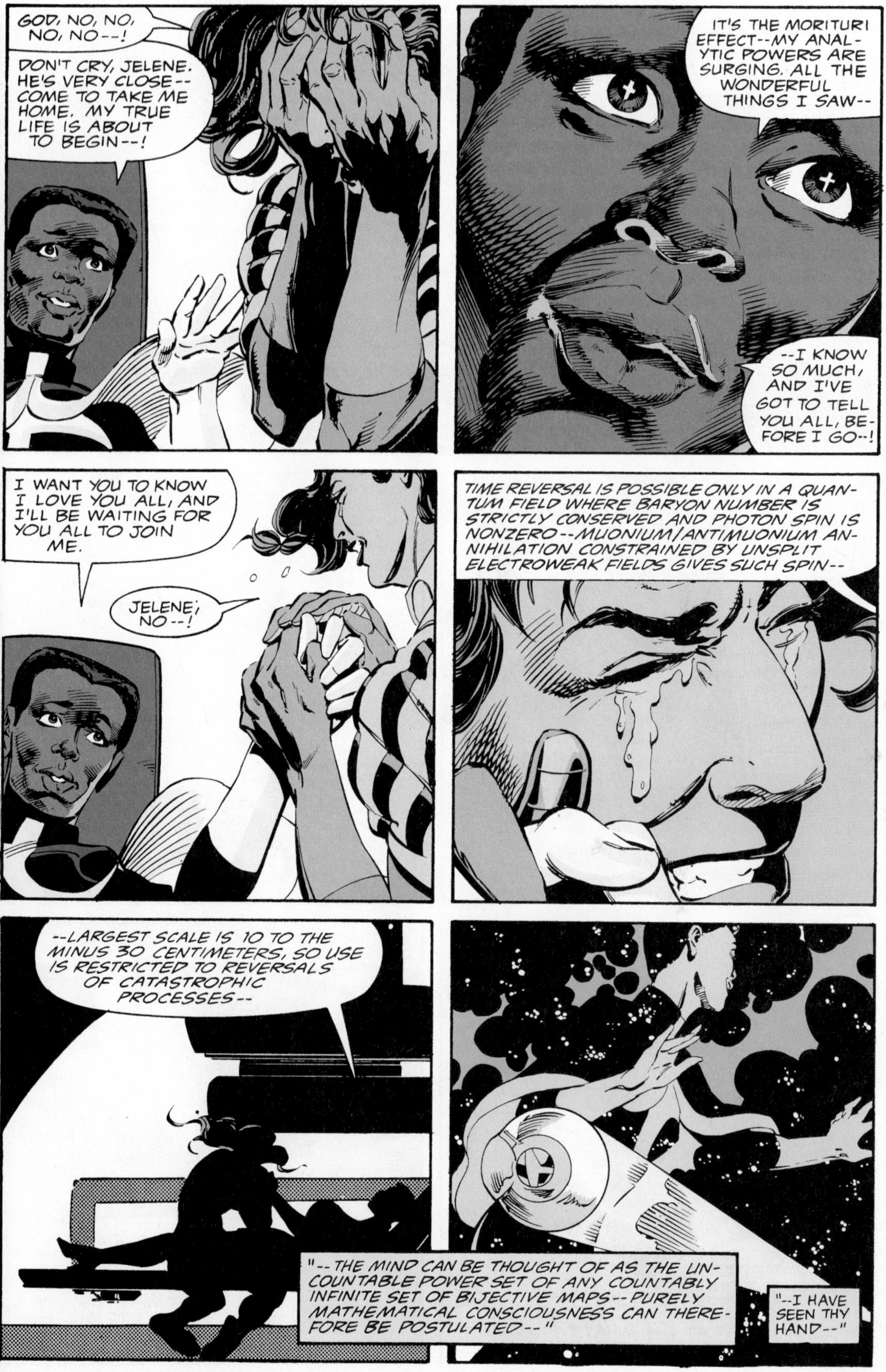
GOD, NO, NO, NO, NO--!
DON'T CRY, JELENE. HE'S VERY CLOSE--COME TO TAKE ME HOME. MY TRUE LIFE IS ABOUT TO BEGIN--!
IT'S THE MORITURI EFFECT--MY ANALYTIC POWERS ARE SURGING. ALL THE WONDERFUL THINGS I SAW--
--I KNOW SO MUCH, AND I'VE GOT TO TELL YOU ALL, BEFORE I GO--!
I WANT YOU TO KNOW I LOVE YOU ALL, AND I'LL BE WAITING FOR YOU ALL TO JOIN ME.
JELENE; NO--!
TIME REVERSAL IS POSSIBLE ONLY IN A QUANTUM FIELD WHERE BARYON NUMBER IS STRICTLY CONSERVED AND PHOTON SPIN IS NONZERO--MUONIUM/ANTIMUONIUM ANNIHILATION CONSTRAINED BY UNSPLIT ELECTROWEAK FIELDS GIVES SUCH SPIN--
--LARGEST SCALE IS 10 TO THE MINUS 30 CENTIMETERS, SO USE IS RESTRICTED TO REVERSALS OF CATASTROPHIC PROCESSES--
"--THE MIND CAN BE THOUGHT OF AS THE UNCOUNTABLE POWER SET OF ANY COUNTABLY INFINITE SET OF BIJECTIVE MAPS--PURELY MATHEMATICAL CONSCIOUSNESS CAN THEREFORE BE POSTULATED--"
"--I HAVE SEEN THY HAND--"

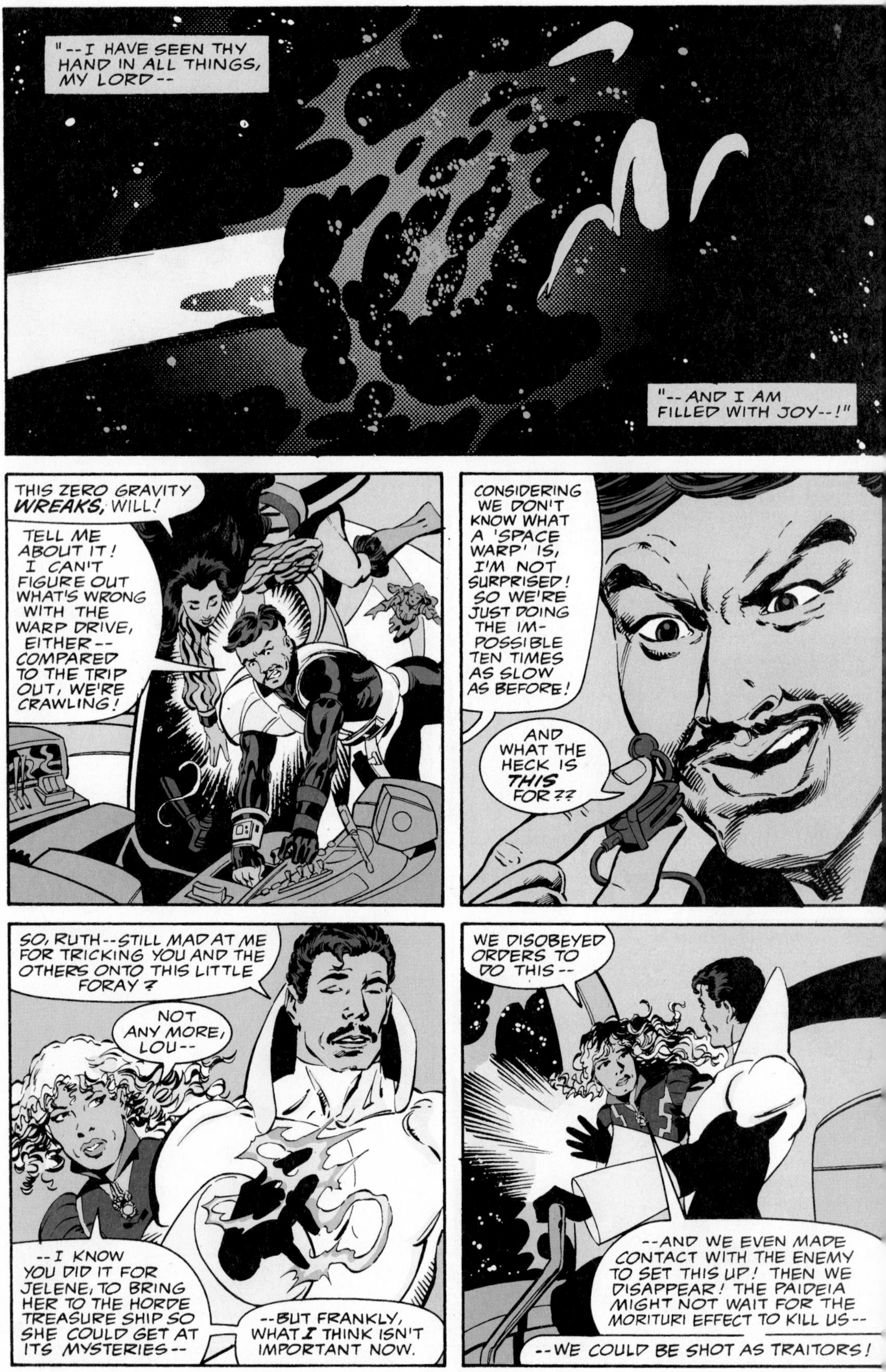
"--I HAVE SEEN THY HAND IN ALL THINGS, MY LORD--
"--AND I AM FILLED WITH JOY--!"
THIS ZERO GRAVITY WREAKS, WILL!
TELL ME ABOUT IT! I CAN'T FIGURE OUT WHAT'S WRONG WITH THE WARP DRIVE, EITHER--COMPARED TO THE TRIP OUT, WE'RE CRAWLING!
CONSIDERING WE DON'T KNOW WHAT A 'SPACE WARP' IS, I'M NOT SURPRISED! SO WE'RE JUST DOING THE IM-POSSIBLE TEN TIMES AS SLOW AS BEFORE!
AND WHAT THE HECK IS THIS FOR??
SO, RUTH--STILL MAD AT ME FOR TRICKING YOU AND THE OTHERS ONTO THIS LITTLE FORAY?
NOT ANY MORE, LOU--
--I KNOW YOU DID IT FOR JELENE, TO BRING HER TO THE HORDE TREASURE SHIP SO SHE COULD GET AT ITS MYSTERIES--
--BUT FRANKLY, WHAT I THINK ISN'T IMPORTANT NOW.
WE DISOBEYED ORDERS TO DO THIS--
--AND WE EVEN MADE CONTACT WITH THE ENEMY TO SET THIS UP! THEN WE DISAPPEAR! THE PAIDEIA MIGHT NOT WAIT FOR THE MORITURI EFFECT TO KILL US--
--WE COULD BE SHOT AS TRAITORS!

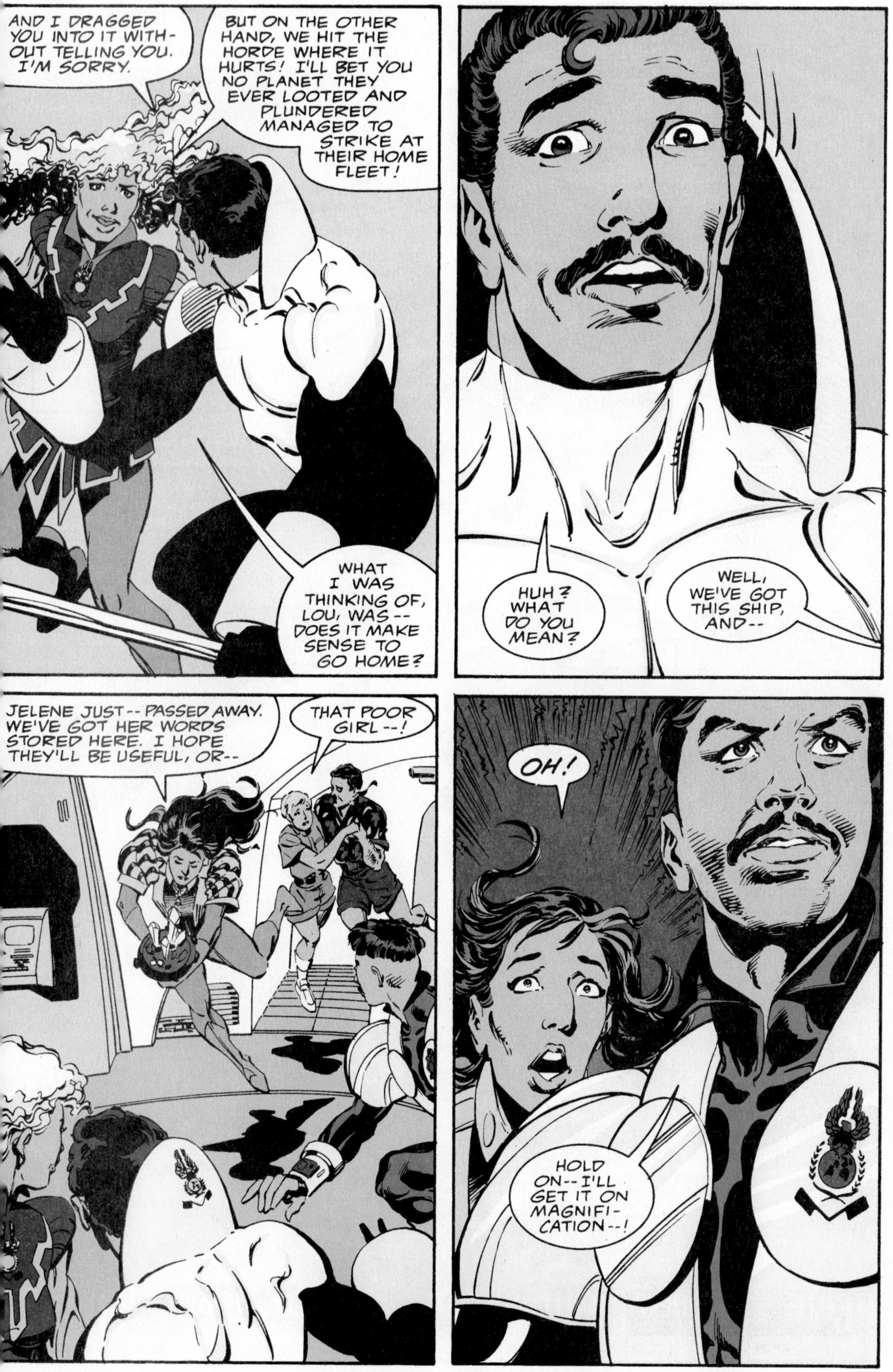
AND I DRAGGED YOU INTO IT WITH-OUT TELLING YOU. I'M SORRY.
BUT ON THE OTHER HAND, WE HIT THE HORDE WHERE IT HURTS! I'LL BET YOU NO PLANET THEY EVER LOOTED AND PLUNDERED MANAGED TO STRIKE AT THEIR HOME FLEET!
WHAT I WAS THINKING OF, LOU, WAS-- DOES IT MAKE SENSE TO GO HOME?
HUH? WHAT DO YOU MEAN?
WELL, WE'VE GOT THIS SHIP, AND--
JELENE JUST-- PASSED AWAY. WE'VE GOT HER WORDS STORED HERE. I HOPE THEY'LL BE USEFUL, OR--
THAT POOR GIRL--!
OH!
HOLD ON--I'LL GET IT ON MAGNIFI-CATION--!

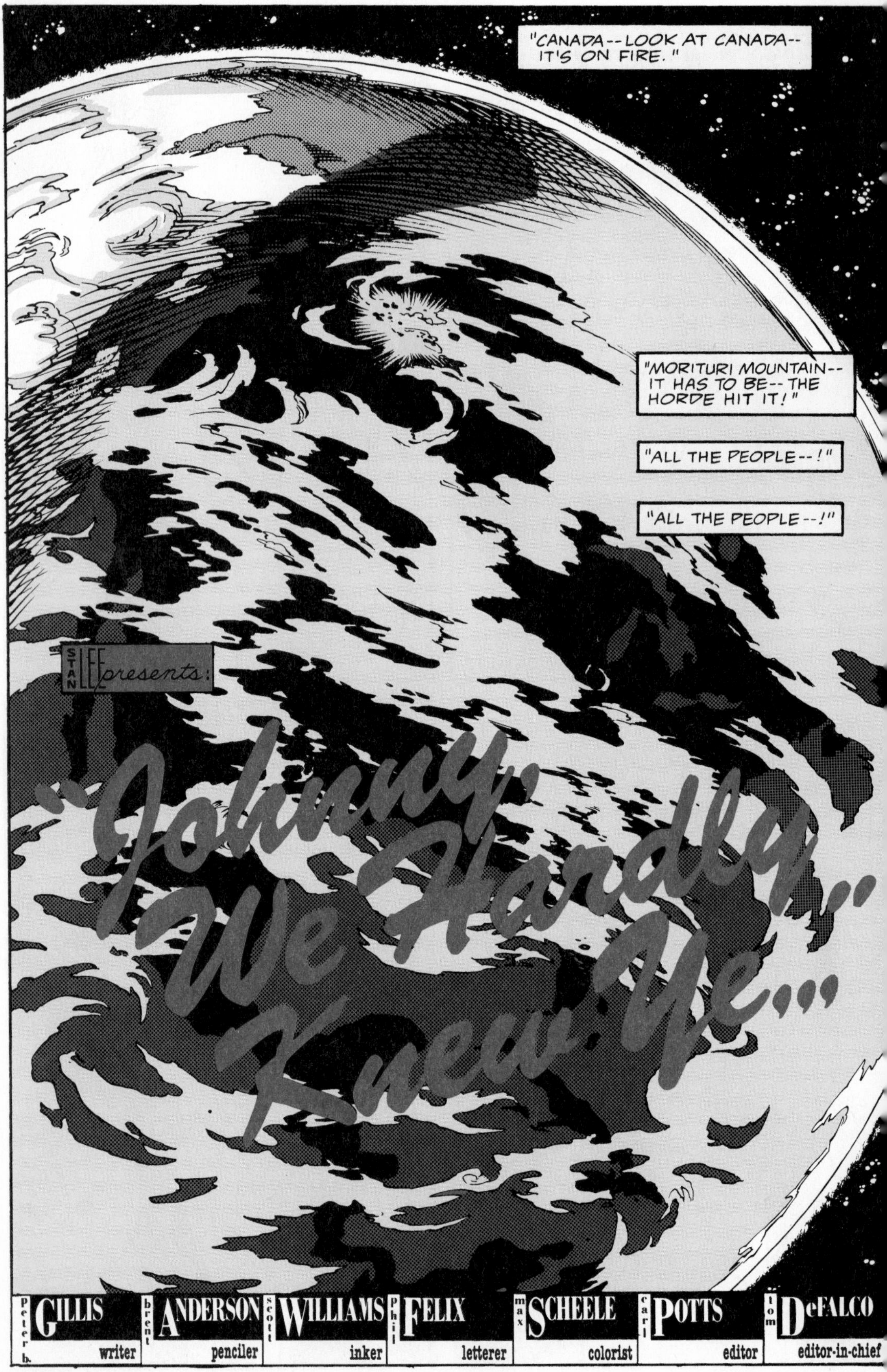
"CANADA--LOOK AT CANADA--
IT'S ON FIRE."
"MORITURI MOUNTAIN--
IT HAS TO BE--THE
HORDE HIT IT!"
"ALL THE PEOPLE--!"
"ALL THE PEOPLE--!"
STAN LEE presents:
"Johnny We Hardly Knew Ye..."
peter b. GILLIS writer
brent ANDERSON penciler
scott WILLIAMS inker
phil FELIX letterer
max SCHEELE colorist
carl POTTS editor
tom DeFALCO editor-in-chief

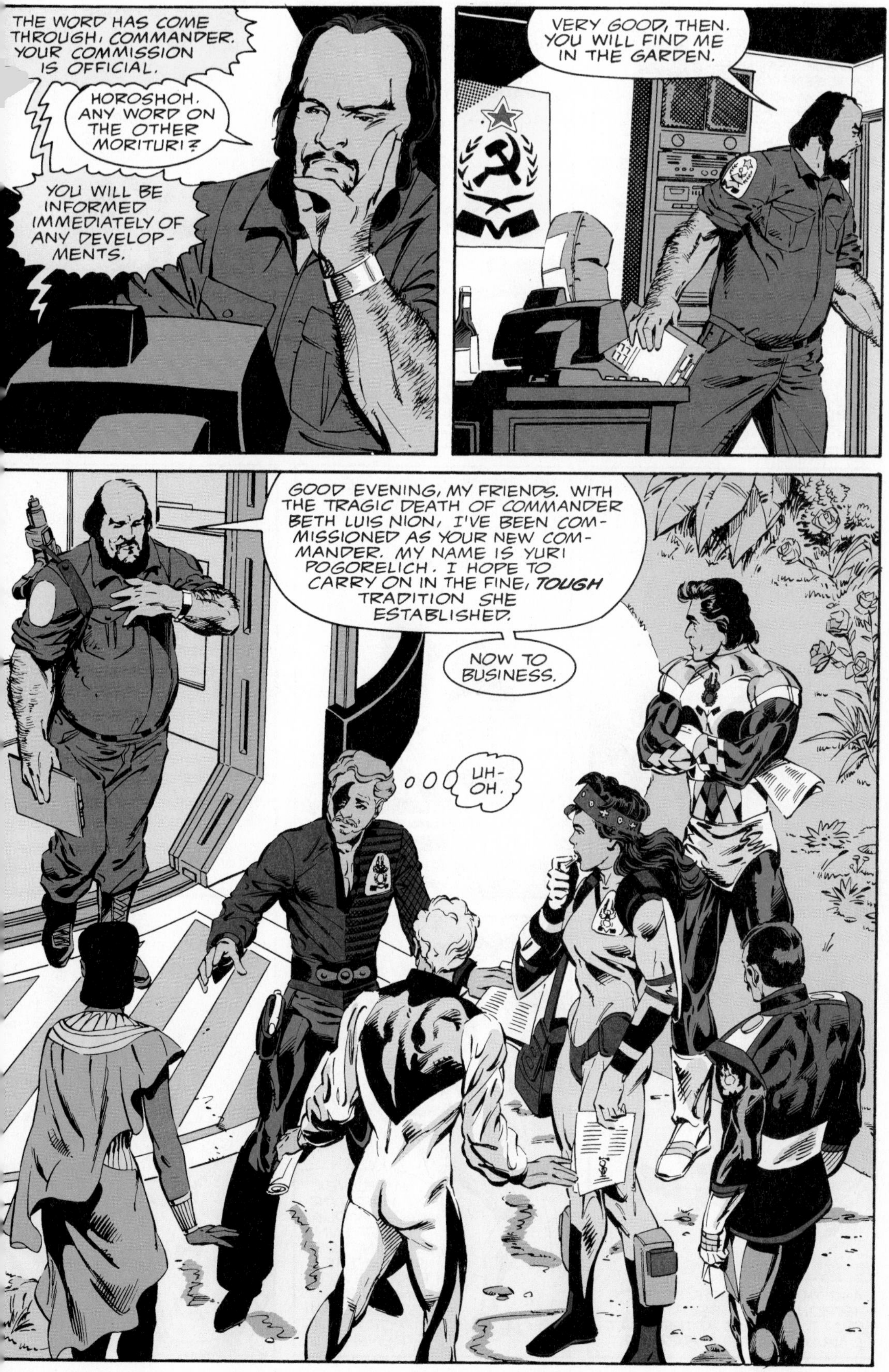
THE WORD HAS COME THROUGH, COMMANDER. YOUR COMMISSION IS OFFICIAL.
HOROSHOH. ANY WORD ON THE OTHER MORITURI?
YOU WILL BE INFORMED IMMEDIATELY OF ANY DEVELOPMENTS.
VERY GOOD, THEN. YOU WILL FIND ME IN THE GARDEN.
GOOD EVENING, MY FRIENDS. WITH THE TRAGIC DEATH OF COMMANDER BETH LUIS NION, I'VE BEEN COMMISSIONED AS YOUR NEW COMMANDER. MY NAME IS YURI POGORELICH. I HOPE TO CARRY ON IN THE FINE, TOUGH TRADITION SHE ESTABLISHED.
NOW TO BUSINESS.
UH-OH.

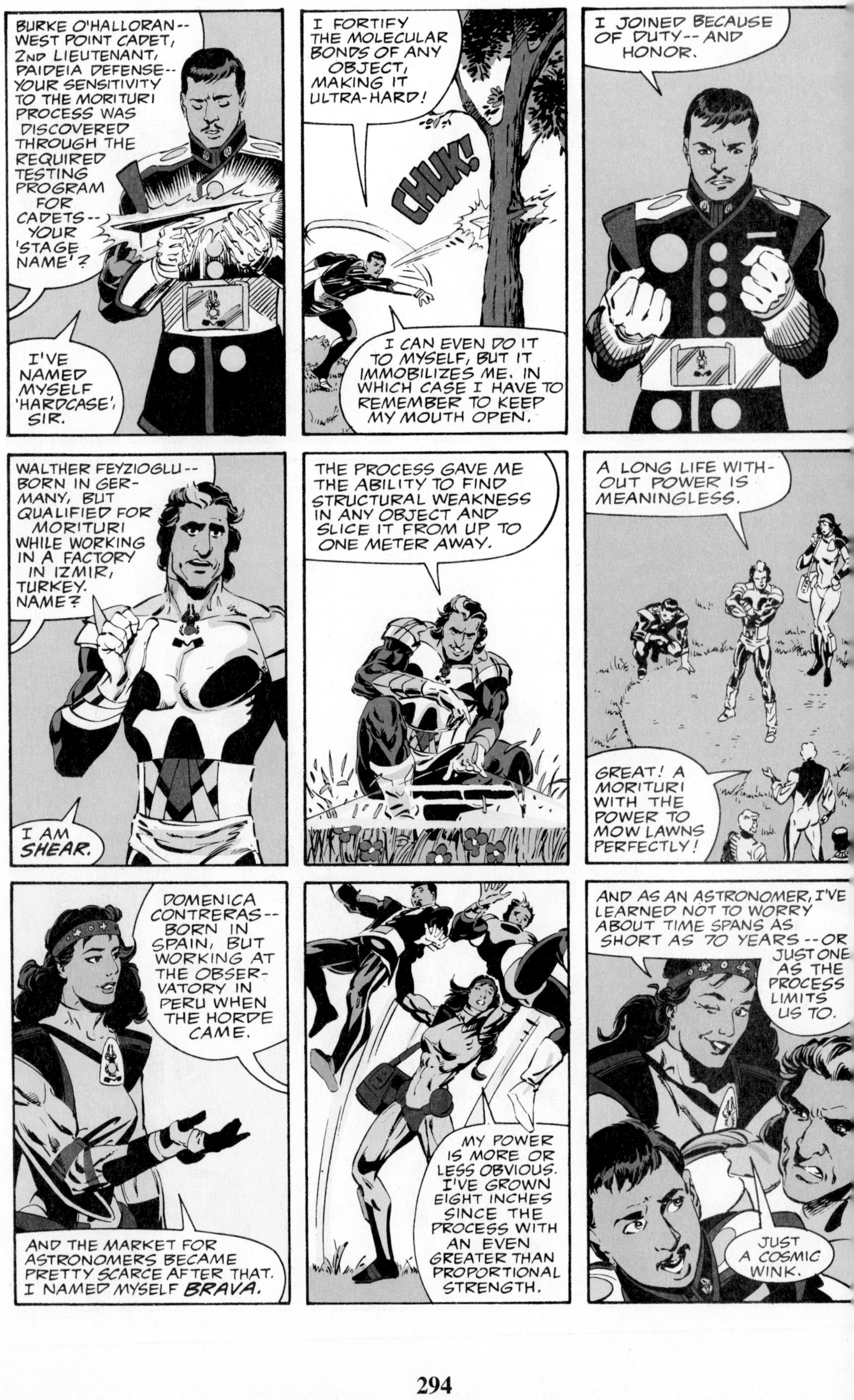
BURKE O'HALLORAN-- WEST POINT CADET, 2ND LIEUTENANT, PAIDEIA DEFENSE-- YOUR SENSITIVITY TO THE MORITURI PROCESS WAS DISCOVERED THROUGH THE REQUIRED TESTING PROGRAM FOR CADETS-- YOUR 'STAGE NAME'?
I'VE NAMED MYSELF 'HARDCASE', SIR.
I FORTIFY THE MOLECULAR BONDS OF ANY OBJECT, MAKING IT ULTRA-HARD!
CHUK!
I CAN EVEN DO IT TO MYSELF, BUT IT IMMOBILIZES ME. IN WHICH CASE I HAVE TO REMEMBER TO KEEP MY MOUTH OPEN.
I JOINED BECAUSE OF DUTY-- AND HONOR.
WALTHER FEYZIOGLU-- BORN IN GERMANY, BUT QUALIFIED FOR MORITURI WHILE WORKING IN A FACTORY IN IZMIR, TURKEY. NAME?
I AM *SHEAR*.
THE PROCESS GAVE ME THE ABILITY TO FIND STRUCTURAL WEAKNESS IN ANY OBJECT AND SLICE IT FROM UP TO ONE METER AWAY.
A LONG LIFE WITHOUT POWER IS MEANINGLESS.
GREAT! A MORITURI WITH THE POWER TO MOW LAWNS PERFECTLY!
DOMENICA CONTRERAS-- BORN IN SPAIN, BUT WORKING AT THE OBSERVATORY IN PERU WHEN THE HORDE CAME.
AND THE MARKET FOR ASTRONOMERS BECAME PRETTY SCARCE AFTER THAT. I NAMED MYSELF *BRAVA*.
MY POWER IS MORE OR LESS OBVIOUS. I'VE GROWN EIGHT INCHES SINCE THE PROCESS WITH AN EVEN GREATER THAN PROPORTIONAL STRENGTH.
AND AS AN ASTRONOMER, I'VE LEARNED NOT TO WORRY ABOUT TIME SPANS AS SHORT AS 70 YEARS --OR JUST ONE AS THE PROCESS LIMITS US TO.
JUST A COSMIC WINK.

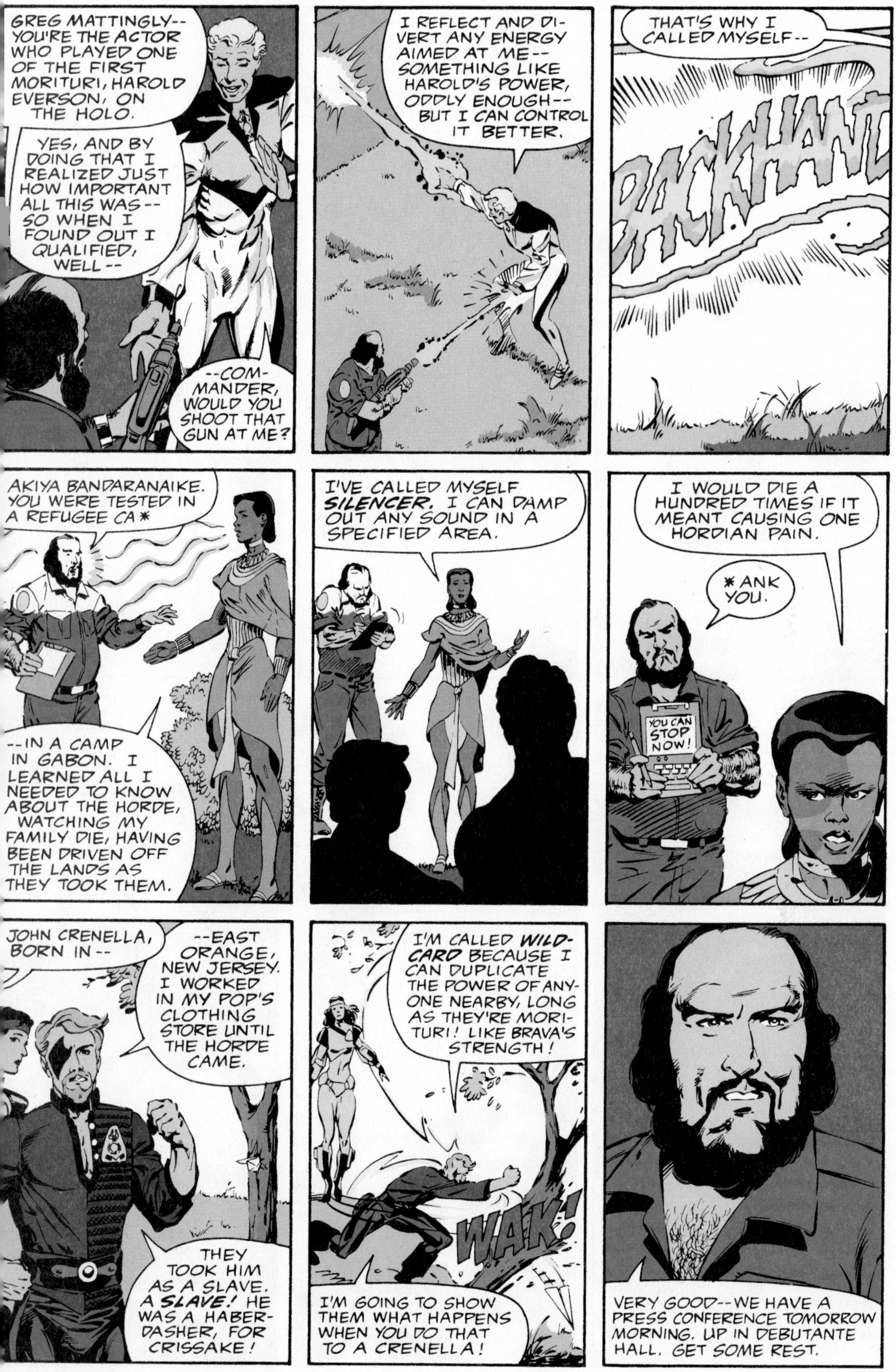
GREG MATTINGLY-- YOU'RE THE ACTOR WHO PLAYED ONE OF THE FIRST MORITURI, HAROLD EVERSON, ON THE HOLO.
YES, AND BY DOING THAT I REALIZED JUST HOW IMPORTANT ALL THIS WAS-- SO WHEN I FOUND OUT I QUALIFIED, WELL--
--COMMANDER, WOULD YOU SHOOT THAT GUN AT ME?
I REFLECT AND DIVERT ANY ENERGY AIMED AT ME-- SOMETHING LIKE HAROLD'S POWER, ODDLY ENOUGH-- BUT I CAN CONTROL IT BETTER.
THAT'S WHY I CALLED MYSELF--
BACKHAND
AKIYA BANDARANAIKE. YOU WERE TESTED IN A REFUGEE CA*
--IN A CAMP IN GABON. I LEARNED ALL I NEEDED TO KNOW ABOUT THE HORDE, WATCHING MY FAMILY DIE, HAVING BEEN DRIVEN OFF THE LANDS AS THEY TOOK THEM.
I'VE CALLED MYSELF SILENCER. I CAN DAMP OUT ANY SOUND IN A SPECIFIED AREA.
I WOULD DIE A HUNDRED TIMES IF IT MEANT CAUSING ONE HORDIAN PAIN.
*ANK YOU.
YOU CAN STOP NOW!
JOHN CRENELLA, BORN IN--
--EAST ORANGE, NEW JERSEY. I WORKED IN MY POP'S CLOTHING STORE UNTIL THE HORDE CAME.
THEY TOOK HIM AS A SLAVE. A SLAVE! HE WAS A HABERDASHER, FOR CRISSAKE!
I'M CALLED WILDCARD BECAUSE I CAN DUPLICATE THE POWER OF ANYONE NEARBY, LONG AS THEY'RE MORITURI! LIKE BRAVA'S STRENGTH!
WAK!
I'M GOING TO SHOW THEM WHAT HAPPENS WHEN YOU DO THAT TO A CRENELLA!
VERY GOOD--WE HAVE A PRESS CONFERENCE TOMORROW MORNING. UP IN DEBUTANTE HALL. GET SOME REST.

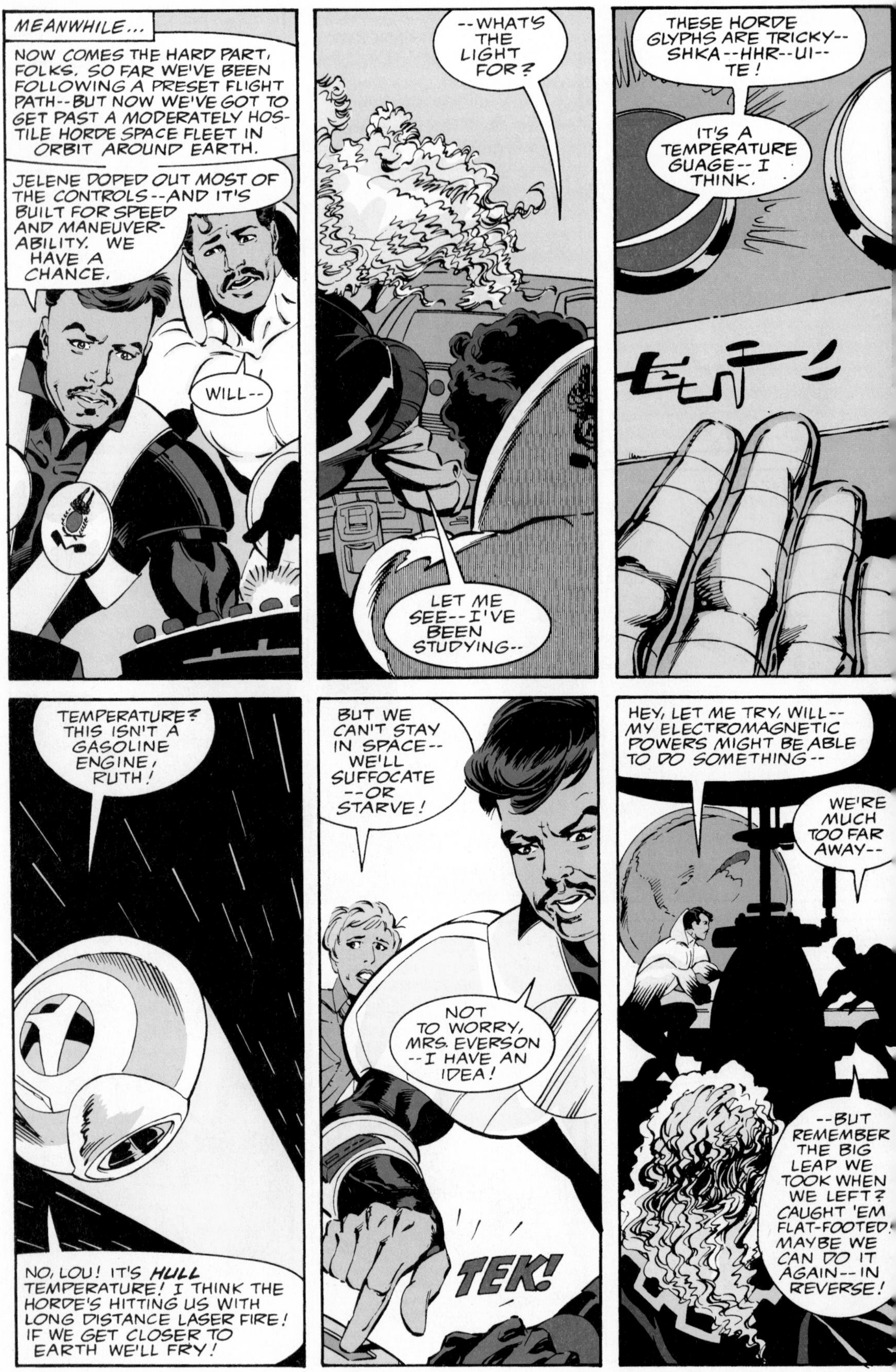
MEANWHILE...
NOW COMES THE HARD PART, FOLKS. SO FAR WE'VE BEEN FOLLOWING A PRESET FLIGHT PATH--BUT NOW WE'VE GOT TO GET PAST A MODERATELY HOSTILE HORDE SPACE FLEET IN ORBIT AROUND EARTH.
JELENE DOPED OUT MOST OF THE CONTROLS--AND IT'S BUILT FOR SPEED AND MANEUVERABILITY. WE HAVE A CHANCE.
WILL--
--WHAT'S THE LIGHT FOR?
LET ME SEE--I'VE BEEN STUDYING--
THESE HORDE GLYPHS ARE TRICKY--SHKA--HHR--UI--TE!
IT'S A TEMPERATURE GUAGE--I THINK.
TEMPERATURE? THIS ISN'T A GASOLINE ENGINE, RUTH!
NO, LOU! IT'S HULL TEMPERATURE! I THINK THE HORDE'S HITTING US WITH LONG DISTANCE LASER FIRE! IF WE GET CLOSER TO EARTH WE'LL FRY!
BUT WE CAN'T STAY IN SPACE--WE'LL SUFFOCATE--OR STARVE!
NOT TO WORRY, MRS. EVERSON--I HAVE AN IDEA!
TEK!
HEY, LET ME TRY, WILL--MY ELECTROMAGNETIC POWERS MIGHT BE ABLE TO DO SOMETHING--
WE'RE MUCH TOO FAR AWAY--
--BUT REMEMBER THE BIG LEAP WE TOOK WHEN WE LEFT? CAUGHT 'EM FLAT-FOOTED. MAYBE WE CAN DO IT AGAIN--IN REVERSE!

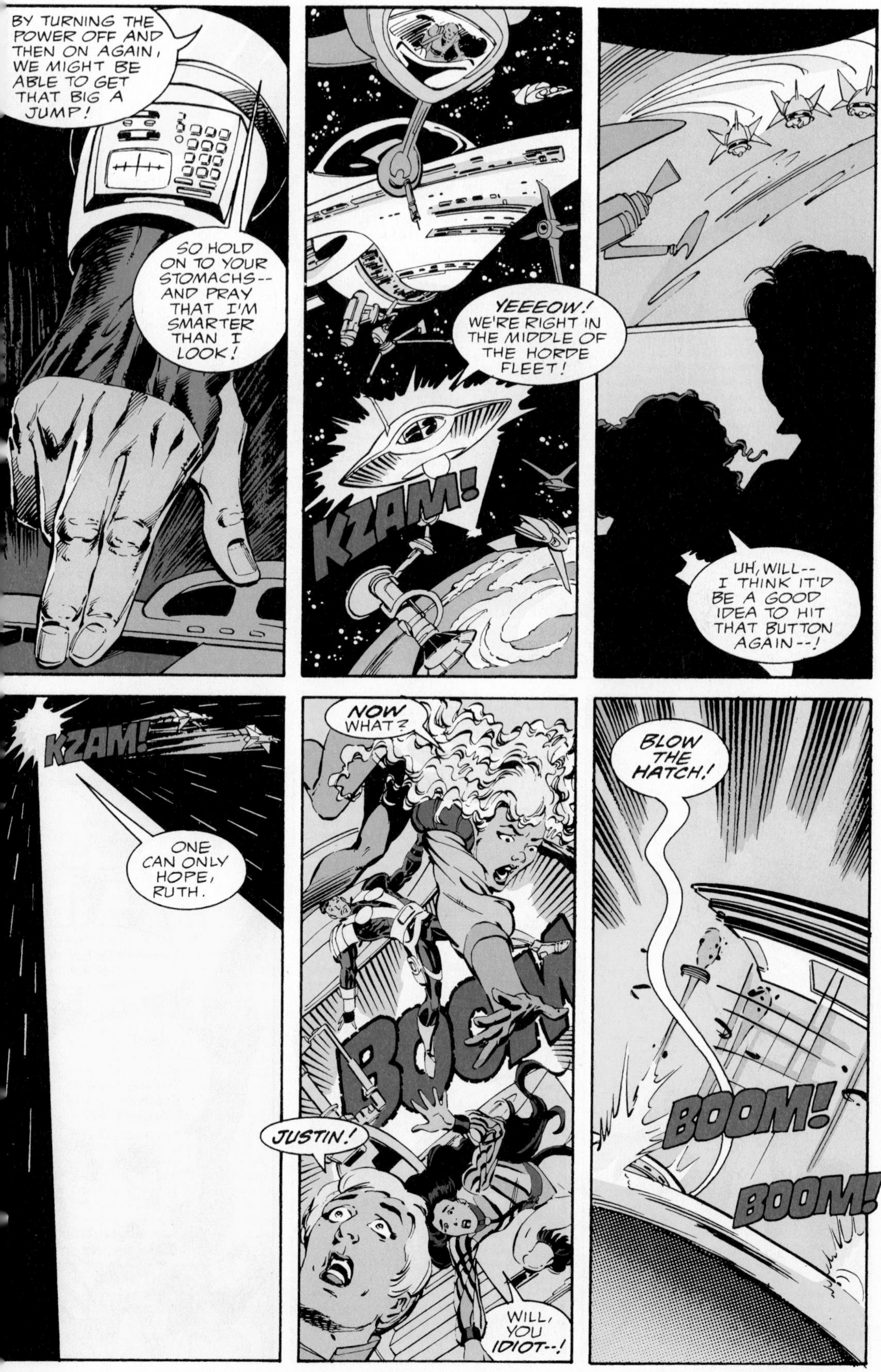
BY TURNING THE POWER OFF AND THEN ON AGAIN, WE MIGHT BE ABLE TO GET THAT BIG A JUMP!
SO HOLD ON TO YOUR STOMACHS-- AND PRAY THAT I'M SMARTER THAN I LOOK!
YEEEOW! WE'RE RIGHT IN THE MIDDLE OF THE HORDE FLEET!
KZAM!
UH, WILL-- I THINK IT'D BE A GOOD IDEA TO HIT THAT BUTTON AGAIN--!
KZAM!
ONE CAN ONLY HOPE, RUTH.
NOW WHAT?
BOOM
JUSTIN!
WILL, YOU IDIOT--!
BLOW THE HATCH!
BOOM!
BOOM!

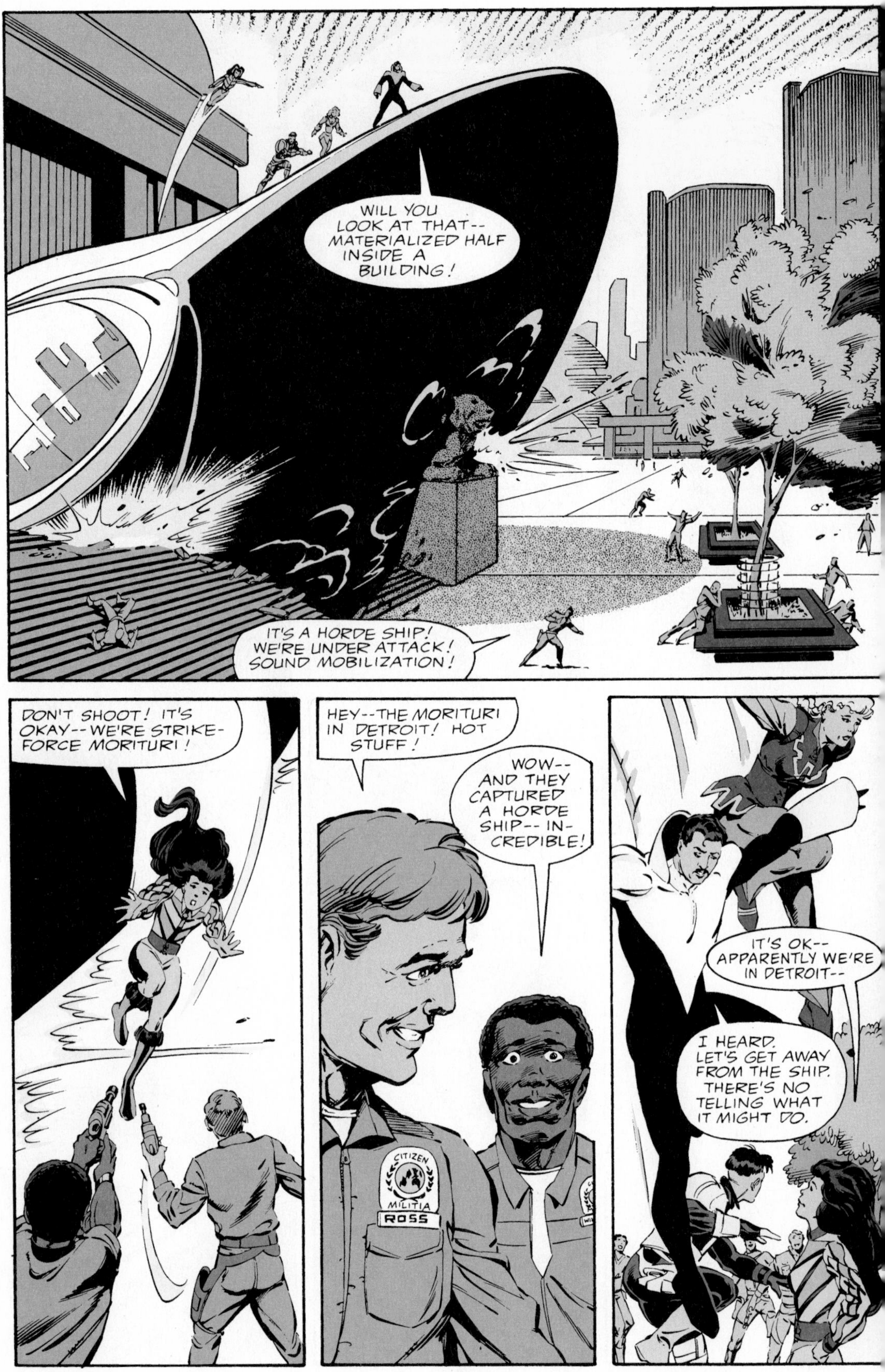
WILL YOU LOOK AT THAT-- MATERIALIZED HALF INSIDE A BUILDING!
IT'S A HORDE SHIP! WE'RE UNDER ATTACK! SOUND MOBILIZATION!
DON'T SHOOT! IT'S OKAY--WE'RE STRIKE-FORCE MORITURI!
HEY--THE MORITURI IN DETROIT! HOT STUFF!
WOW-- AND THEY CAPTURED A HORDE SHIP-- IN-CREDIBLE!
CITIZEN MILITIA
ROSS
IT'S OK-- APPARENTLY WE'RE IN DETROIT--
I HEARD. LET'S GET AWAY FROM THE SHIP. THERE'S NO TELLING WHAT IT MIGHT DO.

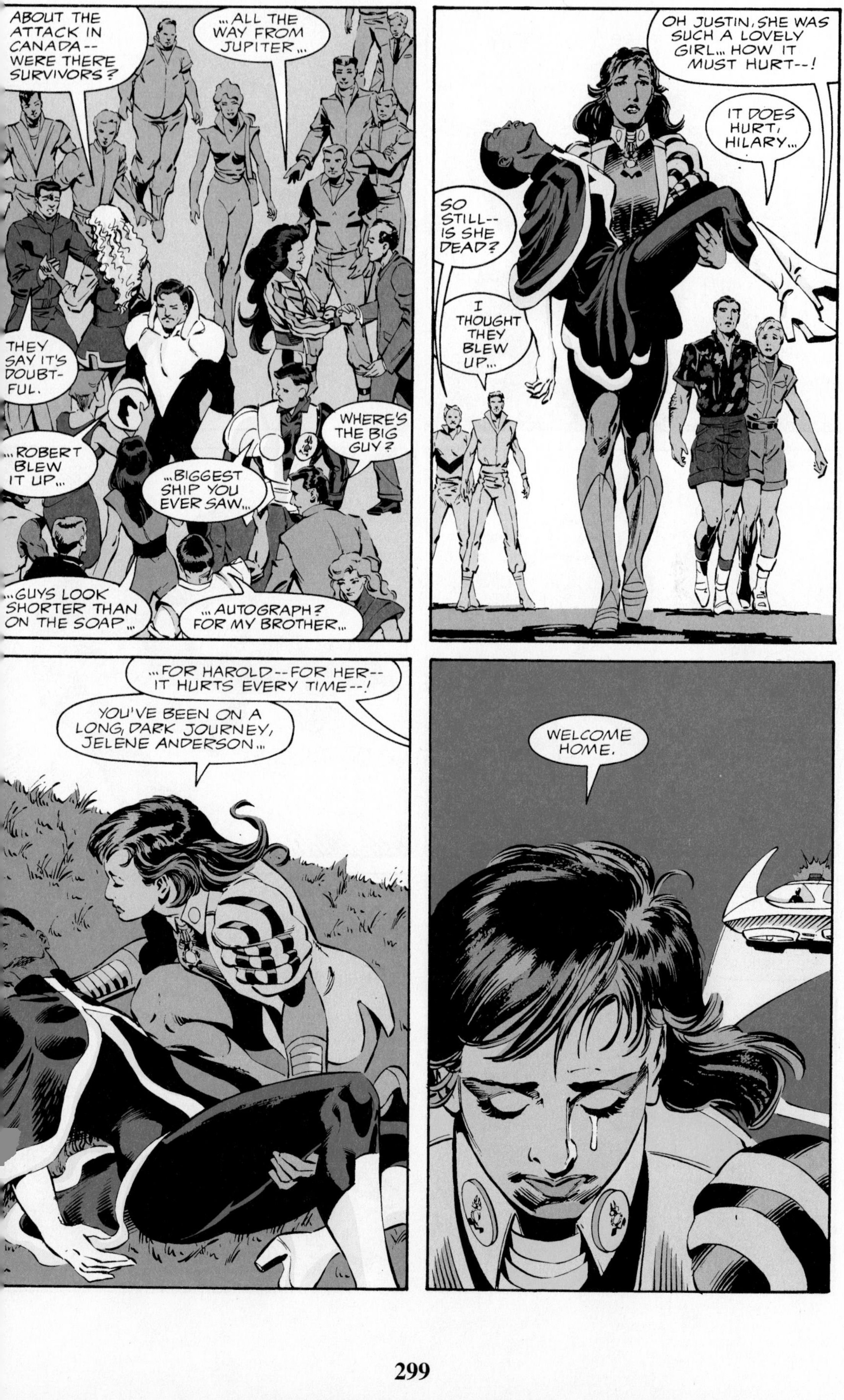
ABOUT THE ATTACK IN CANADA-- WERE THERE SURVIVORS?
...ALL THE WAY FROM JUPITER...
THEY SAY IT'S DOUBTFUL.
...ROBERT BLEW IT UP...
WHERE'S THE BIG GUY?
...BIGGEST SHIP YOU EVER SAW...
...GUYS LOOK SHORTER THAN ON THE SOAP...
...AUTOGRAPH? FOR MY BROTHER...
OH JUSTIN, SHE WAS SUCH A LOVELY GIRL... HOW IT MUST HURT--!
IT DOES HURT, HILARY...
SO STILL-- IS SHE DEAD?
I THOUGHT THEY BLEW UP...
...FOR HAROLD--FOR HER-- IT HURTS EVERY TIME--!
YOU'VE BEEN ON A LONG, DARK JOURNEY, JELENE ANDERSON...
WELCOME HOME.

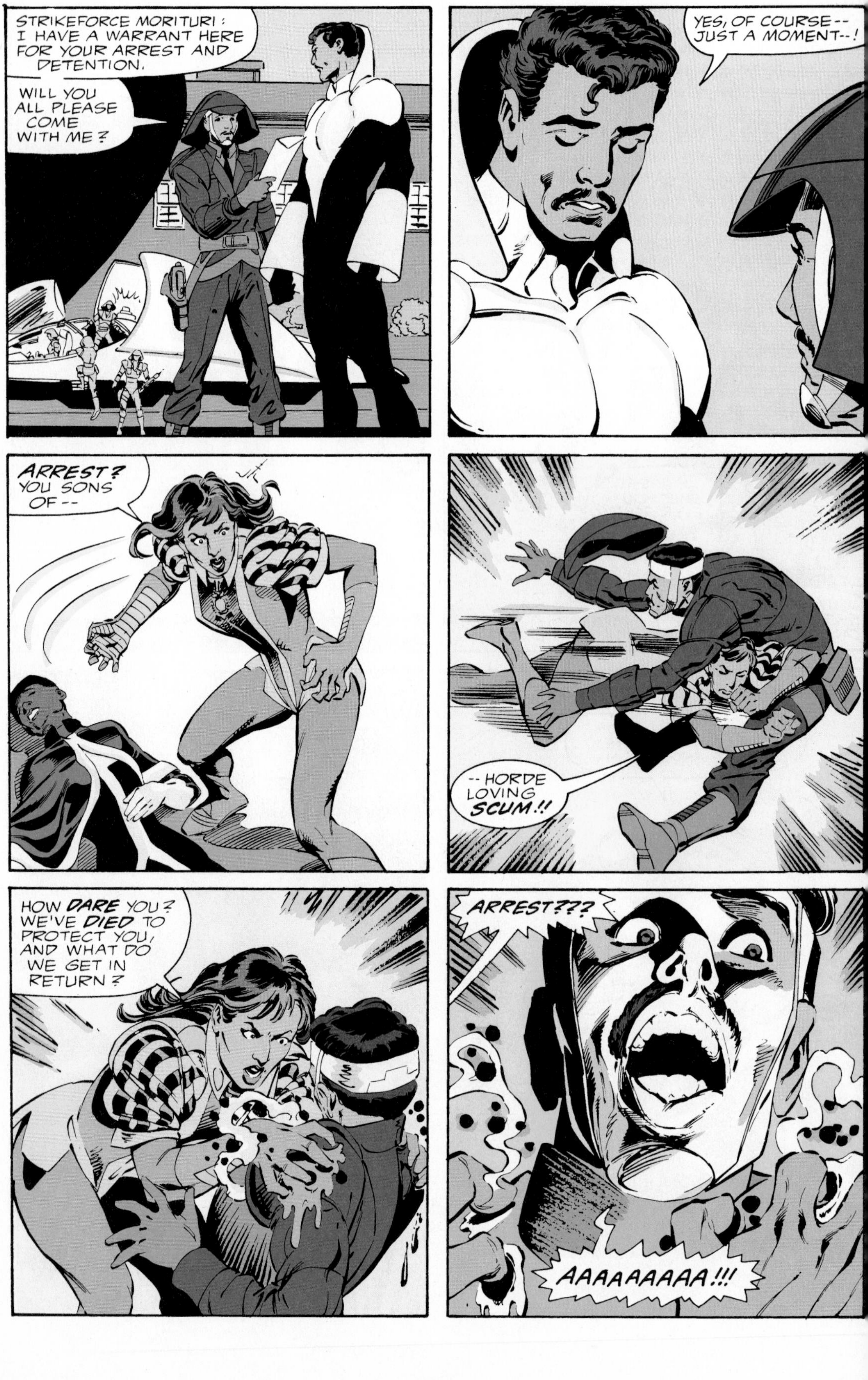
STRIKEFORCE MORITURI: I HAVE A WARRANT HERE FOR YOUR ARREST AND DETENTION.
WILL YOU ALL PLEASE COME WITH ME?
YES, OF COURSE -- JUST A MOMENT--!
ARREST? YOU SONS OF --
-- HORDE LOVING SCUM!!
HOW DARE YOU? WE'VE DIED TO PROTECT YOU, AND WHAT DO WE GET IN RETURN?
ARREST???
AAAAAAAAA!!!

WHAT AM I DOING? I'M SORRY!

I DIDN'T MEAN TO HU*UUUNGH!*

AAAAAAAAAAAA!

ANIMAL!

ALINE, STOP IT!

EVERYBODY INTO THE COP FLIER! WE'RE GETTING OUT OF HERE!

IT LOOKS LIKE WE DON'T HAVE ANY CHOICE!

I'LL BROADCAST A LITTLE ANGER TO COVER OUR ESCAPE!

HEY-- THAT COP SHOT A MORITURI!

GET 'EM!

I'LL TEMPORARILY BLIND THE ONES ON THE GROUND-- WILL, GET THE DRIVER!

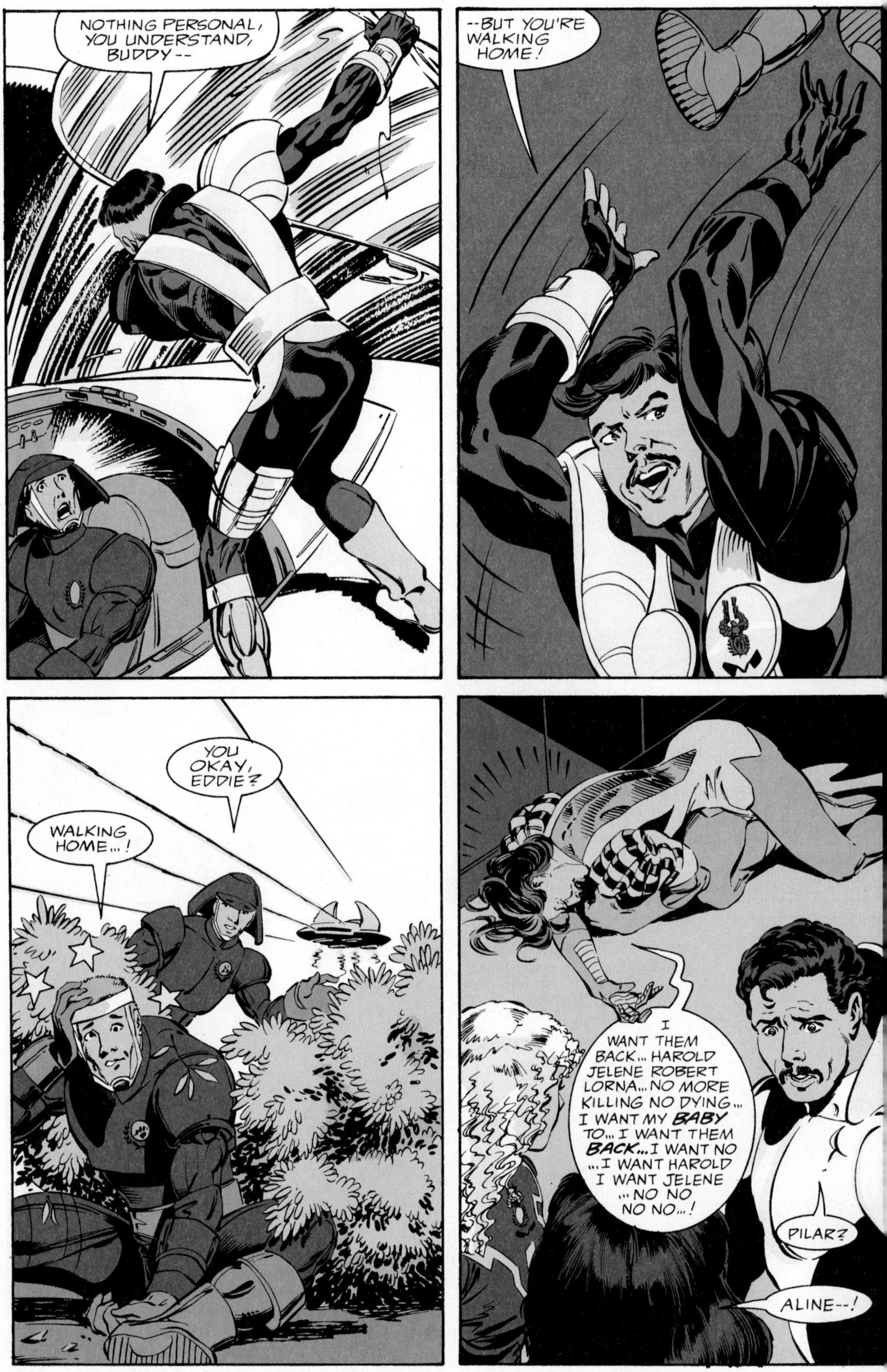
NOTHING PERSONAL, YOU UNDERSTAND, BUDDY--
--BUT YOU'RE WALKING HOME!
YOU OKAY, EDDIE?
WALKING HOME...!
I WANT THEM BACK... HAROLD JELENE ROBERT LORNA... NO MORE KILLING NO DYING... I WANT MY BABY TO... I WANT THEM BACK... I WANT NO ...I WANT HAROLD I WANT JELENE ...NO NO NO NO...!
PILAR?
ALINE--!

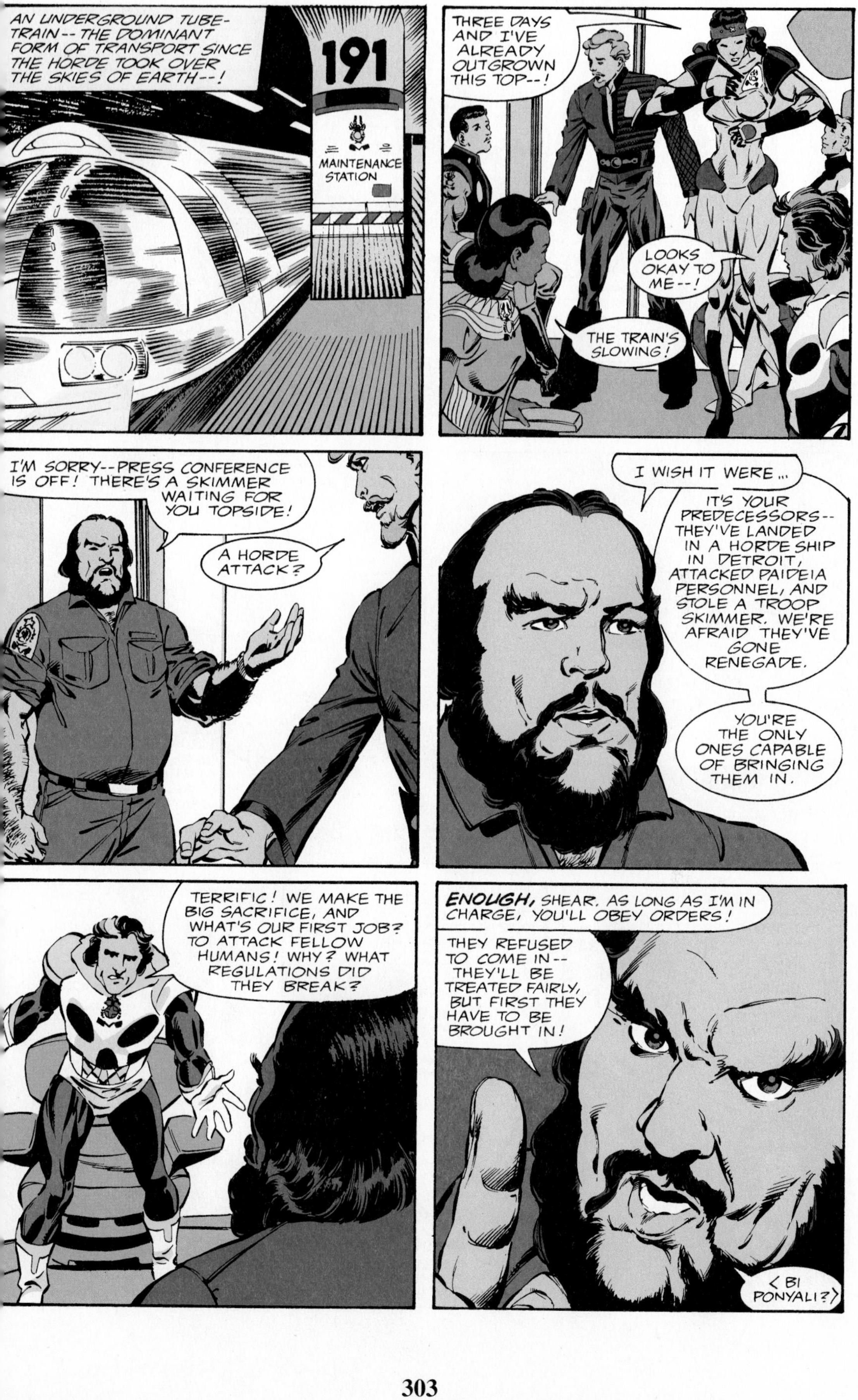

AN UNDERGROUND TUBE-TRAIN -- THE DOMINANT FORM OF TRANSPORT SINCE THE HORDE TOOK OVER THE SKIES OF EARTH --!
191
MAINTENANCE STATION
THREE DAYS AND I'VE ALREADY OUTGROWN THIS TOP--!
LOOKS OKAY TO ME--!
THE TRAIN'S SLOWING!
I'M SORRY--PRESS CONFERENCE IS OFF! THERE'S A SKIMMER WAITING FOR YOU TOPSIDE!
A HORDE ATTACK?
I WISH IT WERE...
IT'S YOUR PREDECESSORS-- THEY'VE LANDED IN A HORDE SHIP IN DETROIT, ATTACKED PAIDEIA PERSONNEL, AND STOLE A TROOP SKIMMER. WE'RE AFRAID THEY'VE GONE RENEGADE.
YOU'RE THE ONLY ONES CAPABLE OF BRINGING THEM IN.
TERRIFIC! WE MAKE THE BIG SACRIFICE, AND WHAT'S OUR FIRST JOB? TO ATTACK FELLOW HUMANS! WHY? WHAT REGULATIONS DID THEY BREAK?
ENOUGH, SHEAR. AS LONG AS I'M IN CHARGE, YOU'LL OBEY ORDERS!
THEY REFUSED TO COME IN-- THEY'LL BE TREATED FAIRLY, BUT FIRST THEY HAVE TO BE BROUGHT IN!
<BI PONYALI?>

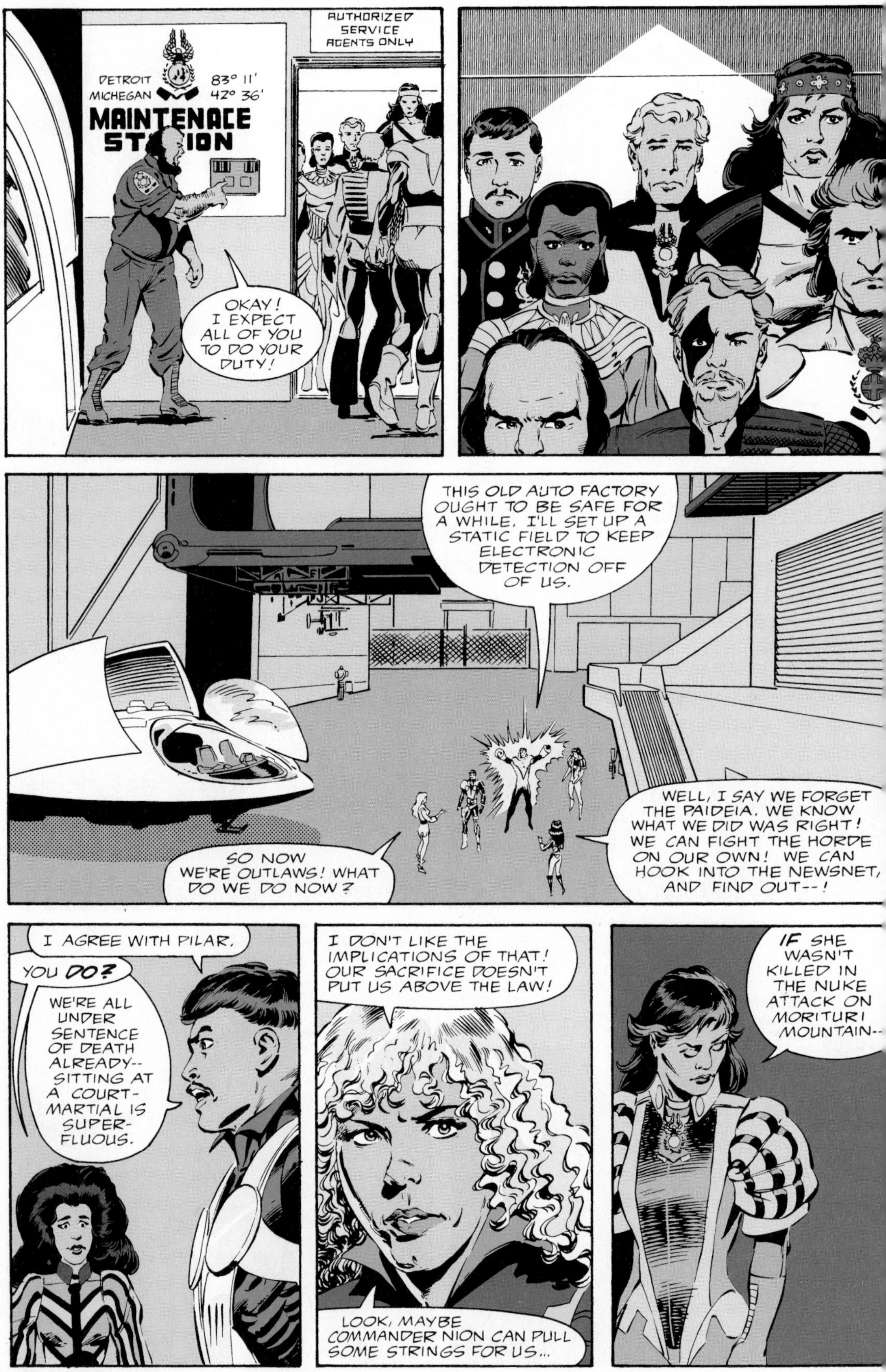
AUTHORIZED SERVICE AGENTS ONLY
DETROIT MICHEGAN 83° 11' 42° 36'
MAINTENACE STATION
OKAY! I EXPECT ALL OF YOU TO DO YOUR DUTY!
THIS OLD AUTO FACTORY OUGHT TO BE SAFE FOR A WHILE. I'LL SET UP A STATIC FIELD TO KEEP ELECTRONIC DETECTION OFF OF US.
SO NOW WE'RE OUTLAWS! WHAT DO WE DO NOW?
WELL, I SAY WE FORGET THE PAIDEIA. WE KNOW WHAT WE DID WAS RIGHT! WE CAN FIGHT THE HORDE ON OUR OWN! WE CAN HOOK INTO THE NEWSNET, AND FIND OUT--!
I AGREE WITH PILAR.
YOU DO?
WE'RE ALL UNDER SENTENCE OF DEATH ALREADY-- SITTING AT A COURT-MARTIAL IS SUPER-FLUOUS.
I DON'T LIKE THE IMPLICATIONS OF THAT! OUR SACRIFICE DOESN'T PUT US ABOVE THE LAW!
LOOK, MAYBE COMMANDER NION CAN PULL SOME STRINGS FOR US...
IF SHE WASN'T KILLED IN THE NUKE ATTACK ON MORITURI MOUNTAIN--

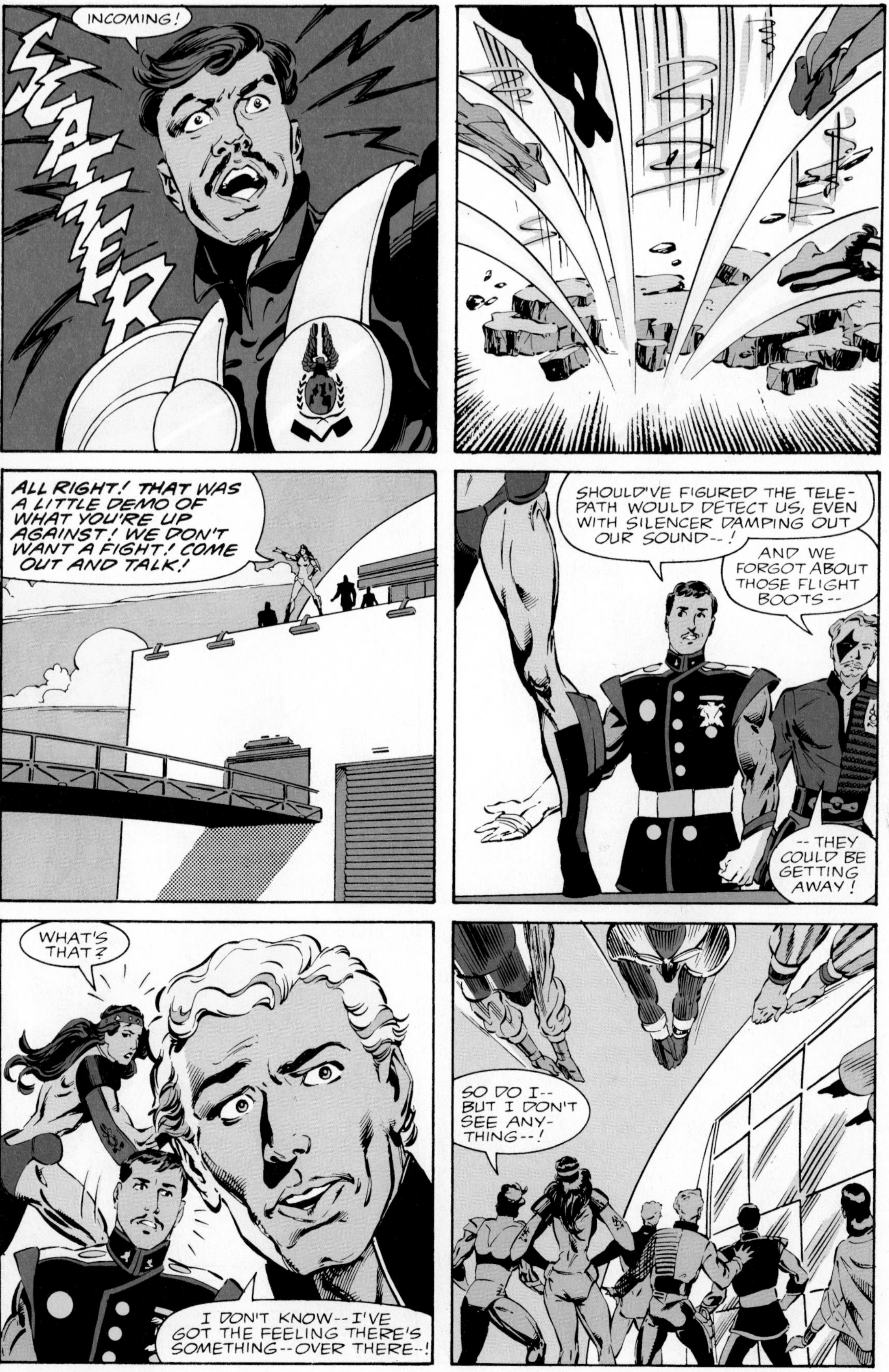
INCOMING!
SCATTER
ALL RIGHT! THAT WAS A LITTLE DEMO OF WHAT YOU'RE UP AGAINST! WE DON'T WANT A FIGHT! COME OUT AND TALK!
SHOULD'VE FIGURED THE TELE-PATH WOULD DETECT US, EVEN WITH SILENCER DAMPING OUT OUR SOUND--!
AND WE FORGOT ABOUT THOSE FLIGHT BOOTS--
--THEY COULD BE GETTING AWAY!
WHAT'S THAT?
I DON'T KNOW--I'VE GOT THE FEELING THERE'S SOMETHING--OVER THERE--!
SO DO I--BUT I DON'T SEE ANY-THING--!

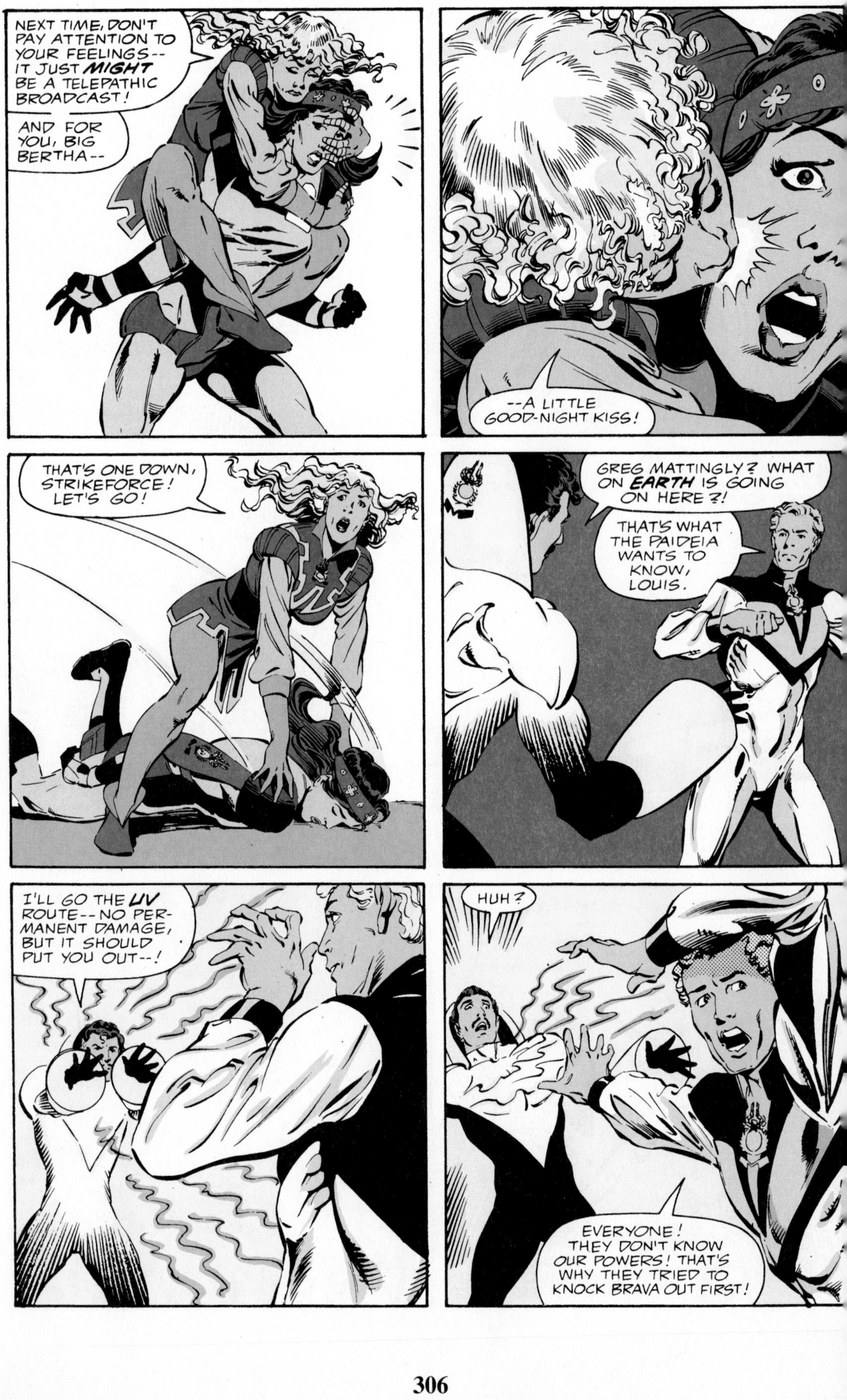
NEXT TIME, DON'T PAY ATTENTION TO YOUR FEELINGS-- IT JUST MIGHT BE A TELEPATHIC BROADCAST!
AND FOR YOU, BIG BERTHA--
--A LITTLE GOOD-NIGHT KISS!
THAT'S ONE DOWN, STRIKEFORCE! LET'S GO!
GREG MATTINGLY?! WHAT ON EARTH IS GOING ON HERE?!
THAT'S WHAT THE PAIDEIA WANTS TO KNOW, LOUIS.
I'LL GO THE UV ROUTE--NO PERMANENT DAMAGE, BUT IT SHOULD PUT YOU OUT--!
HUH?
EVERYONE! THEY DON'T KNOW OUR POWERS! THAT'S WHY THEY TRIED TO KNOCK BRAVA OUT FIRST!

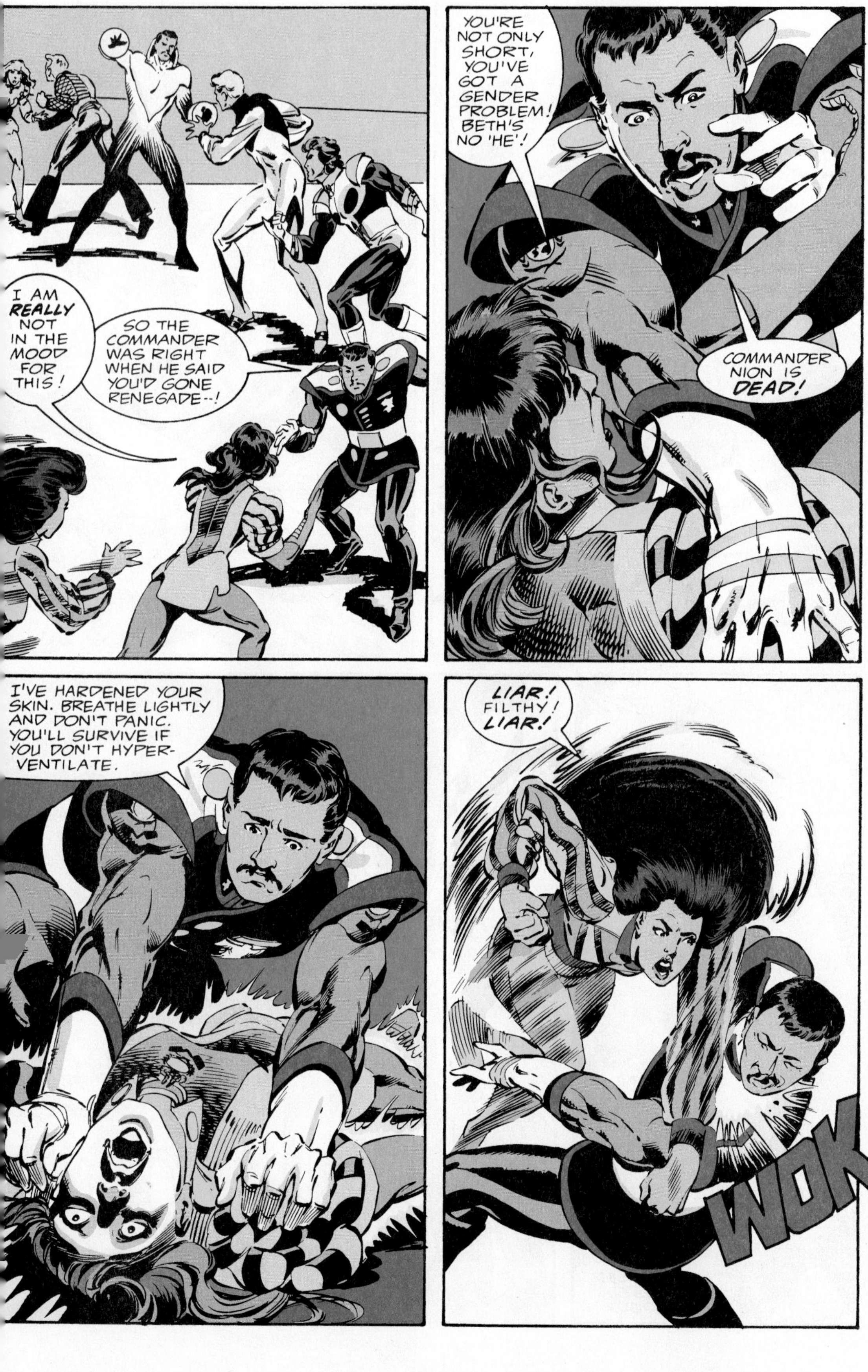
I AM REALLY NOT IN THE MOOD FOR THIS!
SO THE COMMANDER WAS RIGHT WHEN HE SAID YOU'D GONE RENEGADE--!
YOU'RE NOT ONLY SHORT, YOU'VE GOT A GENDER PROBLEM! BETH'S NO 'HE'!
COMMANDER NION IS DEAD!
I'VE HARDENED YOUR SKIN. BREATHE LIGHTLY AND DON'T PANIC. YOU'LL SURVIVE IF YOU DON'T HYPER-VENTILATE.
LIAR! FILTHY! LIAR!
WOK

YOU *TAKE THAT BAC※*

BRAVA MAY BE OUT BUT I CAN STILL BORROW HER POWER!

CRENELLA, YOU *MORON!*

THEY HAVE FLIGHT BOOTS-- *WE DON'T!*

WHERE'S ALINE?

DOWN THERE, SOMEWHERE! WE'VE GOT TO GET HER UP--!

BURKE! HERE! I NEED YOU!

IT'S CALLED *GLASS*, FEYZIOGLU.

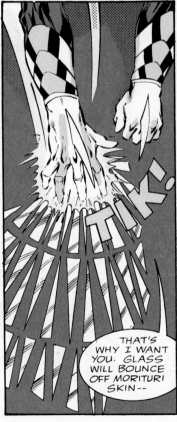

K-TAK!

THAT'S WHY I WANT YOU. GLASS WILL BOUNCE OFF MORITURI SKIN--

--BUT NOT AFTER HARDCASE GETS THROUGH WITH IT. MY APOLOGIES.

O'HALLORAN

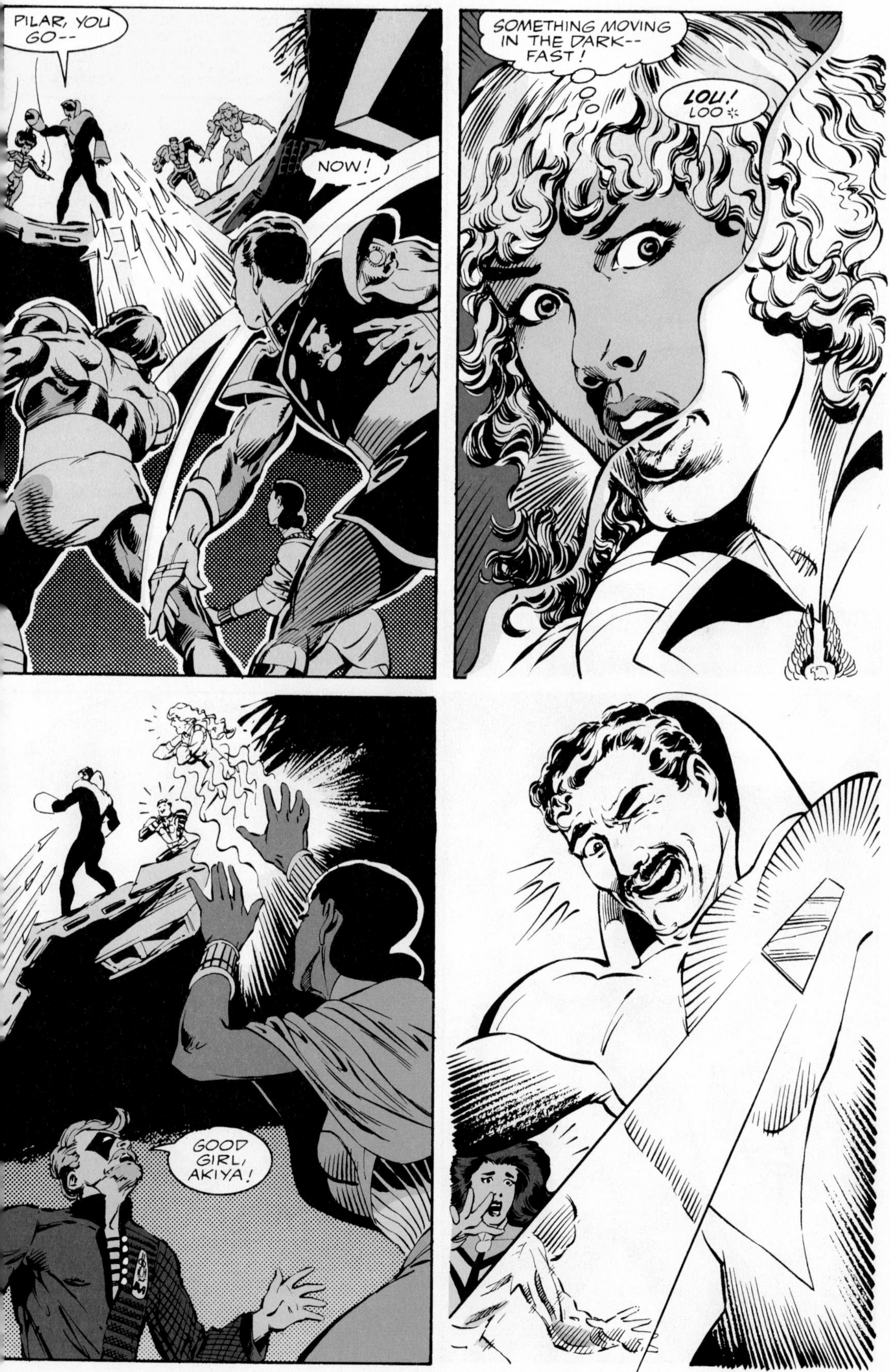
PILAR, YOU GO--
NOW!
SOMETHING MOVING IN THE DARK-- FAST!
LOU! LOO
GOOD GIRL, AKIYA!

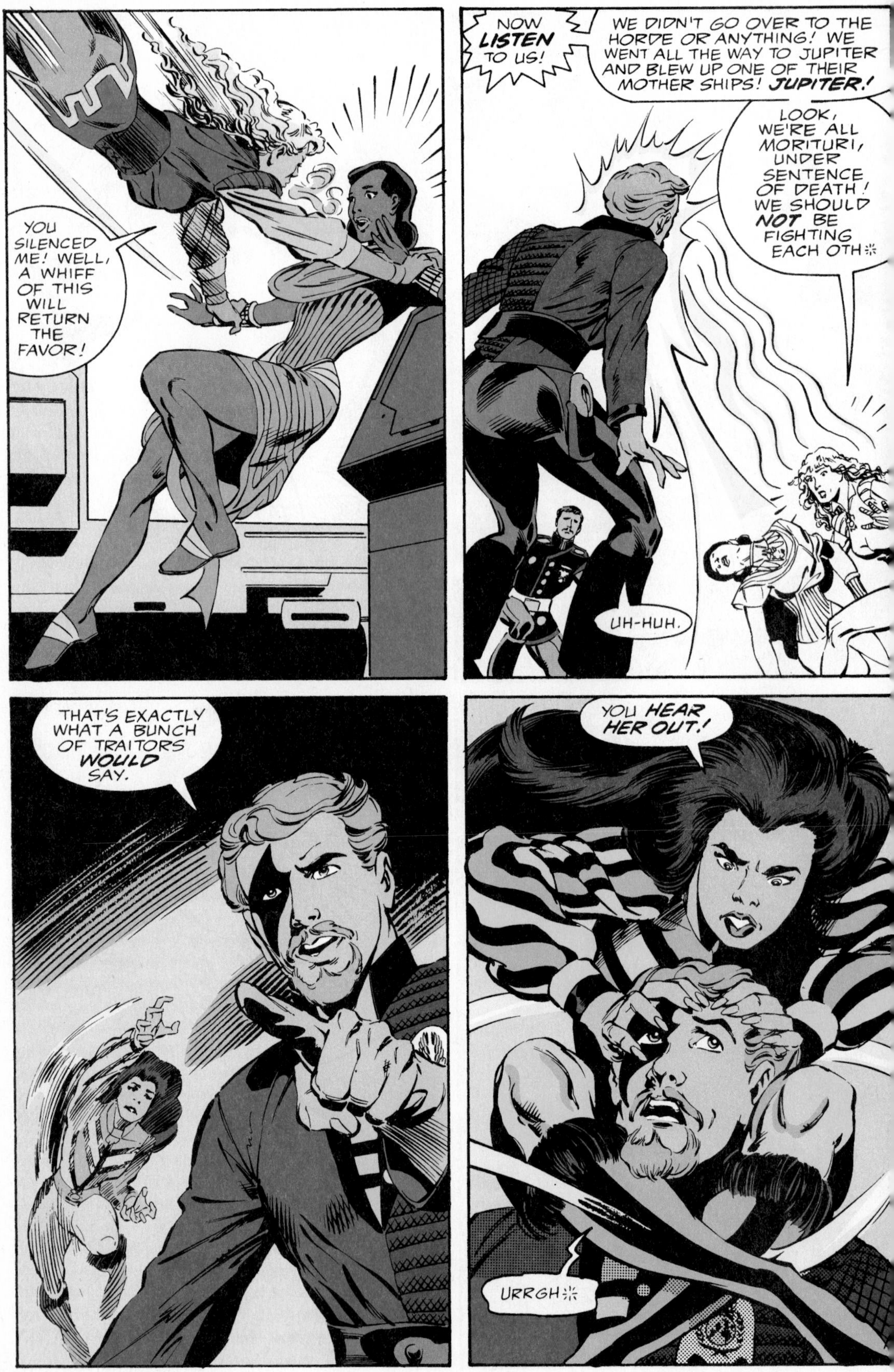
YOU SILENCED ME! WELL, A WHIFF OF THIS WILL RETURN THE FAVOR!
NOW LISTEN TO US!
WE DIDN'T GO OVER TO THE HORDE OR ANYTHING! WE WENT ALL THE WAY TO JUPITER AND BLEW UP ONE OF THEIR MOTHER SHIPS! JUPITER!
LOOK, WE'RE ALL MORITURI, UNDER SENTENCE OF DEATH! WE SHOULD NOT BE FIGHTING EACH OTH※
UH-HUH.
THAT'S EXACTLY WHAT A BUNCH OF TRAITORS WOULD SAY.
YOU HEAR HER OUT!
URRGH※

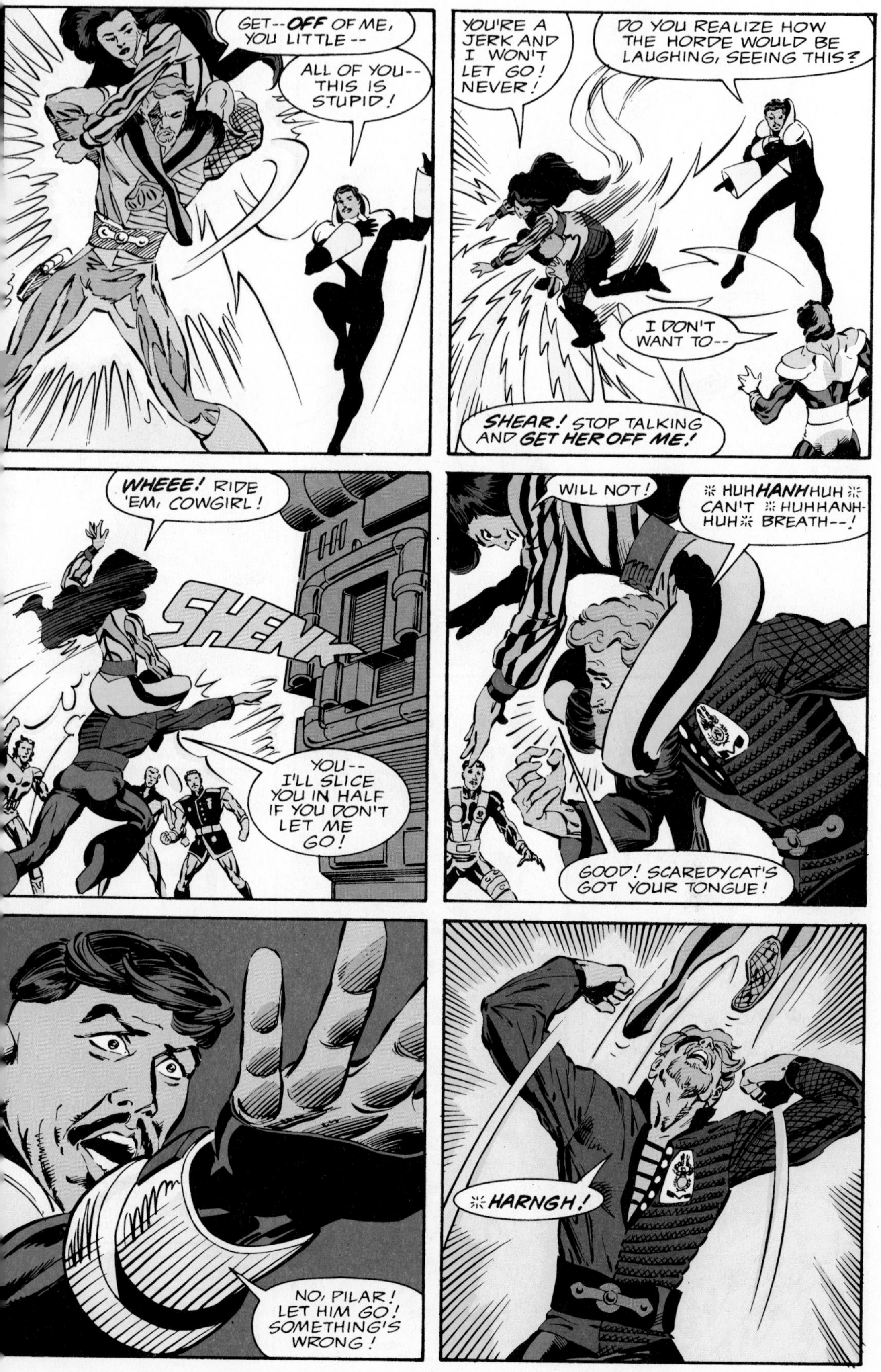
GET--OFF OF ME, YOU LITTLE--
ALL OF YOU-- THIS IS STUPID!
YOU'RE A JERK AND I WON'T LET GO! NEVER!
DO YOU REALIZE HOW THE HORDE WOULD BE LAUGHING, SEEING THIS?
I DON'T WANT TO--
SHEAR! STOP TALKING AND GET HER OFF ME!
WHEEE! RIDE 'EM, COWGIRL!
SHENK
YOU-- I'LL SLICE YOU IN HALF IF YOU DON'T LET ME GO!
WILL NOT!
HUHHANHHUH CAN'T HUHHANH-HUH BREATH--!
GOOD! SCAREDYCAT'S GOT YOUR TONGUE!
NO, PILAR! LET HIM GO! SOMETHING'S WRONG!
HARNGH!

BLESSED BE-- HE WASN'T JOKING!

AH HUH * HAH * HUH *

NO *

NO * IT'S * TOO SOON *

I'VE ONLY * HAD * WEEKS--*

WEEKS *

ALAINE

HELLLPLPLLLLLLLLLLLL

"HE CRAWLED TO ME-- LYING HERE HELPLESS-- HE'S MELTING--!"

"WHY DID HE TAKE MY POWER AT THE LAST MOMENT?"

"MY POWER--"

"OH DEAR LORD HE'S, DYING MY DEATH--!"

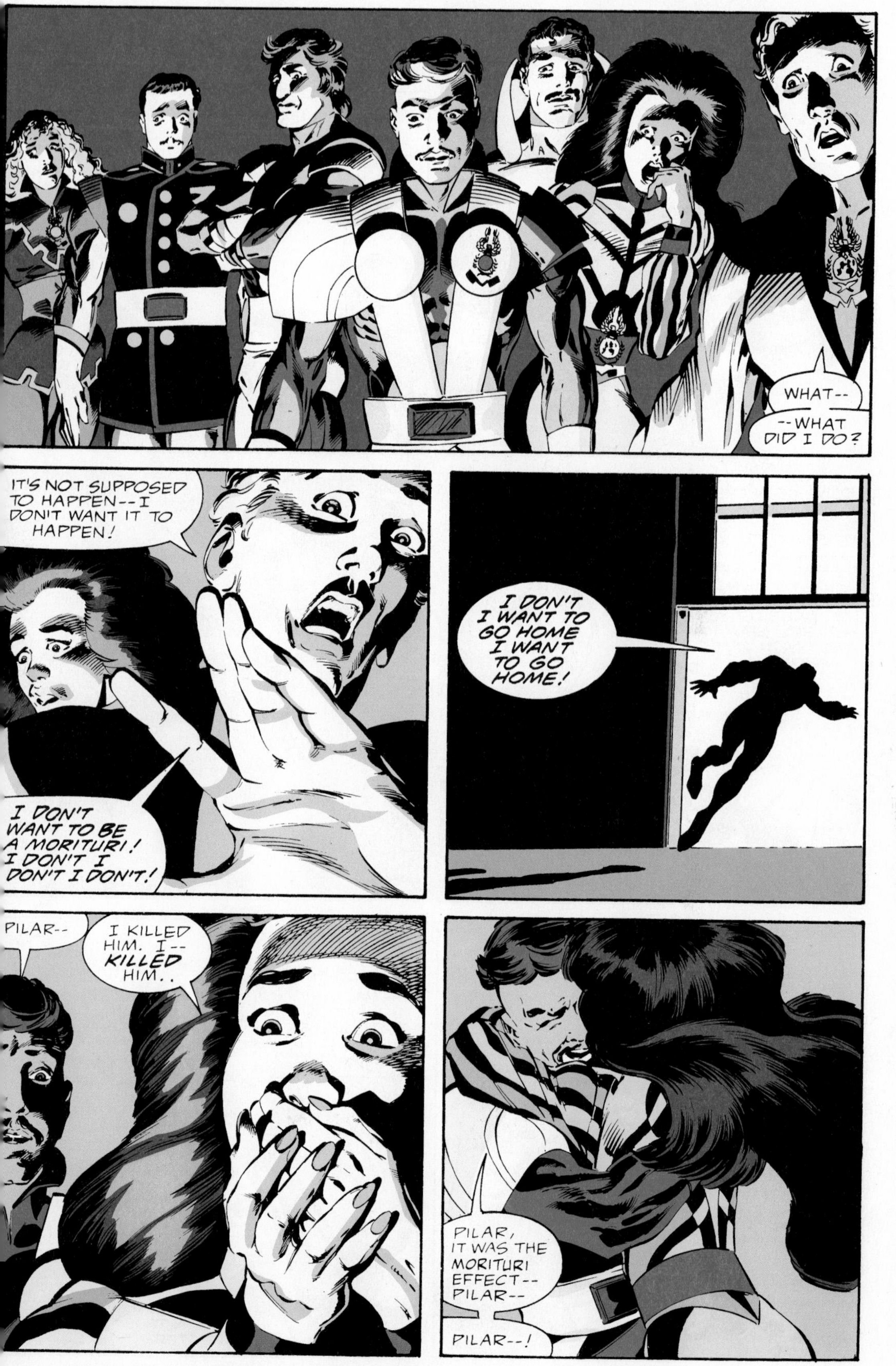
WHAT--
--WHAT DID I DO?
IT'S NOT SUPPOSED TO HAPPEN--I DON'T WANT IT TO HAPPEN!
I DON'T WANT TO BE A MORITURI! I DON'T I DON'T I DON'T!
I DON'T I WANT TO GO HOME I WANT TO GO HOME!
PILAR--
I KILLED HIM. I-- KILLED HIM..
PILAR, IT WAS THE MORITURI EFFECT-- PILAR--
PILAR--!

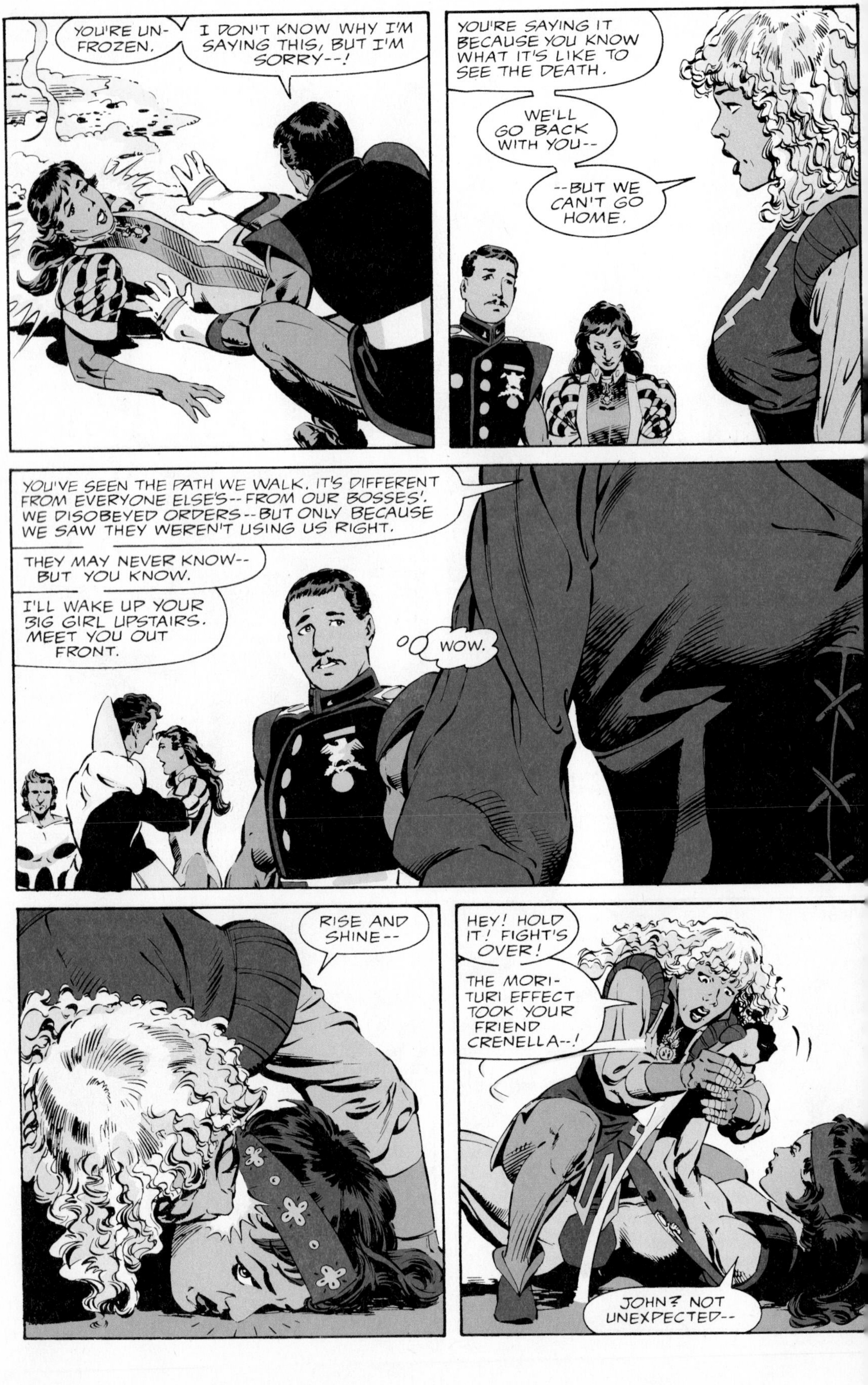
YOU'RE UN-FROZEN.
I DON'T KNOW WHY I'M SAYING THIS, BUT I'M SORRY--!
YOU'RE SAYING IT BECAUSE YOU KNOW WHAT IT'S LIKE TO SEE THE DEATH.
WE'LL GO BACK WITH YOU--
--BUT WE CAN'T GO HOME.
YOU'VE SEEN THE PATH WE WALK. IT'S DIFFERENT FROM EVERYONE ELSE'S--FROM OUR BOSSES'. WE DISOBEYED ORDERS--BUT ONLY BECAUSE WE SAW THEY WEREN'T USING US RIGHT.
THEY MAY NEVER KNOW--BUT YOU KNOW.
I'LL WAKE UP YOUR BIG GIRL UPSTAIRS. MEET YOU OUT FRONT.
WOW.
RISE AND SHINE--
HEY! HOLD IT! FIGHT'S OVER!
THE MORI-TURI EFFECT TOOK YOUR FRIEND CRENELLA--!
JOHN? NOT UNEXPECTED--

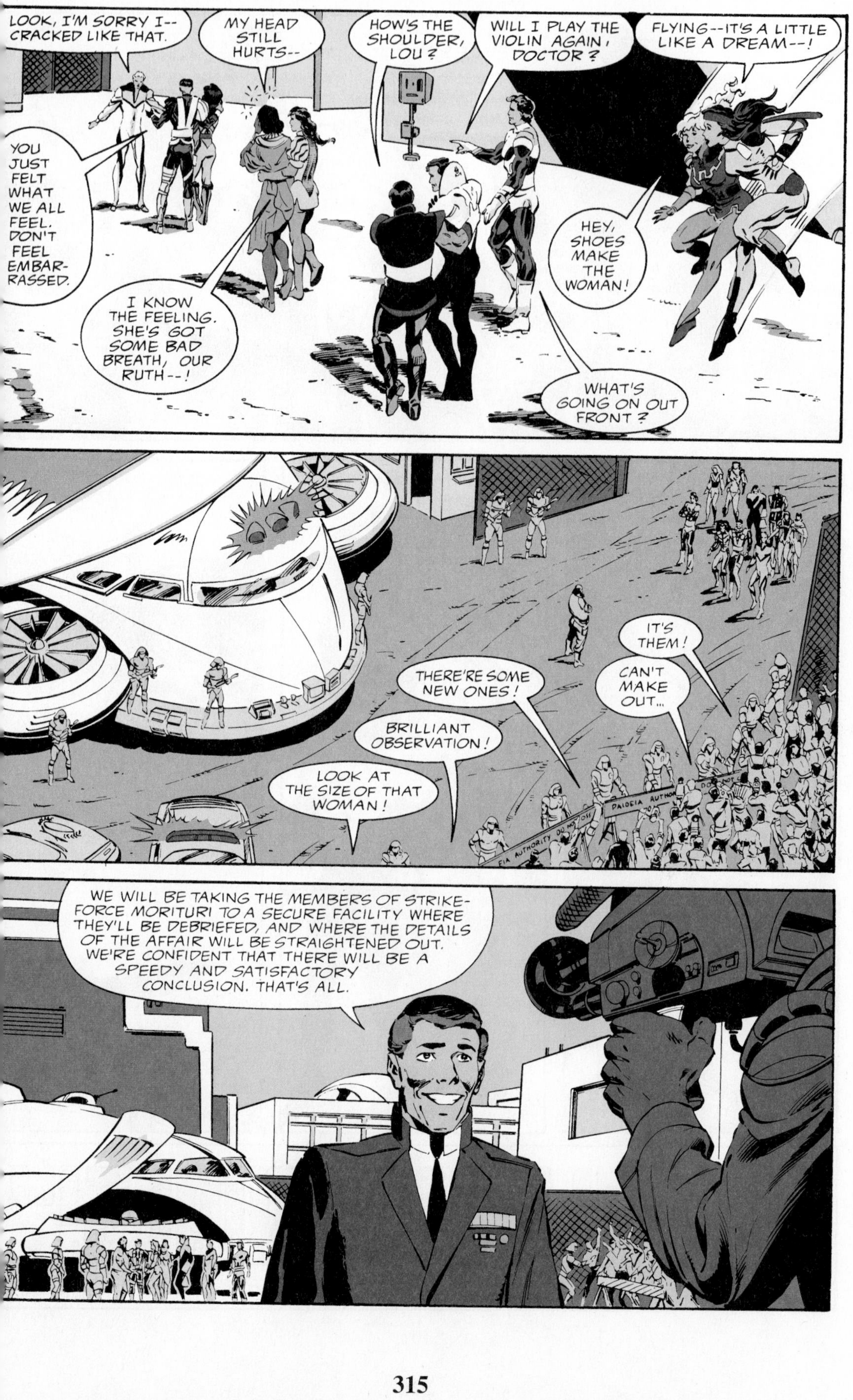
LOOK, I'M SORRY I-- CRACKED LIKE THAT.
YOU JUST FELT WHAT WE ALL FEEL. DON'T FEEL EMBAR-RASSED.
MY HEAD STILL HURTS--
I KNOW THE FEELING. SHE'S GOT SOME BAD BREATH, OUR RUTH--!
HOW'S THE SHOULDER, LOU?
WILL I PLAY THE VIOLIN AGAIN, DOCTOR?
WHAT'S GOING ON OUT FRONT?
FLYING--IT'S A LITTLE LIKE A DREAM--!
HEY, SHOES MAKE THE WOMAN!
IT'S THEM!
CAN'T MAKE OUT...
THERE'RE SOME NEW ONES!
BRILLIANT OBSERVATION!
LOOK AT THE SIZE OF THAT WOMAN!
WE WILL BE TAKING THE MEMBERS OF STRIKE-FORCE MORITURI TO A SECURE FACILITY WHERE THEY'LL BE DEBRIEFED, AND WHERE THE DETAILS OF THE AFFAIR WILL BE STRAIGHTENED OUT. WE'RE CONFIDENT THAT THERE WILL BE A SPEEDY AND SATISFACTORY CONCLUSION. THAT'S ALL.

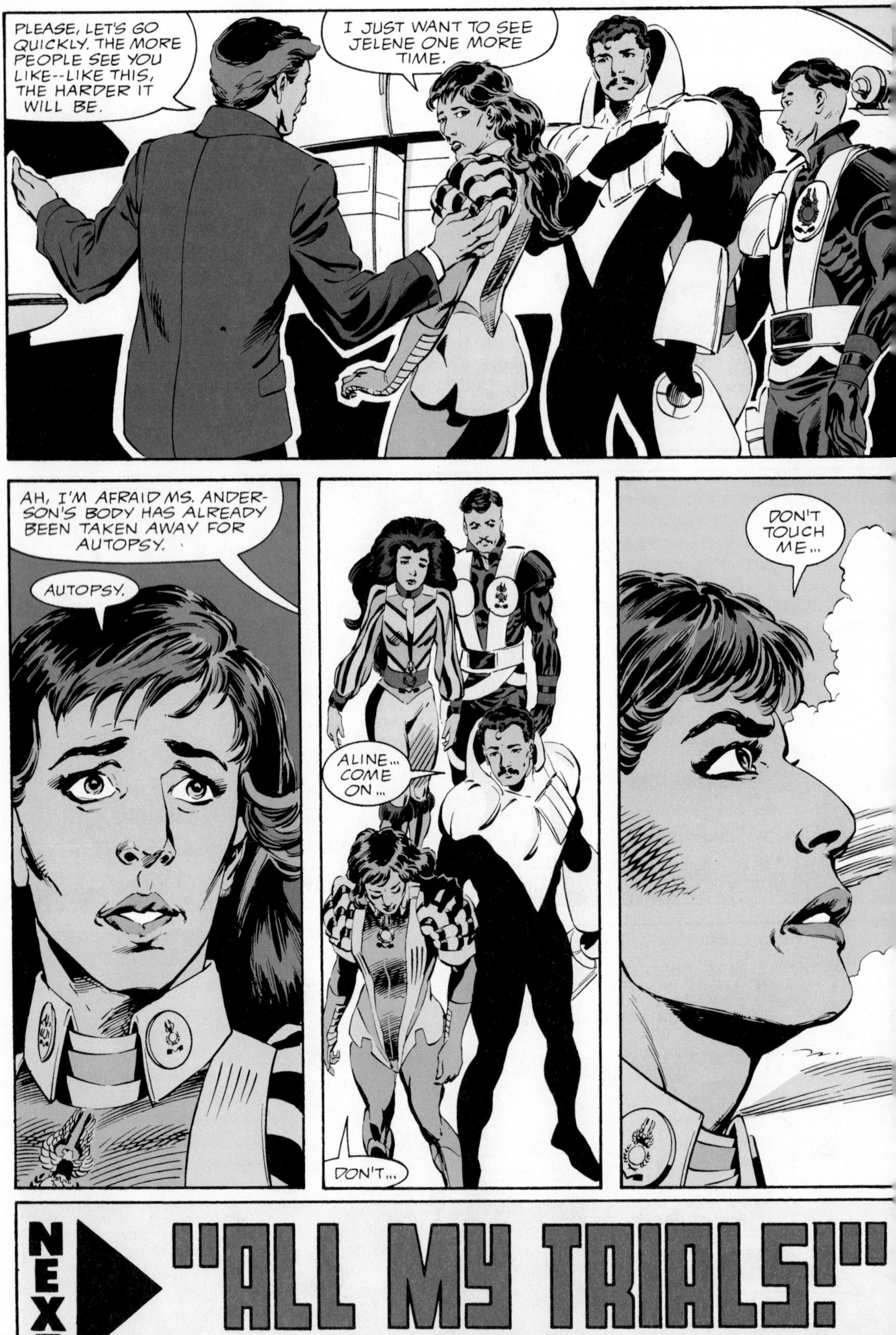
PLEASE, LET'S GO QUICKLY. THE MORE PEOPLE SEE YOU LIKE--LIKE THIS, THE HARDER IT WILL BE.
I JUST WANT TO SEE JELENE ONE MORE TIME.
AH, I'M AFRAID MS. ANDERSON'S BODY HAS ALREADY BEEN TAKEN AWAY FOR AUTOPSY.
AUTOPSY.
ALINE... COME ON...
DON'T...
DON'T TOUCH ME...
NEXT
"ALL MY TRIALS!"
ON SALE IN THIRTY DAYS!
'NUFF SAID!

THE OFFICIAL Strikeforce: MORITURI HANDBOOK

THE PAIDA

With the attainment of nuclear disarmament in the 21st century and the Compact of Brienz between the major powers, The Paideia Institute began to exercise more of a significant role in human affairs. Originally established as an education reform organization, it started to function, with the final dissolution of the long-moribund United Nations, as a mediation and arbitration service among large corporations and later states. By mid-century, having mediation contracts with all 50 United States, all the Canadian Provincesa, members of the European Community and the Soviet Socialist Republics, the Paideia became by the back door what so many on Earth had sought for so long: a World Government. The African and Asian nations made the Paideia's hegemony complete.

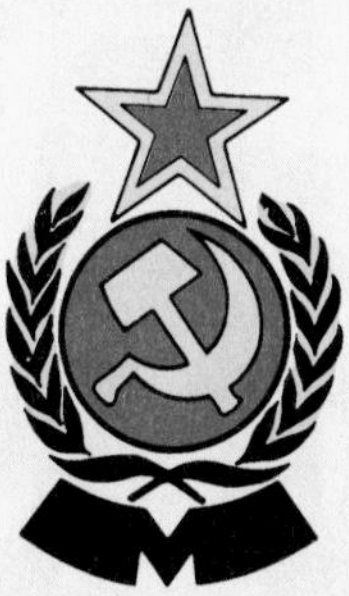

USSR

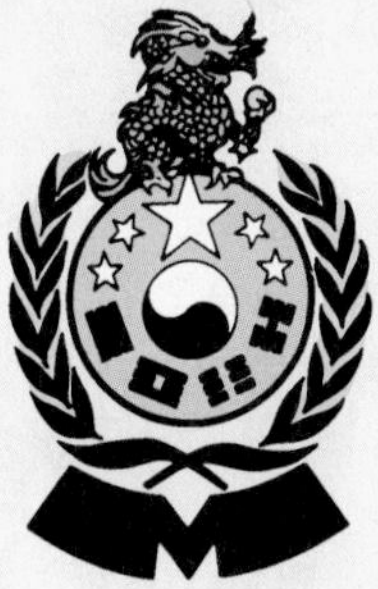

ASIA

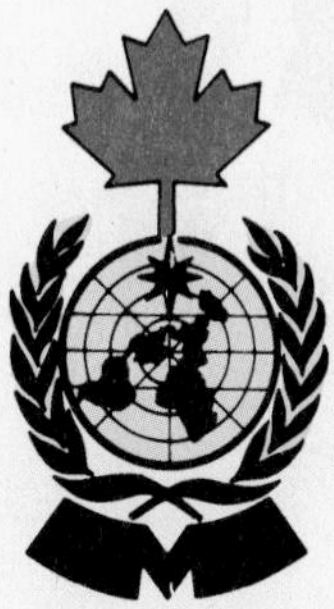

CANADA

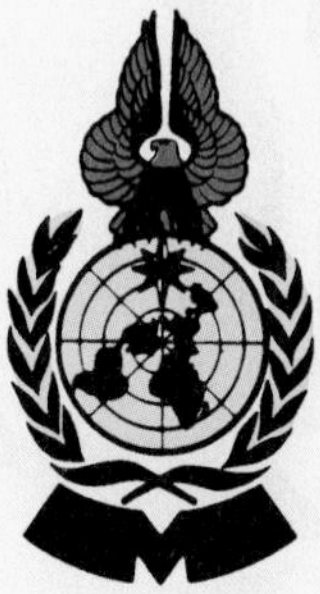

AMERICAS

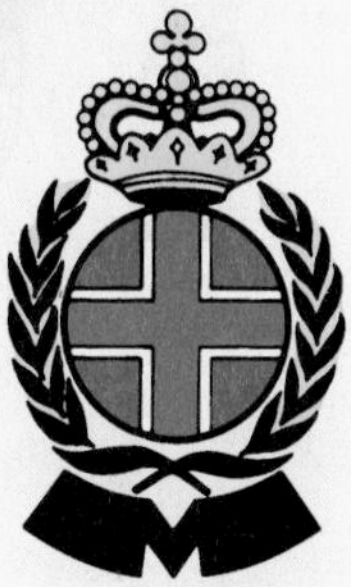

EUROPE

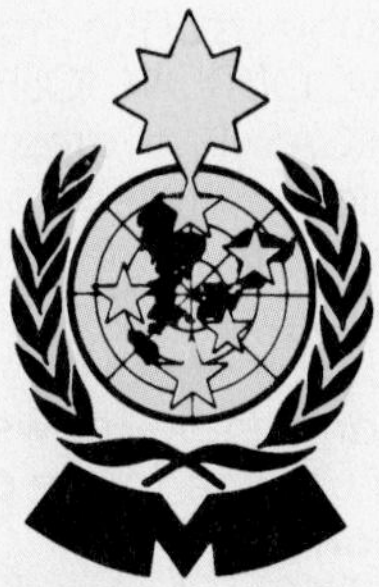

AUSTRALIA AND OCEANIA

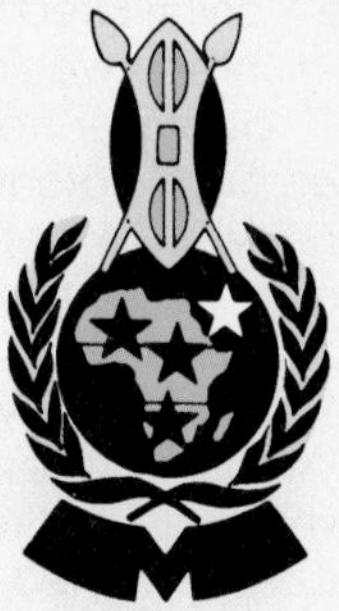

AFRICA

While acknowledging the principle of self determination of all sovereign states, the Paideia was the first organization to be effective as a policeman in world affairs. Whether the *Pax Humana* that the Paideia effected could last for more than one or two generations was made a moot question by the arrival of the Horde on Earth. It quickly became the coordinating authority for Earth's defenses, with full emergency powers.

text: PETER B. GILLIS art: BRENT ANDERSON

THE OFFICIAL Strikeforce: MORITURI HANDBOOK

THE BLACK WATCH

Shortly after the Morituri Effect was discovered by Dr. Kimmo Tuolema, it was decided that a set of five volunteers would be chosen as the first subjects of the process. They were CLINTON ROGERS, a farmer from Decatur, Kansas; WOODROW JOSHUA GREEN, an industrial designer from Toronto, Ontario, BRUCE HIGASHI, a stress therapist from Hiroshima, Japan. All had been veterans of the Paideia Armed Forces during the invasion. They became the team that the world knew as the Black Watch: two other volunteers, AARON RAY LEONARD and PATRICIA LYNNE SOBRERO did not live through the ordeal in the biowar facility nicknamed 'the Garden' that served to stimulate the survivors' powers. While they developed super strength and energy powers, the fact they were all above what was later recognized as the optimum age for the process (which is around 18) probably shortened their life spans more than usual.

Their first and only mission was an attack on the Horde's earthbound command post situated in Cape Town, South Africa. In the attack, the Hordian First In The Field was killed by Rogers, who was in turn killed by the Hordian Forces. Woodrow Joshua Green and Bruce Higashi escaped, but Woodrow succumbed to the massive fatal rejection known as the Morituri Effect. The escape ship crashed, and the site was hit by a Horde nuclear weapon in retaliation. It is assumed that Hogashi perished in that explosion.

text: PETER B. GILLIS art: BRENT ANDERSO

ROLL OF HONOR

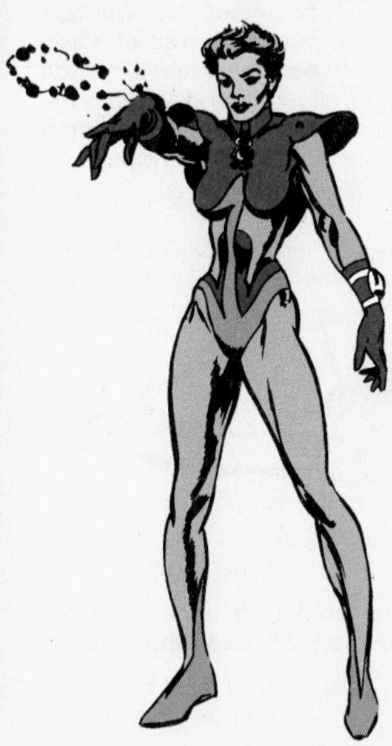

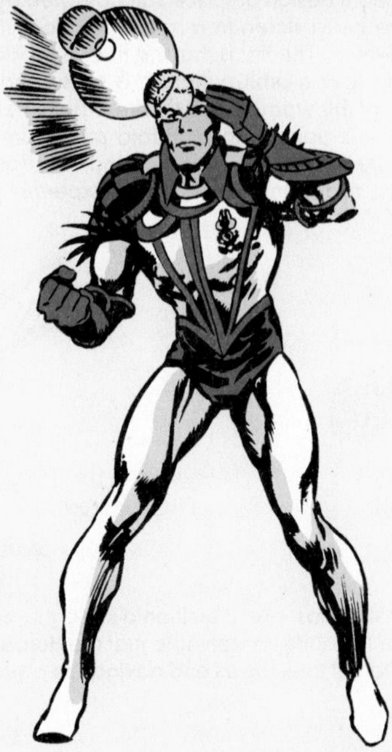

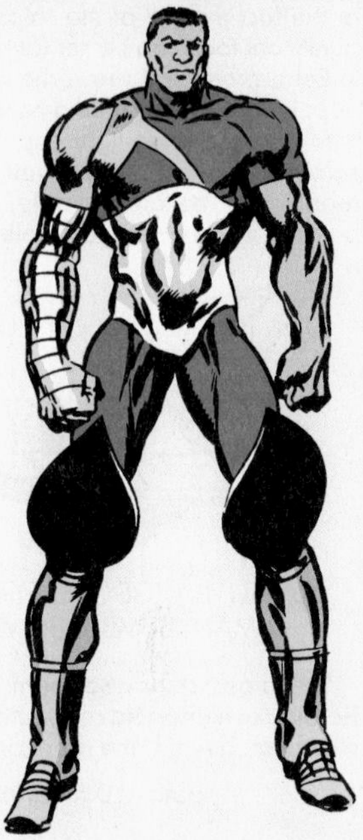

Everson, Harold—**VIKING**

Raeburn, Lorna—**SNAPDRAGON**

Greenbaum, Robert—**MARATHON**

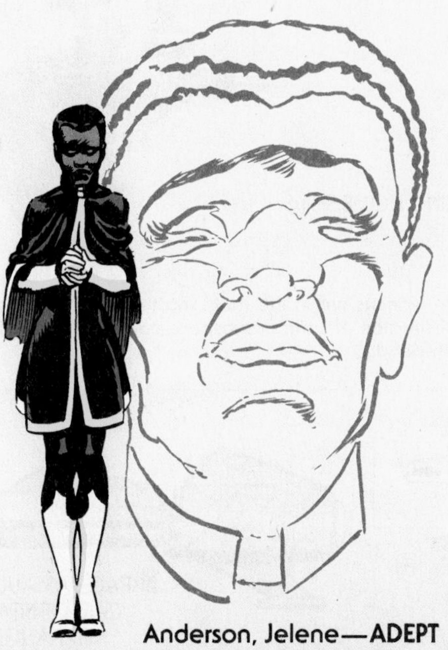

"Death is their price, their sacrifice, their glory: Memory is our gift, our tribute, our solemn duty."

Anderson, Jelene—**ADEPT**

text: PETER B. GILLIS art: BRENT ANDERSON

THE OFFICIAL *Strikeforce:* MORITURI HANDBOOK

HORDE SPACECRAFT

There seems to be no single dominant design of spacecraft operated by the Horde. This is undoubtedly due to the fact that all of the ships have been stolen from the civilizations that the Hordians plundered. A few significant facts can be set forth, however. The first is that the fleet is divided up into two groups: the warships in Earth orbit, and the remainder in Jovian orbit, where it is presumed that the preponderance of Horde population lives, including nearly all of the women and children. The smallest craft seem to be suborbital craft with no faster-than-light capability: it is apparently standard procedure not to allow warp drives into the combat zone for fear of their capture. Whatever their provenance, Hordian spacecraft have their controls modified to be quite simple, owing to the lack of technical expertise prevalent in the warrior class, and perhaps in the race as a whole.

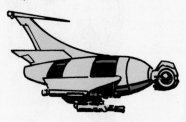

SMALL-RANGE (SUB-ORBITAL) 2-MAN "BUMBLE BOMBER"

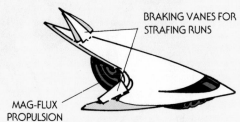

BRAKING VANES FOR STRAFING RUNS
MAG-FLUX PROPULSION

SMALL-RANGE (SUB-ORBITAL) "DART SHIP"

The largest ships also seem to be the most alien, built on a scale that seems to have little to do with either Hordian or humanoid configurations. It is quite conceivable that the Horde know very little about these ships in particular, beyond the mere operation of their drives and navigation equipment.

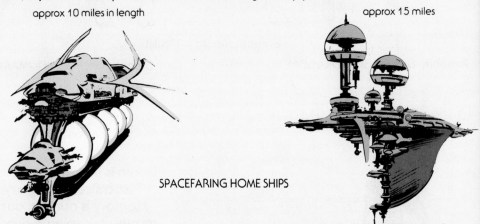

approx 10 miles in length

approx 15 miles

SPACEFARING HOME SHIPS

This said, it must be emphasized that the Horde warriors are in the main masterful combat pilots and extremely deadly in any confrontation. With the destruction of Earth's aerospace capability in the first few weeks of the invasion, this has made them extremely deadly.

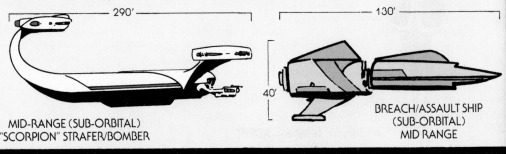

290'

MID-RANGE (SUB-ORBITAL) "SCORPION" STRAFER/BOMBER

130'
40'

BREACH/ASSAULT SHIP (SUB-ORBITAL) MID RANGE

text: PETER B. GILLIS art: BRENT ANDERSON & C

THE OFFICIAL *Strikeforce:* MORITURI HANDBOOK

KNOWN SUBSIDIARY ALIEN RACES

It is not unexpected that the Horde should have taken slaves in their interstellar wanderings. To date, however, only a few of the races the Horde conquered have become known to the Paideia, undoubtedly due to the unwillingness to take unfriendly (if pacified) aliens into a combat situation. The races are as follows.

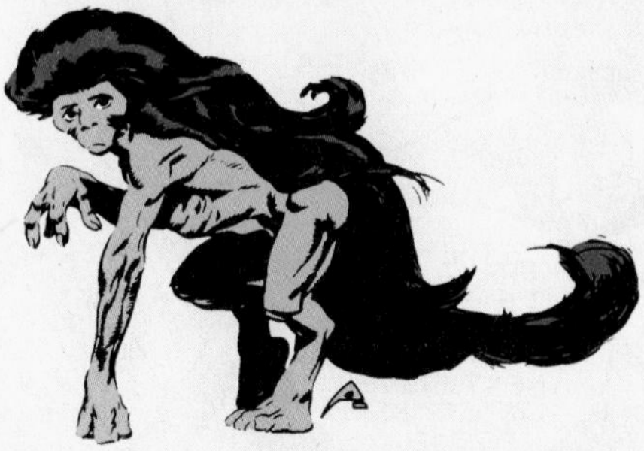

THE MELLIDAR. These small quadrupeds are intelligent and perhaps sentient. About the size of a large cat or dog and covered with soft fur, they seem to exercise no useful function in Horde society, though they have been observed on many occasions. The Horde conceivably keep them as pets.

HEALERS: These are semi-amorphous, tentacular creatures with the facility for healing wounds. Hordians have been seen carrying these creatures from time to time. Whether they are indigenous to the Horde's planet of origin is unknown, though they seem well adapted to serving the Horde. When in contact with humans, the results are catastrophic: the Healer will cause radical skin growth that quickly seals up all orifices and causes death by suffocation.

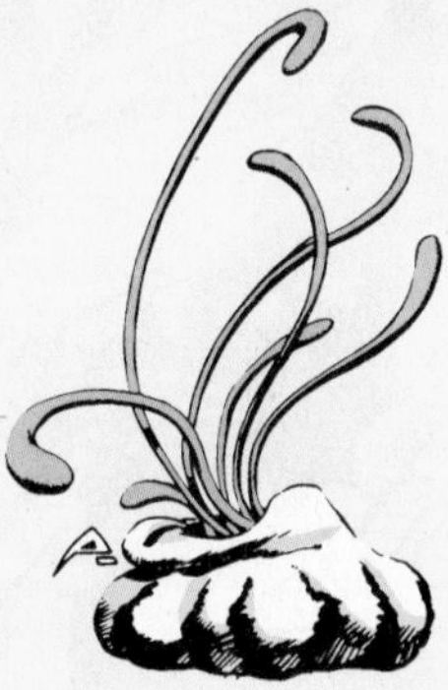

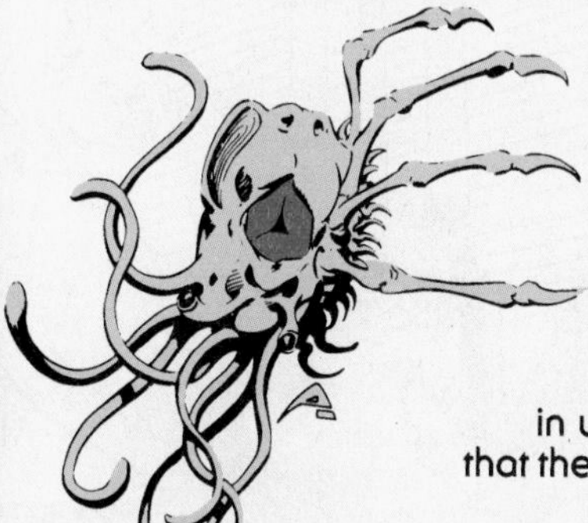

TRANSLATORS: Tentacular, but with a three-part circular mouth, these highly specialized beings seem to be trainable in translation from the Hordian into any number of human languages. The skills of these creatures seem to vary from individual to individual, from crude word-for-word translation to smooth idiomatic speech. They are not widely in use among the Hordians warriors, which leads us to believe that they are quite rare.

THE TALL ONES: Very little is known about these aliens, and it is quite conceivable that none survive. Indeed, a few images are the only evidence for their existence. Nonetheless, their role is a signal one: they were the aliens who first made contact with the then-planet-bound Horde. They mean to induct the Hordians into an interstellar brotherhood — and were completely unprepared for the brutality with which they were received. The Tall Ones were slaughtered, their ships taken, even though the Hordians at that stage were roughly at a stage of development comparable to 21st century Earth. No evidence of any interstellar brotherhood beyond these images has been found, and there is no way of knowing just where that civilization or group of civilizations may be found. By all indications the Horde have no nostalgic sentiment toward their home planet: indeed, they seem to denigrate it severely.

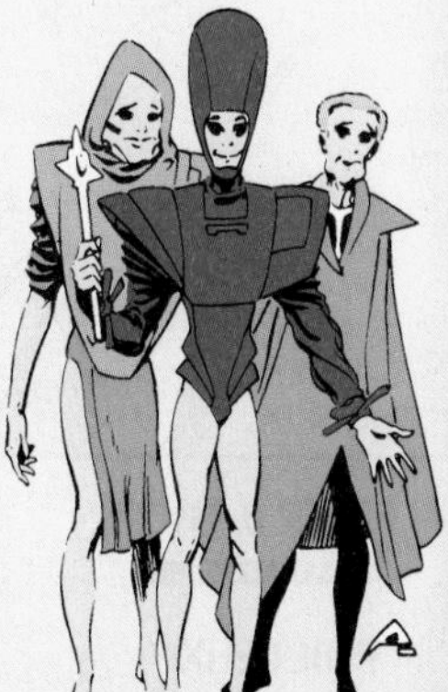

text: PETER B. GILLIS art: BRENT ANDERSON

HERE IT IS! "HOW PETER & BRENT CREATE (& DESTROY) STRIKEFORCE MORITURI"

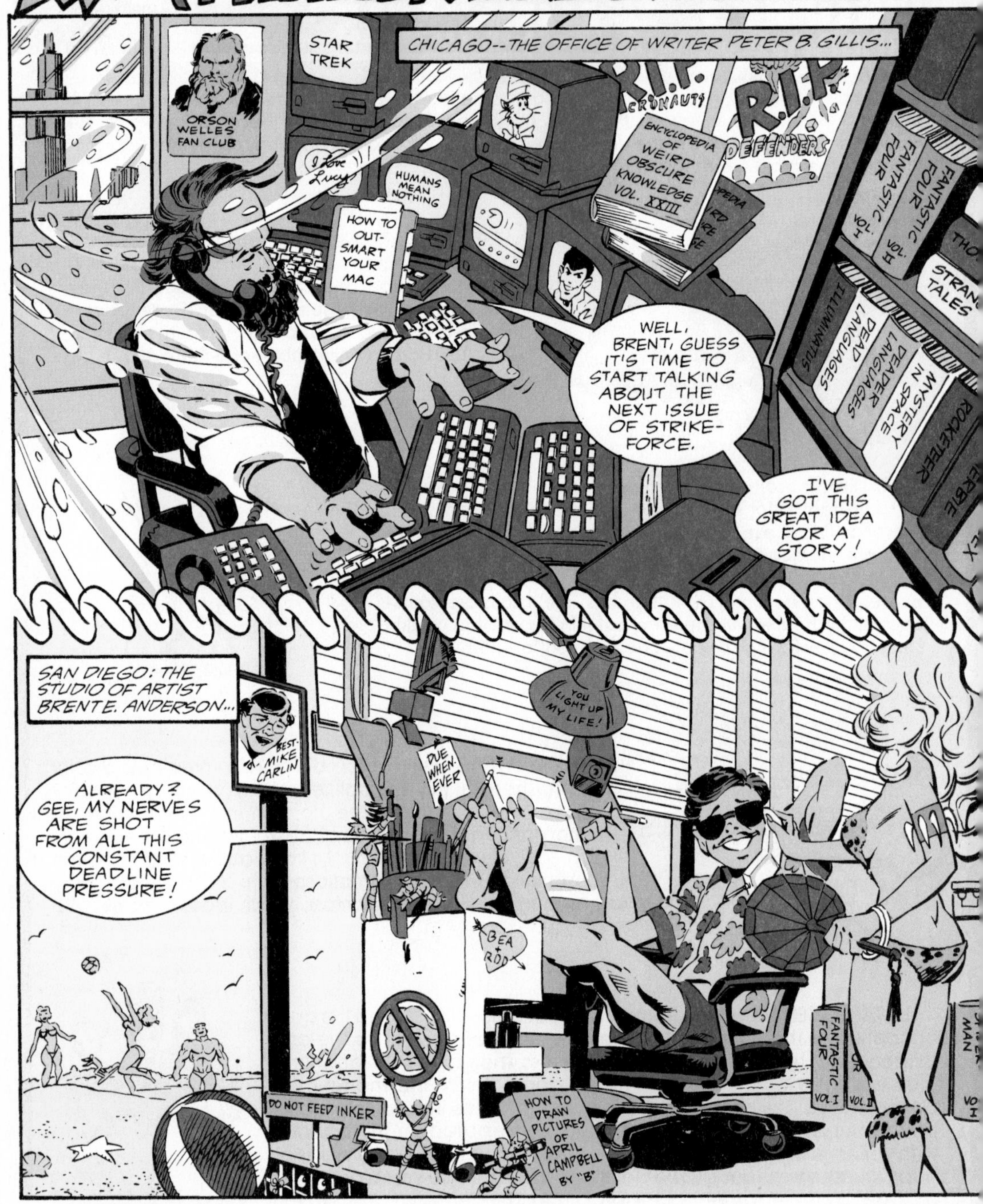

CHICAGO--THE OFFICE OF WRITER PETER B. GILLIS...
STAR TREK
ORSON WELLES FAN CLUB
R.I.P. CRONAUTS
R.I.P. DEFENDERS
ENCYCLOPEDIA OF WEIRD OBSCURE KNOWLEDGE VOL. XXIII
I Love Lucy
HUMANS MEAN NOTHING
HOW TO OUT-SMART YOUR MAC
FANTASTIC FOUR VOL. I
FANTASTIC FOUR VOL. II
STRANGE TALES
ILLUMINATUS
DEAD LANGUAGES
DEADER LANGUAGES
MYSTERY IN SPACE
ROCKETEER
WELL, BRENT, GUESS IT'S TIME TO START TALKING ABOUT THE NEXT ISSUE OF STRIKE-FORCE.
I'VE GOT THIS GREAT IDEA FOR A STORY!
SAN DIEGO: THE STUDIO OF ARTIST BRENT E. ANDERSON...
BEST- MIKE CARLIN
YOU LIGHT UP MY LIFE!
DUE WHEN-EVER
ALREADY? GEE, MY NERVES ARE SHOT FROM ALL THIS CONSTANT DEADLINE PRESSURE!
BEA + ROD
DO NOT FEED INKER
HOW TO DRAW PICTURES OF APRIL CAMPBELL BY "B"
FANTASTIC FOUR VOL. I

PETER B. GILLIS mumbles

BRENT E. ANDERSON scrawls

SCOTT WILLIAMS blots

PHIL FELIX scratches

CHRISTIE SCHEELE stains

CARL POTTS meddles

TOM DeFALCO meddles in chief

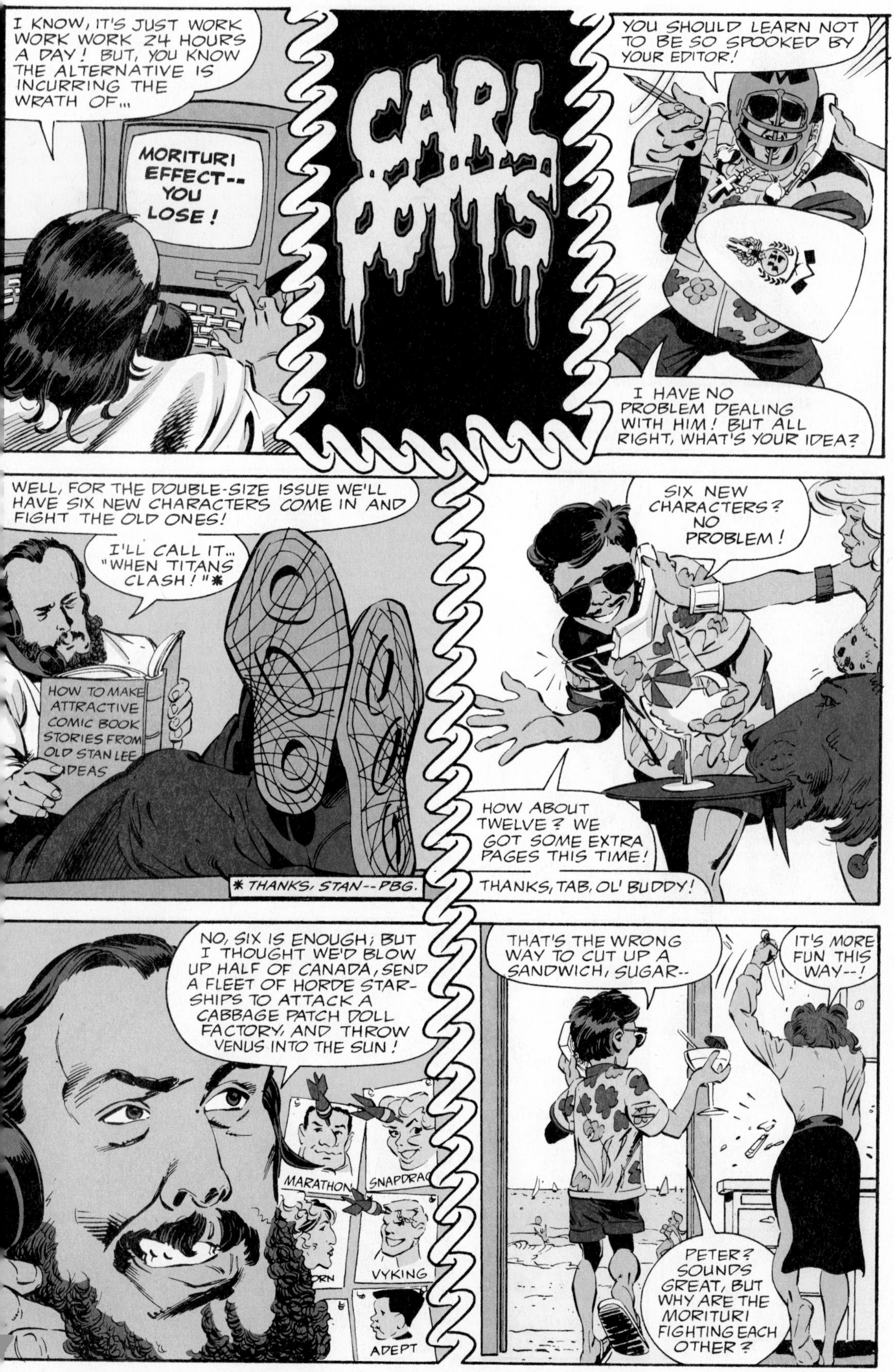

I KNOW, IT'S JUST WORK WORK WORK 24 HOURS A DAY! BUT, YOU KNOW THE ALTERNATIVE IS INCURRING THE WRATH OF...
MORITURI EFFECT-- YOU LOSE!
CARL POTTS
YOU SHOULD LEARN NOT TO BE SO SPOOKED BY YOUR EDITOR!
I HAVE NO PROBLEM DEALING WITH HIM! BUT ALL RIGHT, WHAT'S YOUR IDEA?
WELL, FOR THE DOUBLE-SIZE ISSUE WE'LL HAVE SIX NEW CHARACTERS COME IN AND FIGHT THE OLD ONES!
I'LL CALL IT... "WHEN TITANS CLASH!"*
HOW TO MAKE ATTRACTIVE COMIC BOOK STORIES FROM OLD STAN LEE IDEAS
*THANKS, STAN--PBG.
SIX NEW CHARACTERS? NO PROBLEM!
HOW ABOUT TWELVE? WE GOT SOME EXTRA PAGES THIS TIME!
THANKS, TAB, OL' BUDDY!
NO, SIX IS ENOUGH; BUT I THOUGHT WE'D BLOW UP HALF OF CANADA, SEND A FLEET OF HORDE STAR-SHIPS TO ATTACK A CABBAGE PATCH DOLL FACTORY, AND THROW VENUS INTO THE SUN!
MARATHON
SNAPDRAG
VYKING
ADEPT
THAT'S THE WRONG WAY TO CUT UP A SANDWICH, SUGAR--
IT'S MORE FUN THIS WAY--!
PETER? SOUNDS GREAT, BUT WHY ARE THE MORITURI FIGHTING EACH OTHER?

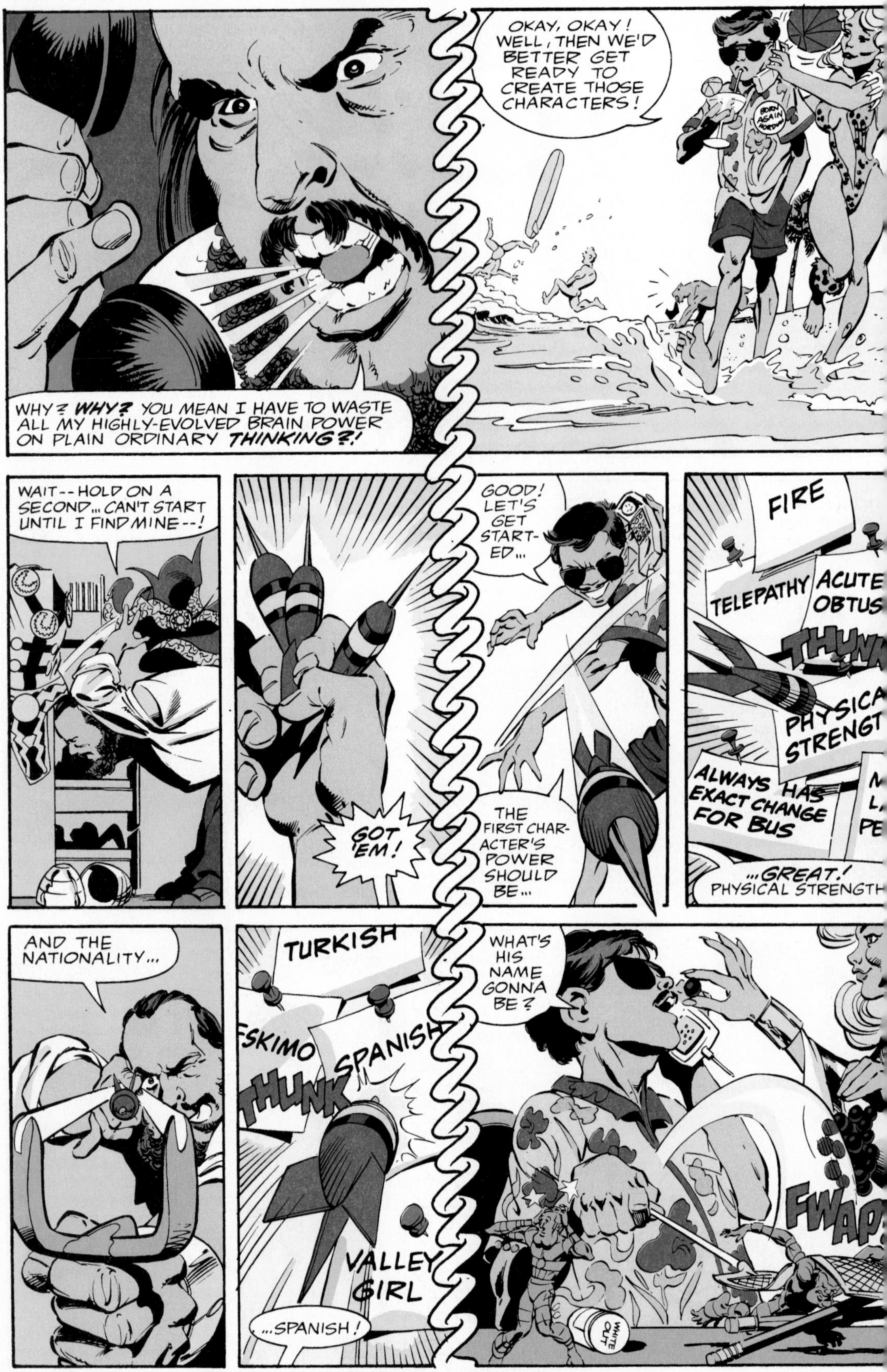
OKAY, OKAY! WELL, THEN WE'D BETTER GET READY TO CREATE THOSE CHARACTERS!
BORN AGAIN
WHY? WHY? YOU MEAN I HAVE TO WASTE ALL MY HIGHLY-EVOLVED BRAIN POWER ON PLAIN ORDINARY THINKING?!
WAIT--HOLD ON A SECOND... CAN'T START UNTIL I FIND MINE--!
GOT 'EM!
GOOD! LET'S GET START-ED...
THE FIRST CHAR-ACTER'S POWER SHOULD BE...
FIRE
TELEPATHY
ACUTE OBTUS
THUNK
PHYSICA STRENGT
ALWAYS HAS EXACT CHANGE FOR BUS
...GREAT! PHYSICAL STRENGTH
AND THE NATIONALITY...
TURKISH
ESKIMO
SPANISH
THUNK
VALLEY GIRL
...SPANISH!
WHAT'S HIS NAME GONNA BE?
FWAP
WHITE OUT

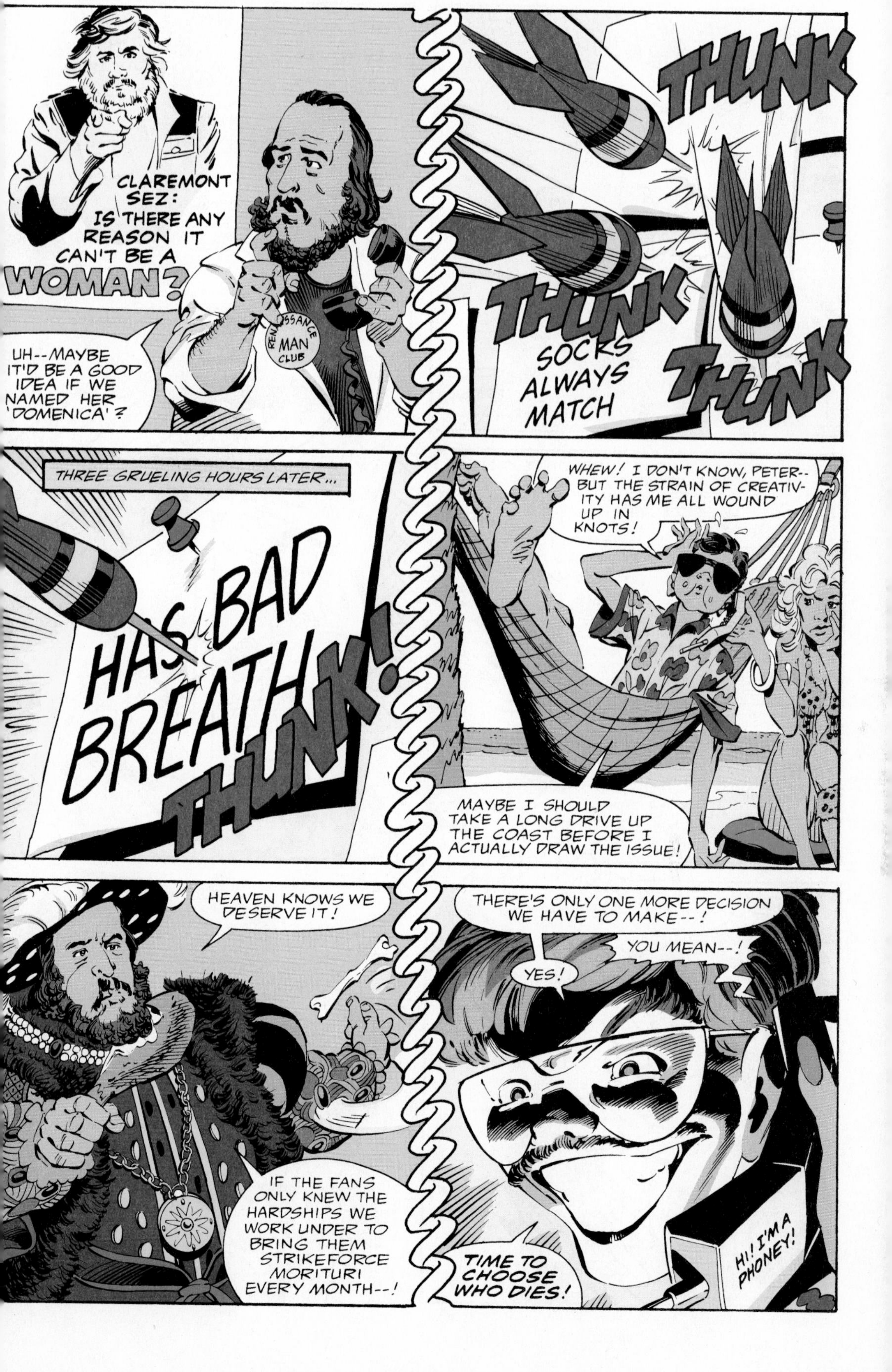

CLAREMONT SEZ: IS THERE ANY REASON IT CAN'T BE A WOMAN?
UH--MAYBE IT'D BE A GOOD IDEA IF WE NAMED HER 'DOMENICA'?
RENAISSANCE MAN CLUB
THUNK
THUNK
SOCKS ALWAYS MATCH
THUNK
THREE GRUELING HOURS LATER...
HAS BAD BREATH
THUNK!
WHEW! I DON'T KNOW, PETER--BUT THE STRAIN OF CREATIVITY HAS ME ALL WOUND UP IN KNOTS!
MAYBE I SHOULD TAKE A LONG DRIVE UP THE COAST BEFORE I ACTUALLY DRAW THE ISSUE!
HEAVEN KNOWS WE DESERVE IT!
IF THE FANS ONLY KNEW THE HARDSHIPS WE WORK UNDER TO BRING THEM STRIKEFORCE MORITURI EVERY MONTH--!
THERE'S ONLY ONE MORE DECISION WE HAVE TO MAKE--!
YOU MEAN--!
YES!
TIME TO CHOOSE WHO DIES!
HI! I'M A PHONEY!

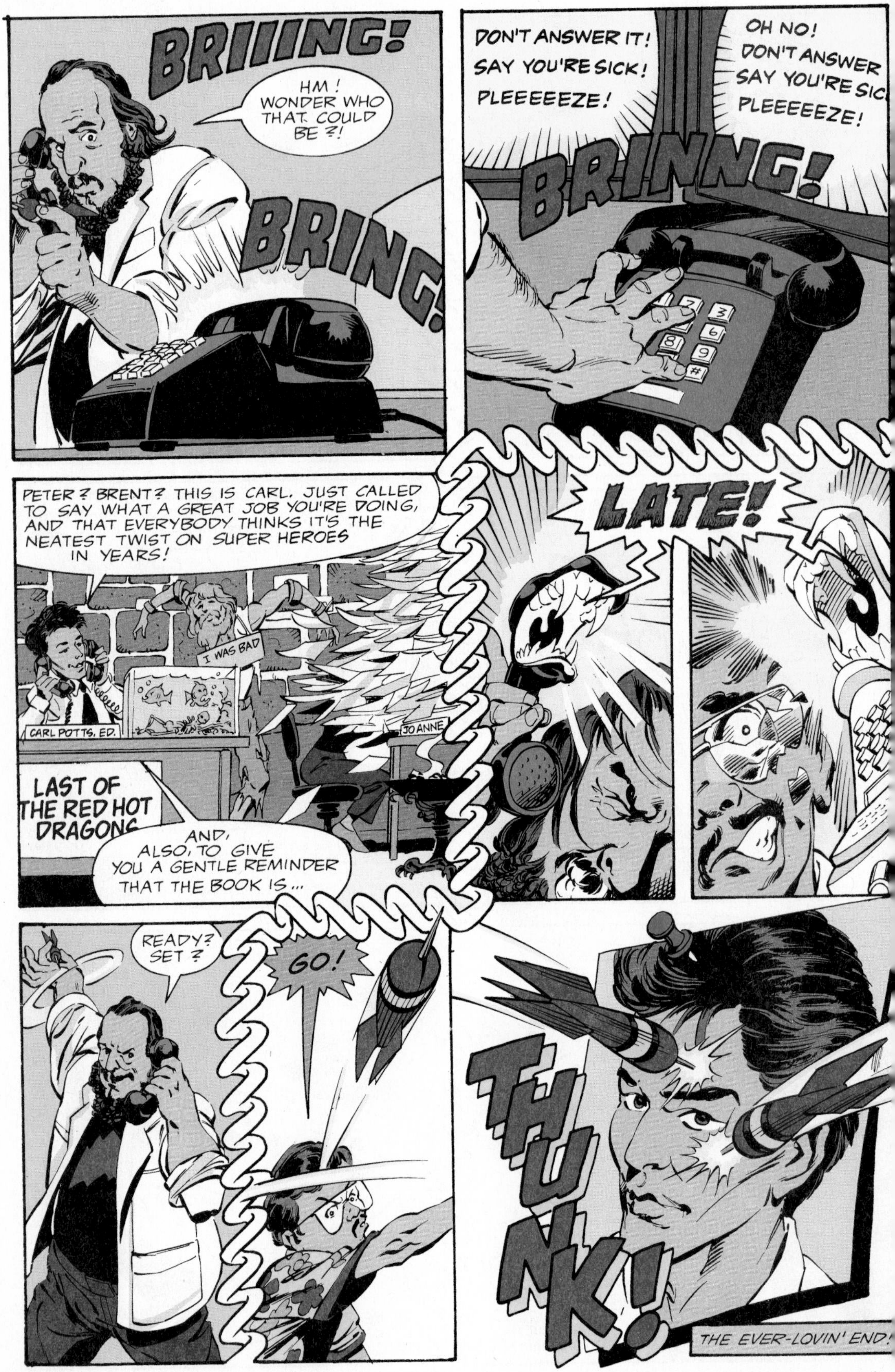
BRIIING!
HM! WONDER WHO THAT COULD BE ?!
BRING!
DON'T ANSWER IT! SAY YOU'RE SICK! PLEEEEEZE!
OH NO! DON'T ANSWER SAY YOU'RE SIC PLEEEEEZE!
BRINNG!
PETER? BRENT? THIS IS CARL. JUST CALLED TO SAY WHAT A GREAT JOB YOU'RE DOING, AND THAT EVERYBODY THINKS IT'S THE NEATEST TWIST ON SUPER HEROES IN YEARS!
I WAS BAD
CARL POTTS, ED.
JO ANNE
LAST OF THE RED HOT DRAGONS
AND, ALSO, TO GIVE YOU A GENTLE REMINDER THAT THE BOOK IS...
LATE!
READY? SET ?
GO!
THUNK!
THE EVER-LOVIN' END!

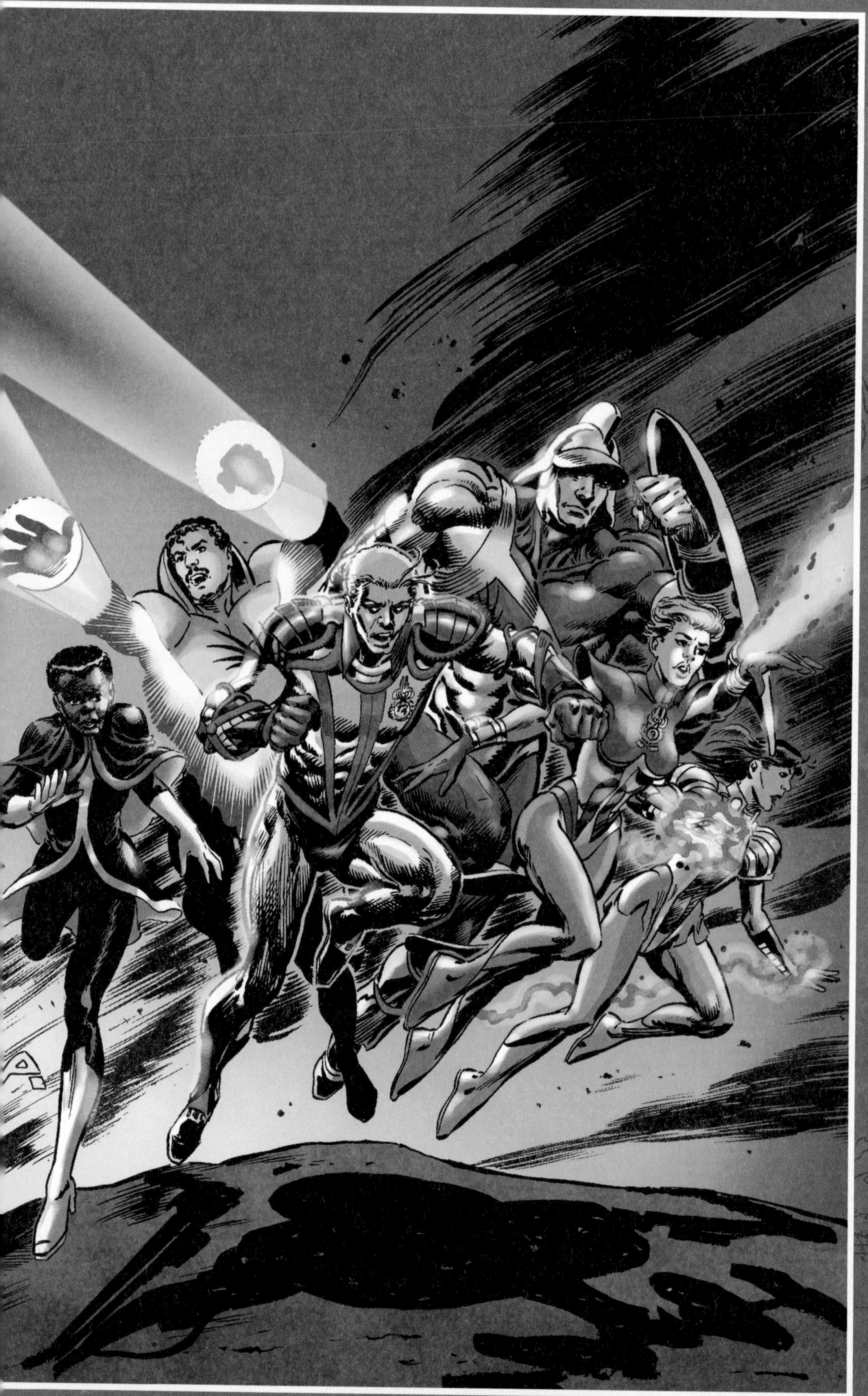

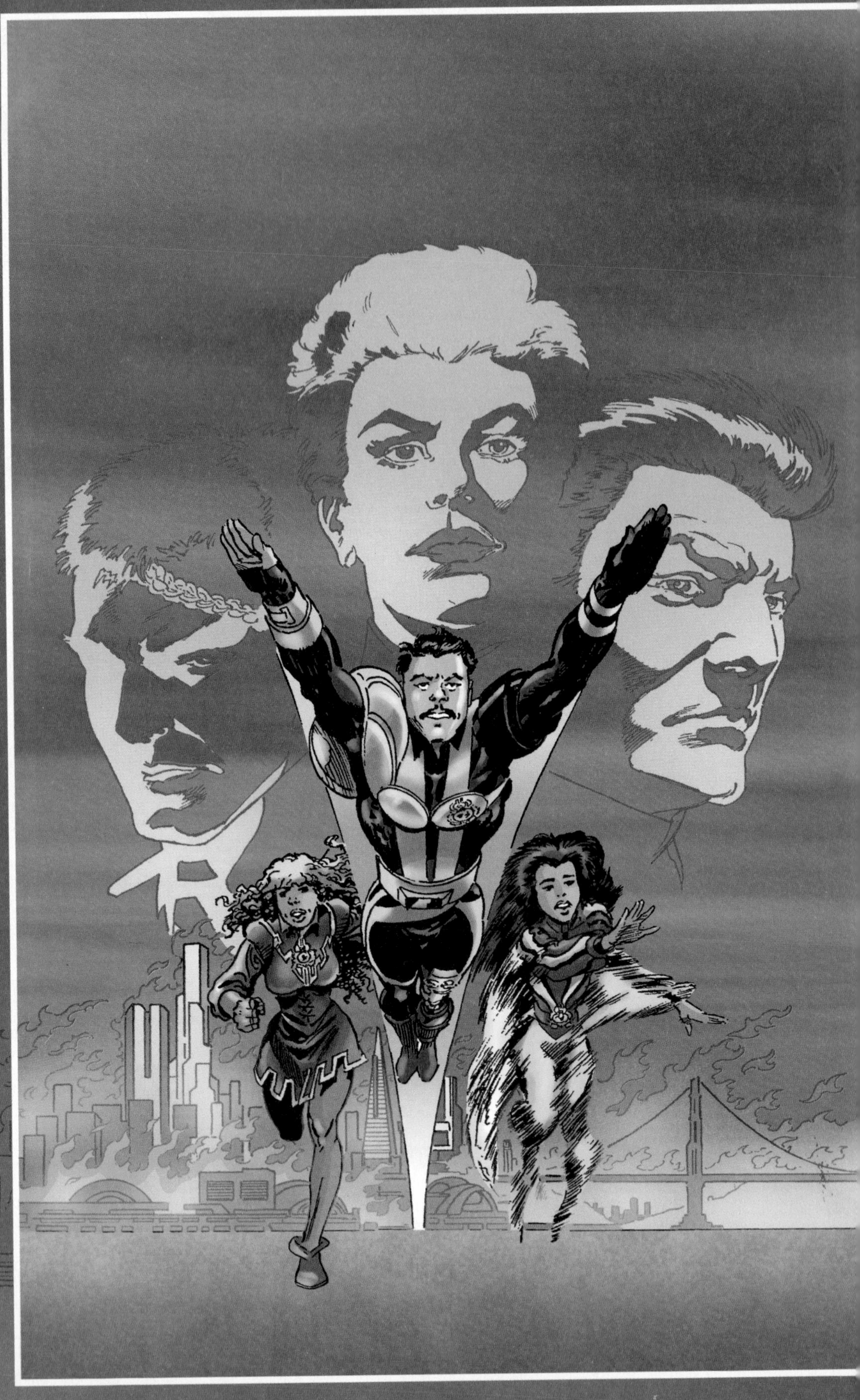